# Komm mit!

## HOLT GERMAN LEVELS 1, 2, and 3

### SO SAGT MAN DAS!

**Making plans**

You have been using the **möchte**-forms (*would like to*) to express
**Er möchte Musik hören.** You can also use **wollen** (*to want to*).

Talking to someone:

    **Heiko, was willst du machen?**

Talking about someone:

    **Wohin will Birte gehen?**

Talking about yourself:

    **Ich will in ein Caf**

    **Sie will ins Schw**

## A ROAD MAP TO PROFICIENCY

**K**omm mit!'s **functionally driven scope and sequence** gives students reasons to communicate. As a result, they develop proficiency in the four language **skills** (listening, speaking, reading, and writing) and build their critical-thinking skills.

    Plus, Komm mit! presents **grammar** in context to support the functions, enhancing your students' ability to communicate with accuracy and confidence.

*George's movie schedule*

# JOURNEY AT A REALISTIC PACE

*Komm mit!*'s **manageable chapters** set a realistic pace, so you and your students can complete each level of this three-level program in one year—without sacrificing language development.

*Komm mit!*'s **spiraling** of functions, vocabulary, and grammar increases your students' retention of newly acquired language and presents opportunities for using the language in various situations. And, with only 60 to 70 active **vocabulary** words per chapter, your students can use the core vocabulary with greater ease, yet still personalize their own communication.

Best of all, *Komm mit!*'s variety of activities, strategies, and supplementary materials **meets individual student needs**—ensuring the success of all students.

Schon bekannt
Ein wenig *G*rammatik

Monika could say of Katja:

> **Katja will am Freitag in die Stadt gehen.** *or*
> **Am Freitag will Katja in die Stadt gehen.**

You have seen this type of word order before—in **Kapitel 2**, when you learned about German word order:

> **Wir spielen um 2 Uhr Fußball.**
> **Um 2 Uhr spielen wir Fußball.**

What is the position of the verbs in all four of these sentences[1]?

## WORTSCHATZ

**Wohin gehen?   Was machen?** Lies, was Katja und Julia planen! Julia sagt: „Katja und ich, wir wollen ..."

in ein Café gehen,
ein Eis essen

ins Schwimmbad gehen,
baden gehen

ins Kino gehen,
einen Film sehen

## EXPLORE CULTURE

**D**evelop your students' appreciation of the German-speaking world with **Komm mit!**'s **authentic** dialogues, interviews, realia, photos, and videos. **Komm mit!**'s strong cross-cultural perspective enriches students' understanding of the **multicultural** nature of the German-speaking world.

shown 75% of actual size

### In der Freizeit

What do you think students in Germany like to do when they have time to spend with their friends? We have asked a number of students from different places this question, but before you read their responses, write down what you think they will say. Then read these interviews and compare your ideas with what they say.

LANDESKUNDE

## EIN WENIG LANDESKUNDE

The prices on German menus include the tip. However, most people will round the check up to the next mark or to the next round sum, depending on the total of the bill.

*Had a great time!*

# YOU'RE READY FOR ANYTHING!

Lesson plans, activities, strategies, scripts, and more highlight the Teacher's Edition, providing a **variety of instructional materials**.

Chapter Resource blackline masters—including realia, situation cards, and listening activities—are **organized by chapter** for ease of use. Students sharpen their language skills as they see and hear German in context via **integrated technology**: the high-interest audio program and on-location **videos** they'll have fun with while they learn.

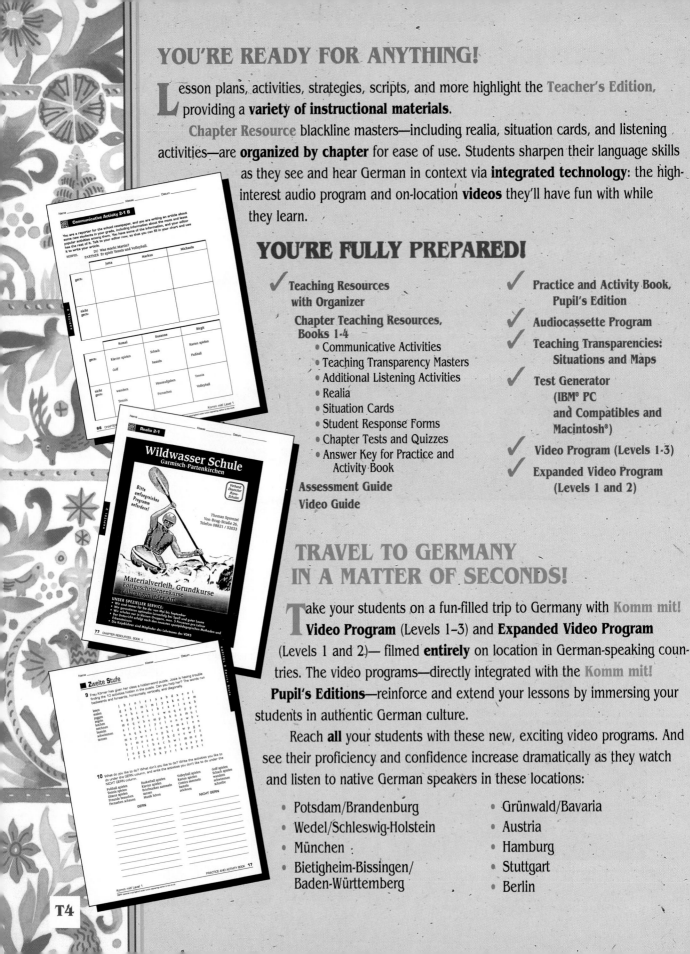

# YOU'RE FULLY PREPARED!

✓ **Teaching Resources with Organizer**

**Chapter Teaching Resources, Books 1-4**
- Communicative Activities
- Teaching Transparency Masters
- Additional Listening Activities
- Realia
- Situation Cards
- Student Response Forms
- Chapter Tests and Quizzes
- Answer Key for Practice and Activity Book

**Assessment Guide**

**Video Guide**

✓ **Practice and Activity Book, Pupil's Edition**

✓ **Audiocassette Program**

✓ **Teaching Transparencies: Situations and Maps**

✓ **Test Generator (IBM® PC and Compatibles and Macintosh®)**

✓ **Video Program (Levels 1-3)**

✓ **Expanded Video Program (Levels 1 and 2)**

# TRAVEL TO GERMANY IN A MATTER OF SECONDS!

Take your students on a fun-filled trip to Germany with Komm mit! **Video Program** (Levels 1–3) and **Expanded Video Program** (Levels 1 and 2)— filmed **entirely** on location in German-speaking countries. The video programs—directly integrated with the Komm mit! **Pupil's Editions**—reinforce and extend your lessons by immersing your students in authentic German culture.

Reach **all** your students with these new, exciting video programs. And see their proficiency and confidence increase dramatically as they watch and listen to native German speakers in these locations:

- Potsdam/Brandenburg
- Wedel/Schleswig-Holstein
- München
- Bietigheim-Bissingen/ Baden-Württemberg
- Grünwald/Bavaria
- Austria
- Hamburg
- Stuttgart
- Berlin

# Komm mit!

## Holt German

### Level 1

TEACHER'S EDITION

**HOLT, RINEHART AND WINSTON**
*Harcourt Brace & Company*

**Austin** • New York • Orlando • Chicago • Atlanta • San Francisco • Boston • Dallas • Toronto • London

Printed in the United States of America

ISBN 0-03-032522-6

3  4  5  6  7  041  99  98  97  96  95

**For permission to reprint copyrighted material, grateful acknowledgment is made to the following sources:**

*allmilmö Corporation:* Advertisement, "Best in Germany-Best in America," from *Metropolitan Home,* Special Edition, The Best of Winners!: Fall 1991, p. 9.

*Baars Marketing GmbH:* Advertisement, "Das haben Sie jetzt daron," from *Stern,* Nr. 27, p. 103, June 25, 1992.

*Bauconcept:* Advertisement, "Die Oase in der City!," from *Südwest Presse: Schwäbisches Tagblatt,* Tübingen, July 14,1990.

*Bertelsmann Club:* Advertisement and front cover, "Die Firma," from *Bertelsmann Club,* March 1993, p. 9.

*Bundesverband der Phonographischen Wirtschaft E. V.:* "Singles" from *Bravo,* 40/1993, p. 75, September 30, 1993. MUSIKMARKT TOP-Single-Charts, put together at the request of the Federal Sound Association of Media Control (Bundesverbandes Phono von Media Control).

*C & A Mode:* Advertisement, "C & A: SCHNUPPER PREISE," March 1992, p. 18.

*Columbia Tristar Home Video GmbH & CO. KG:* "Groundhog Day," from *K-Tips,* June, 1993, p. 8.

*Commerzbank:* Logo and "Umrechnungstabelle: Stand: Febr. '93" (exchange rate card).

*Crash Discothek:* Advertisement, "Crash," from *in münchen,* July 25–August 8, 1991, no. 30/31.

*Deike-Press-Bilderdienst:* Game, "Skat," from *Südwest Presse: Schwäbisches Tagblatt,* Tübingen July, 1990.

*Deutscher Wetterdienst:* "Das Wetter" from *Frankfurter Allgemeine: Zeitung für Deutschland,* June 9, 1993, no. 131/23D.

*EMI April Music Inc.:* "Kino" by Rolf Brendel. Copyright © 1984 by Edition Hate/EMI Songs Musikverlag. All Rights Controlled and Administered by EMI April Music Inc. All Rights Reserved. International Copyright Secured.

*Winfried Epple:* Advertisement, "Gute Laune," by Wertobjekte Immobilien Epple (Wie) from *Südwest Presse: Schwäbisches Tagblatt,* Tübingen, July 14, 1990.

*Frankfurter Allgemeine:* "Das Wetter" from *Frankfurter Allgemeine: Zeitung Für Deutschland,* June 9, 1993, no. 131/23D.

*Die Gilde Werbeagentur GmbH:* Advertisement, "Butaris," from *Petra,* June 1992, p. 197.

*Dr. Rudolf Goette GmbH:* Advertisements, "Dienstag, 26. Januar" and "Dienstag, 25, Mai," from *Pro-Arte: Konzerte '93.*

*Gräfe und Unzer Verlag GmbH, München:* Recipe, "Pikanter Quark," from *Das große Vollkorn Kochbuch,* p. 126. Copyright © by Gräfe und Unzer GmbH, München. "Dallmayr", and photograph of "Münchens ältestes 'Schlaraffenland': Feinkost Dallmayr," "Das Wetter" (weather chart), "Der Besondere Tip," and photograph of "Feuchtfröhliche Gaudi ohnegleichen: Isarfloßfahrten" from "Englischer Garten," and photograph "Der Englische Garten ist Europas größte Großstadt-Grünanlage" from "Januar Fasching," "Ludwig Beck," "Medizinische Versorgung," from "Olympiapark," and photograph "Olympiapark: Der Schauplatz der XX." and from "Peterskirche, St. Peter" from *MERIAN live!: München,* pp. 30, 31, 39, 42, 80, 95, 112, 119, and 120.

*Hamburg Tourist Board:* Advertisement, "Tag u. Nacht," from *Hotels und Restaurants 93/94,* Hamburg Das Tor zur Welt.

These acknowledgments continued on page 365, which is an extension of the copyright page.

## CONTRIBUTING WRITERS

**Ulrike Puryear**
Austin, TX
Mrs. Puryear wrote background information, activities, and teacher suggestions for all chapters of the Teacher's Edition.

**Dorothea Bruschke**
Parkway School District
Chesterfield, MO
Mrs. Bruschke wrote activities and teacher suggestions for Chapters 1 and 6 of the Teacher's Edition.

## CONSULTANTS

The consultants conferred on a regular basis with the editorial staff and reviewed all the chapters of the Level 1 Teacher's Edition.

**Dorothea Bruschke**
Parkway School District
Chesterfield, MO

**Diane E. Laumer**
San Marcos High School
San Marcos, TX

**Patrick T. Raven**
School District of Waukesha
Waukesha, WI

**Rolf Schwägermann**
Stuyvesant High School
New York, NY

**Jim Witt**
Grand Junction High School
Grand Junction, CO

## FIELD TEST PARTICIPANTS

**Eva-Marie Adolphi**
Indian Hills Middle School
Sandy, UT

**Connie Allison**
MacArthur High School
Lawton, OK

**Linda Brummet**
Redmond High School
Redmond, WA

**Dennis Bergren**
Hest High School
Madison, WI

**M. Beatrice Brusstar**
Lincoln Northeast High School
Lincoln, NE

**Jane Bungartz**
Southwest High School
Fort Worth, TX

**Devora D. Diller**
Lovejoy High School
Lovejoy, GA

**Margaret Draheim**
Wilson Junior High School
Appleton, WI

**Kay DuBois**
Kennewick High School
Kennewick, WA

**Elfriede A. Gabbert**
Capital High School
Boise, ID

**Petra A. Hansen**
Redmond High School
Redmond, WA

**Christa Hary**
Brien McMahon High School
Norwalk, CT

**Ingrid S. Kinner**
Weaver Education Center
Greensboro, NC

**Diane E. Laumer**
San Marcos High School
San Marcos, TX

**J. Lewinsohn**
Redmond High School
Redmond, WA

**Linnea Maulding**
Fife High School
Tacoma, WA

**Judith A. Nimtz**
Central High School
West Allis, WI

**Jane Reinkordt**
Lincoln Southeast High School
Lincoln, NE

**Elizabeth A. Smith**
Plano Senior High School
Plano, TX

**Elizabeth L. Webb**
Sandy Creek High School
Tyrone, GA

## PROFESSIONAL ESSAYS

*Using Portfolios in the Foreign Language Classroom*
**Jo Anne S. Wilson**
Consultant
Glen Arbor, MI

*Teaching Culture*
**Nancy A. Humbach**
Miami University
Oxford, Ohio

**Dorothea Bruschke**
Parkway School District
Chesterfield, MO

*The Student-Centered Classroom*
**Patrick T. Raven**
School District of Waukesha
Waukesha, WI

*Learning Styles and Multi-Modality Teaching*
**Mary B. McGehee**
Louisiana State University
Baton Rouge, LA

*Higher-Order Thinking Skills*
**Audrey L. Heining-Boynton**
The University of North Carolina at Chapel Hill, NC

## AUTHOR

**George Winkler**
Austin, TX

Mr. Winkler developed the scope and sequence and framework for the chapters, created the basic material, selected realia, and wrote activities.

## CONTRIBUTING WRITERS

**Margrit Meinel Diehl**
Syracuse, NY

Mrs. Diehl wrote activities to practice basic material, functions, grammar, and vocabulary.

**Carolyn Roberts Thompson**
Abilene, TX

Mrs. Thompson was responsible for the selection of realia for readings and for developing reading activities.

## CONSULTANTS

The consultants conferred on a regular basis with the editorial staff and reviewed all the chapters of the Level 1 textbook.

**Maria Beck**
University of North Texas
Denton, TX

**Dorothea Bruschke**
Parkway School District
Chesterfield, MO

**Ingeborg R. McCoy**
Southwest Texas State University
San Marcos, TX

**Patrick T. Raven**
School District of Waukesha
Waukesha, WI

## REVIEWERS

The following educators reviewed one or more chapters of the Pupil's Edition.

**Jerome Baker**
Columbus East High School
Columbus, IN

**Angela Breidenstein**
Robert Lee High School
San Antonio, TX

**Nancy Butt**
Washington and Lee High School
Arlington, VA

**Frank Dietz**
University of Texas at Austin
Austin, TX

**Connie Frank**
John F. Kennedy High School
Sacramento, CA

**Don Goetz**
West High School
Davenport, IA

**Joan Gosenheimer**
Franklin High School
Franklin, WI

**Jacqueline Hastay**
Lyndon Baines Johnson High School
Austin, TX

**Leroy Larson**
John Marshall High School
Rochester, MN

**Diane E. Laumer**
San Marcos High School
San Marcos, TX

**Carol Masters**
Edison High School
Tulsa, OK

**Linnea Maulding**
Fife High School
Tacoma, WA

**Linda Miller**
Craig High School
Janesville, WI

**Doug Mills**
Greensburg Central Catholic High School
Greensburg, PA

**John Scanlan**
Arlington High School
Arlington, OR

**Rolf Schwägermann**
Stuyvesant High School
New York, NY

**Mary Ann Verkamp**
Hamilton South Eastern High School
Indianapolis, IN

**Jim Witt**
Grand Junction High School
Grand Junction, CO

## FIELD TEST PARTICIPANTS

We express our appreciation to the teachers and students who participated in the field test. Their comments were instrumental in the development of this book.

**Eva-Marie Adolphi**
Indian Hills Middle School
Sandy, UT

**Connie Allison**
MacArthur High School
Lawton, OK

**Dennis Bergren**
West High School
Madison, WI

**Linda Brummett**
Redmond High School
Redmond, WA

**M. Beatrice Brusstar**
Lincoln Northeast High School
Lincoln, NE

**Jane Bungartz**
Southwest High School
Fort Worth, TX

**Devora D. Diller**
Lovejoy High School
Lovejoy, GA

**Margaret Draheim**
Wilson Junior High School
Appleton, WI

**Kay DuBois**
Kennewick High School
Kennewick, WA

**Elfriede A. Gabbert**
Capital High School
Boise, ID

**Petra A. Hansen**
Redmond High School
Redmond, WA

**Christa Hary**
Brien McMahon High School
Norwalk, CT

**Ingrid S. Kinner**
Weaver Education Center
Greensboro, NC

**Diane E. Laumer**
San Marcos High School
San Marcos, TX

**J. Lewinsohn**
Redmond High School
Redmond, WA

**Linnea Maulding**
Fife High School
Tacoma, WA

**Judith A. Nimtz**
Central High School
West Allis, WI

**Jane Reinkordt**
Lincoln Southeast High School
Lincoln, NE

**Elizabeth A. Smith**
Plano Senior High School
Plano, TX

**Elizabeth L. Webb**
Sandy Creek High School
Tyrone, GA

# ACKNOWLEDGMENTS

We are very grateful to the German students who participated in our program and are pictured in this textbook. We wish to express our thanks also to the parents who allowed us to photograph these young people in their homes and in other places. There are a number of teachers, school administrators, and merchants whose cooperation and patience made an enormous difference in the quality of these pages; we are grateful to them as well.

## MAIN CHARACTERS

**Brandenburg:** Daniel Hartmann, Handan Hasbolat, Timo Krause, Cordula Nowak, Hannelore Tehrani, Taraneh Tehrani, Constantin Trettler

**Schleswig-Holstein:** Sigried Becker, Marc Duncker, Will Roger Föll, Julianne Grimm, Johan-Michel Menke, Holger Müller, Constanze Russek, Nalan Sönmez

**München:** Benedict Böhm, Veronika Böhm, Mark Ikusz, Marianne Kramel, Stefan Seyboth, Sandra Zlinac

**Baden-Württemberg:** Gesa Grossekathöfer, Cordula von Hinüber, Astrid Junius, Kai Katuric, Oliver Meyer, Darius Schabasian, Gisela Simon, Karl-Heinz Simon

## TEACHERS AND FAMILIES

Cordula and Eduard Böhm, Monika and Eckhard von Hinüber, Anke Kjer-Peters, Heidi Reich, Helena and Herbert Russek, Gisela and Karl-Heinz Simon, Renate and Dieter Sprick, Jutta and Jochen Thassler, Bärbel and Johann Trettler

## SCHOOLS

Bismarck-Gymnasium, Hamburg; Drei Linden Oberschule, Berlin; Ellental-Gymnasium, Bietigheim-Bissingen; Helene-Lange-Gymnasium, Hamburg; Johann-Rist-Gymnasium, Wedel

# TEACHER'S EDITION

## Contents

# Komm mit!

## Come along—to a world of new experiences!

*Komm mit!* offers you the opportunity to learn the language spoken by millions of people in several European countries and around the world. Let's find out about the countries, the people, and the German language.

TEACHING SUGGESTIONS FOR THE VORSCHAU............T64–T71

## Vorschau

## Komm mit nach
## *Brandenburg!*

# KAPITEL 1
## *Wer bist du?*.....16

TEACHING SUGGESTIONS FOR THE
SCHLESWIG–HOLSTEIN LOCATION OPENER..........87A–87B

Komm mit nach

# *Schleswig-Holstein!*

LOCATION FOR KAPITEL 4,5,6.....88

TEACHING SUGGESTIONS FOR KAPITEL 4............91A–91R

KAPITEL 4

## *Alles für die Schule!* . . . . . 92

T14

T15

Komm mit nach

# München!

## KAPITEL 7
### Zu Hause helfen . . . . . 168

T16

## Komm mit nach
# Baden-Württemberg!

## KAPITEL 10
# Kino und Konzerte . . . . 244

T18

# Cultural References

## POINTS OF INTEREST

## RECIPES

# To The Teacher

$S$ ince the early eighties, we have seen significant advances in modern foreign language curriculum practice: (1) a redefinition of the objectives of foreign language study involving a commitment to the development of proficiency in the four skills and in cultural awareness; (2) a recognition of the need for longer sequences of study; (3) a new student-centered approach that redefines the role of the teacher as facilitator and encourages students to take a more active role in their learning; (4) the inclusion of students of all learning abilities.

The new Holt, Rinehart and Winston foreign language programs take into account not only these advances in the field of foreign language education but also the input of teachers and students around the country.

## PRINCIPLES AND PRACTICES

As nations become increasingly interdependent, the need for effective communication and sensitivity to other cultures becomes more important. Today's youth must be culturally and linguistically prepared to participate in a global society. At Holt, Rinehart and Winston, we believe that proficiency in a foreign language is essential to meeting this need.

*The primary goal of the Holt, Rinehart and Winston foreign language programs is to help students develop linguistic proficiency and cultural sensitivity. By interweaving language and culture, our programs seek to broaden students' knowledge of other languages while at the same time deepening their appreciation of other cultures.*

We believe that all students can benefit from foreign language instruction. We recognize that not everyone learns at the same rate or in the same way; nevertheless, we believe that all students should have the opportunity to acquire language proficiency to a degree commensurate with their individual abilities.

*By appealing to a variety of learning styles, the Holt, Rinehart and Winston foreign language programs are designed to accommodate all students.*

We believe that effective foreign language programs should motivate students. Students deserve an answer to the question they often ask, "Why are we doing this?" They need to have goals that are interesting, practical, clearly stated, and attainable.

*The Holt, Rinehart and Winston foreign language programs promote success. They present relevant content in manageable increments that encourage students to attain achievable functional objectives.*

We believe that proficiency in a foreign language is best nurtured by programs that encourage students to think critically and to take risks when expressing themselves in the language. We also recognize that students should strive for accuracy in communication. While it is important that students have a knowledge of the basic structures of the language, it is also important that they go beyond simple manipulation of forms.

*Holt, Rinehart and Winston's foreign language program reflects a careful progression of activities that guides students from comprehensible input of authentic language through structured practice to creative, personalized expression. This progression, accompanied by consistent re-entry and spiraling of functions, vocabulary, and structures, provides students with the tools and the confidence to express themselves in their language.*

Finally, we believe that a complete program of foreign language instruction should take into account the needs of teachers in today's increasingly demanding classrooms.

*At Holt, Rinehart and Winston we have designed programs that offer practical teacher support and provide multiple resources to meet individual learning and teaching styles.*

**T26**

# Using Portfolios in the Foreign Language Classroom

*The promise of portfolios is one of a more realistic and accurate way to assess the process of language teaching and learning.*

A communicative, whole-language approach describes today's foreign language instruction. This approach requires methods of assessment that closely parallel the daily teaching and learning strategies in the proficiency-oriented classroom. We know that language acquisition is a process. Portfolios are process-oriented and provide for authentic assessment of both learning and instruction.

## What Is a Portfolio?

A portfolio is a purposeful, systematic, and organized collection of a student's work. It shows the student's efforts, progress, and achievements for a given period of time, usually a semester or a school year. The portfolio is a tool to assist you in developing a student profile. It may be used as a basis for periodic evaluation, for final grades, for overall evaluation, even for placement. It may also be used to enhance or provide alternatives to traditional assessment measures, such as formal tests, quizzes, class participation, and homework.

## Why Use Portfolios?

Portfolios are of great benefit to both students and teachers, because they

- **Are ongoing and systematic.** A language learner acquires skill in the language by trial and error. A portfolio reflects the real-world process of production, assessment, revision, and reassessment. It parallels the natural rhythm of learning.

- **Offer an incentive to learn.** Students have a vested interest in creating their portfolios because portfolios give them the opportunity to showcase their ongoing efforts and tangible achievements. Students select the work to be included and have a chance to revise, perfect, evaluate, and explain the contents.

- **Are sensitive to individual needs.** There is a wide diversity in the pace and manner of language development. Language learners bring varied abilities to the classroom and do not acquire skills in a uniformly neat and orderly fashion. Portfolios offer a way of personalizing and individualizing assessment that responds to this diversity.

- **Provide documentation of language development.** Language learning is a process. The material in a student portfolio is evidence of student progress in this process. The contents of the portfolio make it easier for you to discuss student progress with the students as well as with parents and others interested in the student's progress.

- **Offer multiple sources of information.** A portfolio presents a way to collect and analyze information from multiple sources that reflect a student's efforts, progress, and achievements in the language. This information gives valuable feedback to both teachers and students that allows them to assess and improve both the teaching and learning processes.

## Portfolio Components

For the foreign language portfolio to be of value, it should include both oral and written work, student self-evaluation, and documentation of teacher observation. For example, a Level One portfolio might contain audio tapes of a student's description of family members or the acting out of an everyday situation, such as shopping for clothing. Writing samples could include a shopping list or labeling of items pictured on a poster or sketch of a classroom setting. Teacher observation should be included in the portfolio, too, perhaps in the form of brief, non-evaluative, anecdotal comments of student performance written on adhesive notes.

## The Oral Component

The oral component of a portfolio might be an audio or video cassette. It may contain both rehearsed and extemporaneous dialogues and monologues. For a rehearsed speaking activity, give a specific communicative task that students can personalize according to their individual interests (for example, ordering a favorite meal in a restaurant).

Rehearsing with other members of the class gives students an opportunity for peer coaching and revision prior to the final recording. For an extemporaneous speaking activity, first acquaint students with some possible topics for discussion or the specific task they will be expected to perform. (For example, tell them they will be asked to discuss a picture showing a sports activity or a restaurant scene.)

### The Written Component

Portfolios offer an excellent opportunity to incorporate process-writing strategies into the foreign language classroom. Evidence of the writing process—documentation of prewriting brainstorming, multiple drafts, and peer comments—should be included along with the finished product.

Involve students in the selection of a writing task. At the beginning levels of learning, the task might include some structured writing in the target language, such as labeling or listing. Evidence of cultural sensitivity can be included in pieces written by the student in English. Keeping a journal in the target language is also a valuable way for students to see progress in their ability to use the written language. Letter-writing is another appropriate way for students to become involved in the writing process. Final drafts of a specific writing assignment could even be displayed on bulletin boards or reproduced in a newsletter.

### Student Self-Evaluation

Students are not only major contributors of material to their portfolios, but they should also be involved in critiquing and evaluating their portfolios as well. It is appropriate that students monitor their own progress; therefore, the process and procedure for student self-evaluation should be considered in planning the contents of the portfolio. Students should work with you and their peers to design the exact format. Self-evaluation encourages them to think about what they are learning (content), how they learn (process), why they are learning (purpose), and where they are going in their learning (goals).

### Teacher Observation

A crucial component of a foreign language portfolio is documentation of teacher observations. Results of these systematic, regular, and ongoing observations are placed in the portfolio only after discussing them with the student. They are not intended to be evaluative, but rather to provide expert-witness feedback on the process of language learning.

With portfolios, you become a distanced observer of student behavior, recording observations with an established set of criteria that has been developed earlier with input from the student. Observation techniques may include the following:

- Jotting notes in a journal to be discussed with the student and then placed in the portfolio
- Using a checklist of observable behaviors such as the willingness to take risks when using the target language, demonstrations of strategic or linguistic competence, and an indication of the degree to which the learner is engaged in the linguistic task

- Making observations on adhesive notes that can be easily placed in folders
- Recording anecdotal comments, during or after class, using a small hand-held voice-activated cassette recorder.

What about subjectivity? The reality of subjectivity is present whenever the human element, however appropriate, is a part of evaluation. Nothing should be placed in a permanent portfolio that cannot be substantiated. Knowledge of the criteria you use in your observation gives students a framework for their performance. You are the expert in the classroom. Your expert observation, with appropriate documentation, utilizes your professional skills in a way that is missing from traditional testing methods.

### How Are Portfolios Evaluated?

The portfolio should reflect the process of student learning over a specific period of time. At the beginning of that time period, determine the criteria by which you will assess the final product and convey them to the students. Make this evaluation a collaborative effort by seeking students' input as you formulate these criteria and your instructional goals.

Students need to understand that evaluation based on a predetermined standard is but one phase of the assessment process; demonstrated effort and growth are just as important. As you consider correctness and accuracy in both oral and written

work, also consider the organization, creativity, and improvement revealed by the student's portfolio over the time period. The portfolio provides a way to monitor the growth of a student's knowledge, skills, and attitudes. The contents should show the student's efforts and progress, as well as achievements.

## How to Implement Portfolios

Teacher/teacher collaboration is as important to the implementation of portfolios as teacher/student collaboration. Confer with your colleagues to determine the answers to questions such as the following: What kinds of information do you want to see in the student portfolio? How will the information be presented? What is the purpose of the portfolio? Will it be used for grading, placement, or a combination of both? What are the criteria for evaluating the portfolio? Answers to these and other questions can help create a strong foreign language department and foster a departmental cohesiveness and consistency that will ultimately benefit the students.

## The Promise of Portfolios

As teachers and students work together to develop portfolios and to decide how they will be used, there is a high degree of student involvement. This involvement promises renewed student enthusiasm for learning and improved achievement. As students compare portfolio pieces done early in the year with work produced later, they can take pride in their progress as well as reassess their motivation and work habits.

Portfolios also provide a framework for periodic assessment of teaching strategies, programs, and instruction. They offer schools a tool to help solve the problem of vertical articulation and accurate student placement. The promise of portfolios is one of a more realistic and accurate way to assess the process of language teaching and learning that is congruent with the strategies that should be used in the proficiency-oriented classroom.

*Komm mit!* supports the *use of portfolios* in the following ways:

**The Pupil's Edition**
▶ Includes numerous oral and written activities that can be easily adapted for student portfolios.

**The Teacher's Edition**
▶ Identifies in the *Portfolio Assessment* feature activities that may serve as portfolio items.

**The Ancillary Program**
▶ Includes in the *Assessment Guide* criteria for evaluating portfolios.

# Teaching Culture

*We must integrate culture and language in a way that encourages curiosity, stimulates analysis, and teaches students to hypothesize.*

Ask students what they like best about studying a foreign language. Chances are that learning about culture, the way people live, is one of their favorite aspects. Years after language study has ended, adults remember with fondness the customs of the target culture, even pictures in their language textbooks. It is this interest in the people and their way of life that is the great motivator and helps us sustain students' interest in language study.

That interest in other people mandates an integration of culture and language. We must integrate culture and language in a way that encourages curiosity, stimulates analysis, and teaches students to hypothesize and seek answers to questions about the people whose language they are studying. Teaching isolated facts about how people in other cultures live is not enough. This information is soon dated and quickly forgotten. We must attempt to go a step beyond and teach students that all behavior, values, and traditions exist because of certain aspects of history, geography, and socio-economic conditions.

There are many ways to help students become culturally knowledgeable, and to assist them in developing an awareness of differences and similarities between the target culture and their own. Two of these approaches involve critical thinking, that is, trying to find reasons for a certain behavior through observation and analysis, and relating these observations to larger cultural patterns.

## First Approach: Questioning

The first approach involves *questioning* as the key strategy. At the earliest stages of language learning, students learn ways to greet peers, elders, strangers, as well as the use of **du, ihr,** and **Sie.** Students need to consider questions such as: How do German-speaking people greet each other? Are there different levels of formality? Who initiates a handshake? What's considered a good handshake? Each of these questions leads students to think about the values that are expressed through words and gestures. They start to "feel" the other culture, and at the same time, understand how much of their own behavior is rooted in their cultural background.

Magazines, newspapers, advertisements, and television commercials are all excellent sources of cultural material. For example, browsing through a German magazine, one finds an extraordinary number of advertisements for health-related products. Could this indicate a great interest in staying healthy? To learn about customs involving health, reading advertisements can be followed up with viewing videos and films, or by interviewing native speakers or people who have lived in German-speaking countries. Students might want to find answers to questions such as: "How do Germans treat a cold? What is their attitude toward fresh air? Toward exercise?" This type of questioning might lead students to discover that some of the popular leisure-time activities, such as **einen Spaziergang machen** or **eine Wanderung machen,** are related to health consciousness.

An advertisement for a refrigerator or a picture of a German kitchen can provide an insight into practices of shopping for food. Students first need to think about the refrigerator at home, take an inventory of what is kept in it, and consider when and where their family shops. Next, students should look closely at a German refrigerator. What is its size? What could that mean? (Smaller refrigerators might mean that shopping takes place more often, stores are within walking distance, and people eat more fresh foods.)

Food wrappers and containers also provide cultural insight. For example, in German-speaking countries, bottled water is preferred to tap water even though tap water is safe to drink in most places. Why, then, is the rather expensive bottled water still preferred? Is it a tradition stemming from a time when tap water was not pure? Does it relate to the Germans' fondness of "taking the waters," i.e., drinking fresh spring water at a spa?

## Second Approach: Associating Words with Images

The second approach for developing cultural understanding involves *forming associations of words with the cultural images they suggest.* Language and culture are so closely related that one might actually say that language is culture. Most words, especially nouns, carry a cultural connotation. Knowing the literal equivalent of a word in another language is of little use to students in understanding this connotation. For example, **Freund** cannot be translated simply as *friend,* **Brot** as *bread,* or **Straße** as *street.* The German word **Straße,** for instance, carries with it such images as people walking, sitting in a sidewalk café, riding bicycles, or shopping in specialty stores, and cars parked partly over the curb amid dense traffic. There is also the image of **Fußgängerzone,** a street for pedestrians only.

When students have acquired some sense of the cultural connotation of words—not only through explanations but, more importantly, through observation of visual images—they start to discover the larger underlying cultural themes, or what is often called deep culture.

These larger cultural themes serve as organizing categories into which individual cultural phenomena fit to form a pattern. Students might discover, for example, that Germans, because they live in much more crowded conditions, have a great need for privacy (cultural theme), as reflected in such phenomena as closed doors, fences or walls around property, and shutters on windows. Students might also discover that love of nature and the outdoors is an important cultural theme as indicated by such phenomena as flower boxes and planters in public places, well-kept public parks in every town, and people going for a walk or hiking.

As we teach culture, students learn to recognize elements not only of the target culture but also of their American cultural heritage. They see how elements of culture reflect larger themes or patterns. Learning what makes us Americans and how that information relates to other people throughout the world can be an exciting discovery for a young person.

As language teachers, we are able to facilitate this discovery of our similarities with others as well as our differences. We do not encourage value judgments about others and their culture, nor do we recommend adopting other ways. We simply say to students, "Other ways exist. They exist, just as our ways exist, due to our history, geography, and what our ancestors have passed on to us through traditions and values."

---

*Komm mit!* develops *cultural understanding and cultural awareness* in the following ways:

**The Pupil's Edition**

▶ Informs students about daily life in German-speaking countries through culture notes.

▶ Provides deeper insight into cultural phenomena through personal interviews in the **Landeskunde** section.

▶ Helps students associate language and its cultural connotations through authentic art and photos.

**The Teacher's Edition**

▶ Provides additional cultural and language notes.

▶ Suggests critical thinking strategies that encourage students to hypothesize, analyze, and discover larger underlying cultural themes.

**The Ancillary Program**

▶ Includes realia that develops cultural insight by serving as catalyst for questioning and discovery.

▶ Offers activities that require students to compare and contrast cultures, as well as to find reasons for certain behavior.

# Implementing Komm mit! in the Middle Grades

**R**emember that planning a variety of tactile, kinesthetic, and visual activities that invite participation will help students be successful.

Students in the middle grades are at different levels of cognitive development than are high school and elementary students. In addition, middle school students are at markedly different levels of development from one another and have many different learning styles. Many sixth and seventh graders, especially, are tactile and kinesthetic, with a particular need for opportunities for movement. Seventh and eighth graders are more capable of formal cognitive operations and are increasingly preoccupied with social issues. They need and demand to know that what they learn in school relates to their lives. For all middle school students, self-esteem can be particularly fragile because of the many developmental changes they are undergoing.

The wide variety of activities in the various components of *Komm mit!* Level 1 enables teachers to adapt the many materials to their students' needs.

## Scheduling

*Komm mit!* Level 1 can best be taught as a two-year program in the middle grades. Covering six chapters and two Location Openers each year allows five to six weeks for each chapter. This scheduling affords ample time to include varied activities that the diversity of the students demands.

## Instruction

A number of proposals for teaching **Kapitel 3** are presented below as examples of activities especially well suited to middle school students. Many of these suggestions are either directly excerpted or adapted from those in the *Teacher's Edition* and ancillary materials. As you plan your own lessons, remember that planning a variety of tactile, kinesthetic, and visual activities that invite participation will help students be successful. Remember, too, that varying the type of activity often within each class and offering students choices will augment enthusiasm and motivation.

## Los geht's!

Visual and concrete learners enjoy and learn from the videos. Show them the video segment **Los geht's!** without sound and ask them to watch for things that seem to be different in Germany.

- After briefly discussing what they think happened in the segment, write the title **Nach der Schule** on the board, and then draw three sets of spokes branching from the themes **Was wir tun, Was wir essen,** and **Was wir trinken.** Ask the students in English about what they like to do after school, and put their answers into German in the word webs on the board. Creating the web personalizes the material, makes it visual, and also helps students anticipate what they are about to see and hear as the video is presented a second time.
- As suggested on p. 63H, the activities that follow **Los geht's!** on p. 68 can be completed in cooperative learning groups after viewing the video.
- Occasionally, have groups briefly speculate about what will happen in the **Fortsetzung** before showing it. This activity is fun and encourages the students to anticipate what they may see and hear.

## Erste Stufe

Before beginning the **Erste Stufe,** offer students a concrete, hands-on project. For example, share with them a list of foods and beverages that you would like to have as props in the classroom for presentations and role-playing, and have them sign up to make the life-size prop of their choice, using chenille stems, construction paper, fabric, papier-maché, plastic cups, and more. Have them make more than one of whatever they choose so that you will have props for all of the cooperative learning groups.

- To introduce the **Wortschatz** on p. 71, give each group a basket full of props, and then use TPR as suggested on p. 63J. Call on one student from each group as you request each prop.
- The **möchte**-forms are introduced on p. 71; Activity 11 on p. 72 provides a brief opportunity to practice them. Another opportunity particularly suited to visual, kinesthetic, and social learners is a team game requiring dry erase boards, dry erase markers preferably of the low odor variety, and rags. Show a glass of mineral water and ask **Was möchtet ihr trinken?** The cooperative learning groups work silently as teams to write **Wir möchten ein Glas Mineralwasser, bitte,** or **Wir möchten ein Mine-**

**ralwasser.** The student in each group who has possession of the board when the question is given should write the first word of an appropriate response and then pass the materials to the next person. That person can choose either to correct the one word that has been written or to add the word that should follow. The third student, in turn, may choose either to correct a word or to add the word that should follow. Allow a designated amount of time to pass, and then award each group a point for each word correctly written.

- Have students use the props they made to do Activity 12 on p. 72.
- The students very much enjoy seeing and hearing kids close to their own ages in the **Landeskunde** segments, and the activities in the Activity Masters define clear tasks for them to accomplish as they listen.

## Zweite Stufe

In the **Zweite Stufe**, students learn to describe bedrooms and the furniture in them; personalize the material by asking students how they would like to furnish their bedrooms if money were no object.

- Presenting the grammar introduced on p. 75 and elsewhere in the book in the way suggested on p. 63L encourages students to draw their own inferences, and this process promotes self-esteem as it encourages students to use higher-order thinking skills and empowers them to construct their own knowledge.
- Many learners in the middle grades especially enjoy games such as the opposites game suggested on p. 63M which involves movement.
- A number of activities present-

ed in the teacher's suggestions, such as Activitiy 15 on p. 63L, Activity 18 on p. 63M, and the Suggested Project on p. 63E, are suitable for middle school students.

## Dritte Stufe

In the **Dritte Stufe,** students learn to describe people and talk about family members. To introduce the new vocabulary, talk about and show pictures of your own family as you put the words for relations onto the board in a family tree. Instead of simply using chalk, color code the new words according to whether they refer to male or female relations.

- Have students work in groups to ask one another about their families using possessives, pronouns, and the new vocabulary for describing people. To help students organize their notes on what they learn from one another, prepare a grid like the one proposed in Group Work suggestion for Activity 20 on p. 63O.

- The numbers 21-100 are introduced on p. 79, and p. 63O suggests playing Bingo. Model the game by playing as a class, then break into small groups to allow more students to be callers and thus practice pronouncing the new vocabulary.
- Seventh grade students especially enjoy playing Buzz when they can stand at their desks until they are eliminated, and addition games such as the one on p. 63O can also be good fun.
- A number of activities presented in the teacher's suggestions, such as **Anwendung 8c** on p. 85, Activity 20, *Chapter Resources Book 1*, p. 146, the TPR game and the game of *Twenty Questions* on p. 63P, are suitable for the middle school students.

*Komm mit!* addresses the *needs of learners in the middle grades* in the following ways:

### The Pupil's Edition
▶ Offers a sequence of activities in each **Stufe** that guides students from structure practice to open-ended activities promoting personalized, meaningful expression.
▶ Provides tips in the **Lerntrick** and **Lesetrick** features that help students become autonomous learners.
▶ Includes a **Zum Lesen** section at the end of each chapter that offers prereading, reading, and postreading activities to help students develop reading strategies.
▶ Features many photos and drawings.

### The Teacher's Edition
▶ Proposes a variety of activities that target auditory, kinesthetic, tactile, and visual learners; features many cooperative learning activities.
▶ Offers **Family Link** suggestions that younger students enjoy.
▶ Presents game ideas at the beginning of each chapter that can easily be made active and can often be used just as well with other chapters.

### The Ancillary Program
▶ The extensive ancillary program provides both extensive auditory and visual exposure to the language and many activities that help learners simplify complex learning tasks.

T33

# Learning Styles and Multi-Modality Teaching

*I*ncorporating a greater variety of teaching and learning activities to accommodate the learning styles of all students can make the difference between struggle and pleasure in foreign language learning.

The larger and broader population of students who are enrolling in foreign language classes brings a new challenge to foreign language educators, calling forth an evolution in teaching methods to enhance learning for all our students. Educational experts now recognize that every student has a preferred sense for learning and retrieving information: visual, auditory, or kinesthetic. Incorporating a greater variety of teaching and learning activities to accommodate the learning styles of all students can make the difference between struggle and pleasure in foreign language learning.

## Accommodating Different Learning Styles

A modified arrangement of the classroom is one way to provide more effective and more enjoyable learning for all students. Rows of chairs and desks must give way at times to circles, semicircles, or small clusters. Students may be grouped in fours or in pairs for small group work, cooperative work, or peer teaching. It is important to find a balance of arrangements, thereby providing the most comfort in varied situations.

Since auditory, kinesthetic, and visual learners will be present in the class, and also because every student's learning will be enhanced by a multi-sensory approach, lessons must be directed toward all three learning styles. Any language lesson content may be presented auditorially, visually, and kinesthetically.

Visual presentations and practice may include the chalkboard, charts, posters, television, overhead projectors, books, magazines, picture diagrams, flash cards, bulletin boards, films, slides, or videos. Visual learners need to see what they are to learn. Lest the teacher think he or she will never have the time to prepare all those visuals, Dickel and Slak (1983) found that visual aids generated by students are more effective than ready-made ones.

Auditory presentations and practice may include stating aloud the requirements of the lesson, oral questions and answers, paired or group work on a progression of oral exercises from repetition to communication, tapes, CDs, dialogues, and role-playing. Jingles, catchy stories, and memory devices using songs and rhymes are good learning aids. Having students record themselves and then listen as they play back the cassette allows them to practice in the auditory mode.

Kinesthetic presentations entail the students' use of manipulatives, chart materials, gestures, signals, typing, songs, games, and role-playing. These lead the students to associate sentence constructions with meaningful movements.

## A Sample Lesson Using Multi-Modality Teaching

A multi-sensory presentation on greetings might proceed as follows. As the teacher begins oral presentation of greetings and introductions, he or she simultaneously shows the written forms on transparencies, with the formal expressions marked with an adult's hat, and the informal expressions marked with a baseball cap. The teacher then distributes cards with the hat and cap symbols representing the formal or informal expressions. As the students hear taped mini-dialogues, they hold up the appropriate card to indicate whether the dialogues are formal or informal. On the next listening, the students repeat the sentences they hear. A longer taped dialogue follows, allowing students to hear the new expressions a number of times. The students next write from dictation several sentences containing the new expressions. They may work in pairs, correcting each other's work as they "test" their own understanding of the lesson at hand. Finally, students respond to simple questions using the appropriate formal and informal responses cued by the cards they hold.

For additional kinesthetic input, members of the class come to the front of the room, each holding a hat or cap symbol. As the teacher calls out situations, the students play the roles, using gestures and props appropriate to the age group they are portraying. Non-cued, communicative role-playing

with props further enables the students to "feel" the differences between formal and informal expressions.

## Helping Students Learn How to Use Their Preferred Mode

Since we require students to perform in all language skills, part of the assistance we must render is to help them develop strategies within their preferred learning modes to carry out an assignment in another mode. For example, visual students hear the teacher assign an oral exercise and visualize what they must do. They must see themselves carrying out the assignment, in effect watching themselves as if there were a movie going on in their heads. Only then can they also hear themselves saying the right things. Thus, this assignment will be much easier for the visual learners who have been taught this process, if they have not already figured it out for themselves. Likewise, true auditory students, confronted with a reading/writing assignment, must talk themselves through it, converting the entire process into sound as they plan and prepare their work. Kinesthetic students presented with a visual or auditory task must first break the assignment into tasks and then work their way through them.

Students who experience difficulty because of a strong preference for one mode of learning are often unaware of the degree of their preference. In working with these students, I prefer the simple and direct assessment of learning styles offered by Richard Bandler and John Grinder in their book *Frogs into Princes,* which allows the teacher and student to quickly determine how the student learns. In an interview with the

student, I follow the assessment with certain specific recommendations of techniques to make the student's study time more effective.

It is important to note here that teaching students to maximize their study does not require that the teacher give each student an individualized assignment. It does require that each student who needs it be taught how to prepare the assignment using his or her own talents and strengths. This communication

between teacher and student, combined with teaching techniques that reinforce learning in all modes, can only maximize pleasure and success in learning a foreign language.

## References

Dickel, M.J. and S. Sleek. "Imaging Vividness and Memory for Verbal Material." *Journal of Mental Imagery 7*, i(1983):121-6

Bandler, Richard, and John Grinder. *Frogs into Princes,* Real People Press, Moab, Utah. 1978

*Komm mit!* accommodates *different learning styles* in the following ways:

**The Pupil's Edition**
▶ Presents basic material in video, audio, and printed format.
▶ Includes role-playing activities and a variety of multi-modality activities.

**The Teacher's Edition**
▶ Provides suggested activities for auditory, visual, and kinesthetic learners.
▶ Offers Total Physical Response activities.

**The Ancillary Program**
▶ Meets individual needs of students with additional reinforcement activities in a variety of modes.

# Higher-Order Thinking Skills

*I*ntroduce students to the life skills they need to become successful, productive citizens in our society.

Our profession loves acronyms! TPR, ALM, OBI, and now the HOTS! HOTS stands for **h**igher-**o**rder **t**hinking **s**kills. These thinking skills help our students listen, speak, read, write, and learn about culture in a creative, meaningful way, while providing them with necessary life skills.

## What Are Higher-Order Thinking Skills?

Higher-order thinking skills are not a new phenomenon on the educational scene. In 1956, Benjamin Bloom published a book that listed a taxonomy of educational objectives in the form of a pyramid similar to the one in the following illustration:

**Bloom's Taxonomy of Educational Objectives**

Evaluation
Synthesis
Analysis
Application
Comprehension
Knowledge

**Knowledge** is the simplest level of educational objectives, and is not considered a higher-order thinking skill. It requires the learner to remember information without having to fully understand it. Tasks that students perform to demonstrate knowledge are recalling, identifying, recognizing, citing, labeling, listing, reciting, and stating.

**Comprehension** is not considered a higher-order thinking skill either. Learners demonstrate comprehension when they paraphrase, describe, summarize, illustrate, restate, or translate.

Foreign language teachers tend to focus the most on knowledge and comprehension. The tasks performed at these levels are important because they provide a solid foundation for the more complex tasks at the higher levels of Bloom's pyramid. However, offering our students the opportunity to perform at still higher cognitive levels provides them with more meaningful contexts in which to use the target language.

When teachers incorporate **application, analysis, synthesis,** and **evaluation** as objectives, they allow students to utilize **higher-order thinking skills.**

**Application** involves solving, transforming, determining, demonstrating, and preparing.

**Analysis** includes classifying, comparing, making associations, verifying, seeing cause and effect relationships, and determining sequences, patterns, and consequences.

**Synthesis** requires generalizing, predicting, imagining, creating, making inferences, hypothesizing, making decisions, and drawing conclusions.

Finally, **evaluation** involves assessing, persuading, determining value, judging, validating, and solving problems.

Most foreign language classes focus little on higher-order thinking skills. Some foreign language educators mistakenly think that all higher-order thinking skills require an advanced level of language ability. Not so! Students can demonstrate these skills by using very simple language available even to beginning students. Also, higher-order thinking tasks about the target culture or language can be conducted in English. The use of some English in the foreign language classroom to utilize higher cognitive skills does not jeopardize progress in the target language.

Higher-order thinking skills prepare our students for more than using a foreign language. They introduce students to the life skills they need to become successful, productive citizens in our society. When we think about it, that *is* the underlying purpose of education.

## Why Teach Higher-Order Thinking Skills?

There is already so much to cover and so little time that some teachers may question the worth of adding this type of activities to an already full schedule. Yet we know from experience that simply "covering" the material does not help our students acquire another language.

BY AUDREY L. HEINING-BOYNTON

Incorporating higher-order thinking skills in the foreign language classroom can help guide students toward language acquisition by providing meaningful experiences in a setting that can often feel artificial.

Also, we now know that employing higher-order thinking skills assists all students, including those who are at risk of failing. In the past, we felt that at-risk students were incapable of higher-order thinking, but we have since discovered that we have been denying them the opportunity to experience what they are capable of doing and what they need to do in order to be successful adults.

### Sample Activities Employing Higher-Order Thinking Skills

There are no limitations to incorporating higher-order thinking skills into the foreign language classroom. What follows are a few sample activities, some of which you may already be familiar with. Use *your* higher-order thinking skills to develop other possibilities!

### Listening

**HOTS:** Analysis
**Tasks:** Patterning and sequencing
**Vocabulary Needed:** Three colors
**Materials Required:** Three colored-paper squares for each student

After reviewing the colors, call out a pattern of colors and have the students show their comprehension by arranging their colored pieces of paper from left to right in the order you give. Then have them finish the pattern for you. For example, you say: **rot, grün, blau, rot, grün, blau, rot, grün,...** now what color follows? And then what color?

This is not only a HOTS activity; it also crosses disciplines. It reviews the mathematical concept of patterning and sequencing. You can have the students form patterns and sequences using any type of vocabulary.

### Reading

**HOTS:** Synthesis
**Tasks:** Hypothesizing and imagining
**Vocabulary Needed:** Determined by level of students
**Materials Required:** Legend or short story
After the students have read the first part of the story, have them imagine how the story would end based on the values of the target culture.

### Speaking

**HOTS:** Evaluation
**Tasks:** Assessing and determining value
**Vocabulary Needed:** Numbers 0-25, five objects students would need for school
**Materials Required:** Visuals of five school-related objects with prices beneath them

Tell students that they each have twenty-five dollars to spend on back-to-school needs. They each need to tell you what they would buy with their money.

### Writing

**HOTS:** Analysis
**Tasks:** Classifying
**Vocabulary Needed:** Leisure activities
**Materials Required:** Drawings of leisure activities on a handout

From the list of activities they have before them, students should write the ones that they like to do on the weekend. Then they should write those that a family member likes to do. Finally, students should write a comparison of the two lists.

### Commitment to Higher-Order Thinking Skills

Teaching higher-order thinking skills takes no extra time from classroom instruction since language skills are reinforced during thinking skills activities. What teaching higher-order thinking skills does require of teachers is a commitment to classroom activities that go beyond the knowledge/comprehension level. Having students name objects and recite verb forms is not enough. Employing HOTS gives students the opportunity to experience a second language as a useful device for meaningful communication.

*Komm mit!* encourages *higher-order thinking* in the following ways:

**The Pupil's Edition**
▶ Develops higher-order thinking skills through a variety of activities.

**The Teacher's Edition**
▶ Includes the feature *Thinking Critically* that requires students to draw inferences, compare and contrast, evaluate, and synthesize.

**The Ancillary Program**
▶ Incorporates higher-order thinking skills in activities that help students use the language in a creative, meaningful way.

# Professional References

The Professional References section provides you with information about many resources that can enrich your German class. Included are addresses of German government and tourist offices, pen pal organizations, subscription agencies, and many others. Since addresses change frequently, you may want to verify them before you send your requests.

## PEN PAL ORGANIZATIONS

The Student Letter Exchange will arrange pen pals for your students. For the names of other pen pal groups, contact your local chapter of AATG. There are fees involved, so be sure to write for information.

**Student Letter Exchange**
630 Third Avenue
New York, NY 10017
(212) 557-3312

## EMBASSIES AND CONSULATES

**Embassy of the Federal Republic of Germany**
4645 Reservoir Rd. N.W.
Washington, D.C. 20007-1998
(202) 298-4000

**Consulate General of the Federal Republic of Germany**
460 Park Avenue
New York, NY 10022
(212) 308-8700
*(also in Atlanta, Boston, Chicago, Detroit, Houston, Los Angeles, San Francisco, Seattle)*

**Embassy of Austria**
3524 International Court N.W.
Washington, D.C. 20008
(202) 895-6700

**Austrian Consulate General**
950 Third Avenue
New York, NY 10022
(212) 737-6400
*(also in Los Angeles and Chicago)*

## CULTURAL AGENCIES

For historic and tourist information and audiovisual materials relating to Austria, contact:

**Austrian Institute**
11 East 52nd Street
New York, NY 10022
(212) 759-5165

Material on political matters is available from **Bundeszentrale für politische Bildung,** a German federal agency.

**Bundeszentrale für politische Bildung**
Berliner Freiheit 7
53111 Bonn, GERMANY
(0228) 5150

For free political, cultural, and statistical information, films, and videos, contact:

**German Information Center**
950 Third Avenue
New York, NY 10022
(212) 888-9840

For various materials and information about special events your classes might attend, contact the **Goethe Institut** nearest you. For regional locations, contact:
**Goethe Haus, German Cultural Center**
1014 Fifth Avenue
New York, NY 10028
(212) 439-8700

The **Institut für Auslandsbeziehungen** provides cultural information to foreigners. The institute offers books and periodicals on a limited basis as well as a variety of two- and three-week professional seminars which allow educators to learn about the people, education, history, and culture of German-speaking countries.

**Institut für Auslandsbeziehungen**
Charlottenplatz 17
70173 Stuttgart, GERMANY
(0711) 22250

**Inter Nationes**, a nonprofit German organization for promoting international relations, supplies material on all aspects of life in Germany (literature, posters magazines, press releases, films, slides, audio and video tapes, records) to educational institutions and organizations abroad.

**Inter Nationes**
Kennedyallee 91-103
53175 Bonn, GERMANY
(0228) 8800

## TOURIST BUREAUS

Write to the following tourist offices for travel information and brochures.

**German National Tourist Office**
122 East 42nd St. 52nd Floor
New York, NY 10168
(212) 661-7200
*(also in Chicago and San Francisco)*

**Deutsche Zentrale für Tourismus e.V.**
Beethovenstraße 69
60325 Frankfurt, GERMANY
(0611) 75720

## PROFESSIONAL ORGANIZATIONS

The two major organizations for German teachers at the secondary school level are:

**American Council on the Teaching of Foreign Languages (ACTFL)**
6 Executive Plaza
Yonkers, NY 10701
(914) 963-8830

**American Association of Teachers of German (AATG)**
112 Haddontowne Court
Suite 104
Cherry Hill, NJ 08034
(609) 795-5553

## PERIODICALS

Listed below are some periodicals published in German. For the names of other German magazines and periodicals contact a subscription agency.

**Deutschland-Nachrichten**, a weekly newsletter available in both German and English, is published by the German Information Center *(see address under Cultural Agencies)*.

**Goethe Haus** *(see address under Cultural Agencies)* publishes **Treffpunkt Deutsch**, a magazine of information, bibliographies, and ideas for teachers.

**Bundeszentrale für politische Bildung** *(see address under Cultural Agencies)* publishes **Politische Zeitung (PZ)**, a quarterly magazine covering issues of social interest.
The Austrian Press and Information Service publishes a monthly newsletter. Write to:
**Austrian Information**
3524 International Court N.W.
Washington, D.C. 20008

**Juma** classroom magazine is a free publication to which you can subscribe. You can order multiple copies.

**Redaktion Juma**
Frankfurter Straße 128
51065 Köln, GERMANY
(0221) 693061

## SUBSCRIPTION SERVICES

German magazines can be obtained through subscription agencies in the United States. The following companies are among the many which can provide your school with subscriptions:

**EBSCO Subscription Services**
P.O. Box 1943
Birmingham, AL 35201-1943
(205) 991-6600

**Continental Book Company**
8000 Cooper Ave. Bldg. 29
Glendale, NY 11385
(718) 326-0560

## MISCELLANEOUS

**(ADAC) Allgemeiner Deutscher Automobil Club**
Am Westpark 8
81373 München, GERMANY
(089) 76760

For students who want to find a summer job in Germany, write to:

**Zentralstelle für Arbeitsvermittlung**
Dienststelle 2122
Postfach 170545
60079 Frankfurt, GERMANY
(069) 71110
*(Applicants must have a good knowledge of German.)*

For international student passes and other student services contact:

**CIEE Student Travel Services**
205 E. 42nd Street
New York, NY 10017
(212) 661-1414
*(has branch offices in several other large cities)*

# Scope and Sequence: German Level 1

**VORSCHAU**
- Das Alphabet
- Wie heißt du?
- Im Klassenzimmer
- Die Zahlen von 0 bis 20

**KAPITEL 1   WER BIST DU?**

**Functions:**
- Saying hello and goodbye
- Asking someone's name and giving yours
- Asking who someone is
- Talking about places of origin
- Talking about how someone gets to school

**Grammar:**
- Forming questions
- Definite articles **der, die, das**
- Subject pronouns and **sein**

**Culture:**
- Greetings
- Using **der** and **die** in front of people's names
- Map of German states and capitals
- **Wie kommst du zur Schule?**

**Re-entry:**
- Asking someone's name
- Numbers 0-20
- Geography of German-speaking countries

**KAPITEL 2   SPIEL UND SPASS**

**Functions:**
- Talking about interests
- Expressing likes and dislikes
- Saying when you do various activities
- Asking for an opinion and expressing yours
- Agreeing and disagreeing

**Grammar:**
- The singular subject pronouns and present tense verb endings
- The plural subject pronouns and verb endings
- The present tense of verbs
- Inversion of time elements
- Verbs with stems ending in **d, t, n,** or **-eln**

**Culture:**
- Formal and informal address
- **Was machst du in deiner Freizeit?**
- German weekly planner

**Re-entry:**
- Question formation
- Greetings
- Expressions **stimmt/stimmt nicht** used in a new context

**KAPITEL 3   KOMM MIT NACH HAUSE!**

**Functions:**
- Talking about where you and others live
- Offering something to eat and drink and responding to an offer
- Saying please, thank you, and you're welcome
- Describing a room
- Talking about and describing family members
- Describing people

**Grammar:**
- The **möchte**-forms
- Indefinite articles **ein, eine**
- The pronouns **er, sie, es,** and **sie**
- The possessive adjectives **mein, dein, sein,** and **ihr**

**Culture:**
- The German preference for **Mineralwasser**
- **Wo wohnst du?**

**Re-entry:**
- Definite articles **der, die, das**
- Asking someone's name and age
- Asking who someone is
- Talking about interests

**KAPITEL 4   ALLES FÜR DIE SCHULE!**

**Functions:**
- Talking about class schedules
- Using a schedule to talk about time
- Sequencing events
- Expressing likes, dislikes, and favorites
- Responding to good news and bad news
- Talking about prices
- Pointing things out

**Grammar:**
- The verb **haben**
- Usings **Lieblings-**
- Noun plurals

**Culture:**
- The German school day
- 24-hour time system
- The German grading system
- **Was sind deine Lieblingsfächer?**
- German currency

**Re-entry:**
- Numbers
- Likes and dislikes: **gern**
- Degrees of enthusiasm
- The pronouns **er, sie, es,** and **sie**

**KAPITEL 5   KLAMOTTEN KAUFEN**

**Functions:**
- Expressing wishes when shopping
- Commenting on and describing clothes
- Giving compliments and responding to them
- Talking about trying on clothes

**Grammar:**
- Definite and indefinite articles in the accusative case
- The verb **gefallen**
- Direct object pronouns
- Separable prefix verbs
- Stem-changing verbs **nehmen** and **aussehen**

**Culture:**
- Exchange rates
- German store hours
- German clothing sizes
- **Welche Klamotten sind „in"?**

**Re-entry:**
- Numbers and prices
- Colors
- Pointing things out
- Expressing likes and dislikes
- Asking for and expressing opinions
- The verb **aussehen**

**KAPITEL 6   PLÄNE MACHEN**

**Functions:**
- Starting a conversation
- Telling time and talking about when you do things
- Making plans
- Ordering food and beverages
- Talking about how something tastes
- Paying the check

**Grammar:**
- The verb **wollen**
- The stem-changing verb **essen**

**Culture:**
- Clocks on public buildings
- **Was machst du in deiner Freizeit?**
- Tipping in Germany

**Re-entry:**
- Expressing time when referring to schedules
- Vocabulary: School and freetime activities
- Inversion of time elements
- Sequencing events
- Accusative case
- The verb **nehmen**
- Using **möchte** to order food

## KAPITEL 7   ZU HAUSE HELFEN

**Functions:**
- Extending and responding to an invitation
- Talking about how often you do things
- Offering help and explaining what to do
- Talking about the weather

**Grammar:**
- The modals **müssen** and **können**
- The separable prefix verb **abräumen**
- The accusative pronouns
- Using present tense to refer to the future

**Culture:**
- **Was tust du für die Umwelt?**
- German weather map and weather report
- Weather in German-speaking countries

**Re-entry:**
- Separable prefix verbs
- Time clauses
- Vocabulary: Free-time activities
- Using numbers in a new context, temperature

## KAPITEL 8   EINKAUFEN GEHEN

**Functions:**
- Asking what you should do
- Telling someone what to do
- Talking about quantities
- Saying you want something else
- Giving reasons
- Saying where you were and what you bought

**Grammar:**
- The modal **sollen**
- The **du**-commands
- The conjunctions **weil** and **denn**
- The past tense of **sein**

**Culture:**
- Specialty shops and markets
- **Was machst du für andere Leute?**
- Weights and measures
- German advertisements

**Re-entry:**
- The **möchte**-forms
- Numbers used in a new context, weights and measures
- Responding to invitations
- Vocabulary: Activities
- Vocabulary: Household chores

## KAPITEL 9   AMERIKANER IN MÜNCHEN

**Functions:**
- Talking about where something is located
- Asking for and giving directions
- Talking about what there is to eat and drink
- Saying you do/don't want more
- Expressing opinions

**Grammar:**
- The verb **wissen**
- The verb **fahren**
- The formal commands with **Sie**
- The phrase **es gibt**
- Using **kein**
- The conjunction **daß**

**Culture:**
- The German **Innenstadt**
- **Was ißt du gern?**
- Map of a German neighborhood
- **Imbißstube** menu
- **Leberkäs**

**Re-entry:**
- Vocabulary: Types of stores
- **Du**-commands
- Vocabulary: Food items
- Indefinite articles: accusative case

## KAPITEL 10   KINO UND KONZERTE

**Functions:**
- Expressing likes and dislikes
- Expressing familiarity
- Expressing preferences and favorites
- Talking about what you did in your free time

**Grammar:**
- The verb **mögen**
- The verb **kennen**
- The stem-changing verb **sehen**
- The phrase **sprechen über**
- The stem-changing verbs **lesen** and **sprechen**

**Culture:**
- The German movie rating system
- A German pop chart
- German movie ads
- **Welche kulturellen Veranstaltungen besuchst du?**
- German upcoming events poster
- German best-seller lists
- German video-hits list
- Popular German novels

**Re-entry:**
- Expressing likes and dislikes
- The verb **wissen**
- The stem-changing verb **aussehen**
- Vocabulary: Activities
- The stem-changing verbs **nehmen** and **essen**
- Talking about when you do things

## KAPITEL 11   DER GEBURTSTAG

**Functions:**
- Using the telephone in Germany
- Inviting someone to a party
- Talking about birthdays and expressing good wishes
- Discussing gift ideas

**Grammar:**
- Introduction to the dative case
- Word order in the dative case

**Culture:**
- Using the telephone
- Saints' days
- German good luck symbols
- **Was schenkst du zum Geburtstag?**
- German gift ideas

**Re-entry:**
- Numbers 0-20
- Time and days of the week
- Months
- Accusative case
- Vocabulary: Family members

## KAPITEL 12   DIE FETE (Wiederholungskapitel)

**Functions (Review):**
- Offering help and explaining what to do
- Asking where something is located and giving directions
- Making plans and inviting someone to come along
- Talking about clothing
- Discussing gift ideas
- Describing people and places
- Saying what you would like and whether you do or don't want more
- Talking about what you did

**Grammar (Review):**
- the verb **können**; the preposition **für**; accusative pronouns; and **du**-commands
- the verb **wissen** and word order following **wissen**
- the verbs **wissen** and **müssen**; word order
- nominative and accusative pronouns; definite and indefinite articles
- dative endings
- the nominative pronouns **er, sie, es,** and **sie** (pl); possessive pronouns
- the **möchte**-forms; **noch ein** and **kein**

**Culture:**
- **Spätzle** and **Apfelküchle**
- **Mußt du zu Hause helfen?**
- German gift ideas
- Photos from furniture ads
- Menu from an **Imbißstube**

# Scope and Sequence: German Level 2

## KAPITEL 1   BEI DEN BAUMANNS
### (Wiederholungskapitel)
**Functions (Review):**
- Asking for and giving information about yourself and others; describing yourself and others; expressing likes and dislikes; identifying people and places
- Giving and responding to compliments; expressing wishes when buying things
- Making plans; ordering food; talking about how something tastes

**Grammar (Review):**
- Present tense forms of verbs
- Present tense forms of **haben** and **sein**
- The possessive adjectives **mein, dein, sein,** and **ihr** (nominative)
- The **möchte**-forms

**Culture:**
- A typical family — love of pets, music, flowers
- Meeting with friends in a café
- Students' favorite things

**Re-entry:**
- Expressions of time, sequence, enthusiasm
- Expressions describing people, sports, activities,
- School subjects, clothing, and food

## KAPITEL 2   BASTIS PLAN
### (Wiederholungskapitel)
**Functions (Review):**
- Expressing obligations; extending and responding to an invitation; offering help and telling what to do
- Asking and telling what to do; telling you need something else; telling where you were and what you bought
- Discussing gift ideas; expressing likes and dislikes; expressing likes, preferences, and favorites; saying you do or don't want more

**Grammar (Review):**
- The present tense forms of **müssen, können, sollen,** and **mögen**
- Clauses introduced by **weil** and **denn**
- Personal pronouns: accusative case
- The possessives **mein, dein, sein,** and **ihr** (accusative)

- The familiar commands
- The past tense forms of **sein**
- The dative case of the possessives **mein, dein, sein,** and **ihr**
- **kein,** nominative and accusative
- **noch ein,** nominative and accusative

**Culture:**
- Family breakfast in the kitchen, discussing plans for the day
- Tasks assigned to children; helping the grandparents
- Coffee and cake in the afternoon
- Presents to take when invited

**Re-entry:**
- Expressions of frequency, degrees of liking
- Expressions for chores, groceries, stores, presents, movies, and events.

## KAPITEL 3   WO WARST DU IN DEN FERIEN?
**Functions:**
- Reporting past events, talking about activities
- Reporting past events, talking about places
- Asking how someone liked something; expressing enthusiasm or disappointment, responding enthusiastically or sympathetically

**Grammar:**
- The conversational past with **haben** and **sein**
- The past tense of **haben** and **sein**
- The prepositions **an** and **in** with dative-case forms to express location
- Personal pronouns, dative case

**Culture:**
- Getting to know Frankfurt, Dresden, and an Austrian village more closely — typical sights and foods
- Vacations

**Re-entry:**
- Expressions of time and frequency
- Expressing likes and dislikes
- Names for activities and interests, and names for sights in a city or village

## KAPITEL 4   GESUND LEBEN
**Functions:**
- Expressing approval and

disapproval
- Asking for information and responding emphatically or agreeing with reservations
- Asking and telling what you may and may not do

**Grammar:**
- Reflexives verbs (accusative)
- **jeder, jede, jedes** (nominative, accusative, dative)
- **dürfen,** present tense
- The verb **schlafen** (**schläft**)

**Culture:**
- The Germans' concern for fitness and a healthful diet

**Re-entry:**
- Expressions of place, time, frequency, and quantity
- Expressions of place and activities
- Giving reasons
- **für** and the accusative
- **daß**-clauses
- **kein**

## KAPITEL 5   GESUND ESSEN
**Functions:**
- Expressing regret and downplaying; expressing scepticism and making certain
- Calling someone's attention to something and responding
- Asking for specific information; expressing preference and strong preference

**Grammar:**
- **dieser, diese, dieses** (nominative, accusative, dative)
- The possessives (summary)
- **welcher, welche, welches** (nominative, accusative, dative)
- The preposition **zu**

**Culture:**
- Students, breaks during the morning, and what they can consume during break
- A typical breakfast and lunch

**Re-entry:**
- Expressions related to school supplies and foods
- Giving reasons
- the forms of **mögen**
- **was für ein**
- **kein**
- **gefallen** and **schmecken**

## KAPITEL 6   GUTE BESSERUNG!
**Functions:**
- Inquiring about someone's

health and responding; making suggestions
- Asking about and expressing pain
- Asking for and giving advice; expressing hope

**Grammar:**
- The inclusive command (**wir**-command)
- Verbs used with dative case forms
- Reflexive verbs (dative)
- The verbs **sich (etwas) brechen, sich waschen, messen**

**Culture:**
- Students doing homework together
- Health issues among German students
- The **Apotheke** and the **Drogerie**

**Re-entry:**
- Expressions of time and frequency
- Reflexive (accusative)
- Dative-case forms
- The modals **sollen** and **müssen**

## KAPITEL 7   STADT ODER LAND?

**Functions:**
- Expressing preference and giving a reason
- Expressing wishes
- Agreeing with reservations; justifying your answers

**Grammar:**
- Comparative forms of adjectives
- The verb **sich wünschen**
- Adjective endings following **ein**-words
- Adjective endings of comparatives

**Culture:**
- Advantages and disadvantages of living in a town or city versus living in the country
- Rebuilding the new states of Germany
- Fighting noise pollution

**Re-entry:**
- Names of places; names of rooms
- Descriptive adjectives
- **weil**-clauses (giving reasons)

## KAPITEL 8   MODE—JA ODER NEIN?

**Functions:**
- Describing (clothes)
- Expressing interest, disinterest, and indifference
- Making and accepting compliments; persuading and dissuading

**Grammar:**
- Adjective endings after **der** and **dieser**-words
- The verb **tragen** *to wear*
- Further uses of the dative case

**Culture:**
- What's "in" and what's "out"
- Young people's interest in fashions

**Re-entry:**
- Adjective endings after **ein**-words
- names of colors used as adjectives

## KAPITEL 9   WOHIN IN DIE FERIEN?

**Functions:**
- Expressing indecision; asking for and making suggestions
- Expressing doubt, conviction, and resignation
- Asking for and giving directions

**Grammar:**
- Two-way prepositions, accusative
- Expressing direction: the prepositions **nach, an, in** and **auf**
- Expressing direction and location (Summary)
- Prepositions followed by dative case forms
- **ob**-clauses
- Superlatives with adjective endings

**Culture:**
- German vacations
- Favorite vacation spots

**Re-entry:**
- Inclusive commands
- **daß**-clauses
- adjective endings
- sequencing of events

## KAPITEL 10   DEINE INTERESSEN?

**Functions:**
- Asking about and expressing interest
- Asking for and giving permission; asking for information and giving an opinion
- Expressing surprise, agreement and disagreement; talking about plans

**Grammar:**
- Verbs with prepositions
- **da**-compounds and **wo**-compounds
- The future tense with **werden**

**Culture:**
- Television in Germany
- German cars

**Re-entry:**
- Comparatives
- Personal pronouns, first and second persons
- Word order in clauses

## KAPITEL 11   OMA GEBURTSTAG

**Functions:**
- Asking about someone's wishes and expressing yours
- Ordering a meal, making suggestions
- Proposing a toast

**Grammar:**
- The **würde**-forms
- The **hätte**-forms
- Unpreceded adjectives

**Culture:**
- Celebrating birthdays
- How to order in a restaurant
- Typical meals on a menu

**Re-entry:**
- **mögen**
- Comparative forms, esp. **gern, lieber, am liebsten**, and **gut, besser, am besten**

## KAPITEL 12   AUS DEN FERIEN ZURÜCK

- Review of major functions and grammar

**Functions:**
- Giving directions
- Making suggestions
- Expressing wishes
- Expressing likes, dislikes, and preferences
- Asking about someone's wishes
- Inquiring about someone's injuries
- Expressing admiration
- Reporting past events

**Grammar:**
- The perfect
- The modal verbs
- Word order
- Adjectives after **dieser**- and **ein**-words
- Comparatives and superlatives
- Reflexive verbs
- Verbs with prepositions

**Culture:**
- Friends get together for a backyard party
- Preparation of food and the type of foods served at a get-together
- What students wear at such a get-together
- Where Germans spend their vacations

# Scope and Sequence: German Level 3

**KAPITEL 1** reviews major functions and grammar presented in the first half of **Komm mit!** German 2

**KAPITEL 2** reviews major functions and grammar presented in the second half of **Komm mit!** German 2

## KAPITEL 3  AUSSEHEN: WICHTIG ODER?
**Functions:**
**Attitudes and opinions**
•Asking and giving opinions
•Explaining and justifying
**Feelings and emotions**
•Admitting something; expressing regret
•Expressing sympathy and resignation
**Attitudes and opinions**
•Expressing purpose and giving reasons
•Giving advice
**Grammar:**
**Da**-compounds and **wo**-compounds
More uses of the infinitive
Some uses of dative case forms
**Culture:**
Attitudes toward fashion, health, and fitness; type of diet; food trends
Centers of fashion in Germany, and importance of fashion to young people; influence of USA
Description of young women in Germany today–attitudes, interests, goals
**Re-entry:**
Reflexive verbs
Uses of the infinitive

## KAPITEL 4  VERHÄLTNIS ZU ANDEREN
**Functions:**
**Attitudes and opinions**
•Agreeing; expressing reservations
**Exchanging information**
•Asking for clarification and more information
**Attitudes and opinions**
•Giving advice; introducing another point of view
•Speculating on how things might be

**Grammar:**
Verbs used as nouns
Relative clauses
Describing things and people: the genitive case
**Culture:**
Relationship of young people to parents and friends; how and with whom they spend their time
Attitudes toward other people–those who choose to dress and behave differently, people from other countries, people for different social backgrounds
Problems between parents and young people
**Re-entry:**
Prepositions with the dative case
**Da**-compounds used to anticipate a clause

## KAPITEL 5  RECHTE UND PFLICHTEN
**Functions:**
**Attitudes and opinions**
•Expressing possibility
•Saying you wouldn't know what to do
•Expressing what you would have done (but didn't)
•Indicating that you're not sure
**Expressing information**
•Reporting what had to be done
**Expressing information**
•Saying that something is going on right now
•Reporting past events
•Expressing doubt, uncertainty
**Feelings and emotions**
•Expressing surprise, relief, resignation
**Grammar:**
The past perfect
The past tense of modals (the imperfect)
**Culture:**
Coming of age: rights and responsibilities; requirements for getting a driver's license
Choosing between military service or an alternative service
Comparing life of young people today with life when their grandparents were young
**Re-entry:**
The **könnte**-forms

## KAPITEL 6  MEDIEN: STETS GUT INFORMIERT?
**Functions:**
**Exchanging information**
•Asking to take a position; asking for reasons
•Narrating past events
•Accepting, rejecting, and changing the subject; reproaching
**Attitudes and opinions**
•Expressing opinions
**Feelings and emotions**
•Expressing surprise, annoyance, and frustration
**Grammar:**
Narrative past (imperfect) and conversational past (perfect)
Superlative forms of adjectives
**Culture:**
Young people and the media
School newspapers and student government in Germany
Content and goals of a student newspaper
**Re-entry:**
Comparing things

## KAPITEL 7  OHNE REKLAME GEHT ES NICHT
**Functions:**
**Feelings and emotions**
•Expressing annoyance
**Exchanging information**
•Comparing
•Giving examples
**Attitudes and opinions**
•Eliciting, expressing agreement
**Exchanging information**
•Expressing conviction, uncertainty, and what seems to be
•Repeating what you've heard
**Grammar:**
**derselbe, dieselbe, dasselbe**
Determiners of quantity
Introducing relative clauses with **was** and **wo**
**irgendein** and **irgendwelche**
Other words preceded by **irgend-**
**Culture:**
Advertising in Germany
A class discusses advertising–types of ads, their audience, effectiveness, and ethics
Young people express opinions about advertising

Re-entry:
Reflexive constructions
daß-clauses

## KAPITEL 8  WEG MIT DEN VORURTEILEN!

Functions:

**Feelings and emotions**
•Expressing surprise, disappointment, annoyance/displeasure
**Attitudes and opinions**
•Making assumptions
**Persuading**
•Suggesting/recommending; warning

Grammar:

Subordinating conjunctions
The subordinating conjunctions als, weil, and denn
Verbs with prefixes (Summary)

Culture:

Young Germans discuss their impressions of the USA and how their impressions were formed
Young Americans explore their preconceived impressions of Germany and how their views of other people were changed
Students respond to the term "patriotism"

Re-entry:

Verbs with separable prefixes
Command forms of verbs

## KAPITEL 9  UNSERE UMWELT, UNSERE VERANTWORTUNG

Functions:

**Feelings and emotions**
•Expressing concern, fear
**Attitudes and opinions**
•Making accusations
•Expressing wishes

**Persuading**
•Saying what could or should be done
**Persuading**
•Asking and telling what to do
•Expressing possibility
•Making exhortations
**Attitudes and opinions**
•Making hypotheses

Grammar:

Subjunctive forms of können, müssen, dürfen, sollen, and sein
Conditional sentences

Culture:

Concerns about the environment
What is being done at home, in the schools, and in the community to protect the environment and raise public awareness of problems

Re-entry:

The passive

## KAPITEL 10  DIE KUNST ZU LEBEN

Functions:

**Feelings and emotions**
•Expressing preference and possibility
•Expressing envy
**Feelings and emotions**
•Expressing happiness and sadness
**Exchanging information**
•Describing customary occurrence

Grammar:

Prepositions with the genitive case
Choosing the passive voice (Summary)

Culture:

Cultural activities and interest of young people in Germany
A school class goes to the ballet

Going to a concert
Re-entry:
The genitive case
wo-compounds and da-compounds

## KAPITEL 11  DEINE WELT IST DEINE SACHE

Functions:

**Attitudes and opinions**
•Expressing determination and indecision
•Expressing importance and unimportance
**Attitudes and opinions**
•Expressing certainty; refusing and rejecting
•Expressing fulfillment in the future
**Feelings and emotions**
•Expressing relief

Grammar:

Verbs with prepositions
The perfect infinitive with modals and werden

Culture:

Young people discuss their plans for after graduation
Hopes and goals for the future- young people discuss how they would like their lives to be
Young people talk about their future

Re-entry:

Infinitive constructions
The future tense

## KAPITEL 12 EIN BLICK IN DIE ZUKUNFT (WIEDERHOLUNG)

Reviews major functions and grammar presented in Chapters 3 through 11 of **Komm mit!** German 3

# The Pupil's Edition

*Proficiency is the goal of language instruction in Komm mit! Every chapter begins with authentic situations that model communicative needs common among young people: ordering from a menu, asking someone for a date, shopping for clothes. In the ensuing situations, students learn the functions, vocabulary, and grammar that support natural expression. They also become interested, involved, and responsive—in short, they answer the invitation to Komm mit! and to communicate.*

## An Overview

The **Komm mit!** Pupil's Edition opens with **Vorschau**, a preliminary chapter that invites students to explore the geography and culture of the German-speaking nations. This motivating, colorful preview of the benefits—and fun—of learning German starts the year on a positive, exciting note.

Following the **Vorschau**, Chapters 1-11 provide a carefully sequenced program of balanced skills instruction in the four key areas of listening, speaking, reading, and writing. In addition, every chapter is rich in authentic culture and language. Most chapter photographs were taken on location and reflect the characters and settings featured in the videos that accompany *Komm mit!*

Chapter 12 is a review of the first year's study of German. It provides an opportunity to reinforce skills and remediate deficiencies before the end of the school year. This opportunity to pause and reflect on what has been learned provides closure and gives students a sense of accomplishment and renewed purpose.

At the end of the *Pupil's Edition*, a Reference Section summarizes functions, grammar rules, and pronunciation features for quick reference. It also provides a list of Additional Vocabulary as well as German>English and English>German glossaries. Throughout the year, students are encouraged to consult the Reference Section to review and expand their choices of functional expressions, vocabulary, and structures.

## Activity-Based Instruction

In *Komm mit!*, language acquisition is an active process. From the first day, students are using German. Within each lesson, a progression of activities moves students from discrete point use of language to completely open-ended activities that promote personalized, meaningful expression. This sequence allows students to practice receptive skills before moving on to language production. It is this carefully articulated sequence that ensures success.

## A Guided Tour

On the next several pages, you will find a guided tour of *Komm mit!* On these pages, we have identified for you the essential elements of the textbook and the various resources available. If, as you are using *Komm mit!*, you encounter any particular problems, please contact your regional office for information or assistance.

In Komm mit!, Level 1, students visit four locations. Each locale is introduced with photographs, text and authentic cultural video footage shot at the location site.

Inset maps show the location within Germany and its relationship to neighboring countries. *The Teacher's Edition* suggests activities that strengthen students' understanding of the geography of the region.

KAPITEL 1, 2, 3

Komm mit nach

## Brandenburg!

### Brandenburg

**Population:** 2.64 million
**Area:** 29,056 square kilometers (11,216 square miles), approximately as large as the state of Maryland
**Capital:** Potsdam (140,000 inhabitants)
**Cities:** Cottbus, Brandenburg, Frankfurt an der Oder
**Rivers:** Oder, Havel, Spree
**Canals:** Oder-Spree-Kanal, Rhin-kanal, Elbe-Havel-Kanal
**Lakes:** Ruppiner See, Werbellinsee, Schwielochsee, Plauer See
**Industries:** Textiles, machinery, cement, porcelain, farming, forestry, petroleum, coal
**Favorite local dishes:** lentil soup, chicken fricassee

Photo ① : Die Terrassen von Schloß Sanssouci in Potsdam

The almanac provides economic, demographic, political, and geographic information.

Coats of arms for each location introduce the symbols identified with these regions.

### Brandenburg

*Brandenburg, the heartland of former Prussia, is a state characterized by vast flat sandy lands, hundreds of beautiful lakes, and large wooded areas consisting mostly of fir trees. A trip through the towns in Brandenburg reveals stately buildings and churches in characteristic red brick, waiting to be restored to their former beauty.*

② Castle Branitz in Cottbus, built in 1772, now a museum, is situated in a magnificent nineteenth-century park.

⑤ Cecilienhof Palace, built between 1913 and 1917. Here the Allied powers signed the Potsdam Agreement in 1945.

⑥ A ship hoist at Niederfinow on the Oder-Havel canal. Canal barges, like the one pictured here, transport bulk goods, such as coal, sand or gravel.

*The students in the following three chapters live in the Potsdam area. Potsdam is the capital of Brandenburg. In 1993, Potsdam celebrated its 1000th birthday. The city became famous when Frederick the Great decided to establish his summer residence there and built Sanssouci Palace.*

⑦ Ahmet, Jens, Handan, Tara, Holger, and Steffi invite you to Potsdam.

③ A marble statue of Frederick the Great, sculpted by Joseph Uphues.

④ The new wing of Sanssouci Palace, built in 1747 and remodeled between 1771 and 1775. In the background the recently renovated **Historische Mühle.**

Each location opener introduces the students who will be our hosts as we visit their home towns.

Two pages of photographs illustrate German life in towns, cities, and countryside.

# Chapter Opener

Each chapter is organized around a topic with intrinsic appeal for teenagers—school, sports, leisure activities. As the topic is developed through a variety of situations, students will learn and practice the functions necessary for real-life communication.

## LIVELY PHOTOGRAPHS
Colorful pictures shot on location illustrate authentic scenes tied to the chapter theme.

## REALISTIC SITUATIONS
Each chapter topic is immediately placed in a realistic context, a situation that encourages exploration and interest.

KAPITEL

# 4
## Alles für die Schule!

**W**hen a new school year begins, students are often curious about their friends' classes: When do they meet? Which ones are their favorites? What school supplies do they need? There are some similarities and some differences in what students in German-speaking countries and in the U.S. experience in school. Let's find out what they are.

**In this chapter you will learn**
- to talk about class schedules; to use a schedule
- to talk about time; to sequence events
- to express likes, dislikes, and favorites; to respond to good news and bad news
- to talk about prices; to point things out

**And you will**
- listen to German-speaking students talk about their schedules
- read ads for school supplies and become familiar with German money
- write a report card for yourself in German
- find out what German students have to say about school

① Wann habt ihr Sport?

② Was kosten die Hefte?

③ Am Freitag haben wir Mathe.

92 *zweiundneunzig*

*dreiundneunzig* 93

## APPROPRIATE FUNCTIONS
Students are immediately alerted to the functions they will be learning and the outcomes expected from their study. This clear statement of objectives helps students to focus and organize.

# Los geht's!

The first step in every chapter is to provide authentic cultural and linguistic input. In each opening episode situations are developed that will require students to generate language as they discuss the characters' actions and motives.

## 1 Was passiert hier?
Do you understand what is happening in the **Foto-Roman**? Check your comprehension by answering these questions. Don't be afraid to guess.
1. What plans have Julia and Katja made for the afternoon?
2. What is Heiko going to do?
3. Where do the three friends meet Michael?
4. Why does Michael apologize to Katja? How does Katja react?

## 2 Genauer lesen
Reread the conversations. Which words or phrases do the characters use to
1. ask how someone is doing
2. talk about time
3. name food or drinks
4. tell a waiter they want to pay
5. apologize

## 3 Was paßt zusammen?
Match each statement or question on the left with an appropriate response on the right.
1. Wie geht's denn?
2. Wohin gehst du?
3. Wie spät ist es jetzt?
4. Wer bekommt den Cappuccino?
5. Ich möchte zahlen.

a. Er ist für mich.
b. So lala.
c. Das macht zusammen vierzehn Mark zehn.
d. Viertel nach drei.
e. Zu Katja.

## 4 Was fehlt hier?
Based on the **Foto-Roman** that you've just read, complete each of the sentences below with an appropriate item from the list.

bekommt, Eis, möchte, Hausaufgaben, einen Eisbecher, Stimmt, zahlen, halb

Katja und Julia machen zuerst die __1__. Dann wollen sie in ein Café gehen, ein __2__ essen. Sie wollen so um __3__ fünf gehen. Im Café fragt der Kellner: „Was __4__ ihr?" Katja __5__ einen Cappuccino. Julia sagt: „Ich bekomme __6__, Fruchteis." Michael will gehen. Er sagt: „Ich möchte __7__, bitte." Der Kellner sagt: „Vierzehn Mark zehn." Und Michael antwortet, „Fünfzehn Mark. __8__ schon."

**Café am Markt**
| | |
|---|---|
| Nudelsuppe | DM 4,50 |
| Käsebrot | 5,20 |
| Wurstbrot | 5,60 |
| Wiener mit Senf | 5,80 |
| Pizza | 8,00 |
| Apfelkuchen | 2,00 |
| Eis | 1,10 |
| Mineralwasser | 3,50 |
| Kaffee | 4,20 |
| Cola | 3,00 |

## 5 Und du?
Look at the menu from the **Café am Markt**. Which items are foods, and which are beverages? If you were with your friends at the **Café am Markt**, what would you order? Make a list, including the prices.

144 *hundertvierundvierzig* KAPITEL 6 Pläne machen

**RECEPTIVE SKILLS**
Recognition activities following the opening story reinforce receptive skills. Students work with the episode—exploring the new language presented, relating it to their own experiences, and making new combinations based on their accumulated language base.

**AUTHENTIC INPUT**
The natural language and situations of the conversations build interest and provide language models. Auditory and visual learners also have access to both video and audio recordings of the dialogue.

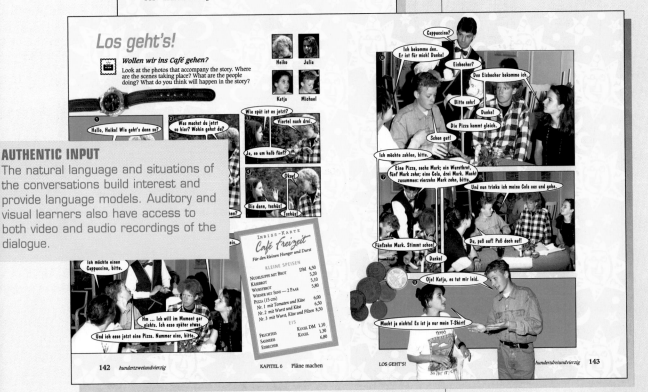

142 *hundertzweiundvierzig* KAPITEL 6 Pläne machen

LOS GEHT'S! *hundertdreiundvierzig* 143

T49

# Stufen

Each chapter is divided into three Stufen, short manageable lessons that provide a carefully planned progression of activities. Within each Stufe, activities are sequenced from structured practice to open-ended communication in individual, pair, and group activities that accommodate many different learning styles.

## FORM FOLLOWS FUNCTION

Grammatical structures that support the communicative functions appear under the headings **Grammatik** and **Ein wenig Grammatik**. This carefully planned integration of grammar with a communicative purpose helps students communicate with increasing accuracy.

## VOCABULARY IN CONTEXT

Theme-related, functional vocabulary is presented visually in the **Wortschatz** and then re-entered in the activities of the **Stufe**.

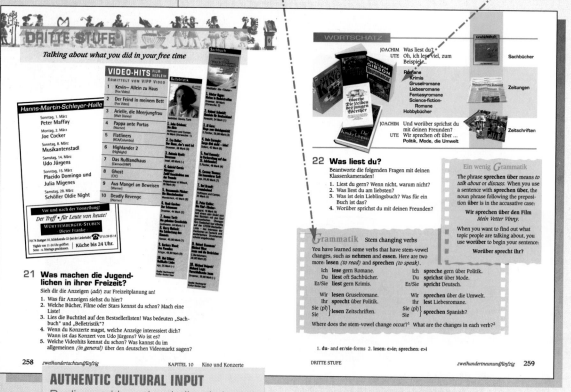

## AUTHENTIC CULTURAL INPUT

Realia provide authentic linguistic and cultural input. Students gain cultural insight and increasing confidence in their ability to read and comprehend authentic material.

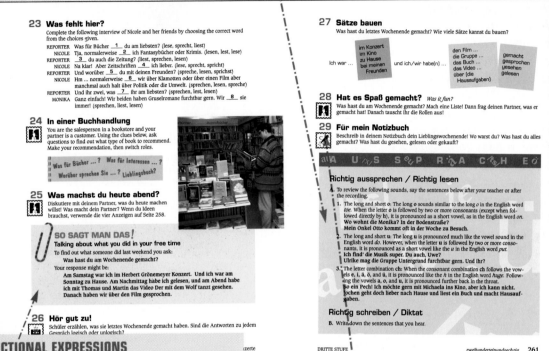

### 23 Was fehlt hier?

Complete the following interview of Nicole and her friends by choosing the correct word from the choices given.

REPORTER  Was für Bücher __1__ du am liebsten? (lese, sprecht, liest)
NICOLE  Tja, normalerweise __2__ ich Fantasybücher oder Krimis. (lesen, lest, lese)
REPORTER  __3__ du auch die Zeitung? (liest, sprechen, lesen)
NICOLE  Na klar! Aber Zeitschriften __4__ ich lieber. (lese, sprecht, spricht)
REPORTER  Und worüber __5__ du mit deinen Freunden? (spreche, lesen, sprichst)
NICOLE  Hm ... normalerweise __6__ wir über Klamotten oder über einen Film aber manchmal auch halt über Politik oder die Umwelt. (sprechen, lesen, spreche)
REPORTER  Und ihr zwei, was __7__ ihr am liebsten? (sprechen, lest, lesen)
MONIKA  Ganz einfach! Wir beiden haben Gruselromane furchtbar gern. Wir __8__ sie immer! (sprechen, liest, lesen)

### 24 In einer Buchhandlung

You are the salesperson in a bookstore and your partner is a customer. Using the clues below, ask questions to find out what type of book to recommend. Make your recommendation, then switch roles.

Was für Bücher ... ?  Was für Interessen ... ?
Worüber sprechen Sie ... ? Lieblingsbuch?

### 25 Was machst du heute abend?

Diskutiere mit deinem Partner, was du heute machen willst! Was macht dein Partner? Wenn du Ideen brauchst, verwende die vier Anzeigen auf Seite 258.

**SO SAGT MAN DAS!**

Talking about what you did in your free time

To find out what someone did last weekend you ask:
Was hast du am Wochenende gemacht?

Your response might be:
Am Samstag war ich im Herbert Grönemeyer Konzert. Und ich war am Sonntag zu Hause. Am Nachmittag habe ich gelesen, und am Abend habe ich mit Thomas und Martin das Video Der mit dem Wolf tanzt gesehen. Danach haben wir über den Film gesprochen.

### 26 Hör gut zu!

Schüler erzählen, was sie letztes Wochenende gemacht haben. Sind die Antworten zu jedem Gespräch logisch oder unlogisch?

### 27 Sätze bauen

Was hast du letztes Wochenende gemacht? Wie viele Sätze kannst du bauen?

Ich war ...  | im Konzert / im Kino / zu Hause / bei meinen Freunden | und ich/wir habe(n) ... | den Film ... / die Gruppe ... / das Buch ... / das Video ... / über (die Hausaufgaben) | gemacht / gesprochen / gesehen / gelesen

### 28 Hat es Spaß gemacht? *Was it fun?*

Was hast du am Wochenende gemacht? Mach eine Liste! Dann frag deinen Partner, was er gemacht hat! Danach tauscht ihr die Rollen aus!

### 29 Für mein Notizbuch

Beschreib in deinem Notizbuch dein Lieblingswochenende! Wo warst du? Was hast du alles gemacht? Was hast du gesehen, gelesen oder gekauft?

## AUSSPRACHE

### Richtig aussprechen / Richtig lesen

A. To review the following sounds, say the sentences below after your teacher or after the recording.

1. The long and short o: The long o sounds similar to the long o in the English word *toe*. When the letter o is followed by two or more consonants (except when followed directly by h), it is pronounced as a short vowel, as in the English word *on*.
Wo wohnt die Monika? In der Bodenstraße?
Mein Onkel Otto kommt oft in der Woche zu Besuch.

2. The long and short u: The long u is pronounced much like the vowel sound in the English word *do*. However, when the letter u is followed by two or more consonants, it is pronounced as a short vowel like the u in the English word *put*.
Ich find' die Musik super. Du auch, Uwe?
Ulrike mag die Gruppe Untergrund furchtbar gern. Und ihr?

3. The letter combination ch: When the consonant combination ch follows the vowels e, i, ä, ö, and ü, it is pronounced like the h in the English word *huge*. Following the vowels a, o, and u, it is pronounced further back in the throat.
So ein Pech! Ich möchte gern mit Michaela ins Kino, aber ich kann nicht.
Jochen geht doch lieber nach Hause und liest ein Buch und macht Hausaufgaben.

### Richtig schreiben / Diktat

B. Write down the sentences that you hear.

# Landeskunde

Landeskunde *is an integrated approach to culture that enriches students' cultural awareness and language skills. These informal, spontaneous interviews with people of all ages illustrate aspects of daily life in German-speaking countries. The* Landeskunde *is also available in both audio and video formats, and this allows students to sharpen their listening and pronunciation skills by becoming familiar with a variety of regional dialects.*

**PREPARING TO LISTEN**
A brief introduction presents the topic and explains the subject of the interview.

**AUTHENTIC LANGUAGE**
The names and photographs of each of the people interviewed remind students that the views expressed and the language used are real. As students listen to people from various regions and countries, they will heighten their awareness of differences in attitudes and interests, as well as speech.

**REINFORCING COMPREHENSION**
Questions following the interviews encourage students to compare and contrast the opinions of the people interviewed and to consider how their views match or differ from those of Americans. This cross-cultural analysis builds personal as well as global understandings.

## EIN WENIG LANDESKUNDE

Although there are many large, modern supermarkets in Germany, many people still shop in small specialty stores or at the open-air markets in the center of town. Many Germans shop frequently, buying just what they need for one or two days. Refrigerators are generally much smaller than in the United States, and people prefer to buy things fresh.

**CULTURAL AWARENESS**
The **Ein wenig Landeskunde** are small cultural notes that appear wherever useful to explain some point of German culture that might be puzzling to an American teenager.

# Zum Lesen

**Even reluctant readers will be motivated by the eye-catching format and appealing realia of Zum Lesen. These intriguing lessons help students develop reading skills and simultaneously acquire more information about German life.**

## READING TIPS

The **Lesetrick** notes provide useful hints that ease reading anxieties and develop valuable reading strategies.

## INNOVATIVE ACTIVITIES

Activities suggest the use of pertinent skills such as skimming or looking for visual clues. Questioning strategies become more complex as students master a variety of skills.

## REALIA

Students build reading confidence by working with authentic materials such as German recipes, travel brochures, entertainment guides, or excerpts from newspapers and magazines.

A system of icons is used throughout the *Pupil's Edition* to identify activities that are specifically designed to promote certain skills or that might be particularly useful in pair or group work.

# Anwendung

The end-of-chapter review, Anwendung, offers the same level of interest and challenge as the instructional pages. Students are engaged in a series of activities that measure their ability to comprehend and generate language.

**Listening**

This icon indicates the listening activities that range from global comprehension to discrete tasks. Teachers can use the audiocassette for authentic input or read from the scripts available in the *Teacher's Edition* interleaf before each chapter.

**Writing**

*Komm mit!* offers a variety of writing activities, many of which are intended to be placed in the student's *Notizbuch*. Teachers may decide how formal they wish the *Notizbuch* or journal to be, but students who are able to look back at their own writing periodically are reassured and encouraged by seeing their own growth and improvement.

## COMPLETE SKILLS REVIEW
Each **Anwendung** covers all four skill areas: listening, speaking, reading, and writing. These activities require students to recombine language and are a true measure of their growth in proficiency.

**Pair Work**

Activities with this icon are ideal for pair work. It may be helpful to assign pairs for a certain period of time, preferably a week or two. This also promotes students' social growth as they learn to interact with a variety of people.

**Group Work**

Group activities are particularly successful in alleviating students' stress and inhibitions. Students will benefit from being assigned to groups at times and allowed to choose their own groups at others. The choice of how these groups will report is the teacher's, and direction lines may be varied so that groups report orally or in writing, or both.

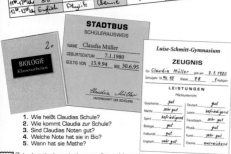

## ROLE-PLAYING
Every chapter review culminates in a **Rollenspiel**. These dramatic activities encourage students to use language in imaginative and creative expression.

## SPIRALED CHAPTER OBJECTIVES

Questions in the margins recall the communicative functions found at the beginning of each chapter. Each activity reveals students' strengths and points out areas for possible improvement.

## Kann ich's wirklich?

*This self-check page allows students to gauge their progress and gives them a true sense of accomplishment. After its successful completion, students can move ahead with confidence.*

## HELPFUL PAGE REFERENCES

Page numbers tell students where to find the essential functional expressions, grammar, and vocabulary they may need to complete each task.

## VOCABULARY LISTS

The **Wortschatz** page provides a comprehensive list of the words and expressions targeted in the chapter. Divided by **Stufe** and arranged in semantic fields, this vocabulary list can be used for reference, review, or study.

---

### KANN ICH'S WIRKLICH?

**Can you extend and respond to an invitation? (p. 174)**

**1** How would you invite a friend to go

 a. to a movie  b. to a Café  c. shopping  d. swimming

**2** Accept or decline the following invitations. If you decline, give a reason why you can't go.

 a. Wir gehen jetzt in eine Disko. Komm doch mit!
 b. Ich muß in die Stadt gehen. Möchtest du mitkommen?
 c. Wir spielen jetzt Tennis. Kannst du mitkommen?

**Can you express obligation using müssen? (p. 174)**

**3** Say that the people below have to do the things indicated.

Bernd    Leyla    Pedro und Felipe    Karin

**Can you talk about how often you have to do things? (p. 178)**

**4** How would you ask a classmate how often he or she has to

 a. washes the windows    c. clears the table
 b. vacuums               d. does the dishes

**5** How would you tell a classmate how often you have to do each of the things above?

**Can you offer help and tell someone what to do using expressions with "für"? (p. 179)**

**6** How would you ask a classmate if you could help him or her? How would you ask two classmates?

**7** Using **können**, explain to each of these people what they can do to help you:

 a. Sara: das Geschirr spülen
 b. Silke und Peter: das Zimmer aufräumen
 c. Markus: das Bett machen
 d. Claudia und Daniel: den Tisch decken

**8** How might a friend respond if he or she agreed to do some chores for you?

**Can you talk about the weather? (p. 183)**

**9** How would you tell a classmate what the weather is like today? How would you tell him or her the weather forecast for tomorrow?

**10** How would you tell someone new to your area what the weather is like in

 a. January    c. June      e. December
 b. March      d. October

190 *hundertneunzig*        KAPITEL 7  Zu Hause helfen

---

### WORTSCHATZ

**ERSTE STUFE**

**EXTENDING AND RESPONDING TO INVITATIONS**
mitkommen (sep)  *to come along*
Komm doch mit!  *Why don't you come along!*
Ich kann leider nicht.  *Sorry, I can't.*
Das geht nicht.  *That won't work.*

**EXPRESSING OBLIGATION**
tun  *to do*
helfen  *to help*

zu Hause helfen  *to help at home*
müssen  *to have to*
ich muß ...  *I have to...*
mein Zimmer aufräumen (sep)  *clean up my room*
Staub saugen  *vacuum*
den Müll sortieren  *sort the trash*
den Rasen mähen  *mow the lawn*
die Katze füttern  *feed the cat*
den Tisch decken  *set the table*
den Tisch abräumen (sep)  *clear the table*

das Geschirr spülen  *wash the dishes*
die Blumen gießen  *water the flowers*
das Bett machen  *make the bed*
meine Klamotten aufräumen  *pick up my clothes*
die Fenster putzen  *clean the windows*
Ich habe keine Zeit.  *I don't have time.*

**ZWEITE STUFE**

**SAYING HOW OFTEN YOU HAVE TO DO THINGS**
Wie oft?  *How often?*
nie  *never*
manchmal  *sometimes*
oft  *often*
immer  *always*
einmal, zweimal, dreimal ...  *once, twice, three times...*
in der Woche  *a week*
im Monat  *a month*

jeden Tag  *every day*

**ASKING FOR AND OFFERING HELP AND TELLING SOMEONE WHAT TO DO**
können  *can, to be able to*
Was kann ich für dich tun?  *What can I do for you?*
Kann ich etwas für dich tun?  *Can I do something for you?*
Du kannst ...  *You can...*

Gut! Mach' ich!  *Okay! I'll do that!*
für  *for*
Für wen?  *For whom?*
mich  *me*
dich  *you*
uns  *us*
euch  *you (pl)*

**OTHER USEFUL WORDS AND EXPRESSIONS**
ungefähr  *about, approximately*

**DRITTE STUFE**

**TALKING ABOUT THE WEATHER**
Was sagt der Wetterbericht?  *What does the weather report say?*
Wie ist das Wetter?  *How's the weather?*
Es ist...  *It is...*
 heiß  *hot*
 warm  *warm*
 kühl  *cool*
 kalt  *cold*
 trocken  *dry*
 naß  *wet*
 sonnig  *sunny*

wolkig  *cloudy*
der Schnee  *snow*
Es schneit.  *it's snowing*
der Regen  *rain*
Es regnet.  *it's raining*
das Eis  *ice*
das Gewitter  *thunder-storm*
Die Sonne scheint.  *The sun is shining.*
heute  *today*
morgen  *tomorrow*
heute abend  *this evening*
Wieviel Grad haben wir?  *What's the temperature?*
der Grad  *degree (s)*

zwei Grad  *two degrees*
der Monat, -e  *month*
der Januar  *January*
im Januar  *in January*
 Februar  *February*
 März  *March*
 April  *April*
 Mai  *May*
 Juni  *June*
 Juli  *July*
 August  *August*
 September  *September*
 Oktober  *October*
 November  *November*
 Dezember  *December*

WORTSCHATZ        *hunderteinundneunzig* **191**

# The Teacher's Edition

*The* Komm mit! *Teacher's Edition is designed to help you meet the increasingly varied needs of today's students by providing an abundance of suggestions and strategies. The Teacher's Edition includes the pages of the Pupil's Edition, with annotations, plus interleaf pages before each location and chapter opener.*

## Using the Location Opener Interleaf

Preceding each location opener is a two-page interleaf section with specific background information on each photograph. In addition, teaching suggestions help you motivate students to learn more about the history, geography, and culture of German-speaking countries.

## Using the Chapter Interleaf

The Chapter Interleaf includes background information, a list of resources, additional culture notes, and suggestions on how to motivate students, present material, and adapt activities to accommodate different learning styles.

### Getting Started

At the beginning of each chapter you'll find a chapter overview chart, listening scripts, a suggested project, and several games.

**Chapter Overview** outlines the chapter in a concise chart that includes the functions, grammar, and culture presented in each **Stufe**, as well as a list of corresponding resource materials. The re-entry column lists previously presented material that is recycled in the chapter.

**Textbook Listening Activities Scripts** provide scripts of the recorded chapter listening activities for your reference or use in class.

**Suggested Project** proposes an extended four-skills activity based on the theme of the chapter or the location opener.

**Games** allow students to apply and reinforce the functions, structures, vocabulary, and culture in an informal, non-threatening atmosphere.

### Teaching Cycle

For each **Stufe**, a logical instructional sequence enables you to:

**motivate** students by personalizing and contextualizing the topic;

**teach** the functions, vocabulary, structures, and culture with a variety of approaches;

**close** each **Stufe** with activities that combine the communicative goals;

**assess** students' progress with a quiz and/or performance assessment.

The teaching cycle contains the following sections:

## Meeting Individual Needs

The following features suggest alternate approaches to help you address the diverse needs and abilities of students.

**Visual, Auditory, Tactile, Kinesthetic Learners** benefit from activities that accommodate their unique learning styles.

**A Slower Pace** provides ideas to break the presentation of information into smaller steps to facilitate comprehension.

**Challenge** includes creative, open-ended activities that encourage students to extend their reach.

## Making Connections

To help students appreciate their membership in a global community, suggestions for linking German with other disciplines and cultures appear under the following categories:

**Math (History, . . .)**
   **Connections** relate the chapter topic to other subject areas, making German relevant to the students' experiences.

**Multicultural Connection** compares and contrasts the language and culture of German-speaking countries with those of other parts of the world.

**Community/Family Link** encourages students to seek opportunities for learning outside of the classroom by interacting with neighbors and family members.

## Developing Thinking Skills

**Thinking Critically** helps students develop their higher-order thinking skills by drawing inferences, comparing and contrasting, analyzing, and synthesizing.

## Establishing Collaborative Learning

**Cooperative Learning** allows students to work in small groups to attain common goals by sharing responsibilities.

## Actively Involving Students

**Total Physical Response** techniques visually and kinesthetically reinforce structures and vocabulary.

## Teaching *Zum Lesen*

Teacher's notes in **Zum Lesen** offer prereading, reading, and post-reading activities to help students develop reading strategies and improve comprehension.

# Komm Mit! Ancillaries

*The* Komm mit! *Holt German program offers a state of the art ancillary package that addresses the concerns of today's teachers. Because foreign language teachers are providing for all types of students, our ancillaries are designed to accommodate all learners. The* Komm mit! *ancillary materials are innovative, relevant to students' lives, and full of variety and fun.*

## Teaching Resources with Professional Organizer

HRW has taken an innovative approach to organizing our **Teaching Resources**. The *Komm mit!* ancillaries are conveniently packaged in time-saving **Chapter Resources** books with a **Teaching Resource Organizer**. Each Chapter Resources book puts a wealth of resources at your fingertips!

### Chapter Resources, Books 1-4

♦ Oral communication is the language skill that is most challenging to develop and test. The *Komm mit!* **Situation Cards** and **Communicative Activities** are designed to help students develop their speaking skills and give them opportunities to communicate in a variety of situations.

♦ **Additional Listening Activities**, in combination with the textbook audiocassette program, provide students with a unique opportunity to actively develop their listening comprehension skills in a variety of authentic contexts.

♦ The *Komm mit!* **Realia** reproduce real documents to provide your students with additional language practice in authentic cultural contexts. Included with the **Realia** are suggestions for their use.

♦ The **Student Response Forms** are provided for your convenience. These copying masters enable you to reproduce standard answer forms for the listening activities in the textbook.

♦ The *Komm mit!* **Assessment Program** responds to your requests for a method of evaluation that is fair to all students, and that encourages students to work toward realistic, attainable goals. The **Assessment Program** includes the following components:
  ♦ Three **Quizzes** per chapter (one per **Stufe**)
  ♦ One **Chapter Test** per chapter; each **Chapter Test** includes listening, speaking, reading, writing, and culture. Part of each test can be corrected on ScanTron®.

♦ Also included in the *Chapter Resources:*
  ♦ **Teaching Transparency Masters** for use in a variety of activities
  ♦ **Listening Scripts** for the Additional Listening Activities and the Assessment Program
  ♦ **Answer Key** for the *Practice and Activity Book*

### Assessment Guide

The **Assessment Guide** describes various testing and scoring methods. This guide also includes:
  ♦ **Portfolio Assessment** suggestions and rubrics
  ♦ **Speaking Tests** to be used separately or as part of the Chapter Test
  ♦ A cumulative **Midterm Exam**
  ♦ A comprehensive **Final Exam**

### Teaching Resource Organizer

A tri-fold binder helps you organize the ancillaries for each chapter.

Name _____ Klasse _____ Datum _____

**Teaching Transparency Master 2-1**

**Im Herbst ...**

**Im Winter ...**

**Im Sommer ...**

**Im Frühling ...**

Komm mit! Level 1                    Chapter Resources, Book 1 **69**

HRW material copyrighted under notice appearing earlier in this work.

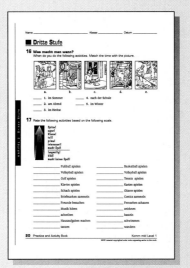

## Teaching Transparencies

The **Teaching Transparencies** benefit the visual learner as well as all students. These colorful, situational transparencies add variety and focus to your classroom. The **Chapter Resources** books include suggestions to help you integrate the 24 transparencies and two full-color map transparencies into your lesson plans.

## Audiocassette Program

The listening activities in the **Audiocassette Program** help students develop their listening and pronunciation skills by providing opportunities to hear native speakers of German in a variety of authentic situations and to practice the sounds of the language.

## Practice and Activity Book

The **Practice and Activity Book** is filled with imaginative, challenging activities that will motivate students to learn German. In addition, there are exercises that reinforce the grammatical structures. Extension activities allow students to explore culture and language in a personally relevant context.

## Test Generator

The **Test Generator** is a software program that enables you to create customized worksheets, quizzes, and tests for each chapter in *Komm mit!* The **Test Generator** is available for IBM® PC and Compatibles and Macintosh® computers

T59

# Komm mit! Video

Komm mit! *Video Program* and Komm mit! *Expanded Video Program bring the German speaking world right into your classroom! Filmed entirely on location in Germany and Austria, these video programs feature native speakers of German in realistic, high-interest situations.*

Video is the ideal medium for providing authentic input and increasing proficiency in German. With the **Video Program** and **Expanded Video Program,** students both see and hear speakers of German interacting with one another naturally in realistic settings. Students' comprehension of authentic speech is enhanced by the rich visual cues that the video provides. Moreover, the video is entertaining as well as educational.

## *Komm mit!* Video Program

The **Video Program** correlates directly with the *Komm mit!* Pupil's Edition:

♦ **Chapter Opener** Filmed on location in the chapter setting, these images preview the chapter theme and reflect the functions and vocabulary of the chapter. This dynamic collage of people in real situations is a motivating introduction to the chapter.

♦ **Los geht's! Act I** A contemporary, dramatic episode, thematically linked to the chapter, models the functional expressions, vocabulary, and grammar, and also spirals material from previous chapters in new contexts. This video episode can be used either as the primary or supplemental means of presenting the chapter.

♦ **Landeskunde** Authentic interviews with native speakers of German on a variety of cultural topics complement the information presented in the chapter. German culture comes to life as real people talk about themselves, their country, and their way of life.

# Komm mit! Expanded Video Program

Komm mit! *Expanded Video Program offers the teacher an even wider variety of video materials, directly related to the textbook, which will enhance and expand students' proficiency in the German language and their knowledge of people, places, and culture.*

The Expanded Video Program includes all of the material provided in the Video Program, and more.

♦ **Location Opener** A narrated tour of the region presented in the Location Opener expands students' acquaintance with the geography and people of that area.

♦ **Los geht's!** Act II continues the dramatic episode begun in Act I to further motivate and challenge students. The episodes of **Los geht's!** Act I end in ways that suggest several possible sequels. In **Act II**, the dramatic episodes continue the story lines and resolve the situations. **Act II** not only provides additional high-interest input related to the functions and vocabulary of each chapter, but also offers opportunities for students to go a step beyond. Confidence and proficiency increase as Act II spirals functions, vocabulary, and structures from previous chapters and previews content of upcoming chapters.

♦ **Landeskunde** interviews are presented in their entirety and additional people are interviewed in the **Expanded Video Program**. These interviews with a wide variety of native speakers of German give students exposure to regional variations in speech, the diversity of the German people, and varying points of view. This assortment of interviews from the German-speaking countries enriches students' appreciation of German culture.

♦ **Video realia** provide short segments of video that include authentic footage from German television, music videos, news broadcasts, commercials, and more. Students will gain confidence as they realize that they can understand and enjoy material not expressly designed for language learners, but produced for native speakers of German!

## Komm mit! Video Guide

*Komm mit!* Video Guide provides background information and suggestions for pre- and post-viewing activities for all portions of the **Video Program** and the **Expanded Video Program**. In addition, the **Video Guide** contains a transcript and synopsis of each **Los geht's!** dramatic episode, a supplemental vocabulary list, and reproducible student activity sheets.

# Chapter 3 Sample Lesson Plan

| DAILY PLANS | RESOURCES |
|---|---|
| **DAY 1**    OBJECTIVE: **To find out about homes and families of German-speaking students** | |
| Chapter Opener, pp. 64-65 Discussion<br>**Los Geht's!** pp. 66-67:<br>  Motivating Activity, p. 63H<br>  Basic Material: **Bei Jens zu Hause!**<br>  **Was passiert hier?** 1, p. 68<br>  **Genauer lesen** 2, p. 68<br>  **Stimmt oder stimmt nicht?** 3, p. 68<br>  Activity 4, p. 68<br>Closure: Discussion<br>Assign: Activity 5, p. 68 | *Video Program* OR *Expanded*<br>*Video Program*, Videocassette 1<br>*Video Guide*, **Kapitel 3**<br>*Textbook Audiocassette* 2A<br><br><br><br><br>*Practice and Activity Book* |
| **DAY 2**    OBJECTIVE: **To talk about where you live** | |
| **Erste Stufe**, p. 69<br>  Presentation: **So sagt man das! / Wortschatz**, p. 63I<br>  Activity 6, p. 70<br>  Activity 8, p. 70<br>  **Landeskunde**, p 73: Discussion<br>  Assignment: Activity 7, p. 70 | *Textbook Audiocassette* 2A<br>*Chapter Resources*, Book 1<br>*Video Program* OR *Expanded*<br>*Video Program*, Videocassette 1<br>*Video Guide*, **Kapitel 3**<br>*Practice and Activity Book* |
| **DAY 3**    OBJECTIVE: **To offer food and drink and to respond to an offer** | |
| Presentation: **Wortschatz** (p 71), p. 63I<br>Presentation: **So sagt man das!** (p 70), p. 63I<br>Activity 9, p. 71: Discussion<br>Presentation: **Grammatik** (p. 71), p. 63J<br>Activity 10, p. 71<br>Presentation: **So sagt man das!** (p. 72), p. 63J<br>Activity 12, p. 72<br>Assess, p 63K<br>Closure, p. 63K<br>Assignment: Activity 11, p. 72 | *Textbook Audiocassette* 2A<br>*Chapter Resources*, Book 1<br><br><br><br><br><br><br><br>*Practice and Activity Book* |
| **DAY 4**    OBJECTIVE: **To describe a room** | |
| Quiz: **3-1**<br>**Zweite Stufe**, p. 74<br>  Motivating Activity, p. 63L<br>  Presentation: **Wortschatz** (p. 74), p. 63L<br>  Activity 13, p. 74<br>  Presentation: **So sagt man das!** (p. 75),p. 63L<br>  Assignment: Activity 14, p. 75 | *Chapter Resources*, Book 1<br>*Assessment Items*,<br>  *Audiocassette* 7A<br>*Textbook Audiocassette* 2A<br><br><br>*Practice and Activity Book* |
| **DAY 5**    OBJECTIVE: **To describe a room** | |
| Presentation: **Grammatik** (p. 75), p. 63L<br>Activities 15, 16, 17, pp. 75-76<br>Assess, p. 63M<br>Game, p. 63M<br>Closure, p. 63M<br>Assignment: Activity 18, p. 76 | *Chapter Resources*, Book 1<br><br><br><br><br>*Practice and Activity Book* |

## DAY 6

**OBJECTIVE:** To talk about family members

Quiz: 3-2
**Dritte Stufe**, p. 77
  Motivating Activity, p. 63N
  Presentation: **Wortschatz** (p. 77), p. 63N
  Activity 19, p. 77
  Activity 20, p. 78
  Presentation: **So sagt man das!** (p. 78), p. 63N
  Assignment: Activity 21, p. 78

*Chapter Resources*, Book 1
*Assessment Items,*
  *Audiocassette* 7A
*Textbook Audiocassette* 2A

*Practice and Activity Book*

## DAY 7

**OBJECTIVE:** To use additional numbers and to describe people

Presentation: **Wortschatz** (p. 79), p. 63O
Activities **a.** and **b.** (Wortschatz), p. 79
Activity 22, p. 79
Activity 23, p. 79
Presentation: **Wortschatz/So sagt man das!** p. 80, p. 63O
Activities 25, 26, 27, pp. 80-81
Assess, p. 63P
Game, p. 63P
Closure, p. 63P
Assignment: Activity 24, p. 79

*Textbook Audiocassette* 2A
*Chapter Resource*, Book 1

*Practice and Activity Book*

## DAY 8

**OBJECTIVE:** To read German classified ads

Quiz: **3-3**
Presentation: **Aussprache**, (p. 81), p. 63P
  Diktat, p. 63D
Presentation: **Zum Lesen**, (pp. 82-83), p. 63P
Activities 1-6, Discussion pp. 82-83
Assignment: Activity 7, p.83

*Chapter Resources*, Book 1
*Assessment Items,*
  *Audiocassette* 7A
*Texbook Audiocassette* 2A

*Practice and Activity Book*

## DAY 9

**OBJECTIVE:** To use what you have learned, to prepare for the Chapter Test

**Anwendung** (pp. 84-85), p. 63R
  Activities 1, 2, 4, and 6 a, p.84
**Kann ich's wirklich?**, p. 86
Assignment: **Wortschatz**, p.87

*Textbook Audiocassette* 2A
*Chapter Resources*, Book 1
*Video Program* OR *Expanded
Video Program*, Videocassette 1
*Video Guide*, **Kapitel 3**

## DAY 10

**OBJECTIVE:** To assess progress

**Kapitel 3** Chapter 3 Test

*Chapter Resources*, Book 1
*Assessment Items,*
  *Audiocassette* 7A
*Assessment Guide*, **Kaptel 3**

# VORSCHAU, pp.1-11 *Chapter Overview*

Annette von Droste-Hülshoff

Matterhorn, southwest of Zermatt

CHAPTER OVERVIEW

# VORSCHAU, pp.1-11
## *Suggested Project*

*In this activity students will consider their reasons for studying German (motivation) and set personal objectives and goals. Students will share their ideas with the class in creative poster presentations that can also be used to decorate the classroom and provide motivation later in the semester. This project should be done in English.*

## MATERIALS

✂ **Students may need**
- Poster board
- construction paper
- scissors
- glue
- tape
- old magazines
- travel brochures

## Outline

Students should address the following areas in their poster presentations:

**Motivation**   What are two or three major reasons you are learning German (may be social, academic, or professional)?

**Objectives**   What are two or three realistic objectives you would like to achieve in this class this semester?

**Long-Term Goals**   What are your long-term goals for learning German?

## SUGGESTED SEQUENCE

1. Talk to students about the importance of being aware of motivation and setting objectives and goals for language learning. Mention that initial motivations, objectives, and goals are likely to change throughout the learning process. You may want to share your own "story" with students, explaining the reasons you began to learn German, and describing how your motivation, objectives, and goals changed over the years.

2. Describe the project and assign a date for the oral presentations. Write the project questions on the board, or distribute a project assignment sheet. Be sure to set a time limit for presentations.

3. Go over each of the project questions and elicit a few example answers from the class. If no one has any ideas at first, you might want to give a few of the examples listed here as suggestions.

   a. Motivation (reasons for learning)—need foreign language credit to graduate, need foreign language for college or future career, have German relatives, like German food, want to learn about German culture, etc.

   b. Objectives—be able to carry on a simple conversation in German, be able to write a letter to a German-speaking pen pal, get a B in this class, etc.

   c. Long-Term Goals—test out of foreign language requirement in college, speak fluently enough to order a meal at a German restaurant, travel in German-speaking countries, study at a German university, etc.

Stress that students should be honest with themselves, even if their motivation, objectives, and goals are not as romantic or intellectual as they think might be expected.

4. Give students some time in class to brainstorm and begin organizing ideas.

5. Students create their posters based on their personal motivations, objectives, and goals. Encourage students to be as creative as they want to be, using words, photos, drawings, etc. to express themselves. This can be done in class or as homework.

6. Students make their presentations to the class, showing their posters and explaining their motivation, objectives, and goals.

## GRADING THE PROJECT

The purpose of this project is to encourage students to think about why they are learning German, and what kinds of outcomes they expect. Because of the personal nature of the project, it would be counterproductive to assign a grade to the subjective content of the project. Instead, grading should focus on completion (were all aspects of the assignment completed?), presentation, and creativity.

Suggested point distribution (total=100 points)

| | |
|---|---|
| Completion of assignment | 40 |
| Poster and presentation | 40 |
| Creativity | 20 |

# Vorschau, pages 1-11

## Teacher Notes

- The **Vorschau** is meant to be an introduction to the study of German. Students should not be expected to fully master the material. We recommend spending no more than three class periods on the **Vorschau.**
- The script for Activity 1 can be found on p. 15D.

## *U*sing the Photographs and Maps, *pp. 1-3*

▶ *page 1*

### Motivating Activity

Ask students to brainstorm and write down their ideas about the following question: "What comes to mind when you think of the German-speaking countries or the German language?" Examples: German cars, foods, tennis players, etc.

### Background Information

① This photograph depicts the city of Innsbruck. It was the site of the 1964 and 1976 Winter Olympics.

② This photograph depicts the Matterhorn. For more information, see notes on p. T68.

③ This photograph depicts the castle Wartburg in Eisenach, Germany. The Wartburg was commissioned in 1067 by Ludwig der Springer. According to legend, he is said to have exclaimed, **"Wart Berg, du sollst mir eine Burg werden!"**, hence the name Wartburg. The castle is situated 400 meters high on a rocky slope, and in its 900-year history, it has never been besieged, conquered, or destroyed. The Wartburg is not the biggest or most beautiful of all German castles, but it is as well known and as frequently visited as Ludwig's famous castle Neuschwanstein in Bavaria. Martin Luther went into hiding at Wartburg in 1521 under the alias "Junker Jörg." During the time he was at Wartburg, Luther translated the Bible. This interior section of the Wartburg was built in the **Fachwerk** style. **Fachwerk** is a building style

consisting of a framework of straight and crosstimbered beams in which the area between the beams is filled in with clay or bricks. This style of architecture reached its high point in the 16th and 17th centuries.

## Teaching Suggestion

1 Before students listen to the cassette, ask them to locate the countries where German is spoken. Then ask them to also point out the capital of each country.

## Background Information

1 After students have done Activity 1, you might want to tell them about the following landmark. **Unter den Linden**: a street located between the Brandenburg Gate and Marx-Engels-Place and considered for the past 250 years to be the most beautiful street in Berlin.

## Music Connection

1 Ask students if they know a very famous composer who lived in Salzburg. (Mozart) Ask them if they can mention some of his works. (Examples: **Eine kleine Nachtmusik,** and operas such as **Die Zauberflöte, Don Giovanni**)

## Thinking Critically

- **Observing** Have students scan the map on p.1 and identify two geographical features (lakes, rivers, mountains, islands, coastlines, etc.) that also occur in the students' own geographic region. Next, ask them to identify two features that are unfamiliar.

▶ *pages 2-3*

## Geography Connection

Ask students to locate the rivers that were mentioned in Activity 1: **der Rhein, die Donau, die Elbe,** and **die Oder.** Ask them why these rivers play such an enormous role in the country's economy. (transportation, commerce, etc.) Can they think of rivers in the United States of similar importance? (Mississippi, Missouri, Saint Lawrence, Ohio)

## Geography Connection

The activity on p. 1 gave students examples of well-known ski resorts. Give students examples such as **St. Moritz** and **Zermatt** and have students find them on a map.

 **Multicultural Connection**

Point out to students that Liechtenstein is a monarchy led by **Fürst Hans Adam II**. Ask students what other countries have a monarch. (Examples: Japan, Morocco, England, Sweden, Monaco, Belgium, The Netherlands, Denmark) Ask students if they know what type of government the other German-speaking countries have. (parliamentary democracies)

# $\mathcal{U}$sing the Photographs, pp. 4-5

▶ *page 4*

## Background Information

① Germany's highways are choking with traffic, and the sky is crowded with air traffic during the day (many cities do not permit flights in and out of their airports after 10 PM and before 6 AM). Therefore, trains are a vital part of Germany's infrastructure. The ICE, the Intercity-Express, which is considerably faster than the automobile and therefore competitive with the airlines, began service in 1991. It runs between western Germany's largest cities. In order to accommodate speeds up to 280 km/h or 173 mi/h and to make the rails as straight as possible, new railroad beds had to be built, along with new bridges and tunnels. Billions of marks have been invested in this undertaking so far, and indications are that these trains will be successful and profitable. Since reunification, Germany has planned to invest another 56 billion marks for rebuilding the infrastructure in the states in the east and to reconnect them to the states in the west. Sixty percent of this amount, about 33 billion marks, will be spent on new rail lines to cut travel time, for example, between Hannover and Berlin from nearly four hours to 105 minutes.

**Culture Note** Tell students that the railway system is the largest transportation enterprise in Germany. It is currently owned and operated by the federal government but will soon be privatized.

② The **Brandenburger Tor** was built between 1788 and 1791 by architect Carl Gotthard Langhans and first named **Friedenstor.** It was modeled after the Propylaea of the Acropolis in Athens, Greece. It is the only one remaining of 18 original gates in Berlin.

**Culture Note** City walls originated in medieval times when many cities in Europe erected them as a defense against invaders. Gates became important because they were the only ways to enter and leave the towns. As cities expanded beyond the confines of the original walls, the walls were often torn down, but many of the gates survived.

**Multicultural Connection** Have students compare the Brandenburg Gate to similar structures in other parts of the world. Examples might be the Great Wall of China and the fortifications of Zimbabwe in Africa. The Great Wall of China is a 30-ft. high fortification that runs for 1,500 miles from the Yellow Sea westward deep into central Asia. In the 3rd century B.C., Shih Huang Ti, the first emperor of united China, connected a number of existing walls into a single system to keep out barbarian tribes. The Great Wall remains the largest structure ever built. Zimbabwe (Bantu for "stone dwelling") was a large fortified city, now in ruins, located southeast of Nyanda in the modern African country of Zimbabwe. Between the 11th and the 15th centuries, Zimbabwe, with its impressive fortifications was the center of a large empire.

③ Liechtenstein's history dates back as far as 800 B.C., but the principality was not officially founded until 1719. The country's government is headed by a male-line monarch. The present head, Prince Hans Adam II, shares the governmental power with the Liechtenstein parliament, which is elected directly by the public. Despite its small size (comparable to Washington D.C.), Liechtenstein is one of the most highly industrialized countries. It has a population of 30,000. The capital, Vaduz, with a population of approximately 5,000, is the seat of government and the residence of the monarch and his family. The largest number of visitors to Liechtenstein come from Switzerland, Germany, and the United States, primarily for the alpine sports.

④ The State Opera in Vienna (**Wiener Oper**) was built in the 1860s and faithfully reconstructed after it was destroyed in World War II. Performance season is September through June with performances daily.

⑤ The Matterhorn (14,691 ft/4,478 m) is a mountain located along the border between Switzerland and Italy. It owes its German name (it is called Mont Cervin in French and Monte Cervino in Italian) to the Swiss village of Zermatt (Zer**matt**/**Matt**erhorn) located 6 mi/10 km from the mountain.

**Geography Connection** Have students look up the height of the Matterhorn in an encyclopedia or an atlas. (14,691 ft/4,478 m) Ask them to compare this peak to some American mountains. Examples: Pikes Peak in Colorado 14,110 ft/4,301 m; Mount Shasta in California 14,162 ft/4,316 m; Mount McKinley in Alaska 20,320 ft/6,194 m, the highest in the United States and in North America

**Multicultural Connection** Like the Matterhorn, other mountains across the world have become identified with a particular culture or country. Mount Fuji in Japan, for example, is often used as a symbol of the Japanese people and culture. Your students may be able to suggest other mountains that are closely identified with a particular country or culture. Examples: Olympus in Greece; Kilimanjaro in Tanzania; Popocatépetl in Mexico; Everest in Nepal; Etna in Italy

▶ *page 5*

## Teaching Suggestion

Have students look at the pictures on p. 5. Ask them which ones they recognize. What can they tell you about them? Which areas of "culture" do these people represent? (science, music, literature, sports, psychology, etc) Ask students if they know of any other famous German-speaking people.

### ❖ For Individual Needs

**Challenge** Have students choose a famous German-speaking person and write a short report explaining this person's contribution. Students may also give an oral presentation about that person. Afterwards, reports may be displayed on the bulletin board.

## *T*eaching Das Alphabet,
*p. 6*

## Teaching Suggestion

**2** After students have listened to the rhyme, let them practice spelling their names. (Later when students have chosen their German names, you could ask them to spell them out as well.) As students get more comfortable with the sounds, they can then play the following game for auditory learners.

### ♟ Game

Divide the class into two teams. One person from each team comes up to the board. As you spell a word in German, the contestants write each letter on the board. Each student who spells the word correctly wins a point for his or her team. At the conclusion of each round, have students spell the words aloud.

## Language Note

**3** The abbreviations in Activity 3 stand for the following: **VW=Volkswagen; BMW=Bayerische Motoren Werke; BRD=Bundesrepublik Deutschland; ADAC=Allgemeiner Deutscher Automobil Club; BASF=Badische Anilin- und Soda-Fabrik.**

## Teacher Note

**3** Here are some other frequently used abbreviations: **Kfz=Kraftfahrzeug** (*motor vehicle*); **LKW= Lastkraftwagen** (*semitrailer*); **DSB=Deutscher Sportbund** (*German athletic association*).

## *T*eaching Wie heißt du?
*p. 7*

## Teaching Suggestion

**4** After the listening activity, distribute index cards to be used as name tags by the students. Before students choose a German name, address the girls in class and slowly read them the list of female names. While the girls are choosing their names, address the boys in the class and read all the male names to them. Then go around the class

and repeat any names that students have problems with as they decide on their names. For additional names have students look on p. 325.

# Teaching Im Klassenzimmer, p. 8

## Teaching Suggestion

7 Have signs with the corresponding German words on them taped to key objects in the classroom. Point to the signs as you pronounce the names of the objects. Repeat them several times. Remove signs shortly before doing Activity 7b.

 **For Individual Needs**

8 **Kinesthetic Learners** Explain to students the expressions **Bitte zeig auf ...! Bitte zeigt auf ...!** to prepare for the following TPR activity. Model the appropriate action by repeating the command and carrying it out. Then motion for the class to imitate the action. Repeat commands several times. Example: **Zeig .../ Zeigt .../ auf die Tafel/ auf den Schreibtisch/ auf Kelly/ auf Steve**, etc.

**TPR** **Total Physical Response**

A simple way to introduce the **Ausdrücke fürs Klassenzimmer** is to teach them through TPR. Model the commands for the students and then have them follow your commands.

# Teaching Die Zahlen, p. 9

## Motivating Activity

9 Write the following numbers on the board: **24.8.79** (birthday given in order of date, month, and year); **24109 Kiel** (zip code of Kiel); **0431/ 322370** (area code and phone number). Then ask students what they think the numbers correspond to. Students don't need to know how to say the numbers in German. This should only show them that numbers can be used in different ways in different countries. Tell students that after the reunification zip codes changed from 4 to 5 digits in 1993. This eliminated duplicate zip codes in the former two Germanys.

## Teaching Suggestion

9 Ask students to look at the handwritten numbers on the page and to compare the way Germans write numbers with the way people do in the United States.

## Language Note

Here's a German rhyme you might want to teach your students: 1, 2, 3, 4, **das Glück gehört mir!** This rhyme is often recited when somebody sees a chimney sweep. Chimney sweeps are said to bring good luck to the person who sees them.

 **For Individual Needs**

**Kinesthetic Learners** Bring a ball (soccer ball, tennis ball, etc.) to class. Throw the ball to individual students and ask them to bounce the ball as many times as the number between 0 and 20 that you call out in German. (If you call out **dreizehn**, the student bounces the ball 13 times.) You could also ask the student or the whole class to count aloud in German while the ball is being bounced. As a variation to this game students could pass or throw the ball from person to person—the person catching the ball says the next number in the sequence.

**For Individual Needs**

10 **Auditory Learners** After students have completed Activity 10c, ask them to stand up. Read off a list of your students' phone numbers, which you might have recorded on the first day of class. (If you don't have a list, ask your students to write their phone numbers on a slip of paper before beginning this activity.) When a student hears his or her number, he or she can sit down.

## Reteaching: Numbers and Letters

Write the following German license plates on the board and have students read them aloud. This will help students review numbers, letters, and abbreviations. You might want to go over the abbreviations quickly first and point out that license plates in Germany always indicate the city where the car was registered.

| | |
|---|---|
| KI – AM  199 | (Kiel) |
| M – FB  345 | (München) |
| K – NM  028 | (Köln) |
| NMS – CG  607 | (Neumünster) |

Preliminary Chapter  **T69**

# $\mathcal{U}$sing Why Study German?
## p. 10

###  Culture Notes

- Between 1830 and 1890, more than one-fourth of all immigrants to the United States were German. The peak years for German immigration were 1881-90 when 1,452,970 Germans came to America. In America, most Germans settled in the German triangle, an area bounded by the three cities of Saint Louis, Cincinnati, and Milwaukee; however, German settlers could also be found across the country in places as distant as Anaheim, California and areas around San Antonio, Texas. At one point, there were seventy-four daily and nearly four hundred weekly German newspapers published in America.

- In addition to such institutions of American life as kindergartens and delicatessens, the immigrants from Germany made other significant contributions ranging from the Kentucky rifle, a mainstay of colonial frontiersmen, to the Conestoga wagons in which pioneers moved west.

- Ironically, two of the most famous German-Americans, John "Blackjack" Pershing and Dwight D. Eisenhower, rose to national prominence because of their military leadership in World Wars I and II—against German forces. For additional information on German immigration, you may wish to consult *Coming to America: A History of Immigration and Ethnicity in American Life,* by Roger Daniels. © 1990 by Visual Education Corporation.

### Thinking Critically

**Drawing Inferences**   Ask students why they think some Germans decided to leave Germany and immigrate to the United States. Ask them when most Germans came to the United States. (Examples: overcrowding in Germany and availability of land in the United States; religious and political persecution; large influx of German immigrants from mid 19th century to World War I)

### Geography Connection

Have students look at a map of the United States and look for other cities with German names.

### Language Note

Ask students if they can think of any other German words that have been incorporated into the English language. Examples: **Holstein, Gesundheit, Muesli, Sauerkraut, Fahrvergnügen, Kaffeeklatsch,** etc.

### Teaching Suggestion

You might want to give students extra credit for doing the following assignment. Have the whole class make a bulletin board display of famous German-Americans. Here are a few suggestions: Levi Strauss, Wernher von Braun, John Jacob Astor, Friedrich Wilhelm von Steuben, Maximilian Berlitz, Henry Kissinger, and Arnold Schwarzenegger, who is of Austrian descent. Students could group these famous people according to categories, for example, sports, politics, science, etc.

### Thinking Critically

**Drawing Inferences**   Have students pair up and brainstorm additional careers in which German or any other foreign language would be necessary or be a valuable asset. They should make a list of the careers.

### Community Link

If possible you might ask some guest speakers to come to your class and talk about the importance of German in their careers.

### Group Work

Ask students to look through the classified ad section of a major newspaper and look for advertised jobs which require another language. This should be done at home. Or you may want to collect the ads yourself and make them available to the class. Next put students in groups of 3 or 4 and give each group 3 or 4 ads. Each student in the group looks at every ad, and students as a group collect the following data: job title, job description, qualifications needed, and name of business or organization offering the job. Have every group present its list of jobs to the class, and the whole class can vote on the job for which they would most like to apply.

## Teacher Note

There are many German-owned companies throughout the United States, with a large number of them located in New York, California, Illinois, Georgia, Texas, and New Jersey. Thus the demand for German language proficiency is high.

## Teaching Suggestion

Tell students that part of learning a language is also learning about the people who speak it. Knowledge of current events is therefore an asset. Ask students always to be on the look-out for news from any of the German-speaking countries, whether it is from TV or the newspaper. If they see or hear of news, they should report it briefly in class the next day. Students can also be encouraged to bring in newspaper clippings or short summaries of news reports. You can display these on a special bulletin board in your classroom labeled **Nachrichten aus deutschsprachigen Ländern.** Give extra credit for student participation in this ongoing project.

## History Connection

- Ask students what the abbreviation UN stands for. Ask them what the purpose of the United Nations is.

- Ask students if they know when the Berlin Wall came down. (Nov. 9, 1989) Ask them what this symbolizes and what the historical significance of this event is.

## Thinking Critically

**Drawing Inferences**   Ask students to talk about other areas they think might change as a result of the events in the early nineties in Germany and the rest of Europe (reunification of Germany, division of Czechoslovakia, dissolution of the Soviet Union, the war in Yugoslavia, etc.). Discuss with students some of the ways they might be affected directly by these events. Examples: new textbooks, maps, history books, etc.

## Using Tips for Studying German, p. 11

## Teaching Suggestions

- After introducing students to the paragraph on speaking, suggest that students always greet you and the other German students in German, even outside the classroom.

- For additional authentic listening, provide students occasionally with popular German songs and accompanying lyrics.

- Tell students that an excellent way to "connect" is in the oral and written portfolios they will soon start developing and the **Notizbuch** they will keep throughout the year. These will provide opportunities to experiment with the language. For more information on portfolios, please refer to the essay on pp. T27–29 and the *Assessment Guide.* The **Notizbuch** is a personal diary in which students will be asked to write in German. There will be at least one **Notizbuch** activity per chapter.

- If you have access to magazines, newspapers, or any other realia from German-speaking countries, make them available to your students. This will provide students with additional authentic input. Look on pp. T38–39 for useful addresses where you can obtain such information.

# Vorschau

*German is the native language of nearly 100 million people in Austria, Germany, Switzerland, Liechtenstein, and parts of France and Italy. It is an official language of Luxembourg and is used as a second language by many other people in central Europe.*

DÄNEMARK

*Nordsee*

*Ostsee*

Hamburg

Bremen

*Elbe*

*Havel*

*Oder*

POLEN

*Weser*

Berlin

*Ems*

BUNDESREPUBLIK

Potsdam

NIEDER-
LANDE

*Rhein*

*Oder*

*Spree*

Düsseldorf

DEUTSCHLAND

Leipzig

*Elbe*

*Neisse*

Bonn

RUHRGEBIET

*Saale*

Dresden

BELGIEN

*Mosel*

Frankfurt

*Main*

TSCHECHISCHE REPUBLIK

*Rhein*

*Neckar*

LUXEM-
BURG

Stuttgart

*Donau*

SLOWAKEI

FRANKREICH

*Rhein*

SCHWARZWALD

*Isar*

Linz

*Donau*

*Inn*

*Traun*

München

Wien

*Rhein*

A L P E N

Zugspitze

Salzburg

Eisenstadt

Basel Zürich

Bregenz

*Salzach*

ÖSTERREICH

*Ems*

*Aare*

St.Gallen

Vaduz

Innsbruck

A L P E N

Luzern

Chur

Graz

UNGARN

Bern

SCHWEIZ

Davos

Großglockner

*Rhône* Interlaken

A L P E N

St.Moritz

Großvenediger

Eiger

Klagenfurt

Zermatt

ITALIEN

LIECHTENSTEIN

SLOWENIEN

Matterhorn

KROATIEN

② Matterhorn, Schweiz

① Innsbruck, Österreich

③ Wartburg, Deutschland

## 1 Komm mit! *Come along!*

You are now going to take a trip to the German-speaking countries of **Deutschland, Österreich, Schweiz,** and **Liechtenstein.** As you listen to a description of these countries, try to locate on the map the places mentioned. When you have finished, do the following activities.

Possible answers: Frankreich, Niederlande, Belgien

1. Find and identify:
   a. a non-German-speaking country west of Germany
   b. a river that runs through Germany, Austria, and Hungary
      Donau (Danube)
   c. a city in northern Germany; in Austria; in Liechtenstein

   Some possible answers Hamburg, Bremen, Kiel; Wien, Salzburg; Vaduz

2. a. Look at the map on page 2. What three German cities have the status of city-states? Hamburg, Bremen, Berlin
   b. Look at the map on page 3. What is the name of the mountain peak southwest of Zermatt, Switzerland? Matterhorn

EUROPA

NORWEGEN
SCHWEDEN LETTLAND
DÄNEMARK LITAUEN
GROSSBRITANNIEN
IRLAND
NIEDER-
LANDE POLEN
BEL. DEUTSCHLAND
LUX. TSCHECH. REP.
SLOWAKISCHE REP.
ÖSTERREICH UNGARN
SCHWEIZ
FRANKREICH LIECH. SLOWENIEN
KROATIEN BOSNIEN-
HERZEGOWINA SERBIEN
SPANIEN ITALIEN
AND.
PORTUGAL ALB.

# Map of the Federal Republic of Germany

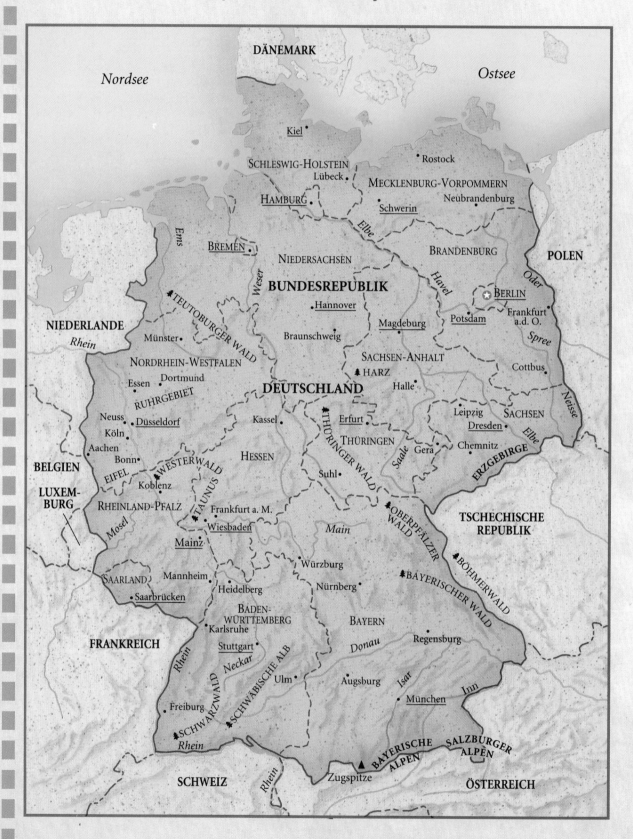

DÄNEMARK

Nordsee

Ostsee

Kiel

Rostock

SCHLESWIG-HOLSTEIN

Lübeck

MECKLENBURG-VORPOMMERN

HAMBURG

Neubrandenburg

Schwerin

Ems

BREMEN

NIEDERSACHSEN

BRANDENBURG

POLEN

Weser

BUNDESREPUBLIK

Elbe

Havel

Oder

BERLIN

Hannover

Frankfurt a.d. O.

TEUTOBURGER WALD

NIEDERLANDE

Magdeburg

Potsdam

Rhein

Münster

Braunschweig

Spree

NORDRHEIN-WESTFALEN

SACHSEN-ANHALT

Essen

Dortmund

HARZ

Cottbus

RUHRGEBIET

DEUTSCHLAND

Halle

Neuss

Düsseldorf

Kassel

Erfurt

Leipzig

SACHSEN

Köln

THÜRINGEN

Dresden

Neisse

Aachen

Bonn

WESTERWALD

HESSEN

THÜRINGER WALD

Gera

Chemnitz

Elbe

BELGIEN

EIFEL

Suhl

Saale

ERZGEBIRGE

Koblenz

TAUNUS

LUXEM-
BURG

RHEINLAND-PFALZ

Frankfurt a. M.

OBERPFÄLZER
WALD

TSCHECHISCHE
REPUBLIK

Mosel

Wiesbaden

Main

Mainz

Würzburg

BÖHMERWALD

SAARLAND

Mannheim

Nürnberg

BAYERISCHER WALD

Saarbrücken

Heidelberg

BADEN-
WÜRTTEMBERG

BAYERN

Karlsruhe

Donau

Regensburg

FRANKREICH

Stuttgart

SCHWÄBISCHE ALB

Rhein

Neckar

Ulm

Augsburg

Isar

München

Inn

Freiburg

SCHWARZWALD

SALZBURGER
ALPEN

Rhein

BAYERISCHE
ALPEN

SCHWEIZ

Rhein

Zugspitze

ÖSTERREICH

# Map of Liechtenstein, Switzerland, and Austria

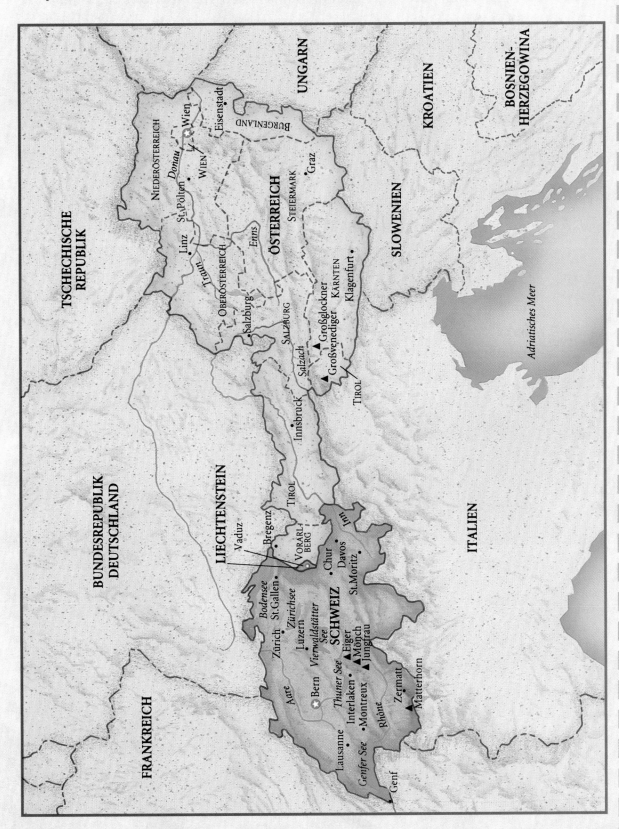

*There are many things that may come to mind when you hear of places like Germany, Switzerland, Austria, and Liechtenstein. As you can see from these photos, life in these countries ranges from the very traditional to the super modern.*

**1** ICE, Intercity-Express

**2** Brandenburg Gate in Berlin

**3** Liechtenstein

**4** State Opera in Vienna

**5** Matterhorn, southwest of Zermatt

*Through the centuries, in areas as diverse as science and sports, literature and psychology, German-speaking women and men have made invaluable contributions, both in their own countries and abroad.*

### Albert Einstein

**1**

**Albert Einstein** (1879-1955) revolutionized physics with his theory of relativity. In 1933 he emigrated to the United States and began a lifetime teaching career at the Institute for Advanced Study in Princeton, New Jersey.

### Steffi Graf

**2**

**Ludwig van Beethoven** (1770-1827) is perhaps the best known composer of classical music. Though his hearing grew increasingly impaired, he composed his greatest masterpieces during the last years of his life.

### Ludwig Van Beethoven

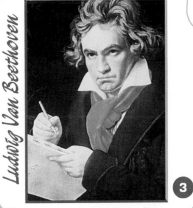

**3**

**Steffi Graf** (1969-), one of the top-ranked tennis players in the world, has won a number of major tournaments, including the Grand Slam Championship in 1988.

### Annette von Droste-Hülshoff

**4**

**Günter Grass** (1927-) is a major figure in contemporary German literature. Many of his works are controversial and deal with such issues as Germany's struggle with its Nazi past. Two well-known works are **Die Blechtrommel** and **Katz und Maus**.

### Günter Grass

**5**

**Annette von Droste-Hülshoff** (1797-1848) was one of the leading women writers of nineteenth-century Germany. She is remembered for both her poetry and her prose, her best-known work being the novella **Die Judenbuche**.

### Sigmund & Anna Freud

**6**

**Sigmund Freud** (1856-1939) is the founder of modern psycho-analysis. His theories of the unconscious, neuroses, and dreams have had a lasting impact on psychology. His daughter, **Anna Freud** (1895-1982), helped develop the study of child psychology.

# Das Alphabet

## 2 Richtig aussprechen *Pronounce correctly*

The letters of the German alphabet are almost the same as those in English but the pronunciation is different. Listen to the rhyme, and learn the alphabet the way many children in German-speaking countries learn it. Then pronounce each letter after your teacher or after the recording.

a b c d e,
**der Kopf tut mir weh,**

f g h i j k,
**der Doktor ist da,**

l m n o,
**jetzt bin ich froh,**

p q r s t,
**es ist wieder gut, juchhe!**

u v w x,
**jetzt fehlt mir nix,**

y z,
**jetzt geh' ich ins Bett.**

There are a few more things you should remember about German spelling and pronunciation.
  **a.** The letter ß (Eszett) is often used in place of the "double s" (ss) in German spelling. However, the ß cannot always be substituted for the "double s", so it is important that as you build your German vocabulary you remember which words are spelled with ß.
  **b.** Many German words are spelled and pronounced with an umlaut (¨) over the **a, o,** or **u** (**ä, ö, ü**). The umlaut changes the sound of the vowels, as in **Käse, Österreich,** and **grün.** You will learn more about the use of the umlaut in the **Aussprache** sections of the book.

## 3 Deutsche Abkürzungen *German abbreviations*

Listen to how these common abbreviations are pronounced in German.

VW   BMW   USA   BRD   ADAC   BASF

# Wie heißt du?

**4  Hör gut zu!**  *Listen carefully*

a. Listen and try to figure out what these students are saying.

> Hallo! Wie heißt du?
>
> Ich heiße Robert. Und du? Wie heißt du?
>
> Ich heiße Monika.

b. Below are some popular first names of German girls and boys. Listen to how they are pronounced.

**Vornamen für Mädchen**

Daniela
Marina   Michaela   Nicole
Ute   Silke   Ulrike   Karin

Birgit   Christine   Julia   Inge
Christiane   Claudia   Gisela
Antje   Kristin   Katja
Sara

**Vornamen für Jungen**

Mark   Sven   Jörg
Holger   Stefan   Jochen
Christof   Michael   Jens   Benjamin

Peter   Daniel   Andreas   Manfred
Uwe   Christian   Alexander
Sebastian

c. Pick a German name for yourself and practice pronouncing it.

**5  Namenkette**  *Name chain*

One student begins the "name chain" by asking the name of the person next to him or her. That student answers and then asks the next person until everyone has had a turn. Students who wish to do so may use the German name they chose in Activity 4c above.

BEISPIEL   *EXAMPLE*   **Ich heiße Antje. Wie heißt du?**

**6  Wie heißt mein Partner?**  *What's my partner's name?*

In this book you will be asked many times to work with a partner to find out new information and to practice the new things you are learning. Find a partner who sits near you and ask that person his or her name. Then he or she will ask you.

# Im Klassenzimmer *In the classroom*

## 7 Was ist das? *What's that?*

a. As you look at the picture to the right, listen to the way the names of the classroom objects are pronounced.

b. Pick one of the objects in the illustration and write the German word for it on an index card. When your teacher calls out that object, place your card next to the correct object in your classroom.

c. Take turns asking a partner what the different objects in the classroom are called. As you point to something, you will ask: **Was ist das?** and your partner will answer in German.

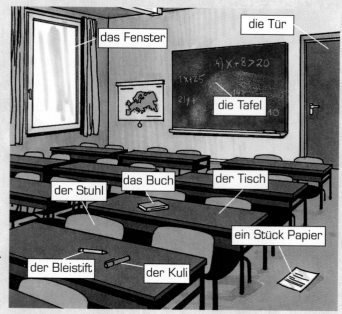

die Tür
das Fenster
die Tafel
das Buch
der Tisch
der Stuhl
ein Stück Papier
der Bleistift
der Kuli

## Ausdrücke fürs Klassenzimmer

*Expressions for the classroom*

Here are some common expressions your teacher might use in the classroom:

Öffnet eure Bücher auf Seite ... !  *Open your books to page...*
Nehmt ein Stück Papier!  *Take out a piece of paper.*
  einen Bleistift!  *a pencil.*
  einen Kuli!  *a pen.*
Steht auf!  *Stand up.*
Setzt euch!  *Sit down.*
Hört zu!  *Listen.*
Schreibt euren Namen!  *Write down your names.*
Paßt auf!  *Pay attention.*
Geht an die Tafel!  *Go to the chalkboard.*

Here are some phrases you might want to use when talking to your teacher.

Wie sagt man ... auf deutsch?  *How do you say... in German?*
Was bedeutet ...?  *What does...mean?*
Wie bitte?  *Excuse me?*

## 8 Simon sagt ... *Simon says...*

Look over the classroom expressions for a few minutes. Now your teacher will give everyone in the class instructions in German, but you should do only what your teacher says if he or she first says **Simon sagt ...**

BEISPIEL    LEHRER(IN)  Simon sagt, steht auf!
                        *Everyone in the class stands up.*

# Die Zahlen von 0 bis 20

## 9 Hör gut zu! *Listen carefully!*

Listen to how the numbers below are pronounced. Then read each number.

| 0 | 1 | 2 | 3 | 4 | 5 | 6 | 7 | 8 |
|---|---|---|---|---|---|---|---|---|
| null | eins | zwei | drei | vier | fünf | sechs | sieben | acht |

| 9 | 10 | 11 | 12 | 13 | 14 | 15 |
|---|----|----|----|----|----|----|
| neun | zehn | elf | zwölf | dreizehn | vierzehn | fünfzehn |

| 16 | 17 | 18 | 19 | 20 |
|----|----|----|----|----|
| sechzehn | siebzehn | achtzehn | neunzehn | zwanzig |

## EIN WENIG LANDESKUNDE
*(About the country and the people)*

Look again at how the numbers are written in German. Pay particular attention to the numbers  1 and 7.

When using hand signals to indicate numbers or when counting on their fingers, Germans use the thumb to indicate one, the thumb and the index finger to indicate two, and so on. How do you indicate numbers with your fingers?

## 10 Wir üben mit Zahlen! *Practicing with numbers*

a. Each person in the class will count off in sequence: first student **eins**, second student **zwei**, etc. When you reach 20, start again with number one.
b. With a partner, count aloud the girls, then the boys in your class.
c. Tell your partner your phone number one digit at a time. Your partner will write it down, say it back to you, and then tell you his or her telephone number.

## 11 Zahlenlotto *Number Game*

Draw a rectangle and divide it into sixteen squares as shown. Number the squares randomly, using numbers between 0 and 20. Use each number only once. Your teacher will call numbers in random order. As you hear each number, mark the corresponding square. The winner is the first person to mark off four numbers in a vertical, horizontal, or diagonal row.

| 8 | 2 | 5 | 13 |
|---|---|---|----|
| 7 | 1 | 6 | 4 |
| 9 | 10 | 3 | 19 |
| 18 | 11 | 16 | 12 |

# Why Study German?

Germantown, Pennsylvania

$\mathscr{C}$an you guess how many Americans trace all or part of their ethnic background to Germany, Austria, or Switzerland? — 10 million? 30 million? 50 million? If you guessed 50 million, you were close! Forty-nine million people, or about 20% of the population, reported that they were at least partly of German, Swiss, or Austrian descent.

Germans were among the earliest settlers in the United States. In 1683, the first group arrived from Krefeld and founded Germantown, Pennsylvania. Since 1683 more than seven million German-speaking immigrants have come to this country.

United Nations
General Assembly

Everywhere, there are reminders of those early settlers: towns such as Hanover, North Dakota; Berlin, Wisconsin; and Potsdam, New York; and German family names such as Klein, Meyer, and Schneider are very common. Many traditions, such as the Christmas tree and the Easter bunny, as well as many words and phrases, like *pumpernickel, noodle, wurst, dachshund,* and *kindergarten*, and those "typically American" foods such as hamburgers, pretzels, and frankfurters were brought over by German-speaking immigrants and have become part of our everyday life and language.

Perhaps German will play an important role in your future. Many exciting jobs and careers require knowledge of a foreign language, and many employers consider it to be a great asset. You could use German in many ways in your future — as a teacher, librarian, lawyer, buyer for a large company, economist, writer, publisher, financial expert, reporter, translator, sportscaster — and, of course, tour guide, to name just a few possibilities. More than 1,200 American companies have offices in the German-speaking countries, and over 140,000 Americans live and work there. German is particularly useful in technological fields. Many high-tech companies name German as the language they would prefer prospective employees to have studied.

Above all, NOW is a great time to discover German. Dramatic changes are taking place all over Europe. With the disappearance of the "iron curtain" you can now travel freely in the former German Democratic Republic (East Germany), where travel was greatly restricted for over 40 years. History-making events, like the fall of the Berlin Wall and the reunification of Germany, make this an exciting and interesting time to be learning the language and learning more about the people of the German-speaking countries. So, **komm mit** (*come along*), and let's learn German!

November, 1989:
The Fall of the
Berlin Wall

# Tips for Studying German

Most likely, you decided to study German so that you can learn to *speak* the language. This book is designed around conversational expressions (in the **SO SAGT MAN DAS!** boxes), that will help you do just that. The vocabulary (**WORTSCHATZ**) and grammar (**Grammatik**) are intended to expand your language skills so that you can say what you really want to say.

## Speak

To get the best results from instruction in German, practice speaking aloud every day. Talking with classmates and your teacher is an easy and fun way to practice. Don't be afraid to experiment! And remember: It's okay to make mistakes! It's a natural part of learning a language.

## Practice

Studying for short periods each day is the best way to keep on top of things. As with most subjects, it is much easier to remember things in small pieces than in large ones. Cramming for hours the night before a test will not work. Remember, you did not learn English by staying up all night once when you were two years old!

## Listen

Listening to a new language is one of the best ways to learn it. You probably won't be able to understand everything you hear, but don't be frustrated. You are actually absorbing many things even though you don't realize it. When you are asked to listen for certain information, think of it as a detective game. Listen for possible clues, catch what you can, and enjoy it!

## Expand

You will need to get a notebook for your German class. In this **Notizbuch** you will be asked periodically to write information that pertains to you personally. You can use this information when you are asked to say or write something about yourself. There are also many ways to increase your contact with German outside of class. You might be able to find someone living near you who speaks German or find German programs on TV. There are also many German magazines and newspapers in stores and libraries in the United States. Don't be afraid to try to read them! You will not understand every word you read, but that's okay—you don't need to. You can usually tell what a story or article is about from the words you do recognize.

## Connect

When you study vocabulary, use the new words in a sentence or phrase. When you are trying to learn whole phrases or sentences, use them in a conversation. For example, if the phrase is a question, supply an answer, and if the phrase is a statement, think of a question that would fit with it. When you are learning new grammar points, always use them in sentences as part of a larger conversation.

## Have fun!

Above all, remember to have fun! The more you try, the more you will learn. By studying German you are opening the door to many exciting discoveries about the German-speaking countries and the people who live there.

## [CD] Location Opener

# *Brandenburg, pages 12–15*
### *Expanded Video Program, Videocassette 1*

## *U*sing the Photograph,
### *pp. 12-13*

### Background Information

Sanssouci Palace was built between 1745 and 1747 by the famous German architect Georg Wenzeslaus von Knobelsdorff as a summer residence for the Prussian king, Friedrich II (**Friedrich der Große**). Located at the foot of a hill with a view of Potsdam, it is considered one of the finest examples of German rococo architecture. On either side of the base of the six-terraced entrance to the palace are statues of Venus and Mercury. In the **Marmorsaal** (marble hall), statues of Venus, Urania, and Apollo represent the arts and sciences.

### Language Note

French was the language used at the court of King Friedrich II. The name he chose for his palace comes from the French *sans souci*, which means *worry free*.

### Thinking Critically

**Comparing and Contrasting**   Ask students if they know of other impressive palaces in the world (the Palace of Versailles, France; the Winter Palace in St. Petersburg, Russia)

## *U*sing the Almanac and Map,
### *p. 13*

A coat of arms was originally painted on a knight's shield or armor so that his allies could distinguish him in battle. Over time, the study of coats of arms (called *heraldry*) became a complicated field, as coats of arms became more elaborate and formalized. The crest of the state of Brandenburg shows a red eagle on a white background. This links the state to the medieval territory **Mark Brandenburg.** When Brandenburg was a part of Prussia, the eagle was black.

### Terms in the Almanac

- **Cottbus** (128,000 inhabitants): an important center of chemical and power production

- **Brandenburg** (95,000 inhabitants): city dating back to the 6th century when it was called Brennabor. It is the home of the impressive St. Peter and Paul Cathedral, which was built between 1165 and 1240.

- **Frankfurt an der Oder** (88,000 inhabitants): an old trading and university city. Heinrich von Kleist (1777-1811), one of the greatest German dramatists, studied here.

- **Linseneintopf:** lentil stew made with bacon, leeks, carrots, potatoes, and pork sausage

- **Hühnerfrikassee:** chicken dish made with white asparagus, mushrooms, capers, and calf's tongue, and served on rice

### Using the Map

- Have students use the map on p. 2 to identify the German states that border on Brandenburg. (Mecklenburg-Vorpommern, Sachsen-Anhalt, Sachsen) You may also want to use Map Transparency 1.

- Have students identify the country that shares a border with Brandenburg. (Poland)

- Have students locate the Oder, the Havel, and the Spree rivers.

- Have students locate the cities of Potsdam, Cottbus, and Frankfurt an der Oder.

- Ask students if they have ever heard of Frankfurt. Ask them why the city of Frankfurt in Brandenburg adds the words **an der Oder** to its name. Students should infer that the name of the river the city is built on has been added to the name of Frankfurt. One reason for doing this is to distinguish Frankfurt am Main from Frankfurt an der Oder.

- Have students locate the city of Frankfurt am Main and compare its location to that of Frankfurt an der Oder.

### History Connection

In July and August of 1945, at the end of World

War II, the world centered its attention on Potsdam, when Churchill (later, Atlee) of Great Britain, Stalin of the Soviet Union, and U.S. President Truman negotiated the Potsdam Agreement in the Cecilienhof Palace. Under the Potsdam agreement Germany was divided into four **Besatzungszonen** *(occupation zones)*, one of which was to be controlled and overseen by U.S. forces.

## Geography Connection

Have students look up Germany in an atlas and compare its size to that of the United States. Then ask students to locate the state of Maryland, which is approximately the same size as Brandenburg, and compare its size to the rest of the United States and to the students' own state.

## *I*nterpreting the Photo Essay, pp. 14-15

② **Schloß Branitz** is located 2 km east of Cottbus. This two-story baroque building, dating back to 1772, was renovated around 1850 by architect Gottfried Semper for Hermann Fürst von Pückler Muskau (1785-1871), who used it as his residence. Today it serves as the **Bezirksmuseum** *(district museum)*.

③ **Friedrich II.** (**Friedrich der Große**) was born in 1712 in Berlin and died in 1786 in Potsdam. He became king of Prussia after the death of his father, **Friedrich Wilhelm I.**, in 1740. Friedrich considered himself a servant to the state (**erster Diener meines Staates**). He loved the arts and encouraged science, philosophy, and free thinking, though only to the extent that it would not overstep his own interests. He led the Prussian army in several wars, including the Seven Years' War. During his reign Prussia became a major European power. The marble statue pictured here stands in front of the **Östliches Gärtnerhaus** on the grounds of Sanssouci Palace. It was sculpted by Joseph Uphues in 1899.

④ The wing of the Sanssouci Palace known as the **Neue Kammern** is a later addition to the palace. It was built by the original architect of Sanssouci, Knobelsdorff, in 1747. It was later rebuilt from 1771 to 1775 to become a guest house with separate apartments.

⑤ **Schloß Cecilienhof** was completed in 1917 and was occupied by the Hohenzollern royal family until 1945. At the end of World War II the family fled from Stalin's Red Army but managed to take all the furnishings. In the summer of 1945 this site was chosen for the negotiations of the Potsdam Agreement. The palace had to be refurnished quickly to enable the delegation to live and work there. The **Tagesraum** with the famous **Runder Tisch** (the round table at which the delegates worked), as well as the studies that Churchill, Truman, and Stalin each occupied, are in their original condition and are open to the public.

• **History Connection** Ask students if they can think of another famous location in Europe where a peace treaty was finalized and signed. (the Palace of Versailles in France where the Treaty of Versailles was signed in 1919 to mark the end of World War I)

⑥ The **Schiffshebewerk** in Niederfinow is an important ship hoist that was built to connect the two rivers Oder and Havel by way of the **Oder-Havelkanal.** This hoist enables ships to travel despite elevation differences during the course of a waterway. The hoist operates much like an elevator. It lifts the ship in a huge water-filled trough from one level to the other.

• **Drawing Inferences** Ask students why they think countries spend so much money and energy building locks and hoists. Ask them how commerce benefits from locks and hoists. (Locks and hoists facilitate ship travel by cutting time. Centers of trade are often located near waterways, and the hoists and locks provide ships with easy access for loading and transporting goods within a country or between countries.)

⑦ The students here attend the **Dreilinden Gymnasium** in Potsdam. Five of them were born in the Berlin area: Jens (top right), Tara (middle row left), Holger (middle row right), Steffi (bottom right), and Handan (bottom left). Ahmet (top left) was born in Turkey but has spent all his life in Germany. His parents are of Italian and Turkish descent. Jens, Holger, and Steffi have native German parents. Handan's parents are Turkish, and Tara has an Iranian father and a German mother.

# Komm mit nach

# Brandenburg!

# Brandenburg

**Population:** 2.64 million

**Area:** 29,056 square kilometers (11,216 square miles), approximately as large as the state of Maryland

**Capital:** Potsdam (140,000 inhabitants)

**Cities:** Cottbus, Brandenburg, Frankfurt an der Oder

**Rivers:** Oder, Havel, Spree

**Canals:** Oder-Spreekanal, Rhinkanal, Oder-Havelkanal

**Lakes:** Ruppiner See, Werbellinsee, Schwielochsee, Plauer See

**Industries:** Textiles, machinery, cement, porcelain, farming, forestry, petroleum, coal

**Favorite local dishes:** Lentil soup, chicken fricassee

Photo ① : Die Terrassen von Schloß Sanssouci in Potsdam

# Brandenburg

*Brandenburg, the heartland of former Prussia, is a state characterized by vast flat sandy lands, hundreds of beautiful lakes, and large wooded areas consisting mostly of fir trees. A trip through the towns in Brandenburg reveals stately buildings and churches in characteristic red brick, waiting to be restored to their former beauty.*

② Castle Branitz in Cottbus, built in 1772, now a museum, is situated in a magnificient nineteenth-century park.

③ A marble statue of Frederick the Great, sculpted by Joseph Uphues.

④ The new wing of Sanssouci Palace, built in 1747 and remodeled between 1771 and 1775. In the background the recently renovated **Historische Mühle.**

⑤ Cecilienhof Palace, built between 1913 and 1917. Here the Allied powers signed the Potsdam Agreement in 1945.

⑥ A ship hoist at Niederfinow on the **Oder-Havel-Kanal**. Canal barges, like the one pictured here, transport bulk goods, such as coal, sand, or gravel.

*The students in the following three chapters live in the Potsdam area. Potsdam is the capital of Brandenburg. In 1993, Potsdam celebrated its 1000th birthday. The city became famous when Frederick the Great decided to establish his summer residence there and built Sanssouci Palace.*

⑦ Ahmet, Jens, Handan, Tara, Holger, and Steffi invite you to Potsdam.

# Kapitel 1: Wer bist du? *Chapter Overview*

| **Los geht's!** *pp. 18-20* | Vor der Schule, p. 18 | | | *Video Guide* |
|---|---|---|---|---|
| | **FUNCTIONS** | **GRAMMAR** | **CULTURE** | **RE-ENTRY** |
| **Erste Stufe** *pp. 21-24* | •Saying hello and goodbye, *p. 21* •Asking someone's name and giving yours, *p. 22* •Asking who someone is, *p. 23* | •Forming questions, *p. 23* •Definite articles **der, die, das,** *p. 24* | •**Ein wenig Landeskunde:** Greetings, *p. 21* •**Ein wenig Landeskunde:** Using **der** and **die** in front of people's names, *p. 24* | Asking someone's name, *p. 22* (from **Vorschau**) |
| **Zweite Stufe** *pp. 25-27* | Asking someone's age and giving yours, *p. 25* | Subject pronouns and the verb **sein**, *p. 26* | Map of German states and capitals, *p. 27* | •Numbers 0-20, *p. 25* (from **Vorschau**) •Geography of German-speaking countries, *p. 27* (from **Vorschau**) |
| **Dritte Stufe** *pp. 28-33* | •Talking about where people are from, *p. 28* •Talking about how someone gets to school, *p. 30* | | Landeskunde: **Wie kommst du zur Schule?** *p. 31* | |
| **Aussprache** *p. 33* | The long vowels **e, ä, ü, ö**, the letter **w**, the letter **v** | | | Diktat: *Textbook Audiocassette* 1 A |
| **Zum Lesen** *pp. 34-35* | **Postkarten aus den Ferien** Reading Strategy: Using visual clues to determine meaning | | | |
| **Review** *pp. 36-39* | •Anwendung, *p. 36* •Kann ich's wirklich? *p. 38* •Wortschatz, *p. 39* | | | |
| **Assessment Options** | **Stufe Quizzes** •*Chapter Resources,* Book 1   **Erste Stufe,** Quiz 1-1   **Zweite Stufe,** Quiz 1-2   **Dritte Stufe,** Quiz 1-3 •*Assessment Items, Audiocassette* 7 A | | **Kapitel 1 Chapter Test** •*Chapter Resources,* Book 1 •*Assessment Guide,* Speaking Test •*Assessment Items, Audiocassette,* 7 A   **Test Generator, Kapitel 1** | |

*Video Program* **OR** *Textbook Audiocassette* 1 A
*Expanded Video Program,* Videocassette 1

| **RESOURCES** Print | **RESOURCES** Audiovisual |
| --- | --- |

*Textbook Audiocassette* 1 A

*Practice and Activity Book*
*Chapter Resources,* Book 1
  •Communicative Activity 1-1
  •Additional Listening Activity 1-1 . . . . . . . . . . . . . . . . *Additional Listening Activities, Audiocassette* 9 A
  •Student Response Form
  •Realia 1-1
  •Situation Card 1-1
  •Teaching Transparency Master 1-1 . . . . . . . . . . . *Teaching Transparency* 1-1
  •Quiz 1-1. . . . . . . . . . . . . . . . . . . . . . . . . . . . . *Assessment Items, Audiocassette* 7 A

*Textbook Audiocassette* 1 A

*Practice and Activity Book*
*Chapter Resources,* Book 1
  •Additional Listening Activity 1-2 . . . . . . . . . . . . . . . *Additional Listening Activities, Audiocassette* 9 A
  •Additional Listening Activity 1-3 . . . . . . . . . . . . . *Additional Listening Activities, Audiocassette* 9 A
  •Student Response Form
  •Realia 1-2
  •Situation Card 1-2
  •Quiz 1-2. . . . . . . . . . . . . . . . . . . . . . . . . . . . . *Assessment Items, Audiocassette* 7 A

*Textbook Audiocassette* 1 A

*Practice and Activity Book,*
*Chapter Resources,* Book 1
  •Communicative Activity 1-2
  •Additional Listening Activities 1-4, 1-5, 1-6 . . . . . . . . *Additional Listening Activities, Audiocassette* 9 A
  •Student Response Form
  •Realia 1-3
  •Situation Card 1-3
  •Teaching Transparency Master 1-2 . . . . . . . . . . . . . . *Teaching Transparency* 1-2
  •Quiz 1-3. . . . . . . . . . . . . . . . . . . . . . . . . . . . . *Assessment Items, Audiocassette* 7 A
*Video Guide.* . . . . . . . . . . . . . . . . . . . . . . . . . . . . . . *Video Program/Expanded Video Program,* Videocassette 1

*Video Guide.* . . . . . . . . . . . . . . . . . . . . . . . . . . . . . . *Video Program/Expanded Video Program,* Videocassette 1

**Alternative Assessment**
  •Performance Assessment,  •Portfolio Assessment
  *Teacher's Edition*  Written: **Zweite Stufe,** Activity 20, *Pupil's Edition,* p. 26, *Assessment*
    **Erste Stufe,** p. 15K  *Guide*
    **Zweite Stufe,** p. 15M  Oral: **Anwendung,** Activity 2, *Pupil's Edition,* p. 36, *Assessment Guide*
    **Dritte Stufe,** p. 15Q  •**Notizbuch,** *Pupil's Edition,* p. 33; *Practice and Activity Book,* p. 145

CHAPTER OVERVIEW

# Kapitel 1: Wer bist du?
## Textbook Listening Activities Scripts

## Erste Stufe

### Activity 6, p. 21

1. — Hallo! Bist du neu hier?
   — Ja, ich heiße Ilse. Grüß dich.

2. — Guten Morgen! Bitte setzt euch!
   — Guten Morgen, Herr Gerber!

3. — Ich muß jetzt los.
   — Na, bis dann, Salmun.
   — Tschüs, Martin!

4. — Da kommt die Leyla. Morgen, Leyla!
   — Hallo! Wie geht's?

5. — Morgen ist Training.
   — Ja. Ich komm' auch. Tschüs!
   — Tschau!

### Activity 9, p. 23

1. — Heißt du Antje?
   — Ja, ich heiße Antje.

2. — Wie heißt der Junge?
   — Er heißt Kemal. Er ist neu hier.

3. — Heißt das Mädchen da Ute?
   — Nein, sie heißt Sabine.

4. — Wie heißt du denn?
   — Ich heiße Hans.

### Activity 11, p. 24

1 — Wer ist das da?
   — Das ist die Katrin.

2 — Und wer ist das?
   — Das ist Frau Möller.

3. — Wer ist denn das?
   — Das ist die Deutschlehrerin.

4. — Wer ist das?
   — Das ist der Mathelehrer, Herr Scholz.

5. — Wer ist das?
   — Das ist Frau Bach, die Deutschlehrerin.

6. — Wer ist das?
   — Das ist doch die Silke.

7. — Wer ist das?
   — Er heißt Christian Hansen.

8. — Und wer ist das?
   — Hm, das ist der Jens.

## Zweite Stufe

### Activity 15, p. 25

HOLGER  Wie alt ist Handan? Ist sie 15?
AHMET  Ja. Ich glaube, sie ist schon 15.
HOLGER  Und sag mal, Ahmet, wie alt bist du eigentlich?
AHMET  Ich bin sechzehn.
HOLGER  Sechzehn? Bin ich auch. Und wie alt sind denn die Renate und der Jens?
AHMET  Renate ist erst 14, aber der Jens ist schon 16 Jahre alt.

### Activity 17, p. 26

1. — Tag! Ich heiß' Ulrike, und ich bin vierzehn.

2. — Wer ist der Junge da drüben?

3. — Wer ist denn das? Stefan?

4. — Sind Helmut und Jens auch schon hier?

5. — Ist Frau Bach die neue Sportlehrerin?

## Dritte Stufe

### Activity 22, p. 28

JÖRG  Ja also, ich heiß' Jörg Schulze, und ich komm' aus Berlin.
KEMAL  Ich heiße Kemal Acar und bin ziemlich neu hier in Düsseldorf.
WIEBKE  Ich bin die Wiebke Jansen und wohne in Hamburg.
BRIGITTE  Ja, und ich bin Brigitte Dennhöffer und komm' halt aus München.
MELINA  Grüß Gott! Ich bin die Melina Kiritsis und komm' aus Stuttgart.

### Activity 27, p. 30

Die Heike kommt meistens mit dem Moped, und der Philipp kommt eigentlich immer mit der U-Bahn. Die Annette dagegen kommt mit dem Bus, und die Sara kommt auch mit dem Bus. Der Michael fährt mit dem Rad. Und ich . . . na ja, meine Mutter bringt mich oft mit dem Auto.

## Diktat, *p. 33*

You will hear two students, Jochen and Stefan, talking about another student. First, listen to what they are saying, then write down their conversation. Who are they talking about?

JOCHEN Hallo, grüß dich, Stefan! Wer ist das Mädchen da?

STEFAN Das ist die Erika.

JOCHEN Wie alt ist sie denn?

STEFAN Vierzehn.

JOCHEN Und woher kommt sie?

STEFAN Aus Österreich. Ich glaube Wien.

## *A* nwendung
### Activity 1, p. 36

MARIA Hallo, Ich heiße Maria, bin 16 Jahre alt und komme aus Wien.

MARTIN Ich bin der Martin. Ich bin 14 und komm' aus Berlin.

FRAU BACH Ich bin die Frau Bach. Ich bin eine Deutschlehrerin hier. Ich bin 29 Jahre alt und komme aus Brandenburg.

TARA Also, ich heiße Tara. Ich bin 14 und komme aus der Stadt Potsdam.

## *V* orschau
### Activity 1, p. 1

The Federal Republic of Germany, **die Bundesrepublik Deutschland,** is a land of contrasts and striking diversity. A divided country for almost 50 years, Germany was reunited in 1990 under one government. This relatively small country has something for everyone. In the east is cosmopolitan **Berlin,** the capital of Germany once again. A highly industrial region known as the **Ruhrgebiet** is in the west, and in the south lie the foothills of the **Alpen,** where rural traditions are still strong.

When visiting **Berlin** you can see the famous **Brandenburger Tor** and what's left of the **Mauer.** You can also visit the **Alexanderplatz,** the hub of former **Ost-Berlin,** or take a stroll down **Unter den Linden,** a famous boulevard. The **Freistadt** of **Hamburg,** home of Germany's largest port, is in the north. In southwestern Germany you will find the spectacular **Schwarzwald.** East of the **Schwarzwald,** tucked away in the foothills of the Alps along Germany's southern border, is another great attraction, **Neuschwanstein,** Ludwig the Sec-

ond's most famous castle. Directly on the border between Germany and Austria towers the **Zugspitze,** the tallest mountain in the German Alps.

Germany's rivers play an important role in its economy. If you travel to the western part of the country, you will see the famous **Rhein** river. In the south flows the **Donau,** and to the east are the **Elbe** and the **Oder.** To the north lie the **Nordsee** and the **Ostsee,** two major seas critical to Germany's economy and industry. Germany is surrounded by nine countries in all: **Polen, die Tschechische Republik, Österreich, die Schweiz, Frankreich, Luxemburg, Belgien, die Niederlande,** and **Dänemark.**

Southeast of Germany you will see **Österreich.** Two Austrian cities that you have probably heard about, **Salzburg** and **Wien,** host well-known music festivals every year. Other Austrian attractions are the **Großglockner** and the **Großvenediger,** the highest mountains in the Austrian Alps. Austria is also known for its many magnificent palaces and castles, such as the **Schönbrunn** near **Wien,** as well as its picturesque villages and colorful traditions. Although most Austrians live in the countryside, fully one-fifth of the population resides in **Wien,** the capital. **Wien** lies on the **Donau,** one of the most important and beautiful rivers in Europe. Other important Austrian cities are **Innsbruck, Salzburg,** and **Graz.**

**Die Schweiz,** which lies southwest of Germany across the **Rhein** river, is the land of the **Alpen.** Switzerland is famous for its breathtaking scenery and towering peaks, like the **Eiger** or **Matterhorn.** It is also known for its luxurious ski resorts, like **St. Moritz** or **Zermatt**—and of course, Swiss cheese, fine chocolates, and quality watches. The capital of Switzerland is **Bern.** Other important cities are **Zürich, Luzern,** and **Basel.** Switzerland has four official languages, German, French, Italian, and Romansch. Sixty percent of the population speaks German.

The principality of **Liechtenstein** is one of the smallest countries in the world. It is smaller in area than Washington, DC. In the west, the **Rhein** river forms **Liechtenstein**'s border with Switzerland, with which it has very close cultural and economic ties. **Vaduz** is the capital of **Liechtenstein.**

As you can see from this brief trip through **Deutschland, Österreich, die Schweiz,** and **Liechtenstein,** the German-speaking countries are rich in natural beauty, and have fascinating traditions and exciting cultures. You are probably eager to learn more about these countries and the language spoken there. So **Komm mit!** Let's learn German!

# Kapitel 1: Wer bist du?
## *Suggested Project*

*In this activity students will create a travel brochure (or a poster) for a German city. It will be written and presented in English.*

## SITUATION

Tell students to imagine that the German Club's itinerary for the upcoming trip to Germany has all been planned except for the last day. The task for the club members is to choose their favorite city and convince the other members that this is where they should spend their last day in Germany. Have students prepare and present a travel brochure for this city. The brochure should be a persuasive presentation of things to see and do in the selected city. This project can be done individually or in small groups, depending on class size and the number of cities to choose from.

## MATERIALS

✂ **Students may need**
- *poster board*
- *glue*
- *pictures and other available realia.*
- *scissors*
- *tape*

## SUGGESTED CITIES

Hamburg, Berlin, München, Heidelberg, Freiburg, Bremen, Lübeck, Dresden, Leipzig, or any other city, subject to teacher's approval.

## SUGGESTED TOPICS

Students must provide the following information for their visual and oral presentation:

**Location: Bundesland;** geographic location

**Statistics:** population, size; commercial interests

**History:** brief synopsis of city's history

**Points of Interest:** What is there to see? Why do people want to go to this city? What will this group of teenagers be able to do there?

**Unusual/interesting facts**

## SUGGESTED SEQUENCE

1. Decide on individual or group work depending on your class size and time allotment for this activity.

2. Let students choose the city for their brochure.

3. Ask students to do research by looking up information in the school library or the local library, using almanacs, world reference books, or travel magazines. They can also visit local travel agencies that always have a variety of brochures and guides on Germany.

   For further information, and if time permits, information can be obtained from different organizations listed on pp. T38-39 of the *Teacher's Edition.* The German National Tourist Office might be especially good for this project.

4. Have students compile all their information and materials (including pictures) and begin to organize it.

5. Have students make a brief written outline of how they plan to present their city. Provide general feedback and suggestions if necessary.

6. Have students complete their project.

7. On the day of the presentation, have the students make a short presentation to the rest of the class. After all travel brochures have been presented and submitted they will be displayed.

8. As the final step, have all students vote on the city they would like to visit on this imaginary trip to Germany.

Suggestion: Set a time limit for the presentations. (2-3 minutes each)

## GRADING THE PROJECT

Since this project's objective is to introduce students to Germany and its cities and is to be presented in English, the grade should be based on the students' research, presentation, and creativity.

Suggested point distribution (total = 100 points)

| | |
|---|---|
| Content/Subject Matter | 40 |
| Presentation | 40 |
| Creativity | 20 |

# Kapitel 1: Wer bist du?

# *Games*

*On this page you will find suggestions for games in which students practice some of the functions, structures, vocabulary, and cultural features studied in Chapter 1. When planning your lessons for this chapter, remember that games such as these are not only a fun part of the students' classroom experience, but are also effective in motivating students to practice and review the material in this chapter and other chapters.*

## CITY CONNECTIONS

*The objective of this game is to familiarize students with the geography of Germany and the names of the cities.*

**Materials** You will need enlarged copies of the map of Germany on p. 2, two highlighters or colored pens, and a set of game cards.

**Procedure** Before the game, prepare at least 30 index cards. On each card write the name of two German cities (Example: **München** and **Stuttgart**) on the same side on the card. Divide the cards into 2 sets of 15 cards each. You will need one set of cards and a map per team. Divide the class into 2 teams. Tape the enlarged map copies on opposite ends of the chalkboard. Then place the two sets of cards on a table at the front of the class face down along with the colored pens. A student from each group comes to the table and takes the top card from his or her team's stack of cards then takes the card to the team's map without looking at it. When you give the signal, the two students get to look at their card, and each says the names of the cities on the card. They then find the two cities and draw a line between them. Set a time limit per card of 20 seconds. If the student correctly connects the two cities on the card, he or she returns the card to the teacher and sits down. If the student cannot locate the cities or make the correct connections within the time allowed, the card goes back to the bottom of the stack. The student then sits down. The next person from each team continues with the next card in their stack. Set a time limit of five minutes for the game. At the end of the game, both teams (or the teacher) count up all the cards they have correctly used (2 points per card - 1 per city). Add up all points, and the team with the most points wins.

## AROUND THE WORLD

*This is a fast vocabulary review game that is easy to set up and fun for the students.*

**Materials** You will need flashcards with pictures of vocabulary items.

**Note** Before the start of the game, let the class know that all students will be asked to write down as many vocabulary words as they can remember after the game.

**Procedure** Students sit in rows. The first student in the first row stands beside the desk of the second student in the row. They will compete. The teacher holds up a flashcard with a picture of a vocabulary item. The first one of the two competing students to name correctly the item on the flashcard wins. The student who named the word first continues down the row to compete with the next student. The other student sits down. A round is complete after each person has had a turn. Play as many rounds as you and your students would like. The winner is the student who has passed the most desks in the course of the game. As you play, make sure you show the flashcard to the whole class. All students should clearly see the word on the flashcard so they can be thinking about the words.

GAMES

# Kapitel 1: Wer bist du?
## *Lesson Plans, pages 16-39*

## *U*sing the Chapter Opener, pp. 16-17

### Motivating Activity

Before starting with the Chapter Opener have students introduce themselves in English. You might want to start by following this model: Hello! My name is ___. I am the German teacher. I'm from ___. I'm ___ years old (up to teacher's discretion ). Have students follow your model. Tell students that by the end of this lesson they will be able to repeat this activity in German.

### Teaching Suggestion

① Ask students if they can tell by looking at the picture where the German teenagers are.

### Teacher Note

① The students in the photo are on their break on the supervised school grounds (**Schulhof**).

### Thinking Critically

**Comparing and Contrasting** Ask students if they can name the different activities German students take part in during their break (basketball, table tennis). Ask them what American students typically do during their breaks or at lunch time at school. Are their activities similar to those of the German students?

###  Culture Note

② Students often ask each other how they get to school. Most German students ride their bikes while many walk or take public transportation. Some older students ride a moped or drive a car. German teenagers must be 16 to get an operator's license for a moped and 18 to get a license to drive a car.

### Thinking Critically

**Observing** After students have looked at the captions of the three pictures, ask them if they have noticed anything different about the written German language. (capitalization) What words are capitalized in the three sentences besides the beginning words? (nouns: **Tag, Jahre, Moped, Schule**)

### Teaching Suggestion

Have students make a list of 5-10 German words (excluding names of people or places) which are capitalized in German. Students should use their knowledge of the **Vorschau** and the Brandenburg Location Opener on pp. 12-15. Have several students go to the board to write some of their words.

###  Culture Note

Summer vacation is much shorter in Germany (maximum 6 weeks) than in the United States. However, students do get fall, Christmas and spring breaks which last about 2 weeks each. The dates for the summer vacation will differ from **Bundesland** to **Bundesland** so as not to overload the highways of the country at any given time with vacationing families and other travelers. You might also want to point out to students that workers in Germany get at least six weeks off every year. That means that parents can often have time off at the same time as their children.

### Focusing on Outcomes

After doing the motivating activity, have students preview the learning outcomes listed on p. 17. NOTE: Each of these outcomes is modeled in the video and evaluated in **Kann ich's wirklich?** on p. 38.

# *T*eaching Los geht's!
## pp. 18-20

### Resources for Los geht's!

- *Video Program* **OR**
  *Expanded Video Program,* Videocassette 1
- *Textbook Audiocassette* 1 A
- *Practice and Activity Book*

▶ **pages 18-19**

### Video Synopsis

This segment of the video takes place on the first day of school, as several friends (Tara, Jens, and Ahmet) get to know a new student (Holger). The student outcomes listed on p. 17 are modeled in the video: saying hello and goodbye, asking someone's name and giving yours; asking who someone is, asking someone's age and giving yours, talking about where people are from, and talking about how someone gets to school.

### Motivating Activity

To help students prepare for the content and functions modeled in the pictures, ask them what typically happens on the first day of school. How do they talk to old friends? Do they talk in a casual or formal manner? What about new students? What do they usually talk about?

### Teaching Suggestions

- To prepare students for the text, do the prereading activity on p.18 at the top of the **Foto-Roman.** Next, have them look for any visual clues, cognates, etc. to help them figure out what the scenes are about.

- Have students listen to the text while looking at the photos, or have them watch this segment of the video. Remind them that they do not need to understand every word. They should try to get the gist of what is happening in the story. Have them match visual clues with words or phrases that they hear.

- After students have listened to or read the text, ask them to tell you who these people are. Have them tell you one fact about each person.

###  Culture Notes

- It is typical for schools in the large cities of the **BRD** to have many students from foreign countries enrolled, especially students from Turkey, Greece, and Italy. The parents or grandparents of these young people went to Germany to find work, and many have settled there permanently.

- German teenagers can get a driver's license for a **Moped** at age 16 and for an automobile at age 18. There are no drivers' education classes offered in school. Instead, teenagers must enroll in a **Fahrschule**. Fees for an automobile license course can be over 2,000 **DM**.

▶ **page 20**

### Teaching Suggestion

**2** Have students do this activity in writing. Then put the numbers 1 through 5 on the board and have students come up to write the expressions they found beside the corresponding number.

### For Individual Needs

**2 Challenge** Have students list all the greetings used in the **Foto-Roman.** Then, have them find all the phrases that ask for information.

### Teaching Suggestion

**5** Pair students and let them fill in the blanks together. Next, let them role-play the dialogue to give them a chance to practice pronunciation. Walk around to monitor students reading aloud.

### For Additional Practice

**5** If necessary, let students switch roles for additional practice. You might also ask several pairs to read the conversation aloud at the end of the activity.

### Closure

Refer back to the motivating activity from the Chapter Opener on p.15 G in which students introduced themselves in English. Now have students introduce themselves in German by telling their name, their age, and saying where they are from or where they live.

# *T*eaching Erste Stufe,
## *pp. 21-24*

---

### Resources for Erste Stufe

*Practice and Activity Book*
*Chapter Resources,* Book 1
- Communicative Activity 1-1
- Additional Listening Activity 1-1
- Student Response Form
- Realia 1-1
- Situation Card 1-1
- Teaching Transparency Master 1-1
- Quiz 1-1

*Audiocassette Program*
- *Textbook Audiocassette* 1 A
- *Additional Listening Activities, Audiocassette* 9 A
- *Assessment Items, Audiocassette* 7 A

---

▶ **page 21**

## *MOTIVATE*

### Teaching Suggestion

Before starting with the **Erste Stufe,** let students list all the ways we greet and say goodbye to one another in English. Remind them to think of formal and informal expressions and also long and short forms. Put all the expressions on the board or a transparency. Ask students to give an example for when and how each expression may be used. Tell students that the German language also has many different ways to greet and say goodbye to people.

## *TEACH*

### PRESENTATION: So sagt man das!

The German saying "Höflichkeit ist Trumpf" (*courtesy is power*) is often practiced by Germans. Greetings and farewells are therefore a very important part of German culture. With this in mind, introduce the phrases of this function box by walking up to several students and greeting each in a different way and also using the farewell expressions.

### Teaching Suggestion

Tell students that **bis dann** literally means *until then* and that it is generally used as a parting phrase when a specific time has been mentioned

for people to see each other again. It may also simply have the general meaning of *see you later.*

## Teacher Note

Many German teenagers have adopted the American greeting "Hi" instead of **Guten Tag. Tschüs** is more typical for northern Germany and **Tschau** for southern Germany. There are other greetings and farewells not mentioned here which you might want to point out to your students. These greetings are typical of southern Germany: **Grüß dich! Grüß Gott! Servus!** and **Ade!**

## Language Notes

- The initial consonant cluster in **Tschau** or **Tschüs** can be compared to the English initial phoneme in words such as *ch*ina or *ch*ocolate.

- Although many Germans spell the word **Tschüs** with an **ß**, the standard spelling is **Tschüs.**

- After intoducing **Ein wenig Landeskunde** to students, point out the difference between **Morgen** as a greeting and **morgen** meaning *tomorrow* as in **Ist morgen Training?**

## Teacher Note

The listening activities in *Komm Mit!* are designed to help students improve their ability to understand authentic spoken German. They will learn more from the listening tasks throughout the book if they are given *at least* two opportunities to listen. The first time you play the recorded activity, have students put down their pencils and listen carefully. They should write down their answers during the second listening.

▶ **page 22**

## ❖ For Individual Needs

- **Challenge** Pair students and have them greet each other and say goodbye. One of the partners should use the long forms, the other the shorter versions. Have students practice shaking hands while greeting each other and saying goodbye. Tell them their handshake must be firm, since a handshake is seen as a reflection of character.

- **A Slower Pace** Make up (or have students make up) index cards with greetings and goodbyes, especially the longer, more formal ones. Allow students to refer to the cards when they want to use a different greeting.

## PRESENTATION: So sagt man das!

Introduce the phrases from the **So sagt man das!** function box briefly. Have students use their name tags from Activity 8 and have them work in groups of 2 or 3 using functions and phrases such as introducing themselves and asking questions.

Example:
Student A: **Wie heißt du?**
Student B: **Ich heiße _____. Und du?**
Student A: **Ich heiße_____.**
  (points to another student in class):
  **Wie heißt sie ?**
Student B: **Sie heißt _____.**

## Language Note

The /ch/ sound in **Mädchen** can be compared to the English /h/ in words such as *humid, huge, human.*

▶ *page 23*

## Thinking Critically

**Comparing and Contrasting**   Before introducing the **Grammatik** box, ask students to list as many interrogative pronouns in English as they can, and write them on the left side of the board or on a transparency. Then, ask students what type of question starts with these pronouns. (open-ended question) Ask students what other type of question there is. (yes/no question) Ask them for an example of a yes/no question, and write it opposite the interrogative pronouns. Then present the **Grammatik** box. Students should realize that the concepts of open-ended and yes/no questions also exist in German.

## Game

**10**   Divide the class into two teams. The first student on Team A identifies himself or herself saying **Ich heiße** ... and then points to a student on the same team asking **Wer ist das?** The first student on Team B must give the correct name. If the answer is correct, the student stays in the game. If it is incorrect, the student is out. Continue in this way, alternating teams.

## PRESENTATION: So sagt man das!

Introduce the four pictures with their captions to your students. Then, point to one of the students in your class, and ask the rest of the class **Wer ist das**? The class should follow the model and respond in a chorus **Das ist der/die _____.**

▶ *page 24*

## PRESENTATION: Grammatik

- Before explaining the **Grammatik** box to students, point out that the grammatical definition of an article doesn't always correspond to the natural gender of a given noun, therefore we speak in terms of grammatical gender. **Der, die, das** have one equivalent in English, *the.*

- The word **Mädchen** is neuter because of the diminutive suffix **-chen**. It comes from the middle high German word **maget**, which means *unmarried, young.*

### Multicultural Connection

Ask students if they know of any other languages that have more than one way of saying *the.* (French has **le** and **la**; Spanish has **el** and **la**)

### For Individual Needs

**A Slower Pace**   Some students might have trouble with the grammatical term *definite article*. Try explaining that the definite article points out and refers to one or more "definite" or particular things of a group or class. Contrast the English definite and indefinite articles and usage, for example: "This is the president" and "This is a president."

**12 Challenge**   After students have completed the dialogue, ask them to rewrite it changing all names of people and places.

**13 Tactile Learners**   Have students make a blank seating chart of the class or have copies of one available. Have students work in pairs filling in the names of their classmates. Each of the partners points to different students asking **Wer ist das Mädchen?** or **Wie heißt der Junge?** Have students keep this chart for future activities.

## Game

**14** For this game each student should bring two or three different pictures of famous people. A student stands in front of the class or at his or her desk and holds up a picture. It should be visible to everybody. The student asks the class **Wer ist das?** or **Wie heißt er/sie?** The student who correctly answers the question first gets to show his or her picture to the class and ask the class to identify the person in that picture. Continue until everyone has shown at least one picture.

## CLOSE

### Focusing On Outcomes

Refer students back to the learning outcomes listed on p. 17. Students should recognize that they are now able to say hello and goodbye, ask someone's name and give theirs, and ask who someone is.

## ASSESS

- **Performance Assessment** Write the following statements on a transparency or on the board. Have students form the question that would elicit each statement as an answer. This can be done orally or in writing.

  1. Ich heiße Martin. (Wie heißt du?)
  2. Er heißt Hans. (Wie heißt er/der Junge/der Mann?)
  3. Das ist die Nina. (Wer ist das?)
  4. Sie heißt Frau Siegel. (Wie heißt sie/die Frau?)
  5. Nein, er heißt Thomas. (Heißt er Peter?/Heißt der Junge Peter?)
  6. Das ist Herr Heppt. (Wer ist das?)
  7. Das ist die Monika. (Wer ist das?)
  8. Ja, er heißt Stefan. (Heißt er/der Junge Stefan?)
  9. Sie heißt Lise. (Wie heißt sie/das Mädchen/die Frau?)
  10. Das ist Frau Schleifer, die Englischlehrerin. (Wer ist das?)

- Quiz 1-1, *Chapter Resources,* Book 1

# Teaching Zweite Stufe, pp. 25-27

## Resources for Zweite Stufe

*Practice and Activity Book*
*Chapter Resources,* Book 1
- Additional Listening Activities 1-2, 1-3
- Student Response Form
- Realia 1-2
- Situation Card 1-2
- Quiz 1-2

*Audiocassette Program*
- *Textbook Audiocassette* 1 A
- *Additional Listening Activities, Audiocassette* 9 A
- *Assessment Items, Audiocassette* 7 A

▶ **page 25**

## MOTIVATE

### Building on Previous Skills

Quickly review the numbers in the **Wortschatz** box by having the whole class count to 20, then backwards from 20 to 0. Repeat until the class seems warmed up. Then get a large ball and have a maximum of 21 students stand in a circle. Assign each student a number between 0 and 20. The first student calls out a number **Wo ist Nummer 5?** The person who was assigned number 5 answers **Ich bin 5.** The first student throws the ball to number 5 who then calls out another number, and so on.

## TEACH

### TPR Total Physical Response

Practice the numbers using some of the expressions presented in the **Vorschau.** Give students the following commands.

**Juan und Sam, schreibt die Nummer 13 an die Tafel!**

**Carol und Felicia, nehmt 2 Bücher!**

**Reggie und Bob, öffnet eure Bücher auf Seite 19!**

**Leticia und Suzy, nehmt 3 Kulis!**

## For Individual Needs

**Challenge** Ask students to create and write elementary math problems between the numbers 0 and 20 using the following kinds of expressions: **Was ist eins plus drei?** or **Wieviel ist sieben minus drei?** Have individual students call out their math problems, and the rest of the class give the correct answer in German.

## PRESENTATION: So sagt man das!

After introducing the new phrases, walk around the classroom and ask individual students questions from this function box. Have them reply using the appropriate answer from the box.

## For Additional Practice

Have students turn to classmates around them and ask them their ages.

▶ **page 26**

## Teaching Suggestion

Before introducing the **Grammatik** box, tell students that subject pronouns are words used only to replace nouns and noun phrases, often to avoid repetitiveness (pronoun = "for the noun"). Walk around the classroom addressing the students using the verb **sein.** Example: **Ich bin die Deutschlehrerin. Wer bist du?**

## For Additional Practice

**17** If you think your students need more practice, add these sentences: **Sabine und ich sind 14. Ahmet, bist du aus der Türkei? Wo ist Herr Möller? Wolfgang ist aus Berlin. Irene und Dieter sind nicht hier.**

## Teaching Suggestion

**18/19** Work through Activities 18 and 19 with the entire class, eliciting answers from individual students to monitor their understanding and usage of the verb **sein.**

## For Additional Practice

**18** Have students write out the same conversation but use people in their class and change ages accordingly. If they have to ask an age they should do so in German.

**For Individual Needs**

**19 Challenge** Have students first say how old the people in the pictures are, then add a negative. Example: **Steffi ist fünfzehn, nicht vierzehn. Melanie und Katja sind sechzehn, nicht siebzehn.**

**20 A Slower Pace** On the board or transparency provide students with a sample of an introduction and then have them proceed with the activity.

 **Portfolio Assessment**

**20** You might want to use Activity 20 as a written portfolio item for your students. See *Assessment Guide,* Chapter 1.

▶ *page 27*

 **For Individual Needs**

**Tactile Learners** Have students draw a map of the **BRD** with labels on all the German states and the bordering countries, using heavy stock paper. Have students cut out the different states as well as Austria and Switzerland. Using the map like a puzzle, have students practice in pairs or small groups, naming the state or country and putting it in the right place.

## Geography Connection

Have students bring in maps of Europe and ask them to write down the names of all the countries that border Germany. Have them also name the waters that border the country and finally have them list three major German rivers.

 **Culture Note**

Switzerland is made up of 26 **Kantone** and Austria of 9 **Bundesländer.**

## CLOSE

### Teaching Suggestion

Have students take out the seating chart they made in the **Erste Stufe** when they filled in the names of their classmates. Let them go around the class again. They should ask the question **Wie alt bist du?** and add the answer under the correct name. Afterwards, call on several students and ask them the age of some of the students they questioned.

## Focusing on Outcomes

Refer students back to the learning outcomes listed on p. 17. Students should recognize that they are now able to ask someone's age and give theirs.

## ASSESS

• **Performance Assessment** On a transparency show the following sentence fragments and call on students to form complete sentences. You might also have students write several answers in full sentences on the chalkboard. Then correct sentences on the board if there are any mistakes.

| | | |
|---|---|---|
| ich | ist | 15 |
| du | bin | 14 |
| er | bist | 16 |
| sie(pl.) | sind | 12 |
| Peter | | 13 |
| Maria | | |
| sie | | |

• Quiz 1-2, *Chapter Resources,* Book 1

*Answers, p. 27*

**a** There are 16 **Bundesländer:** Schleswig-Holstein, Niedersachsen, Nordrhein-Westfalen, Rheinland-Pfalz, Hessen, Saarland, Baden-Württemberg, Bayern, Thüringen, Sachsen, Sachsen-Anhalt, Brandenburg, Mecklenburg-Vorpommern, Hamburg, Berlin, and Bremen.

**b** Schleswig-Holstein: Kiel; Niedersachsen: Hannover; Nordrhein-Westfalen: Düsseldorf; Rheinland-Pfalz: Mainz; Hessen: Wiesbaden; Saarland: Saarbrücken; Baden-Württemberg: Stuttgart; Bayern: München; Thüringen: Erfurt; Sachsen: Dresden; Sachsen–Anhalt: Magdeburg; Brandenburg: Potsdam; Mecklenburg-Vorpommern: Schwerin; Hamburg: Hamburg; Berlin: Berlin; Bremen: Bremen

**c** Baden-Württemberg borders on Switzerland. Bayern borders on Austria.

**d** Bern; Wien

# *T*eaching Dritte Stufe,
## pp. 28-33

## Resources for Dritte Stufe

*Practice and Activity Book*
*Chapter Resources,* Book 1
- Communicative Activity 1-2
- Additional Listening Activities 1–4, 1-5, 1-6
- Student Response Form
- Realia 1-3
- Situation Card 1-3
- Teaching Transparency Master 1-2
- Quiz 1-3

*Audiocassette Program*
- *Textbook Audiocassette* 1 A
- *Additional Listening Activities, Audiocassette* 9 A
- *Assessment Items, Audiocassette* 7 A

▶ *page 28*

## *MOTIVATE*
### Building on Previous Skills

Pair students and provide each group with a copy of a map of Germany. Have the names of at least 15 cities blanked out on the map but numbered and put those 15 cities on the board or on a transparency in random order. You might want to include cities such as Potsdam, Essen, Stuttgart, Düsseldorf, etc. Pairs must correctly fill the blanks on their copy of the map in a given amount of time. To review the results, call out the number and have students give you the name of the corresponding city. If using a copy of the map in the book, have students tell you in which **Bundesland** the corresponding city is located. This activity will help familiarize students with German geography.

## *TEACH*
### PRESENTATION: So sagt man das!

Introduce the new phrases of the **So sagt man das!** box by asking either/or questions or yes/no questions such as **Woher kommt der amerikanische Präsident, (Bill Clinton)? Aus Indiana oder Arkansas? Ist Arnold Schwarzenegger aus Österreich?** Students should be able to infer the meaning of the questions through contextual guessing, especially if many cognates are used.

## Teaching Suggestion

**23** On the overhead projector, list the key questions that students will need for their pair work. **Wer ist das?** or **Wie heißt er/sie? Wie alt ist er/sie? Woher ist er/sie?** or **Woher kommt er/sie?**

▶ *page 29*

## Teaching Suggestion

**24** Practice with students the pronunciation of all the city names before playing the game with partners. First read the one syllable names, then practice the two syllable names. Note that the stress in these names is always on the first syllable except for Berlin and Schwerin. Then, practice the three syllable names where the stress varies. In Magdeburg, Düsseldorf, and Wiesbaden, the stress is on the first syllable, in Hannover and Saarbrücken, it is on the second syllable.

## ◆ For Individual Needs

**25 Challenge**   Let each student take scrap paper and write a note similar to Birgit's about themselves. Ask students to only use their initials or their German name, and to print clearly when they write their notes because others must be able to read them. Put all notes in a hat and redistribute them among students. Let each student read one note to the class and see if they know who wrote the note. This is also a good way for students to learn about their classmates and remember their German names.

## Teaching Suggestion

After introducing the **Sprachtip** box have students make and keep a list of connectors. Connectors will be helpful for the students' **Notizbuch** entries as well as the oral and written portfolios.

## Language Note

Words such as **ach ja, ja klar,** and **denn** are also called "flavoring words." They help the language sound more natural and flowing. Students should also keep a list of these words.

▶ *page 30*

## Thinking Critically

**Comparing and Contrasting** Before introducing the **Wortschatz** box, ask students the following questions: How do American students typically get to school? Can you think of a reason why the U.S. public schools provide school bus transportation for most students? How do you think German students get to school every day? Why aren't there school buses in Germany? (Germany has a sophisticated public transportation network that already accommodates students, thus eliminating the need for a separate system.)

## For Individual Needs

**Visual Learners** Introduce the **Wortschatz** box using flashcards with pictures and asking either/or and yes/no questions. Example: While holding up a picture of a bus ask students: **Ist das ein Bus?** or **Ist das ein Bus oder ein Auto?**

## Culture Note

It is quite common for German students who use the public transportation system to obtain a weekly, monthly, or annual pass (**Wochen-, Monats,-** or **Jahreskarte**). These passes allow unlimited rides for a discounted fare.

## Teaching Suggestion

After introducing the **Wortschatz** box, practice with students the phrases denoting means of transportation by grouping all phrases with **mit dem...** together. Then practice **mit der U-Bahn** and **zu Fuß.**

## PRESENTATION: So sagt man das!

To help students with the pronunciation of the expressions of the **So sagt man das!** function box have students practice in pairs. Have one student ask the question and the other student give the answer. Monitor students and make corrections if needed.

## For Individual Needs

**27 A Slower Pace** Have students make a list of the students' names from the **Wortschatz** box before listening to this activity.

▶ *page 31*

## PRESENTATION: Landeskunde

### Teacher Note

The interviews are recorded on audiocassette and videocassette.

### Geography Connection

Have students locate Bietigheim and Berlin in an atlas.

### Thinking Critically

- **Drawing Inferences** Ask students to compare the way these students get to school. How does the size of the town affect the way students travel to school? (Students in a large city such as Berlin must rely on the subway and buses because their schools are often far away from where they live. Also, it might not always be safe for students to ride their bikes to school in large cities because of the heavy traffic.)
- **Drawing Inferences** Ask students if they can infer the age of Tim and Sandra by the way they get to school. What types of transportation do they use that would be an indication of their age? (Tim is at least 16 years old because he rides a moped and Sandra must be at least 18 years old because she sometimes drives her car to school.)

### Teaching Suggestion

If possible, obtain a poster or booklet featuring road signs by writing to the German Automobile Club (**ADAC**) or the German Tourist Office. Share this information with your class. Can students guess the meaning of some of the signs? Which ones are similar to those used in the United States?

### Background Information

Germans must be at least 18 years old in order to obtain a driver's license. Since the mandatory drivers' education courses are extremely expensive, many young people must wait even longer. When they have completed their course work, they must then pass a written exam and a road test. Once a license has been issued, it is good for life.

## Thinking Critically

**Comparing and Contrasting** Ask students to name the steps involved in getting a driver's license in the United States. What is the cost? How long is the license valid?

 **Culture Note**

American students often want to know if they can drive in Germany if they are 16. The answer is no. Most rental car agencies require drivers to be at least 21 and ask foreign drivers for a valid driver's license and often an International Driving Permit.

## Teacher Note

Mention to your class that the **Landeskunde** will also be included in Quiz 1-3 given at the end of the **Dritte Stufe**.

▶ *page 32*

## Teacher Note

**28** **Versteckte Sätze** activities will be recurring activities throughout the chapters of the book. There are many possible sentences that can be made. It is up to the teacher to set limits on the number and type of sentences.

 **For Individual Needs**

**28** **Visual Learners** Have each student come up with at least 3 sets of sentences (questions and answers) and write them on a sheet of paper. If time permits let some students put their sentences on the board.

## Language Note

Point out to students that a **Gymnasium** is a school and not a *gymnasium*. It's a false cognate.

## Group Work

**29** Have students form groups of three. Ask each group to prepare a 10- to 12-line conversation between two young people, one of them a new student in school. Give each group of students an overhead transparency. Have them write the conversation on it, leaving a blank line for each question that needs to be asked but writing in the answer. The other groups should then try to complete the conversation orally. Each conversation has to make sense. All people in the group must be able to supply the missing question if asked to do so.

▶ *page 33*

## Teaching Suggestion

**31** Have students use the seating chart they made earlier and add information on how each student gets to school. When all boxes are filled in, ask students what they found out about how their classmates get to school. Ask students about survey totals: **Wie viele Schüler kommen mit dem Bus? mit dem Rad?** etc.

## PRESENTATION: Aussprache

Remind students that German vowels are pronounced with more muscular tension. Many English and German vowel sounds are similar, but not exactly the same.

- **ä/e** There is no glide with this sound. The short vowels **ä/e** will be introduced in Chapter 5.

- **ü** Remind students that an umlaut over a letter indicates a change in sound. You may want to point out that the **ü** sound can also be represented by a **y** in such words as **Lyrik** and **Mythos**. Students will learn the short **ü** in Chapter 8.

- **ö** This sound can also be represented by **oe** in such words as **Goethe**. Students will learn the short **ö** in Chapter 8.

## Teaching Suggestion

Before starting the **Diktat**, tell students to number the sentences from one to six as they write down what they hear. Once finished, ask six students each to write one sentence on the board. Then call on those same six students to read their sentences and ask the rest of the class if the sentences need any corrections.

## *CLOSE*

**Game** Play the game *City Connections*. See p. 15F for the procedure.

## Focusing On Outcomes

Refer students back to the learning outcomes listed on p. 17. Students should recognize that they are now able to talk about where people are from and talk about how someone gets to school.

DRITTE STUFE

ZUM LESEN

## ASSESS

- **Performance Assessment** Ask one student to tell where he or she is from using the verb **kommen.** Then ask another student to repeat what the first student said using the verb **sein.** Repeat this activity with several students. Example:

  Student A: **Ich komme aus Dallas.**

  Student B: **Sie ist aus Dallas.**

- Quiz 1-3, *Chapter Resources*, Book 1

## Teaching Zum Lesen,
*pp. 34-35*

### Reading Strategy

The targeted strategy in this reading is using visual clues to determine the subject of a reading. Students should learn about this strategy before doing Question 1. Students will also be asked to skim for the gist, scan for specific information, answer questions to show comprehension, and transfer what they have learned.

## PREREADING

### Motivating Activity

Ask students about their impressions of German-speaking countries, where they might like to visit, when they would like to go and why. What kind of souvenirs would they like to bring back?

### Thinking Critically

**Drawing inferences** Looking at the map of Germany on p. 2, can students think of which places could be popular vacationing spots and why? (oceans, mountains, historical places, etc.)

### Teacher Note

Questions 1-4 are prereading activities.

## READING

### Skimming and Scanning

Remind students that most of the time when they read postcards like these, they are looking either for the global picture (skimming) to get an idea about the entertainment possibilities, or for specific information (scanning) such as the words that are used for greetings or the names of the cities the people are writing from. When students do Activities 5 and 6, they will be using the strategies of skimming and scanning. In Activities 7-10, students are reading for comprehension.

### Cooperative Learning

Put students in groups of 4. Ask them to choose a discussion leader, a recorder, a proofreader, and an announcer. Give students a specific amount of time in which to complete Activities 5-10. Monitor group work as you walk around, helping students if necessary. At the end of the activity call on each group announcer to read his or her group's results. You can decide whether or not to collect their work for a grade at the end of the activity.

## POST-READING

### Teacher Note

Activities 11a and b are postreading tasks that will show whether students can apply what they have learned.

### Closure

Tell students to return to their cooperative learning groups and have them compose their own postcard from the **Ferienort** of their choice. They should use the postcards they studied as a guide. Have them write their postcard on a large piece of construction paper, read it to the class, and hang it up on the wall at the end of the activity. This can also be graded as part of the cooperative learning activity.

Hallo Rita!
Herzliche Grüße aus dem Schwarzwald!
Das Wetter ist prima - warm und sonnig. Wir schwimmen, wandern, und spielen Tennis, Volleyball, Minigolf!
Bis bald!

Monika

Rita Meyer
Gartenstraße 2
14482 Potsda

## *U*sing Anwendung,
### pp. 36-37

 **For Individual Needs**

**1 A Slower Pace** Write the names of the people in random order on the board or on a transparency. Students will then have only two pieces of information to listen for.

 **Portfolio Assessment**

**2** You might want to use Activity 2 as an oral portfolio item for your students. See *Assessment Guide*, Chapter 1.

### Teaching Suggestions

• Have all students get out their seating chart one final time and ask each student to introduce one person in class giving all the information collected about him or her.

**4** Hand out index cards and have students use them as their own **Schülerausweise**. Students can add their picture to make them look more authentic. If possible, laminate all cards and either display on class bulletin board or have students keep them in their folders.

## *K*ann ich's wirklich?
### p. 38

This page is intended to prepare students for the test. It is a brief checklist of the major points covered in the chapter. The students should be reminded that it is a checklist only and not necessarily everything that will appear on the test.

## *U*sing Wortschatz,
### p. 39

### Teaching Suggestion

Since this is the first **Wortschatz** presented to the students, you might want to point out to students that they can practice the vocabulary by working with a partner. One of the partners keeps his or her book open and asks the other student for the German or the English equivalent of a certain expression or word. Partners can switch off after a given number of words or after each **Stufe**.

### Game

**Preparation** The day before the game, have students write each word or expression from the **Wortschatz** on pieces of paper, cutting each word into its letter components. Then have students put the fragments of each word or phrase into a numbered envelope. Go around to each student and write the corresponding expression on a separate sheet of paper beside the number. Collect all envelopes. All this should be done a day ahead of this game, as making the envelopes and recording the expressions will take up time. Make as many envelopes as there are students in the class. To help you prepare for this game, you can ask students of one class to help you prepare the envelopes for the other class.

**Procedure** Pair students with one sheet of paper between them then distribute envelopes to each group. Students mark the number of the envelope they just received on their paper. Give the signal to open the envelope and set a specific time, such as 20 seconds per envelope, to unscramble the content and write the word or expression beside its number. When the teacher says "stop" students must immediately return the letters to the envelope and pass it onto the next group who will try to unscramble it. You may want to have each group receive 10 envelopes. The group with the most correct words or expressions wins.

### Teacher Note

Give the **Kapitel 1** Chapter Test, *Chapter Resources, Book 1*.

KAPITEL

# 1 Wer bist du?

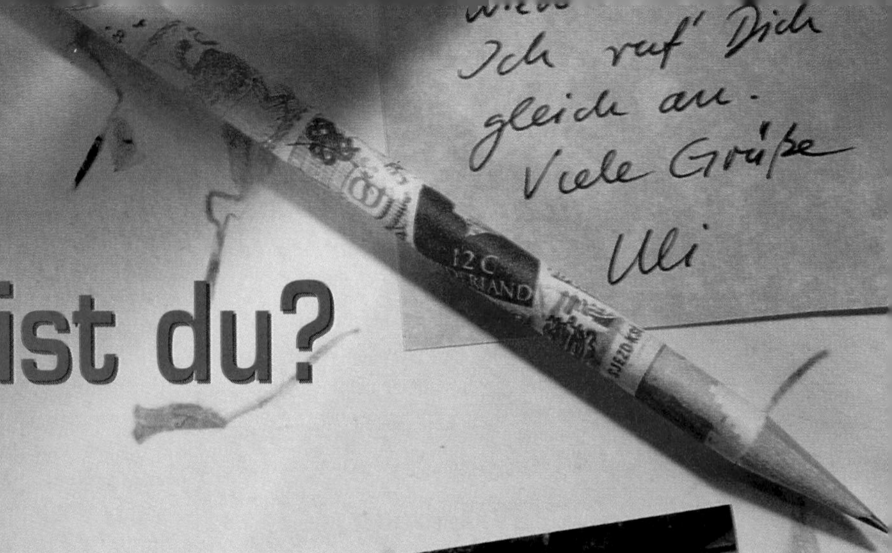
Ich ruf' Dich
gleich an.
Viele Grüße
Uli

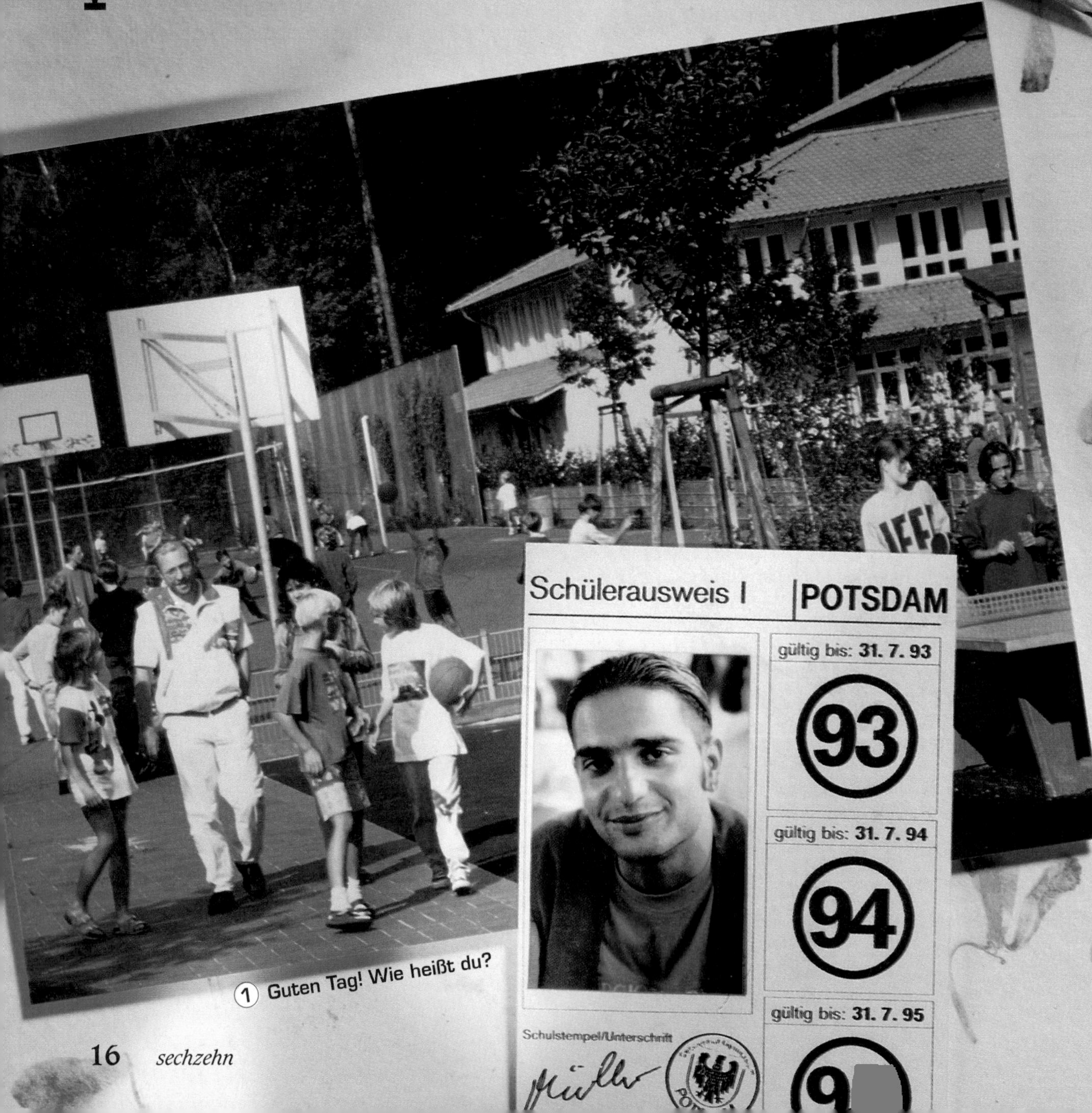
Schülerausweis I
POTSDAM
gültig bis: 31. 7. 93
93
gültig bis: 31. 7. 94
94
gültig bis: 31. 7. 95
9
Schulstempel/Unterschrift

① Guten Tag! Wie heißt du?

**W**hen summer vacation is over and school begins, students look forward to seeing old friends and meeting new ones. What is the first day of school like for you? What do you look forward to?

## In this chapter you will learn

- to say hello and goodbye; to ask someone's name and give yours; to ask who someone is
- to ask someone's age and give yours
- to talk about where people are from; to talk about how someone gets to school

## And you will

- listen to some students introduce themselves telling their names, ages, and where they are from
- read a letter from a pen pal
- write a short letter introducing yourself to a pen pal
- learn where the German states and their capitals are located; find out how students in German-speaking countries get to school

② Ich komme mit dem Moped zur Schule.

③ Ich bin 16 Jahre alt. Und du?

# Los geht's!

## Vor der Schule

Look at the photos that accompany the story. Where and when do you think these scenes are taking place? What clues tell you this?

Jens

Tara

Holger

Ahmet

**①**

- Hallo, Jens!
- Hallo!
- Ist das dein Moped?
- Ja.
- Super! Klasse!
- Jetzt komme ich immer mit dem Moped zur Schule.
- Ach ja! Du bist jetzt sechzehn!

**②**

- Hallo! Wer bist du denn? Bist du neu hier?
- Ja, ich bin neu hier.
- Und wie heißt du?
- Ich heiße Holger.
- Und ich bin Jens. Tag!

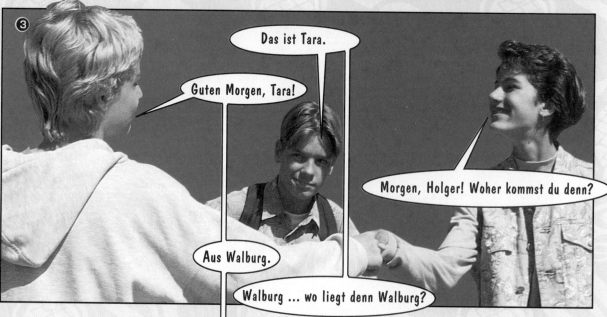

**③**

- Das ist Tara.
- Guten Morgen, Tara!
- Morgen, Holger! Woher kommst du denn?
- Aus Walburg.
- Walburg ... wo liegt denn Walburg?
- In Hessen.

## 1 Was passiert hier? *What's happening here?*

Do you understand what is happening in the **Foto-Roman**? Check your comprehension by answering these questions. Don't be afraid to guess.

1. What happens at the beginning of the story?
2. Why is Jens' age important?
3. What do you learn about the new student?
4. What information does Ahmet have for Jens? What "team" do you think they are talking about?

1. Students greet each other, Tara sees that Jens has a new moped.
2. Sixteen is the minimum required age to drive a moped.
3. Holger is from Walburg in Hessen.
4. Ahmet and Jens have practice tomorrow at 3 pm. A soccer team

## 2 Genauer lesen *Reading for detail*

Reread the conversations. Which words or phrases do the characters in the **Foto-Roman** use to

1. greet each other        1. Guten Morgen, Hallo, Morgen
2. ask someone's name       2. Wie heißt du?
3. ask where someone is from     3. Woher kommst du denn?
4. ask where a place is      4. Wo ist denn ...?
5. say goodbye      5. Tschüs.

## 3 Stimmt oder stimmt nicht? *Right or wrong?*

Are these statements right or wrong? Answer each one with either **stimmt** or **stimmt nicht**. If a statement is wrong, try to state it correctly.

1. Jens ist jetzt sechzehn und kommt mit dem Moped zur Schule.
2. Ahmet ist neu in der Schule.
3. Walburg ist in Bayern.
4. Tara und Holger haben morgen Training.
5. Ahmet kommt aus der Türkei.

1. Stimmt.
2. Stimmt nicht. Holger ist neu.
3. Stimmt nicht. Walburg ist in Hessen.
4. Stimmt nicht. Jens und Ahmet haben morgen Training.
5. Stimmt.

## 4 Wer macht was? *Who is doing what?*

What have you learned about each of these students? Match the descriptions on the right with the names on the left, then read each completed sentence.

1. Holger   d
2. Tara   c
3. Jens   a
4. Ahmet   b

a. ...ist jetzt sechzehn und kommt mit dem Moped zur Schule.
b. ...ist der beste Mann im Team.
c. ...buchstabiert den Namen von Ahmet.
d. ...ist neu in der Schule.

## 5 Wer bist du denn? *Who are you?*

Using words from the box, complete this conversation between two new students.

ULRIKE  Hallo! Ich __1__ Ulrike. Wer bist __2__ denn? Bist du __3__ hier?   *heiße   du   neu   komme*

GUPSE  Ja, ich heiße Gupse. Ich __4__ aus der Türkei. __5__ kommst du?   *Woher*

ULRIKE  __6__ Hessen.   *Aus*

GUPSE  Schau mal! __7__ ist das?   *Wer*

ULRIKE  Das ist die Birgit. Sie __8__ sechzehn und kommt __9__ dem Moped zur Schule. Toll, was?   *ist   mit*

Word box: mit   Woher   heiße   ist   Wer   Aus   du   neu   komme

*Saying hello and goodbye; asking someone's name and giving yours; asking who someone is*

## SO SAGT MAN DAS! *Here's how you say it!*

### Saying hello and goodbye

Saying hello:

**Guten Morgen!** *Good morning!*
**Morgen!** *Morning!*
**Guten Tag!** *Hello!*
**Tag!**
**Hallo!** } *Hi!*
**Grüß dich!**

Saying goodbye:

**Auf Wiedersehen!** *Goodbye!*
**Wiedersehen!** *Bye!*

**Tschüs!**
**Tschau!** } *Bye!*
**Bis dann!** *See you later!*

---

**6** ## Hör gut zu! *Listen carefully*

Listen to the following people greet each other or say goodbye. For each exchange you hear, write whether it is a **hello** or a **goodbye**.

1. Hello
2. Hello
3. Goodbye
4. Hello
5. Goodbye

## EIN WENIG LANDESKUNDE
*(About the country and the people)*

**Guten Morgen!** and **Guten Tag!** are standard greetings and can be used in almost any social situation. With whom do you think you might use the abbreviated forms **Morgen!** and **Tag!**? The phrases **Hallo!** and **Grüß dich!** are casual and are generally used with friends and family. **Grüß dich!** is heard more in southern Germany and Austria. **Auf Wiedersehen!**, **Wiedersehen!**, and **Tschüs!** are all ways of saying goodbye. Which of the three do you think would be the most formal? If you were going to greet a fellow student and good friend, and then say goodbye, which phrases would you use?

Grüß dich, Klaus!

Guten Tag, Frau Müller!

Auf Wiedersehen, Herr Kießling!

Tschau, Silvia!

## 7 Hallo!

Here you see some friends greeting each other and saying goodbye. Match the exchanges with the appropriate pictures.

a.

b.

c.

d.

1. —Tschüs, Lisa!  c.
   —Tschau, Christian!
2. —Wiedersehen, Frau Weber!  a.
   —Auf Wiedersehen, Peter!

3. —Tag, Alexander! Sebastian!  d.
   —Tag, Julia!
4. —Guten Morgen, Herr Koschizki!  b.
   —Morgen, Elisabeth!

## 8 Freunde begrüßen

*Greeting friends*

Make a name tag for yourself, using your own name or one chosen from the list in the **Vorschau.** Get together with a few of your classmates. For more German first names, turn to page 325 in the back of your book. Greet and say goodbye to each other, using the names on the tags. Don't forget to greet and say goodbye to your teacher.

Was sagt Anna zum Monster mit den drei Köpfen?

---

## SO SAGT MAN DAS! *Here's how you say it!*

### Asking someone's name and giving yours

When you meet a new student you'll want to find out his or her name.

You ask:
  **Wie heißt du?**

You might also ask:
  **Heißt du Holger?** *Is your name Holger?*

To ask a boy's name:
  **Wie heißt der Junge?**
  **Heißt der Junge Ahmet?**
    *Is that boy's name Ahmet?*

To ask a girl's name:
  **Wie heißt das Mädchen?**
  **Heißt das Mädchen Ulrike?**

The student responds:
  **Ich heiße Holger.**

  **Ja, ich heiße Holger.**

  **Der Junge heißt Ahmet.**
  **Ja, er heißt Ahmet.**

  **Das Mädchen heißt Steffi.**
  **Nein, sie heißt Steffi.**

---

## 9 Hör gut zu! *Listen carefully*

To complete these conversations, match each exchange you hear with the correct illustration.

1. b
2. d
3. c
4. a

*Ich heiße Hans*

**a.**

*Ja, ich heiße Antje*

**b.**

*Nein. Sie heißt Sabine*

**c.**

*Er heißt Kemal. Er ist neu hier.*

**d.**

---

*G*rammatik    Forming questions

There are several ways of asking questions in German. One way is to begin with a question word (interrogative) such as **wie** *(how)*. Some other question words are: **wer** *(who)*, **wo** *(where)*, and **woher** *(from where)*.

Look at the questions below. How are they different from questions such as **Wie heißt der Junge?**[1] What is the position of the verb in these questions?[2]

| | |
|---|---|
| **Heißt du Holger?** | **Ja, ich heiße Holger.** |
| **Heißt das Mädchen Kristin?** | **Nein, sie heißt Antje.** |

---

## 10 Wie heißt er? Wie heißt sie?

How well do you remember the names of your classmates? When someone asks you: **Wie heißt das Mädchen?** or **Wie heißt der Junge?**, give the name of the person referred to. For practice, use complete sentences.

---

### SO SAGT MAN DAS!

#### Asking who someone is

To find out someone else's name you ask:    **Wer ist das?**
The response might be:

**Das ist die Moni.**

**Das ist der Stefan.**

**Das ist Herr Gärtner, der Deutschlehrer.**

**Das ist Frau Weigel, die Biologielehrerin.**

---

1. These questions anticipate *yes* or *no* as a response.   2. The verb will always be at the beginning of a *yes/no* question.

ERSTE STUFE        *dreiundzwanzig*   **23**

## *G*rammatik  The definite articles **der**, **die**, and **das**

German has three words for *the:* **der**, **die**, and **das**, called *definite articles.* These words tell us to which class or group a German noun belongs. Words that have **der** as the article, such as **der Junge** *(the boy),* are masculine nouns. Words that have the article **die**, such as **die Lehrerin** *(the female teacher),* are feminine nouns. The third group of nouns have the article **das**, as in **das Mädchen** *(the girl),* and are neuter nouns. You will learn more about this in **Kapitel 3.**

| **der**—words (masculine) | **die**—words (feminine) | **das**—words (neuter) |
|---|---|---|
| **der Junge** | | **das Mädchen** |
| **der Lehrer** | **die Lehrerin** | |
| **der Deutschlehrer** | **die Deutschlehrerin** | |

## 11 **Hör gut zu!** *Listen carefully!*

Holger is asking Jens and Tara about various people in the class. Listen and decide whether the person they are talking about is male or female.

1. Female 2. Female 3. Female 4. Male 5. Female 6. Female 7. Male 8. Male

## 12 **Wie heißt der Junge?**

Holger is trying to learn the names of everyone in his class. He asks Tara for help. Rewrite the conversation, filling in the missing definite articles **der**, **die**, or **das**.

| | HOLGER | Wie heißt der Junge? | Der |
|---|---|---|---|
| Der | TARA | __1__ Junge heißt Uwe. __2__ Uwe kommt aus München. | Der |
| | HOLGER | Und __3__ Mädchen? | das |
| Das | TARA | __4__ Mädchen heißt Katja. __5__ Katja kommt aus Hamburg. | Die |
| | HOLGER | Und wie heißt __6__ Lehrerin? | die |
| | TARA | __7__ Lehrerin heißt Frau Möller. | Die |

### EIN WENIG LANDESKUNDE

In casual speech, the definite articles **der** and **die** are often used with first names (**Das ist die Tara. Das ist der Jens.**). This practice occurs more often in southern Germany, Austria, and Switzerland than in northern Germany. **Der** and **die** are also often used with the last names of celebrities and other well-known people. How would you refer to **Steffi Graf**?

**LERNTRICK**

In English, we know that the word "the" signals a noun. In German, we use **der**, **die**, and **das** in much the same way. Remember that in German, every time you learn a new noun, you must also learn the definite article (**der**, **die**, or **das**) that goes with it.

## 13 **Wer sind meine Mitschüler?**

*Who are my classmates?*

Now team up with a classmate and ask each other the names of other students in the class. Be sure to use all of the ways of asking you have learned.

## 14 **Ratespiel** *Guessing Game*

Bring in pictures of well-known people and ask your classmates to identify them.

## Asking someone's age and giving yours

### SO SAGT MAN DAS!

**Asking someone's age and giving yours**

To find out how old someone is, you might ask:

**Wie alt bist du?**

You might get responses like these:

> **Ich bin vierzehn Jahre alt.**
> *I am 14 years old.*
> **Ich bin vierzehn.**
> **Vierzehn.**

**Nein, ich bin vierzehn.**

**Bist du schon fünfzehn?**
*Are you already 15?*
**Wie alt ist der Peter?**
**Und die Monika? Ist sie auch fünfzehn?**

**Er ist fünfzehn.**

**Ja, sie ist auch fünfzehn.**

Can you identify the verbs in the different examples?[1] Why do you think the verbs change?[2]

---

## WORTSCHATZ

**Do you remember the numbers you learned in the Vorschau?**

| | | | | | | | | | | | |
|---|---|---|---|---|---|---|---|---|---|---|---|
| 0 | null | 1 | eins | 2 | zwei | 3 | drei | 4 | vier | 5 | fünf |
| 6 | sechs | 7 | sieben | 8 | acht | 9 | neun | 10 | zehn | 11 | elf |
| 12 | zwölf | 13 | dreizehn | 14 | vierzehn | 15 | fünfzehn | 16 | sechzehn | 17 | siebzehn |
| 18 | achtzehn | 19 | neunzehn | 20 | zwanzig | | | | | | |

---

## 15 Hör gut zu!

Holger wants to get to know his new classmates, so he asks Ahmet how old everyone is. Listen to their conversation and write down the ages of the students below.

Handan: ═══  Ahmet: ═══  Renate: ═══  Jens: ═══

ist 15          ist 16          ist 14          ist 16

## 16 Wir stellen vor *Introducing*

Ask your partner's name and age and then introduce him or her to the rest of the class.

---

1. The verbs are **bist, bin, ist**.  2. The verbs change because the subjects of the sentences change.

## *G*rammatik   Subject pronouns and the verb **sein** *(to be)*

The phrases **ich bin, du bist, er ist, sie ist,** and **sie sind** each contain a subject pronoun corresponding to the English *I, you, he, she,* and *they,* and a form of the verb **sein** *(to be)*: *I am, you are, he is, she is, they are.* **Sein** is one of the most frequently used verbs in German.*

| | | |
|---|---|---|
| Ich | **bin** | dreizehn. |
| Du | **bist** | auch dreizehn. |
| Karola<br>Sie } | **ist** | vierzehn. |
| Jens<br>Er } | **ist** | sechzehn. |
| Ahmet und Holger<br>Sie } | **sind** | sechzehn. |

## 17 Hör gut zu!

Listen to the following sentences and determine if Ulrike is talking about herself, about one other person, or about more than one person.

1. self   2. one person   3. one person   4. more than one   5. one person

| | about self | about one person | about more than one person |
|---|---|---|---|
| 1 | | | |
| 2 | | | |

## 18 Wie alt sind sie?

Fill in the missing forms of **sein** in this conversation between Ahmet and Holger.

HOLGER   Sag mal, wie alt __1__ du?   bist
AHMET   Ich __2__ 16.   bin
HOLGER   Du __3__ 16? Ich auch. Und wie alt __4__ Tara und Jens?   bist; sind
AHMET   Tara __5__ 14, und Jens __6__ 16.   ist; ist

## 19 Wie alt sind die Jungen und Mädchen?

Say who these people are and how old they are.

Steffi, 15
**Steffi ist fünfzehn.**

Melanie und Katja, 16
**Melanie und Katja sind sechzehn.**

Björn, 16
**Björn ist sechzehn.**

Karola, 14
**Karola ist vierzehn.**

## 20 Zum Schreiben   *Writing*

You are preparing for a conversation with an exchange student from Germany. Write in German the questions you want to ask in order to find out the student's name and age. Then write how you would answer those questions yourself.

*There are three other forms of **sein** you will learn about and practice later: **wir sind** *(we are)*, **ihr seid** *(you are, plural)* and **Sie sind** *(you are, formal)*.

The **Bundesrepublik Deutschland** (*Federal Republic of Germany*) is made up of **Bundesländer** (*federal states*). Each **Bundesland** has a **Hauptstadt** (*capital*) and its own regional government. The **Bundesrepublik Deutschland** is abbreviated **BRD**.

a. How many **Bundesländer** are there? Make a list of them.
b. Write the **Hauptstadt** beside the name of each **Bundesland**.
c. Which **Bundesland** borders Switzerland? Austria?
d. What are the **Hauptstädte** of Switzerland and Austria?

Kiel ·
SCHLESWIG-HOLSTEIN

MECKLENBURG-VORPOMMERN

Schwerin ·

HAMBURG

· BREMEN

NIEDERSACHSEN

BRANDENBURG

Potsdam · BERLIN

**Wiebke Jansen, 16**

**Jörg Schulze, 19**

Hannover ·

Magdeburg ·

NORDRHEIN-WESTFALEN

**Kemal Acar, 15**

SACHSEN-ANHALT

· Düsseldorf

Dresden ·

Erfurt ·

THÜRINGEN

SACHSEN

HESSEN

· Wiesbaden

RHEINLAND-PFALZ

Mainz ·

SAAR-LAND

Saar-brücken ·

· Stuttgart

BAYERN

**Melina Kiritsis, 18**

BADEN-WÜRTTEMBERG

· München

Wien ☻

**Brigitte Dennhöffer, 19**

Zürich ·

SCHWEIZ

Bern ☻

LIECHTENSTEIN

· Vaduz

ÖSTERREICH

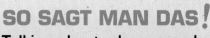

# DRITTE STUFE

*Talking about where people are from; talking about how someone gets to school*

## SO SAGT MAN DAS!

### Talking about where people are from

To find out where someone is from you might ask:

**Woher kommst du?** *or*
**Woher bist du?**
**Bist du aus Deutschland?**

The other person might respond:

**Ich komme aus Texas.**
**Ich bin aus Texas.**
**Nein, ich bin aus Wisconsin.**

To find out where someone else is from you ask:

**Und Herr Gärtner, der Deutschlehrer, woher ist er?**
**Kommt die Inge auch aus Österreich?**

**Er ist aus Österreich.**
**Nein, sie kommt aus Thüringen.**

What do you think the question word **woher** is equivalent to in English?[1]

## 22 Hör gut zu!

Look at the map on page 27 as you listen to the five students introducing themselves. For each introduction, write the name of the student who is speaking and where he or she is from.

1. Jörg Schulze - Berlin 2. Kemal Acar - Düsseldorf 3. Wiebke Jansen - Hamburg 4. Brigitte Dennhöffer - München 5. Melina Kiritsis - Stuttgart

## 23 Woher sind sie?

a. Look at the photos of the people on page 27. Take turns asking and telling your partner about each person pictured, mentioning name, age, and where that person is from.

b. Ask your partner where he or she is from, and your partner will ask you. Be prepared to share your partner's answer with the class.

c. One student begins by calling on a classmate. That person says his or her name, age, and where he or she is from, then calls on someone else.

1. **Woher?** asks the question *From where?*

## 24 Rate mal

Choose one of the **Landeshauptstädte** from the box below and write it down. The city you choose is your imaginary hometown. Your partner will try to guess where you are from. If he or she guesses incorrectly, you can say **Nein, ich komme nicht aus ...** After your partner guesses correctly, switch roles and guess where your partner is from.

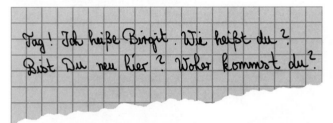

Erfurt    Magdeburg    Mainz    Dresden    Berlin

Düsseldorf    Saarbrücken    Hannover    Wiesbaden

Hamburg    Bremen

Kiel    Stuttgart    Potsdam    Schwerin    München

## 25 Woher kommst du?

A classmate, Birgit, slips Holger the following note in class.

Tag! Ich heiße Birgit. Wie heißt du?
Bist Du neu hier? Woher kommst du?

What does Holger write back to her?
Write his note. Possible answers include: **Ich heiße Holger.**
**Ich bin neu hier. Ich komme aus Walburg.**

### SPRACHTIP

There are many short words in German that you can use to connect your ideas and to make your German sound more natural. Some of these words are: **und** *(and),* **auch** *(also),* **jetzt** *(now),* and **schon** *(already).*

The teenagers in the **Foto-Roman** also used some other expressions: **Also, einfach!** *(That's easy!);* **Ach ja!** *(Oh, yeah!);* **Ja klar!** *(Of course.);* and **Prima!** *(Great!).* Look back at the conversations in the **Foto-Roman** and see how these words were used.

## 26 Zum Schreiben  *Writing*

a. Choose three of the students shown on the map on page 27 as possible pen pals and write three sentences about each of them, telling their names, ages, and where they are from.

b. Exchange papers with a partner and read your partner's sentences. Is everything written correctly? Make corrections on your partner's paper and he or she will do the same on your paper.

c. Now write a few sentences about yourself that you might use in a letter to one of these people, giving the same information.

Wie kommen die Mädchen und Jungen zur Schule?

Annette kommt **mit dem Bus.**

Michael kommt **mit der U-Bahn.**

Philipp kommt **mit dem Rad.**

Sara kommt **zu Fuß.**

Meine Mutter bringt mich **mit dem Auto.**

Und Heike kommt **mit dem Moped.**

## 27 Hör gut zu!

Based on the information given in the **Wortschatz**, determine whether the statements you hear are right or not. List the names you hear and write beside the name **stimmt** if the information is correct or **stimmt nicht** if it is incorrect. Heike: stimmt  Philipp: stimmt nicht  Annette: stimmt
Sara: **stimmt nicht**  Michael: **stimmt nicht**  ich: **stimmt**

### SO SAGT MAN DAS!

#### Talking about how someone gets to school

To find out how someone gets to school you ask:

> **Wie kommst du zur Schule?**
> **Kommt Ahmet zu Fuß zur Schule?**
> **Wie kommt Ayla zur Schule?**
> **Und wie kommt der Wolfgang zur Schule?**

The responses might be:

> **Ich komme mit dem Rad.**
>
> **Nein, er kommt auch mit dem Rad.**
> **Sie kommt mit dem Bus.**
>
> **Er kommt mit der U-Bahn.**

# Wie kommst du zur Schule?

In Germany, many people of all ages ride bicycles—to school, to work, even to do their shopping. Why do you think this might be so? In addition to bicycles, there are a number of other possibilities available to German students for getting to and from school. Students who are at least 16 can drive a **Moped,** 14-year-olds can ride **Mofas,** and students 18 or over can get a driver's license for a car. We asked several students around Germany about how they get to school; here are their responses.

**LANDESKUNDE**

**Christina,** *Bietigheim*

„Ich heiße Christina, bin 17 Jahre alt und komme mit dem Leichtkraftrad zur Schule."

**Johannes,** *Bietigheim*

„Also, ich heiße Johannes Hennicke, bin 12 Jahre alt und fahre jeden Morgen mit dem Fahrrad zur Schule."

**Sonja,** *Berlin*

„Ich heiße Sonja Wegener. Ich bin 17 Jahre alt. Ich fahre meistens mit der U-Bahn zur Schule, aber im Sommer fahr' ich mit dem Fahrrad."

**Tim,** *Berlin*

„Ich heiße Tim Wiesbach und komme mit meinem Moped jeden Tag, wenn das Wetter mitspielt, zur Schule."

**Sandra,** *Berlin*

„Ich heiße Sandra Krabbel. Ich geh' auf die Max-Beckmann-Oberschule, und meistens fahr' ich mit dem Bus, ganz selten auch mit dem Fahrrad, und jetzt neuerdings auch manchmal mit dem Auto, aber nur sehr selten."

1. Christina-motorbike
Johannes-bicycle
Sonja-subway/bicycle
Tim-moped
Sandra-bus/bicycle/car

**A.**
1. How do these students get to school? List the names of the students that were interviewed, then beside each name write the way that each student gets to school.
2. Look at the list you made, and try to determine where these students might live: in a large city? in a suburb? etc. First discuss this question with a partner, then together explain to the rest of the class how you came to the conclusions that you did.
3. The photo above is fairly typical for a German city. What do you notice about it? Is the German city in the photo similar to or different from a city in the United States? What conclusions can you draw about possible differences in transportation in Germany and in the United States?

**B.** Ask several of your classmates how they get to school, and decide together if there are differences between the way American students get to school and the way German students get to school. Write a brief essay discussing this question.

## 28 Versteckte Sätze  *Hidden sentences*

How many questions and answers can you form?

Possible answers include:
Wie kommst du zur Schule?
Wie kommt der Jens zur Schule?
Wie kommen Ahmet und Holger zur
Schule?

**a. Viele Fragen**  *A lot of questions*

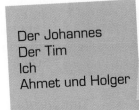

Wie

kommst
kommen
kommt

die Sonja
der Jens
du
Ahmet und Holger

zur Schule?

**b. Viele Antworten**  *A lot of answers*

Der Johannes
Der Tim
Ich
Ahmet und Holger

komme
kommen
kommt

mit dem Rad.
mit dem Bus.
zu Fuß.
mit dem Moped.
mit dem Auto.
mit der U-Bahn.

Der Tim kommt mit
dem Rad.
Ich komme zu Fuß.
Ahmet und Holger kom-
men mit der U-Bahn.

## 29 Wer ist neu?

Can you complete this conversation between
Susanne and Manfred, two students at
Tara's school? (More than one question
may be possible!)

SUSANNE  Tag! ====?  Bist du neu hier?
MANFRED  Ja, ich bin neu hier.
SUSANNE  ====?  Wie heißt du?
MANFRED  Ich heiße Manfred.
SUSANNE  Und ====?  Woher kommst du?
MANFRED  Aus Saarbrücken.

*Inge kommt mit dem Moped.*
MANFRED  ====?  Wie heißt das Mädchen?
SUSANNE  Das ist Inge.
MANFRED  ====?  Ist die Inge sechzehn?
SUSANNE  Ja, Inge ist sechzehn und kommt
immer mit dem Moped zur
Schule. ====?  Kommst du mit dem Moped zur Schule?
MANFRED  Nein, ich komme mit dem Rad zur Schule.

Which one is the new student? How does he or she get to school?  Manfred; by bicycle
(mit dem Rad)

## 30 Interview

Write eight questions like the ones you came up with in Activity 29. Be sure to use questions beginning with question words, as well as yes/no questions. Then, working with a
partner, use the questions you wrote to interview each other.

## 31 Eine Umfrage  *A survey*

a. Form small groups. Each of you will take a turn asking the person to your right how he or she gets to school.

b. Now take turns reporting to the whole class on how the classmate you asked gets to school. As everyone reports, one person will make a chart on the board. Discuss the survey results with the class.

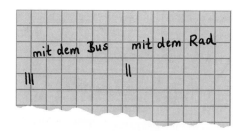

## 32 Für mein Notizbuch  *For my notebook*

As your first entry in your **Notizbuch**, write something about yourself. Include your name (or your German name), your age, where you are from, and how you get to school.

---

# AUSSPRACHE

## Richtig aussprechen / Richtig lesen
*Pronounce correctly / Read correctly*

A. To practice the following sounds, say the words and sentences below after your teacher or after the recording.

1. The letters **ä** and **e**: The long **ä** and **e** are pronounced much like the long *a* in the English word *gate*.
   **Mädchen, dem, zehn  /  Das Mädchen kommt mit dem Bus.**

2. The letter **ü**: To pronounce the long **ü**, round your lips as if you were going to whistle. Without moving your lips from this position, try to say the vowel sound in the English word *bee*.
   **Grüß, begrüßen, Tschüs  /  Grüß dich, Klaus! Tschüs, Ahmet!**

3. The letter **ö**: To pronounce the long **ö**, round your lips, then without moving your lips from this position, try to say the vowel sound in the English word *bay*.
   **Hör, Österreich  /  Inge kommt aus Österreich.**

4. The letter **w**: The letter **w** is pronounced like the *v* in the English word *viper*.
   **wer, wo, woher, wie  /  Woher kommt Uwe? Aus Walburg?**

5. The letter **v**: The letter **v** is usually pronounced like the *f* in the English word *fish*.
   **vier, vor, von, viele  /  Er ist vierzehn, und Volker ist fünfzehn.**

## Richtig schreiben / Diktat  *Write correctly / Dictation*

B. Write down the sentences that you hear.

# ZUM LESEN

## Postkarten aus den Ferien

1. Look at the pictures as well as the format of these texts. What kinds of texts are they? informal notes/postcards

2. What do you think **Postkarten aus den Ferien** means? The format of the texts should help you guess what the word **Postkarten** means. Once you know that, ask yourself: When do people usually write texts like this? How does the answer to this question help you understand what the words **aus den Ferien** mean?

3. Have you ever written to someone while you were on vacation? What did you write about?

4. With a friend, write down some phrases you use when you write to friends on vacation.

5. Which **Postkarte** mentions a lot of activities?
   5. The card from the Schwarzwald

Schwarzwald

Hallo Rita!
Herzliche Grüße aus dem Schwarzwald!
Das Wetter ist prima – warm und sonnig. Wir schwimmen, wandern, und spielen Tennis, Volleyball, Minigolf.
Bis bald!
Monika

Rita Meyer
Gartenstraße 21
14482 Potsdam

London

Liebe Frau Polgert!
How do you do? Ich bin in London und finde die Stadt und die Engländer ganz phantastisch! Ich lerne viel Englisch.
Herzliche Grüße!
Ihre Claudia Bach

Fr. Anja Polgert
Vogelsangstr. 39
14478 Potsdam
Germany

Brandenburger Tor, Berlin

Liebe Omi! Lieber Opi!

Ich bin mit meiner
Schulklasse in Berlin
– eine tolle Stadt, echt
super!
Wir kommen am Freitag
wieder zurück.
Liebe Grüße
    Euer Bernhard

Gerhart u. Friede Schnitzler
Eichenstr. 7
14489 Potsdam

6. Which words in these texts are types of greetings or farewells?

7. To whom are these texts written? What clues tell you how well the writers know the people to whom they are writing? Which **Postkarte** is probably written to a teacher? How can you tell?

8. Where is each person writing from? Why are they there? If they do not state the reason directly, what phrases help you infer why they are there?

9. What is the weather like where Monika is?

10. Why does Claudia use an English expression in her **Postkarte?** Do you think she is enjoying herself? How do you know?

11. Write a postcard in German based on one of the following activities:

   a. You and a friend have stayed with a German family while on vacation. After you leave, write a postcard to your host family, telling them where you are and how you like it.

   b. Assume you are in Germany for the first time. Write a postcard to a friend who knows some German.

6. **Hallo, herzliche Grüße, Bis bald!, Liebe Grüße.**

7. The one from London: to a teacher; from the **Schwarzwald:** to a friend; the one from Berlin: to relatives.

Liebe(r) ...
   Ich bin in ═══ .
Hier ═══ es sehr
schön. ═══ ist eine
interessante Stadt.
    Herzliche ═══

8. London-vacation, **Schwarzwald**-vacation, Berlin-school trip

9. warm and sunny.

10. She is writing to her English teacher.

**1** Listen to four people talking about themselves. Write their names on a piece of paper, then beside each name write the person's age and where he or she is from.

Maria, 16, Wien     Frau Bach, 29, Brandenburg
Martin, 14, Berlin     Tara, 14, Potsdam

**2** **a.** Say hello to a classmate. Ask his or her name, age, and where he or she is from.

   **b.** Introduce yourself to the class, giving your name, age, and where you are from. Then introduce the classmate you just met.

**3** Read the letter below and complete the activities that follow.

> Eisenach, den 10. Februar 1994
>
> Lieber Ralph!
> Ich heiße Mandy Gerber. Ich bin aus Eisenach.
> Das ist in Thüringen. Ich bin vierzehn Jahre
> alt. Wie alt bist Du? Bist Du auch vierzehn?
> Bitte, schreib mir und schick auch ein Foto von
> Dir! Viele Grüße
>                                   Mandy

**a.** Make a list of things Mandy tells about herself.

a. Name, hometown (Eisenach), age (14)
b. Wie alt bist du? Bist du schon vierzehn?

**b.** What does Mandy want to know? Make a list of her questions.

**4** Look at the **Schülerausweis** (*school identification card*) to the right and answer the questions that follow.

   **a.** To whom does this **Schülerausweis** belong?

   **b.** When was this person born?

   **c.** Where does this person live?

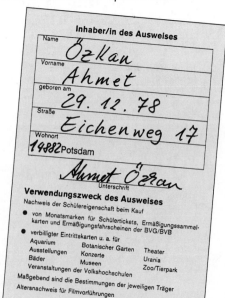

Inhaber/in des Ausweises
Name: Özkan
Vorname: Ahmet
geboren am: 29. 12. 78
Straße: Eichenweg 17
Wohnort: 14882 Potsdam
Unterschrift: Ahmet Özkan

**Verwendungszweck des Ausweises**
Nachweis der Schülereigenschaft beim Kauf

- von Monatsmarken für Schülertickets, Ermäßigungssammel-karten und Ermäßigungsfahrscheinen der BVG/BVB
- verbilligter Eintrittskarten u. a. für
  Aquarium          Botanischer Garten    Theater
  Ausstellungen     Konzerte              Urania
  Bäder             Museen                Zoo/Tierpark
  Veranstaltungen der Volkshochschulen

Maßgebend sind die Bestimmungen der jeweiligen Träger
Altersnachweis für Filmvorführungen

**5** If you were an exchange student in one of the German-speaking countries, you would receive a **Schülerausweis**. Using the example to the right as a model, create a **Schülerausweis** for yourself, filling in all the required information.

4. a. Ahmet Özkan
   b. December 29, 1978
   c. Eichenweg 17, 14882 Potsdam

6 Look at the picture below with a partner and take turns with your classmates telling how the people in the illustration get to school.

Ralf

Sara

Herr
Müller

Peter

Andreas

Mehmet

 7 Write a letter to a pen pal in Germany like the one Mandy wrote to Ralph on
page 36. Use the information you wrote about yourself from Activity 26c to
help you.

 8

## R O L L E N S P I E L

You and some of your friends have been designated to introduce the
"exchange students" on page 31.

a. Working as a group, prepare statements that you can use in your
introductions. Remember to give as much information as possible
about each student, including name, age, where he or she is from
and how he or she gets to school. Include anything else that
might be of interest to the class.

b. Using the pictures, present the visiting exchange students to the
class.

**Can you greet people and say goodbye? (p. 21)**

**1** How would you say hello and goodbye to the following people?

    **a.** a classmate         **b.** your principal

    a. Hallo! Tschau! Tschüs!     b. Guten Tag! Auf Wiedersehen! Guten Morgen!

**Can you give your name and ask someone else's? (p. 22)**

**2** How would you introduce yourself to a new student and ask his or her name?
Ich heiße … Wie heißt du?

**Can you ask and say who someone is? (p. 23)**

**3** **a.** How would you ask who someone is? Say who these students are.
Wer ist das?

Das ist (die) …    Tara      Das ist (der) …    Jens      Das ist (der) …    Holger      Das ist (der) …    Ahmet

**Can you supply the correct definite articles (der, die, das) for the nouns you have learned in this chapter? (p. 24)**

**4** Complete Birgit's explanation to Holger about who everyone is, using the articles **der, die,** and **das**.

    <u>Der</u> Junge da? Er heißt Helmut. Und <u>das</u> Mädchen heißt Monika. <u>Der</u> Lehrer heißt Herr Becker. Und <u>die</u> Deutschlehrerin heißt Frau Hörster.

**Can you ask someone's age and tell yours? (p. 25)**

**5** **a.** How would you ask a classmate his or her age and say how old you are? Wie alt bist du? Ich bin [vierzehn].

    **b.** Say how old the following students are. Silke ist fünfzehn. Dirk ist dreizehn. Marina und Susi sind vierzehn.

    Silke, 15      Dirk, 13      Marina und Susi, 14

**Can you ask where someone is from and tell where you are from? (p. 28)**

**6** How would you ask a classmate where he or she is from? Woher kommst du?

**7** Say where the following students are from. Make statements with both **kommen** and **sein**.

    **a.** Nicole, Brandenburg      **c.** Mark, Niedersachsen
    **b.** Britte und Andreas, Sachsen-Anhalt

Nicole kommt aus Brandenburg. Mark ist aus Niedersachsen. Britte und Andreas kommen aus Sachsen-Anhalt.

**8** How would you tell someone where you are from? Ich komme aus …

**Can you say how someone gets to school? (p. 30)**

**9** How would you ask a classmate how he or she gets to school? How might he or she respond? Wie kommst du zur Schule? Ich komme mit …

    Say how these people get to school:

    **a.** Steffi, bicycle      **b.** Petra and Ali, moped      **c.** Anna, subway

    a. Steffi kommt mit dem Rad zur Schule.     b. Petra und Ali kommen mit dem Moped zur Schule.     c. Anna kommt mit der U-Bahn zur Schule.

## ERSTE STUFE

### SAYING HELLO AND GOODBYE

Guten Morgen!   *Good morning!*
Morgen!   *Morning!*
Guten Tag!   *Hello!*
Tag!
Hallo!   } *Hi!*
Grüß dich!
Auf Wiedersehen!   *Goodbye!*
Wiedersehen!   *Bye!*
Tschüs!
Tschau!   } *Bye!*
Bis dann!   *See you later!*

### ASKING SOMEONE'S NAME AND GIVING YOURS

heißen   *to be called*
Wie heißt du?   *What's your name?*
Ich heiße ...   *My name is....*
Wie heißt das Mädchen?
   *What's the girl's name?*

Sie heißt ...   *Her name is...*
Wie heißt der Junge?   *What's the boy's name?*
Er heißt ...   *His name is...*
Heißt sie ...?   *Is her name ...?*
ja   *yes*
nein   *no*

### ASKING WHO SOMEONE IS

Wer ist das?   *Who is that?*
Das ist ...   *That's...*
Herr ...   *Mr...*
Frau ...   *Mrs...*
der Lehrer   *teacher (male)*
die Lehrerin   *teacher (female)*
der Deutschlehrer   *German teacher (male)*
die Deutschlehrerin   *German teacher (female)*
die Biologielehrerin   *biology teacher (female)*

der Junge   *boy*
das Mädchen   *girl*

### DEFINITE ARTICLES

der
die   } *the*
das

### OTHER USEFUL WORDS

und   *and*
jetzt   *now*
auch   *also*
schon   *already*
Also, einfach!   *That's easy!*
Ach, ja!   *Oh, yeah!*
Ja, klar!   *Of course!*
Prima!   *Great!*

## ZWEITE STUFE

### ASKING SOMEONE'S AGE AND GIVING YOURS

sein   *to be*
Wie alt bist du?   *How old are you?*
Ich bin 14 Jahre alt.   *I am 14 years old.*

Du bist ...   *you are (sing)*
Er ist ...   *He is...*
Sie ist ...   *She is...*
Sie sind ...   *They are...*

### DIE ZAHLEN VON 0 BIS 20.
See page 25.

### OTHER USEFUL WORDS

Bundesland, ⸚er   *federal state (German)*
Hauptstadt, ⸚e   *capital*

## DRITTE STUFE

### TALKING ABOUT WHERE PEOPLE ARE FROM

kommen   *to come*
Woher bist (kommst) du?   *Where are you from?*
Ich bin (komme) aus ...   *I'm from....*
Sie ist (kommt) aus ...   *She's from....*
Er ist (kommt) aus ...   *He's from....*

Sie sind (kommen) aus ...   *They're from....*

### TALKING ABOUT HOW SOMEONE GETS TO SCHOOL

Wie kommst du zur Schule?   *How do you get to school?*
Ich komme ...   *I come...*
   mit dem Bus   *by bus*
   mit dem Rad   *by bike*
   mit dem Auto   *by car*

mit dem Moped   *by moped*
mit der U-Bahn   *by subway*
zu Fuß   *on foot (I walk)*

### ASKING QUESTIONS

Wer?   *Who?*
Wie?   *How?*
Wo?   *Where?*
Woher?   *From where?*

# Kapitel 2: Spiel und Spaß *Chapter Overview*

| **Los geht's!** pp. 42-44 | Was machst du in deiner Freizeit? *p. 42* | | | *Video Guide* |
|---|---|---|---|---|
| | **FUNCTIONS** | **GRAMMAR** | **CULTURE** | **RE-ENTRY** |
| **Erste Stufe** pp. 45-47 | Talking about interests, *p. 46* | The singular subject pronouns and present tense verb endings, *p. 46* | | Question formation, *pp. 45-47* (from **Kapitel 1**) |
| **Zweite Stufe** pp. 48-52 | Expressing likes and dislikes, *p. 48* | •The plural subject pronouns and verb endings, *p. 48* <br> •The present tense of verbs, *p. 50* | •**Ein wenig Landeskunde:** Formal and informal address, *p. 50* <br> •**Landeskunde: Was machst du gern?** *p. 52* | Greetings, *p. 51* (from **Kapitel 1**) |
| **Dritte Stufe** pp. 53-57 | •Saying when you do various activities, *p. 53* <br> •Asking for an opinion and expressing yours, *p. 55* <br> •Agreeing and disagreeing, *p. 56* | •Inversion of time elements, *p. 54* <br> •Verbs with stems ending in **d, t,** or **n,** *p. 55* <br> •Verbs that end in **-eln,** *p. 56* | German weekly planner, *p. 54* | Expressions **stimmt/stimmt nicht** used in a new context, *p. 56* (from **Kapitel 1**) |

| **Aussprache** p. 57 | The vowel combination **ie,** the vowel combination **ei,** the letter **j,** the letter **z** | **Diktat:** *Textbook Audiocassette* 1B |
|---|---|---|
| **Zum Lesen** pp. 58-59 | **Was machen wir am Wochenende?** Reading Strategy: Scanning for specific information | |
| **Review** pp. 60-63 | •Anwendung, *p. 60* <br> •Kann ich's wirklich? *p.62* <br> •Wortschatz, *p. 63* | |

| **Assessment Options** | **Stufe Quizzes** <br> •*Chapter Resources,* Book 1 <br>   Erste Stufe, Quiz 2-1 <br>   Zweite Stufe, Quiz 2-2 <br>   Dritte Stufe, Quiz 2-3 <br> •*Assessment Items, Audiocassette* 7A | **Kapitel 2 Chapter Test** <br> •*Chapter Resources,* Book 1 <br> •*Assessment Guide,* Speaking Test <br> •*Assessment Items, Audiocassette* 7 A <br><br> **Test Generator, Kapitel 2** |
|---|---|---|

*Video Program* **OR**
*Expanded Video Program,* Videocassette 1

*Textbook Audiocassette* 1 B

| **RESOURCES** Print | **RESOURCES** Audiovisual |
|---|---|

*Textbook Audiocassette* 1 B

*Practice and Activity Book*
*Chapter Resources,* Book 1
- Communicative Activity 2-1
- Additional Listening Activity 2-1 . . . . . . . . . . . . . *Additional Listening Activities, Audiocassette* 9 A
- Additional Listening Activity 2-2 . . . . . . . . . . . . . *Additional Listening Activities, Audiocassette* 9 A
- Student Response Form
- Realia 2-1
- Situation Card 2-1
- Teaching Transparency Master 2-1 . . . . . . . . . . . . *Teaching Transparency* 2-1
- Quiz 2-1 . . . . . . . . . . . . . . . . . . . . . . . . . . . . . *Assessment Items, Audiocassette* 7 A

*Textbook Audiocassette* 1 B

*Practice and Activity Book*
*Chapter Resources,* Book 1
- Additional Listening Activity 2-3 . . . . . . . . . . . . . *Additional Listening Activities, Audiocassette* 9 A
- Additional Listening Activity 2-4 . . . . . . . . . . . . . *Additional Listening Activities, Audiocassette* 9 A
- Student Response Form
- Realia 2-2
- Situation Card 2-2
- Quiz 2-2 . . . . . . . . . . . . . . . . . . . . . . . . . . . . . *Assessment Items, Audiocassette* 7 A
*Video Guide.* . . . . . . . . . . . . . . . . . . . . . . . . . . . . . .*Video Program/Expanded Video Program,* Videocassette 1

*Textbook Audiocassette* 1 B

*Practice and Activity Book*
*Chapter Resources,* Book 1
- Communicative Activity 2-2
- Additional Listening Activity 2-5 . . . . . . . . . . . . . *Additional Listening Activities, Audiocassette* 9 A
- Additional Listening Activity 2-6 . . . . . . . . . . . . . *Additional Listening Activities, Audiocassette* 9 A
- Student Response Form
- Realia 2-3
- Situation Card 2-3
- Teaching Transparency Master 2-2 . . . . . . . . . . . . *Teaching Transparency* 2-2
- Quiz 2-3 . . . . . . . . . . . . . . . . . . . . . . . . . . . . . *Assessment Items, Audiocassette* 7 A

*Video Guide.* . . . . . . . . . . . . . . . . . . . . . . . . . . . . . .*Video Program/Expanded Video Program,* Videocassette 1

**Alternative Assessment**
- Performance Assessment, *Teacher's Edition*
  **Erste Stufe,** p. 39J
  **Zweite Stufe,** p. 39M
  **Dritte Stufe,** p. 39P
- Portfolio Assessment
  Written: **Zweite Stufe,** *Teacher's Edition,* p. 39L; *Assessment Guide*
  Oral: **Anwendung,** *Teacher's Edition,* p. 39R; *Assessment Guide*
- **Notizbuch,** *Pupil's Edition,* p. 51; *Practice and Activity Book,* p. 146

# Kapitel 2: Spiel und Spaß
# *Textbook Listening Activities Scripts*

## Erste Stufe
### Activity 6, p. 45

HOLGER  Du Stefan, was machst du denn in deiner Freizeit?

STEFAN  Ich? Also, ich spiele eigentlich sehr oft Klavier.

HOLGER  Und die Anne, was macht sie so?

STEFAN  Ich glaub', sie spielt sehr viel Basketball.

HOLGER  Und Helena? Was macht sie gern in ihrer Freizeit?

STEFAN  Helena spielt oft Golf. Sie spielt gar nicht schlecht.

HOLGER  Und was macht der Jörg?

STEFAN  Der Jörg? Der spielt fast immer nur Fußball. Er spielt in demselben Team wie der Ahmet und der Jens.

## Zweite Stufe
### Activity 12, p. 48

1.  GABI  Tag Karin, Tag Ute! Was macht ihr beide denn?

    UTE  Ach, wir spielen Karten. Spielst du mit?

2.  GABI  Mensch, Ralf! Spielst du auch mit den andern Karten?

    RALF  Nein, ich geh' jetzt Volleyball spielen. Karten spiele ich ja nicht so gern.

3.  GABI  Du, Susanne, ich möchte gern Schach spielen. Spielst du mit mir?

    SUSANNE  Tut mir leid, Gabi. Schach spiele ich wirklich nicht gern.

4.  GABI  He, Jochen und Sabine! Ihr seid ja noch hier! Was macht ihr denn?

    JOCHEN  Wir hören uns gleich die neueste Kassette von Ina Deter an.

5.  GABI  Und du, Ahmet? Du spielst doch gern Schach. Spielst du vielleicht Schach mit mir?

    AHMET  Natürlich, gern!

### Activity 15, p. 50

MICHAEL  Was machen wir denn, Claudia? Was machst du gern?

CLAUDIA  Ich zeichne eigentlich sehr gern. Und du?

MICHAEL  Nö, ich zeichne nicht so gern. Ich sammle lieber Briefmarken — aber ich schwimm' gern und oft. Schwimmst du?

CLAUDIA  Nein, nicht so gern. Ich finde schwimmen langweilig. Ich höre aber sehr gern Musik und finde Fernsehenschauen auch ganz interessant. Und du? Hörst du gern Musik? Oder schaust du gern Fernsehen?

MICHAEL  Musik höre ich schon gern — aber Fernsehen finde ich langweilig.

CLAUDIA  Dann hören wir eben Musik!

MICHAEL  Gut! Gehen wir zu Birgit? Sie hat immer die neuesten CDs!

### Activity 16, p. 51

1.  MONIKA  Guten Tag, Herr Weber! Was machen Sie?

    H. WEBER  Guten Tag, Monika! Das Wetter ist so schön, da geh' ich jetzt ein bißchen wandern.

    MONIKA  Wie schön! Ich wander' auch sehr gern.

2.  ANNE  Grüß dich, Andreas! Stefan, Antje und ich gehen jetzt tanzen. Kommst du mit?

    ANDREAS  Nee, Tanzen mag ich nicht so gern.

3.  FR. SCHILLING  Guten Tag, Ayla!

    AYLA  Guten Tag, Frau Schilling! Spielen Sie heute wieder Tennis?

    FR. SCHILLING  Ja, natürlich! Tennis spiel' ich ja jeden Tag.

# Dritte Stufe

## Activity 22, p. 54

USCHI  Was ich am Wochenende so mache? Hmm—
ich besuche oft Freunde. Und dann während
der Woche, so nach der Schule, spiel' ich oft
Basketball mit meinen Freunden. Basteln tu'
ich viel am Nachmittag, besonders wenn das
Wetter schlecht ist. Am Abend höre ich dann
manchmal Musik, Kassetten und CDs. Im
Frühling spiele ich gern Volleyball mit Freunden und so. Und im Sommer schwimme ich
sehr gern, wenn ich Zeit habe. Aber am liebsten wander' ich, das mache ich besonders
gern im Herbst.

## Activity 30, p. 56

1. YASMIN  Ich finde Wandern toll.
   AHMET  Ich auch, Yasmin. Besonders im Frühling.
2. YASMIN  Aber Basteln ist so langweilig.
   AHMET  Das finde ich gar nicht.
3. YASMIN  Na ja, Schwimmen mache ich lieber.
   AHMET  Stimmt! Schwimmen macht viel Spaß!
4. YASMIN  Aber am liebsten gehe ich in die Disko
tanzen.
   AHMET  Ich nicht. Tanzen ist blöd.
5. YASMIN  He! Diese Musik ist super! Einfach
stark!
   AHMET  Ja, das finde ich auch.

## Diktat, p. 57

Silvia and Julia are talking about what they like to
do in their free time. First listen to what they are
saying, then write down their conversation.

SILVIA  Du, Julia was machst du gern am
Wochenende?

JULIA  Ach, ich wandere gern. Und du, Silvia, was
machst du so am Wochenende?

SILVIA  Ich zeichne gern und ah . . . ich spiele
Volleyball.

JULIA  Volleyball spiele ich auch gern. Aber ich
spiel' nicht sehr gut.

SILVIA  Wirklich? Wie findest du Fußball? Ich find's
toll.

JULIA  Ja, ich auch.

# Anwendung

## Activity 1, p. 60

1. (Telefon klingelt)
   — Ahmet Özkan
   — Hallo Ahmet! Hier ist Tara! Willst du mit mir
nach der Schule Tennis spielen?
   — Ja, klar — um 4 Uhr, geht das?

2. — Du Steffi! Was machst du heute nachmittag?
   — Ich spiel' Volleyball — unser Team spielt
heute um 2.

3. — Tag, Katja! Was machst du am Wochenende?
   — Also, Steffi, Holger und ich gehen wandern.
Kommst du mit?
   — Nein, danke. Ich hab' zu viel zu tun.

## Activity 2, p. 60

Also, der Sporti hat wirklich viele Interessen. Er
spielt Basketball, Volleyball und Fußball. Er ist
auch ziemlich musikalisch und spielt seit fünf
Jahren Gitarre. Er kann auch ein bißchen Klavier
spielen. Tanzen macht dem Sporti natürlich Spaß.
Tennis spielt er immer im Frühling und im Herbst,
und im Sommer wandert er gern. Er malt auch
gern. Fernsehenschauen findet er blöd, da spielt er
schon lieber Karten mit Freunden.

Die Sporti ist auch sehr aktiv. Sie spielt in einem
Volleyballteam, in einem Basketballteam und in
einem Fußballteam. Ihre Familie wandert immer
gern im Sommer. Sie lernt gerade Eishockey spielen, das findet sie nicht ganz einfach. Sie geht nicht
oft mit Freunden in die Disko zum Tanzen. Sie
findet die Musik zu laut. Aber zu Hause Musik
hören oder Fernsehenschauen macht Spaß. Sie
mag auch Schach spielen, Freunde besuchen und
basteln.

# Kapitel 2: Spiel und Spaß
## *Suggested Project*

*In this activity students will prepare posters for homecoming at their school and decorate the hallway in the Foreign Language area with sports posters in German. It is a great way to advertise the big game and promote school spirit. Since this project will take several days to complete, you may want to break it into smaller components.*

## MATERIALS

✂ **Students may need**
- poster boards
- photographs
- pictures from magazines
- tape
- markers
- scissors
- glue

## SUGGESTED TOPICS

school athletes
a particular sport
activities surrounding homecoming
school motto and mascot
the coach
cheers
band/musical instruments

## SUGGESTED OUTLINE

Students can use their own drawings, magazine cut-outs, and/or computer creations. If students describe team members, for example, they should include their names, pictures, information obtained through interviews, etc.

## SUGGESTED SEQUENCE

1. Working in groups of two or three, students choose a theme for their poster and decide on a title for it.

2. Students make a list of the German words to be used on their posters. Since students still have a very limited vocabulary, you can refer them to the vocabulary section at the end of the book and help them with difficult words.

3. Students begin working on their posters by putting on the title and arranging all their materials.

4. Students share their posters with the class in short oral presentations.

## GRADING THE PROJECT

Since this project is designed not only to spark students' enthusiasm for the language but also to involve students in a major school activity, the grade should encompass the students' research, preparation, and originality.

Suggested point distribution (total=100 points)

| | |
|---|---|
| Content | 30 |
| Appearance | 15 |
| Correct usage of grammar | 20 |
| Originality | 10 |
| Presentation | 25 |

Be sure to display the students' posters in time for the big event.

PROJECT

# Kapitel 2: Spiel und Spaß
 *Games*

## WORD SCRAMBLE

*This game is especially good for tactile learners. The objective is for students to be able to construct at least five German words from scrambled letters.*

**Materials**   You will need 10 small squares of paper for each student.

**Procedure**   Divide the class into two teams. Each person looks up a German word from the **Wortschatz** on p. 63. Limit the number of letters in each word to 10. The students then write each letter that makes up that word on one of the pieces of paper. After everybody is finished, team members exchange their letters with a person on the other team. Students immediately try to arrange the letters in the correct order. Students who unscramble a word before their counterparts can each win a point for their team.

## KETTENSPIEL

*This game, which helps students review vocabulary and practice third person conjugations, is good for auditory learners.*

**Procedure**   Begin by saying: **Am Wochenende besuche ich Freunde.** The first student then says: **Am Wochenende besucht sie Freunde, und ich spiele Fußball.** The second student repeats what has already been said in the third person and adds his or her own comment to the sentence. This "chain" continues until the last student has finished his or her sentence. This game focuses not only on vocabulary but also verb conjugation and word order.

## MEMORY

*This game, in which students try to match German vocabulary words with their English definitions, is good for visual learners.*

**Materials**   You will need large index cards numbered 1-50, markers, and some tape.

**Procedure**   Tape 50 numbered index cards in rows of five on the chalkboard so that you can lift them up and write words underneath. Write 25 words from the **Wortschatz** under 25 of the cards at random. Write the English definitions under the other 25 cards. Divide the class into two teams. The first student calls out a number in German, and the teacher raises the index card and says the word for everybody to hear. Then the student must call out one more number to try to find the definition in the opposite language. If the student finds it, his or her team gets a point and gets another turn. Otherwise the opposite team has its turn. Each student must remember which words are under which number without any help from team members.

# Kapitel 2: Spiel und Spaß
## *Lesson Plans, pages 40-63*

## $\mathcal{U}$sing the Chapter Opener, *pp. 40-41*

### Motivating Activity

Go around the classroom and ask your students to talk about the activities they enjoy outside of school. What are their hobbies and interests? You may want to begin this discussion by talking about your own free time activities.

###  Multicultural Connection

Ask students whether they can name typical sports and recreational activities of other countries that might not be as typical or as popular in the United States. Examples: England: rugby, field hockey; Canada: ice hockey, curling; Nigeria: cricket; Germany: soccer, tennis; Norway: cross-country skiing

### Thinking Critically

① **Comparing and Contrasting** The girls in this photo are on their way to play tennis. Ask if any students play tennis. If they do, or know someone who does, ask them what they wear to play. Do they wear the same types of outfits as the students in the picture?

###  Culture Note

① It is very common for students to ride their bikes almost everywhere they go. German cities and towns are generally less "spread out" than those in America, so bikes are a more viable form of transportation. There are also special bicycle paths in most cities. The students in this picture are probably going to play tennis at a court that is relatively close to their homes.

###  Multicultural Connection

② Soccer is the most popular team sport in many countries around the world, including the German-speaking countries. Like American children, German children play on soccer teams, but large numbers of teenagers and adults also enjoy playing for fun and competition. The World Cup, **Fußballweltmeisterschaft,** brought soccer fans from all over the world to the United States in 1994.

### Teaching Suggestion

③ Find out if any students collect stamps or have pen pals, friends, or relatives that they write to in other countries. If so, ask them to bring stamps to show to the class.

### Thinking Critically

③ **Drawing Inferences** Ask students why certain commemorative stamps are printed (Example: the *Elvis stamp*). See if students can think of any people, places, or events that might be commemorated on stamps in German-speaking countries. (Examples: classical music composers such as Beethoven, Brahms; German reunification; music festivals; buildings such as cathedrals and other historical landmarks, etc.)

### Focusing on Outcomes

Have students preview the learning outcomes listed on p. 41. **NOTE:** Each of these outcomes is modeled in the video and evaluated in **Kann ich's wirklich?** on p. 62.

# Teaching Los geht's!
## pp. 42-44

### Resources for Los geht's!

- *Video Program* OR
  *Expanded Video Program,* Videocassette 1
- *Textbook Audiocassette* 1 B
- *Practice and Activity Book*

▶ **pages 42-43**

### Video Synopsis

In this segment of the video, Holger finds his new friends Tara, Jens, and Ahmet, playing a card game in the school yard. They ask Holger about his hobbies and interests and discover they share many, but not all, of the same interests. The student outcomes listed on p. 41 are modeled in the video: talking about interests, expressing likes and dislikes, talking about when one does various activities, asking for and expressing opinions, and agreeing and disagreeing.

### Motivating Activity

Tell the class that German students enjoy a variety of card games, such as **Mau-Mau** played with a regular deck of cards, or popular board games like **Mensch ärgere dich nicht, Dame,** and **Mühle.** Have students ask a partner about games, sports, or activities they enjoy. Let students briefly report to the rest of the class what they found out. This activity will be repeated in German in Activity 10 on p. 47.

### Group Work

This activity can be done as an advance organizer in preparation for the **Foto-Roman.** Have students working in pairs or groups of three look at the story and make a list of cognates and any other words they might recognize. They should not look up any words in the **Wortschatz** or the vocabulary section at the back of the book. Ask several students to come to the board and list the words they found and were able to identify.

### Teaching Suggestion

Have students listen to the text while looking at the photos, or have them watch this segment of the video. Remind students that they do not need to understand every word. They should try to get the gist of what is happening in the story. Have them match visual clues with words or phrases that they hear.

▶ **page 44**

### For Individual Needs

**3  A Slower Pace**   Rather than having students look back at the dialogue, have this activity prepared on a transparency. Then have students look at the pictures in the story on pp. 42-43.

## *T*eaching Erste Stufe, *pp. 45-47*

ERSTE STUFE

### Resources for Erste Stufe

*Practice and Activity Book*
*Chapter Resources,* Book 1
- Communicative Activity 2-1
- Additional Listening Activities 2-1, 2-2
- Student Response Form
- Realia 2-1
- Situation Card 2-1
- Teaching Transparency Master 2-1
- Quiz 2-1

*Audiocassette Program*
- *Textbook Audiocassette* 1 B
- *Additional Listening Activities, Audiocassette* 9 A
- *Assessment Items, Audiocassette* 7 A

▶ *page 45*

## *MOTIVATE*

### Teaching Suggestion

To help students prepare for the content and functions modeled in the **Erste Stufe**, put the following chart headings on the board or on a transparency.

SPORTS          HOBBIES          INSTRUMENTS

Ask students to name their interests from these categories and use the information they give you to fill in the chart on the board or on a transparency.

## *TEACH*

### PRESENTATION: Wortschatz

To introduce the vocabulary and the activities presented in the illustrations you'll need pictures of the vocabulary items (basketball, tennis ball, etc.) or the actual objects if you have them available. Present the vocabulary as follows: hold up a soccerball and say: **Das ist ein Fußball**. Hold up a basketball and say: **Das ist ein Basketball**. Continue with all vocabulary items. In the next step hold up a tennis ball and ask: **Ist das ein Golfball?** to elicit a student response of **Ja** or **Nein**. If you want students to produce the new vocabulary, proceed one level further by asking either/or questions such as **Ist das eine Gitarre oder ein Klavier?**

### Teacher Note

**Und dann noch ...** boxes contain optional vocabulary, which is meant to help students personalize their conversations, and writing. Students will not be expected to produce these words on tests or quizzes. Additional vocabulary arranged by topic is presented on pp. 321-35 of the *Pupil's Edition*.

▶ *page 46*

### ◆ For Individual Needs

**7 Visual Learners**   Prepare several cutout pictures from magazines (large enough for students to see) of other activities with cognate names such as golf, yoga, ballet, etc. After reading the **Lerntrick** on p. 45 with students, hold up the pictures and have students say and write down the name of the activity.

### PRESENTATION: So sagt man das!

In German, tell students what sports, interests, or hobbies you enjoy. (Example: **Ich spiele gern Volleyball. Ich spiele nicht Basketball.**) Next, ask several students yes/no questions: **Maria, spielst du Klavier?** and so on. Finally, ask the class either/or questions such as **Spielt Maria Klavier oder Gitarre?**

### PRESENTATION: Ein wenig Grammatik

1. Have students list the subject pronouns they learned in Chapter 1 (**ich, du, er, sie, sie** *pl*). Write the pronouns on the board or a transparency as students call them out to you.

2. For each subject pronoun, add the verb **spielen** in its correct form. Ask students to try to differentiate between the stems and the endings for each form of **spielen**. You could also have one student come to the front and underline the verb endings.

▶ *page 47*

## For Additional Practice

**10** Have students name the activities associated with famous international or national sport celebrities or musicians. Have them include local people and fellow schoolmates as well.

Examples: **Michael Jordan spielt Basketball.**
**José Canseco spielt Baseball.**
**Monica Seles spielt Tennis.**
**Branford Marsalis spielt Saxophon.**

 ## For Individual Needs

• **11 A Slower Pace** Rather than having students write an article, have them write two or three sentences about the activities of each person they interviewed.

• **Kinesthetic Learners** Divide the class into two teams to play this game practicing the **du**-form of the verbs students have learned. Have each team make a list of at least ten sentences using **du,** and write them on separate sheets of paper. Examples: **Du spielst Karten. Du spielst Gitarre.** Then, alternating between teams, a member of one team draws a sentence from the pile written by the other team and acts it out in front of his or her group. If the members of his or her team can guess the activity they get a point; if not, the team forfeits a point, and it is the other team's turn. Two points can be earned: one for naming the correct activity and one for using the correct verb ending in their answer. Example: **Du spielst Karten.** or **Sie spielt Karten.**

## Reteaching: Verb endings

To reteach the verb endings, use a transparency and fill in the following columns:

| subject pronouns or names | infinitives studied up to this point | activities |
|---|---|---|

Example:

| Maria | spielen | Volleyball |
|---|---|---|
| Hans | machen | Schach |
| Ich | hören | Sport |
| Du | | Musik |
| Wir | | |

Have students form complete sentences based on this information orally or in writing. Let students write their sentences on the board.

❖ ## For Individual Needs

**Visual Learners** Collect several pictures of various activities from calendars, post cards, magazines, etc. Distribute one picture to each student and have each student show and tell his or her activity to the class.
Example: **Der Mann hier spielt Golf.**
**Das ist Fechten.**

## Focusing on Outcomes

Refer students back to the learning outcomes listed on p. 41. Students should recognize that they are now able to talk about interests.

*ASSESS*

• **Performance Assessment** Give each student a piece of paper with the name of a well-known athlete or musician on it. Call on the individual students and ask them to tell the rest of the class who their person is and what he or she does. Example: **Boris Becker spielt Tennis.**

• Quiz 2-1, *Chapter Resources,* Book 1

**ERSTE STUFE**

# Teaching Zweite Stufe, pp. 48-52

## Resources for Zweite Stufe

*Practice and Activity Book*
*Chapter Resources,* Book 1
- Additional Listening Activities 2-3, 2-4
- Student Response Form
- Realia 2-2
- Situation Card 2-2
- Quiz 2-2

*Audiocassette Program*
- *Textbook Audiocassette* 1 B
- *Additional Listening Activities, Audiocassette* 9 A
- *Assessment Items, Audiocassette* 7 A

▶ **page 48**

## MOTIVATE

### Teaching Suggestion

Ask students if there are any activities that they participate in during the school year, in their PE class for example, that they like and look forward to, and if there are any they do not like. Let students tell you in English about the activities they like and dislike. On the board, write down what students tell you about their activities. (Example: Michael: -soccer, +golf) Use these notes for presenting **So sagt man das!**

## TEACH

### PRESENTATION: So sagt man das!

Using the notes you wrote on the board during the motivating activity, point to the activities on the board and use them to model the expressions in the function box.

Example: **Michael spielt nicht gern Fußball. Er spielt gern Golf.**

## PRESENTATION: Ein wenig Grammatik

Walk around the classroom and address two or more students at a time asking questions related to sports or other interests. Use verbs such as **machen, schwimmen, spielen, hören,** and **tanzen.** Example: **Macht ihr gern Sport? Tanzt ihr gern?** Students should answer using **wir.** Example: **Ja, wir tanzen gern.**

▶ **page 49**

## PRESENTATION: Wortschatz

Demonstrate some of the activities pictured mimicking someone reading a book, writing a letter, etc. Then ask yes/no questions such as **Höre ich Musik?** Once you feel students understand the vocabulary, ask either/or questions such as **Höre ich Musik oder schaue ich Fernsehen?** To practice additional pronouns, ask students to volunteer to mimic one of the activities. Then, you can ask yes/no or either/or questions such as **Schwimmt er? Wandert sie oder tanzt sie?**

▶ **page 50**

## PRESENTATION: Ein wenig Landeskunde

When explaining the two forms of *you* in the **Ein wenig Landeskunde** box, you might want to give students some language history. For example, you may want to explain the historical development of the formal **Sie.** During the medieval period when German nobility became quite taken with French culture, they began to model the French formal address, **vous.** From the late 17th century on the formal **Sie** was incorporated into the German language.

ZWEITE STUFE

## PRESENTATION: Grammatik

Write a simple sentence such as **Er schwimmt** on the board or on a transparency. Ask students how they would translate this sentence into English. Once students understand that three different English sentences can be expressed by one German sentence (*He swims. He is swimming. He does swim.*), ask them to review the verb endings of the present tense by giving examples for each subject pronoun with the verb **schwimmen.**

▶ page 51

## For Additional Practice

**16** Read the following five sentences to the class and have students indicate orally or on paper whether the people talking know each other well or not.

**Wann spielen Sie denn Tennis, Frau Köhler?**

**Komm mit, Brigitte!**

**Sie spielen aber sehr gut Klavier, Fräulein Schmidt.**

**Mach bitte die Tür zu! Mir ist kalt.**

**Kommt ihr mit? Wir wollen tanzen gehen.**

## Teaching Suggestions

**17** Make students aware of the addition of the *e* in the **du-, er/sie,-** and **ihr-** forms of **zeichnen.** To help students remember, have them try to say these forms without the *e*: **zeichnst, zeichnt.** This will show them that these words cannot easily be pronounced without the *e*. This will be covered in the **Dritte Stufe** of this chapter.

**17** Have students create new sentences by moving each group of subjects one picture to the right.

## 📁 Portfolio Assessment

You might want to use the following activity as a written portfolio item for your students. Have students work in pairs. One partner is the reporter and the other is a famous singer or actor. The reporter wants to find out about the star's interests and activities for an upcoming news special. Have students write down this conversation and present it to the class. See *Assessment Guide*, Chapter 2.

▶ page 52

## 📼 PRESENTATION: Landeskunde

### Teaching Suggestion

As an advance organizer to the **Landeskunde** interviews, ask students if they are familiar with German sports. Do they know which are popular? (The three most popular sports are soccer, gymnastics, and tennis.)

### Geography Connection

In the Chapter 1 **Landeskunde,** students were asked to locate Bietigheim and Berlin in an atlas. Ask them now to look up the location of Hamburg to prepare them for the next activity.

### Thinking Critically

**Drawing Inferences** Given the location and the geography of Berlin and Hamburg, ask students if they can think of some sports that might be popular in those areas. (bike riding because there are few hills and sailing because of the proximity of water) Ask students if they can think of one sport that would not be possible in these areas. (skiing or mountain climbing)

### Teaching Suggestion

Before having students read, listen to, or watch the interviews, you might want to introduce them to the following vocabulary: **angucken** (*to watch or to look at something or someone*) **fernsehen** (*to watch television — as alternative to* **Fernsehen schauen**) **Trimm-Dich-Pfad** (*fitness trail with suggested activities marked along its path*)

ZWEITE STUFE

## Background Information

**Trimm-Dich** means *get fit* or *get yourself into shape*. **Trimm-Dich-Pfade** are well-marked fitness trails that can be found all across Germany. They encourage people of all ages to integrate activities such as pushups and situps in their walk or run. The length of the trails varies anywhere from 1 to 3 km, and each station has clearly marked signs to explain the activities.

###  Multicultural Connection

If students have the opportunity, they should interview foreign exchange students and teachers from other countries to find out what activities are popular in that particular country and culture. Students should share their findings with the class.

## CLOSE

### Teaching Suggestion

Tell students to imagine they are in Potsdam on an exchange and their host family is making suggestions of what to do and see around town. Using the activities mentioned, they should respond by telling their host family what they like and do not like to do.

**Schloß Sanssouci besuchen.**

**Im Bornstedter See schwimmen.**

**Ein Konzert in der Nikolaikirche hören.**

**In den Rehgarten mit dem Rad fahren.**

**Ins Filmmuseum gehen.**

Example: **Ich besuche Schloß Sanssouci nicht gern.**

### Focusing On Outcomes

Refer students back to the learning outcomes listed on p. 41. They should realize that they are now able to express likes and dislikes.

## ASSESS

- **Performance Assessment**   Divide the class into two groups and put a *Tic-Tac-Toe* game on the chalkboard or on a transparency. Have teams take turns creating complete sentences or questions using the verbs in their correct forms. If a team is able to make a correct statement or question with a particular verb, that team can mark an X or an O in that space.

| machen | fahren | joggen |
|---|---|---|
| schwimmen | tanzen | besuchen |
| sammeln | schreiben | spielen |

X: **Ich sammle Briefmarken.**
O: **Wir schreiben Briefe.**

- Quiz 2-2, *Chapter Resources*, Book 1

# *T*eaching Dritte Stufe,
## pp. 53-57

### Resources for Dritte Stufe

*Practice and Activity Book*
*Chapter Resources,* Book 1
- Communicative Activity 2-2
- Additional Listening Activities 2-5, 2-6
- Student Response Form
- Realia 2-3
- Situation Card 2-3
- Teaching Transparency Master 2-2
- Quiz 2-3

*Audiocassette Program*
- *Textbook Audiocassette* 1 B
- *Additional Listening Activities, Audiocassette* 9 A
- *Assessment Items, Audiocassette* 7 A

▶ *page 53*

## *MOTIVATE*

### Teaching Suggestion

Ask students at what times during the week or weekend they are involved in their various activities. Is anybody involved in any activities outside of school? Take a quick survey in class to find out who participates in after-school activities and who belongs to a club that is not associated with school.

## *TEACH*

### PRESENTATION: So sagt man das!

Write the time expressions from this box on the board or on a transparency and write several verbs in their infinitive forms next to them. On the far right side, make a column of subject pronouns.

Example:

nach der Schule   schwimmen   ich

Go over the new vocabulary from the **So sagt man das!** function box and ask students to take out a sheet of paper and write three or four original sentences. Let students read them aloud in class.

### Language Note

**Herbst** might look more familiar to students if they think of the English word *harvest.* The German word has its origin in its verb form **herbsten,** to *harvest grapes,* which refers to **Weinbau** (wine-growing).

▶ *page 54*

###  For Individual Needs

**24 Challenge**   Tell students to imagine that new neighbors have moved in across the street and are unfamiliar with the neighborhood. Have the students come up with as many suggestions as they can for activities and things to do in their town during the different seasons. Write the names of the seasons on the board and have students come up and write their ideas.

Example:

| Frühling | Winter | Sommer | Herbst |
|----------|--------|--------|--------|
| reiten | Ski laufen | Baseball spielen | wandern |

### PRESENTATION: Grammatik

Write several sentences in fragments on cardboard or construction paper. Hand out the pieces to students who will go to the front of the class and hold their cards for the class to see. Have one other student manipulate the students into the correct positions to form a complete sentence with all pieces in the correct order. Then ask the student who is holding the time element to move to a different position and let the manipulator make all other necessary changes. Use a new set of students for the next sentence.

Example: **Im Winter spielen wir oft Eishockey.**
              1            2        3    4      5

          **Wir spielen im Winter oft Eishockey.**
           3       2        1        4      5

## Building on Previous Skills

Ask students to turn to the map of Europe on p. 1 and imagine that they are travelling through one or more of the German-speaking countries with friends for one year. Have them write sentences about what they do during the different seasons.

Example: **Im Winter laufen wir Ski in Österreich.**
**Im Herbst spielen wir Fußball.**
**Im Sommer fahre ich an die Ostsee.**
**Im Frühling besuchen wir den Schwarzwald.**

▶ page 55

###  For Individual Needs

**28 A Slower Pace** Have students write their new sentences in large print and then cut out each word. Ask them to put the sentence strips into an envelope and give it to you. After you number each envelope, distribute one envelope to each student. Have each student recreate one sentence. Check the sentences and let students read them aloud.

▶ page 56

## PRESENTATION: So sagt man das!

Students may recognize the expressions **stimmt** and **stimmt nicht** from the activity in the **Los geht's!** part of Chapter 1. Have students compare the meaning of **stimmt** and **stimmt nicht** in the context of the **Los geht's!** activity and in the context of agreeing and disagreeing in this **So sagt man das!** function box.

###  For Individual Needs

**29 Challenge** Call on one student and ask him or her to express his or her opinion about an activity or interest. Have this student call on another student who must disagree with the opinion expressed. Then call on another student to start again.

Example:

| | |
|---|---|
| Teacher: | Tom, wie findest du Briefmarken-sammeln? |
| Tom: | Ich finde Briefmarkensammeln sehr langweilig. Und du, Lori? |
| Lori: | Aber ich finde Briefmarkensam-meln interessant. |

## PRESENTATION: Ein wenig Grammatik

As a follow-up to **So sagt man das!**, write the following statements on the board or on an overhead transparency:
**Basteln ist blöd.**
**Ich finde Segeln langweilig.**
**Comics sammeln macht keinen Spaß.**
Ask students to disagree with these statements and to say that they do these activities often. Guide them to responses like the following:
**Stimmt nicht! Ich bastle oft.**
**Stimmt nicht! Ich segle oft.**
**Stimmt nicht! Ich sammle Comics gern.**
Write these responses to the original statements and ask students to analyze the verb forms in relation to the infinitive **basteln.**

## For Additional Practice

**31** After students have rewritten the letter, tell them to underline all verbs in the letter. Let them tell you what the verbs mean and how each is being used. (Example: **fragst** means *ask* and is used in the **du**-form with an **-st** ending.)

###  Culture Note

**Brieffreundschaften** among young people are very popular in Germany. There is always a long list of ads in all the youth magazines. If any of your students are interested in finding a German-speaking pen pal write to the *Student Letter Exchange* in New York. The address is on p. T38.

▶ *page 57*

## PRESENTATION: Aussprache

- **ie** Remind students that like all German vowels, this sound is pronounced with more muscular tension in the mouth than English vowels. The English comparison is not an exact match. Also, students often confuse the pronunciation of the German vowels **ei** and **ie** with the English pronunciation. To help them "unlearn" this tendency, remind them to pronounce the second letter in each combination as if it were the English *i* as in *mine* and *e* as in *me*.

- **ei** Like German vowels, this diphthong is pronounced with more tension in the mouth than English vowels. This sound is sometimes written **ai**, **ay**, or **ey**.

## Reteaching: Word order

Create new sentence strips or reuse the numbered envelopes with sentence strips inside (from the slower-paced Activity 28). You will need one for each student. Give students 30 seconds per envelope to put together a complete sentence. Ask students to write their sentences on a sheet of paper with the number from the envelope in front of the sentence. When the time is up, students pass their envelope to the next person. By the end of the activity, every student should have at least six sentences written down. Students can take turns calling out the sentence that corresponds to each number. As the sentences are read, each student will be able to check his or her sentences.

## CLOSE

### Teaching Suggestion

Have two students work together to plan weekend activities. For each activity one student suggests and is excited about, the other student should disagree and suggest something different. In the end they should both agree on five activities.

### Focusing On Outcomes

Refer students back to the outcomes listed on p. 41. Students should recognize that they are now able to say when they do various activities, ask for an opinion and express theirs, and agree and disagree.

## ASSESS

- **Performance Assessment** Check students' comprehension by calling out the following sentences and having students respond with either **stimmt** or **stimmt nicht.**

 **Am Wochenende gehen wir gern in die Schule.**
 **Die Deutschen spielen sehr gern Fußball.**
 **Unsere Basketballmannschaft ist Spitze!**
 **Wir gehen jetzt ins Museum.**
 **Ich spiele gern Schach und Mau-Mau.**
 **Wir finden Rockmusik toll.**
 **Ich besuche meine Freunde gern.**

- Quiz 2-3, *Chapter Resources,* Book 1

**ZUM LESEN**

# $\mathcal{T}$eaching Zum Lesen, pp. 58-59

## Reading Strategy

The targeted strategy in this reading is scanning for specific information. Students should learn about this strategy before doing Question 1. Students will also be asked to skim for the gist, answer questions to show comprehension, and transfer what they have learned.

## *PREREADING*

### Motivating Activity

Point out to students that Germans are very active and pursue many organized after-school and after-work activities. Have students bring the weekend newspaper section in which upcoming events are publicized. Ask them to make a list of various activities and any important information given for such events.

### Teacher Note

There are prereading questions in the **Lesetrick** box.

## *READING*

###  Cooperative Learning

Put students in groups of four. Ask them to choose a discussion leader, a recorder, a proofreader, and an announcer. Give students a specific amount of time in which to complete Activities 1–5. Monitor group work as you walk around, helping students if necessary. At the end of the activity, call on each group announcer to read his or her group's results. You can decide whether or not to collect their work for a grade at the end of the activity.

### For Individual Needs

**A Slower Pace**   Before working with all the ads on the page, group students to work with just one or two ads at a time. Each group should have three tasks: find the name of the activities, find the dates and times they take place, and make a list of the words they recognize. Students can report their findings to the class.

## *POST-READING*

### Teacher Note

Questions 6–7 are post-reading tasks that will show whether students can apply what they have learned.

### Teaching Suggestion

After completion of the **Zum Lesen** activities, have the students create an announcement for an upcoming event with the following German proverb as the jumping-off point: **Wer rastet, der rostet!** (*Use it or lose it!*)

Example: participate in the next 10k run.

You may want to supply paper, scissors, and colored pens to help students get started. Have students display their ads in the classroom.

# Schach

**Nr. 2743 – Dr. Siegfried Brehmer**
„Schachexpress" 1948

Matt in zwei Zügen

Weiß: Kb8, De7, Tb7, Ld6, Sd3 (5)
Schwarz: Kc6, Del, Ta5, Th4, Lh2, Lh3, Sc3, Sg3, Ba7, d5, d7, e5, h6 (13)

*Liebe (Lieber) ═══!*
*Morgen habe ich viel vor. Am Vormittag ═══.*
*Später ═══. Am Abend gehe ich zum Sommerfest.*
*Dort ═══. Bevor ich ins Bett gehe, ═══.*
*Dein(e)*

# Using Anwendung,
## p. 60-61

### Motivating Activity

**1** Have one student describe another student in German class by talking about his or her interests and dislikes to the rest of the class without naming or looking at that student. After the student has completed his or her description, the rest of the class can only ask yes/no questions to find out who is being described.

### (TPR) Total Physical Response

Have students demonstrate their understanding of given commands by performing the appropriate elements. First, have students imitate the appropriate responses to new commands. Once students seem comfortable, you can have them follow your commands individually or as a group. For this activity you will need a deck of cards, a chess board, and a tennis racket.

#### Commands

**Steht auf!**

**Setzt euch!**

**Zeigt auf den Tisch!**

**Zeigt auf den Stuhl!**

**Zeigt auf die Lehrerin/den Lehrer!**

**Zeigt auf die Spielkarten!**

**Zeigt auf das Schachbrett!**

**Zeigt auf den Tennisschläger!**

**Leg das Schachbrett auf den Tisch!**

**Leg die Spielkarten auf den Stuhl!**

**Leg den Tennisschläger auf das Schachbrett!**

**Gib der Lehrerin/dem Lehrer den Tennisschläger!**

### Portfolio Assessment

You might want to use the following activity as an oral portfolio item for your students. Have each student come up with at least three different questions for a survey about popular activities and interests. Each student will then interview a set number of people, other than German class students (parents, siblings, neighbors, librarian) for his or her survey. The student then records his or her questions and findings in German and reports them to class.

Example: What is your favorite weekend activity?

See *Assessment Guide,* Chapter 2.

### For Additional Practice

**5** Tell students that a new exchange student from a German-speaking country is attending the next German Club meeting. Ask them to help you introduce him or her by writing a paragraph providing the following information: name, age, where he or she is from, what school he or she goes to, and his or her likes and dislikes.

# Kann ich's wirklich?
## p. 62

This page is intended to prepare students for the test. It is a brief checklist of the major points covered in the chapter. The students should be reminded that it is a checklist only and not necessarily everything that will appear on the test.

# Using Wortschatz,
## p. 63

### Game

• Play the game **Kettenspiel** to review Chapter 2 vocabulary and third person conjugations. See p. 39 F for the procedure.

• Play the game *Memory* to review Chapter 2 vocabulary. See p. 39F for the procedure.

### Teacher Note

Give the **Kapitel 2** Chapter Test, *Chapter Resources*, Book 1.

# 2 Spiel und Spaß

1 Was machst du denn in deiner Freizeit?

Teenagers in German-speaking countries enjoy their spare time in many ways. They play sports and games, pursue various interests and hobbies, listen to music, and get together with their friends. Does this sound like what you and your friends do in your free time? How are the leisure time activities you like to do similar to the ones mentioned above? How are they different?

## In this chapter you will learn

- to talk about interests
- to express likes and dislikes
- to say when you do various activities; to ask for an opinion and express yours; to agree and disagree

## And you will

- listen to German students talk about sports and other activities
- read excerpts from German newspapers and magazines
- write a brief introduction for a visiting student from Germany
- find out what people in German-speaking countries do in their free time

② Fußball finde ich super!

③ Ich sammle gern Briefmarken.

# Los geht's!

**Holger** **Jens** **Tara**

**Steffi** **Ahmet**

## Was machst du in deiner Freizeit?

Look at the photos that accompany the story.
What are the people in each picture doing?
What do you think Holger might be telling
them about himself?

**①**

Was spielt ihr denn da?

Was fragst du?

Ich frage, was ihr da spielt.

Karten.

Ja, das sehe ich. Aber was spielt ihr?

Wir spielen Mau-Mau.

Wer gewinnt?

Tara und Ahmet, wie immer!

**②**

Du gewinnst auch manchmal.

Aber ihr mogelt oft.

Was? Wir mogeln nicht.

Du bist nur sauer, weil du verlierst.

**③**

Spielst du auch Karten, Holger?

Ja, aber nicht so gern.

Was machst du denn sonst in deiner Freizeit?

Tja, hm ... Fußball, ich geh'* oft schwimmen, im Winter lauf' ich Ski, ich ...

**④**

Was noch? Hast du andere Interessen?

Na, klar! Ich sammle Briefmarken. Und ich höre gern Musik.

Spielst du ein Instrument?

Ja, ich spiele Gitarre.

---

* Frequently in spoken German, the e-ending on the ich-form of the verb is omitted.
In writing this is indicated by an apostrophe.

## 1 Was passiert hier?

Do you understand what is happening in the **Foto-Roman**? Check your comprehension by answering these questions. Don't be afraid to guess!

1. What are Ahmet, Tara, and Jens doing at the beginning of the story?
2. Which sports does Holger play? What other interests does Holger mention?
3. Why is Tara teasing Holger? What does she say to him?
4. How does Holger feel at the end of the story? What does he say that lets you know how he feels?

1. playing cards
2. soccer, swimming, skiing; stamp collecting, listening to music, playing the guitar
3. He thinks tennis is boring. „**Aber schade, du findest Tennis langweilig.**"
4. He is annoyed. „**So ein Mist!**"

## 2 Genauer lesen

Reread the conversations. Which words or phrases do the characters use to

1. ask what someone likes to do in his or her free time
2. say they like to listen to music
3. ask if someone plays an instrument
4. ask if someone has other interests
5. tell what their favorite sport is
6. say that they do something often
7. say that they find something boring

Possible answers:
1. Was machst du denn in deiner Freizeit?
2. Ich höre gern Musik.
3. Spielst du ein Instrument?
4. Hast du andere Interessen?
5. Mein Lieblingssport ist...
6. Ich gehe oft schwimmen.
7. Tennis find' ich langweilig.

## 3 Was paßt zusammen? *What goes together?*

Jens and Tara ask Holger what he does in his free time. Match each question on the left with an appropriate response on the right.

1. Spielst du Karten? c.
2. Was machst du in deiner Freizeit? d.
3. Hast du auch andere Interessen? b.
4. Spielst du ein Instrument? e.
5. Spielst du auch Tennis? a.

a. Nein, Tennis finde ich langweilig.
b. Ja, ich sammle Briefmarken und höre gern Musik.
c. Ja, aber ich spiele Karten nicht so gern.
d. Ich spiele Fußball, ich geh' schwimmen, und im Winter lauf' ich Ski.
e. Ja, ich spiele Gitarre.

## 4 Welches Wort paßt? *Which word fits?*

Based on the story you just read and heard, complete each of the sentences below with an appropriate word from the box.

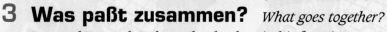

Karten Musik sammelt langweilig Tennis spielen

Tara, Ahmet und Jens spielen gern __1__. Holger __2__ lieber Briefmarken und hört auch gern __3__. Holger findet Tennis __4__, aber Tara findet den Sport super. __5__ ist Taras Lieblingssport. Tara und Steffi __6__ oft Tennis.

1. Karten 2. sammelt 3. Musik 4. langweilig 5. Tennis 6. spielen

## 5 Wer macht was?

What have you learned about these students? Match the statements with the people they describe.

1. Tara — 1. c
2. Ahmet — 2. e
3. Holger — 3. b
4. Jens — 4. a
5. Steffi — 5. d

a. verliert oft beim Kartenspielen.
b. spielt Karten nicht gern.
c. findet Holger nett.
d. spielt oft mit Tara Tennis.
e. gewinnt oft beim Kartenspielen.

# ERSTE STUFE

*Talking about interests*

JENS  Was machst du in deiner Freizeit?
UTE   Ich mache viel Sport. Ich spiele ...

Fußball

Basketball

Volleyball

Tennis

JENS  Spielst du auch Golf?
UTE   Nein, ich spiele nicht Golf.
JENS  Spielst du ein Instrument?
UTE   Ja klar! Ich spiele ...

JENS  Hast du auch andere Interessen?
UTE   Ja, ich spiele auch...

Gitarre

Klavier

Karten

Schach

**Und dann noch . . .**

Schlagzeug     Flöte     Trompete

**LERNTRICK**

Look for cognates when you read. Cognates are words that look similar and have the same meaning in German and English. Some are identical, for example, *tennis* and **Tennis**. Others differ slightly in spelling, such as *trumpet* and **Trompete**. How many cognates can you find in the **Wortschatz**?

## 6  Hör gut zu!

Using the drawings above as a guide, listen as Holger asks what his classmates do in their free time. First write the name of any activity you hear mentioned. Then, listen again for the students' names. This time, write each student's name beside the activity he or she does.

Stefan spielt Klavier; Anne spielt Basketball; Helena spielt Go...

## 7 Bildertext    1. Fußball 2. Karten 3. Schach 4. Gitarre 5. Klavier

Complete the following description of Ahmet's free time activities, using the pictures as cues.

Ahmet spielt oft __1__  . Mit Tara und Jens spielt er oft __2__  , aber

__3__ 🨒 spielt er nicht so gern.  Er spielt auch zwei Instrumente: er spielt

__4__ 🎸 , und er spielt auch __5__ 🎹 , aber das spielt er nicht so gut.

---

## SO SAGT MAN DAS!
### Talking about interests

If you want to know what a friend does in his or her free time, you might ask:

**Was machst du in deiner Freizeit?**
**Spielst du Volleyball?**
*Do you play volleyball?*
**Was macht Steffi?**
**Spielt sie auch Volleyball?**

**Toll! Und Jens? Spielt er auch Volleyball?**

You might get these responses:

**Ich spiele Gitarre.**
**Ja, ich spiele Volleyball.** *or*
**Nein, ich spiele nicht Volleyball.**
**Sie spielt Tennis und Basketball.**
**Ja, ich glaube, sie spielt oft Volleyball.**

**Nein, er spielt nicht Volleyball.**

---

### Ein wenig *Grammatik*

In the sentences above that use **spielen,** the subject pronouns change as different people are addressed or talked about. A question addressed to one person uses **du**. The response to such a question uses **ich**. What pronouns do you use in German when you talk about a female? a male?[1] As the subject pronoun changes, the forms of the verb also change: **ich spiele, du spielst, er/sie spielt**. The part of the verb that does not change is the *stem*. What is the stem of **spielen**?[2] In the two boxes below, match the verb endings with the pronouns.[3]

| du | ich | er | sie |
|---|---|---|---|

| -t | -st | -t | -e |
|---|---|---|---|

## 8 Was fehlt hier?

Holger wants to know what some of his classmates do in their free time. Supply the correct endings of the verbs.

1. HOLGER  Mach═══ du oft Sport? -st
   HEIKE  Ja, ich mach═══ viel Sport! -e
   HOLGER  Was spiel═══ du denn alles? -st
   HEIKE  Ich spiel═══ Fußball, -e
   Volleyball und auch Tennis.

2. HOLGER  Und Werner?
   Was mach═══ er gern? -t
   HEIKE  Er spiel═══ gern Klavier. -t
   HOLGER  Spiel═══ Gabi auch Klavier? -t
   HEIKE  Nein. Sie spiel═══ Gitarre. -t

1. sie; er  2. spiel-  3. du:st  ich:e  er:t  sie:t

## 9 Fragen und Antworten  *Questions and answers*

Steffi is trying to find people to play a game with her. Complete her conversation with Tara by filling in the missing lines with an appropriate question or answer from the boxes. Which game do they decide to play? Do all the girls like that game?

> Spielt die Elisabeth auch?

> Na klar! Basketball ist Klasse!

> Nein, aber sie spielt Volleyball.

> Spielst du auch Volleyball?

STEFFI  Hallo, Tara! Sag mal, spielst du Basketball?
TARA  ===  **Na klar! Basketball ist Klasse!**
STEFFI  ===  **Spielt die Elisabeth auch?**
TARA  Ja, Elisabeth spielt auch.
STEFFI  Und die Sybille?
TARA  ===  **Nein, aber sie spielt Volleyball.**
STEFFI  Und du? ===  **Spielst du auch Volleyball?**
TARA  Ja, ich spiele auch Volleyball. Und Elisabeth auch.
STEFFI  Prima! Also spielen wir heute Volleyball!  Volleyball; yes

## 10 In meiner Freizeit …

Using the **Wortschatz** shown on page 45, write down three things you do in your free time. Tell these activities to your partner, and then ask if he or she does them, too.

BEISPIEL  DU  **Ich spiele …**
**Und du?**

PARTNER  **Ja, ich spiele auch …** *or*
**Nein, ich spiele nicht …**

## 11 Ein Interview

a. You are a reporter for the school newspaper and are interviewing students about their interests. Get together with two other classmates and ask them questions in German to find out what they do in their free time. Then switch roles.
b. After you talk to two classmates, write what you learned, so that your article can be ready for the next edition.

BEISPIEL  DU  **Was …?**
(JOHN)  **Ich spiele Fußball und Basketball, und …**
YOU WRITE  **John spielt Fußball und Basketball, und …**

> Und dann noch…
>
> Baseball
> Handball
> Videospiele
> Tischtennis
> Brettspiele

## SO SAGT MAN DAS!

### Expressing likes and dislikes

To find out what someone likes
or doesn't like to do, you ask:

**Was machst du gern, Ahmet?**
**Schwimmst du gern?**
   *Do you like to swim?*
**Steffi, Tara, was macht ihr gern?**

The responses might be:

**Ich spiele gern Fußball.**
**Nein, nicht so gern.**

**Wir schwimmen sehr gern.**
   *We like to swim very much.*

To talk about what others like to do,
you say:

   **Tara und Steffi schwimmen gern.** *or*
   **Sie schwimmen gern.**

### Ein wenig *G*rammatik

In the question **Was macht ihr gern?** two people are addressed directly; the subject pronoun is **ihr**. The response to this question is also plural and uses **wir**: **Wir schwimmen gern.** The endings added to the verb stem with **ihr** and **wir** are **-t** and **-en**: **Schwimmt ihr? Ja, wir schwimmen gern.**

   When you are talking *about* two or more people, use the plural pronoun **sie**. What ending is added to the verb stem when the pronoun **sie** is used?[1]

   In the two boxes below, can you match the verbs and pronouns correctly?[2]

bist  schwimmt  machen
spielen  komme

sie (pl)  du  ich  wir  ihr

## 12  Hör gut zu!

Gabi is trying to find someone to do something with her. Listen as she talks with her friends and determine if she is speaking to one person or more than one. Then figure out what game Gabi wants to play and who finally plays it with her.

1, 4 - more than one;  2, 3, 5 - one;  chess, Ahmet
1. **-en** 2. Answers will vary. Possible answers: **sie machen, du bist, ich komme, wir spielen, ihr schwimmt**

|   | one | more than one |
|---|-----|---------------|
| 1 |     |               |
| 2 |     |               |

## 13 **Was fehlt hier?** *What's missing?*

Complete the following conversation between Ahmet and Holger with **ihr**, **wir**, or **sie** (pl).

HOLGER Tag Jens, Ahmet! Was macht __1__ jetzt?

JENS UND AHMET __2__ spielen jetzt Fußball. Was machst du?

HOLGER Steffi, Uwe und ich hören Musik. __3__ hören Country sehr gern. Ich glaube, Tara und Stefan kommen auch. __4__ hören Country auch gern. Und __5__? Hört __6__ das gern? 1. ihr 2. Wir 3. Wir 4. Sie 5. ihr 6. ihr

JENS UND AHMET Na klar!

UWE Sag mal, was machst du gern?
STEFAN Oh, ich ...

**sammle Briefmarken und Comics**

**zeichne**

**bastle viel**

UWE Und ihr, Christiane und Ulrike?
CHRISTIANE Tja, wir ...

**besuchen Freunde**

**schauen Fernsehen**

**hören Musik**

UWE Und deine Freunde, Katharina und Sven? Was machen sie?
CHRISTIANE Sie ...

**schwimmen**

**tanzen**

**wandern**

**Und dann noch ...**

Wir ...

lesen    malen

kochen   schreiben

fahren Rad   laufen Ski

laufen Rollschuh   joggen

segeln   reiten

## 14 Mix-Match: Viele Interessen  *A lot of interests*

Complete Jutta's description of her and her friends' free time activities by matching the following phrases to form complete sentences.

1. Ich besuche ... c.
2. Und ich spiele ... f.
3. Uwe und ich schauen ... b.
4. Christiane hört ... e.
5. Jörg sammelt ... a.
6. Und Peter und Uwe, sie ... d.

a. Briefmarken
b. Fernsehen.
c. Freunde.
d. schwimmen sehr gern.
e. Musik gern.
f. Fußball gern.

## 15 Hör gut zu!

Two of Tara's friends, Claudia and Michael, are trying to figure out what to do today. Listen to their conversation and write down which activities Claudia likes, which ones Michael likes, and what they finally decide to do together.  Musik hören

Claudia: Zeichnen, Musik hören, Fernsehen schauen; Michael: Briefmarken sammeln, schwimmen, Musik hören;

## *G*rammatik   The present tense of verbs

The statements and questions you have been practicing all refer to the present time and have verbs that are in the present tense. In English there are three ways to talk about the present tense, for example, *I play, I am playing,* or *I do play*. In German there is only one verb form to express the present tense: **ich spiele.**

All verbs have a basic form, the form that appears in your word lists (**Wortschatz**) or in a dictionary. This form is called the infinitive. The infinitive of all verbs in German has the ending -**en** as in **spielen** or -**n**, as in **basteln.** When a verb is used in a sentence with a subject, the verb is conjugated. That means that the -**en** (or -**n**) of the infinitive is replaced with a specific ending. The ending that is used depends on the noun or pronoun that is the subject of the verb.

The following chart summarizes these different verb forms using **spielen** as a model.

| Ich | spiele | } | | Wir | spielen | } | |
|---|---|---|---|---|---|---|---|
| Du | spiel**st** | } Tennis. | | Ihr | spiel**t** | } Tennis. | |
| Holger (Er) | spiel**t** | | | Holger und | | | |
| Tara (Sie) | | | | Tara (Sie, pl) | spielen | | |

Almost all German verbs follow this pattern. Two verbs that you already know—besides **spielen**—are **kommen** and **machen.**

When speaking to adults who are not family members or relatives, you must use the formal form of address: **Sie. Sie** is used with the verb form ending in -**en,** the same form used with **wir** and **sie** (plural). It is always capitalized.

**Spielen Sie Tennis, Herr Meyer?**
**Wie heißen Sie?**
**Woher sind Sie, Frau Schmidt?**

### EIN WENIG LANDESKUNDE

Germans tend to be more formal than Americans, and teenagers rarely call adults by their first names. While there are no hard and fast rules about using **du** and **Sie,** it is safer to err in the direction of being too formal. If people want you to call them **du,** they will tell you.

## 16 Hör gut zu!

As you listen to these conversations, decide whether the speakers are talking to someone they know well, or someone they don't know so well.
1. not very well
2. very well
3. not very well

| | very well | not very well |
|---|---|---|
| 1 | | |
| 2 | | |

## 17 Bilder-Quiz

Using the photos as cues, take turns with a partner saying what the following people do in their free time.

Wir ... **Wir hören Musik.**
Du ... **Du hörst Musik.**
Sie (*you*, formal) ...
**Sie hören Musik.**

Klaus ... **Klaus zeichnet.**
Du ... **Du zeichnest.**
Ihr ... **Ihr zeichnet.**

Ahmet und Holger ...
Ich ... **Ahmet und Holger**
Sie (pl) ... **sammeln Comics.**
**Ich sammle Comics.**
**Sie sammeln Comics.**

Das Mädchen ...
Der Junge ...
Ihr ... **Das Mädchen spielt Gitarre.**
**Der Junge spielt Gitarre.**
**Ihr spielt Gitarre.**

## 18 Frag mal deinen Lehrer! *Ask your teacher!*

Ask your teacher about his or her interests. Work with a partner and write down five questions to ask, for example, **Spielen Sie Tennis? Hören Sie gern Musik?**

## 19 Was machst du gern?

Look at the vocabulary on pages 45 and 49 again. Tell your partner five things you like to do and two that you do not like to do. Then your partner will do the same. Make a list of your partner's likes and dislikes and circle the items you both like and dislike.

## 20 Für mein Notizbuch

Write down some things you like to do in your **Notizbuch**. For the names of any activities not listed on pages 45 and 49, refer to the Additional Vocabulary section on page 321 in the back of your book. These are words and expressions you can use whenever you're asked about your own interests.

## 21 Was macht ihr gern?

Work with two or four other classmates. Students in your group should pair off, leaving one person to be IT (**ES**). Using German, each pair should decide on one activity they both like to do. The person who is IT has to find out what that activity is by asking questions: **Spielt ihr gern Volleyball? Besucht ihr gern Freunde?** Students should answer truthfully with **Nein, wir ... nicht gern ...** or, when IT guesses correctly, **Ja, wir ... gern ...** The person who is IT reports each pair's activity to the class. Take turns being IT.

## Was machst du gern?

What kinds of interests do you think German teenagers might enjoy? What sports do you play? What interests do you have? Make a list of the things you like to do in your free time. Then, read what these teenagers said about their free time activities.

**Michael,** *Hamburg*

„Ich mach' also am liebsten in meiner Freizeit Basketballspielen oder ausgehen, so in Diskos mit meinen Freunden oder auch Fahrrad fahren."

**Björn,** *Hamburg*

„Tja, ich sitze eigentlich ziemlich oft vor dem Computer. Ich seh' auch gerne fern oder guck' mir ein Video an. Dann fahr' ich ganz gerne Rad und schwimme auch manchmal ganz gerne."

**Christina,**
*Bietigheim*

„Ich les' gern, ich hör' gern Musik und ich fahr' gern Moped."

**Heide,** *Berlin*

„Ich mach' dreimal in der Woche Sport. Da jogg' ich vier Kilometer mit Trimm-Dich-Pfad, dann fahr' ich auch noch Fahrrad, danach so eine Stunde mit einem Freund."

**Elke,** *Berlin*

„Ich spiele jetzt gern Volleyball. Im Sommer surf' ich, und im Winter geh' ich mit meinen Eltern nach Österreich Ski laufen."

**A.** 1. Work with a partner. Make a list of what each person interviewed likes to do. Organize your answers in a chart with the headings **Sport** and **andere Interessen**. After making your chart, what can you say about the personality of each person interviewed?

2. Answer the following questions with your classmates. Look back at the list of interests you made for yourself before reading. What are some similarities and differences between the free time activities teenagers in the German-speaking countries like to do, and what teenagers like to do where you live? What do you think students in German-speaking countries imagine that teenagers in the United States like to do? Where do they probably get their ideas?

**B.** You and your partner are exchange students in Potsdam and have been asked to come up with a plan of activities for an afternoon at a local **Jugendzentrum** (youth center). There will also be some other exchange students there, so you will need to plan activities that most everyone will enjoy. Make your plan on a large piece of paper or poster board with a lot of color (you could even cut some pictures out of magazines). Then present your activity plans to the class.

*Saying when you do various activities; asking for an opinion and expressing yours; agreeing and disagreeing*

## SO SAGT MAN DAS!

### Saying when you do various activities

To find out when people do things, you might ask:

They might tell you:

**Was machst du nach der Schule?**
*What do you do after school?*

**Am Nachmittag mache ich Sport.**
*In the afternoon I play sports.*

**Und am Abend mache ich die Hausaufgaben und schaue Fernsehen.** *In the evening I do my homework and watch television.*

**Und am Wochenende? Was machst du am Wochenende?**

**Tja, am Wochenende besuche ich Freunde.**

**Was machst du im Sommer?**
*What do you do in the summer?*

**Im Sommer wandere ich gern.**

What do you notice about the responses in this box? Do they all begin with the subject?[1] What do you observe about the position of the subject in these sentences? What is the position of the verb in all the sentences?[2]

## WORTSCHATZ

### Wann machst du das?

im Frühling

im Sommer

im Herbst

im Winter

---

1. These sentences begin with a time expression, rather than with the subject. 2. The verb is in second position, followed by the subject.

## 22 Hör gut zu!

You will hear one of Holger's new classmates, Uschi, talk about when she does various activities. First, write the activities as you hear them mentioned, then match the activities with the phrases that tell when Uschi does them.

**a.** im Frühling Volleyball

**b.** am Wochenende
Freunde besuchen

**c.** im Herbst wandern

**d.** am Nachmittag
basteln

**e.** im Sommer schwimmen

**f.** am Abend Musik hören

## 23 Wann ...?

Based on the page from Tara's weekly planner, answer the following questions.

1. Was macht Tara nach der Schule?
2. Wann wandert sie?
3. Wann besucht sie Steffis Familie?
4. Wann spielt sie Fußball?

1. Sie spielt Basketball.   3. Am Abend.
2. Am Wochenende.   4. Am Samstag

## 24 Wann machst du das?

List five activities you like to do and when you do them.

## 25 Zum Schreiben

Using complete sentences, write a description of what activities you like to do and when you like to do them. Use the list you made in Activity 24.

**MAI**

15. Montag

16. Dienstag

17. Mittwoch   7.00 – Steffi u. Ahmet besuchen

18. Donnerstag   2.00 – Basketball

19. Freitag

20. Samstag   2.00 – Fußball mit Joachim

21. Sonntag   3.00 – wandern mit Ahmet u. Jens

## *Grammatik* Word order: verb in second position

As you noticed on page 53, German sentences do not always begin with the subject. Often another word or expression (**nach der Schule, im Sommer**) is the first element. What happens to the verb in such cases?[1]

| Wir | spielen | nach der Schule | Fußball. |
| Nach der Schule | spielen | wir | Fußball. |
| Tara und Steffi | besuchen | im Sommer | Freunde. |
| Im Sommer | besuchen | Tara und Steffi | Freunde. |

## 26 Für mein Notizbuch

Exchange the sentences you wrote in Activity 25 with a partner. Check each other's sentences to make sure that the verbs are in second position and that all the verbs have the proper endings. Then trade papers back again, after you and your partner have made corrections or changes. You may want to modify some of your sentences, putting something else besides the subject at the beginning for a little variety. When you have finished, write your corrected sentences in your **Notizbuch**.

1. The verb is in second position, even when something other than the subject begins the sentence.

## 27 Und was machst du?

Ask your partner what he or she does at various times. Then switch roles. Use the phrases in the boxes below to help you answer your partner's questions. Be prepared to report your partner's answers to the class.

Some possible answers:
**Am Wochenende besuche ich Freunde.**
**Im Sommer schwimme ich.**
**Nach der Schule höre ich Musik.**
**Im Sommer spielt er Fußball.**
**Am Abend macht er Hausaufgaben.**
**Im Herbst spielt sie Basketball.**

am Wochenende
am Nachmittag
am Abend
nach der Schule
im Herbst
im Sommer
im Winter
im Frühling

Hausaufgaben machen
Freunde besuchen
Fernsehen schauen
Musik hören
Karten spielen
Basketball spielen
Fußball spielen
schwimmen

## SO SAGT MAN DAS!
### Asking for an opinion and expressing yours

To find out what someone thinks about something, you might ask:

**Wie findest du Tanzen?**

**Und wie findet Georg Tanzen?**

Some possible responses are:

**Ich finde Tanzen langweilig.** *I think dancing is boring.*
**Tanzen ist Spitze!** *Dancing is great!*
**Tanzen macht Spaß.** *Dancing is fun.*
**Er findet Tanzen langweilig.**

## *G*rammatik   Verbs with stems ending in **d, t** or **n**

**Finden** and other verbs with stems ending in **d, t** or **n** do not follow the regular pattern in the **du**- and **er/sie**-forms. These verbs add -**est** to the **du**-form (**du findest**) and -**et** to the **er/sie**- and **ihr**- forms (**er/sie findet, ihr findet**). Another verb that follows this pattern is **zeichnen** (**du zeichnest, er/sie zeichnet, ihr zeichnet**). You will learn more about these verbs later.

## 28 Blöd oder Spitze?

Express your opinion about the following activities. You may choose expressions from the list.

1. Ich finde Briefmarkensammeln ...
2. Fernsehen ist ...
3. Musik hören ist ...
4. Basteln finde ich ...
5. Wandern finde ich ...
6. Volleyball ...
7. Freunde besuchen ...
8. Schach ...

Some possible answers:
**Musik hören ist toll!**
**Freunde besuchen macht Spaß!**
**Schach ist langweilig!**
**Basteln finde ich prima!**

### Degrees of enthusiasm

Spitze!
super!
Klasse!
toll!
prima!
interessant!
macht Spaß!

langweilig!
blöd!
macht keinen Spaß!

## 29 Wie findest du …?

Ask your partner his or her opinion of three activities. Then switch roles. Be prepared to report your partner's opinions to the class.

## SO SAGT MAN DAS!

### Agreeing and disagreeing

If someone expresses an opinion such as **Ich finde Volleyball langweilig**, you might agree:

**Ich auch!** *or*
**Das finde ich auch.**

Or you might disagree:

**Ich nicht!** *or*
**Das finde ich nicht.**

If someone makes a statement like **Basteln ist blöd!** you might agree:

**Stimmt!**

or disagree:

**Stimmt nicht!**

---

### Ein wenig Grammatik

Verbs that end in **-eln**, like the verb **basteln**, change in the **ich**-form: the **e** drops from the verb stem, and the verb becomes **ich bastle**. Can you guess what the **ich**-form of **segeln** is?[1]

## 30 Hör gut zu!

Listen to the conversation between Ahmet and a friend as they discuss free time activities. Do they agree or disagree? About what? 1, 3, 5 agree / 2, 4 disagree

## 31 Ein Brief

You have just written the letter on the right to your pen pal in Germany. Unfortunately, on the way to the post office it started to rain and your letter got a little smeared. Rewrite the letter, fixing all the smeared words.

*Liebe Katja*

*Du fragst, was wir in den USA spielen. Ja, wir spielen auch Fußball und wir spielen Basketball. Im Winter laufen wir Ski, und im Sommer gehen wir schwimmen. ... ihr auch Fußball?*

*Wir machen viel Sport. Ich, zum Beispiel, fahre gern Rad. Im Sommer gehe ich wandern, und ich spiele viel Tennis. Ich finde Tennis toll! Du auch? Meine Freunde und ich — ja, wir hören Musik, und am Nachmittag spielen wir immer Volleyball.*

*Was macht Ihr in Deutschland?*

*Dein(e)...*

Liebe Katja!
Du fragst, was wir in den USA spielen. Ja, wir spielen Fußball und wir spielen auch Basketball. Im Winter laufen wir Ski, und im Sommer gehen wir schwimmen. Spielt ihr auch Fußball?
 Wir machen viel Sport. Ich, zum Beispiel, fahre gern Rad. Im Sommer gehe ich wandern, und ich spiele viel Tennis. Ich finde Tennis toll! Du auch? Meine Freunde und ich — ja, wir hören Musik, und am Nachmittag spielen wir immer Volleyball.
 Was macht Ihr in Deutschland?
Dein(e) ...

1. **Ich segle.**

## 32 Und deine Meinung? *And your opinion?*

1. List six activities and write your opinion of each one next to it.
2. Work with a partner. Ask your partner what he or she thinks of each activity on your list. Agree or disagree with your partner's opinion. When you disagree, express your own opinion.
3. Respond to your partner's list.
4. Which activities do you and your partner agree on? Which ones don't you agree on? Make a list and be prepared to report to the class.

## 33 Zum Schreiben

In this chapter you have learned a lot about how Germans spend their free time. Imagine you are Katja and respond to the letter on page 56. Refer to the **Landeskunde** for ideas.

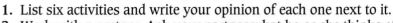

###  Richtig aussprechen / Richtig lesen

A. To practice the following sounds, say the words and sentences below after your teacher or after the recording.

1. The letter combination **ie:** The vowel combination **ie** sounds much like the long *e* in the English word *me*.
   **spielen, viel, vier / Sie und ihre sieben Brüder spielen Klavier.**

2. The letter combination **ei:** The vowel combination **ei** is pronounced like the long *i* in the English words *mine* and *shine*.
   **schreiben, deiner, Freizeit / Heike findet Zeichnen langweilig.**

3. The letter **j:** The letter **j** is pronounced like the *y* in the English word *yes*. In words borrowed from other languages, such as **Jeans**, the **j** is pronounced as it is in English.
   **Jens, Jürgen, Junge / Wer ist der Junge? Der Junge heißt Jens.**

4. The letter **z:** The letter **z** is pronounced like the consonant combination *ts* as in the English word *hits*.
   **zur, zehn, zwölf / Zwei und zehn sind zwölf.**

### Richtig Schreiben / Diktat

B. Write down the sentences that you hear.

# ZUM LESEN

## *Was machen wir am Wochenende?*

1. Scan the articles for the following information: **a) 30. Juni, 17-24 Uhr**

   a. the day and time when you can hear a jazz concert in the **HAP-Grieshaber-Halle**

   b. the number of hot air balloon clubs in Hessen **b) 6**

   c. the three kinds of bands that will perform at the UNI summer festival **c) Big Band, jazz, dance**

   Did you have to read every word of the ad in order to find that information?

2. You live in Eningen and have friends visiting for the weekend. They are interested in jazz, so you want to take them to the jazz festival. Now you will need to get more specific information.

   a. How many groups can you hear at the festival? Where are the groups from?

   a) 5 groups, Reutlingen, Stuttgart, **Ungarn**

### Immer mehr machen mit

Immer mehr Leute unterschiedlichen Alters begeistern sich fürs Ballonfahren. Bei den sechs hessischen Ballon-Clubs, die die luftige Fahrt auch für Vereinsgäste anbieten, ist ein Jahr Wartezeit für die Aufnahme in den Club die Regel. Im März dieses Jahres war Stuttgart Ziel des 22. Deutschen Freiballonfahrertages.

### Eninger HOT JAZZ Festival

**Am 30. Juni von 17–24 Uhr in der HAP-Grieshaber-Halle**

Mit  Tante Frieda's Jazz Kränzchen, Reutlingen
All Star Groove, Stuttgart
Royal Garden Ramblers, Stuttgart
Stuttgarter Dixieland All Stars
Budapest Ragtime Orchestra, Ungarn

**Hallenbewirtschaftung mit Faßbier und kleineren Speisen.**

Eintrittskarten sind zu 20.– DM bei allen Zweigstellen der Kreissparkasse Reutlingen und »Sigi's Jazz House«, Im Bebenhäuser Hof, Reutlingen sowie an der Abendkasse zu 25.– DM erhältlich.

Hallenöffnung: 16.00 Uhr

### Skat

Die Karten in Mittelhand: Kreuz-Bube, Pik-Bube, Herz-Bube, Karo-Bube, Kreuz-As, Herz-As, Dame, Pik-König, Dame, 9 Vorhand paßt nach ausgereiztem Null ouvert Hand. Mittelhand spielt kurzentschlossen Pik Solo Hand, doch das Spiel endet, obwohl es kaum begonnen hat, mit 60:60 Augen. Die Gewinnchancen für einen Grand Hand waren sicher größer, doch käme es hierbei auch auf den Kartensitz bei der Gegenpartei an. Schließlich reizte Vorhand bis 59, und es war nicht auszuschließen, daß Vorhand im Besitz der restlichen Pikkarten sein konnte. Vorhand führt in zwei roten Farben (4+5 K.) 24 Augen, dazu eine schwarze Lusche. Hinterhand führt in zwei schwarzen Farben (1+6 K.) 17, dazu in einer roten Farbe 18 Augen.

3. Possible answers: **Tanz, Musik. Die Uni. 23. Juni, 19 Uhr, Neue Aula, Geschwister-Scholl-Platz. Eintritt frei.**

5. **Potsminton- Badminton. (003733) 458317**

6. Possible answers: **ich spiele Tennis/ich gehe wandern Karten/Schach/ich höre Musik/ich schaue Fernsehen/ ich spiele**

# Potsminton

## BADMINTON-TURNIER

**Sonntag, 24. Juni 1990, von 11.00 bis 16.00 Uhr**

Vom Freizeitsportler bis zum Aktiven bieten wir für jeden etwas. Hobby-Sportler können alles Wichtige über Federball und Badminton erfahren. Aktiven Spielern verrät unser Fachtrainer Hasso Böttcher Tricks und Kniffe oder gibt Tips für das individuelle Training.

Natürlich können Sie auch unsere Court's einfach nur mal testen.

Leihschläger liegen für Sie bereit!

Potsminton/Potsdam Sport-Center
Brandenburger Str. 73
14467 Potsdam
Telefon (003733) 458317

Potsminton

# UNI

23. Juni

19.00 Uhr

# Sommerfest

- Eintritt frei - Bewirtung -

**-Neue Aula-Geschwister-Scholl-Platz**

**Festsaal**
- Workshop Orchester der Tübinger Musiktage
- Tanzband Die Piccolos
- Vorführgruppe Elementarer Tanz
- Die hüpfenden und tanzenden Tonnen
- Modern- und Jazz-Tanzgruppe des Sportinstituts

**Neue Aula Foyer**
- Big Band Such Over Sky

**Geschwister-Scholl-Platz**
- Neckartown-Jazzband

**Bar**
- Karl Springer - Piano

# Schach

**Nr. 2743 – Dr. Siegfried Brehmer**
„Schachexpress" 1948

Matt in zwei Zügen

Weiß: Kb8, De7, Tb7, Ld6, Sd3 (5)
Schwarz: Kc6, Del, Ta5, Th4, Lh2, Lh3, Sc3, Sg3, Ba7, d5, d7, e5, h6 (13)

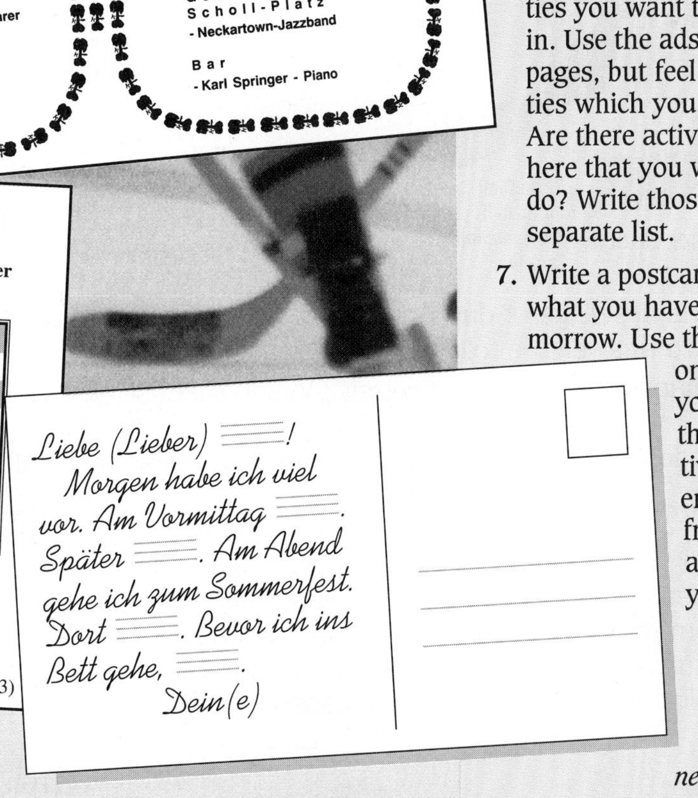

Liebe (Lieber) ___!
Morgen habe ich viel vor. Am Vormittag ___. Später ___. Am Abend gehe ich zum Sommerfest. Dort ___. Bevor ich ins Bett gehe, ___.
Dein(e)


b. How much will the tickets cost if you buy them at the **Kreissparkasse** in Reutlingen? How much will they cost if you wait and buy them on the evening of the performance? How early can you enter the concert hall? b) 20 DM, 25 DM, 16 Uhr

3. What would you and your friends probably be interested in if you wanted to attend the **UNI Sommerfest**? Can you figure out who is sponsoring this event? When will the event take place (time and date) and where? How much will it cost to get into the festival?

> **Weißt du noch?** *Remember?* You will often be able to use visual clues to figure out the meaning of a text.

4. List any visual clues on this page that help you determine the meaning of the texts. Skat, chess

5. If your friends would like to learn badminton better, where should they go? What telephone number should they call?

6. With a friend, make a list of places you want to go or activities you want to participate in. Use the ads on these two pages, but feel free to add activities which you particularly enjoy. Are there activities mentioned here that you would not want to do? Write those activities on a separate list.

7. Write a postcard to a friend about what you have planned for tomorrow. Use the partial sentences on the postcard as your guide, filling in the blanks with activities that you enjoy. Use words from the newspaper ads or other words you have learned.

1. Ahmet und Tara/Tennis/vier Uhr
2. Steffi/Volleyball/zwei Uhr
3. Steffi, Holger, Katja/wandern/am Wochenende

**1** You will hear several people talk about their interests and activities. Take notes as you listen, then answer the questions **Wer? Was? Wann?** for each conversation

**2 a.** Listen to the description of **der Sporti** and **die Sporti** pictured below. Write down any sports and activities that are mentioned but **not** pictured.

**b.** Pick one of the **Sportis** below and tell your partner everything the **Sporti** does. Your partner will tell you about the other **Sporti**.

der Sporti

Basketball
Volleyball
Klavier spielen
Tanzen

wandern
Fernsehschauen

die Sporti

Volleyball
Tanzen
Musik hören

Freunde besuchen
basteln

**3** Look at the drawings of **der Sporti** and **die Sporti** above and use them for clues to answer the following questions.

**a.** Was machst du in deiner Freizeit? Wann machst du das? Was machst du nicht?

**b.** Wie findest du das alles? Zum Beispiel, wie findest du Fußball, Tennis, usw.?

**4** Everyone in class will write on a slip of paper the German name for an activity presented in the chapter. Put all the slips of paper into a small box, then get into two teams. Two students, one from each team, together draw a slip of paper from the box. These two "mimes" will act out the activity, and the teams will take turns guessing what they are doing. The first person to guess right wins a point for his or her team. Guesses must be in this form: **Ihr spielt Tennis!**

5 Read the following student profiles. Working with a partner, take turns choosing one of the people pictured below and telling your partner about that person's name, age and interests.

Nicole König, 14
Hamburg
Tennis und Volleyball
spielen, zeichnen,
Freunde besuchen

Martin Braun, 16
Düsseldorf
Fußball und Gitarre
spielen, Briefmarken
sammeln, wandern

Julia Meier, 15
Ludwigsburg
schwimmen, Klavier
spielen, basteln, Schach
spielen, Musik hören

6 Working in groups of three, interview each member of your group and write descriptions like the ones above. First, decide together which questions you need to ask. Then, while one person interviews another, the third writes down the information on a separate piece of paper, leaving out the person's name. When the whole class is finished, put the descriptions in a box and take turns drawing them and telling the class about that person. Your classmates will guess who is being described.

7 One of the students pictured above is visiting your school, and you have to introduce him or her at a German club meeting. Write down what you are going to say in complete sentences.

8

## R O L L E N S P I E L

Get together with two of your classmates and act out the following situation.

It's Friday after school. You and two of your friends are really bored, and you are trying to find something fun to do. Discuss the activities that each of you likes, then try to find several that you can do together. Make a plan that includes several different activities and discuss when you want to do them. Be prepared to report your plans to the class.

# KANN ICH'S WIRKLICH?

**Can you ask about someone's interests, report them, and tell your own? (p. 46)**

Some possible answers:
Spielst du ...? Was machst du in deiner Freizeit? Schwimmst du? Sammelst du ...?

**1** How would you ask a classmate about interests, using the verbs **spielen, machen, schwimmen,** and **sammeln**?

**2** How would you report someone else's interests?

a. Susanne: tanzen, wandern, Gitarre spielen
b. Jörg: Golf spielen, basteln, zeichnen
c. Johannes: Schach spielen, Freunde besuchen
d. Uschi: Fernsehen schauen, Musik hören, Karten spielen

a) Susanne tanzt/ wandert/ spielt Gitarre
b) Jörg spielt Golf/bastelt/zeichnet
c) Johannes spielt Schach, besucht Freunde
d) Uschi schaut Fernsehen, hört Musik, spielt Karten

**3** How would you tell some of the things you do?

**Can you ask what others like to do and don't like to do, report what they say, and tell what you and your friends like and don't like to do? (p. 48)**

**4**
a. How would you say what activities you like and don't like to do?
  a) Possible answers: Ich spiele gern Fußball. Ich schwimme nicht so gern.
b. How would you ask a classmate what he or she likes to do and report that information to someone else?
  b) Was machst du gern? \ Possible answers: Sie spielt gern Klavier/schwimmt gern.
c. How would you ask these people what they like to do and then report what they say?
  c) Katharina und Ute, was macht ihr gern? Sie schwimmen gern. Sie spielen Schach gern. / Sie hören Musik gern.
  **Katharina und Ute: schwimmen, Schach spielen, Musik hören**
d. How would you ask your teacher if he or she plays basketball or chess, or if he or she collects stamps?
  d) Spielen Sie Basketball? Spielen Sie Schach? Sammeln Sie Briefmarken?

**Can you say when you do various activities? (p. 53)**

**5** How would you say that you
a. watch TV after school
  a) Nach der Schule schaue ich Fernsehen.
b. play soccer in the afternoon
  b) Am Nachmittag spiele ich Fußball.
c. go hiking in the spring
  c) Im Frühling wandere ich.
d. swim in the summer
  d) Im Sommer schwimme ich.

**6** How would you ask a classmate what he or she thinks of
a. tennis   b. music   c. drawing   d. hiking
  Wie findest du Tennis, Musik, Zeichnen, wandern?

**Can you ask for an opinion, agree, disagree and express your own opinion? (pp. 55, 56)**

**7** Agree or disagree with the following statements. If you disagree, express your opinion. Answers will vary. Possible answers: a. Das finde ich auch.
  b. Stimmt nicht. Basteln ist blöd.
a. Schach ist langweilig.
b. Basteln macht Spaß.
c. Briefmarkensammeln ist interessant.
d. Tennis ist super!
  c. Stimmt!   d. Das finde ich nicht. Tennis ist langweilig.

**8** How would you express your opinion of the following activities:
a. Fußball spielen
b. Briefmarkensammeln
c. wandern
d. schwimmen
Answers will vary. Possible answers:
a. Fußball spielen ist Spitze.
b. Briefmarkensammeln ist langweilig.
c. Wandern ist prima.
d. Schwimmen ist super.

## ERSTE STUFE
### TALKING ABOUT INTERESTS

**Was machst du in deiner Freizeit?** *What do you do in your free time?*

**Machst du Sport?** *Do you do sports?*

**machen** *to do*

**spielen** *to play*

**Ich spiele Fußball.** *I play soccer.*
  **Basketball** *basketball*
  **Volleyball** *volleyball*
  **Tennis** *tennis*
  **Golf** *golf*
**Spielst du ein Instrument?** *Do you play an instrument?*
**Ich spiele Klavier.** *I play the piano.*
  **Gitarre** *guitar*
  **Karten** *cards*

  **Schach** *chess*
**Hast du andere Interessen?** *Do you have other interests?*

### OTHER USEFUL WORDS AND PHRASES

**viel** *a lot, much*
**nicht** *not, don't*
**andere** *other*
**Ich glaube...** *I think...*
**oft...** *often*

---

## ZWEITE STUFE
### EXPRESSING LIKES AND DISLIKES

**gern (machen)** *to like (to do)*
**nicht gern (machen)** *to not like (to do)*
**nicht so gern** *not to like very much*

### ACTIVITIES

**Briefmarken sammeln** *to collect stamps*
**Comics sammeln** *to collect comics*

**Freunde besuchen** *to visit friends*
**Fernsehen schauen** *to watch TV*
**Musik hören** *to listen to music*
**zeichnen** *to draw*
**basteln** *to do crafts*
**schwimmen** *to swim*
**tanzen** *to dance*
**wandern** *to hike*

### PRONOUNS

**ich** *I*    **wir** *we*
**du** *you*    **ihr** *you (pl)*

**er** *he*    **sie** *they*
**sie** *she*    **Sie** *you (formal)*

### OTHER USEFUL WORDS AND PHRASES

**so** *so*
**sehr** *very*
**Sag mal,...** *Say,...*
**Tja...** *Hm...*

---

## DRITTE STUFE
### SAYING WHEN YOU DO VARIOUS ACTIVITIES

**die Hausaufgaben machen** *to do homework*
**Wann?** *When?*
  **nach der Schule** *after school*
  **am Nachmittag** *in the afternoon*
  **am Abend** *in the evening*
  **am Wochenende** *on the weekend*
  **im Frühling** *in the spring*
  **im Sommer** *in the summer*
  **im Herbst** *in the fall*
  **im Winter** *in the winter*

### EXPRESSING OPINIONS

**Wie findest du (Tennis)?** *What do you think of (tennis)?*
**Ich finde (Tennis) ...** *I think (tennis) is...*
  **Spitze!** *super!*
  **super!** *super!*
  **Klasse!**
  **prima!** } *great! terrific!*
  **toll!**
  **interessant** *interesting*
  **langweilig** *boring*
  **blöd** *dumb*

**(Tennis) macht Spaß.** *(Tennis) is fun.*
**(Tennis) macht keinen Spaß.** *(Tennis) is no fun.*

### AGREEING AND DISAGREEING

**Ich auch.** *Me too.*
**Ich nicht.** *I don't./Not me!*
**Stimmt!** *That's right! True!*
**Stimmt nicht!** *Not true!*
**Das finde ich auch.** *I think so too.*
**Das finde ich nicht.** *I disagree.*

# Kapitel 3: Komm mit nach Hause! *Chapter Overview*

| **Los geht's!** pp. 66-68 | Bei Jens zu Hause! p. 66 | | | *Video Guide* |
|---|---|---|---|---|
| | **FUNCTIONS** | **GRAMMAR** | **CULTURE** | **RE-ENTRY** |
| **Erste Stufe** pp. 69-73 | •Talking about where people live, *p.69* <br>•Offering something and responding to an offer, *p. 70* <br>•Saying please, thank you, you're welcome, *p.72* | •The **möchte-**forms, *p. 71* <br>•Indefinite articles **ein, eine,** *p. 72* | Ein wenig Landeskunde: The German preference for **Mineralwasser,** *p. 71* | |
| **Zweite Stufe** pp. 74-76 | Describing a room, *p. 74* | The pronouns **er, sie, es,** and **sie** *pl, p. 75* | **Landeskunde:** Wo wohnst du? *p. 73* | Definite articles **der, die, das,** p.74 (from **Kapitel 1**) |
| **Dritte Stufe** pp. 77-81 | •Talking about family members, *p. 78.* <br>•Describing people, *p. 80* | The possessive adjectives **mein, dein, sein,** and **ihr,** *pp. 78 and 79* | | Asking someone's name and age, pp. 78 and 85; asking who someone is, p. 78 (from **Kapitel 1**); talking about interests, pp. 84 and 85 (from **Kapitel 2**) |
| **Aussprache** p. 81 | The long vowel **o,** the long vowel **u,** the letters **s, ss,** and **ß** | | | Diktat: *Textbook Audiocassette* 2 A |
| **Zum Lesen** pp. 82-83 | Wo wohnst du denn? <br>Reading Strategy: Using root words | | | |
| **Review** pp. 84-87 | •Anwendung, *p. 84* <br>•Kann ich's wirklich? *p.86* <br>•Wortschatz, *p. 87* | | | |

| **Assessment Options** | **Stufe Quizzes** <br>•*Chapter Resources,* Book 1 <br>    **Erste Stufe,** Quiz 3-1 <br>    **Zweite Stufe,** Quiz 3-2 <br>    **Dritte Stufe,** Quiz 3-3 <br>•*Assessment Items, Audiocassette* 7 A | **Kapitel 3 Chapter Test** <br>•*Chapter Resources,* Book 1 <br>•*Assessment Guide,* Speaking Test <br>•*Assessment Items, Audiocassette* 7 A <br>**Test Generator, Kapitel 3** |
|---|---|---|

| | |
|---|---|
| *Video Program* **OR** *Expanded Video Program,* Videocassette 1 | *Textbook Audiocassette* 2 A |

| RESOURCES Print | RESOURCES Audiovisual |
|---|---|
| | *Textbook Audiocassette* 2 A |

*Practice and Activity Book*
*Chapter Resources,* Book 1
- Communicative Activity 3-1
- Additional Listening Activity 3-1 . . . . . . . . . . . . . . *Additional Listening Activities, Audiocassette* 9 A
- Additional Listening Activity 3-2 . . . . . . . . . . . . . . *Additional Listening Activities, Audiocassette* 9 A
- Student Response Form
- Realia 3-1
- Situation Card 3-1
- Quiz 3-1 . . . . . . . . . . . . . . . . . . . . . . . . . . . . . . *Assessment Items, Audiocassette* 7 A

*Textbook Audiocassette* 2 A

*Practice and Activity Book*
*Chapter Resources,* Book 1
- Additional Listening Activity 3-3 . . . . . . . . . . . . . . *Additional Listening Activities, Audiocassette* 9 A
- Additional Listening Activity 3-4 . . . . . . . . . . . . . . *Additional Listening Activities, Audiocassette* 9 A
- Student Response Form
- Realia 3-2
- Situation Card 3-2
- Teaching Transparency Master 3-1 . . . . . . . . . . . . . *Teaching Transparency* 3-1
- Quiz 2-2 . . . . . . . . . . . . . . . . . . . . . . . . . . . . . . *Assessment Items, Audiocassette* 7 A

*Video Guide.* . . . . . . . . . . . . . . . . . . . . . . . . . . . . . . . *Video Program/Expanded Video Program,* Videocassette 1

*Textbook Audiocassette* 2 A

*Practice and Activity Book*
*Chapter Resources,* Book 1
- Communicative Activity 3-2
- Additional Listening Activity 3-5 . . . . . . . . . . . . . . *Additional Listening Activities, Audiocassette* 9 A
- Additional Listening Activity 3-6 . . . . . . . . . . . . . . *Additional Listening Activities, Audiocassette* 9 A
- Student Response Form
- Realia 3-3
- Situation Card 3-3
- Teaching Transparency Master 3-2 . . . . . . . . . . . . . *Teaching Transparency* 3-2
- Quiz 3-3 . . . . . . . . . . . . . . . . . . . . . . . . . . . . . . *Assessment Items, Audiocassette* 7 A

*Video Guide.* . . . . . . . . . . . . . . . . . . . . . . . . . . . . . . . *Video Program/Expanded Video Program,* Videocassette 1

**Alternative Assessment**
- Performance Assessment, *Teacher's Edition*
  **Erste Stufe,** p. 63K
  **Zweite Stufe,** p. 63M
  **Dritte Stufe,** p. 63P

- Portfolio Assessment
  Written: **Zum Lesen,** Activity 7, *Pupil's Edition,* p. 83, *Assessment Guide*
  Oral: **Anwendung,** Activity 1, *Pupil's Edition,* p. 84, *Assessment Guide*
- **Notizbuch,** *Pupil's Edition,* p. 79; *Practice and Activity Book,* p. 147

# Kapitel 3: Komm mit nach Hause!
# Textbook Listening Activities Scripts

## Erste Stufe

### Activity 6, p. 70

1. Ich wohne in der Bahnhofstraße. Von der Schule ist das gar nicht weit. Also, ich komm' immer zu Fuß zur Schule.

2. Ich wohne in der Stadt Berlin. Da gibt es zu viele Autos, da komm' ich halt immer mit der U-Bahn zur Schule. Das ist einfacher.

3. Ich wohne auf dem Land. Wenn das Wetter gut ist, komme ich mit dem Rad zur Schule.

4. Ich wohne in einem Vorort von Potsdam. Die Schule ist nicht weit von hier, da komm' ich also meistens mit dem Moped.

### Activity 9, p. 71

JENS   Tag, Tara! Tag, Ahmet! Kommt 'rein. Der Holger ist auch grad hier.

TARA   Hallo, Holger!

JENS   Ja, ihr zwei! Möchtet ihr auch etwas zu essen und trinken?

AHMET  Ja klar! Zuerst möchte ich aber doch ein Mineralwasser.

JENS   Und du, Tara? Was kann ich dir holen?

TARA   Ja, also vielleicht ein Stück Kuchen und einen Orangensaft, bitte.

JENS   Und du, Ahmet? Was möchtest du essen? Auch ein Stück Kuchen?

AHMET  Nein, Danke. Ich möchte lieber etwas Obst.

JENS   Gut. Ich bin gleich wieder da!

## Zweite Stufe

### Activity 13, p. 74

AHMET  Du, die Möbel sind aber schön, Steffi!

STEFFI Meinst du? Die Stereoanlage ist neu, aber das Regal ist schon ziemlich alt. Und schau mal da! Der Schrank ist eigentlich auch ganz schön. Ich habe viel Platz darin.

AHMET  Der Schreibtisch ist aber groß! Das finde ich ganz praktisch.

STEFFI Ja, ich auch. Nur der Stuhl ist etwas zu klein dafür. Und mein Bett, na ja, das ist ganz bequem. Es gefällt mir sehr.

# Dritte Stufe
## Activity 20, p. 78

1. Ich heiße Anja, und meine Mutter heißt Johanna. Meine Tante wohnt auch bei uns. Sie heißt Tante Lore. Ich hab' auch einen Bruder. Das ist der Rolf und er ist elf. Mein Großvater, also der Opa, wohnt ganz in der Nähe, in der Holstenstraße.

2. Ich heiße Werner und wohne bei meinem Vater in Berlin. Mein Vater heißt Franz. Meine Großmutter und mein Großvater wohnen auch in Berlin, auch gar nicht weit von hier. Ich habe eine Schwester, die Ute. Sie studiert an der Uni hier. In Dahlem, das ist ein Vorort von Berlin, da wohnt mein Onkel. Er heißt Gerhard.

3. Ich heiße Christa. Meine Mutter heißt Christiane, und mein Vater heißt Frank. Wir wohnen alle in Potsdam. Meine Tante und mein Onkel wohnen auf dem Land, außerhalb von Potsdam. Ich habe auch einen Cousin, Karl, der ist zweiundzwanzig. Und mein Bruder Peter wohnt in Hamburg, wo er studiert.

## Activity 22, p. 79

TARA Du, Steffi, sag mal, wie alt ist eigentlich deine Kusine, die Anna?

STEFFI Sie ist schon zweiundzwanzig.

TARA Und wie alt sind denn deine Eltern?

STEFFI Ja also, meine Mutter ist dreiundvierzig, und mein Vater, der ist fünfundvierzig. Hier ist ein Photo von Onkel Florian, hm . . . ich glaub', er ist schon fünfzig.

TARA Und ist das dein Cousin?

STEFFI Ja, das ist mein Cousin Bernhard. Er ist sechsundzwanzig. Seine Mutter, also meine Tante, ist einundfünfzig. Mein Großvater heißt Gerd. Er ist schon siebzig! Und meine Großmutter, die Oma Hannah, ist auch schon siebenundsechzig.

## Diktat, p. 81

You will hear Stefan and Uwe talking. First listen to what they are saying, then write down their conversation.

STEFAN Hier ist mein Zimmer.

UWE Die Couch ist aber bequem.

STEFAN Wirklich? Sie ist schon sehr alt. Was möchtest du trinken?

UWE Eine Cola oder Limo, bitte.

STEFAN Und auch etwas zu essen?

UWE Ja, ich möchte ein Stück Kuchen.

STEFAN Also, hier ist deine Limo und der Apfelkuchen. Noch warm.

UWE Danke.

# Anwendung
## Activity 4, p. 84

Das hier ist mein Zimmer. Die Couch ist ziemlich neu und wirklich sehr schön, nicht? Das Regal dagegen ist aber alt und einfach zu klein! Ich finde, es ist häßlich. Nun, das Bett ist relativ groß und sehr bequem. Leider ist der Schreibtisch ein bißchen zu klein und nicht sehr praktisch. Der Stuhl ist auch schon alt und etwas unbequem. Aber meine Stereoanlage ist neu und super! Eine tolle Anlage, nicht wahr? Ich finde mein Zimmer sehr modern, was meinst du?

## Activity 7c, p. 85

Das Mädchen heißt Sonja Schmidt. Sie ist 16 Jahre alt und wohnt in Wedel. Das ist ein Vorort von Hamburg. Sie wohnt in der Bachstraße 4. Sie hat wirklich viele Interessen. Sie malt gern, Landschaftsszenen und so. Sie mag gern basteln am Abend. Am Wochenende geht sie auch gern radfahren mit Freunden, wenn das Wetter schön ist.

# Kapitel 3: Komm mit nach Hause!
## *Suggested Project*

*In this activity students will design, furnish, label, and describe their dream house. The project could be called* **Mein Traumhaus.** *You will probably want to begin this project after students have covered the vocabulary and functions introduced in the* **Zweite Stufe.**

## MATERIALS

✄ **Students may need**
- *old magazines*
- *weekend edition of newspapers*
- *catalogs*
- *poster board*
- *scissors*
- *glue*
- *markers*

## SUGGESTED SEQUENCE

1. Ask each student to plan the design of his or her dream house by gathering ideas from pictures from the home section of weekend newspapers, home magazines, furniture and decorating catalogs, etc.

2. Students paste the pictures they have chosen on poster boards.

3. Students make small German labels for each piece of furniture pasted on the posterboard. (Example: **die Stereoanlage**) You might want to provide additional vocabulary or make dictionaries available. Some additional vocabulary words are provided on p. 322 in the *Pupil's Edition.*

4. After students have designed, furnished, and labeled their dream house, ask them to write a paragraph describing their house. Where is it located? Supply necessary phrases such as **Ferienhaus am Meer, in den Bergen,** etc. What are the colors of the different rooms and of the outside of the house?

5. Students present their project and read their written work to the class, a smaller group, or a partner.

6. Display the projects in your class or in the foreign language area.

## GRADING THE PROJECT

Suggested point distribution (total=100 points)

| | |
|---|---|
| Poster content and appearance | 30 |
| Written paragraph | 30 |
| Oral presentation | 30 |
| Originality | 10 |

## FAMILY LINK

Ask students to share their project with their family. Students should teach the German words used for furniture to interested family members.

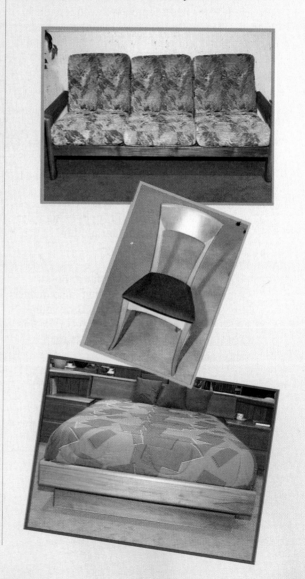

# Kapitel 3: Komm mit nach Hause!
 *Games*

## WORTBILDER

*In this game, students practice the vocabulary from p. 87 by identifying words represented by* **Wortbilder.** *It is especially helpful for tactile learners.*

**Procedure** Divide the class into two teams. Each team decides how to draw several pictures of words from the **Wortschatz** on p. 87 **(Wortbilder).** Have a student from Team 1 draw his or her **Wortbild** on the board. Team 2 has a set amount of time (determined by the teacher) to guess what the picture stands for. If Team 2 guesses the word correctly, that team scores, and it is that team's turn to draw another **Wortbild.** If a team gets five points in a row, it is automatically the other team's turn.

Example:

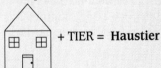

+ TIER = **Haustier**

## LOTTO

*This game is especially good for helping auditory learners practice numbers.*

**Procedure** Prepare game cards by drawing an empty grid with five rows and five columns that you can photocopy and distribute to students. Also, write the numbers one through one hundred on small pieces of paper. Give each student one game card and a small handful of dried beans to use as game markers. Have students fill in their game cards with random numbers between one and one hundred. Put the slips of paper with the numbers into a hat or other container. Draw numbers one at a time and call them out in German. Students should mark any numbers they have on their card with a bean. The first student to get five in a row down, across, or diagonally, wins. If you have time, you can continue the game until one student has marked all the numbers on his or her card. You can give small prizes to the first five students to get five in a row and a "grand prize" to the student who gets "black-out."

## DAS SUBJEKT FEHLT!

*This game can be used at any time to review the vocabulary of the* **Stufe** *you are working on.*

**Procedure** Prepare strips of paper large enough to write one sentence on each. Write a German sentence on each strip of paper, omitting the subject. (Example: _____ **ist sehr unbequem.**) Use the vocabulary of the specific **Stufe** you're working on. Place all slips of paper into a hat. Divide the class into two groups. Alternating between groups, have each group member pull a sentence from the hat, read the incomplete sentence aloud, add an appropriate subject, and read the completed sentence aloud to the class. For the example above, the student could reply **Die Couch ist sehr unbequem.** If the subject fits and is grammatically correct, the student scores a point for his or her group. The game continues until each student has pulled a slip from the hat and made a complete sentence. The group with the most points wins.

GAMES

# Kapitel 3: Komm mit nach Hause!
## *Lesson Plans, pages 64-87*

## Using the Chapter Opener, pp. 64-65

### Motivating Activity

If American students were asked where they live, how might they describe the physical features of:

a. the area they live in

b. their neighborhood

c. their home?

### Geography Connection

① Have students locate Potsdam in relationship to Berlin on the map on p. 2 and guess which waterway this bridge most likely crosses. (**Havel** river)

### Background Information

① The **Glienicker Brücke,** spanning the river Havel, connects the two cities of Potsdam and Berlin. The Havel is 337 km long and runs into the Elbe river.

### Thinking Critically

② **Observing**  Ask students about the photo of the four teenagers standing in front of a house. Can students tell from certain clues in the picture how many families might live in the house? (two, the two doorbells underneath the intercom indicate that it's a **Zweifamilienhaus**) Ask students what purpose the intercom (**Lautsprecher**) serves. (The house is closed off from the street by the iron gate which is most likely locked. Visitors need the intercom to identify themselves to the person in the apartment.) Ask students how the tenants of the apartment receive their mail. (The mail slot is located right beneath the doorbell.)

② **Comparing and Contrasting**  Ask students how they receive their mail. (post office box, mail box on their property, lobby of the building, etc.) In Germany, private homes almost always have a mail slot built into their front door.

###  Culture Note

② Privacy is very important to Germans. Homes are often protected by hedges, fences, or gates in front of the property as well as in the back.

### Thinking Critically

③ **Comparing and Contrasting**  Ask students what rooms they like to receive their friends in when they come to visit. Do the students serve food or soft drinks? If so, what do they typically serve? In German-speaking countries it is customary to serve guests cake if they arrive in the afternoon.

③ **Observing**  Can students guess the time of day in this picture? It is probably between 3 and 4 P.M., a time of day typically called **Kaffeezeit.**

### Multicultural Connection

Germans like to make time for **Kaffeezeit** on a daily basis. Where else around the world is a routine break typical during the afternoon? (Example: Great Britain: afternoon tea)

### Focusing on Outcomes

After doing the motivating activity at the beginning of the chapter opener, have students preview the learning outcomes listed on p. 65. **NOTE:** Each of these outcomes is modeled in the video and evaluated in **Kann ich's wirklich?** on p. 86.

# Teaching Los geht's!
## pp. 66-68

### Resources for Los geht's!

- *Video Program* **OR**
  *Expanded Video Program,* Videocassette 1
- *Textbook Audiocassette* 2 A
- *Practice and Activity Book*

▶ **pages 66-68**

### Video Synopsis

In this segment of the video Jens invites Holger to his house after school. The boys have a snack, and Jens shows Holger his room. Later Jens' cousin comes to visit, and Holger is surprised to find that Jens' cousin is Tara. The student outcomes listed on p. 65 are modeled in the video: Talking about where you and others live, offering something to eat and drink and responding to an offer, saying please, thank you, and you're welcome, describing a room, talking about family members, and describing people.

### Background Information

In the **Foto-Roman,** Holger tells Jens that he lives in Babelsberg. The suburb Babelsberg is known for its park and castle (built 1834-1849). The prince and later emperor, **Wilhelm I,** used this as his summer residence.

### Motivating Activity

Tell students that German homes are different from American homes because of physical as well as cultural differences between the two countries. Have students look at the photos from the story **Bei Jens zu Hause** and let them list all the things they notice that seem different to them. (Examples: kitchen, entrance hall, living room, Jens' room)

### Thinking Critically

**Drawing Inferences**  Ask students if they can think of a reason why Germans have doors to every room in a house (including the kitchen and living room) and why the doors are usually kept closed. (Doors are closed for privacy, which is very important, since space is limited.)

▶ **page 68**

### Cooperative Learning

Put students in groups of four. Ask them to choose a discussion leader, a recorder, a proofreader, and an announcer. Give students a specific amount of time in which to complete Activities 1-5. Monitor group work as you walk around, helping students if necessary. At the end of the activity, call on each group announcer to read his or her group's results. You can decide whether or not to collect their work for a grade at the end of the activity.

### For Individual Needs

**3 Challenge**  Have each student write down a statement which would require a **stimmt** or **stimmt nicht** response. Ask one or two students to read their sentences to the class and ask the class to respond. Example: **Wir gehen am Abend in die Schule. Stimmt nicht.**

**5 Visual Learners**  Before students do this activity have them match the sentences to the appropriate pictures. Then proceed with Activity 5.

### Closure

Ask students if they can name three similarities and three differences between German homes and American homes from the pictures on pp. 64-67.

LOS GEHT'S!

**ERSTE STUFE**

# Teaching Erste Stufe,
*pp. 69-73*

## Resources for Erste Stufe

*Practice and Activity Book*
*Chapter Resources,* Book 1
- Communicative Activity 3-1
- Additional Listening Activities 3-1, 3-2
- Student Response Form
- Realia 3-1
- Situation Card 3-1
- Quiz 3-1
*Audiocassette Program*
- *Textbook Audiocassette* 2 A
- *Additional Listening Activities, Audiocassette* 9 A
- *Assessment Items, Audiocassette* 7 A

▶ *page 69*

## MOTIVATE
### Teaching Suggestion
When people ask where you live, there are many possible answers, for example, in the United States, in California, in the country, or in the city. Ask students how they would answer the question "Where do you live?"

## TEACH
### PRESENTATION: So sagt man das!
To teach the verb **wohnen** use the verb in context as you give examples of several famous people and the places where they live. Example: **Der amerikanische Präsident wohnt in Washington, D.C. Steffi Graf wohnt in Deutschland.**

### PRESENTATION: Wortschatz
Have students infer the meaning of this vocabulary through contextual guessing. Give examples such as **Los Angeles ist eine große Stadt. Beverly Hills ist ein Vorort von Los Angeles. Rodeo Drive ist eine Straße in Beverly Hills. Old Mac-Donald wohnt auf dem Land.** If necessary, draw a simple map on the board or on a transparency as you present your examples.

 **Culture Note**
Potsdam (142,900 inhabitants) is located on the river Havel at the site of an early settlement near the **Alter Markt** that dates back as early as 993. The settlement didn't expand until the 16th century when it became the second residence for Prussian kings such as King Friedrich I and Friedrich Wilhelm I.

▶ *page 70*

 **For Individual Needs**
**7 Challenge** Put the following words on the board for the students to refer to (in addition to the **Wortschatz** on p. 69) as they work in pairs on this activity: **wohnen; Vorort = Vorstadt; weit von hier; in der Nähe von; in der ____ Straße; Wohnung; Haus; Zweifamilienhaus.** Quickly explain these words so students will be able to use them for the activity.

 **Culture Note**
Germans have a different way of numbering the floors in buildings. If you live on the ground floor you live on the **Erdgeschoß**, the second floor is called **erster Stock,** the third floor is called **zweiter Stock,** etc. Example: **Ich wohne im ersten Stock.**

### PRESENTATION: So sagt man das!
Ask individual students what they would like to eat or drink. Example: **Jill, was möchtest du trinken?** (You can add a drinking gesture to your question to help visual learners.) They can either point to the item they would like or try to use the food vocabulary in the **Wortschatz.**

► *page 71*

## PRESENTATION: Wortschatz

Introduce the food vocabulary using the TPR method. You could check with the home economics teachers to see if they have plastic props or food posters to help with your presentation. First, tell students the name of each item as you point to it. Then, point to a student in the class and give the following command: **Bob, eine Limo, bitte!** Your student should bring you the bottle of lemon soda. Then, point to a second student and give another command: **Susan, ein Glas Orangensaft, bitte!** Susan should bring you the glass of orange juice. Repeat your TPR commands until all the vocabulary items have been used. If you don't have access to props, use pictures.

 ## For Individual Needs

**Auditory Learners**   After introducing the two parts of the **Wortschatz**, ask several students to respond to the following questions: **Was möchtest du gern essen? Was möchtest du gern trinken?**

## PRESENTATION: Grammatik

Ask students to look at the **Foto-Roman** on pp. 66-67. Point to the dialogue in which **möchte** is used. Then ask students if they can give an English translation for the phrases.

► *page 72*

## For Additional Practice

**11**  Tell students to imagine they have invited their partner to their house for the weekend. Students should find out what their partner would like to do, to eat, and to drink. Have students write down their partner's responses. Select one or two pairs to report to the class.

## PRESENTATION: So sagt man das!

Ask students to list typical expressions in English they would use to respond when someone serves them food or drink. How does the person serving the food or drink respond? Make a list on the board of the expressions the students come up with. Tell students that in German there are also several ways to thank somebody or say *you're welcome.* You might want to point out to students that the word **bitte** is also used in other contexts:
**Bitte?** *(Pardon me?)*
**Bitte?** *(May I help you?)*
**Bitte!** *(Here you go!)*

## For Additional Practice

**12**  Have each group make a skit based on Activity 12, and present it to the class. Encourage students to use props.

► *page 73*

## PRESENTATION: Landeskunde

### Teaching Suggestion

After students have seen the video segment or listened to the tape, ask five students to each read one of the interviews aloud for pronunciation practice.

### Thinking Critically

• **Drawing Inferences**   Ask students to observe how Jasmin and Thomas each state where they go to school. Have students compare the two expressions and find differences (**ich gehe in die ...** versus **ich bin an der ...** )

• **Drawing Inferences**   Ask students to review Dominick's statement about where he lives. What is Pinneberg (a suburb) and what does that say about the size of the city of Hamburg? (It's a large city. Its current population is 1,634,000.)

Erste Stufe  **63J**

**ERSTE STUFE**

## Background Information

In the 1960s, when Germany was in need of a larger labor force than it could supply from within, it opened its doors to foreign workers. These workers were invited to leave their own countries to work in Germany. They came mainly from countries such as Turkey, Italy, Greece, and Portugal, where recruiting offices had been set up initially. The foreign workers are often referred to as **Gastarbeiter** (*guest-workers*).

## History Connection

Can students think of some reasons why Germany was in need of a larger labor force at this time in history? (After World War II, Germany needed to rebuild its economy, but because of losses in World War II, could not supply adequate manpower to handle the rapidly growing economy.)

## Teacher Note

Mention to your students that the **Landeskunde** will also be included in Quiz 3-1 given at the end of the **Erste Stufe**.

## *CLOSE*

### Teaching Suggestion

Have students tell you what they would like to eat and drink when they get home from school today using the verb **möchte**.

### Focusing on Outcomes

Refer students back to the outcomes listed on p. 65. Students should recognize that they are now able to talk about where they and others live, offer something to eat and drink and respond to an offer, and say *please, thank you,* and *you're welcome.*

## *ASSESS*

• **Performance Assessment** Have students form groups of 3 to role-play an afternoon gathering at someone's house. The host should offer a variety of snacks and beverages. The two guests should take some time to decide what they would like, asking about the choices before they make up their minds.

• Quiz 3-1, *Chapter Resources,* Book 1

# *T*eaching Zweite Stufe,
*pp. 74-76*

## Resources for Zweite Stufe

*Practice and Activity Book*
*Chapter Resources,* Book 1
- Additional Listening Activities 3-3, 3-4
- Student Response Form
- Realia 3-2
- Situation Card 3-2
- Teaching Transparency Master 3-1
- Quiz 3-2

*Audiocassette Program*
- *Textbook Audiocassette* 2 A
- *Additional Listening Activities, Audiocassette* 9 A
- *Assessment Items, Audiocassette* 7 A

▶ *page 74*

## *MOTIVATE*

### Teaching Suggestion

Ask students how they would like to furnish their rooms if they had the money to make any changes they wanted to.

## *TEACH*

### PRESENTATION: Wortschatz

You might want to introduce the adjectives in this vocabulary box by describing specific objects in your classroom. Point to a small book and say: **Das Buch ist klein.** Point to a large book and say: **Das Buch ist groß.** Continue by asking yes/no questions such as **Ist der Tisch klein?** Then extend your questions by asking either/or questions. Example: **Ist die Tafel klein oder groß?**

 **For Individual Needs**

**13   A Slower Pace**   Before students listen to the dialogue, review the vocabulary for this activity. Do this by showing pictures and asking yes/no and either/or questions.
Examples:
**Ist das eine Stereoanlage? Nein.**
**Ist das ein Schrank oder ein Bett? Ein Bett.**
**Ist dieser Stuhl bequem oder unbequem? Bequem.**

▶ *page 75*

### PRESENTATION: So sagt man das!/Grammatik

Use classroom objects to teach students how to replace nouns with pronouns. Example: Hold the small book you used in the presentation of the **Wortschatz** on p. 74 and say **Das Buch ist klein. Es ist klein.** Then write the sentence on the board or on a transparency. Give students an example of each gender and let them draw inferences as to what pronouns can replace certain nouns.

### Teacher Note

You might want to point out to students that **die Möbel** *(furniture)* is plural in German, although it is singular in English. They should be aware that there are many nouns like this in German, as well as others that are singular in German and plural in English. Example: **die Hose** *(pants)*

 **For Individual Needs**

**15   A Slower Pace**   Supply students with the vocabulary needed to do this task: **Stühle, Tische, Bücherregale,** etc.

**ZWEITE STUFE**

## ♜ Game

Divide the class in half. The teacher calls out an adjective. (Example: **alt**) The first person on team A responds with the opposite (**neu**). If the answer is wrong the other team gets a turn. Call out a set number of adjectives. The team with the higher score wins.

▶ **page 76**

## Teaching Suggestion

**18** At this point the project described on p. 63E should be introduced and explained.

## CLOSE

## Teaching Suggestion

Ask students about Jens' room in Babelsberg.

    **Wie findest du sein Zimmer?**
    **Was findest du gut/nicht gut in Jens' Zimmer?**

Point out to students that names ending in **s** or **z** that are used in the possessive (as **Jens' Zimmer**) are pronounced following this model: **"Jenses" Zimmer, "Heinzes" Mutter, "Klauses" Vater.**

##  Culture Notes

- Germans have a proverb which appropriately describes their feeling for their homes, no matter what size it might be: **Klein, aber mein!**

- German **Kinderzimmer** and **Schlafzimmer** never have built-in closets as do bedrooms in the United States. Therefore, you will always find a **Kleiderschrank,** and perhaps also a **Kommode** (*dresser*) in a bedroom.

## Focusing On Outcomes

Refer students back to the outcomes listed on p. 65. They should recognize that they are now able to describe a room.

## ASSESS

- **Performance Assessment** Have students prepare a short oral description of the furniture in their bedroom at home. They should describe the contents of the room as well as the color, level of comfort, and size of the furniture.

- Quiz 3-2, *Chapter Resources,* Book 1

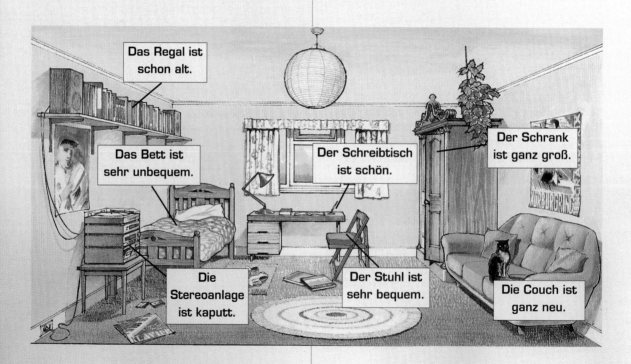

Das Regal ist schon alt.

Das Bett ist sehr unbequem.

Die Stereoanlage ist kaputt.

Der Schreibtisch ist schön.

Der Stuhl ist sehr bequem.

Der Schrank ist ganz groß.

Die Couch ist ganz neu.

ZWEITE STUFE

# *T*eaching Dritte Stufe,
## *pp. 77-81*

### Resources for Dritte Stufe

*Practice and Activity Book*
*Chapter Resources,* Book 1
- Communicative Activity 3-2
- Additional Listening Activities 3-5, 3-6
- Student Response Form
- Realia 3-3
- Situation Card 3-3
- Teaching Transparency Master 3-2
- Quiz 3-3

*Audiocassette Program*
- *Textbook Audiocassette* 2 A
- *Additional Listening Activities, Audiocassette* 9 A
- *Assessment Items, Audiocassette* 7 A

▶ **page 77**

## *MOTIVATE*

### Teaching Suggestion

Have students talk about their family, the people with whom they live, or the family members from a popular movie or TV show. List as many words as possible that show family relationships. Examples: mother, father, cousin, aunt, uncle .

## *TEACH*

### PRESENTATION: Wortschatz

Before introducing the vocabulary in this box, give each student a generic family tree chart with blank lines. Put the vocabulary of the **Wortschatz** box in random order on the board. If they don't know the name of or have a relative for a particular spot, students should pick a likely name. Ask students to fill in the names of their family members or fantasy family members as best they can using the vocabulary on the board. (Example: **Die Tante: Shirley**) Then show the class a transparency with a sample family tree and introduce each of the family members in German. Example: **Das ist meine Mutter, Cindy. Und das ist mein Vater, Lawrence.** Then have students go back to their charts and correct whatever mistakes they might have made.

### Teaching Suggestion

The following vocabulary might be helpful for talking about **Jens und seine Familie: der Familienstammbaum** (*family tree*); **die Familienforschung** (*genealogy*); **der Vetter** (*another word for male cousin*); **der Vorfahre** (*ancestor*)

 ### Culture Notes

- Just as in the United States, German children have informal names by which they call their parents. For example, the mother can be called **Mama, Mami,** or **Mutti,** and the father can be called **Papa, Papi,** or **Vati.**

- Point out to students the two words for male cousin **(Cousin, Vetter). Cousin** is pronounced as the French pronounce it [KUZĒ] and is used more frequently than **Vetter.** It is an example of the influence of the French language on the German language.

▶ **page 78**

### PRESENTATION: So sagt man das!

Ask students to take out the family tree they made at the beginning of the **Dritte Stufe.** Ask them questions about their family using the expressions in this function box.

### PRESENTATION: Ein wenig Grammatik

Use the transparency you made showing a family tree and reintroduce some of the members. Make sure that each of the statements you make is also written at the bottom of the transparency.
Examples:
**Das ist meine Tante Lucy.**
**Das ist mein Onkel Paul.**
**Das ist mein Cousin Gary.**
Ask students why **mein(e)** has two different forms in the sentences you just pointed out. What conclusions can they draw?

## Group Work

Using the family trees they made, have students ask each other questions about their families and talk about them, giving as much information as they can using possessives and pronouns.

### For Individual Needs

**20 Visual Learners** Make copies of the transcript available to students after they have listened to the three friends talking about their families. Let students use the transcript as they complete the chart.

## Group Work

**20** Personalize this activity by having students in pairs or groups of three ask questions about each other's families and pets. Students should feel free to make up names for relatives and pets. Students should take notes and be able to report to the class about their partners' responses.

▶ page 79

## PRESENTATION: Wortschatz

Use these additional activities to practice and review numbers.

- Ask these questions:
  1. **Wie schnell darf man in der Stadt mit dem Auto fahren?** or **Wie schnell ist dein Auto?**
  2. **Wie viele Sterne sind auf der amerikanischen Flagge?**
  3. **Was ist deine Telefonnummer?**
  4. **Wie viele Jungen und Mädchen sind in dieser Klasse?**
  5. **Was ist die Notrufnummer?** (Write the number 911 on the board.)
  6. **Welche Schuhgröße hast du?**
- Play German Bingo (**Lotto**) with the numbers 0-100. See p. 63F for the procedure.

## Game

Draw a large tree on the board. At the end of each branch draw a box containing the word for a number. (Example: **einundzwanzig**) The object is to see who can add the total of all the leaves (never higher than 100 for this **Stufe**) first and accurately. To prepare ahead of time, this can be drawn on a transparency.

## Language Note

Point out the fact that one and seven are written differently in German than in English.

|  | English | German |
|---|---|---|
| one | 1 | *1* |
| seven | 7 | *7* |

## Teaching Suggestion

Make conversion tables available on a handout or on a transparency including the metric system, temperature in Celsius, and clothing sizes. This will allow you to ask some more questions using numbers.

▶ page 80

## PRESENTATION: Wortschatz

To teach the expressions of this vocabulary box, begin by describing yourself. Then describe individual students to the rest of the class.

## Teacher Note

You might want to point out to students the difference between **Er hat eine Glatze** and *He is bald*.

## For Additional Practice

Tell students to imagine their family is having a big family reunion where not everybody knows everybody else. Therefore, attending members are asked to give a short personal introduction. Ask students to describe themselves to the rest of the family.

## ♜ Game

Divide the class into two groups and, alternating between groups, choose one person to come to the front. Show this person a name (of a fellow classmate, teacher, celebrity, etc.) on an index card. Alternating between teams, students will try to guess the identity of the secret person by asking yes/no questions. If the answer to a question is yes, the team gets another turn; if the answer is no, the other team gets a turn. The team who guesses the correct name wins.

> Example: Boris Becker
> **Ist es ein Mann? Ja.**
> **Ist er alt? Nein.**
> **Spielt er Musik? Nein.**
> **Hat er rote Haare? Ja.**
> **Hat er eine Brille? Nein.**

## ⓉⓅⓇ Total Physical Response

Give commands to the class or to individual students. Use vocabulary from this and previous chapters focusing on furniture in the classroom, some parts of the body (**Augen, Haare**), etc.
Example:
**Leg das Buch auf den Tisch!**
**Gib Sara Lee die Brille!**
**Zeig auf eine Schülerin, die braune Haare hat!**

▶ *page 81*

## PRESENTATION: Aussprache

Remind students that German vowels require more tension in the mouth than the English and they do not glide. To illustrate this point, and as ongoing remedial work, contrast the German word **Boot** with the English *boat*.

## Reteaching: Family members

• Give all students a blank copy of a basic family tree. Have them fill in names and relationships of their own family or of one they create.

• **Group Work**  Let students cut out magazine pictures of famous people and create a "unique" tree showing imaginary relationships between the celebrities. Students should write sentences about the relationships they have created. Ask one or two groups to read them aloud.

## *CLOSE*

### Teaching Suggestion

Show students pictures of famous people and ask them to describe the pictures.
*or*
Ask students to compare the characteristics of a young member of their family with an older member (age, appearance, etc.).

### Focusing on Outcomes

Refer students back to the outcomes listed on p. 65. They should recognize that they are now able to talk about family members and describe people.

## *ASSESS*

• **Performance Assessment**  Ask students to describe orally or in writing:

  a. a fantasy girlfriend or boyfriend (what would he or she look and be like?)

  b. their best friend.

  Students must give the name and age and describe the physical appearance, the interests, and the likes and dislikes of the person they choose.

• Quiz 3-3, *Chapter Resources,* Book 1

## *Teaching Zum Lesen,* pp. 82-83

### Reading Strategy

The targeted strategy in this reading is the use of root words to help determine the meaning of new words. Students should learn about this strategy before doing Questions 1 and 2. Students will also be asked to use visual clues, skim for the gist, scan for specific information, answer questions to show comprehension, and transfer what they have learned.

ZUM LESEN

## PREREADING

### Motivating Activity

You will need several samples of ads from the classified section on rental properties and real estate. Ask students what kind of information is provided in the classified ad section for rental/real estate properties. Write students' responses on the board. What kinds of information would they want to know about a place when they decide to live on their own?

### Teaching Suggestion

**2** Help your students guess intelligently about the meanings of these words by giving them certain clues. Example: adding -**ung** to the stem of a verb frequently makes a noun (**bilden: Bildung; erfahren: Erfahrung**)

### Teaching Suggestion

Have your students guess what these ads are about. Ask them when they might need the information found in ads like these. Once they have told you that the ads have to do with places to live, ask them 1) where one might find ads like these; 2) what kinds of places are generally advertised in such ads (houses, apartments, etc.); and 3) what kinds of information might be important in such ads. (You are leading students to mention size, price, price per square foot, location, etc.)

### Thinking Critically

**Comparing and Contrasting** Have students scan the ad (**Wohnung**) and ask them to take a look at the address. How does the German way of writing an address differ from the American? (See Culture Note.)

 ### Culture Note

In a German address, the name of the street always comes before the street number, and the equivalent of zip codes (**Postleitzahl**) comes before the name of the city.

### Language Note

Vorwahl = telephone area code

### Teacher Note

Activities 1 and 2 are prereading activities.

## READING

### Group Work

Ask students to get into groups of three or four. Assign each group an ad and have students make a list of all the words they recognize. Let them write their words on the board or on a transparency and tell the class what they found.

 ### Culture Note

In Germany, the *size* of a home is determined by the number of rooms. If somebody is looking for a 3-bedroom house or apartment, with a living room and dining room, he or she must look for a **5-Zimmer-Haus** or **Wohnung**. Bathrooms, kitchen, and hall areas are not included in the room count.

### Thinking Critically

**Comparing and Contrasting** In several ads the price is listed. How does the German way of writing prices differ from the American? (See Culture Note.)

 ### Culture Note

Germans use a space or a period to separate millions, thousands, and hundreds. The comma sets off the decimal fraction. Put the following examples on the board and point out the differences to students:

American way: $100,035,000.40
German way: DM100.035.000,40
     *or* DM100 035 000,40

### Teacher Note

None of the ads offer an apartment for rent. That's because there is a shortage of apartments in many cities and especially in university cities such as Tübingen.

## POST-READING

### Teacher Note

Activities 7a and 7b are post-reading tasks that will show whether students can apply what they have learned.

 ### Portfolio Assessment

**7** You may want to use Activity 7 as a written portfolio item. See *Assessment Guide,* Chapter 3.

## Closure

Ask students which words caught their eye in the ads they just read and why.

### Answers to Activity 1

Ads describing houses and apartments; Ads looking for a place to live

Wohnen (to live somewhere): Wohnung (apartment), Eigentumswohnung (condominium)

### Answers to Activity 2

1. b
2. c
3. d
4. a

### Answers to Activity 3

Ads describing houses and apartments: Bauconcept, Gute Laune, Auf dem Lande, Tübingen-Lustnau; Ads looking for a place to live: Wohnung (Verlag J. C. B. Mohr), In/um Tübingen

### Answers to Activity 4

a. Auf dem Lande

b. Tübingen-Lustnau am Herrlesberg

c. Immobilien-Kurcz

### Answers to Activity 5

a. 1-Fam. Haus in Remmingsheim, DM 458 000,-

b. 1-Zi-Apartment, Tü-Osterberg, DM 145 000,-

c. Einfamilienhaus "Auf dem Lande" have 7 ½ rooms

d. 1-Fam.-Haus in Remmingsheim, 174m²

e. 1-Zi-Apartment, Tü-Osterberg, 32 m²

f. 1-Zi-Apartment, Tü-Osterberg, 3½ -Zi-Wohnung (Bauconcept ad), Einfamilienhaus "Auf dem Lande", 2-Zi-Eigentumswohnung.

## Using Anwendung, pp. 84-85

### Portfolio Assessment

1 You might want to use Activity 1 as an oral portfolio item for your students. See *Assessment Guide,* Chapter 3.

## For Individual Needs

4 **Visual Learners** Before they listen to the tape, have students look at the three pictures of Tara's room. Ask students to describe at least one of the rooms to re-familiarize themselves with the vocabulary they are about to hear. As students produce relevant vocabulary, write those words on the board.

## Teaching Suggestion

6 Before doing Activity 6, decide on a set number of questions for the reporter. You might want to give examples of what should be included (name, physical description, age, hobbies/interests, address, telephone number).

## Kann ich's wirklich?
### p. 86

This page is intended to prepare students for the test. It is a brief checklist of the major points covered in the chapter. The students should be reminded that it is a checklist only and not necessarily everything that will appear on the test.

## Using Wortschatz,
### p. 87

### Game

Play **Lotto** to review numbers. See p. 63F for the procedure.

### Teaching Suggestions

• Use flash cards to review the vocabulary for describing a room, eating, and drinking.

• Use a large family tree poster to review family vocabulary.

### Teacher Note

Give the **Kapitel 3,** Chapter Test *Chapter Resources,* Book 1.

# Komm mit nach Hause!

**❶** Ich wohne in Potsdam.

Students in German-speaking countries often go straight home after school—to eat, to do their homework, or to be with their families. What do you and your friends usually do after school? Let's find out more about teenagers in German-speaking countries — their after-school activities, their rooms, and their families.

## In this chapter you will learn

- to talk about where you and others live; to offer something to eat and drink and respond to an offer; to say please, thank you, and you're welcome
- to describe a room
- to talk about family members; to describe people

## And you will

- listen to a description of someone's room
- read personal profiles of students in German-speaking countries
- write a description of a real or imaginary family, based on a family tree that you will make
- find out about the homes and families of German-speaking students

② Das ist meine Kusine Handan.

③ Möchtest du ein Stück Kuchen?

# Los geht's!

Jens

Tara

Holger

Mutti

### Bei Jens zu Hause!

Look at the photos that accompany the story and try to guess where Jens and Holger are. What are they doing? What do you think they are talking about?

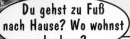

**①**

Du gehst zu Fuß nach Hause? Wo wohnst du denn?

In der Kopernikusstraße.

Wo ist denn die?

In Babelsberg.

Ich wohn' auch da in der Nähe. Möchtest du mit mir nach Hause kommen?

Ja, prima!

**②**

Hallo, Mutti! Wo bist du?

Hier oben! Ich komme gleich runter.

**③**

Du, Mutti, das ist Holger, ein Klassenkamerad. Er ist neu.

Guten Tag, Frau Hartmann!

Guten Tag, Holger!

**④**

Möchtet ihr etwas trinken? Oder etwas essen?

Was möchtest du, Holger?

Ach, ich möchte ... ich trinke eine Cola.

Und ich ein Mineralwasser. Haben wir noch Kuchen, Mutti?

Ich glaube ja.

**⑤**

Hier, deine Cola und dein Kuchen.

Danke!

Bitte!

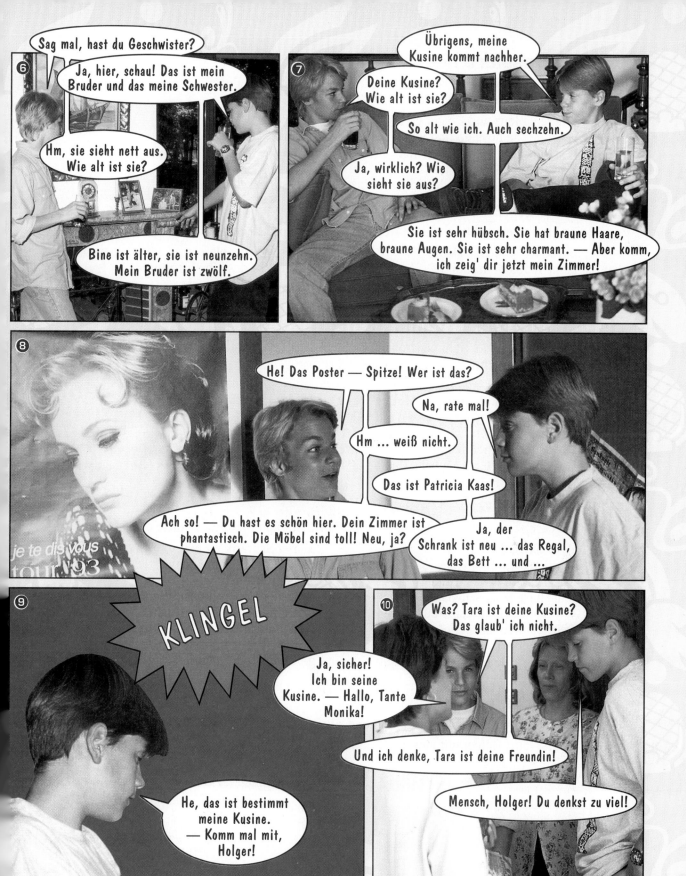

## 1 Was passiert hier?

Do you understand what is happening in the **Foto-Roman**? Check your comprehension by answering these questions. Don't be afraid to guess.

1. Where do Jens and Holger go together after soccer practice? to Jens' house
2. What do the boys do first when they get home? greet Jens' mother, have a snack
3. What kinds of photos does Jens show Holger? family photos
4. How does Holger like Jens' room? very much
5. Who comes to visit? Why do you think Holger is surprised? Tara, Jens' cousin; he thought she was Jens' girlfriend

## 2 Genauer lesen

Reread the conversations. Which words or phrases do the characters use to

1. introduce someone else   1. Das ist ...
2. name foods or drinks   2. Eine Cola; Mineralwasser; Kuchen
3. name family members   3. Mutter („Mutti"), Bruder, Schwester, Kusine
4. describe people   4. hübsch; braune Augen, braune Haare; charmant
5. name or describe furniture   5. Der Schrank ist neu; das Regal; das Bett

## 3 Stimmt oder stimmt nicht?

Are these statements right or wrong? Answer each one with either **stimmt** or **stimmt nicht**. If a statement is wrong, try to state it correctly.

1. Holger geht mit Jens nach Hause.  stimmt
2. Frau Hartmann ist Holgers Mutter.  stimmt nicht; die Mutter von Jens
3. Holger trinkt eine Cola und ißt ein Stück Kuchen.  stimmt
4. Jens hat zwei Geschwister: einen Bruder und eine Schwester.  stimmt
5. Der Bruder ist neunzehn, und die Schwester ist zwölf.  stimmt nicht; Der Bruder ist zwölf, die Schwester ist neunzehn.
6. Holger hat auch eine Kusine. Sie heißt Tara.  stimmt nicht; Tara ist die Kusine von Jens

## 4 Was paßt zusammen?

Match each statement or question on the left with an appropriate response on the right.

1. Wo wohnst du?  c
2. Mutti, das ist Holger.  g
3. Möchtest du etwas trinken?  e
4. Jens, hast du Geschwister?  b
5. Wie sieht deine Kusine aus?  f
6. Dein Zimmer ist schön! Sind die Möbel neu?  a
7. Ich denke, Tara ist deine Freundin!  d

a. Der Schrank ist neu.
b. Ja, das ist meine Schwester, und das ist mein Bruder.
c. In der Kopernikusstraße.
d. Nein, sie ist meine Kusine.
e. Ich möchte eine Cola, bitte!
f. Sie ist sehr hübsch.
g. Guten Tag, Holger!

## 5 Nacherzählen

Put the sentences in logical order to make a brief summary of the **Foto-Roman**.

1. Zuerst fährt Holger mit Jens nach Hause.

5 Und dann zeigt er Holger sein Zimmer.

2 Frau Hartmann sagt Holger „Guten Tag".

4 Er zeigt Holger Fotos von der Familie.

6 Zuletzt kommt Tara, die Kusine von Jens.

3 Und Jens gibt Holger eine Cola und ein Stück Kuchen.

*Talking about where you and others live; offering something to eat and drink and responding to an offer; saying please, thank you, and you're welcome*

## SO SAGT MAN DAS!

### Talking about where you and others live

To find out where someone lives,
you ask:

**Wo wohnst du?**

**Wo wohnt der Jens?**

The responses might be:

**Ich wohne in Los Angeles.** *or*
**In Los Angeles.**

**Er wohnt in Babelsberg.** *or*
**In Babelsberg.**

How would you ask someone where Tara lives?[1]

## WORTSCHATZ

AHMET  Wo wohnst du?
MITSCHÜLER  Ich wohne …

Michaela

in der Stadt

AHMET  Wohnt ihr **weit von hier?**
GÜNTHER  Nein, ich wohne **in der Nähe.**
ANDREA  Ja, ich wohne **weit von hier.**

Andrea

auf dem Land

Dieter

in Babelsberg, das ist ein Vorort von Potsdam

Günther

in der Brunnenstraße

---

1. Wo wohnt (die) Tara?

## 6 Hör gut zu!

You will hear four students talk about where they live. Match each description with one of the pictures below.   1c 2b 3a 4d

a.   b.   c.   d.

## 7 Wo wohnen die Schüler?

Ahmet wants to know where these students live. Answer his questions using the pictures as cues.

1. Wo wohnt die Sara?
   **auf dem Land**

2. Wo wohnt der Georg? **in der Poststraße**

3. Wo wohnen Jürgen und Simone? **in der Stadt**

4. Wo wohnt die Anja?
   **in einem Vorort**

## 8 Wer wohnt wo?

Ask your partner where he or she lives, then switch roles. Describe where you live in as much detail as you can, using the phrases you learned in the **Wortschatz** box. Be prepared to tell the class as much as you can about where your partner lives.

### SO SAGT MAN DAS!

**Offering something to eat and drink and responding to an offer**

Often, when friends come over, you ask what they would like to eat and drink.

You might ask:

   **Was möchtest du trinken?**

   **Was möchte Holger trinken?**

To offer several friends something to eat, you might ask:

   **Was möchtet ihr essen?**

Can you figure out what **möchte** means?[1]

The response might be:

   **Ich möchte ein Mineralwasser trinken.**

   **Er möchte im Moment gar nichts.**

The response might be:

   **Wir möchten ein Stück Kuchen, bitte.**

1. *would like to*

**Was möchtet ihr trinken?**     **Und was möchtet ihr essen?**

**Eine Cola, bitte!**

**Ein Glas Orangensaft.**

**Ein Stück Kuchen, bitte!**

**Ich möchte Obst.**

**Ein Mineralwasser.**

**Ein Glas Apfelsaft.**

**Ein paar Kekse.**

**Danke, nichts!**

## 9 Hör gut zu!

Tara: **Kuchen, Orangensaft**
Ahmet: **Obst, Wasser**

Ahmet and Tara come over to Jens' house. Listen to their conversation with Jens and write down what each one would like to eat and drink.

## 10 Was möchtest du?

Look at the pictures in the **Wortschatz** box above and ask your partner what he or she would like to eat and drink. Then switch roles.

### EIN WENIG LANDESKUNDE

If someone asks for **ein Glas Wasser, ein Glas Mineralwasser** will be served. Germans rarely drink tap water, considering it to be unhealthy. In addition, Germans very rarely use ice cubes in cold drinks, even in cafés and restaurants.

### *G*rammatik    The **möchte**-forms

The **möchte**-forms express what you *would like* or *would like* to do. They are often used with another verb, but if the meaning is obvious, the second verb can be omitted.

**Ich möchte ein Glas Orangensaft trinken.**
**Ich möchte Obst essen.**
**Ich möchte Obst.**

Here are the forms of **möchte:**

Ich **möchte** eine Limo.          Wir **möchten** Kekse.
Du **möchtest** Saft?              Ihr **möchtet** nichts?
Sie/Er **möchte** Kuchen.          Sie(pl) ⎫
                                   Sie    ⎬ **möchten** auch Kuchen.

# 11 Was möchten sie alle?

Say what everyone would like using the words and pictures as cues.

1. Wir ...

möchten eine Cola.

2. Ihr ...

möchtet ein Glas
Orangensaft.

3. Er ...

möchte Obst.

4. Du ...

möchtest ein paar
Kekse.

5. Ich ...

möchte ein Glas
Apfelsaft.

6. Jens und
Holger ... möchten ein
Stück Kuche

## SO SAGT MAN DAS!

### Saying please, thank you, and you're welcome

To say *please*, you can simply say **bitte**. You can also add **bitte** to a request: **Ich möchte eine Limo, bitte.**

Here are several ways to say thank you:
- **Danke!**
- **Danke sehr!**
- **Danke schön!**

Here are several ways to say you're welcome:
- **Bitte!**
- **Bitte sehr!**
- **Bitte schön!**

# 12 Snacks für deine Freunde

Role-play the following situation with three classmates. Use as many forms of **möchte** as possible. You have invited three friends home for a snack after school. One friend will help you get the snack ready by asking the other two "guests" what they would like to eat and drink. After they answer, your helper will tell you what everyone would like. When you have finished, switch roles until everyone has been the "host" and the "helper."

### Ein wenig *G*rammatik

Some of the names for the various snack items pictured on page 71 are preceded by either **ein** or **eine**. What do you think these words mean?[1] Now look at the words below.

- **ein Junge**
- **ein Stück (Kuchen)**
- **eine Limo**

Why are there different forms of **ein**?[2]

### LERNTRICK

You don't always have to respond to a question with a whole sentence. Sometimes a word or phrase is enough:
**Was möchtest du trinken? — Ich möchte eine Limo, bitte!** or simply **Eine Limo, bitte!**

### Und dann noch ...

eine Limo    eine Tasse Kaffee    eine Tasse Tee
eine Banane    eine Orange    ein Stück Melone

---

1. **Ein** and **eine** mean *a, an*. 2. Masculine and neuter nouns are preceded by **ein**, feminine nouns by **eine**.

## Wo wohnst du?

We asked several teenagers where they live. Before you read their interviews, write where you live, using as much detail as you can. Two of these teenagers were not born in Germany. Can you guess who they are?

**Dominick,** *Hamburg*

„Ich heiss' Dominick Klein. Ich bin zwölf Jahre alt und wohn' in Hamburg, also Pinneberg."

**Thomas,** *München*

„Ich heiße Thomas Schwangart. Ich wohne in München. Ich bin an der Reichenau-Schule und komme aus Italien."

**Jasmin,** *München*

„Ich heiße Jasmin und bin fünfzehn. Ich geh' in die Reichenau-Schule. Und äh ... ich wohne in München, und äh ... ich komme aus der Türkei."

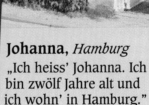

**Johanna,** *Hamburg*

„Ich heiss' Johanna. Ich bin zwölf Jahre alt und ich wohn' in Hamburg."

**Ingo,** *Hamburg*

„Ich wohn' hier in der Nähe, also in der Gustav-Falke-Straße. Es ist zehn Minuten von hier."

**A.** 1. Write the name of each person interviewed and what each person says about where he or she lives.
2. Now look at what you wrote earlier. Did any of these teenagers say where they live in the same way you did? If so, which ones? What seems to be the most natural response to the question **Wo wohnst du?** Is this also your first response?
3. Discuss these questions with your classmates: Who are the two teenagers not born in Germany? Where are they from? Did you pick the right people before you read the interviews? What influenced your choice? Considering that two out of these five teenagers were not born in Germany, what can you infer about the ethnic makeup of German society in the large cities?

**B.** There are many ethnic groups represented in German society: Turks, Italians, Greeks, and many Eastern Europeans, just to name a few. Italian, Greek, Chinese, Indonesian and Thai foods have become very popular with native Germans. Why do you think some of these ethnic groups might be attracted to Germany? How does this compare with the situation in the United States? Discuss these questions with your classmates and then write a brief essay answering these questions.

# ZWEITE STUFE

*Describing a room*

## Jens zeigt Holger sein Zimmer.

HOLGER  Deine Möbel sind schön!

JENS  Ja, wirklich? Schau!

Das Regal ist schon alt.

Das Bett ist sehr unbequem.

Der Schreibtisch ist schön.

Der Schrank ist ganz groß.

Die Stereoanlage ist kaputt.

Der Stuhl ist sehr bequem.

Die Couch ist ganz neu.

groß – klein
bequem – unbequem
alt – neu
schön – häßlich
kaputt

If **bequem** means *comfortable*, what does **unbequem** mean? What do you think the word **häßlich** means? **Groß** means *large*; what do you think **klein** means? The word **neu** looks like what word in English? What is its opposite?  uncomfortable; ugly; small; new; old

---

### Schon bekannt
### Ein wenig *G*rammatik

In **Kapitel 1** you learned that there are three classes of German nouns: masculine, feminine, and neuter. The definite articles **der, die,** and **das** tell which class the noun belongs to:

> **der Schrank**  *masculine*
> **die Couch**  *feminine*
> **das Bett**  *neuter*

## 13  Hör gut zu!

Listen as Steffi describes her room to Ahmet, and match each piece of furniture on the left with the appropriate adjective on the right.

1. die Stereoanlage  d  **a.** bequem
2. der Schrank  b  **b.** schön
3. das Regal  e  **c.** groß
4. der Schreibtisch  c  **d.** neu
5. der Stuhl  f  **e.** alt
6. das Bett  a  **f.** klein

## Describing a room

To describe your room, you might say:

**Die Stereoanlage ist alt. Sie ist auch kaputt!**
**Das Bett ist klein aber ganz bequem.** *or*
**Das Bett ist klein, aber es ist ganz bequem.**

A friend might ask:                              You might respond:
**Ist der Schreibtisch neu?**          **Ja, er ist neu, aber der Stuhl ist alt.**

What do you think the words **er, sie,** and **es** refer to?[1] What is the English equivalent?[2] Why are there three different words that mean the same thing?[3]

Possible answers include:
Die Couch ist bequem, aber alt. Das Bett is neu, aber unbequem.
Der Stuhl ist sehr groß, aber alt.

## 14 Versteckte Sätze

How many sentences can you make using the words in the boxes? Use the picture of Jens' room on page 74 for clues.

BEISPIEL    **Die Couch ist neu, aber unbequem.**

| Die Couch | | bequem | | alt |
|---|---|---|---|---|
| Der Schrank | | häßlich | | neu |
| Das Bett | | klein | | bequem |
| Das Regal | ist | ganz unbequem | aber | unbequem |
| Der Schreibtisch | | schon alt | | schön |
| Die Stereoanlage | | schon kaputt | | häßlich |
| Das Zimmer | | neu | | groß |
| Der Stuhl | | ganz schön | | klein |
| | | sehr groß | | kaputt |

## Grammatik    Pronouns

**Er, sie,** and **es** are called pronouns. **Er** refers to a masculine noun, **sie** to a feminine noun, and **es** to a neuter noun.

*masculine*     **Der Schreibtisch** ist neu. *or* **Er** ist neu.
*feminine*       **Die Stereoanlage** ist kaputt. *or* **Sie** ist kaputt.
*neuter*          **Das Regal** ist häßlich. *or* **Es** ist häßlich.

The pronoun **sie** is also used to refer to a plural noun.

*plural*          **Die Möbel** sind schön. *or* **Sie** sind schön.

## 15 Im Klassenzimmer

Describe your classroom and some of the furniture in it.

1. The nouns mentioned in the preceding sentences.  2. Here, **er, sie** and **es** are all equivalent to *it*.  3. The nouns they refer to belong to different noun classes, i.e., masculine, feminine, and neuter..

## 16 Was fehlt hier?

1. Das  2. es  3. Die  4. sie  5. Das  6. es  7. Der
8. er  9. Die  10. Sie  11. Der  12. er  13. das  14. Es
15. Die  16. Sie

Jens has seen Holger's new room and is talking to Steffi about it. Complete his description by filling in the correct article and pronoun.

___1___ Zimmer ist sehr groß, und ___2___ ist ganz schön. ___3___ Couch ist schön, und ___4___ ist auch neu. ___5___ Bett ist ziemlich klein, aber ___6___ ist sehr bequem. ___7___ Schrank ist wirklich alt, und ___8___ ist sehr groß. ___9___ Stereoanlage ist super! ___10___ ist ganz neu. ___11___ Schreibtisch ist groß, aber ___12___ ist leider häßlich. Und dann noch ___13___ Regal. ___14___ ist auch sehr groß. ___15___ Möbel sind wirklich toll. ___16___ sind Klasse!

## 17 Wie findest du das Zimmer?

Use one of these adjectives to describe the items below to your partner. Your partner may agree or disagree. Then switch roles.

DU **Der Schreibtisch ist sehr schön.**
PARTNER **Ja, stimmt! Er ist sehr schön.** *or* **Was? Er ist ganz häßlich!**

bequem   alt   kaputt
unbequem   häßlich
neu
klein   groß   schön

a.

b.

c.

d.

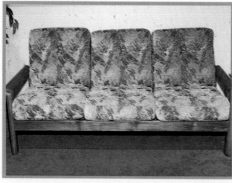

e.

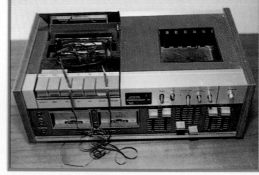

f.

## 18 Zum Schreiben: Mein Zimmer

Draw a diagram of your room or a room you would like to have. Label the pieces of furniture. Then write a few sentences describing your room. If you need extra vocabulary, turn to page 322.

## Talking about family members; describing people

### WORTSCHATZ

**Jens und seine Familie**

die Großmutter (Oma)
*Ella*

der Großvater (Opa)
*Georg*

meine Großeltern

meine Eltern
die Mutter
*Monika*

der Vater
*Dieter*

die Tante
*Hannelore*

der Onkel
*Amir*

*Jens*

meine Geschwister
die Schwester
*Sabine*

der Bruder
*Andreas*

die Kusine
*Tara*

der Cousin
*Tawan*

die Katze
*Fritzi*

der Hund
*Harras*

meine Haustiere

**Und dann noch ...**

| | |
|---|---|
| Stiefmutter | *stepmother* |
| Stiefvater | *stepfather* |
| Stiefschwester | *stepsister* |
| Stiefbruder | *stepbrother* |
| Halbschwester | *half sister* |
| Halbbruder | *half brother* |

## 19 Familienquiz

1. Monika und Dieter
2. Sabine und Andreas
3. Hannelore

Answer the following questions about Jens' family.

1. Wie heißen Sabines Mutter und Vater?
2. Wie heißen die Geschwister von Jens?
3. Wer ist die Schwester von Dieter?
4. Wie heißt Dieters Vater? Georg

5. Wer ist der Onkel von Sabines Bruder? Amir
6. Wer ist die Kusine von Tawan? Sabine
7. Wer ist der Bruder von Taras Mutter? Dieter
8. Wie heißen die Haustiere? Fritzi und Harras

## 20 Hör gut zu!

1. Christa (6)   2. Werner   3. Anja
4. Werner   5. no

Make a chart like the one below, listing all of the new vocabulary from Jens' family tree. Then listen as three friends of Jens' describe their families. Every time you hear a family member mentioned put a check next to the correct vocabulary word.

After listening to the descriptions, try to answer these questions.

1. Who mentions the most family members?
2. Who does not mention the mother?
3. Who mentions an aunt but not an uncle?
4. Who mentions an uncle but not an aunt?
5. Do any of the three friends mention pets? If so, who mentions them?

|  | Anja | Werner | Christa |
|---|---|---|---|
| der Vater |  |  |  |
| die Mutter |  |  |  |
| der Bruder |  |  |  |

## SO SAGT MAN DAS!

### Talking about family members

To find out about someone's family you might ask:

**Ist das deine Schwester?**
**Wie alt ist sie?**
**Und dein Bruder? Wie heißt er?**
**Wie alt ist er?**
**Und wer ist der Mann?**
**Und die Frau?**
**Wo wohnen deine Großeltern?**

The responses might be:

**Ja, das ist meine Schwester.**
**Sie ist einundzwanzig.**
**Mein Bruder heißt Robert.**
**Er ist schon dreiundzwanzig.**
**Das ist mein Opa.**
**Das ist meine Oma.**
**In Köln.**

What is the difference between **dein** and **deine**? **Mein** and **meine**? What do the words mean? When is each one used?

## 21 Deine Familie und meine Familie

Steffi and Tara are looking at photos of their families. Complete their conversation by filling in the blanks with **mein/meine** or **dein/deine**.

TARA   Ist das __1__ Schwester? *deine*

STEFFI   Ja, das ist Angelika.

TARA   Wie alt ist __2__ Schwester? *deine*

*Meine* STEFFI   __3__ Schwester ist zwanzig. Und das
*mein*   ist __4__ Bruder. Er ist einundzwanzig.

TARA   Und sind das __5__ Großeltern? *deine*

STEFFI   Ja, das ist __6__ Oma, und das ist *meine*
   __7__ Opa. Ist das __8__ Vater? *mein; dein*

TARA   Nein, das ist __9__ Onkel Dieter. Und *mein*
   das hier ist __10__ Tante Monika. *meine*

STEFFI   Ist das __11__ Kusine? *deine*

TARA   Ja, das ist __12__ Kusine, die Sabine. *meine*
   Und das ist __13__ Cousin, Jens. *mein*

STEFFI   Na klar!

### Ein wenig *G*rammatik

The words **dein** and **deine** *(your)* and **mein** and **meine** *(my)* are called *possessives*.

masculine (**der**)
neuter (**das**) } **mein, dein**

feminine (**die**)
plural (**die**) } **meine, deine**

These words are similar to **ein** and **eine**. Because of this similarity, **mein** and **dein** are often called **ein**-words.

To talk about the ages of various family members, you need to review **die Zahlen von 0 bis 20** and learn **die Zahlen von 21 bis 100.**

| | | | | | | | |
|---|---|---|---|---|---|---|---|
| 21 | einundzwanzig | 26 | sechsundzwanzig | 30 | dreißig | 70 | siebzig |
| 22 | zweiundzwanzig | 27 | siebenundzwanzig | 40 | vierzig | 80 | achtzig |
| 23 | dreiundzwanzig | 28 | achtundzwanzig | 50 | fünfzig | 90 | neunzig |
| 24 | vierundzwanzig | 29 | neunundzwanzig | 60 | sechzig | 100 | hundert |
| 25 | fünfundzwanzig | | | | | | |

**a.** With your classmates, count aloud to one hundred, first by tens, then by fives, then by twos. Students take turns leading the counting.

**b.** Make up simple math problems with no results greater than 100. Working with a partner, ask each other the problems you each wrote down and see how fast you can solve them. Some words you may need are **und** *(plus)*, **minus** *(minus)*, **mal** *(times)*, and **durch** *(divided by)*.

---

## 22  Hör gut zu

Listen as Steffi tells Tara more about her family. First list the names of the family members in the order you hear them. Then listen a second time and write their ages beside their names.

> die Kusine Anna     die Tante     der Vater
> der Onkel Florian     der Großvater
> die Großmutter   die Mutter   der Cousin Bernhard

die Kusine Anna, 22
die Mutter, 43
der Vater, 45
der Onkel Florian, 50
der Cousin Bernhard, 26
die Tante, 51
der Großvater Gerd, 70
die Großmutter Hannah, 67

---

## 23  Wer ist das? Wie alt ist er? Wie alt ist sie?

Bring some photos of family members to class, or if you like, bring in pictures from magazines and create a make-believe family. Show the photos to your partner, and he or she will ask you questions about them. Then switch roles. When you have finished, tell your classmates what you learned about one of your partner's relatives.

BEISPIEL  **Sein(e)** *(His)* ...
**Ihr(e)** *(Her)*...

### Ein wenig *G*rammatik

The words **sein** *(his)* and **ihr** *(her)* are also possessives. They take the same endings as **mein** and **dein.**

| | |
|---|---|
| *masculine* **(der)** *neuter* **(das)** | **sein, ihr** |
| *feminine* **(die)** *plurals* **(die)** | **seine, ihre** |

---

## 24  Für mein Notizbuch

Write four sentences in which you tell about two of your favorite family members or people who are close to you.

**Steffi zeigt Tara ein Fotoalbum. Steffi:**

Meine Mutter hat lange, rote Haare und grüne Augen. Sie spielt gern Schach.

Mein Vater hat braune Haare und blaue Augen. Er spielt sehr gut Klavier.

Und mein Bruder Ralf ist ein-undzwanzig. Er hat kurze, blonde Haare und hat eine Brille. Er schwimmt sehr gern.

Meine Großmutter Marie ist fünfundsechzig. Sie hat weiße Haare und blaue Augen. Sie hört gern Musik.

Und meine Kusine Anna ist zweiundzwanzig. Sie hat kurze, schwarze Haare und braune Augen. Sie geht oft wandern.

Mein Onkel Florian hat eine Glatze und grüne Augen. Er hat auch eine Brille. Er sammelt gern Briefmarken.

## 25 Steffis Familie

Working with your partner, create a chart of the characteristics of Steffi's family. Write the names of the various family members across the top and their characteristics underneath using the categories, **Alter, Haarfarbe, Augenfarbe,** and **Interessen.**

### SO SAGT MAN DAS!

**Describing people**

If you want to know what someone looks like, you might ask:

**Wie sieht dein Bruder aus?**

If you are asking about more than one person, you say:

**Wie sehen deine Großeltern aus?**

The response might be:

**Er hat lange, blonde Haare und braune Augen.**

**Mein Opa hat weiße Haare und grüne Augen. Und meine Oma hat graue Haare und blaue Augen.**

## 26 Wie sieht Steffis Familie aus?

Referring to the chart you and your partner made for Activity 25, try to answer the following questions about Steffi's family.

1. Wer hat blaue Augen?`   Vater, Großmutter Marie
2. Wie alt ist Steffis Bruder? Und ihre Kusine?   21; 22
3. Wie sieht Onkel Florian aus?   Glatze, grüne Augen, Brille
4. Was macht die Mutter in der Freizeit? Der Vater? Anna?   spielt Schach; spielt Klavier; wandert
5. Wie sehen die Eltern aus?   Mutter: lange, rote Haare, grüne Augen. Vater: braune Haare, blaue Augen
6. Wer hat schwarze Haare?   Anna
7. Wer hat kurze Haare? Lange Haare?   Anna und Ralf, die Mutter (Grossmutter, Vater, Onkel)
8. Wie alt ist die Großmutter? Wie sieht sie aus?   65; weiße Haare, blaue Augen
9. Wer hat eine Brille?   Onkel Florian, Mutter, Ralf

## 27 Rate mal!

Pick one person in the room and think about how you might describe him or her to someone else. Your partner will ask you questions and try to guess whom you have chosen. Then switch roles.

BEISPIEL   PARTNER   **Hat diese Person blonde Haare?**

auA  U /x/ S Se?uP  R A  C/ts/H  E Ö

## Richtig aussprechen / Richtig lesen

A. To practice the following sounds, say the words and sentences below after your teacher or after the recording.

1. The letter **o**: The long **o** is pronounced much like the long *o* in the English word *oboe*, however the lips are more rounded.

   **Obst, Moped, schon  /  Wo wohnt deine Oma?**

2. The letter **u**: The long **u** is similar to the vowel sound in the English word *do*, however the lips are more rounded.

   **Stuhl, super, Kuchen  /  Möchtest du ein Stück Kuchen?**

3. The letters **s, ß, ss**: When the letter **s** begins a word or syllable and is followed by a vowel, it is pronounced like the *z* in the English word *zebra*. In the middle or final position of a syllable, the letter s sounds similar to the *s* in the English word *post*. The letters ß and **ss** are also pronounced this way.

   **so, sieben, Sonja  /  Deine Kusine sieht sehr hübsch aus.**
   **aus, das, es  /  Die Couch ist zu groß und ganz häßlich.**

## Richtig schreiben / Diktat

B. Write down the sentences that you hear.

*Wo wohnst du denn?*

Answers to these activities in TE Interleaf, p. 63Q

1. What do you think the classified ads are about? You know the word **wohnen**. Does knowing the meaning of **wohnen** help you understand the ads? Make a list of words built on the stem of **wohnen** (**wohn-**) and try to guess what they mean.

2. Working with a partner, match these German words with their English equivalents. Remember to look for the root words.

   1. **Wochenendheimfahrerin**
   2. **Eigentumswohnung**
   3. **Einfamilienhäuser**
   4. **Grundstück**

      a. *plot (of land)*
      b. *someone who goes home on the weekend*
      c. *condominium*
      d. *single-family homes*

3. There are two types of ads on this page: ads describing available houses and apartments, and ads placed by people looking for a place to live. Can you figure out

Bauvorhaben
**Gösstraße – Tübingen**

**Die Oase in der City!**

z. B. 1½ Zimmer-Wohnung, Südloggia, Garage, großzügiger Grundriß mit 34 m² Wohnfläche: **DM 171 620,–**

z. B. 3½ Zimmer-Wohnung, großer Südbalkon, herrliche Aussicht. 62 m² Wohnfläche, Garage: **DM 287 100,–**

## BAUCONCEPT
**Der leistungsstarke Immobilien-Spezialist.**

Rufen Sie uns an: Mo – Fr 7.30 bis 20.00 , Sa. 8.00 bis 16.00
Telefon: (0 70 31) 87 70 91

### Auf dem Lande
Großzügiges Einfamilienhaus mit Einliegerwohnung in Remmingsheim. Allerbeste Ausstattung mit wertvollen Einbauten und offenem Kamin. Insg. 174 m² Wfl. bei 7 1/2 Zimmern, gepflegtes Grundstück mit 3,5 Ar, Garage und Autoabstellplätze, sofort beziehbar.

DM 458 000.–

### 2-Zi.-Eigentumswohnung
(Baujahr 1985) in Entringen, sofort beziehbar, 52 m² Wohnfläche, Einbauküche, Balkon, Keller, Stellplatz.

DM 190 000.–

## Für den neuen Chefredakteur unserer ‚Juristenzeitung' suchen wir eine

# Wohnung

Im Idealfall ist sie ruhig gelegen in Tübingen oder näherer Umgebung, hat 3 bis 4 Zimmer – und ist bald zu beziehen.

Kompromisse sind sicher möglich. Bitte schreiben Sie oder rufen Sie an und fragen Sie nach Herrn Lesch.

*Verlag J.C.B. Mohr (Paul Siebeck)*
*Wilhelmstraße 18, 72074 Tübingen*
*Telefon 07071 – 26064*

---

---

which ads fit into each of these categories?

4. Which ads would be most interesting to these people:
   a. a large family wanting to buy a house
   b. a couple in Tübingen-Lustnau looking for a condominium
   c. the owner of several rental properties, looking for prospective tenants

5. Working with a partner, try to find the following information.
   a. the most expensive house or apartment
   b. the least expensive house or apartment
   c. the house or apartment with the most rooms
   d. the house or apartment with the most square meters of living space
   e. the house or apartment with the least amount of living space
   f. the places that have either a garage or a space to park a car

6. If you were looking for a place to live, which of these ads would appeal to you the most? Be prepared to tell (in English) why you would choose one place over another.

7. a. Assume that you are going to Germany for a year and need a place to live. Write an ad in German that summarizes what you need.
   b. Many Americans and Europeans swap houses for several weeks at a time, so that they can live in a different culture without having to pay enormous hotel expenses. Imagine that you are going to take part in such an **Austausch** (*exchange*). Using the format of these ads, write a classified ad for your home that you could place in a German newspaper.

1 You are at your partner's house in the afternoon. Your partner offers you something to eat and drink, and you say what you would like using **möchte**. Then ask your partner what he or she would like. Write the conversation and act it out together.

2 Write a brief physical description of your partner on a 3x5 card. Find out his or her age and where he or she lives and include that information, as well. Everyone will put his or her description in a box. Students will take turns drawing cards and reading the information aloud while the other students take turns guessing who it is.

3 At a party last week you met someone you really like. You learned a lot about the person, but you don't know how to get in touch with him or her. Write a short paragraph describing him or her that you could pass along to your friends. Include the person's age, name, where he or she lives, his or her interests, and a physical description.

4 Listen to Tara's description of her room and indicate which of the drawings below matches the description you hear.

a.           b.           c.

5 Using the adjectives to the right, describe your room to your partner. He or she will draw a sketch based on your description. Then switch roles.

> neu   alt   häßlich   groß   kaputt
> schön   bequem   unbequem   klein

6 You would like to put a personal ad in a teen magazine.

a. Your partner is a reporter for the magazine and will interview you. Unfortunately, no photo can be found, so you must give a complete description of yourself. Your partner will ask questions and take down the information. Then switch roles. When you are the reporter, be prepared to share with the class the information you obtained.

b. Now write your partner's ad the way it will appear in the magazine. Your partner will write yours. Use the profiles on page 85 as models.

**7** These personal profiles appeared in a magazine for teenagers.

   **a.** Read each profile.

**Bettina Schilling**
Schulstraße 27
60594 Frankfurt a.M.
14 J.
Interessen: Musik, Klavier,
Reiten, Schwimmen

**Peter Fischer**
Körtestraße 8
10967 Berlin
15 J.
Interessen: Wandern,
Musik, Fußball

**Helmut Heine**
Königstraße 24
39116 Magdeburg
16 J.
Interessen: Radfahren,
Basteln, Comics sammeln

   **b.** Choose one of the profiles above and describe the person in the profile using complete sentences.

   **c.** Now listen to Holger's description of a girl named Sonja whom he read about in a magazine. Based on what he says, with which of the students above would Sonja have the most in common?  Helmut Heine

**8** **a.** Bring in photos of your family or clip out photos of a family from magazines.

   **b.** Write a few sentences about each family member, telling his or her age, where he or she lives, some interests he or she has, and a brief physical description.

   **c.** Make a poster of your family tree (**Stammbaum**) using your photos. You can use Jens' family tree on page 77 as a model. Label each family member and write at least one sentence about that person below his or her picture.

   **d.** Show your family tree to the class. After you've told your classmates a little about your family, they will ask you more questions about various family members.

**9**

## R O L L E N S P I E L

Two friends whom you have not seen for a while come to your house after school. First, offer your friends something to eat and drink, then show them your room. You have recently made some changes, so the three of you talk about your furniture. Then your conversation turns to family. Take turns describing various family members, what they look like, and what their interests are. Write out the conversations and practice them. Then role-play them in front of the class.

**Can you talk about where people live? (p. 69)**

**1** How would you ask a classmate where he or she lives and tell him or her where you live? *Wo wohnst du? Ich wohne in …*

**2** Say where the following people live:

*a. wohnt auf dem Land*
*b. wohnt in der Hegelstraße*

a. Thomas (Land)
b. Britte (Hegelstraße)
c. Marian und Karl (Brauhausberg, Vorort von Potsdam)
d. Renate (Köln)
e. Sabine und Rolf (Stadt: Bismarckstr.)

*c. wohnen in Brauhausberg, ein Vorort von Potsdam*
*d. wohnt in Köln*
*e. wohnen in der Stadt; in der Bismarckstraße*

**Can you offer something to eat and drink (using möchte) and respond to an offer? (p. 70)**

**3** How would you ask a classmate what he or she would like to eat and drink? How would you ask more than one classmate? How would you tell a classmate that you would like a lemon-flavored soda? *Was möchtest du essen/trinken? Was möchtet ihr essen/trinken? Ich möchte eine Limo.*

**4** If you and some of your classmates were at a friend's house, how would you help your friend by telling her or him what everyone was having for a snack?

a. Anna, eine Cola
b. Martin und Klaus, ein Stück Kuchen
c. Nicole und Jörg, ein paar Kekse
d. Ayla, Obst

*a. möchte*
*b. möchten*
*c. möchten*
*d. möchte*

**Can you say please, thank you, and you're welcome? (p. 72)**

**5** How would you ask your friend politely for a few cookies? How would you thank him or her? How would he or she respond? *Ich möchte ein paar Kekse, bitte. Danke! Bitte schön!*

**Can you describe a room? (p. 75)**

**6** How would you describe these pieces of furniture? Make two sentences about each one using the correct pronoun **er, sie, es,** or **sie** (pl) in the second sentence.

*a. Der Schrank ist alt und häßlich. Er ist groß.*
*b. Das Bett ist klein und bequem. Es ist neu.*

a. der Schrank (*old, ugly, large*)
b. das Bett (*small, comfortable, new*)
c. die Möbel (*beautiful, new, large*)
d. die Couch (*old, ugly, broken*)

*c. Die Möbel sind schön und neu. Sie sind groß. d. Die Couch ist alt und häßlich. Sie ist kaputt.*

**Can you talk about family members? (p. 78)**

**7** How would you tell a classmate about five of your family members, giving their relationship to you, their names, and their ages?

**8** How would you describe the people below?

**Can you describe people? (p. 80)**

**9** How would you ask a classmate what his or her brother, sister, grandfather, parents, and cousins (male and female) look like?

## ERSTE STUFE

### TALKING ABOUT WHERE YOU LIVE

**nach Hause gehen** *to go home*
**wohnen** *to live*
**Wo wohnst du?** *Where do you live?*
  **in der Stadt** *in the city*
  **auf dem Land** *in the country*
  **ein Vorort von** *a suburb of*
  **weit von hier** *far from here*
  **in der Nähe** *nearby*
  **in der ... Straße** *on . . . Street*

### THINGS TO EAT AND DRINK

**möchten** *would like (to)*
**essen** *to eat*
**Was möchtest du essen?** *What would you like to eat?*
  **ein Stück Kuchen** *a piece of cake*
  **Obst** *fruit*
  **ein paar Kekse** *a few cookies*
**trinken** *to drink*
**Was möchtest du trinken?**
  *What would you like to drink?*
  **ein Glas Apfelsaft (Orangensaft)** *a glass of apple juice (orange juice)*
  **eine Cola** *cola*

**ein Glas (Mineral) Wasser** *a glass of (mineral) water*
**Nichts, danke!** *Nothing, thank you!*
**Im Moment gar nichts.** *Nothing at the moment (right now).*

### SAYING PLEASE, THANK YOU, AND YOU'RE WELCOME

**Bitte!** *Please!*
**Danke!** *Thank you!*
**Danke (sehr) (schön)!** *Thank you (very much)!*
**Bitte (sehr) (schön)!** *You're (very) welcome!*

## ZWEITE STUFE

### DESCRIBING A ROOM

**das Zimmer, -** *room*
**die Möbel (pl)** *furniture*
  **der Schrank, ¨e** *cabinet*
  **der Schreibtisch, -e** *desk*
  **die Stereoanlage, -n** *stereo*
  **die Couch, -en** *couch*
  **das Bett, -en** *bed*
  **das Regal, -e** *bookcase, shelf*
  **der Stuhl, ¨e** *chair*

**neu** *new*
**alt** *old*
**klein** *small*
**groß** *big*
**bequem** *comfortable*
**unbequem** *uncomfortable*
**schön** *pretty, beautiful*
**häßlich** *ugly*
**kaputt** *broken*

### PRONOUNS

**er** *he, it*
**sie** *she, it*
**es** *it*
**sie (pl)** *they*

### OTHER USEFUL WORDS AND EXPRESSIONS

**ganz** *really*
**aber** *but*

## DRITTE STUFE

### TALKING ABOUT THE FAMILY

**die Familie, -n** *family*
**Das ist ...** *That's...*
  **die Mutter, ¨** *mother*
  **der Vater, ¨** *father*
  **die Schwester, -n** *sister*
  **der Bruder, ¨** *brother*
  **die Großmutter, ¨ (Oma)** *grandmother*
  **der Großvater, ¨ (Opa)** *grandfather*
  **die Tante, -n** *aunt*
  **der Onkel, -** *uncle*
  **die Kusine, -n** *cousin (female)*
  **der Cousin, -s** *cousin (male)*
  **das Haustier, -e** *pet*
  **der Hund, -e** *dog*

  **die Katze, -n** *cat*
  **der Mann, ¨er** *man*
  **die Frau, -en** *woman*
**Das sind ...** *These are...*
  **die Eltern (pl)** *parents*
  **die Geschwister (pl)** *brothers and sisters*
  **die Großeltern (pl)** *grandparents*

### DIE ZAHLEN VON 21 BIS 100
**see page 79**

### DESCRIBING PEOPLE

**Wie sieht er aus?** *What does he look like?*
**Wie sehen sie aus?** *What do they look like?*

**lange (kurze) Haare** *long (short) hair*
**rote (blonde, schwarze, weiße, graue, braune) Haare** *red (blonde, black, white, gray brown) hair*
**blaue (grüne, braune) Augen** *blue (green, brown) eyes*
**eine Glatze haben** *to be bald*
**eine Brille** *a pair of glasses*

### POSSESSIVES

**dein, deine** *your*
**mein, meine** *my*
**sein, seine** *his*
**ihr, ihre** *her*

## 📼 Location Opener

# Schleswig-Holstein, pages 88-91

**Expanded Video Program, Videocassette 2**

## Using the Photograph, pp. 88-89

### Background Information

The **Holstentor** (Holsten Gate) was built in 1478 as part of a system of walls designed to protect the city of Lübeck from possible invaders. Near the gate are the original salt storehouses (**Salzspeicher** 16th -18th century). At its height, Lübeck was the trading center of the Hanseatic League and was one of the largest cities in Germany.

### Thinking Critically

**Drawing Inferences** Lübeck was once a center of the very important salt trade. Ask students to brainstorm some reasons why salt was such an important commodity for the countries around the Baltic Sea. (Salt was not only used to preserve food products such as meats and fish but was also necessary for the production of leather.)

### Geography Connection

Have students locate the city of Lübeck on a map and try to explain why the building of the **Stecknitzkanal** was such an important achievement. (It connects the city of Lübeck with the **Lübecker Bucht**, which leads into the Baltic Sea.)

### Language Note

The saying above the gate is **Concordia domi foris pax.** Ask students what language that is, (Latin) and whether they can translate the phrase or any part of it. (*Harmony at home and peace at the marketplace*) Point out that *marketplace* during this time period referred to commerce between cities. Ask students why they think Latin would be used on a German structure such as this gate. (See following Culture Note.)

### 🌐 Culture Note

Because of the enormous political and cultural importance of the Roman Empire, as well as the use of Latin by the Roman Catholic Church, Latin became the international language of Europe during the Middle Ages. Latin was also the language of higher learning, and most books during this time were written in Latin.

## Using the Almanac and Map, p. 89

 Schleswig-Holstein's vertically split coat of arms tells us about the two parts of this state, Schleswig and Holstein. Schleswig is represented by two lions on a gold background (related to the three lions on the coat of arms of Denmark). The symbol of Holstein is a silver nettle leaf on a red background.

### Terms in the Almanac

- **Matjes:** salted filets of young herring that are considered a great delicacy in northern Germany

- **Rote Grütze:** a very popular dessert in northern Germany made from a variety of berries and usually served with whipped cream

### Using the Map

- Have students use the map on p. 2 to identify the German states that border Schleswig-Holstein. You may also want to use Map Transparency 1. (Hamburg, Niedersachsen, Mecklenburg-Vorpommern)

- Have students compare the industries of Schleswig-Holstein with those of Brandenburg (see p. 13). Why are there differences? (different geographical locations)

- What other country shares a border with Schleswig-Holstein? (Denmark)

- Have students locate the Elbe and Eider rivers in an atlas.

- Have students locate the **Inseln** mentioned in the almanac and identify the bodies of water in which they are located. (Helgoland, Sylt, and Föhr are in the North Sea; Fehmarn is in the Kieler Bucht.)

# Interpreting the Photo Essay, pp. 90-91

② **Drawing Inferences** Ask students where lighthouses are typically situated and how the need for them has changed over the years. (Lighthouses are usually located along coastlines to provide visual landmarks and safety for ship traffic. Today many lighthouses are no longer manned and are operated automatically. With the technological advances of navigation equipment the need for lighthouses has decreased.)

③ **Teaching Suggestion** Have students locate the island Sylt on a map. Mention to students that this island is the largest of the North Frisian islands. In 1925 the island was connected with the mainland when the 11 km long **Hindenburgdamm** was built. Only trains can cross the dam, but cars can travel across on the trains.

- **Background Information** The traditional farm houses of northern Germany have roofs made of native reeds. This type of roof provides warmth but is often a fire hazard.

- **Drawing Inferences** Ask students why houses are built differently throughout the United States. (Houses had to be built according to local climates and building materials that were available.) Have students give a few examples of different architectural styles in the United States. Ask them why they think reeds were a popular choice of roofing material for the coastal areas. (a material readily available in that area)

- **Background Information** The beach chairs shown here are large hooded wicker baskets that can seat two people comfortably. They can be found on many North Sea and Baltic Sea beaches. These chairs can be rented by the day, week, or month and provide both a sense of privacy on a crowded beach and some protection against the weather.

④ Kiel, named after the Old German word for bay, is the gateway to Scandinavia and known as **die Stadt der frischen Winde.** Kiel annually hosts the **Kieler Woche,** one of the world's greatest yachting events.

- **Comparing and Contrasting** Ask students what cities in the United States (also close to water) can be compared to Kiel. (Examples: Galveston, Texas; Mare Island, north of San Francisco; Norfolk, Virginia; Mobile, Alabama) Like Kiel, these cities are major ports and have attracted shipping and other industries.

⑤ **Drawing Inferences** A **Reepschläger** is a rope-maker. Given the location of Wedel, ask students to guess what the ropes that were originally manufactured in this house were used for. (For those working on the Elbe river, ropes were needed not only for fishing equipment but for tying down and pulling ships.)

- **Culture Note** It is not unusual for business owners to live in the building where their business is located. The proprietor of the **Teestube** lives upstairs. The feather bed and pillow are put onto the windowsill in the morning to be aired out.

⑥ Almost every town and city in Germany has a certain day on which vendors set up their stands in a central location. It usually opens around 6:00 in the morning and lasts until the early afternoon. Florists, farmers, seafood vendors, and vendors of many other types of items sell their goods in the open-air market.

- **Background Information** The statue of the knight Roland is not unique to Wedel, but can be found on pillars in front of city halls and in market places all over Germany. Roland is always depicted with a shield and sword and symbolizes that a city fought for its independence and became a "free" city.

## Group Work

Have students working in small groups study the pictures. They should come up with three questions and/or observations about things that seem different from buildings or landscapes in the United States to share with the class.

⑦ While northern Germans have the reputation of being cool and reserved, the five students from the **Johann-Rist-Gymnasium** do not fit this stereotype. They are outgoing young people with many interests, such as traveling to other countries to improve their language skills. Their school has active exchange programs with schools in France, England, and Russia.

**LOCATION OPENER**

KAPITEL 4, 5, 6

# Komm mit nach

# Schleswig-Holstein!

# Schleswig-Holstein

**Einwohner**: 2,6 Millionen

**Fläche**: 16 000 Quadratkilometer (6 177 Quadratmeilen), ungefähr so groß wie Connecticut

**Landeshauptstadt**: Kiel (257 000 Einwohner)

**Große Städte**: Lübeck, Flensburg, Neumünster

**Flüsse**: Elbe, Eider

**Inseln**: Helgoland, Sylt, Föhr, Fehmarn

**Kanäle**: Nord-Ostsee-Kanal

**Seen**: über 300

**Industrien**: Schiffbau, Ackerbau, Viehzucht

**Beliebte Gerichte**: Matjes, Krabben, Aale, Räucherspeck, Buttermilchsuppe, Rote Grütze

Foto ①: Das Holstentor in Lübeck, Geburtsstadt von Thomas Mann (1875-1955)

# Schleswig-Holstein

*Schleswig-Holstein is the northernmost German state, (**Land**). It is bordered on the west by the North Sea (**Nordsee**), on the east by the Baltic Sea (**Ostsee**), and on the north by Denmark (**Dänemark**). In addition to the dunes, rocky cliffs, tranquil beaches, and fishing villages along its 500-kilometer long coastline, Schleswig-Holstein also has rolling meadows, rich farmland, over 300 lakes and ponds, and beautiful cities, such as Flensburg and Lübeck.*

④ Kiel Week (**Kieler Woche**). Every year some of the best sailors in the world gather here to sail.

③ This north Frisian house with thatched roof (**Reetdach**) is typical for the island of Sylt. Thousands of Germans vacation here every year.

② The Westerhaver Lighthouse (**Leuchtturm**) is surrounded by a type of salty marshland that makes up much of Schleswig-Holstein.

Chapters 4, 5, and 6 take place in the small Holstein town of Wedel. Wedel lies directly on the Elbe, not far from Hamburg, and has a proud heritage as a **Freistadt,** an independent trading town. Among its 30,000 inhabitants are the teenagers you will meet in the next three chapters. They attend the **Johann-Rist-Gymnasium** in Wedel.

⑤ **Das Reepschläger-haus.** At one time, ropes were manufactured in this Frisian house. Today it is a tea-room **(Teestube)** and is one of Wedel's famous landmarks.

⑥ In the open-air market **(Marktplatz)** in Wedel stands a statue of Roland, symbolizing Wedel's ancient rights as a free city.

⑦ Heiko, Katja, Sonja, Julia, and Michael say hello and invite you to join them in Wedel.

# Kapitel 4: Alles für die Schule! *Chapter Overview*

| Los geht's!<br>*pp. 94-96* | Michael kauft Schulsachen, p. 94 | | | *Video Guide* |
|---|---|---|---|---|
| | **FUNCTIONS** | **GRAMMAR** | **CULTURE** | **RE-ENTRY** |
| **Erste Stufe**<br>*pp. 97-101* | •Talking about class schedules, *p. 98*<br>•Using a schedule to talk about time, *p. 99*<br>•Sequencing events, *p. 101* | The verb **haben**, *p. 100* | •**Ein wenig Landeskunde:** The German school day, *p. 98*<br>•**Ein wenig Landeskunde:** The 24-hour time system, *p. 99* | Numbers, *pp. 97, 99, 101, 106, 107* (from **Vorschau** and **Kapitel 3**) |
| **Zweite Stufe**<br>*pp. 102-105* | •Expressing likes, dislikes, and favorites, *p. 102*<br>•Responding to good news and bad news, *p. 104* | Using **Lieblings-**, *p. 102* | •**Ein wenig Landeskunde:** The German grading system, *p. 103*<br>•**Landeskunde: Was sind deine Lieblingsfächer?** *p. 105* | •Likes and dislikes—**gern**, *pp. 102, 104*<br>•Degrees of enthusiasm, *p. 104* (from **Kapitel 2**) |
| **Dritte Stufe**<br>*pp. 106-109* | •Talking about prices, *p. 107*<br>•Pointing things out, *p. 108* | Noun plurals, *p. 106* | **Ein wenig Landeskunde:** German currency, *p. 107* | The subject pronouns **er, sie, es,** and **sie** (pl), *p. 107* |
| **Aussprache**<br>*p. 109* | The diphthongs **eu, äu,** and **au**, the final **b, d,** and **g** | | | Diktat:<br>*Textbook Audiocassette* 2B |
| **Zum Lesen**<br>*pp. 110-111* | **Lernen macht Spaß!**<br>Reading Strategy: Using cognates to determine the meaning of compound words | | | |
| **Review**<br>*pp. 112-115* | •Anwendung, *p. 112*<br>•Kann ich's wirklich? *p.114*<br>•Wortschatz, *p. 115* | | | |
| **Assessment Options** | **Stufe Quizzes**<br>•*Chapter Resources*, Book 2<br>  Erste Stufe, Quiz 4-1<br>  Zweite Stufe, Quiz 4-2<br>  Dritte Stufe, Quiz 4-3<br>•*Assessment Items, Audiocassette* 7 B | | **Kapitel 4 Chapter Test**<br>•*Chapter Resources*, Book 2<br>•*Assessment Guide*, Speaking Test<br>•*Assessment Items, Audiocassette* 7 B<br><br>**Test Generator, Kapitel 4** | |

CHAPTER OVERVIEW

| Video Program **OR** | Textbook Audiocassette 2 B |
| *Expanded Video Program,* Videocassette 2 | |

| **RESOURCES** Print | **RESOURCES** Audiovisual |
|---|---|
| | *Textbook Audiocassette* 2 B |
| *Practice and Activity Book* *Chapter Resources,* Book 2 | |
| • Communicative Activity 4-1 | |
| • Additional Listening Activity 4-1 . . . . . . . . . . . . . . | *Additional Listening Activities, Audiocassette* 9 B |
| • Additional Listening Activity 4-2 . . . . . . . . . . . . . . | *Additional Listening Activities, Audiocassette* 9 B |
| • Student Response Form | |
| • Realia 4-1 | |
| • Situation Card 4-1 | |
| • Teaching Transparency Master 4-1 . . . . . . . . . . . . . | *Teaching Transparency* 4-1 |
| • Quiz 4-1 . . . . . . . . . . . . . . . . . . . . . . . . . . . . . . . | *Assessment Items, Audiocassette* 7 B |
| | *Textbook Audiocassette* 2 B |
| *Practice and Activity Book* *Chapter Resources,* Book 2 | |
| • Communicative Activity 4-2 | |
| • Additional Listening Activity 4-3 . . . . . . . . . . . . . . | *Additional Listening Activities, Audiocassette* 9 B |
| • Additional Listening Activity 4-4 . . . . . . . . . . . . . . | *Additional Listening Activities, Audiocassette* 9 B |
| • Student Response Form | |
| • Realia 4-2 | |
| • Situation Card 4-2 | |
| • Quiz 4-2 . . . . . . . . . . . . . . . . . . . . . . . . . . . . . . . | *Assessment Items, Audiocassette* 7 B |
| *Video Guide.* . . . . . . . . . . . . . . . . . . . . . . . . . . . . . | *Video Program/Expanded Video Program,* Videocassette 2 |
| | *Textbook Audiocassette* 2 B |
| *Practice and Activity Book* *Chapter Resources,* Book 2 | |
| • Communicative Activity 2-2 | |
| • Additional Listening Activity 4-5 . . . . . . . . . . . . . . | *Additional Listening Activities, Audiocassette* 9 B |
| • Additional Listening Activity 4-6 . . . . . . . . . . . . . . | *Additional Listening Activities, Audiocassette* 9 B |
| • Student Response Form | |
| • Realia 4-3 | |
| • Situation Card 4-3 | |
| • Teaching Transparency Master 4-2 . . . . . . . . . . . . . | *Teaching Transparency* 4-2 |
| • Quiz 4-3 . . . . . . . . . . . . . . . . . . . . . . . . . . . . . . . | *Assessment Items, Audiocassette* 7 B |

*Video Guide.* . . . . . . . . . . . . . . . . . . . . . . . . . . . . . *Video Program/Expanded Video Program,* Videocassette 2

**Alternative Assessment**

• Performance Assessment, *Teacher's Edition*
  **Erste Stufe,** p. 91L
  **Zweite Stufe,** p. 91N
  **Dritte Stufe,** p. 91P

• Portfolio Assessment
  Written: **Anwendung,** Activity 6, *Pupil's Edition,* p.113, *Assessment Guide*
  Oral: **Erste Stufe,** Activity 13, *Pupil's Edition,* p. 101 *Assessment Guide*
• **Notizbuch,** *Pupil's Edition,* p. 104; *Practice and Activity Book,* p. 148

# Kapitel 4: Alles für die Schule!
# Textbook Listening Activities Scripts

## Erste Stufe
### Activity 9, p. 99

MICHAEL  Sag mal, Peter, wann hast du denn Musik?

PETER  Am Dienstag um 9 Uhr 45, also gleich nach der Pause.

MICHAEL  Und wann hast du Erdkunde?

PETER  Hm … Erdkunde habe ich am Montag um 8 Uhr — hab' ich ja nicht so gern … das ist einfach zu früh. Dann habe ich auch noch Sport am Montag. Aber Sport ist ja mein Lieblingsfach.

MICHAEL  Und du, Katja? Wann hast du Geschichte?

KATJA  Sehr früh am Freitag — Freitag um 8 Uhr.

MICHAEL  Und Mathe?

KATJA  Oh … am Donnerstag um 9 Uhr 30. Das geht ja noch. Der Mathematiklehrer ist sehr sympathisch, und man lernt viel.

MICHAEL  Wie steht's mit Deutsch?

KATJA  Hm … Deutsch hab' ich am Dienstag um 10 Uhr 45, direkt vor der Pause. Frau Bach ist die Lehrerin. Ich finde sie ganz nett.

MICHAEL  Du, Beate, wann hast du eigentlich Kunst?

BEATE  Am Mittwoch von 12 Uhr 20 bis 13 Uhr 10.

MICHAEL  Und wann hat Hannes Biologie?

BEATE  Ich glaube, am Freitag nach der Pause.

### Activity 10, p. 100

SONJA  Du, Klaus, hast du mittwochs viel zu tun?

KLAUS  Um Gotteswillen ja! Um 8 Uhr habe ich zuerst Mathe. Dann um 8 Uhr 45 habe ich Deutschstunde bei Herrn Rilke. Direkt nach der kleinen Pause, also um 9 Uhr 45, habe ich Englisch, und danach gleich um 10 Uhr 30 Latein. Geschichtsunterricht ist um 11 Uhr 30. Erst in der letzten Stunde, von 12 Uhr 20 bis 13 Uhr 05, habe ich Erdkunde. Ich kann dir sagen, mittwochs habe ich den ganzen Tag viel zu tun. Am Ende bin ich ganz schön kaputt.

## Zweite Stufe
### Activity 17, p. 102

RAINER  Welche Fächer hast du denn gern, Katja?

KATJA  Ich? Tja — ich habe Musik und Latein eigentlich sehr gern. Latein macht viel Spaß und Musik ist Spitze!

RAINER  Und Englisch?

KATJA  Nein, Englisch habe ich nicht so gern, aber Deutsch finde ich nicht schlecht. Ja, ich hab' Deutsch sehr gern.

RAINER  Und, was meinst du ist dein Lieblingsfach?

KATJA  Ich habe so zwei Lieblingsfächer: Geschichte und Erdkunde. Geschichte habe ich am Montag, am Mittwoch und am Donnerstag. Und Erdkunde habe ich am Dienstag. Ich finde den Erdkundelehrer sehr nett. Hast du Erdkunde gern?

RAINER  Es geht. Nicht so sehr, aber Kunst macht Spaß.

KATJA  Wirklich? Das mag ich nicht. Ich finde Kunst langweilig. Na, und Mathe auch. Ich habe Mathe nicht gern, das ist oft schwer.

## Activity 20, *p. 103*

Schau! Heute hab' ich mein Zeugnis bekommen. Meine Schulnoten sind gar nicht mal schlecht! In Mathe habe ich sogar eine Eins! Das ist doch prima, oder? In Physik und Deutsch 'ne Zwei, in Erdkunde eine Drei. Klar, die Drei könnte besser sein! Nur Englisch ist ziemlich schlecht, eine Vier! So was Blödes! Die Note muß das nächste Mal besser werden! Englisch ist aber so langweilig!

## Dritte Stufe
### Activity 25, *p. 107*

JOHANNA Hallo, Daniel!
DANIEL Tag, Johanna!
JOHANNA Was machst du denn hier?
DANIEL Ach ... Ich brauch' ein paar Kulis für die Schule. Entschuldigen Sie? Was kostet dieser Kuli?
VERKÄUFERIN Zwei Mark.
DANIEL Und wo sind ihre Taschenrechner?
VERKÄUFERIN Dort drüben. Auf dem Regal.
JOHANNA Schau mal, Daniel! Die Taschenrechner sind doch toll, was?
DANIEL Ja, so handlich und sehr preiswert. Also, ich glaube, das nehme ich dann.
VERKÄUFERIN Ist das alles für heute?
DANIEL Ja, danke.

## Diktat, *p. 109*

Martin and Anna are talking about Martin's moped and about their school subjects. First listen to what they are saying, then write down their conversation.

ANNA Martin, Tag!
MARTIN Tag, Anna! Wie findest du mein Moped? Es ist neu.
ANNA Spitze! Du bist jetzt sechzehn, nicht?
MARTIN Ja, und jetzt komme ich gern mit dem Moped zur Schule.
ANNA Welche Fächer hast du am Montag?
MARTIN Hm, zuerst habe ich immer Deutsch, dann Mathe und Englisch. Nach der Pause habe ich Chemie. Das ist mein Lieblingsfach.
ANNA Wirklich? In Chemie habe ich nur eine Drei. Mein Lieblingsfach ist Englisch. Da habe ich eine Eins.

## Anwendung
### Activity 7, *p. 113*

Also, es klingelt in zwei Minuten. Bevor ich es vergesse, hier sind einige Schulsachen, die ihr für die Deutschklasse braucht. Schreibt bitte die folgenden Sachen auf: Zuerst braucht ihr ein gutes Deutsch-Englisches Wörterbuch. Natürlich auch Bleistifte. Und ah, ja mindestens einen Kuli, der funktioniert, ja? Außerdem noch zwei Hefte und ach ja ... eine neue, leere Kassette. Ja, ich glaub' das ist alles. Also, bis morgen dann. Auf Wiedersehen!

# Kapitel 4: Alles für die Schule!
## *Suggested Project*

*In this activity students will make a poster outlining some components of the public education systems of Austria, Germany, or Switzerland. This project is designed to be a cooperative learning activity, and students should be grouped accordingly. Each group should have a reader, a writer, a proofreader, and a presenter.*

## MATERIALS

✂ **Students may need**
- *large sheets of paper or construction paper*
- *colored markers*
- *rulers*
- *tape*

## SUGGESTED OUTLINE

Posters should outline differences between the American school system and the school system chosen, such as
- structure (How do the grade levels work?)
- types of schools (**Realschule, Gymnasium,** etc.)
- compulsory age for attending schools
- grading system
- course requirements
- end-of-year exams
- educational tracks chosen by students in secondary education or any other topics the students might find interesting

## SUGGESTED SEQUENCE

1. Once students have been assigned or have chosen a country, each group will begin its research.

2. Students should be given a set time to look for information in their school library. You may also want to supply additional information and have it available for them on reserve. Possible sources for this information are listed on pp. T38 and T39 of the *Teacher's Edition*.

3. Each member of a group should research one or two of the components of the topic.

4. Once all materials have been gathered, each group should make a draft of the information they will put on the poster.

5. The proofreader must ensure correct spelling before the writer creates the final draft.

6. Encourage students to use charts and diagrams as visual aids.

As the final phase of the project, the presenter will present his or her group's project to the class.

## GRADING THE PROJECT

You may want to give individual grades to students based on the assigned research they completed for their group's topic as well as an overall grade for the completed work presented to the class.

Suggested point distribution: (total = 100 points)

| | |
|---|---|
| Correct content information | 25 |
| Oral presentation | 25 |
| Appearance of project | 25 |
| Individual participation | 25 |

# Kapitel 4: Alles für die Schule!
 *Games*

## DER PREIS IST HEISS

*This game can be used to review numbers and to practice concrete vocabulary items from any chapter.*

**Materials**  You will need small pictures depicting the vocabulary you intend to practice (school supplies for this chapter), glue, construction paper or poster board, and index cards.

**Preparation**  To prepare for the game, glue or tape pictures onto cardboard. Write an approximate German price for each item on the back of each card. On a separate index card write two prices for the same object, one of which matches the actual price on the back of the picture and another that is either lower or higher. Place each card face down in front of the corresponding picture.

**Procedure**  The class is divided into two teams, and one student is the host. Each team sends one team member to the front, and the host asks **"Wieviel kostet ...?"** as he or she holds up the item for the two players and the rest of the class to see. Request silence in the classroom as the two players choose between the two prices on the index card. They then write their answer on a notecard. The host asks them to read their answers. If a team member gets the correct price, he or she wins a point for his or her team. If the answer is incorrect, the student does not score a point for the team. The next player from each team comes to the front of the class to take a turn. After all items have been shown or the set time ends, all points are added up. The team with the most points wins.

## ASSOZIATIONSFELD

*This game can be used to review the vocabulary of almost any topic. Topics suggested for this chapter are* **Schulfächer, Schreibwarenladen,** *and hobbies (review topic).*

**Procedure**  Depending on the class size, divide the class into two or more teams. Members of each team form a circle with their chairs and assign one student to be their designated recorder. Announce the topic to the groups and give the signal to start. The members of each team must come up with as many German words as possible that are associated with the topic. The recorder writes down all the suggested words, and each student must ensure that he or she knows the correct spelling. The team members continue to dictate words to their recorder until the teacher calls time. The recorder of each group copies his or her list on the board. After all lists are up, the teacher checks the words for appropriateness and correct spelling. The team with the most appropriate words correctly spelled wins.

## GO FISH

This game must be prepared ahead of time. You will need small cut-out pictures of the vocabulary covered so far and index cards. Glue pictures onto the index cards. If you cannot find a certain picture, draw it on an index card. For one complete deck, you will need four cards of each vocabulary item, but the pictures don't have to match exactly. Each player is dealt five cards, and the remaining cards in the deck are placed on the table face down. Each player must remove from his or her hand all the matching pairs of cards, placing them on the table face up. The dealer begins the game by selecting a player and asking for a card. (Example: **Mary, hast du einen Kuli?** If she has that card she must give it to the person who asked for it who then places his or her matching pair of **Kulis** on the table.) Next, the dealer asks Mary or any other player for another card in his hand and continues as long as he keeps making pairs. If the dealer asks for a card that another player does not have, the dealer has to take a card from the deck. Again, if it matches, the dealer has to place that pair down face up. If the dealer cannot make a match, he keeps that card in his hand, and it is the next player's turn. He or she follows the same steps. The game ends when one player puts down or gives away his or her last card. All players count their pairs, and the player with the most pairs wins.

# Kapitel 4: Alles für die Schule!
## *Lesson Plans, pages 92-115*

## *U*sing the Chapter Opener, pp. 92-93

### Motivating Activity

Have the students think about what would happen if school were several miles from their homes and there were no school buses. How would they get to school? Could they use any public transportation? Discuss the students' responses with them.

###  Culture Note

Mention to your class that German students frequently ride their bikes to school. Books, folders, and other supplies have to be taken to and from school each day because German schools do not have lockers and students cannot leave any belongings in their classrooms.

### Teaching Suggestion

① Ask students to look at the picture and point out things that seem unusual or different to them. Example: German bicycles always have a carrier (**Gepäckträger**) onto which students fasten their heavy school bags.

### Thinking Critically

① **Drawing Inferences**   Ask students if they can think of some reasons why many German students ride their bikes to school. (shorter distances between home and school, few school busses, cost of public transportation, environmental awareness, etc.)

③ **Drawing Inferences**   Ask students to use the visual clues in the picture to guess what she is writing. (a class schedule or **Stundenplan**)

### Focusing on Outcomes

② To get students to focus on the chapter objectives, have them look at the pictures of the school supplies. How would students ask about the prices of each one of those items? Next, have students preview the learning outcomes on p. 93. **NOTE:** each of these outcomes is modeled in the video and evaluated in **Kann ich's wirklich?** on p. 114.

# Teaching Los geht's!
## pp. 94-96

### Resources for Los geht's!

- *Video Program* OR
  *Expanded Video Program,* Videocassette 2
- *Textbook Audiocassette* 2 B
- *Practice and Activity Book*

▶ **pages 94-95**

### 📼 Video Synopsis

A group of friends (Michael, Sonja, Katja, and Heiko) are at school talking about their class schedules and grades. Later, Sonja runs into Michael at a stationery shop where they look at school supplies. The student outcomes listed on p. 93 are modeled in the video: talking about class schedules, using a schedule to talk about time, sequencing events, expressing likes, dislikes, and favorites, responding to good and bad news, talking about prices, and pointing things out.

### Motivating Activity

Ask students to list all the common school supplies that they need, especially at the beginning of a new school year. Where are they most likely to buy these supplies?

### Teaching Suggestion

To get students into the text, first do the prereading activity at the top of p. 94. Have students scan the dialogue of the **Foto-Roman** to look for cognates and any other words they might recognize. Write these words on the board as students call them out. What are they able to tell you from this brief glance about what might be happening in these scenes?

### Teacher Note

You may want to point out to students that the sales tax is already included in the price in Germany. This is why the salesperson does not add tax to the 23 marks Michael is paying for his calculator.

▶ **page 96**

### 🙌 Cooperative Learning

Put students in groups of 4. Ask them to choose a discussion leader, a recorder, a proofreader (proof-reads group's answers before they are turned in), and an announcer. Give students a specific amount of time in which to complete Activities 1-5. Walk around the room monitoring group work, and help students if necessary. At the end of the activity call on each group announcer to read his or her group's results. You can decide whether or not to collect their work for a grade at the end of the activity.

### Closure

Have students compare what they know about the beginning of the German school year with their own experiences in the United States. Does it seem similar or different? Does the similarity surprise them?

# Teaching Erste Stufe,
## pp. 97-101

### Resources for Erste Stufe

*Practice and Activity Book*
*Chapter Resources,* Book 2
- Communicative Activity 4-1
- Additional Listening Activities 4-1, 4-2
- Student Response Form
- Realia 4-1
- Situation Card 4-1
- Teaching Transparency Master 4-1
- Quiz 4-1
*Audiocassette Program*
- *Textbook Audiocassette* 2 B
- *Additional Listening Activities, Audiocassette* 9 B
- *Assessment Items, Audiocassette* 7 B

▶ **page 97**

### *MOTIVATE*

### Teaching Suggestion

Have the students make out their own schedules on 3 x 5 cards. Make an enlarged copy of Heiko and Katja's schedule and put it on an overhead transparency. Ask the students what they notice about the number of subjects Heiko and Katja have as compared to their own. The length of class periods? The number and length of breaks? When does Heiko and Katja's day start and end?

ERSTE STUFE

*TEACH*

## Teaching Suggestion

**6** Ask students what surprises them most about the schedule above Activity 6. (Example: different classes each day, length of school days, two foreign languages, etc)

## Thinking Critically

**Drawing Inferences**    Tell students that they are looking at a typical **Stundenplan.** Ask them if they can determine which of the classes are considered **Hauptfächer** (*major subjects*) and which ones are **Nebenfächer** (*minor subjects*).

 ## Culture Note

Religion is part of the public school curriculum in Germany; there is no separation between church and state. In the first years (grades 5-8) students join the class that represents their denomination (mostly Protestant or Catholic). For any other denomination or religion there are usually special classes. In higher grades (9 and up), religion is taught similarly to social studies in the United States, and students learn about philosophy and the religions practiced around the world.

 ## Multicultural Connection

The students in this chapter don't have school on Saturdays, but many students do in different parts of Germany. Ask students if they know of other countries where classes are sometimes held on Saturdays. (Japan, France, ...)

 ## Total Physical Response

On the board, write the frame of a **Stundenplan** containing only the days and the times. Write the different school subjects on 3 × 5 index cards. Put a small piece of tape on each card. First demonstrate for students as you tell them what you want them to do: **Also, wir machen einen Stundenplan. Ich habe am Montag um 8 Uhr Biologie. Ich nehme das Kärtchen Biologie** (show card) **und hefte es an den richtigen Platz auf dem Stundenplan.** Now give students commands: **Du hast am Diens-** tag um 10 Uhr 30 Mathe. Nimm das Kärtchen und hefte es an den richtigen Platz auf dem Stundenplan! After students have made the **Stundenplan,** have them ask each other questions: **Wann hast du Biologie? Wann hast du Englisch?**

▶ *page 98*

 ## Culture Notes

* Often, a grade-level will be broken down into sections called **Parallelklassen.** For example, if there are 120 ninth-grade students, there might be 4 ninth-grade classes: 9a, 9b, 9c, and 9d. Each student is assigned to one of those classes, and each one has a **Klassenlehrer** (*homeroom teacher*). This teacher teaches at least one of the subjects and also serves as liaison with parents, makes class announcements, etc.

* Most classes are taught in the students' main classroom, and the teachers move from one class to the next. Only science classes, art, music, home economics, and physical education take place in specially equipped rooms.

* Students can always expect homework, since their classes don't meet daily. After students get home from school, they usually spend the early afternoon doing their homework. Extracurricular activities generally start after 4:00 P.M. and can last until 8:00 or 9:00 P.M. depending on the types of activities in which students are involved.

## Teaching Suggestion

**7** Have students look back at the schedule they made for the motivating activity of this **Stufe** and use the back side for their schedule in German. Have one student write his or her schedule on the board. You can use this schedule to present the **So sagt man das!** box "Talking about class schedules."

## PRESENTATION: So sagt man das!

Personalize this function box by using the **Stundenplan** on the board and incorporating the expressions to be taught.

## ♜ Game

Create a **Kreuzworträtsel** (*crossword puzzle*) similar to the sample below using subjects in German.

1. Wir **lesen** *Tom Sawyer*
2. Wir **lernen** a + b = c
3. Wir **lernen** etwas über $H_2O$ und $CO_2$.
4. Wir **lernen** etwas über Mozart und Beethoven.
5. Wir **lernen** etwas über Picasso und Ansel Adams.
6. Wir **lernen** etwas über England, Kanada, Deutschland und China.

```
          4.      1.           5.
      2. M A T H E M A T I K
         U       N           U
         S       G           N
         I       L           S
         K       I           T
                 S          6.
              3. C H E M I E
                 H          R
                            D
                            K
                            U
                            N
                            D
                            E
```

▶ *page 99*

### For Additional Practice

**9** As a second listening activity let students add the names of the students that Michael is addressing.

### Building on Previous Skills

Review the numbers 0-60 with simple math problems. Have a handout with at least 10 problems and let students work in pairs. Each student gets to read five math problems aloud, and then other students take turns answering the problems. This will prepare students for the **So sagt man das!** box "Using a schedule to talk about time."

## PRESENTATION: So sagt man das!

Make a transparency of the **Stundenplan** on p. 97. Using the expressions in the function box on p. 99, talk about when Heiko and Katja have their classes.

## Teaching Suggestions

- Have students make a clock to practice telling 24-hour time in German. They will each need 2 paper plates, brass fasteners, scissors, felt-tip markers, a pencil, a hole-puncher, and a ruler. After students receive supplies, have them draw in pencil a 24-hour clock on one paper plate. If students are not familiar with the 24-hour clock, you may want to remind them that the *13* goes underneath the *1* but is just about half the size. Students then trace the numbers with a felt-tip marker. To make the two hands of the clock, students use the second paper plate and cut two strips about 3/4 of an inch wide, one of which should be 3 inches long and the other about 2 1/2 inches. Next, students punch a hole in the center of the clock and in the end of each of the hands of the clock. Finally, students match the holes of the strips to the hole in the center of the clock and secure the hands with a brass fastener. Have students put their names on the back of their clocks. The clocks will be used in activities to come.

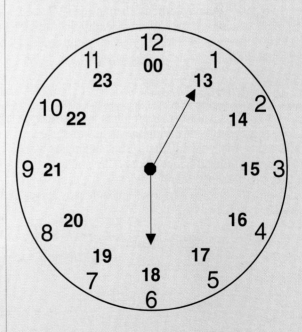

**ERSTE STUFE**

- Have students practice telling time using the **Stundenplan** on p. 97, a TV program guide, and, if available, a German TV program guide or train schedule.
- Have students look at the **Bochum-München** train schedule and see if they can figure out the meaning of 1-2-3-4-5-6-7 under **Verkehrstage**. (days of the week)

▶ *page 100*

## For Additional Practice

**10** After completing the listening activity, have students work in pairs creating sentences that give times for different classes. One student reads the sentence he or she wrote down. Example: **Um 8 Uhr hat er Mathe.** The other student tries to show that time on his or her clock. Tell students to take turns reading their sentences from Activity 10 and showing time on the clocks.

## Teacher Note

**11** You can use the shortened form **um (zehn)** until noon. But you would say **um 13 Uhr** or **um 1 Uhr**, not **um 13**.

## PRESENTATION: Grammatik

Review the regular verb endings from previous chapters. (Example: **lernen**) Then introduce **haben** and its endings. Have students identify the two forms that do not conform to regular conjugation. (**hast, hat**)

###  Culture Note

**12** Unless bad weather prohibits it, students are asked to go outside during the breaks and use this time to socialize with others. Students must remain on the school grounds. Older students (grade varies by school) may leave the school yard during the breaks. At age 18 students may leave whenever they wish.

## Teaching Suggestion

**12** In pairs, have students read the four short conversations aloud.

▶ *page 101*

###  Portfolio Assessment

**13** You might want to suggest this activity as an oral portfolio item for your students. See *Assessment Guide,* Chapter 4.

## PRESENTATION: So sagt man das!

Before introducing the new German words, ask students to name sequencing words they would typically use in English. Do they know what these words are called? (adverbs and prepositions) Tell students that German uses the same kinds of words to make the language flow more naturally. Using the schedule of one of the students in class tell the rest the order of that student's schedule for a particular day using the sequencing words presented.

## Teaching Suggestions

- Recommend that students keep a separate list of sequencing words. Tell them that the list will be useful for written and oral portfolio work as well as for the **Notizbuch** activities.
- If you feel your students can handle more expressions of time and frequency, you might want to introduce other adverbs such as **morgens, heute, nun** (expressions of time), **niemals, immer, oft, manchmal** (expressions of frequency).

###  For Individual Needs

**15 Challenge** In pairs, have students create another dialogue that deals with someone's schedule but uses a different arrangement of subjects and times. Have students cut their dialogues into sentence strips. Have groups exchange their strip stories and recreate the conversation.

## Teaching Suggestion

**16** Call on several students to read their short paragraphs aloud in class. This will give students extra speaking practice without the stress of having to speak spontaneously.

## Reteaching: Talking about schedules

Ask students to look at the **Stundenplan** they made in Activity 7. Go around the classroom asking students questions using the expressions of the **Wortschatz** and **So sagt man das!** boxes of this **Stufe**.

## CLOSE

### Teaching Suggestion

Hand out the clocks that students made earlier in this **Stufe** and ask them to set the clocks as you call out different times. Example: **11 Uhr 45, 23 Uhr 15**, and so on.

### Focusing on Outcomes

Refer students back to the outcomes listed on p. 93. They should recognize that they are now able to talk about class schedules, use a schedule to talk about time, and sequence events.

## ASSESS

- **Performance Assessment** Draw a five-day **Stundenplan** on the board. Call it **Dieters Stundenplan.** Write the German names of all the subjects learned in this **Stufe** on large index cards. Put masking tape on the back of the cards so you can attach them to the chalkboard. Tell individual students to put the subject cards in their correct places on the **Stundenplan** according to your directions. Use sequencing words as well as times in your directions. Example: **Am Montag hat Dieter zuerst Englisch.** Call on different students for each new sentence until you complete the **Stundenplan**.

- Quiz 4-1, *Chapter Resources,* Book 2

## Teaching Zweite Stufe, pp. 102-105

### Resources for Zweite Stufe

*Practice and Activity Book*
*Chapter Resources,* Book 2
- Communicative Activity 4-2
- Additional Listening Activities 4-3, 4-4
- Student Response Form
- Realia 4-2
- Situation Card 4-2
- Quiz 4-2

*Audiocassette Program*
- *Textbook Audiocassette* 2 B
- *Additional Listening Activities, Audiocassette* 9 B
- *Assessment Items, Audiocassette* 7 B

▶ *page 102*

## MOTIVATE

### Teaching Suggestion

Ask the students to think about the grading system used in American schools. What do the grades A, B, C, D, and F stand for? Can they be expressed in alternate ways? How do students express feelings toward each grade? What do they say when they earn an A, B, C, and so on?

## TEACH

### PRESENTATION: So sagt man das!/Ein wenig Grammatik

- Before teaching the expressions in the function box, go around the class and ask students these questions: **Hast du Mathe gern? Welches Fach hast du nicht gern?**

- Tell your class about your own favorite activities and show them pictures if possible. Example: **Ich habe Deutsch gern. Hier ist mein Lieblingsbuch. Ich spiele gern Tennis. Meine Lieblingsshow ist ...**

### For Additional Practice

**17** Have students listen to the recording a second time, and this time have them write down the words Katja uses to describe several of her subjects. (Latein—macht viel Spaß; Musik—Spitze; Deutsch—sehr gern; Kunst—langweilig: Mathe—schwer)

**ZWEITE STUFE**

## Group Work

**19** Have students work in groups of three and make a skit out of this activity. Students should make use of props such as clipboards, microphones, cameras, etc. You might also set a time limit for the interview. This will encourage students to be as succinct with their questions and answers as possible.

▶ *page 103*

## PRESENTATION: Ein wenig Landeskunde

On the chalkboard write the letter symbols used in the American grading system and the number symbols used in the German grading system. Ask students to compare the systems. Here is an approximation:

$1 = A^+$                 $4 = D^+ \Rightarrow C$

$2 = B^+ \Rightarrow A$       $5 = D^- \Rightarrow D$

$3 = C^+ \Rightarrow B$       $6 = F$

 **Culture Note**

If students receive a 5 or 6 in a main subject (**Hauptfach**) they may have to repeat a grade. That is called **sitzenbleiben**. Therefore, school grades are very important. If students are held back more than once, they may be expelled from that school.

 **Multicultural Connection**

Do students know of other grading systems used around the world? Have they met students from other countries who could explain the way they are graded? (Example: In France, students are graded on a scale of 0–20.)

▶ *page 104*

## PRESENTATION: So sagt man das!

Ask two students, one girl and one boy, to read Katja's and Heiko's lines. After each line, ask students what each response could mean and what it is similar to in English.

## For Additional Practice

**22b** Have students create a conversation which contains at least five questions and five expressions of exclamation. Students can then take the conversation one step further by asking: **Was ist dein Lieblingsfach?**

▶ *page 105*

## PRESENTATION: Landeskunde

## Building on Previous Skills

Take a short survey of your students. Ask them to name one thing they like and one thing they dislike about the German school system, based on what they know so far. Have them also give a reason for their opinions. Write students' responses on the board and discuss them.

## Teaching Suggestion

You might want to introduce these expressions before students watch this video segment or listen to the tape:

**die Arbeitslehre**   *work-study class*
**zurechtkommen**   *to manage, succeed in doing something*
**basier'**   (colloquial) *concentrate on something*
**der Leistungskurs**   *concentration on a specific subject in the* **Oberstufe** *of a* **Gymnasium.**

## Thinking Critically

**Drawing Inferences**   Ask students to review Lugana's statement. After saying that she is Greek, why does she add **"und hier geboren."** Remind students of what they learned about **Gastarbeiter** in the **Landeskunde** section of Chapter 3 to help them find an answer. (Lugana's parents were probably one of the many foreign workers, **Gastarbeiter,** who came to Germany during the 1960s. Her family and many other families decided not to return to their homeland and are still living in Germany.)

## Thinking Critically

**Comparing and Contrasting**   Ask students to review Björn's statement. He talks about his interest in his **Informatik** class. What would be the equivalent of this class in the American school system? (computer science class)

## Background Information

• Toward the end of the fourth year at the **Grundschule** (*elementary school*), students, parents, and teachers come together to decide which of the three secondary schools the child should enter. This decision is based largely on academic performance. Although it is possible to change

schools later, this is a very important decision in that it, to some extent, predetermines the future career path of the student.

- You might want to point out to your students that it is important for German **Gymnasiasten** planning to go to a university to get excellent grades in school. Most universities are over-crowded, which means that only a minimum number of students can be accepted, especially in majors such as medicine, dentistry, or pharmacy. Only the students with the best grades are ac-cepted in overcrowded departments.

## Teacher Note

Mention to your students that the **Landeskunde** will also be included in Quiz 4–2 given at the end of the **Zweite Stufe**.

## Reteaching: Responding to good and bad news

Write the numbers 1 through 6 in random order on one side of the board and the written expressions corresponding to German grades (p. 103) on the other side. Ask six students to come up to the board one at a time and have each of them draw a line from the number grade to its correct written expression. (Example: 1 ——— **sehr gut**) In a third column you could also add the expressions from p. 104 and ask another group of students to draw a line between the grade and an appropriate response. (Example: 1 —— **sehr gut** —— **Spitze!**)

## CLOSE

### Teaching Suggestion

On the day of the closure activity, stand by the door and hand a strip of paper to each student with one of the expressions from the **Ein wenig Gram-matik** box on p. 102 (**Lieblingskonzert, Lieblings...**). Once the class is underway ask each student what his or her "**Lieblingsetwas**" is. Ex-ample: **Klaus, was ist dein Lieblingsetwas? Meine Lieblingsmusik ist ...!**

### Focusing on Outcomes

Refer students back to the outcomes listed on p. 93. Students should recognize that they are now able to express likes, dislikes, and favorites and re-spond to good and bad news.

## ASSESS

- **Performance Assessment** Have all students stand up. Give several quick commands based on material introduced in this **Stufe**. Example: **Wenn dein Lieblingsfach Deutsch ist, setz dich, bitte! Wenn du morgen zuerst Englisch hast, schreib deinen Namen an die Tafel!** If anybody is left standing after your series of com-mands, your last command should be: **Setz dich, wenn du heute Deutsch hast!**

- Quiz 4-2, *Chapter Resources,* Book 2

## Teaching Dritte Stufe, pp. 106-109

**Resources for Dritte Stufe**

*Practice and Activity Book*
*Chapter Resources,* Book 2
- Additional Listening Activities 4-5, 4–6
- Student Response Form
- Realia 4-3
- Situation Card 4-3
- Teaching Transparency Master 4-2
- Quiz 4-3
*Audiocassette Program*
- *Textbook Audiocassette* 2 B
- *Additional Listening Activities, Audiocassette* 9 B
- *Assessmet Items, Audiocassette* 7 B

▶ **page 106**

## MOTIVATE

### Building on Previous Skills

Review vocabulary for classroom objects and sup-plies via TPR.

## TEACH

### PRESENTATION: Wortschatz

If possible bring all eight items represented in the **Wortschatz** box to class. Put them on a table in the front of the room. Make eight large index cards and write the name and price for each item on them. Go over the **Wortschatz** several times by pointing to each item and saying the appropriate German

word. When you feel students are ready, ask questions such as: **Was kostet 16, 20 DM? Was kostet sehr viel? Was kostet nicht viel?**

## PRESENTATION: Grammatik

Ask students how plurals are formed in English. The formation of plurals in German often presents a problem for students, even among native Germans. Although there are always exceptions to the rule, there are several patterns that decrease the time of memorization considerably. Refer students to the chart on p. 328 in the back of their books.

 ### For Individual Needs

**Visual Learners**   Write the list of vocabulary words from the **Wortschatz** box on the board. Refer students to the German-English vocabulary pages at the end of the book (pp. 340-354). Write 10 to 15 additional German nouns on the board and have students find the plural of each. Demonstrate the first noun. Example: **das Wörterbuch, die Wörterbücher**

## Thinking Critically

* **Drawing Inferences**   Give these two sentences as samples and ask students how they might be able to tell whether they are looking at a singular or plural noun. **Der Vater spielt Fußball. Die Väter spielen Fußball.** Students should remember that **Vater** is masculine **(der)** and that -**t** is a singular verb ending while -**en** is a plural verb ending.

* **Analyzing**   Ask students what changes occurred in the plural of **Vater.** (umlaut added; plural article **die**)

▶ *page 107*

## Teaching Suggestion

Before presenting **So sagt man das!** refer back to Chapter 1 and ask students what kinds of words subject pronouns replace. (nouns)

## PRESENTATION: So sagt man das!

Use hand gestures (thumbs up/thumbs down) along with newspaper ads to teach **teuer, billig,** and **preiswert.** Use items such as school supplies

that students are familiar with and would know the approximate prices of.

## For Additional Practice

Show the students pictures of jeans, T-shirts, CDs, magazines, and other items they might purchase and tell them how much each item costs. Use pictures of items that are cognates, if possible. Have students respond by saying **Das ist teuer, billig,** or **preiswert.** Students can extend their responses using **ziemlich, sehr,** and **nicht sehr.**

## PRESENTATION: Ein wenig Landeskunde

Bring in the business section of a current newspaper that shows the exchange rates of several different monetary units. Have students convert the prices of the school supplies in the **Wortschatz** box on p. 106 from marks to dollars based on the current exchange rates.

 ### Multicultural Connection

Find out what other currencies students have heard of. Ask them to bring in different coins or bills they might have collected in travels. You might want to make a chart showing the names of countries and their currency. Examples: England, the pound; Russia, the ruble; Japan, the yen; etc.

 ### For Individual Needs

**Challenge**   Can students name the currencies of the other German-speaking countries? Austria—**der Schilling;** Switzerland—**der Schweizer Franken;** Liechtenstein—**der Schweizer Franken**

### ♜ Game

Students now have the vocabulary to play the game **Der Preis ist heiß.** See page 91F for the procedure.

▶ *page 108*

## Teaching Suggestion

**26** Make sure students use expressions such as **teuer, billig,** and **preiswert** in their conversation. Have pairs read their conversation aloud in class.

## PRESENTATION: So sagt man das!

Place a variety of school supplies around the room. Point them out to students using the expressions introduced in the **So sagt man das!** function box.

 **Culture Note**

A **Schreibwarenladen** (*stationery shop*) is a small shop that carries mostly school supplies, some toys and games, wrapping papers, and cards. The owner of the store is the **Schreibwarenhändler (-in)**.

 *page 109*

## For Additional Practice

• Have your students place various school supplies around the room as if they were being displayed in a store. Decide where the front and the back of the store will be. Set up a counter where the salesperson will give information. Have students take turns playing the role of salesperson and customer. The customer will ask where different items are, and the salesperson will say where they are depending on their location in the room.

• Have students "shop" in the **Schreibwarenladen.** They should each buy five different school items. Have them make a list of what they want beforehand. Working in pairs, have them make a map of the store and decide where various supplies are located and where the **Verkäufer(in)** will stand. One student asks the **Verkäufer(in)** where the various items can be found; then the **Verkäufer(in)** helps his or her partner find the items. Remind students to be polite. Have them switch roles.

## PRESENTATION: Aussprache

• **äu/eu** and **au**    You may want to use the following pairs of words to help students learn the **äu/eu** and **au** sounds: loiter/**Leute**, annoy/**Mäuse**, house/**Haus**.

• final **b, d,** and **g**    Tell students to put their hands in front of their mouths as they pronounce the sample words illustrating these sounds. If they pronounce them correctly, they should feel a small burst of air as the sound is released.

## Teacher Note

In the word **Liebling** the final **b** in **Lieb-** is pronounced as /p/. The final **g** in **-ling**, however, is not pronounced as /k/ but sounds similar to the *-ing* ending in English.

## Teaching Suggestion

Have students number each sentence of the **Diktat** as they write down what they hear. Once finished, call on students to write one sentence each on the board. Then call on those same students to read their sentences aloud. The class can make corrections together.

## Reteaching: Pointing things out

Point to several objects in the classroom and ask students questions such as: **Wo ist die Landkarte?** Ask students to respond by telling you where these objects are. (Example: **Sie ist dort drüben!**) Students should use subject pronouns and location adverbs in their responses if possible.

## CLOSE

**Game**
    Play the game **Assoziationsfeld.** See page 91F for the procedure.

## Focusing on Outcomes

Refer students back to the learning outcomes listed on p. 93. Students should recognize that they are now able to talk about prices and point things out.

## ASSESS

• **Performance Assessment**    Collect examples of all the school supplies discussed in this chapter and place them around the room. For each item make an index card with an approximate German price on it and tape it underneath the item. Ask students a two-part question for each labeled item.

Example: **Wo sind die Taschenrechner? Und wieviel kostet der Taschenrechner?** Example: **Sie sind dort drüben. Er kostet 23 Mark.**

• Quiz 4-3, *Chapter Resources,* Book 2

# Teaching Zum Lesen, pp. 110-111

## Reading Strategy

The targeted strategy in this reading is inferring the meaning of compound words by looking at the cognates within the words. Students should learn about this strategy before doing Question 1. As in previous chapters, students will also be asked to skim for the gist, scan for specific information, answer questions to show comprehension, and transfer what they have learned.

## PREREADING

### Motivating Activity

Ask students if they are having trouble in any of their classes or perhaps would like to get some help to catch up on a subject. How would they go about looking for help in their 'problem' subject?

### Teacher Note

Activities 1 and 2 are prereading activities.

### Teaching Suggestion

Before you begin the prereading activities, put the following compound words on the board and ask students for their meaning. **Brieffreund; Deutschbuch; Schreibwarenladen.** Tell students that compounds always take the article of the last noun. Using this information, ask students to tell you what article goes with each of the three nouns on the board.

### Teacher Note

Compound nouns often give students the impression that German has many long words and, therefore, must be difficult. Show students that they can use skills such as recognizing cognates and drawing inferences to make compound words less intimidating. Use one of the compound words listed above to illustrate this point. (**Schreib/waren/laden** or **Brief/freund**)

## READING

### Skimming and Scanning

Draw three columns with the following headings on the board: **Unterricht; Institut Rosenberg; Schulverbund München.** Ask students to skim the readings and come up to the board to write the cognates and other words they recognize under each column head. Quickly go over the three lists. Then proceed with Activities 3-6.

##  For Individual Needs

**A Slower Pace** Ask students to look at each of the small ads and determine what type of tutoring is offered. Allow students to give the answers in English or German. (1. singing 2. math, physics, chemistry 3. piano, keyboard 4. German 5. English)

## Teaching Suggestion

Before having students read the ad for the **Institut Rosenberg,** you might want to introduce the following additional vocabulary:

**Internat** *boarding school*
**Abitur** *school graduation examination that must be passed before students qualify for admission to a university*
**vorbereiten** *to prepare*
**eidgenössisch** *federal, referring to Switzerland*
**Maturitätsprüfung** *term used for* **Abitur** *in Switzerland and Austria*
**gewährleistet** *guaranteed*
**überwacht** *supervised*

## Background Information

After students have read the ad for **Schulverbund München,** tell them that the **Isartor** is a former city gate that dates back to 1330. It was destroyed during World War II and rebuilt from 1946-1971.

## Thinking Critically

- **Analyzing** Can students differentiate the four schools listed? What grade levels are taught at each of the schools?

- **Analyzing** What does the **Institut Rosenberg** offer that the Munich schools do not offer? (Swiss **Maturitätsprüfung,** Italian **Maturitätsprüfung,** preparation for universities in the United States and the United Kingdom)

## Geography Connection

The **Institut Rosenberg** is in St. Gallen. Have students locate **St. Gallen** in an atlas. Given its location (near Lake Constance in Switzerland), what types of activities would students probably find there?

## Teacher Note

The address of the **Institut Rosenberg** includes the country code **CH.** These letters stand for **Confoederatio Helvetica.** This code is used to designate Switzerland.

## POST-READING

## Teacher Note

Activities 6 and 7 are post-reading tasks that will show whether students can apply what they have learned.

## Closure

Using the ads in the reading as a model, have students write a short advertisement for your school or an imaginary school.

# *U*sing Anwendung,
## pp. 112-113

## Teaching Suggestion

**1** So as not to duplicate any items, assign five items to each group and let them make up prices accordingly.

## ◆ For Individual Needs

**5 Tactile Learners**  Instead of writing, have students draw the supplies as they hear them mentioned. Then ask students to tell you the names of the supplies they drew.

• **Visual Learners**  Make sure the classroom items in your class are no longer labeled. As students walk into the classroom, hand each of the students one of the labels. For a warm-up activity ask students to get up and affix the label to the appropriate object in the classroom.

## ■ Portfolio Assessment

**6** You might want to suggest this activity as a written portfolio item for your students. See *Assessment Guide,* Chapter 4.

# *K*ann ich's wirklich?
## p. 114

This page is intended to prepare students for the test. It is a brief checklist of the major points covered in the chapter. The students should be reminded that it is a checklist only and not necessarily everything that will appear on the test.

# *U*sing Wortschatz,
## p. 115

## Teaching Suggestion

Have two students come to the board, one on each side. Call out the English definition of a German noun. The student on the left must write the singular noun with its article and the student on the right must write the plural of the noun with its article. Call new students up for each new noun you want to review.

## ♖ Game

Play the game *Go Fish.* See p. 91F for the procedure.

## Teacher Note

As the students' vocabulary increases you can add pairs of cards to the *Go Fish* game from each **Wortschatz** students study. This will help students review vocabulary from previous chapters.

## ◆ For Individual Needs

**Tactile Learners**  Use sentence strips to practice sentences that include sequencing words. Put the sentence strips into numbered envelopes and have one envelope for each pair of students. Students work together trying to put the sentences back together. Example: **Zuerst spielt Katja Tennis.**

## Teacher Note

Give the **Kapitel 4** Chapter Test, *Chapter Resources, Book 2*

# Alles für die Schule!

① Wann habt ihr Sport?

When a new school year begins, students are often curious about their friends' classes: When do they meet? Which ones are their favorites? What school supplies do they need? There are some similarities and some differences in what students in German-speaking countries and in the U.S. experience in school. Let's find out what they are.

## In this chapter you will learn

- to talk about class schedules; to use a schedule to talk about time; to sequence events
- to express likes, dislikes, and favorites; to respond to good news and bad news
- to talk about prices; to point things out

## And you will

- listen to German-speaking students talk about their schedules
- read ads for school supplies and become familiar with German money
- write a report card for yourself in German
- find out what German students have to say about school

② Was kosten die Hefte?

③ Am Freitag haben wir Mathe.

# Los geht's!

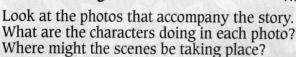

## Michael kauft Schulsachen

Michael    Sonja    Katja    Heiko

Look at the photos that accompany the story.
What are the characters doing in each photo?
Where might the scenes be taking place?

**MICHAEL** Hallo, Leute!

**SONJA** Hallo, Michael!

**MICHAEL** Suchst du denn was?

**KATJA** Ja, wo ist der Stundenplan? Sag,' wann haben wir Mathe?

**MICHAEL** Weiß ich nicht.

**HEIKO** Ah, Mathe ... haben wir nach der Pause, um 9 Uhr 45.

**KATJA** Danke, Heiko! Und was haben wir heute zuerst?

**HEIKO** Zuerst Deutsch, dann Bio, danach Mathe, dann Englisch und Sport.

**SONJA** Du, heute bekommen wir die Mathearbeit zurück.

**MICHAEL** Ich hab' bestimmt wieder eine Vier.

**SONJA** Meinst du?

**MICHAEL** Ja, leider. In Mathe hab' ich immer schlechte Noten.

**SONJA** Schade!

**MICHAEL** Na ja, du bist gut in Mathe.

**SONJA** Ja, ich hab' Mathe gern. Das ist mein Lieblingsfach.

**SONJA** Na, Michael, was machst du denn hier? — Ach, ich seh's: einen Taschenrechner!

**MICHAEL** Schau mal, Sonja! Der Rechner ist toll, nicht?

**SONJA** Ja, du hast recht.

**MICHAEL** Und er ist nicht teuer.

**SONJA** Stimmt! Nur dreiundzwanzig Mark!

| SONJA | Entschuldigung! Wo sind bitte die Hefte und die Bleistifte? |
|---|---|
| VERKÄUFER | Die sind da drüben. |
| SONJA | Und Wörterbücher? |
| VERKÄUFER | Da hinten! |

| VERKÄUFER | Der Rechner, dreiundzwanzig Mark, bitte! |
|---|---|
| MICHAEL | Ach, wie blöd! Jetzt hab' ich nur zwanzig Mark dabei. |
| SONJA | Macht nichts, Michael! Ich geb' dir das Geld. |
| MICHAEL | Oh, das ist sehr nett, Sonja! |

| MICHAEL | Warte, Sonja! |
|---|---|
| SONJA | Was ist los? |
| MICHAEL | So ein Mist! Das ganze Zeug auf der Straße! |
| SONJA | Der Taschenrechner, geht er noch? |
| MICHAEL | Ach wo! Er ist kaputt! So ein Pech! |
| SONJA | So ein Glück! Die Brille ist noch ganz! |

## 1 Was passiert hier?

1. good; Michael gets bad grades.
2. At the stationery store. School supplies.
3. A calculator for math.
4. His calculator breaks, but his glasses are still intact.

Do you understand what is happening in the story? Check your comprehension by answering these questions. Don't be afraid to guess.

1. How is Sonja in math? What about Michael?
2. Where do Sonja and Michael meet again? What kinds of things are they looking for?
3. What does Michael want to buy? Why does he need it?
4. Michael has both bad luck and good luck on the way home. What happens to him?

## 2 Genauer lesen

1. Mathe, Bio, Englisch, Sport
2. Taschenrechner, Hefte, Bleistifte, Wörterbücher
3. Ach, wie blöd, so ein Mist

a. Reread the conversations. Which words or phrases do the characters use to

1. name school subjects
2. name school supplies
3. express annoyance
4. point out something
5. express regret
6. express bad luck; good luck

4. Schau mal, da drüben, dort hinten
5. Schade
6. So ein Pech! So ein Glück!

b. In what three ways are numbers used in the conversations?

time, grades, prices

## 3 Stimmt oder stimmt nicht?

Are these statements right or wrong? Answer each one with either **stimmt** or **stimmt nicht**. If a statement is wrong, try to state it correctly.

3. stimmt nicht; Mathe ist ihr Lieblingsfach.

1. Michael hat immer schlechte Noten in Mathe. 1. stimmt
2. Katja und Heiko haben nach der Pause Deutsch. 2. stimmt nicht; Nach der Pause haben sie Mathe.
3. Sonja hat Mathe nicht gern.
4. Der Rechner ist sehr teuer. 4. stimmt nicht; Der Rechner ko nur 23 Mark.
5. Sonja gibt Michael das Geld. 5. stimmt
6. Die Brille ist kaputt. 6. stimmt nicht; Die Brille ist noch ganz.

## 4 Was paßt zusammen?

Match each statement or question on the left with an appropriate response on the right.

1. Was haben wir zuerst? b
2. Und wann hast du Mathe? e
3. Dieser Taschenrechner ist toll — und nicht teuer. d
4. Ich habe nur 20 Mark dabei. a
5. Schau mal! Der Taschenrechner ist kaputt! c
6. Aber die Brille ist noch ganz. f

a. Macht nichts! Ich gebe dir das Geld.
b. Also, zuerst Deutsch, dann Bio.
c. So ein Pech!
d. Das stimmt! Er kostet nur 23 Mark.
e. Nach der Pause.
f. So ein Glück!

## 5 Nacherzählen

Put the sentences in logical order to make a brief summary of the story.

1. Katja sucht den Stundenplan.

3 Später kommt Michael in einen Schreibwarenladen. Er möchte einen Taschenrechner.

Danach sprechen Sonja und Michael über die Mathearbeit und Michaels Noten. 2

5 Also gibt Sonja Michael das Geld.

Aber er hat nur 20 Mark dabei.

6 Auf dem Weg nach Hause fällt Michaels ganze Zeug auf die Straße. 4

# ERSTE STUFE

*Talking about class schedules; using a schedule to talk about time; sequencing events*

## WORTSCHATZ

Hier ist Heikos und Katjas Stundenplan *(class schedule)*:

Ich wollt, ich wär ein Teppich. Dann könnt ich jeden Morgen liegen bleiben!

QUICK SCHUH

### Stundenplan für

NAME __Katja__   KLASSE __9a__

| ZEIT | MONTAG | DIENSTAG | MITTWOCH | DONNERSTAG | FREITAG | SAMSTAG |
|---|---|---|---|---|---|---|
| 8:00- 8:45 | Deutsch | Deutsch | Mathe | — | Physik | frei |
| 8:45-9:30 | Deutsch | Bio | Deutsch | Physik | Mathe | |
| 9:30-9:45 | Pause | — | — | — | — | |
| 9:45-10:30 | Religion | Mathe | Englisch | Bio | Deutsch | |
| 10:30-11:15 | Bio | Englisch | Latein | Englisch | Latein | |
| 11:15-11:30 | Pause | — | — | — | — | |
| 11:30-12:15 | Latein | Sport | Geschichte | Englisch | Kunst | |
| 12:20-13:05 | Musik | Sport | Erdkunde | Latein | — | |

What do you think the word **Zeit** in the schedule means? What do the other words next to **Zeit** (**Montag**, etc.) refer to? All but four of the class subjects are cognates. Which ones do you recognize?

Kunst          Geschichte          Erdkunde

## 6  Heikos und Katjas Stundenplan

Look at Heiko's and Katja's class schedule and try to answer the following questions in German.

1. On what day(s) do Heiko and Katja have religion? And biology?
2. Which subjects do they have on Tuesday? On Wednesday?
3. On which day(s) do they have art? And history?
4. At what times do Heiko and Katja have math?* On which day(s)?
5. At what time(s) do they have German?

1. Montag; Dienstag und Donnerstag
2. Di: Deutsch, Bio. Mathe, Englisch, Sport. Mi: Mathe Deutsch, Englisch, Latein, Geschichte, Erdkunde
3. Freitag; Mittwoch
4. Am Dienstag von 9:45 bis 10:30, am Mittwoch von 8:00 bis 8:45 und am Freitag von 8:45 bis 9:30.
5. Am Montag von 8:00 bis 9:30, am Dienstag von 8:00 bis 8:45, am Mittwoch von 8:45 bis 9:30, am Freitag von 9:45 bis 10:30.

*To read times from a schedule simply read the numbers and insert **Uhr** between the hour and minutes: 10.30 reads 10 Uhr 30 (zehn Uhr dreißig); 8.45 reads 8 Uhr 45 (acht Uhr fünfundvierzig).

Look at the class schedule. How many different subjects do Heiko and Katja have, and when do they have them? How does this compare to your class schedule?

German schools are also different in that Heiko, Katja, and their classmates stay together for all their classes and, for the most part, in the same classroom. The teachers move from room to room.

What do you think the word **Pause** means, judging by the time alloted for it? Where do you think German students eat lunch? Like you and your friends, students in German-speaking countries have some activities after school: school-sponsored sports, clubs, and social activities. There are, however, fewer such activities in Germany than in the United States.

## 7 Zum Schreiben: Dein Stundenplan

Now make your own class schedule in German. Here are some other subjects you may need to complete your schedule. Turn to page 322 for additional vocabulary.

**Und dann noch ...**

Spanisch, Französisch, Chemie, Chor, Algebra, Informatik, Orchester, Werken, Sozialkunde, Technik, Hauswirtschaft

## SO SAGT MAN DAS!

### Talking about class schedules

If you want to discuss class schedules with your friends, you might ask:

You might get the responses:

**Welche Fächer hast du?**
**Was hast du am Donnerstag?**
**Was hat die Katja am Donnerstag?**

Ich habe Mathe, Bio, Kunst ...
Deutsch, Englisch und Sport.

Sie hat Physik, Bio, Englisch und Latein.

**Julia, Bernd, welche Fächer habt ihr heute nach der Pause?**
**Und was habt ihr am Samstag?**

Wir haben Mathe und Musik.
Wir haben frei!

The word **Fächer** used above means *subjects.* What do you think the equivalent of **welche** is?[1] Could you use **welche** in the second, third and fifth questions? The word **am** always precedes the days of the week. What do you think this word means?[2] With what other time expressions have you already used **am**?[3]

## 8 Welche Fächer hast du?

Using the schedule you created in Activity 7, tell your classmates which subjects you have and when you have them.

1. *which*  2. here: *on*  3. **am Wochenende, am Abend, am Nachmittag**

# 9 Hör gut zu!

Listen carefully as Michael asks his classmates when they have various classes. Match the subjects below with the days of the week in the box to the right.

| a. Bio | b. Musik | c. Kunst | d. Mathe | e. Geschichte |
|---|---|---|---|---|
| am Freitag | am Dienstag | am Mittwoch | am Donnerstag | am Freitag |

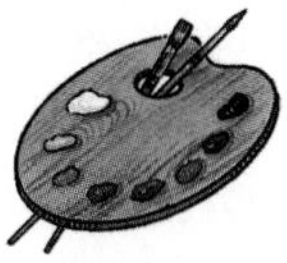

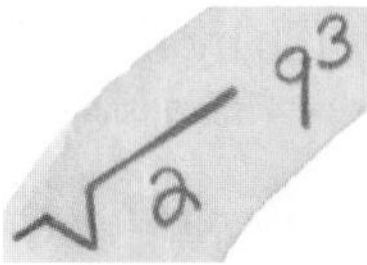

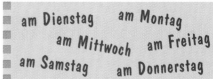
am Dienstag    am Montag
am Mittwoch    am Freitag
am Samstag    am Donnerstag

| f. Erdkunde | g. Sport | h. Deutsch |
|---|---|---|
| am Montag | am Montag | am Dienstag |

## SO SAGT MAN DAS!

### Using a schedule to talk about time

It's the first day of school, and you are curious about when your friends have their classes.

You might ask:

**Wann hast du Erdkunde?**
**Was hast du um 11 Uhr 20?**
**Was hast du von 8 Uhr 45 bis 9 Uhr 30?**
**Und wann hast du Kunst?**

You might get the responses:

**Um 11 Uhr 20.**
**Erdkunde.**

**Ich habe Bio.**
**Um 10 Uhr 30, nach der Pause.**

What do you think **wann** means?[1] How do you answer a question that starts with **wann**?[2] How is the answer to this question different from the answers to questions that begin with **was**? What is the English equivalent of **um**?[3]

## EIN WENIG LANDESKUNDE

Do any of the times in Heiko's and Katja's schedule look unusual to you? When does their last class end? Schedules like this one, and other official schedules, like the train schedule to the right, are based on the 24-hour system of telling time. This system starts immediately after midnight (**00.01 Uhr**) and ends at midnight (**24.00 Uhr**). What time would correspond to 2 P.M.? to 3 P.M? to 8:30 P.M.? What time would you have to board the train in order to get to **Köln**? **Mannheim**?

14.49
15.49

15.49

1. *when* 2. with a time expression 3. here: *at*

### Bochum → München
Hauptbahnhof          Hauptbahnhof

**Preis pro Person in DM. Einfache Fahrt.**
\* Bei Benutzung von EC/IC 6,- DM Zuschlag.
Mögliche Fahrpreisermäßigungen siehe Kapitel „So günstig fahren Sie Bahn".

| ab | Zug | Umsteigen | an | Verkehrstage | Fahrpreis 1. Kl. Fahrpreis 2. Kl. Bemerkungen |
|---|---|---|---|---|---|
| 14.49 | IC 823 | Köln IC Stuttgart EC | 22.11 | 1234567 | |
| 14.49 | IC 823 | Würzburg D | 22.29 | 1234567 | |
| 14.59 | S | Duisburg IC Stuttgart EC | 22.11 | 12345-- | an Werktagen nicht 24., 31. 12. |
| 15.23 | IR 2553 | Kassel-Wilh. ICE | 22.06 | 1234567 | |
| 15.49 | IC 523 | Köln IC Mannheim ICE | 22.17 | 1234567 | |
| 15.49 | IC 523 | Köln IC Karlsruhe IR | 23.40 | 1234567 | |
| 16.22 | IC 517 | | 23.11 | 12345-7 | nicht 24, 12, -2. 1., 9,- 11.4. |
| 16.49 | IC 603 | Mannheim ICE | 23.17 | ------7 | auch 12. 4., nicht 11.4. |

## 10 Hör gut zu!

Listen carefully as Klaus, a friend of Sonja's, talks about the busy schedule he has on Wednesdays. Copy the names of the following subjects onto a piece of paper, then complete his schedule by filling in the times as you hear them.

Mathe    Latein    Englisch    Deutsch    Geschichte    Erdkunde

Mathe 8:00; Deutsch 8:45; Englisch 9:45; Latein 10:30; Geschichte 11:30; Erdkunde 12:20-13:05

## 11 Wann hast du Deutsch?

Working in small groups, take turns asking each other which subjects each of you has and at what times during the day. Remember, you do not need to answer in complete sentences. Sometimes just a phrase will do:

BEISPIEL    PARTNER    **Wann hast du Englisch?**
            DU    **Um 10 Uhr.**    *oder*    **Um 10.**

---

*Grammatik*    The verb **haben**, present tense

Look at the conversation below:

SONJA    **Was hat Katja nach der Pause?**
BEATE    **Sie hat Bio. Und was hast du?**
SONJA    **Ich habe Deutsch.**

What do you notice about **haben** that is different from verbs like **spielen** or **wohnen**?[1] Here are the forms of the verb **haben** (*to have*) in the present tense:

| | | | |
|---|---|---|---|
| Ich | **habe** Mathe. | Wir | **haben** Kunst. |
| Du | **hast** Deutsch. | Ihr | **habt** Geschichte. |
| Er/Sie | **hat** Bio. | Sie (pl) / Sie | **haben** Latein. |

---

## 12 Was sagen die Schüler im Schulhof?

a.

Several students in the **Schulhof** are talking about their schedules. Look at these drawings carefully, and match each conversation with one of the drawings.

1. —Haben Monika und Berndt jetzt Englisch? / Nein, sie haben jetzt Musik.  d
2. —Wann hast du Deutsch? / Nach der Pause.  b
3. —Wann hat Sabine Kunst? / Um 12.  c
4. —Wann habt ihr Physik? / Am Dienstag.  a

b.

c.

d.

1. **haben** is irregular in the **du-** and **er/sie**-forms: **du hast, er/sie hat**

## 13 Ein Interview

a. Prepare a list of questions for your partner in order to find out exactly what his or her schedule is for the semester (which classes he or she has, the times of the classes).

b. Now interview your partner using your list of questions and, as you interview, fill out his or her schedule on another piece of paper. Then your partner will interview you. Compare schedules to see if both of you understood everything correctly.

c. Be prepared to report the information you obtained back to the class.

| Deutsch | 8.05 |
| Geschichte | 8.55 |
| Latein | 9.45 |
| Sport | 10.30 |

### SO SAGT MAN DAS!
#### Sequencing events

You might want to know the order in which your friends have their classes on a certain day.

You might ask:

**Welche Fächer hast du am Freitag?**

If your friend had the schedule above he or she would answer:

**Zuerst hab' ich Deutsch, dann Geschichte, danach Latein, und zuletzt hab' ich Sport.**

What do the words **zuerst, dann, danach,** and **zuletzt** mean?[1]

## 14 Was hast du am Mittwoch?

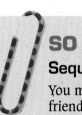

Heiko asks Sonja which classes she has on Wednesday. Working with a partner, put these questions and answers in the appropriate order. Then, together with your partner, read the conversation out loud.

HEIKO   Sonja, was hast du zuerst am Mittwoch?

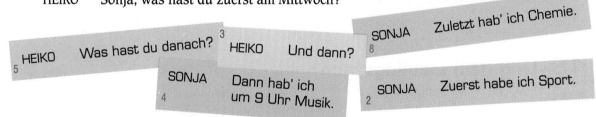

7 HEIKO   Und zuletzt?

6 SONJA   Danach hab' ich Deutsch um 10 und dann Kunst.

SONJA   Zuletzt hab' ich Chemie. 8

5 HEIKO   Was hast du danach? 3 HEIKO   Und dann?

4 SONJA   Dann hab' ich um 9 Uhr Musik.

2 SONJA   Zuerst habe ich Sport.

## 15 Was hast du zuerst? Und zuletzt?

Using the sequencing words **zuerst, dann, danach,** and **zuletzt,** tell your classmates the order in which you have your classes on Monday. You can use **dann** and **danach** several times if you have more than four classes.

## 16 Zum Schreiben

Write a short paragraph describing what you do on a typical Saturday, using some of the activities you learned in **Kapitel 2,** for example, **Tennis spielen, Freunde besuchen,** or **Hausaufgaben machen.** In your description, use the sequencing words you have learned (**zuerst, dann, danach,** and **zuletzt**).

1. *first, then, after that, last of all*

*Expressing likes, dislikes, and favorites; responding to good news and bad news*

## SO SAGT MAN DAS!

### Expressing likes, dislikes, and favorites

In **Kapitel** 2 you learned to say which activities you like and don't like to do using **gern** and **nicht gern**. You might also want to talk about which classes you like and don't like, and which is your favorite.

Your friend might ask you:

**Welche Fächer hast du gern?**
**Was hast du nicht so gern?**
**Und was ist dein Lieblingsfach?**

You might respond:

**Ich habe Kunst und Englisch gern.**
**Chemie.**
**Deutsch, ganz klar!**

## 17 Hör gut zu!

gern: Musik, Latein, Deutsch
nicht gern: Englisch, Kunst, Mathe
Lieblingsfächer: Geschichte, Erdkunde

Listen as Katja describes to Rainer the subjects she is taking. Write down which subjects Katja likes, dislikes, and considers her favorite subjects.

| gern | nicht gern | Lieblingsfächer |
|------|-----------|-----------------|
|      |           |                 |

### Ein wenig Grammatik

**Lieblings-** is a prefix that can be used with many different nouns to indicate favorites. Can you guess what these words mean: **Lieblingsbuch, Lieblings-instrument**, and **Lieblingsfilm**?

## 18 Und dein Lieblingsfach?

Find out which subjects your partner likes and dislikes, and his or her favorite subject. Create a chart like the one you filled out for Activity 17. Using the chart, report the information about your partner back to the class. Remember to use **sein** or **ihr** when you are reporting about your partner's **Lieblingsfach**.

## 19 Trends: Eine Umfrage

Working in small groups, conduct a survey about some of the things teenagers like best. Each member of the group asks two students at least three questions. Use topics from the box to prepare the questions. When you have finished the interviews, prepare a summary in chart form.

Lieblingsbuch     Lieblingsrockgruppe     Lieblingsauto     Lieblingssänger
Lieblingsmusik     Lieblingsfilm     Lieblingslehrer     Lieblingsfarbe

# Zeugnis

für _Michael Hauser_ , Klasse _8b_

geboren am _7. 6. 1978_

Allgemeine Beurteilung: _Muß sich in Latein u. Mathe verbessern!_

Deutsch ..................................... _3_
   mündlich ......... _4_ schriftlich ....... _4_

Geschichte/Sozialkunde ...................... _2_
   Geschichte ......... _2_ Sozialkd ......... _2_

Erdkunde ...................................... _2_

1. Fremdsprache: _Englisch_ _1_
   mündlich ........... _1_ schriftlich ....... _1_

2. Fremdsprache: _Latein_ _5_
   mündlich ........... _5_ schriftlich ....... _5_

**Wahlpflichtfach**

3. Fremdsprache: _Französisch_ _2+_
   mündlich ........... _1_ schriftlich ....... _2_

**Freiwillige Unterrichtsveranstaltungen**

Mathematik ................................ _4_
Physik ..................................... _2_
Chemie ..................................... _2_
Biologie ................................... _3_
Musik ...................................... _1_
Bildende Kunst/
   Bildende Ku...
Sport ......................................

---

befriedigend (*satisfactory*)

sehr gut (*excellent*)

ungenügend (*failing*)

gut (*good*)

ausreichend (*just passing*)

mangelhaft (*unsatisfactory*)

---

## EIN WENIG LANDESKUNDE

Look at Michael's report card. What grades (the numbers) did he get in **Mathe, Erdkunde, Deutsch,** and **Latein?**   4, 2, 3, 5

He was very happy about his geography grade, not too disappointed with the grade in German, very worried about his math grade, and afraid to show his Latin grade to his parents. With this information, can you figure out how the German grading system, which is based on the numbers 1-6 rather than on letters, works? Which numbers go with which descriptions?

---

## 20 Hör gut zu!

Listen as Sonja talks about the grades she received on her last report card. First write down the subjects she mentions in the order you hear them. Then listen again and fill in the **Note** (*grade*) she got for each subject. In which subjects did Sonja do well? In which subjects did she not do so well? Then answer the following questions in German.

1. In which subject did she get the best grade? And the worst?  Mathe; Englisch
2. In which subject did Sonja receive a "satisfactory" grade?  Erdkunde
3. Judging by her grades, which subject do you think Sonja enjoys the most?  Mathe
4. In which subject do you think Sonja needs to study more?  Englisch

## SO SAGT MAN DAS!

### Responding to good news and bad news

You will often want to respond to your friends' good news and bad news. Katja is asking Heiko about his grades. Notice her responses to his answers.

| She asks: | Heiko answers: | Katja responds: |
| --- | --- | --- |
| **Was hast du in Musik?** | **Eine Eins.** | **Toll! Das ist prima!** |
| **In Physik?** | **Eine Drei.** | **Nicht schlecht.** |
| **Und in Englisch?** | **Ich habe bloß eine Vier.** | **Schade! So ein Pech!** |
| **Und Mathe?** | **Eine Fünf.** | **Schade!** |
| | | **Das ist sehr schlecht!** |

Heiko was probably hoping for a better grade in English. What do you think he means by **bloß eine Vier?**[1]

## 21 Logisch oder unlogisch?

Read what these students say about their grades. Does the response in each case make sense? If so, answer **Das ist logisch**, if not, answer **Das ist unlogisch**, and try to think of a response that is more appropriate.

**Degrees of Enthusiasm**

Spitze!
Super!
Toll!
Prima!
Das ist gut!
Nicht schlecht!

---

Schade!
So ein Pech!
Das ist schlecht!
So ein Mist!

1. —Ich habe eine Fünf in Latein!
   —Toll! Das ist gut! _unlogisch_
2. —Du hast eine Vier in Mathe?
   —Ja, das ist blöd, nicht? _logisch_
3. —Englisch ist mein Lieblingsfach. Ich habe eine Zwei.
   —Super! Das ist wirklich gut! _logisch_
4. —In Erdkunde habe ich eine Drei.
   —Hm, nicht schlecht! _logisch_
5. —Und in Deutsch habe ich eine Eins!
   —Ach wie blöd! So ein Pech! _unlogisch_

## 22 Dein Zeugnis

a. Imagine that you are an exchange student in Wedel and have just received your report card for the semester. Design and fill out a German report card for yourself. Write all your subjects and give yourself a grade according to the German grading system.

b. With your report card in hand, have a conversation with a classmate, asking your partner which grades he or she has in various subjects, responding appropriately, and telling him or her about your classes and grades. Use the phrases above in your responses.

## 23 Für mein Notizbuch

Schreib ein paar Sätze über dich und deine Schule! Welche Fächer hast du? Welche Fächer hast du gern? Welche Fächer hast du nicht gern? Was ist dein Lieblingsfach? In welchen Fächern sind deine Noten gut? In welchen sind die Noten nicht so gut?

1. _only a four_ (**ausreichend**)

# Was sind deine Lieblingsfächer?

We asked several teenagers in German-speaking countries what school subjects they have and which ones they like and don't like. Before you read the interviews, make a list of your classes and indicate which ones are your favorites and which ones you don't like very much.

### Jasmin, *München*

„Ich hab' Arbeitslehre — als Lieblingsfach, und Kunst und Mathe mag ich gar nicht; Physik mag ich auch nicht so gerne. Und sonst Sport mag ich noch und dann Englisch, das mag ich auch — das ist auch mein Lieblingsfach, weil ich sehr gern Englisch lernen will."

### Dirk, *Hamburg*

„Ich bin eigentlich genau das Gegenteil von Michael, weil ich ja auch total auf Sprachen basier'. Ich hab' Englisch als Leistungskurs, Spanisch und Französisch hab' ich gehabt. Ich will ja auch mit Sprachen mal was machen, Diplomatie oder so. Mal seh'n!"

### Michael, *Hamburg*

„Ich interessiere mich hauptsächlich für Mathe und Physik und Kunst, also weil ich Architekt werden will. Chemie mag ich überhaupt nicht. Also ich glaube, es ist auch wichtig. Sonst komm' ich mit den meisten Fächern zurecht."

### Lugana, *Bietigheim*

„Okay, ich heiße Lugana, bin Griechin und hier geboren. Bin sechzehn Jahre alt, gehe aufs Ellental-Gymnasium, und Lieblingsfächer sind Englisch und Deutsch."

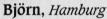

### Björn, *Hamburg*

„In der Schule mag ich am liebsten Physik, Mathematik und Informatik — das ist mit Computern. Das kommt, weil ... ich bin gut in Mathe. Ich arbeite gern an Computern, und ich mag Physik ganz gerne, weil mich die Themen einfach interessieren."

A. 1. What subjects do these teenagers like and dislike? Make a grid.
   2. Which of these teenagers likes the same subjects you do? What are these subjects?
   3. Several of these teenagers give reasons why they like certain subjects. Work with a partner and decide what these reasons are.
   4. Look at the list you made. Try to think of reasons why you like the subjects you indicated. What do your opinions have to do with your future career plans?

B. Do you think teenagers in German-speaking countries start thinking about their future careers earlier than teenagers in the United States do? What can you find in the interviews to support your answer? Discuss the topic with your classmates and then write a brief essay on this question.

## WORTSCHATZ

### Was kosten die Schulsachen im Schul-Shop?

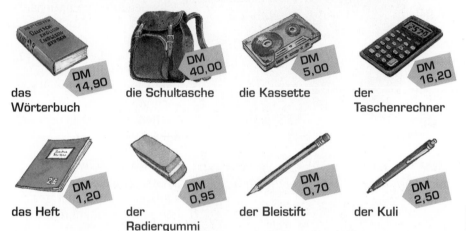

das **Wörterbuch** — DM 14,90

die **Schultasche** — DM 40,00

die **Kassette** — DM 5,00

der **Taschenrechner** — DM 16,20

das **Heft** — DM 1,20

der **Radiergummi** — DM 0,95

der **Bleistift** — DM 0,70

der **Kuli** — DM 2,50

### ACHTUNG SCHULANFAN

Jetzt kaufen — in Ruhe auswä

Unser Schul-Spezial-Angebot
reduzierten Preisen

| | | | jetzt |
|---|---|---|---|
| Bleistifte, 12 Stück | bisher DM | 9,60 | 8, |
| Hefte | bisher DM | 1,60 | 1,2 |
| Kulis, alle Farben | bisher DM | 3,20 | 2,5 |
| Jeans-Taschen | bisher DM | 49,00 | 40, |
| Taschenrechner | bisher DM | 19,50 | 16,2 |
| Stundenpläne | bisher DM | 1,60 | 1,3 |
| Kassetten, 3 Stück | bisher DM | 18,00 | 15,0 |
| Wörterbücher | bisher DM | 16,40 | 14,9 |

**Wo? Im Schul-Shop**

**KAUT-BULLING & CO.** G M & C O

Rolandstr. 30 22880 Wedel - Telefon 04-1

Notice the prices that Germans pay for school supplies. How does this compare with the prices you would pay? How many of each of these supplies do you have with you right now in the classroom?

## 24 Im Schul-Shop

Compare the endings of the words in the school supplies ad with the words printed under each illustration. What do you observe? List the differences and compare your list with that of a classmate. Why do you think the words are written differently?

### *G*rammatik   Noun plurals

As you discovered in Activity 24, there are many different plural endings for German nouns. There is no one rule that tells you which nouns take which endings.

Every German dictionary includes the plural ending of a noun next to the main entry, which is the singular form. In the **Vocabulary** in this book begin-

das **Wort**, ⸚er *word*, 9*
das **Wörterbuch**, ⸚er *dictionary*, 4
der **Wortschatz** *vocabulary*, 1
die **Wortschatzübung**, -en *vocabulary exercise, practice*, 1
**wunderbar** *wonderful*, 11

ning on page 340, you will see entries like those above.

Look up the following words and write sentences using the plural forms of these words:

**der Stuhl, der Keks, die Kassette**

---

* ⸚**er** means that the plural form of **Wort** is **Wörter**.

## 25 Hör gut zu! b-d-a-c

Listen to this conversation between Johanna and Daniel in the stationery store. As you listen, put the four pictures in the correct sequence.

 a.
 b.
 c.
 d.

## SO SAGT MAN DAS!

### Talking about prices

If you and your friend are in a store, you might ask one another about the prices of various items.

You might ask:

**Was kostet der Taschenrechner?**
**Was kosten die Bleistifte?**

Your friend might respond:

**Er kostet nur 23 Mark.**
**Sie kosten 80 Pfennig.**

After you hear the price you might comment to your friend:

**Das ist (ziemlich) teuer!**       *That's (quite) expensive!*
**Das ist (sehr) billig!**          *That's (very) cheap!*
**Das ist (sehr) preiswert!**       *That's a (really) good deal!*

### EIN WENIG LANDESKUNDE

The unit of German currency is the **Deutsche Mark**. How is it abbreviated? How are these prices written differently than prices in the United States? One **Deutsche Mark** has one hundred **Pfennige**. DM 1,00 reads **eine Mark**. DM 0,80 reads **achtzig Pfennig**. DM 2,20 reads **zwei Mark zwanzig**. How would you read DM 1,50? DM 6,70? DM 24,00?

### Schon bekannt
### Ein wenig Grammatik

In **Kapitel 3** you learned that the pronouns **er, sie, es,** and **sie** (pl) can refer to objects: **Die Couch ist neu. Sie ist bequem.** When do you use each of these pronouns?[1]

1. **er** refers to masculine nouns, **sie** to feminine nouns, **es** to neuter nouns, **sie** (pl) to plural nouns.

## 26 Was kostet … ?

You are starting school and need to buy school supplies. You have DM 30,00 to spend. Make a list of the things you need to buy. Your partner is the **Verkäuferin** *(salesclerk)* at the store and will create a price list, using the items and prices in the **Wortschatz** box as cues. Ask your partner how much the items on your list cost, then figure out how much you must spend. Be sure to be polite!

## SO SAGT MAN DAS!

### Pointing things out

When you go to a store, you may need to ask the **Verkäuferin** where various items are located.

| You might ask: | The responses might be: |
|---|---|
| Entschuldigung, wo sind die Schultaschen? | Schauen Sie!* Dort drüben! |
| Und Taschenrechner? Wo finde ich sie? | Dort! |
| Und die Kulis auch? | Nein, sie sind dort drüben! |
| Wo sind bitte die Kassetten? | Kassetten sind da hinten. |
| Und dann noch Hefte. Wo sind die, bitte? | Die sind hier vorn. |

How would the salesperson tell you that the pencils are in the front of the store if he or she were also in the front of the store?[1]

*This is the polite form of **Schau!** that is used among friends. In a store, a salesperson would use the polite form **Schauen Sie!**

## 27 Im Schreibwarenladen

Heiko has asked the **Verkäuferin** where various school supplies are located and what they cost. Complete what the **Verkäuferin** says with the items pictured in the drawing. Be sure to use the correct endings for the plural (including umlauts). More than one answer may be possible.

1. Hefte
2. Taschenrechner
3. Bleistifte
4. Schultaschen
5. Wörterbücher
6. Kassetten
7. Kulis

Bitte, __1__ sind hier vorn. Sie kosten nur DM 2,75. __2__ sind dort drüben und kosten DM 21,00. Das ist sehr preiswert. Und __3__ sind hier vorn. Sie sind im Sonderangebot für nur DM 0,75. __4__ sind auch hier vorn, und __5__ sind da drüben, __6__ sind aber weit da hinten. Oh, und __7__ sind dort drüben. Sie kosten DM 2,95.

1. **Bleistifte sind hier vorn.**

## 28 Eine Werbung *Advertisement*

You are the owner of a store that sells school supplies and you are writing an advertisement to be read over the radio. Make up a name for your store, then pick five school supplies and write an ad describing them.

BEISPIEL **Wir haben Taschenrechner, sie kosten nur 19 Mark 95. Sehr preiswert, nicht? Und Bleistifte nur 85 Pfennig. Super! Die ...**

## 29 Wir brauchen Schulsachen *We need school supplies*

a. Get together with three other classmates and take turns reading the advertisements you wrote in Activity 28. While one person reads, the others will be "listening on the radio" and will write down the various school supplies they hear mentioned and the price of each.

b. Decide with your classmates which store your group will visit. Whoever's store is chosen will play the **Verkäufer** and should set up his or her store (or draw a floorplan). The others will play the customers. The three customers will make a list of all the things they need from the store.

c. Create a conversation between the **Verkäufer** and the customers in the store. The customers ask the **Verkäufer** questions about where the school supplies on their list are located and how much they cost in order to make sure they have heard the ad on the radio correctly. Role-play your scene before the class, using props.

---

**AUSSPRACHE**

## Richtig aussprechen / Richtig lesen

A. To practice the following sounds, say the words and sentences below after your teacher or after the recording.

1. The diphthongs **äu** and **eu**: The diphthongs **äu** and **eu** sound similiar to the *oy* sound in the English word *boy*.
**teuer, deutsch, Verkäufer / Der Verkäufer ist Deutscher.**

2. The diphthong **au**: The diphthong **au** is pronounced much like the *ow* sound in the English word *cow*.
**Pause, schauen, bauen / Ich schaue Fernsehen nach der Pause.**

3. The letters **b**, **d**, and **g**: At the end of a syllable or word, the consonants **b**, **d**, and **g** are pronounced as follows: the letter **b** sounds like the *p* in the English word *map*; the letter **d** is pronounced like the letter *t* in the English word *mat*; and the letter **g** is pronounced like the *k* sound in the English word *make*.
**Liebling, gelb, schreib / Schreib dein Lieblingsfach auf!**
**Rad, Geld, blöd / Ich finde Radfahren blöd.**
**Sag, Montag, Tag / Sag mal, hast du am Montag und Freitag Physik?**

## Richtig schreiben / Diktat

B. Write down the sentences that you hear.

## Institut Rosenberg

Eine der führenden Schweizer Internatsschulen für Mädchen und Jungen seit 1889

# Abitur

Deutsches Abitur im Hause
Vorbereitung für Eidgenössische Maturitätsprüfungen
Vobereitung für das Studium in England und in den USA
Maturità Italiana

Privatunterricht gewährleistet • Überwachtes Studium
Internationale Atmosphäre

### Sportarten:

Tennis • Wasserski • Reiten • Skifahren • Basketball • Volleyball etc.

Auskunft: O. Gademann

Institut Rosenberg • Höhenweg 60 • CH-9000 St.Gallen
Tel. 004171-27 77 77  Fax 004171-27 98 27

**LESETRICK**

**Understanding Compound Words** German has many compound words. Often at least one part of a compound word is a cognate that you will recognize from English. Figuring out the meaning of individual words within a compound will often help you determine the meaning of the entire word.

1. Look at the following words and try to determine what they might mean by looking at the cognates within the compounds. You do not have to know the exact meaning of the compound word, but you can probably come close to figuring it out. For example, you can see that the word **Gesangunterricht** (abbreviated **Gesangunterr.** in the ad) has something to do with singing.
   a. **Keyboardschule** ═══
   b. **Deutschkurse** ═══
   c. **Privatunterricht** ═══
   d. **Volksschule** ═══
   e. **Schulverbund** ═══

2. Work with a partner. Write down the kinds of information you would be looking for if you were looking in the classified ads for a tutor in English.

## SCHULVERBUND PASSAU
### Regensburger Straße 8, 94036 Passau, Tel. 0 851/23 26 71

**—staatlich anerkannt—**

**DONAU-GYMNASIUM**     Seit Sept. '93 zusätzlicher Schulzweig: SPORTGYMNASIUM

**DONAU-REALSCHULE**     Klassen 5-10 (Eintritt nach der 4. Klasse der Volksschule)

**WIRTSCHAFTSSCHULE**     Klassen 7-10 (berufsorientiert)

Passau
**DONAU-VOLKSSCHULE**     Teilhauptschule II, Klassen 7-9

Diese staatlich genehmigten Schulen bieten Schülern eine individuelle, differenzierte Beurteilung und Förderung.
Es gibt keinen Probeunterricht.Während der Probezeit wird die Eignung der Schüler individuell beurteilt.
Die in den letzten 25 Jahren erzielten überdurchschnittlichen Prüfungserfolge bestätigen unser Konzept.

**MAYER-GYMNASIUM**
**MAYER-REALSCHULE**
**DONAU-VOLKSSCHULE**
Klassen 1-4/Teilhauptschule I
Klassen 5+6 angeschl. Kindergarten
**Einschreibung jederzeit möglich!**

**Ganztagsschulen mit Mittagstisch**

Gesangunterr. u. Harmonielehre
☎ (0451) 57328

Dipl.-Physikerin für Mathe, Physik, Chemie
☎ (0451) 13566

Klavier- u. Keyboardschule Müller,
Fachlehrer
☎ 89678

Deutschkurse für Ausländer Probestunde kostenlos, kleine Gruppen, 68 Stunden, DM 500,-
☎ 98105 u. 98287.

Amerikaner erteilt qualifizierten Englischunterricht für Anfänger und Fortgeschrittene. Auch Übersetzungen.
☎ 98120 ab 13 Uhr

3. Scan the ads for the following information:
   a. the telephone number you would call if you wanted singing lessons
   b. what the American wants to tutor
   c. the address of the **Schulverbund Passau**

4. Read the ads and answer the questions about each ad.
   a. Who might be interested in the programs offered by the **Schulverbund?**
   b. Can students eat at the schools in the **Schulverbund?** What tells you this information? Why would they need to?
   c. What new branch of the **Donau-Gymnasium** has been operating since September 1993?
   d. How much does the German course for foreigners cost? How much does a trial class period cost? How long is the course?

   e. In what country is the **Institut Rosenberg** located? Is it a girls' school? What might it prepare you for? Switerzland; no-coed; university studies

5. Write some notes that you could use if you wanted to obtain more information from the school that offers German classes to foreigners. You might want to ask, for example, when and where the class meets.

6. With a partner write a short ad to offer tutoring in whatever you do best. It may be an academic class or a skills-oriented class. Use the classified ads on this page as your model.

7. You are going to be an exchange student in Germany. Which one of these schools would you like to attend. Why? Discuss this with a partner.

3a. 0451-57328   3b. English   3c. **Regensburger Straße 8, 94036 Passau**   4a. students who want an individualized/ alternative program   4b. yes; "**Mittagstisch**"; school lasts all day: "**Ganztagsschulen**   4c. Sportgymnasium 4d. 500 DM; free; 68 instruction hours

# ANWENDUNG

1 Working in small groups, use the ad on page 106 for clues to make up price tags in German for various school supplies in the classroom. Put the tags on the appropriate objects and arrange them as in a store window or as in a store. Now take turns role-playing customer and salesclerk, asking how much things cost and where they are located.

2 What do the items below tell you about the student, Claudia Müller? Use them to answer the questions that follow.

| ZEIT | MONTAG | DIENSTAG | MITTWOCH | DONNERSTAG | FREITAG | SAMSTAG |
|---|---|---|---|---|---|---|
| 7:50 - 8:35 Uhr | Geschichte | Deutsch | Mathe | Deutsch | Latein | frei |
| 8:45 - 9:30 Uhr | Sport | Französisch | Latein | Biologie | Physik | |
| 9:45 - 10:30 Uhr | Mathe | Erdkunde | Deutsch | Mathe | Mathe | |
| 10:40 - 11:25 Uhr | Latein | Kunst | Geschichte | Englisch | Deutsch | |
| 11:40 - 12:25 Uhr | Bio | Kunst | Sport | Sport | Englisch | |
| 12:30 - 13:45 Uhr | Englisch | Physik | Chemie | | Chemie | |

1. Luise-Schmitt-Gymnasium
2. mit dem Bus
3. ja
4. gut (2)
5. Montag 9:45-10:30, Mittwoch 7:50-8:35, Donnerstag 9:45-10:30, Freitag 9:45-10:30

**2+**

BIOLOGIE
Klassenarbeiten

## STADTBUS
### SCHÜLERAUSWEIS

NAME ___Claudia Müller___

GEBURTSDATUM ___7.1.1980___

GÜLTIG VON ___15.9.94___ BIS ___30.6.95___

*Claudia Müller*
UNTERSCHRIFT DES SCHÜLERS

## *Luise-Schmitt-Gymnasium*

### ZEUGNIS

für *Claudia Müller* geb am *7.1.1980*

Schuljahr 19 *94*, *95* Klasse *9 B* *1* Halbjahr

#### LEISTUNGEN
Pflichtunterricht

| | | | | |
|---|---|---|---|---|
| Geschichte.... | *gut* | | Deutsch.......... | *gut* |
| Mathe.......... | *sehr gut* | | Latein............ | *befriedigend* |
| Sport.......... | *befriedigend* | | Französisch... | *sehr gut* |
| Biologie.......... | *gut* | | Physik............ | *gut* |
| Erdkunde..... | *gut* | | Kunst............ | *sehr gut* |
| Englisch........ | *sehr gut* | | Chemie.......... | *ausreichend* |

1. Wie heißt Claudias Schule?
2. Wie kommt Claudia zur Schule?
3. Sind Claudias Noten gut?
4. Welche Note hat sie in Bio?
5. Wann hat sie Mathe?

3 Look at the items in the preceding activity again.
Use the information to write five German sentences about Claudia.

4  Create an activity calendar for yourself in German for the coming Saturday. Include all the things you would like to do and the times you expect to do them. Then, working with a partner, imagine that you ran into him or her after school and are talking about your plans for the weekend. Use the sequencing words **zuerst, dann, danach,** and **zuletzt.** Try to find a time when you are both free and make plans to do something together.

5  Look at the two drawings below. What items can you name in the drawing on the left? What items are missing in the drawing on the right?

BEISPIEL   **Die Bleistifte fehlen**.   *oder*   **Das Heft fehlt**. Die Kassetten, Notizbuch, Bleistifte fehlen.

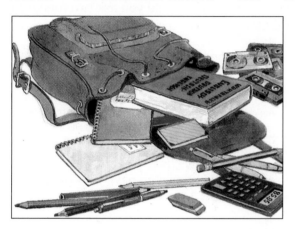
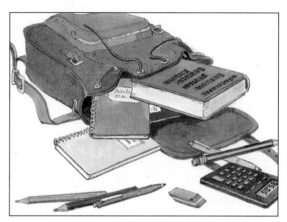

6  Write a letter to your pen pal and tell him or her about school. Write about which classes you have and when, which classes you like or do not like, and which are your favorites. Then write something about how you are doing in various subjects so far.

7  On the first day of school your German teacher is telling you what school supplies you will need. Write them as you hear them mentioned.
Wörterbuch, Bleistifte, Kuli, Hefte, Kassette

8

# R O L L E N S P I E L

With your school supply list from Activity 7 in hand, you go to the school supply store where you run into two friends. Develop a conversation with your two friends and role-play it in front of the class. Make sure to include

a. which classes you have and when

b. which classes you like, dislike and your favorite class

c. grades in some of your classes (make sure your friends respond appropriately)

After your conversation, ask the salesperson where various school supplies are located and what they cost.

**Can you talk about schedules using haben?** (p. 98)

**1** How would you say the following in German: a. Ulrike hat am Mittwoch und Freitag Deut▮

   **a.** Ulrike has German on Wednesday and Friday.
   **b.** Monika and Klaus have history on Tuesday and Thursday.
   **c.** Richard has no classes on Saturday.    b. Monika und Klaus haben am Dienstag und
   c. Richard hat am Samstag frei.     Donnerstag Geschichte.

**2** How would you ask a friend what classes he or she has on Monday? How might he or she respond? How would you ask two friends? How might they respond if they both have the same schedule?

Was hast du am Montag? Ich habe … Was habt ihr am Montag? Wir haben …

**Can you use a schedule to talk about time?** (p. 99)

**3** Say when these people have these classes.

| | | | |
|---|---|---|---|
| **a.** | Martin | 8.30 | Mathe |
| **b.** | Claudia und Ingrid | 9.45 | Latein |
| **c.** | Heiko | 10.20 | Musik |
| **d.** | Michaela und Manfred | 3.00 | Kunst |

a. Martin hat um 8 Uhr 30 Mathe.
b. Claudia und Ingrid haben um 9 Uhr 45 Latein.
c. Heiko hat um 10 Uhr 20 Musik.
d. Michaela und Manfred haben um 3 Uhr Kunst.

**4** How would you tell someone what time you have your German class, using the expression **von … bis** …?   Ich habe von 8 Uhr bis 8 Uhr 45 Deutsch.

**Can you sequence events using zuerst, dann, danach, and zuletzt?** (p. 101)

**5** How would you tell a classmate the sequence of your classes on Thursday?   Am Donnerstag habe ich zuerst …dann…danach…zuletzt

**Can you express likes, dislikes, and favorites?** (p. 102)

**6** How would you say which subjects you like, dislike, and which is your favorite? How would you ask your friend for the same information?   Ich habe … gern. Ich habe … nicht gern.
… ist mein Lieblingsfach.

Welche Fächer ▮ du gern? / nicht gern? / Was ist Lieblingsfach?

**Can you respond to good news and bad news?** (p. 104)

**7** How would you respond if Ahmet, an exchange student at your school, told you:

   **a.** Ich habe eine    **b.** Ich habe eine    **c.** Ich habe eine
      Eins in Bio.         Vier in Latein.       Zwei in Englisch.
      Toll!               So ein Pech!        Prima!

**Can you talk about prices?** (p. 107)

**8** How would you ask a salesperson how much these items cost: calculators, notebooks, erasers, pencils, pens, school bag, dictionaries, and cassettes?   Was kosten die Taschenrechner/ Hefte/ Radiergummis/ Bleistifte/ Kulis/ Schultaschen/ Wörterbücher/ Kassetten?

**9** How would you tell your friend what each of the following items costs? How might he or she comment on the prices?

a. Das Wörterbuch kostet 18 Mark. —Das ist preiswert.

   **a.** Wörterbuch    **b.** Kuli              **c.** Schultasche
      DM 18,00       DM 3,20           DM 24,00

b. Der Kuli kostet 3 Mark 20. — Das ist teuer!    c. Die Schultasche kostet 24 Mark. — Das ist sehr billig!

**Can you point things out?** (p. 108)

**10** Write a conversation in which your friend asks you where several things are located in a store. You point them out and give a general location. Then tell him or her how much they cost.

## ERSTE STUFE

### TALKING ABOUT CLASS SCHEDULES

die Schule, -n* *school*
haben *to have*
er/sie hat *he/she has*
die Klasse, -n *grade level*
der Stundenplan, ¨-e *class schedule*
die Zeit *time*
das Fach, ¨-er *(class) subject*
Welche Fächer hast du? *What (which) subjects do you have?*
Ich habe Deutsch ... *I have German...*
 Bio (Biologie) *biology*

Englisch *English*
 Erdkunde *geography*
 Geschichte *history*
 Kunst *art*
 Latein *Latin*
 Mathe (Mathematik) *math*
 Religion *religion*
 Sport *physical education*

### USING A SCHEDULE TO TALK ABOUT TIME

Wann? *when?*
um 8 Uhr *at 8 o'clock*
von 8 Uhr bis 8 Uhr 45 *from 8 until 8:45*

nach der Pause *after the break*
 am Montag *on Monday*
 Dienstag *Tuesday*
 Mittwoch *Wednesday*
 Donnerstag *Thursday*
 Freitag *Friday*
 Samstag *Saturday*
 Sonntag *Sunday*
Wir haben frei. *We are off (out of school).*

### SEQUENCING EVENTS

zuerst *first*
dann *then*
danach *after that*
zuletzt *last of all*

---

## ZWEITE STUFE

### EXPRESSING LIKES, DISLIKES, AND FAVORITES

gern haben *to like*
nicht gern haben *to dislike*
Lieblings- *favorite*

### GRADES

die Note, -n *grade*

eine Eins (Zwei, Drei, Vier, Fünf, Sechs) grades: *a 1 (2, 3, 4, 5, 6)*

### RESPONDING TO GOOD NEWS AND BAD NEWS

gut *good*
schlecht *bad*
Schade! *Too bad!*

So ein Pech! *Bad luck!*
So ein Mist! *That stinks!/What a mess!*
So ein Glück! *What luck!*

### OTHER WORDS AND PHRASES

Ganz klar! *Of Course!*
bloß *only*

---

## DRITTE STUFE

### SCHOOL SUPPLIES

Das ist/Das sind . . . *That is/Those are*
die Schulsachen (pl) *school supplies*
das Buch, ¨-er *book*
der Kuli, -s *ballpoint pen*
das Wörterbuch, ¨-er *dictionary*
die Schultasche, -n *schoolbag*
der Taschenrechner, - *pocket calculator*
der Radiergummi, -s *eraser*
der Bleistift, -e *pencil*
das Heft, -e *notebook*

die Kassette, -n *cassette*

### TALKING ABOUT PRICES

kosten *to cost*
Was kostet ... ? *How much does . . cost?*
Das ist preiswert. *That's a bargain.*
 billig *cheap*
 teuer *expensive*
das Geld *money*
DM = Deutsche Mark *German mark (German monetary unit)*
die Mark, - *mark*

der Pfennig, - *(smallest unit of German currency; 1/100 of a mark)*

### POINTING THINGS OUT

Schauen Sie! *Look!*
Schau! *Look!*
dort *there*
dort drüben *over there*
da vorn *up there in the front*
da hinten *there in the back*

### OTHER WORDS AND EXPRESSIONS

ziemlich *rather*

*Plural forms will be indicated in this way from now on.

# Kapitel 5: Klamotten kaufen *Chapter Overview*

| **Los geht's!** pp. 118-120 | Was ziehst du an? p. 118 | | | *Video Guide* |
|---|---|---|---|---|
| | **FUNCTIONS** | **GRAMMAR** | **CULTURE** | **RE-ENTRY** |
| **Erste Stufe** pp. 121-124 | Expressing wishes when shopping, *p. 122* | Definite and indefinite articles in the accusative case, *p. 123* | •**Ein wenig Landeskunde:** Exchange rates, *p. 122* •**Ein wenig Landeskunde:** German store hours, *p. 124* | •Numbers and prices, *p. 123* (from **Kapitel 1** and **4**) •Colors, *p. 124* (from **Kapitel 4**) •Pointing things out, *p. 124* (from **Kapitel 4**) |
| **Zweite Stufe** pp. 125-130 | •Commenting on and describing clothes, *p. 125* •Giving compliments and responding to them, *p. 127* | •The verb **gefallen**, *p. 125* •Direct object pronouns, *p. 128* | •**Ein wenig Landeskunde:** German clothing sizes, *p. 126* •**Landeskunde:** Welche Klamotten sind „in"? *p. 130* | •Expressing likes and dislikes, *p. 125* (from **Kapitel 2**) •Asking for and expressing opinions, *p. 129* (from **Kapitel 2**) |
| **Dritte Stufe** pp. 131-133 | •Talking about trying on clothes, *p. 131* | •Separable prefix verbs, *p. 131* •Stem-changing verbs **nehmen**, and **aussehen**, *p. 132* | | The verb **aussehen**, *p. 131* (from **Kapitel 3**) |
| **Aussprache** p. 133 | The short vowels **i**, **ä**, and **e**, the vowel **a**, and the letter combinations **sch**, **st**, **sp** | | | Diktat: *Textbook Audiocassette* 2 B |
| **Zum Lesen** pp. 134-135 | Kleider machen Leute! Reading Strategy: Using what you already know | | | |
| **Review** pp. 136-139 | •Anwendung, *p. 136* •Kann ich's wirklich? *p. 138* •Wortschatz, *p. 139* | | | |
| **Assessment Options** | **Stufe Quizzes** •*Chapter Resources,* Book 2    **Erste Stufe,** Quiz 5-1    **Zweite Stufe,** Quiz 5-2    **Dritte Stufe,** Quiz 5-3 •*Assessment Items, Audiocassette* 7 B | | **Kapitel 5 Chapter Test** •*Chapter Resources,* Book 2 •*Assessment Guide,* Speaking Test •*Assessment Items, Audiocassette* 7 B  **Test Generator, Kapitel 5** | |

| *Video Program* **OR** *Expanded Video Program*, Videocassette 2 | Textbook Audiocassette 3 A |
|---|---|

| **RESOURCES** Print | **RESOURCES** Audiovisual |
|---|---|
| | Textbook Audiocassette 3 A |
| *Practice and Activity Book* *Chapter Resources*, Book 2 &bull;Communicative Activity 5-1 &bull;Additional Listening Activity 5-1 . . . . . . . . . . . . . . &bull;Additional Listening Activity 5-2 . . . . . . . . . . . . . . &bull;Student Response Form &bull;Realia 5-1 &bull;Situation Card 5-1 &bull;Teaching Transparency Master 5-1 . . . . . . . . . . . . . &bull;Quiz 5-1 . . . . . . . . . . . . . . . . . . . . . . . . . . . . . . . | *Additional Listening Activities, Audiocassette* 9 B *Additional Listening Activities, Audiocassette* 9 B *Teaching Transparency* 5-1 *Assessment Items, Audiocassette* 7 B |
| | Textbook Audiocassette 3 A |
| *Practice and Activity Book* *Chapter Resources*, Book 2 &bull;Communicative Activity 5-2 &bull;Additional Listening Activities 5-3, 5-4 . . . . . . . . . . &bull;Student Response Form &bull;Realia 5-2 &bull;Situation Card 5-2 &bull;Teaching Transparency Master 5-2 . . . . . . . . . . . . . &bull;Quiz 5-2 . . . . . . . . . . . . . . . . . . . . . . . . . . . . . . . *Video Guide*. . . . . . . . . . . . . . . . . . . . . . . . . . . . . . . | *Additional Listening Activities, Audiocassette* 9 B *Teaching Transparency* 5-2 *Assessment Items, Audiocassette* 7 B *Video Program/Expanded Video Program*, Videocassette 2 |
| | Textbook Audiocassette 3 A |
| *Practice and Activity Book* *Chapter Resources*, Book 2 &bull;Additional Listening Activity 5-5 . . . . . . . . . . . . . . &bull;Additional Listening Activity 5-6 . . . . . . . . . . . . . . &bull;Student Response Form &bull;Realia 5-3 &bull;Situation Card 5-3 &bull;Quiz 5-3 . . . . . . . . . . . . . . . . . . . . . . . . . . . . . . . | *Additional Listening Activities, Audiocassette* 9 B *Additional Listening Activities, Audiocassette* 9 B *Assessment Items, Audiocassette* 7 B |
| | |
| | |
| *Video Guide*. . . . . . . . . . . . . . . . . . . . . . . . . . . . . . . | *Video Program/Expanded Video Program*, Videocassette 2 |

**Alternative Assessment**
&bull;Performance Assessment, *Teacher's Edition*
    **Erste Stufe**, p. 115 K
    **Zweite Stufe**, p. 115 M
    **Dritte Stufe**, p. 115 O

&bull;Portfolio Assessment
    Written: **Zweite Stufe**, Activity 22, *Pupils Edition*, p. 129, *Assessment Guide*
    Oral: **Dritte Stufe**, Activity 28, *Pupil's Edition*, p. 133, *Assessment Guide*
&bull;**Notizbuch**, *Pupil's Edition*, p. 133; *Practice and Activity Book*, p. 149

**CHAPTER OVERVIEW**

# Kapitel 5: Klamotten kaufen
# *Textbook Listening Activities Scripts*

## *E*rste Stufe
### Activity 6, *p. 121*

Ob flott oder elegant, es ist immer preiswert bei uns, Mode-Mania! Hier finden Sie wirklich alles! Für die Damen haben wir eine große Auswahl an Kleidern und Röcken. Und für den sportlichen Typ: flotte Jogging–Anzüge! Die Blusen aus Leinen und Baumwolle sind gerade im Sonderangebot. Und für ihn haben wir diese Woche auch tolle Sachen, sehr preiswert: schicke Gürtel, zum Beispiel, und bequeme Hemden und Hosen in allen Größen und Farben. Bei Mode-Mania gibt's fesche Sachen für die ganze Familie! Wir sind Montag bis Freitag immer von 10 bis 18 Uhr geöffnet und am Samstag von 10 bis um 14 Uhr. Kommen Sie doch mal vorbei!

### Activity 9, *p. 123*

1. — Was kostet denn der Gürtel, da?
   — Ja also der kostet nur DM 20,00. Sehr preiswert.

2. — Ich möchte den Pulli dort, aber lieber in Rot.
   — So einen Pulli möchte ich auch.

3. — Das T-Shirt kostet nur 10 Mark, nicht?
   — Ja, das T-Shirt ist billig, was?

4. — Du, schau mal! Die Boutique hat die Bluse in Blau.
   — Ehrlich? Die Bluse hat Gaby doch auch, oder nicht?

5. — Du, Sabine, wie findest du den Jogging–Anzug in Grau?
   — Ich finde den einfach toll!

6. — Brauchst du auch eine neue Jacke für den Winter?
   — Ja, eine neue Jacke, vielleicht in Blau, brauch' ich schon.

7. — Die Stiefel in Schwarz da kosten 200 Mark!
   — Wirklich? Die Stiefel sind zu teuer.

8. — Ich suche ein neues Hemd in Grau für meinen Vater, und du?
   — Ich suche ein Hemd in Grün für meinen Bruder.

## *Z*weite Stufe
### Activity 15, *p. 125*

1. Die Schuhe sehen echt blöd aus! Die sind total altmodisch!

2. Die Shorts finde ich ganz fesch! Sie passen gut zu meinem neuen T-Shirt.

3. Die Bluse sieht ja furchtbar aus. Sie gefällt mir wirklich nicht!

4. Hübscher Rock, nicht? So einen möchte ich auch gern haben.

5. Solche Jacken sind zur Zeit in Mode. Ich finde sie super!

### Activity 19, *p. 128*

1. — Der Jogging-Anzug ist total schick, aber etwas zu teuer.
   — Probier' ihn doch trotzdem mal an!

2. — Wie findest du den Rock, da?
   — Ich finde ihn schon schön, aber lieber in Blau!

3. — Ich möchte gern das T-Shirt in Hellgrün.
   — Ja, es ist schick!

4. — Das T-Shirt hier kostet nur 20 Mark.
   — Wirklich? Es ist aber sehr preiswert.

5. — Die Turnschuhe hier sind toll!
   — Ja, sie sind stark.

6. — Möchtest du den Pulli da in Schwarz?
   — Nein, ich möchte ihn wirklich nicht. Die Farbe mag ich einfach nicht.

7. — Wie findest du die Bluse da vorn?
   — Sie ist aber teuer!

# Dritte Stufe
## Activity 23, p. 131

1. VERKÄUFER Ja, stimmt, ... sie ist zwar etwas teuer, aber die Qualität is prima. Der Pulli ist aus Baumwolle. Er steht Ihnen wirklich ausgezeichnet!

   JÜRGEN Finden Sie wirklich?

2. VERKÄUFER Wie paßt denn der Schuh? Drückt er? Vorn haben Sie ja genug Platz.

   JÜRGEN Ja, er paßt eigentlich ganz gut. Welche Größe ist das?

   VERKÄUFER Das hier ist 40. Gefällt Ihnen die Farbe?

3. JÜRGEN Ist die Jeans im Sonderangebot? Ich find' die ja fesch. Gibt's die in meiner Größe?

   VERKÄUFER Einen Moment. Da muß ich mal nachschauen ... Ja, wir haben noch Jeans in Ihrer Größe. Und auch im Angebot, nur DM 45.

4. VERKÄUFER Was darf es noch sein?

   JÜRGEN Danke. Das ist alles. Ich möchte bitte zahlen.

   VERKÄUFER Die Schuhe, die Jacke und die Jeans ... das macht DM 175.

   JÜRGEN Bitte schön. Vielen Dank für Ihre Hilfe.

## Diktat, p. 133

You will hear a description of Katja's and Sonja's trip to a clothing store. First listen to what is said, then write the description.

Katja und Sonja gehen heute zu Mode–Mania. Sie brauchen neue Klamotten für die Fete bei Dieter am Samstag. Zuerst probiert Katja den Rock in Grün an. Er sieht aber scheußlich aus. Dann findet sie Jeans in Schwarz. Die sind wirklich fesch. Und Sonja? Sie findet eine Hose in Dunkelblau und einen Pulli in Weiß. Das paßt alles prima!

# Anwendung
## Activity 5, p. 137

1. Schade! Die Bluse gefällt mir so gut, aber sie ist einfach viel zu groß für mich!

2. Die Jacke gefällt mir schon, aber nicht in der Farbe. Haben Sie die Jacke vielleicht in Braun?

3. Was, 200 Mark? Die Jeans ist ja toll, aber sie ist ja viel zu teuer! So viel kann ich nicht für Jeans bezahlen.

4. Die Hose ist zu lang und auch ein bißchen zu weit. Die sitzt einfach nicht so gut. Haben Sie eine Größe kleiner?

5. Der Pulli in Dunkelgrün ist schick, nur ist das nicht meine Farbe. Meine Lieblingsfarbe ist Blau.

# Kapitel 5: Klamotten kaufen
## *Suggested Project*

*In this activity the class will create a German mail-order clothing catalog featuring teenage clothing. This project should be started after completion of the* **Zum Lesen** *part of this chapter. This project is designed to be carried out with the class divided into eight groups and each group working on one part of the catalog.*

## MATERIALS

✂ **Each group may need**
- *1 sheet of colored construction paper size 16"×20" or poster board*
- *glue*
- *old catalogs and magazines*
- *scissors*
- *colored markers*
- *black pens*

## SUGGESTED CATALOG SECTIONS

Front cover
Sportswear for boys
Sportswear for girls
Formal wear for boys
Formal wear for girls
Shoes
Accessories
Unisex sportswear

## SUGGESTED SEQUENCE

1. Assign groups, depending on the size of your class or number of topics.

2. Assign or allow students to choose the section that each group will work on.

3. Have each group gather materials from old catalogs and magazine ads. If students are not able to find a picture of a certain item but want to include it, they may draw the item.

4. Once they have gathered items, the groups should decide what they want to include in their two-page section of the catalog and make an outline.

5. Students must also prepare a short written description in German for each item in their section of the catalog, including fabric, colors, and sizes available. Each student is responsible for writing at least one of the descriptions. Students may refer to the text on p. 134-135 for helpful vocabulary.

6. Students in each group must proofread each other's descriptions for accuracy before beginning the final lay-out.

7. Have groups complete the assignment by designing their pages in the catalog. Items should be given a letter or number and the corresponding description should be placed near the item.

8. As an option, each group could have a presenter who introduces his or her group's line of clothing.

9. Before the pages are assembled, the class should vote on a name for the catalog and add the name to the front cover.

10. Finally, all pages should be numbered and assembled to resemble an actual catalog. The final product can be displayed on the bulletin board.

## GRADING THE PROJECT

Since the outcome of each section is based on group cooperation and effort, one grade could be given to all members of a group.

Suggested point distribution (total=100 points)

| | |
|---|---|
| Appearance of pages | 25 |
| Accurate descriptions/ correct language usage | 50 |
| Originality | 25 |

# Kapitel 5: Klamotten kaufen
# ♜ *Games*

## ZEICHNE BITTE . . .

*This is a good game to help students practice clothing vocabulary.*

**Procedure**  Divide the class into two teams. The first person from Team A asks a student from the other team to go to the board and draw the clothing item he or she names. Example: **Peter, zeichne bitte einen Gürtel!** The student at the board has a set time limit in which to draw the item. If his or her picture is the correct item, he or she scores a point for the team. If the student draws the wrong item, the team does not receive a point. In either case, players alternate drawing between teams. The team with the highest score at the end of the game wins.

**Family Link**  Students might want to play this game with their younger brothers and sisters. It would give students an opportunity to review the clothing vocabulary while introducing their siblings to the German language.

## WORTBÖGEN

*This game, in which students test their knowledge of vocabulary by identifying "hidden" words, can be played by individuals or in pairs.*

**Preparation**  In preparation for this game you should make several **Wortbögen** (such as the one shown below) using the vocabulary from the **Wortschatz** that you intend to review. Put four or five **Wortbögen** on one sheet of paper and make a copy for each student or pair.

**Procedure**  Give students a time limit for this game depending on how many words are in your **Bögen**. As soon as you give the signal, students try to find as many words as possible within a specific topic. (Examples: clothing, adjectives and separable prefix verbs) Tell students that words must be made up of consecutive letters, and some letters may be used in more than one word. The person or team that finds the most words wins.

**WEIT     HÜBSCH     SCHICK**

# Kapitel 5: Klamotten kaufen
# *Lesson Plans, pages 116-139*

## *U*sing the Chapter Opener,
*pp. 116-117*

### Motivating Activity

Take a survey of students' attitudes towards clothing. Ask students how important clothes are to them on a scale of 1-10. How much time do they spend on average deciding what to wear in the morning? Find out who in the music or entertainment industry dresses in a style they admire and who, in their opinion, dresses the worst.

### Teaching Suggestion

Ask your students to name the articles of clothing in the three pictures. What seems to be popular with girls? (vests)

### Thinking Critically

- **Comparing and Contrasting**   Ask students if they would find the types of clothing items on these pages in American stores. If so, which ones? Also, get students to look for other similarities or differences in the pictures. (Wooden hangers are shown in Picture 2. Most U.S. stores use plastic hangers.)

- **Analyzing**   Germans have a saying: **Kleider machen Leute.** *(Clothes make the person.)* Discuss this phrase with students. Do they agree or disagree?

### ▦ Multicultural Connection

Most countries in the world have some kind of national costume. These are clothes that do not change with fashion trends. Can students think of such costumes and the countries with which they are associated? (Examples: southern Germany and Austria - **Dirndl, Lederhosen;** Japan - kimono; Scotland - kilt **(Schottenröcke)**; Venezuela - liquiliqui; southern Ghana - etam; India - sari) Ask students when such traditional costumes are usually worn. (special occasions such as national holidays, parades, and other festivities)

### Thinking Critically

**Drawing Inferences**   Certain careers require a traditional outfit. Can students think of any reasons for this? (clergy, judges, physicians)

### Focusing on Outcomes

To get students to focus on the chapter objectives listed on p. 117, ask them to tell you when they usually like to go shopping for clothes and with whom they prefer to go. Have them describe a typical shopping trip. What happens from the time they enter a store until they finally buy an item? Then have students preview the learning outcomes listed on p. 117. **NOTE:** Each of these outcomes is modeled in the video and evaluated in **Kann ich's wirklich?** on p. 138.

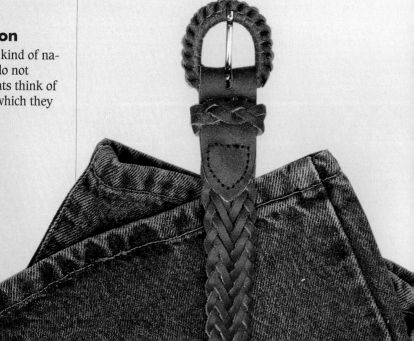

# Teaching Los geht's!
## pp. 118-120

### Resources for Los geht's!

- *Video Program* **OR**
  *Expanded Video Program,* Videocassette 2
- *Textbook Audiocassette* 3 A
- *Practice and Activity Book*

▶ **pages 118-119**

### Video Synopsis

In this segment of the video, Katja and Julia decide to go shopping to buy something to wear to Sonja's party. At **Sport-Kerner** Katja tries on some things and finally buys a T-shirt. The student outcomes listed on p. 117 are modeled in the video: expressing wishes when shopping, commenting on and describing clothes, giving compliments and responding to them, and talking about trying on clothes.

### Motivating Activity

As an advance organizer for the **Foto-Roman,** ask students how they dress when they are invited to a party.

### Teaching Suggestions

- Begin by doing the prereading activity at the top of p. 118.
- Let students scan these conversations for any cognates they might recognize. You could also provide some additional cognates to reinforce the similarities between the two languages. Examples: **der Hut, die Schuhe, die Socken, die Shorts**

### Total Physical Response

For students who might have trouble understanding the scenes, bring to class the clothing items that are part of the **Foto-Roman.** Teach the vocabulary to the class in a short TPR lesson. Ask some students to come to the front of the class, and give each of them commands such as **Zieh den Pulli an!** or **Zieh das T-Shirt an!** To help visual learners, you might want to show the vocabulary words on cards while students are trying on the articles of clothing.

### For Individual Needs

**Tactile Learners** Bring several items of clothing made of different materials, for example, a cotton shirt, a polyester scarf, a wool sweater, a silk blouse, and a rayon skirt. Let students touch and feel the items as you teach the different names of those materials. Extend the activity by asking: **Ist das** (pointing to the wool sweater) **aus Baumwolle?** Students should respond with **Ja** or **Nein.**

▶ **page 120**

### Teaching Suggestion

**3** To practice pronunciation, have students work in pairs and alternate reading the statements and responses. Monitor student activity as you walk around the class.

### Language Note

The word **die Fete** comes from the French word **la fête** *(party)*. The word **Klamotten** is a very casual word used to refer to one's belongings. It is mostly used for items of clothing.

**LOS GEHT'S!**

**ERSTE STUFE**

# 𝒯eaching Erste Stufe,
## pp. 121-124

### Resources for Erste Stufe

*Practice and Activity Book*
*Chapter Resources,* Book 2
- Communicative Activity 5-1
- Additional Listening Activities 5-1, 5-2
- Student Response Form
- Realia 5-1
- Situation Card 5-1
- Teaching Transparency Master 5-1
- Quiz 5-1

*Audiocassette Program*
- *Textbook Audiocassette* 3 A
- *Additional Listening Activities, Audiocassette* 9 B
- *Assessment Items, Audiocassette* 7 B

▶ *page 121*

## MOTIVATE

### ♜ Game

Have all students stand up by giving the command **Steht auf!** Begin with the first student in the front and ask him or her to name any German noun he or she can think of including its article. If the student says the word and article correctly, he or she remains standing. The next student says another noun (students can't use nouns that have already been named). If a student cannot think of a new noun, repeats a noun already used, or names a word that is not a noun, he or she must sit down. (Give the command **Setz dich!**) The last student standing wins the game.

## TEACH

### PRESENTATION: Wortschatz

Have a bag or a suitcase full of clothes and accessories that are part of the **Wortschatz.** Begin by naming the objects and showing them simultaneously. Then ask **ja/nein** questions followed by either/or questions, and finally, short response questions such as **Was ist das?**

## For Individual Needs

**6 Tactile Learners** As students listen to the cassette for the first time, ask them to sketch each article of clothing instead of writing the word. When they have finished drawing all seven items of clothing, ask students to name the items.

▶ *page 122*

## PRESENTATION: Ein wenig Landeskunde

- Ask for a volunteer to check the business section of the newspaper for three to five consecutive days. Have this student bring the exchange tables to class each day. Keep a record of the date and the daily exchange rate for the German mark and the U.S. dollar.

- **Synthesizing** Ask students if they know why the rates change daily. (Rates fluctuate as interest rates change in any given country. Interest rates are tied to everyday events that take place in the country or the world.)

- **Drawing Inferences** As students monitor the changing rates, ask them if they know of any significant events that are currently taking place in Germany or the United States that might be relevant to the fluctuation of the exchange rate.

- **Synthesizing** Ask students what events in the recent past have caused interest rates to go up and consequently increased the value of the mark. (Example: Germany borrowed money to finance German reunification.)

## PRESENTATION: So sagt man das!

- With a collection of clothing in a bag or suitcase, approach a student, tell him or her to imagine that you are a salesperson and ask: **Was möchten Sie? Einen Gürtel oder Jeans?** The student responds: **Ich möchte ...** and takes the appropriate item. Continue the activity, varying the expressions by using those listed in the function box.

- Now ask students to tell you in English what you asked them in the previous activity. Write down the different expressions students give you. Examples: *What would you like?* and *How can I help you?* Tell students that there are different ways of expressing wishes in German, just as there are in English. Point these out in the **So sagt man das!** box.

▶ *page 123*

## PRESENTATION: Grammatik

Since the concept of case is unfamiliar to many students you might want to begin by putting some sentences on the board. Help students identify each part of the sentence. Example: **Die Frau kauft die Bluse. Er möchte das T-Shirt.** Explain to students that the term *case* applies to nouns as well as pronouns. It categorizes their relationship to other parts of the sentence. In order to explain this relationship of sentence parts, grammar notes will traditionally refer to them as the four cases. The case of the subject is also referred to as the nominative case. A noun or pronoun used as a direct object is in the accusative case. Write the following sentences on the board. **Ich kaufe den Pulli. Der Pulli ist rot.** Ask students to label the parts of the sentence. What can they conclude about direct objects and masculine articles ? (**der** changes to **den**)

###  For Individual Needs

**9 A Slower Pace** If students were not able to follow the entire listening activity, write the eight exchanges on a transparency and let students determine the answers.

## Teaching Suggestion

**10** Assign this activity as pair work. Each pair begins by reading the conversation and answering questions 1-3 on a sheet of paper. They then practice reading the conversation aloud. As a final task, have students try to identify the subject and direct object in each sentence. Have them underline the two different sentence parts in two different colors.

### Game

Bring a suitcase and several items of clothing to class. Using the clothing vocabulary from the chapter, have one student start the game by saying the phrase **Ich packe meinen Koffer und nehme ... mit.**, as he or she puts that item of clothing in the suitcase. The following student repeats the sentence, including the first student's addition, and adds his or her own item to the list. The third student adds a third, and, so on. How many pieces of clothing and accessories can students remember?

###  For Individual Needs

**Visual Learners** For additional practice after the game, have a pile of clothing in front of the class. As students repeat items, one student packs the named items in the suitcase, and another student writes the name of each item on the board.

Point out to students that the forms they should use are modeled in the grammar box above, or you may want to write on the board: **der/den, die/die, das/das, ein/einen, eine/eine, ein, ein.**

▶ *page 124*

## For Additional Practice

**13** Assign this to be prepared as a short skit with a set time limit of 1-2 minutes, in which students are encouraged to use props. Students should begin by making a draft of their skit. Offer to check drafts and make suggestions and corrections. Students finalize their skit by drawing up a copy for each player. The performers set up in the front of the class and perform their skit. Use a video camera or tape recorder to record the skits, if possible.

## PRESENTATION: Wortschatz

First teach the colors by showing objects of the colors to be taught. (Examples: flags, crayons, and clothing) Use sentences such as **Der Rock ist grün. Die Flagge ist rot, weiß und blau.** Then, using clothing items, have students ask you for each item in a different color than you are showing. Example: **Haben Sie das auch in Blau?**

###  Culture Note

Shopping hours are regulated all across Germany by federal law. If people need something after hours, they often go into a train station where small vendors provide a limited selection of essential food items.

## Thinking Critically

**Synthesizing**  Ask students to think about some reasons why business hours are so strictly regulated. (This is done mainly to protect the interests of small business owners and their personnel who might be forced to keep long hours to compete with other businesses. Furthermore, the strong influence of labor unions insures tolerable working hours.)

## Reteaching: Colors

Students can make color associations as you ask questions such as **Welche Farbe hat die Sonne? Welche Farbe hat das Gras? Welche Farbe hat das Buch von Rebecca? ... die Hose von ...**

## Reteaching: Nominative and accusative cases

Prepare a chart with the following columns on a transparency.

| Subject/ Pronoun | Verb | Object |
|---|---|---|
| Ich | kaufen | das Buch |
| Susanne | haben | der Pulli |
| Der Junge | nehmen | der Kuli |

Have students use the cues to form complete sentences. Remind students that the masculine article changes in the accusative case. Ask a few volunteers to read their sentences to the class.

## *CLOSE*

### Teaching Suggestion

Ask each student to describe what he or she is wearing today. Students should include accessories and colors.

### Focusing on Outcomes

Refer students back to the learning outcomes listed on p. 117. They should recognize that they are now able to express wishes when shopping.

## *ASSESS*

- **Performance Assessment**  For this activity you will need a spinning color wheel that can be made from paper plates with paper fasteners. Spin the wheel and ask students to name the color the wheel stops on. Ask any students wearing something in that color to name that article of clothing. Example: If the wheel landed on blue, one student might say, **Meine Jacke ist blau, und meine Socken sind auch blau.**

- Quiz 5-1, *Chapter Resources,* Book 2

# *T*eaching Zweite Stufe, pp. 125-130

## Resources for Zweite Stufe

*Practice and Activity Book*
*Chapter Resources, Book 2*
- Communicative Activity 5-2
- Additional Listening Activities 5-3, 5–4
- Student Response Form
- Realia 5-2
- Situation Card 5-2
- Teaching Transparency Master 5–2
- Quiz 5-2

*Audiocassette Program*
- *Textbook Audiocassette* 3 A
- *Additional Listening Activities, Audiocassette* 9 B
- *Assessment Items, Audiocassette* 7 B

▶ *page 125*

## *MOTIVATE*

### Teaching Suggestion

Ask students what phrases they would use to compliment a friend's outfit. What expressions do their parents use to compliment other adults on their clothes?

## *TEACH*

### PRESENTATION: So sagt man das!

Ask students to look back at the **Foto-Roman** on pp. 118-119 and remind them of the functions that are targeted (commenting on and describing clothes, giving compliments and responding to them). Where do students see these functions modeled in the **Foto-Roman**? Have students make a list of the expressions they find.

### For Additional Practice

In order to practice all the new expressions, have students react to you and express their opinions as you put on different pieces of clothing. Try to bring some fashionable items as well as some out-of-fashion pieces to get different reactions.

## PRESENTATION: Ein wenig Grammatik

Suggest that students keep a list with idiomatic expressions for their portfolios and **Notizbücher.**

▶ *page 126*

## PRESENTATION: Wortschatz

Introduce this new vocabulary by emphasizing opposites. Incorporate other examples using pictures, classroom objects, etc. Example: short pencil versus long pencil.

▶ *page 127*

### ◆ For Individual Needs

**17 A Slower Pace** After doing this activity orally in class, assign it as written homework and have students include their opinions about the clothing pictured.

## PRESENTATION: So sagt man das!

Remind students of the motivating activity they did at the beginning of this **Stufe.** See if any of their suggestions are similar to the German expressions introduced in this function box. Explain that intonation plays a big role in how compliments are given and received. Give an example: **Peter, deine Jacke gefällt mir! Wirklich? Wirklich!** As in English, questions and responses have a much different intonation. The speaker's voice goes up at the end of a question, and it remains fairly flat for a response.

▶ *page 128*

## PRESENTATION: Grammatik

Review personal pronouns by giving several examples in which students repeat sentences by replacing sentence parts with pronouns. Have the sentences of this grammar box on the board or on a transparency with the subject and direct objects underlined. Ask students what changes occur when a feminine, neuter, or masculine direct object is replaced by a pronoun. Make a chart of the changes as students name them.

ZWEITE STUFE

ZWEITE STUFE

Examples: Ich finde <u>den Gürtel</u> schick.
Ich finde <u>ihn</u> schick.
Ich finde <u>die Bluse</u> scheußlich.
Ich finde <u>sie</u> scheußlich.
Ich finde <u>das Hemd</u> furchtbar.
Ich finde <u>es</u> furchtbar.

| den | → | ihn |
|-----|---|-----|
| die | → | sie |
| das | → | es  |

 ## For Individual Needs

**19 Challenge**   After students have success-fully matched the articles of clothing with the appropriate adjectives, have them write the seven sentences as accurately as they can recall them. Call on several students to read the sentences aloud.

▶ *page 129*

 ## Portfolio Assessment

**22**   You might want to use this activity as a written portfolio item for your students. See *Assessment Guide,* Chapter 5.

## Reteaching: Direct object pronouns

Make a chart of sentence fragments as in the example below and have students replace nouns with pronouns.

| Sabine | kauft | das Kleid | (das Kleid = es) |
|--------|-------|-----------|------------------|
| **Sie kauft es.** | | | |
| Rolf | möchte | den Kuli | _____ |
| **Er möchte ihn.** | | | |
| Christian | nimmt | die Stiefel | _____ |
| **Er nimmt sie.** | | | |

▶ *page 130*

 ## Presentation: Landeskunde

• Ask students to give a short description of the clothing the four German students are wearing.

• You might want to introduce the following vocabulary to your students before watching the video segment:
**der Body** *bodysuit*
**locker** *loose fitting*
**darüber** *over, on top of*

• After students have seen the video segment or listened to the tape, ask four students to each read one of the interviews aloud for pronunciation practice.

## Multicultural Connection

If possible have students interview foreign exchange students or people they know from other countries. They should try to find out how clothing and clothing styles differ from country to country. Students should share the information they collect with the class.

## Teacher Note

Mention to your students that the **Landeskunde** will also be included in Quiz 5–2 given at the end of the **Zweite Stufe**.

## *CLOSE*

## Game

Divide the class into two teams. Each person will need a piece of paper and a pen or pencil. The first student from Team A writes down an object (Example: item of clothing or classroom object) that is in the classroom and says the game phrase: **Ich sehe was, was du nicht siehst, und es ist...**, inserting a color in the blank. One member from Team B has three guesses to figure out what object the student from Team A is referring to. If the student from Team B guesses correctly, that team gets a point and another turn to guess. If the opposing team does not guess correctly, then that team must ask the question to the other team. The team with the most points at the end of the game wins.

## Focusing on Outcomes

Refer students back to the learning outcomes listed on p. 117. They should recognize that they are now able to describe clothes, and to give and respond to compliments.

## *ASSESS*

• **Performance Assessment**   Ask students to write a short paragraph in which they describe their ideal wardrobe.

• Quiz 5-2, *Chapter Resources,* Book 2

# Teaching Dritte Stufe, pp. 131-133

## Resources for Dritte Stufe

*Practice and Activity Book*
*Chapter Resources*, Book 2
- Additional Listening Activities 5-5, 5-6
- Student Response Form
- Realia 5-3
- Situation Card 5-3
- Quiz 5-3

*Audiocassette Program*
- *Textbook Audiocassette* 3 A
- *Additional Listening Activities, Audiocassette* 9 B
- *Assessment Items, Audiocassette* 7 B

▶ *page 131*

## MOTIVATE

###  Total Physical Response

Prepare a suitcase or bag of clothing for this activity. First pull out each item and review the vocabulary by giving such commands as: **Zeigt auf die Jacke!** Then display all of the items and proceed with other commands using verbs such as **nehmen, geben,** and **bringen.**

## TEACH

### PRESENTATION: So sagt man das!

Use the suitcase of clothes from the TPR activity above to teach the new expressions in the **So sagt man das!** box. Model the phrases first, telling students what you are doing. Then ask students to try on some clothes via TPR: **Probier das T-Shirt an!** Repeat the expressions using several clothing items and involve as many students as possible.

### PRESENTATION: Grammatik

Ask students if they can tell you what the word *prefix* means. (one or more syllables added to the beginning of a word to change its meaning) Ask students to give you some examples in English. (Example: so-cial - *anti*social) Tell students that German has many separable prefix verbs, and ask them to name the verb and the prefix in this example:

**anziehen      Was ziehe ich heute an?**

Continue with the grammar box for more examples.

▶ *page 132*

###  For Individual Needs

**24 Challenge**  Ask students what they would wear to a school dance or a party. Have them respond in German. Example: **Ich ziehe ein Kleid an.**

### For Additional Practice

Once a student has completed the description of his or her outfit in the challenge activity above, ask another student to compliment the outfit.

### Teacher Note

After presenting the **Lerntrick** to students, you may want to have them begin a list of possible prefixes in German. Students can later expand the list as they come across more prefixes in subsequent chapters. Students can start their list with **aus-** and **an-**. You may choose to introduce the following new prefixes immediately: **ab, bei, ein, her, hin, mit, nach, vor.**

### PRESENTATION: Grammatik

Tell students that German has verbs that undergo changes. Usually, the stem of the second and third person singular changes. These verbs and changes must be memorized.

### Teaching Suggestion

**26**  For this activity, students should bring several articles of clothing to class.

### For Individual Needs

**26 Challenge**  One partner provides the context by telling the other partner where he or she will be going (**ins Kino, ins Theater mit den Eltern, ins Café mit Freunden, zum Tennisspiel**). The student then selects the outfit appropriate for the occasion.

**DRITTE STUFE**

▶ *page 133*

## 📁 Portfolio Assessment

**28** You might want to use this activity as an oral portfolio item for your students. See *Assessment Guide,* Chapter 5.

## PRESENTATION: Aussprache

The letter **i** in some instances such as, **ihr, ihm, mir, dir** can also sound much like the *i* in the English word *mean.* Remind students of the other way of pronouncing **ä** and **e** as in the words **spät** and **sehen.** To help students hear the difference between the short and long **a,** contrast the sounds by using word pairs: **Stadt/Staat.**

## Language Note

After presenting the **Aussprache** section to your students, you may want to tell them about a localized dialectal pronunciation of the letter combinations **sp, spr,** and **str,** which can be heard around Hamburg and Hannover. There those initial sounds are pronounced similar to the initial sound of the English word *spit.* A person from Hamburg would pronounce **spucken** as "spucken" not "schpucken."

## Reteaching: Separable prefix verbs

Prepare strips of paper large enough to write one sentence on each. Write the sentences from the **Grammatik** box on p. 131 on the strips. Cut each strip into its sentence components (subject, verb, object, etc.). Divide the class into 6 groups. Each group gets a sentence that it has to put together correctly without using books. One member of each group puts the group's sentence on the board. Students check other groups' sentences for correct word order.

## *CLOSE*

## ♜ Game

This game is much like *Tic-Tac-Toe.* Place a German adjective in each square. Divide the class into two teams. Every time a team member creates a correct sentence using the adjective in one of the squares, an X or O is added to that square. Students must use different subjects and verbs for each sentence.

## Focusing on Outcomes

Refer students back to the learning outcomes listed on p. 117. Students should recognize that they are now able to talk about trying on clothes.

## *ASSESS*

- **Performance Assessment**   Ask individual students to follow commands using the verbs **nehmen, geben, anziehen,** or **anprobieren** and the clothing vocabulary. Example: **Marjorie, zieh den Rock an!**

- Quiz 5-3, *Chapter Resources*, Book 2

# Teaching Zum Lesen,
## pp. 134-135

## Reading Strategy

The targeted strategy in this reading is using what you already know to anticipate the type of information contained in a text.

## PREREADING

### Motivating Activity

Ask students about their favorite stores for buying clothes. What kinds of clothes do these stores sell? Why do students prefer these particular stores?

### Teaching Suggestion

Before doing the prereading activities, you might want to review sizes, abbreviations, the **Deutschmark,** and the expressions found on labels affixed to clothing items.

### Teacher Note

Activities 1 and 2 are prereading activities.

## READING

### Skimming and Scanning

Have students briefly look at all the ads and descriptions and identify words that are also used to describe fashion in English ads. Make a list on the board or a transparency.

### Thinking Critically

**Drawing Inferences**   Ask students to think of some reasons why there are so many  English descriptions used in the ads. (Clothing labels and designer names in English influence the fashion language all over the world.)

### Teacher Note

Students might be curious to find out about the following vocabulary in the **K+L Ruppert** advertisements: **durchgeknöpft** - *buttoned down,* **Vielfalt** - *selection, versatility*

### Cooperative Learning

Put students in groups of four. Ask them to choose a discussion leader, a recorder, a proofreader, and an announcer. Give students a specific amount of time in which to complete Activities 1–10. Monitor group work as you walk around, helping students if necessary. At the end of the activity, call on each group announcer to read his or her group's results. You can decide whether or not to collect their work for a grade at the end of the activity.

### Geography Connection

**K+L Ruppert** lists several cities at the bottom of the ad for women's wear to show where stores can be found. Have students locate some of the cities on a map.

**Umrechnungstabelle**
**USA**
Stand: Febr. '93

| DM | Dollar | Dollar | DM |
|---|---|---|---|
| 1,– | | | |
| 2,– | –,59 | –,10 | –,17 |
| 3,– | 1,18 | –,50 | –,85 |
| 4,– | 1,76 | 1,— | 1,70 |
| 5,– | 2,35 | 2,50 | 4,25 |
| 10,– | 2,94 | 5,— | 8,50 |
| 20,– | 5,88 | 10,— | 17,— |
| 25,– | 11,76 | 20,— | 34,— |
| 30,– | 14,71 | 30,— | 51,— |
| 40,– | 17,65 | 40,— | 68,— |
| 50,– | 23,53 | 50,— | 85,— |
| 75,– | 29,41 | 60,— | 102,— |
| 100,– | 44,12 | 70,— | 119,— |
| 200,– | 58,82 | 80,— | 136,— |
| 250,– | 117,65 | 90,— | 153,— |
| 300,– | 147,06 | 100,— | 170,— |
| 500,– | 176,47 | 200,— | 340,— |
| 750,– | 294,12 | 300,— | 510,— |
| 1.000,– | 441,18 | 400,— | 680,— |
| 2.000,– | 588,24 | 500,— | 850,— |
| | 1.176,47 | 1.000,— | 1.700,— |

1 Dollar (USD) = 100 Cents

Die errechneten Beträge sind nur Annäherungswerte, da die Kurse für An- und Verkauf von Schecks, Noten und Münzen verschieden sind und Schwankungen unterliegen. – Alle Angaben ohne Gewähr

**COMMERZBANK**
Die Bank an Ihrer Seite

ZUM LESEN

## Thinking Critically

**Comparing and Contrasting** The surveys in the reading were taken from *JUMA* magazine, which stands for **Jugendmagazin**. Surveys such as these are quite popular among German-speaking teenagers. Ask students to name a few American youth magazines where they would typically find similar surveys? (Examples: *Teen* and *Seventeen*)

 ## Culture Note

German stores do not have "sales" as frequently as stores in the United States do. The government enforces strict laws, and there are generally only two major sales per year, the **Sommerschlußverkauf** at the end of summer and the **Winterschlußverkauf** at the end of winter. At other times in the year, you might see signs that advertise **Sonderangebote** (*specials*), but you'd rarely see signs that advertise merchandise as 25% or 50% off.

Volker, 16 Jahre
„Das sind meine Sachen: Jeans, Sportschuhe, Kapuzen-Shirt. Ich trage sie, weil sie mir gefallen. Mode interessiert mich nicht."

## POST-READING

## Teacher Note

Activities 11 and 12 are post-reading tasks that will show whether students can apply what they have learned.

 ## Multicultural Connection

Ask teachers of other foreign languages to lend you realia similar to the clothing ads in this reading section. Let your students compare those ads to the German ones. Can they point out five similarities and differences in the way clothing is advertised in those countries?

## Closure

Ask students which of the advertised items in this reading section they would purchase as a present for their brother, sister, mother, or father if they had 100 marks to spend.

*Answers to Activity 4*
reduced prices—**stark reduziert**

*Answers to Activity 5*
interviews/teenager magazine

*Answers to Activity 6*
sixteen/casual clothing/**Jeans, Sportschuhe**

*Answers to Activity 7*
**12 Monate Garantie**

*Answers to Activity 8*
Jeans, athletic shoes, hooded T-shirt/At Kriegbaum's for **DM 12, 90** or **DM 19, 90**/Because of the hood

*Answers to Activity 9*
You can express something through fashion without speaking.

*Answers to Activity 10*
He is interested in brand-name fashion.

# *U*sing Anwendung,
*pp. 136-137*

## Teaching Suggestion

**1** Have students make notes on index cards as they record the patterns and trends for their article. Students can then use these notecards as they write their article. These should be turned in along with the assignment.

###  For Individual Needs

**3 A Slower Pace** Make an enlarged transparency of the conversation. As students provide responses, write them in the blanks on the transparency. When the dialogue is completed, have several pairs of students read the dialogue aloud, practicing pronunciation.

## Teaching Suggestion

**6** Read the fashion review **Das weiße Hemd** to the class as you would hear it in a fashion review on TV or the radio. Ask students to make a list of all the expressions used in the article to describe the clothing.

DAS WEISSE HEMD

Ein weißes Hemd ist das, was Modekenner einen „all time classic" nennen: schick, aber trotzdem leger—ein Basisstück für jede Garderobe. In dieser Saison ist das weiße Hemd das Lieblingskind der Designer, die sich in ihren Variationen gegenseitig übertreffen. Asymmetrisch, geknotet oder aus Leinen, lang oder kurz—zu Jeans, Shorts oder Röcken: alles geht.

# *K*ann ich's wirklich?
*p. 138*

This page is intended to prepare students for the test. It is a brief checklist of the major points covered in the chapter. The students should be reminded that it is a checklist only and not necessarily everything that will appear on the test.

# *U*sing Wortschatz,
*p. 139*

### For Individual Needs

**Visual Learners** Show pictures of actual pieces of clothing, and ask students to name them, including the German articles that accompany the nouns. Point to items around the class and ask students what color they are. Give an adjective such as **lang** and ask students for its opposite by asking: **Was ist das Gegenteil von lang?**

### Game

Play the game **Wortbögen** using as many words from the **Wortschatz** page as possible. See p. 115F for the procedure.

## Teacher Note

Give the **Kapitel 5** Chapter Test, *Chapter Resources,* Book 2.

# Klamotten kaufen

① Ich finde das T-Shirt echt stark.

Teenagers in German-speaking countries usually dress casually, often wearing jeans and T-shirts. They enjoy shopping and talking about clothes and like to follow trends. What kinds of clothes do you and your friends wear? Do you think that clothing styles in the German-speaking countries are similar to those in the United States? Let's find out what teenagers in those countries like to buy.

## In this chapter you will learn

- to express wishes when shopping
- to comment on and describe clothes;
  to give compliments and respond to them
- to talk about trying on clothes

## And you will

- listen to people talk about clothes
- read ads for clothing stores
- write a clothing ad for a newspaper
- find out what teenagers in German-speaking countries like to wear to parties

② Ich brauche ein T-Shirt in Rot.

③ Was ziehst du zu Sonjas Fete an?

# Los geht's!

## Was ziehst du an?

Look at the photos that accompany the story. Who are the people pictured? Where are they at the beginning of the story and where do they go? Based on this information, what do you think they are talking about?

Michael        Katja        Julia

**①**

Was ziehst du denn zu Sonjas Fete an? Rock, Pulli?

Ach was! Ich zieh' meinen Jogging-Anzug an.

Und ich meine Shorts. Ich brauche aber etwas, eine Bluse oder ein T-Shirt. Das ist zu alt und gefällt mir nicht.

Und ich brauche ein Stirnband für meine Haare. Komm, gehen wir zum Sport-Kerner!

**②**

Schau, der Michael!

Hallo, ihr beiden!

Was hast du denn da in der Tüte?

Na, wie gefällt euch mein T-Shirt?

Mensch, scheußlich!

Wirklich? — Also, ich finde es stark!

**③**

Haben Sie einen Wunsch?

Ich suche eine Bluse.

Blusen haben wir in allen Größen und allen Farben. — Hier haben wir etwas für Sie: Toll, nicht?

Haben Sie auch Blusen in Blau?

Natürlich! Hier, in Blau. Größe 40. Paßt bestimmt.

## 1 Was passiert hier?

Do you understand what is happening in the **Foto-Roman**? Check your comprehension by answering these questions. Don't be afraid to guess.

1. What does the word **Fete** mean? Who is having one? 1. Fete means party. Sonja is having a party.
2. What do Katja and Julia still need to do before the **Fete**? 2. go shopping for clothes
3. What does Michael think about his purchase? What do Julia and Katja think of it?
4. Does Katja like the first thing she tries on? What does she say?
5. What does Katja finally buy? Why does she hesitate at first?
6. What do you think about her purchase?

3. Michael likes his T-shirt but Julia and Katja think it's terrible.
4. She doesn't like it and says, „Nein, die Bluse gefällt mir nicht."
5. She buys a T-shirt but hesitates because it is rather expensive.
6. Answers may vary.

## 2 Genauer lesen

Reread the conversations. Which words or phrases do the characters use to

1. name articles of clothing
2. describe or comment on clothing
3. name colors
4. tell a price

3. Blau; weiß.
4. Für 12 Mark. Zweiundvierzig Mark neunzig.
1. Rock, Pulli, Jogging-Anzug, Shorts, Bluse, Stirnband, T-Shirt.
2. Mensch, scheußlich; ich finde es stark; sehr sportlich; sieht toll aus; hundert Prozent Baumwolle; echt toll; lässig.

## 3 Stimmt oder stimmt nicht?

Are these statements right or wrong? Answer each one with either **stimmt** or **stimmt nicht**. If a statement is wrong, try to state it correctly.

1. Julia hat eine Fete.
2. Katja hat Shorts, aber sie braucht eine Bluse.
3. Michael findet sein T-Shirt stark.
4. Katja sucht einen Pulli.
5. Katja möchte die Bluse in Blau haben.
6. Blau ist Katjas Lieblingsfarbe.

1. Sonja hat eine Fete.
2. stimmt
3. stimmt
4. Sie sucht eine Bluse.
5. stimmt
6. Weiß

## 4 Was paßt zusammen?

Match each statement or question on the left with an appropriate response on the right.

1. Was ziehst du zu Sonjas Fete an? e
2. Wie gefällt euch mein T-Shirt? a
3. Haben Sie einen Wunsch? d
4. Wir haben Blusen in allen Farben. c
5. Das T-Shirt kostet 42 Mark 90. f
6. Das ist eine gute Farbe für dich. b

a. Mensch, scheußlich!
b. Weiß ist meine Lieblingsfarbe.
c. Gut! Ich möchte eine Bluse in Blau.
d. Ja, ich suche eine Bluse.
e. Meinen Jogging-Anzug.
f. Das ist teuer!

## 5 Welches Wort paßt?

Based on the **Foto-Roman**, rewrite the following narrative by supplying the missing words.

Katja __1__ eine Bluse für Sonjas Fete und geht mit Julia zum Sport-Kerner. Dort sehen die zwei __2__ den Michael. Er zeigt ihnen sein neues T-Shirt. Katja __3__ das T-Shirt scheußlich, aber Michael findet es __4__. Im Sport-Kerner möchte Katja eine Bluse in __5__ sehen, und sie probiert eine Bluse an. Die Bluse gefällt ihr aber nicht. Die T-Shirts sind aber __6__ sportlich und fesch. Julia findet das T-Shirt mit dem Texas-Motiv ganz toll. Katja __7__ das weiße T-Shirt an, denn Weiß ist Katjas __8__. Sie möchte es nehmen, aber es ist __9__. Am Ende kauft Katja das T-Shirt doch.

1. sucht; 2. Mädchen; 3. findet; 4. stark 5. Blau 6. sehr 7. probiert 8. Lieblingsfarbe 9. teuer

Blau    Lieblingsfarbe    probiert    stark
findet    sehr    sucht    teuer    Mädchen

## WORTSCHATZ

der Rock　　　das Hemd　　　die Stiefel

das Kleid　　　die Hose　　　der Gürtel

die Bluse
die Jacke
die Jeans
die Socke
die Shorts
das T-Shirt
der Pulli (Pullover)
der Jogging-Anzug

die Turnschuhe

### FÜR DAMEN

| | |
|---|---|
| Hosen, Leinenstruktur | 75.- |
| Damenhafte Röcke in Leinenoptik | 55.- |
| T-Shirts, bedruckt, mit Perlen und Pailletten | 38.- |
| Coloured Jeans mit Gürtel | 60.- |
| Bedruckte Blusen mit modischen Details | 55.- |
| T-Shirts mit Applikationen | 35.- |
| <u>YOUNG COLLECTIONS</u> Strickkleider in verschiedenen Formen und Farben | 28.- |

### FÜR HERREN

| | |
|---|---|
| Jacken | 85.- |
| Blouson oder Polo-Shirts, 1/2 Ärmel | 50.- |
| Uni-Socken, Superstretch, 5 Paar | 19.- |
| Seiden-Hemden, sandwashed bedruckt, 1/2 Ärmel | 45.- |
| Streifen-Polo-Shirts, 1/2 Ärmel | 48.- |
| Gymnastik-Shorts | 30.- |

Many clothing items in this ad are cognates. Which ones do you recognize?
Which items are for women, which for men? Which words are used to describe shirts
and T-shirts? What do they mean?

## 6　Hör gut zu!

A certain **Modegeschäft** (*clothing store*) has been doing a lot of advertising lately. As you
listen to one of their radio ads, first write down the items in the order you hear them mentioned. Then figure out which items are for men, and which for women. What does this
store have for "**die ganze Familie**"? Kleider (women); Röcke (women); Jogging-Anzug (women);
Blusen (women); Gürtel (men); Hemden (men); Hosen (men);
The store has „**fesche Sachen für die ganze Familie**".

To the right is an **Umrechnungstabelle** (*conversion table*) for determining how to convert marks to dollars and vice versa. How many dollars will you receive for one mark? How many marks would you receive for one dollar? The table always has a date, because the exchange rate varies from day to day. When was this table printed? Looking at the clothing ad and using the **Umrechnungstabelle**, compare the prices for clothing in Germany with what you pay in the United States. In general, in which country do you think clothes are more expensive? What types of clothes would you expect to be more expensive in Germany than in the United States?

**Umrechnungstabelle**  
**USA**  Stand: Feb

| DM | Dollar | Dollar | |
|---|---|---|---|
| 1,– | –,59 | –,10 | –, |
| 2,– | 1,18 | –,50 | –,8 |
| 3,– | 1,76 | 1,— | 1, |
| 4,– | 2,35 | 2,50 | 4,2 |
| 5,– | 2,94 | 5,— | 8,5 |
| 10,– | 5,88 | 10,— | 17,– |
| 20,– | 11,76 | 20,— | 34,– |
| 25,– | 14,71 | 30,— | 51,– |
| 30,– | 17,65 | 40,— | 68,– |
| 40,– | 23,53 | 50,— | 85,– |
| 50,– | 29,41 | 60,— | 102,– |
| 75,– | 44,12 | 70,— | 119,– |
| 100,– | 58,82 | 80,— | 136,– |
| 200,– | 117,65 | 90,— | 153,– |
| 250,– | 147,06 | 100,— | 170,– |
| 300,– | 176,47 | 200,— | 340,– |
| 500,– | 294,12 | 300,— | 510,– |
| 750,– | 441,18 | 400,— | 680,– |
| 1.000,– | 588,24 | 500,— | 850,– |
| 2.000,– | 1.176,47 | 1.000,— | 1.700,– |

1 Dollar (USD) = 100 Cents

Die errechneten Beträge sind nur Annäherungswerte, da die Kur... für An- und Verkauf von Schecks, Noten und Münzen verschiede... sind und Schwankungen unterliegen. – Alle Angaben ohne Gewäh...

**COMMERZBANK**  
Die Bank an Ihrer Seite

## 7 Wie sind die Preise?

Using the **Umrechnungstabelle** for clues, create a price list for the following items listed in the **Wortschatz** but not in the ad: **Gürtel, Jogging-Anzug, Turnschuhe, Pulli**, and **Stiefel**. Your partner will ask you how much these items cost, and you will answer, using your price list and the ad on page 121. Then switch roles. Be polite!

## 8 Was gibt es im Modegeschäft?

You want to buy something new to wear to your friend's party, but you can't decide what to buy. You have DM 200 to spend. Using the ad on page 121 and your price list, put together three different outfits that would be within your budget. With which outfit would you have the most money left over?

## SO SAGT MAN DAS!

### Expressing wishes when shopping

You have already used the **möchte**-forms to say what you would like to eat and drink. You can use these same forms when you go shopping for other things, such as clothes.

The salesclerk might ask:

**Bitte?** *or*

**Was möchten Sie?**

*or*

**Was bekommen Sie?**

*or*

**Haben Sie einen Wunsch?**

You can respond:

**Ich möchte eine Jacke, bitte!**

**Ich brauche ein T-Shirt.**
*I need a T-shirt.*

**Einen Pulli in Grau, bitte!**
*A sweater in gray, please!*

**Ich suche eine Bluse.**
*I'm looking for a blouse.*

What is the subject of the sentence in each of the salesclerk's questions? Look at the sentence **Einen Pulli in Grau, bitte!** Is there a subject or verb? What do you think is intended?

## *G*rammatik   Definite and indefinite articles, accusative case

Look at the following sentences:

**Der Pulli** kostet 30 Mark.    Möchten Sie **den Pulli**?
**Ein Pulli** kostet 30 Mark.    Möchten Sie **einen Pulli**?

What is the difference between the noun phrases **der Pulli/ein Pulli** on the left and the noun phrases **den Pulli/einen Pulli** on the right?

The noun phrases (**der Pulli/ein Pulli**) on the left are the *subjects* (nominative case) of the sentences. The noun phrases **den Pulli/einen Pulli** on the right are *direct objects* (accusative case) of the sentences. Only articles for masculine nouns change when they are used as direct objects. The articles for feminine, neuter, and plural nouns stay the same:

| | | |
|---|---|---|
| **Das T-Shirt** kostet 10 Mark. | Möchten Sie **das T-Shirt**? | Ja, ich möchte **das T-Shirt**. |
| **Die Jacke** ist schön. | Möchten Sie **die Jacke**? | Ich nehme **die Jacke**. |
| **Die Turnschuhe** kosten 40 Mark. | Möchten Sie **die Turnschuhe**? | Ja, ich möchte **die Turnschuhe**. |

## 9 Hör gut zu!

1. subject  2. direct object  3. subject  4. direct object  5. direct object
6. direct object  7. subject  8. direct object

Listen carefully to these students commenting on different clothes, and decide whether the item of clothing in each exchange is the subject or direct object of the sentences.

## 10 Julia geht einkaufen

Read this conversation between Julia and the salesclerk at **Sport-Kerner**. Look carefully at the conversation and determine what the subject and/or direct object is in each sentence. Then answer the questions that follow.

VERKÄUFERIN  Guten Tag! Haben Sie einen Wunsch?
JULIA  Ich suche einen Rock in Blau. Was kostet der Rock hier?
VERKÄUFERIN  Er kostet nur 60 Mark.
JULIA  Und haben Sie vielleicht auch eine Bluse in Weiß?
VERKÄUFERIN  Ja, die Bluse hier kostet 45 Mark. Wir haben auch das weiße T-Shirt hier im Sonderangebot. Nur 20 Mark. Paßt auch schön zu Röcken.
JULIA  Das T-Shirt ist schön, aber ich brauche ein T-Shirt in Schwarz. Also ich nehme nur den Rock und die Bluse. Danke!

1. She is looking for a blue skirt and a white blouse.
1. What is Julia looking for?
2. Why doesn't she want the T-Shirt?
3. How much is her final purchase?
2. She needs a black T-shirt.    3. 105 marks.

## 11 Was brauchst du?

a. Tell some of your classmates what clothes you need, using the indefinite article when appropriate. Possible answers:
   Ich brauche eine Jacke, ... Socken, ...

| Ich | brauche möchte | Pulli Rock Jeans Hemd T-Shirt Stiefel Gürtel | Turn- schuhe Bluse Kleid Hose Socken Jacke |
|---|---|---|---|

b. Now point to various articles of clothing that your classmates are wearing and say that you would like to have them, using the definite article.
   Answers may include the following:
   Ich möchte den Pulli.  Ich möchte die Hose.  Ich möchte das Hemd.

## 12 Rollenspiel im Kaufhaus

You are in a department store that has many items on sale (**im Sonderangebot**). Make a list of the clothes you would like to buy. Your partner will play the salesperson and ask you what you want and tell you where everything is. In the boxes to the right are some words and phrases you might need.

dort
da drüben
hier vorn
da hinten

der/ein
den/einen
die/eine
das/ein

## 13 Haben Sie das auch in ...?

You didn't find the colors you like at the last store. Ask the salesperson at the new store below if he or she has the items you want in certain colors. Also ask about prices. Then switch roles.

WORTSCHATZ

**Farben!** Haben Sie das auch ...?

in Blau   in Grün   in Weiß   in Hellblau   in Rot

in Dunkelblau   in Braun   in Gelb   in Grau   in Schwarz

## 14 Zum Schreiben: Alles ist im Sonderangebot!

Design your own newspaper ad based on four items in the ad on page 121 or cut out pictures from a magazine. Remember, everything is on sale at your store. Be sure to mention prices and colors in stock. Be prepared to share your ads with the class.

*Commenting on and describing clothes; giving compliments and responding to them*

## SO SAGT MAN DAS!

### Commenting on and describing clothes

If you want to know what someone thinks about a particular item of clothing, you might ask:

**Wie findest du das Hemd?**

You might get positive comments, such as:

**Ich finde es fesch.**
**Es sieht schick aus!**
**Es paßt prima.**
**Es gefällt mir.**

Or you might get negative comments, such as:

**Ich finde es furchtbar.**
**Es sieht blöd aus.**
**Es paßt nicht.**
**Es gefällt mir nicht.**

If the person you ask isn't sure, he or she might say:

**Ich weiß nicht.** *or*
**Ich bin nicht sicher**

## 15 Hör gut zu! 1. Nein 2. Ja 3. Nein 4. Ja 5. Ja

Several students are in a store looking at clothes and talking about what they like and don't like. Determine whether the person speaking likes the item of clothing or not.

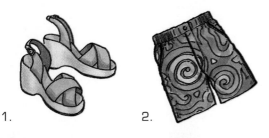

1.
2.
3.
4.
5.

### Ein wenig *G*rammatik

Look at these sentences:

**Wie findest du den Rock?**
**Er gefällt mir.**
**Und die T-Shirts?**
**Sie gefallen mir auch.**

What are the subjects in the two responses?[1] When using the verb **gefallen** to say you like something, you need to know only two forms: **gefällt** and **gefallen**.

**Er/sie/es gefällt mir.** *I like it.*
**Sie (pl) gefallen mir.** *I like them.*

1. er (der Rock), sie (die T-Shirts)

# 16 Wie findest du das?

Look at the items pictured in Activity 15 and ask your partner if he or she likes each item. Then switch roles.

### Nichts paßt!

Das Kleid ist zu lang.

Der Pulli ist viel zu weit.

Die Jacke ist zu groß.

Die Hose ist zu kurz.

Das Hemd ist zu eng.

Die Schuhe sind ein bißchen zu klein.

### HERRENGRÖSSEN

|  | USA | BDR |
|---|---|---|
| Hemden | 13 | 36 |
|  | 15 | 38 |
|  | 16 | 40 |
|  | 17 | 42 |
| Pullover | S | 36-38 |
|  | M | 39 |
|  | L | 40-41 |
|  | XL | 42-44 |
| Anzüge | 34 | 44 |
|  | 36 | 46 |
|  | 40 | 50 |
|  | 44 | 54 |
|  | 46 | 56 |
| Schuhe | 7, 7½ | 40 |
|  | 8 | 41 |
|  | 8½ | 42 |
|  | 9, 9½ | 43 |
|  | 10, 10½ | 44 |
|  | 11, 11½ | 44 |
|  | 12, 12½ | 45 |

### DAMENGRÖSSEN

|  | USA | BDR |
|---|---|---|
| Blusen, Pullover | 8 | 36 |
|  | 10 | 38 |
|  | 12 | 40 |
|  | 14 | 42 |
| Kleider, Mäntel | 8 | 38 |
|  | 10 | 40 |
|  | 12 | 42 |
|  | 14 | 44 |
| Schuhe | 5 | 36 |
|  | 6 | 37 |
|  | 7 | 38 |
|  | 8 | 39 |
|  | 9 | 40 |
|  | 10 | 41 |

## EIN WENIG LANDESKUNDE

German sizes are different from American sizes. However, clothes manufactured in the United States and imported to Germany carry U.S. sizes. For example, jeans are often measured in inches, and T-shirts have the designations **S**, **M**, **L**, **XL**, and **XXL**. Look at the size charts on the right. What size would you take if you were buying German clothes or shoes in Germany?

## 17 Was ist los?

You and a friend are spending the afternoon **in der Innenstadt** (*downtown*). You encounter the people pictured below and discuss their clothing. Take turns describing the clothing pictured to each other. Answers may vary. Examples:
**Der Pulli ist zu lang. Die Schuhe sind zu groß.**

## SO SAGT MAN DAS!

### Giving compliments and responding to them

On numerous occasions you'll want to be able to compliment your friends on their clothes.

You could say:
**Die Jacke sieht lässig aus!** *or*
**Die Jacke gefällt mir!**

The other person might respond:
**Ehrlich?** *or*
**Wirklich?** *or*
**Meinst du?**
**Nicht zu lang (kurz, groß)?**

You could answer:
**Ehrlich!**
**Wirklich!**
**Ja, bestimmt!**
**Nein, überhaupt nicht!**

## 18 Was meinst du?

a. Find five pictures of clothing items in your favorite magazine. Write at least two sentences to describe each item and one sentence to express your opinion about each picture.

fesch   schick   blöd   furchtbar
Spitze   scheußlich          prima
toll     stark     lässig

b. Show your partner the pictures you cut out and ask what he or she thinks of your clothing choices. If your partner compliments you on your choices, respond appropriately.

## *Grammatik*  Direct object pronouns

In **Kapitel 3** you learned that the pronouns **er**, **sie**, **es**, and **sie** (pl) can refer to both people and objects. Look at the following sentences:

**Der Pulli** ist sehr preiswert.          Ich finde **den Pulli** toll.
Ja, **er** ist nicht teuer.                      Ich finde **ihn** auch toll.

What are the pronouns in these sentences? What do you think **er** and **ihn** refer to? **Er**, the pronoun on the left, is the *subject* (nominative case) of the sentence and refers to **der Pulli**. The pronoun **ihn** on the right is the *direct object* (accusative case) of the sentence and refers to **den Pulli**. Only the masculine pronoun changes when it is used as a direct object. The feminine **sie**, neuter **es**, and plural pronoun **sie** stay the same:

**Die Bluse (sie)** ist hübsch.              Ich finde **sie** scheußlich.
**Das Hemd (es)** kostet 40 Mark.         Ich finde **es** teuer.
**Die Stiefel (sie)** sind echt toll!        Aber ich möchte **sie** in Schwarz.

1. subject; **Jogging-Anzug; schick**   2. direct object; **Rock; schön**   3. direct object; **T-Shirt; hellgrün**   4. subject; **T-Shirt; preiswert**
5. subject; **Turnschuhe; stark**   6. direct object; **Pulli; schwarze**   7. direct object; **Bluse; teuer**

## 19  Hör gut zu!

Listen to this conversation between two students who are talking about clothes they want to buy. The first time you hear the conversation, figure out whether the pronouns they mention are subjects or direct objects. Then listen again and match the article of clothing with the words used to describe it.

BEISPIEL  —**Ich finde die blaue Bluse sehr
                    schön. Und du?**
               —**Ja, ich finde sie hübsch.**

|   | Subject | Direct object |
|---|---------|---------------|
| 0 |         | X             |
| 1 |         |               |
| 2 |         |               |

hellgrün  schick
               schwarz
preiswert
teuer      toll
   stark
              schön
hübsch

die Bluse da vorn   der Rock   die blaue Bluse
        das T-Shirt        die Turnschuhe
der Jogging-Anzug   der Pulli   die Bluse

## 20 Welcher Satz paßt?

Katja and Sonja are in a store trying on clothes. Choose the appropriate responses to complete their conversation. Then read the conversation aloud with your partner.

**a** Ich finde ihn toll, aber er ist viel zu lang für dich.

**b** Hm, ich finde sie schön, aber sie paßt nicht.

**c** Bist du sicher? Sie sind sehr teuer.

**d** Ja, es sieht super aus!

SONJA  Wie findest du die Bluse in Rot?
KATJA  ═══. b
SONJA  Meinst du? Wie findest du den Rock hier in Schwarz?
KATJA  ═══. a
SONJA  Ehrlich? So ein Mist! Vielleicht kaufe ich das T-Shirt in Blau.
SONJA  ═══. d
KATJA  Dann kaufe ich das T-Shirt und die Schuhe.
SONJA  ═══. c
KATJA  Ich weiß, aber sie gefallen mir sehr.

## 21 Wie findest du ...?

Find out what your partner thinks about the clothes that Georg and Beate are wearing to Sonja's party. One of you comments on Georg's clothing, and the other on Beate's. When you have finished, switch roles.

Georg

Beate

## 22 Zum Schreiben

With your partner, write a conversation that could go with the picture below. Practice your conversation and be prepared to share it with the class.

# Welche Klamotten sind „in"?

What do you think German students usually like to wear when they go to a party? We asked many students, and here is what some of them said. Listen first, then read the text.

### Sandra,
*Stuttgart*

„Also, wenn ich zu einer Party gehe, dann ziehe ich am liebsten Jeans an und vielleicht einen Body ... und einen weißen Pulli darüber; meistens dann etwas in Blau oder einen weißen Pulli, jetzt, wie grad' eben, denn meine Lieblingsfarben sind doch Blau und Weiß."

### Melina,
*Bietigheim*

„Am liebsten mag ich Jeans, vor allem helle, oder ja so lockere Blusen, kurze halt, und jetzt vor allem T-Shirts, einfarbige; und sie sollen halt schön lang sein und ein bißchen locker. Und ja, meine Lieblingsfarben sind Blau, Apricot oder Rot, Lila auch noch."

### Alexandra,
*Bietigheim*

„Ja, ich zieh' am liebsten Jeans an, und Lieblingsfarben sind dann so Blau oder Pastellfarben, und auf Partys oder so eigentlich immer in Jeans und mal etwas Schöneres oben, in Diskos dann auch, und ab und zu hab' ich mal gern einen Rock."

### Iwan,
*Bietigheim*

„Also, wenn ich auf eine Party gehe, zieh' ich am liebsten ein T-Shirt an und eine kurze Hose. Am liebsten trag' ich Schwarz, so einfach, weil es halt schön aussieht und weil es bequem ist."

A. 1. What items of clothing are mentioned most by these students? Make a list of the clothing each student prefers and list the colors he or she seems to like best.

2. Which of these students would you like to meet and why? Do you and the student you selected have similar tastes in clothes? Explain. What do you generally wear and what are your favorite colors? What do you usually wear to a party?

B. What is your overall impression of the way these German teenagers dress? Compare it with the typical dress for teenagers in the United States. Do you think students in the United States are more or less formal than students in Germany? Why do you think so? Write a brief essay explaining your answer.

## Talking about trying on clothes

## 23 Hör gut zu!

Jürgen goes to a clothing store to find something to wear to Sonja's party. You will hear four short pieces of his conversation with the salesman. On a separate sheet of paper, put the photos in order according to their conversation. c. a. b. d.

a.

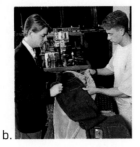

b.

c.

d.

---

## SO SAGT MAN DAS!

### Talking about trying on clothes

When you go shopping for clothes, you will want to try them on.

You might say to the salesperson:

**Ich probiere das T-Shirt an.** *or*      **Ich ziehe das T-Shirt an.**

If you decide to buy it:      If not:

**Ich nehme es.** *or*      **Ich nehme es nicht.** *or*

**Ich kaufe es.**      **Ich kaufe es nicht.**

---

## *G*rammatik    Separable-prefix verbs

The verbs **anziehen** (*to put on, wear*), **anprobieren** (*to try on*), and **aussehen** (*to look, appear*), belong to a group of verbs that have a separable prefix. The prefix is at the beginning of the verb: *an*ziehen, *an*probieren, *aus*sehen. In the present tense, the prefix is separated from the verb and is at the end of the clause or sentence.

**anziehen**

Was **ziehe** ich **an?**

Ich **ziehe** Shorts **an.**

Ich **ziehe** Shorts und ein T-Shirt **an.**

Ich **ziehe** heute Shorts und ein T-Shirt **an.**

Ich **ziehe** heute zu Sonjas Fete Shorts und ein T-Shirt **an.**

Ja, zu Sonjas Fete **ziehe** ich ganz bestimmt Shorts und ein T-Shirt **an!**

---

## 24 Sätze bauen

Build as many sentences as you can.
Be sure to use the correct articles.

| Ich | zieht ... an | Hemd |
| Er | ziehe ... an | gut |
| Bluse | sieht ... aus | blöd |
| Schuhe | sehen ... aus | scheußlich |
| Sie | probiert ... an | Pulli |
| Jogging-Anzug | probiere ... an | Jacke |
| Jeans | | Jeans |
| Gürtel | | |

**LERNTRICK**

A number of German verbs
have prefixes but not all of
them are separable (for example, **gefallen** and **bekommen**).
You can usually recognize separable prefixes if they are
words that can also stand
alone (such as **mit, auf,** and
**aus**) and if they carry the
main stress of the compound
verb. Compare **ánziehen** and
**bekómmen**.

### Ein wenig *G*rammatik

The verbs **nehmen** (*to take*) and **aussehen** (*to
appear, look*) are called stem-changing verbs. In
these verbs, the stem vowel changes in the **du**-
and **er/sie**-forms. These verbs do not follow the
regular patterns of verbs like **spielen**.

Du **nimmst** den Rock.    Du **siehst** gut **aus**!
Er **nimmt** die Jacke.    Sie **sieht** gut **aus**!

You will learn more about these verbs later.

## 25 Was ziehen sie zu Sonjas Fete an?

a. Look at the pictures of clothing below and ask your partner what Julia, Katja, Michael,
and Heiko will wear to Sonja's party. Your partner's responses will be based on the illustrations. Switch roles and vary your responses.

b. You and your partner have been invited to Sonja's party. Ask your partner what he or
she would wear based on the pictures of clothing. Then switch roles.

## 26 Was nimmst du?

You have picked out five items of clothing that you like. Your partner asks you which items
you will try on and which ones you would like to buy. Answer, then switch roles.

## 27 Für mein Notizbuch

For your **Notizbuch** entry, write a paragraph describing what you and your friends usually wear to a party. Describe the kinds of clothes you like and some that you do not like. Describe some of the latest fashions for teens and write what you think about them.

## 28 Im Fernsehen

You work for an ad agency. Get together with two other classmates and write a TV commercial that will convince your audience to shop at a certain clothing store. Be sure to mention prices, colors, and how well the clothes fit and look.

---

au A U /x/ S S eu P R ä A C tsi H E ö

## Richtig aussprechen / Richtig lesen

**A.** To practice the following sounds, say the words and sentences below after your teacher or after the recording.

1. The letter **i:** When the letter **i** is followed by two consonants, it sounds like the short *i* in the English word *pit*.
   **schick, bestimmt, bißchen / Ich finde das Kleid schick. Ehrlich.**

2. The letters **ä** and **e:** The letters **ä** and **e** are pronounced as short vowels when followed by two consonants. They sound similar to the short *e* in the English word *net*.
   **lässig, hell, gefällt / Das fesche Hemd gefällt mir.**

3. The letter **a:** The letter **a** is roughly equivalent to the *a* sound in the English word *father*.
   **haben, lang, Jacke / Wir haben Jacken in allen Farben.**

4. The letter combinations **sch, st,** and **sp:** The consonant combination **sch** is pronounced like the *sh* in the English word *ship*. When the letter **s** is followed by **p** or **t** at the beginning of a syllable, it is also pronounced in this way.
   **schwarz, Turnschuh, Stiefel / Die schwarzen Stiefel sind Spitze!**

## Richtig schreiben / Diktat

**B.** Write down the sentences that you hear.

# *Kleider machen Leute!*

For answers to these questions, see TE interleaf, p. 115Q.

### LESETRICK

**Using what you already know** When you are faced with an unknown text, use what you already know to anticipate the kind of information you might expect to find in the text. It is obvious that these texts are about clothing. Though you may see many words that you do not know, you have read clothing ads in English, and you know that they contain information about prices, styles, sizes, types of material, etc. Watch for this kind of information as you read.

1. Look at a clothing ad from a magazine written in English and make a list of some of the words and expressions that you find in the ad.

2. When you look in a newspaper or magazine for some good buys in clothing, what are some words or phrases that tell you that you would be getting a bargain? Write down some of these English words and phrases.

3. Scan these two pages and write any German words or phrases you find that correspond to the words and phrases you listed in Activities 1 and 2 above. Group the words you find in categories (prices, colors, etc.) and list as many words in each category as you can.

4. Look at the prices of the clothing being advertised. Judging from the photos, are these prices reasonable? Are there prices you could afford? Do you think they are the original prices in all

Ohne Shirts und Shorts geht im Sommer nichts. K + L Ruppert hat für Sie die schönsten ausgesucht. Sagenhafte Vielfalt und sommerleichte Qualitäten. Zu Preisen, die Ihnen passen werden!

[7] **29.-**

**Alex, 16 Jahre**
„Ich trage Schwarz. Ich ändere das nie. Andere Sachen habe ich nicht. Ich glaube, mit Mode kann man etwas erklären, ohne zu reden."

**39**

**Sandra, 16 Jahre**
„Zu meinem braunen Kleid trage ich schwarze Strümpfe und schwarze Schuhe mit Klumpabsatz. Ich ziehe mir auch Sachen an, wenn sie nicht 'in' sind. Es gibt wichtigeres als Mode."

**3**

**Manu, 16 Jahre**
„Meine Jeans und die Lederjacke sind Markenprodukte, keine billigen Kopien. Ich finde das wichtig."

# KRIEGBAUM AKTUELL

*Stark Reduziert!*

**(3)**
**19.90**

**(2)**
**12.90**

2) **Kapuzen-T-Shirts**
100% reine Baumwolle, in vielen Farben sortiert, Größe M-XXL **12.90**

3) **Kapuzen-T-Shirts**
100% reine Baumwolle, top Farben, bedruckt **19.90**

**Volker, 16 Jahre**

„Das sind meine Sachen: Jeans, Sportschuhe, Kapuzen-Shirt. Ich trage sie, weil sie mir gefallen. Mode interessiert mich nicht."

**29.-**

**29.-**

cases? What phrase gives you the information to answer that question?

5. Not all the texts on these pages are ads. What other type of text can you identify? What type of magazine would you expect texts like these to come from?

6. What is the age of the students who are describing their clothing? What generalizations can you make about the clothing of these students? Find words in the text that support your answer.

7. In the ad to the left, what kind of guarantee does **K&L Ruppert** offer for its merchandise?

8. What does Volker wear? Where could he buy a shirt like the one he says he likes to wear? How much would it cost? Do you know why it has that name?

9. What does Alex mean when he says „**Ich glaube, mit Mode kann man etwas erklären, ohne zu reden.**"? (**ohne zu reden**-*without speaking*) Work with a partner and come up with some examples that illustrate this statement.

10. How does Manu differ from Sandra and Volker?

11. You are planning a trip to Germany. Your hosts will meet you at the airport, but they have never seen you. Write them a postcard with a short description of what you look like and what you will be wearing (**Ich trage ...** ).

12. Your club at school is planning a garage sale. Write an ad for the school or local newspaper in which you describe the kinds of clothing you will sell.

**1** You have been hired to write for a German fashion magazine on trends among teens today. Interview your partner about his or her taste in clothes. When you have finished, switch roles and then interview one other person. Find out what clothes they like to wear, what they wear to a party, their favorite color, and their favorite article of clothing. Take notes and write an article in German based on your interviews.

**2** Look at the two display windows for **Mode-Welt.** With a partner compare the two windows and take turns telling each other which items are missing (**fehlen**) from the second window.

**3** What questions would the salesperson and customer have to ask in order to get the responses in this conversation?

| | |
|---|---|
| VERKÄUFERIN | ======? Answers may vary. Example: **Haben Sie einen Wunsch?** |
| KUNDIN | Ich brauche eine Bluse in Weiß. ======? **Was kostet die Bluse hier?** |
| VERKÄUFERIN | Sie kostet DM 43,00. |
| KUNDIN | ======? **Haben Sie die Bluse auch in Gelb?** |
| VERKÄUFERIN | Ja, die haben wir auch in Gelb. |
| KUNDIN | Und ======? **Wie finden Sie die Bluse?** |
| VERKÄUFERIN | Ich finde die Bluse sehr schick. Die hat nicht jeder. |
| KUNDIN | Ich probiere sie mal an. ======? **Paßt sie?** |
| VERKÄUFERIN | Sie paßt prima! |
| KUNDIN | ======? **Nicht zu eng?** |
| VERKÄUFERIN | Nein, die Bluse ist überhaupt nicht zu eng. ======? **Nehmen Sie die Bluse?** |
| KUNDIN | Ja, ich nehme sie. Danke! |

**4** You are in a store looking for some new clothes and your partner, a pushy salesperson, tries to convince you to try on and get clothes that are the wrong color and don't fit. You try them on, and he or she tells you how good they look and how well they fit. You're not so sure. Express your uncertainty and hesitancy. Will you succumb to the pressure in the end and buy the clothes? Develop a conversation based on this scenario and practice it with your partner.

**5** You will hear some conversations in a clothing store. In each case the customer has decided not to buy the item. Determine the reason. Is it the price, the color, or the fit? 1. paßt nicht 2. Farbe 3. Preis 4. paßt nicht 5. Farbe

| | Preis | Farbe | paßt nicht |
|---|---|---|---|
| 1 | | | |
| 2 | | | |

1. A white shirt
2. The reviewer is enthusiastic.

3. It is elegant, yet casual—a basic fashion element. Designers are using it in many ways.

## DAS WEISSE HEMD

Ein weißes Hemd ist das, was Modekenner einen „all time classic" nennen: schick, aber trotzdem leger—ein Basisstück für jede Garderobe. In dieser Saison ist das weiße Hemd das Lieblingskind der Designer, die sich in ihren Variationen gegenseitig übertreffen. Asymmetrisch, geknotet oder aus Leinen, lang oder kurz—zu Jeans, Shorts oder Röcken: alles geht.

**6** Read the fashion review to the right then answer these questions.
   **1.** What clothing item is the fashion editor talking about?
   **2.** Is he or she enthusiastic or skeptical about the item?
   **3.** What does he or she say about the clothing being reviewed?

**7** Find a photo of someone wearing an interesting outfit, and write a review of the clothes he or she is wearing. Share your review with the class.

**8**

# R O L L E N S P I E L

You and two friends are at home trying to find something to wear to a party.
   **a.** One of you is trying on clothes, but you can't find anything that fits or is the right color. Your friends comment on the clothes you try on.
   **b.** Unsuccessful, in the end you all decide to go to the store. Look at the display windows in Activity 2 on page 136 again. Choose one window on which to base your conversation. This time one of you is the salesperson. The other two will be the customers. Ask for items in specific colors. The salesperson will tell you what's available. Will you try the clothes on? How do they look? Will you buy them? Role-play your scene in front of the class using props.

**Can you express wishes when shopping? (p. 122)**

**1** How would a salesperson in a clothing store ask what you would like?
1. Bitte? *or* Was möchten Sie? *or* Was bekommen Sie? *or* Haben Sie einen Wunsch?

**2** How would you answer, saying that you were looking for the following? (Be sure to practice using the articles correctly, and watch out for direct objects.) Ich brauche/suche/möchte ...

a. einen Pulli, bitte.
**a.** a sweater

c. eine Hose in Rot.
**c.** pants in red

e. eine Jacke in Hellgrau.
**e.** a jacket in light gray

**b.** boots in black
b. Stiefel in Schwarz.

**d.** a shirt in brown
d. ein Hemd in Braun.

**f.** a dress in blue
f. ein Kleid in Blau.

**Can you comment on and describe clothing? (p. 125)**

**3** How would you ask a friend what he or she thinks of these clothes:
a. Wie findest du die Jacke?   b. Wie findest du die Schuhe?

a.     b.     c.     d.
c. Wie findest du den Jogging-Anzug?   d. Wie findest du das Hemd?

**4** How might your friend respond positively? Negatively? With uncertainty? Er/Sie/Es gefällt mir. Ich finde ihn/sie/es furchtbar. Ich weiß nicht.

**5** How would you disagree with the following statements by saying the opposite? Use the correct pronoun.   Answers may vary.

**a.** The jacket is too short.
**b.** The shoes are too tight.
**c.** The jogging suit is too small.
**d.** The shirt fits just right.

**e.** I think the belt is terrible.
**f.** I like the tennis shoes.
**g.** I think the dress is too long.
**h.** The skirt looks stylish.

a. Sie ist zu lang.   c. Er ist zu groß.   e. Er ist Spitze.   g. Es ist zu kurz.
b. Sie sind zu groß.   d. Es paßt nicht.   f. Sie gefallen mir nicht.   h. Er ist furchtbar.

**Can you compliment someone's clothing and respond to compliments? (p. 127)**

**6** How would you compliment Katja, using the cues below?

**a.** blouse   **b.** sweater   **c.** T-shirt   **d.** skirt   Answers may vary.
a. Die Bluse gefällt mir!   b. Der Pulli sieht lässig aus!   c. Das T-Shirt ist fesch!   d. Der Rock ist schick!

**7** a. How might Katja respond to your compliments?
b. What would you say next?   a. Ehrlich? *or* Wirklich? *or* Meinst du?
b. Ehrlich! *or* Wirklich! *or* Ja, bestimmt!

**8** How would you tell a friend what the following people are wearing to Sonja's party? (Remember to use **anziehen**!) Answers may vary.

> Jeans   Bluse   T-Shirt
> Shorts   Turnschuhe
> Jogging-Anzug   Gürtel

**a.** Julia   **b.** Katja   **c.** Heiko

a. Julia zieht Jeans und eine Bluse an.   b. Katja zieht Shorts und ein T-Shirt an.   c. Heiko zieht einen Jogging-Anzug an

**Can you talk about trying on clothes? (p. 131)**

**9** How would you tell the salesperson that you would like to try on a shirt in red, pants in white, a sweater in yellow, and a jacket in brown?
Ich möchte ein Hemd in Rot anprobieren./eine Hose in Weiß/einen Pulli in Gelb/eine Jacke in Braun

**10** How would you tell your friend that you will get the shirt, the sweater, and the jacket? (Use **nehmen** or **kaufen**.)
Ich nehme (kaufe) das Hemd, den Pulli und die Jacke.

## ERSTE STUFE

### EXPRESSING WISHES WHEN SHOPPING

**Bitte?**   *Yes?*
**Was bekommen Sie?**
  *What would you like?*
**Haben Sie einen Wunsch?**
  *May I help you?*
**Ich möchte ...**   *I would like...*
**Ich brauche ...**   *I need...*
**Ich suche ...**   *I'm looking for...*
**Einen Pulli in Grau, bitte.**
  *A sweater in gray, please.*
**Haben sie das auch in Rot?**
  *Do you also have that in red?*
**die Farbe, -n**   *color*
  **in Rot**   *in red*

**in Blau**   *in blue*
**in Grün**   *in green*
**in Gelb**   *in yellow*
**in Braun**   *in brown*
**in Grau**   *in gray*
**in Schwarz**   *in black*
**in Weiß**   *in white*
**in Dunkelblau**   *in dark blue*
**in Hellblau**   *in light blue*
**die Klamotten** (pl)   *casual term
  for clothes*
**die Bluse, -n**   *blouse*
**der Rock, ¨e**   *skirt*
**das Kleid, -er**   *dress*
**das Hemd, -en**   *shirt*
**die Jeans, -**   *jeans*
**der Gürtel, -**   *belt*

**die Hose, -n**   *pants*
**die Jacke, -n**   *jacket*
**der Pulli, -s (Pullover,-)**   *sweater*
**der Jogging-Anzug, ¨e**
  *jogging suit*
**das T-Shirt, -s**   *T-shirt*
**der Turnschuh, -e**   *sneaker,
  athletic shoe*
**der Stiefel, -**   *boot*
**die Socke, -n**   *sock*
**die Shorts, -**   *shorts*

### MASCULINE ARTICLES: ACCUSATIVE CASE

**den**   *the*
**einen**   *a, an*

## ZWEITE STUFE

### COMMENTING ON AND DESCRIBING CLOTHES

**Er/Sie/Es gefällt mir.**   *I like it.*
**Sie gefallen mir.**   *I like them.*
**Der Rock sieht ... aus.**   *The skirt
  looks....*
  **hübsch**   *pretty*
  **lässig**   *casual*
  **schick**   *chic, smart*
  **fesch**   *stylish, smart*
  **scheußlich**   *hideous*
  **furchtbar**   *terrible, awful*
**Der Rock paßt prima!**   *The skirt
  fits great!*

**Ich finde den Pulli echt stark!**   *I
  think the sweater is really awesome!*
**Ich bin nicht sicher.**   *I'm not
  sure.*
**Ich weiß nicht.**   *I don't know.*
**die Größe, -n**   *the size*
**zu**   *too*
**viel zu**   *much too*
**ein bißchen**   *a little*
**weit**   *wide*
**eng**   *tight*
**lang**   *long*
**kurz**   *short*

### GIVING AND RESPONDING TO COMPLIMENTS

**Meinst du?**   *Do you think so?*
**ehrlich**   *honestly*
**wirklich**   *really*
**überhaupt nicht**   *not at all*
**bestimmt**   *definitely*
**Nicht zu lang?**   *Not too long?*

### MASCULINE PRONOUN: ACCUSATIVE CASE

**ihn**   *it; him*

## DRITTE STUFE

### TALKING ABOUT TRYING ON CLOTHES

**aussehen** (sep)*   *to look (like),
  appear*
  **er/sie sieht aus**\*\*   *he/she looks*
**anprobieren** (sep)   *to try on*

**anziehen** (sep)   *to put on, wear*
**nehmen**   *to take*
  **er/sie nimmt**   *he/she takes*
**kaufen**   *to buy*

*Verbs with separable prefixes will be indicated with (sep)  \*\*For verbs with stem-vowel changes, the third person singular form will be listed to show you the vowel change that occurs.

# Kapitel 6: Pläne machen *Chapter Overview*

| Los geht's!<br>*pp. 142-144* | Wollen wir ins Café gehen? p. 142 | | | *Video Guide* |
|---|---|---|---|---|
| | **FUNCTIONS** | **GRAMMAR** | **CULTURE** | **RE-ENTRY** |
| **Erste Stufe**<br>*pp. 145-148* | •Starting a conversation, *p. 145*<br>•Telling time and talking about when you do things, *p. 146* | | Pictures of clocks located outside of public buildings, *p. 147* | •Expressing time when referring to schedules, *p. 146* (from **Kapitel 4**)<br>•School and free time activity vocabulary, *p. 148* (from **Kapitel 2** and **4**) |
| **Zweite Stufe**<br>*pp. 149-153* | Making plans, *p. 150* | The verb **wollen**, *p. 150* | **Landeskunde: Was machst du in deiner Freizeit?** *p. 153* | •Inversion of time elements, *p. 151* (from **Kapitel 2**)<br>•Sequencing events, *p. 152* (from **Kapitel 4**) |
| **Dritte Stufe**<br>*pp. 154-157* | •Ordering food and beverages, *p. 154*<br>•Talking about how something tastes, *p. 156*<br>•Paying the check, *p. 156* | The stem-changing verb **essen**, *p. 155* | **Ein wenig Landeskunde:** Tipping in Germany, *p. 157* | •Accusative case, *p. 155* (from **Kapitel 5**)<br>•The verb **nehmen,** *p. 155* (from **Kapitel 5**)<br>•The **möchte**-forms, *p. 155* (from **Kapitel 5**) used in a new context, ordering food |

| **Aussprache**<br>*p. 157* | The letter combination **ch**, the letter **r**, and the final **er** | | | **Diktat:**<br>*Textbook Audiocassette* 3 B |
|---|---|---|---|---|

| **Zum Lesen**<br>*pp. 158-159* | **Wohin in Hamburg?**<br>Reading Strategy: Using context to guess meaning |
|---|---|

| **Review**<br>*pp. 160-163* | •**Anwendung,** *p. 160*<br>•**Kann ich's wirklich?** *p. 162*<br>•**Wortschatz,** *p. 163* |
|---|---|

| **Assessment Options**<br><br>Mid-term Exam,<br>*Assessment Guide Audiocassette* 7 B | **Stufe Quizzes**<br>•*Chapter Resources,* Book 2<br>    **Erste Stufe,** Quiz 6-1<br>    **Zweite Stufe,** Quiz 6-2<br>    **Dritte Stufe,** Quiz 6-3<br>•*Assessment Items, Audiocassette* 7 B | **Kapitel 6 Chapter Test**<br>•*Chapter Resources,* Book 2<br>•*Assessment Guide,* Speaking Test<br>•*Assessment Items, Audiocassette* 7 B<br><br>**Test Generator, Kapitel 6** |
|---|---|---|

Video Program **OR**
Expanded Video Program, Videocassette 2

Textbook Audiocassette 3 B

| RESOURCES Print | RESOURCES Audiovisual |
|---|---|

Textbook Audiocassette 3 B

Practice and Activity Book
Chapter Resources, Book 2
- Communicative Activity 6-1
- Additional Listening Activity 6-1 . . . . . . . . . . . . . . Additional Listening Activities, Audiocassette 9 B
- Additional Listening Activity 6-2 . . . . . . . . . . . . . . Additional Listening Activities, Audiocassette 9 B
- Student Response Form
- Realia 6-1
- Situation Card 6-1
- Teaching Transparency Master 6-1 . . . . . . . . . . . . . Teaching Transparency 6-1
- Quiz 6-1 . . . . . . . . . . . . . . . . . . . . . . . . . . . Assessment Items, Audiocassette 7 B

Textbook Audiocassette 3 B

Practice and Activity Book
Chapter Resources, Book 2
- Communicative Activity 6-2
- Additional Listening Activity 6-3 . . . . . . . . . . . . . . Additional Listening Activities, Audiocassette 9 B
- Additional Listening Activity 6-4 . . . . . . . . . . . . . . Additional Listening Activities, Audiocassette 9 B
- Student Response Form
- Realia 6-2
- Situation Card 6-2
- Quiz 6-2 . . . . . . . . . . . . . . . . . . . . . . . . . . . Assessment Items, Audiocassette 7 B
Video Guide. . . . . . . . . . . . . . . . . . . . . . . . . . . . . .Video Program/Expanded Video Program, Videocassette 2

Textbook Audiocassette 3 B

Practice and Activity Book
Chapter Resources, Book 2
- Additional Listening Activity 6-5 . . . . . . . . . . . . . . Additional Listening Activities, Audiocassette 9 B
- Additional Listening Activity 6-6 . . . . . . . . . . . . . . Additional Listening Activities, Audiocassette 9 B
- Student Response Form
- Realia 6-3
- Situation Card 6-3
- Teaching Transparency Master 6-2 . . . . . . . . . . . . . Teaching Transparency 6-2
- Quiz 6-3 . . . . . . . . . . . . . . . . . . . . . . . . . . . Assessment Items, Audiocassette 7 B

Video Guide. . . . . . . . . . . . . . . . . . . . . . . . . . . . . .Video Program/Expanded Video Program, Videocassette 2

**Alternative Assessment**
- Performance Assessment, *Teacher's Edition*
  **Erste Stufe**, p. 139 K
  **Zweite Stufe**, p. 139 M
  **Dritte Stufe**, p. 139 P
- Portfolio Assessment
  Written: **Zum Lesen**, Activity 6c, *Pupil's Edition*, p. 159, *Assessment Guide*
  Oral: **Dritte Stufe**, Activity 33, *Pupil's Edition*, p. 157, *Assessment Guide*
- **Notizbuch,** *Pupil's Edition*, p. 149; *Practice and Activity Book,* p.150

# Kapitel 6: Pläne machen
# Textbook Listening Activities Scripts

## Erste Stufe

### Activity 6, p. 145

1. — Wie geht's denn?
   — Ach, nicht so besonders gut.
   — Wieso denn?
   — Ich kann mein Geld nicht finden.
   — Na, das tut mir leid. Kann ich dir beim Suchen helfen?

2. — Wie geht's dir denn?
   — Echt schlecht.
   — Darf ich fragen warum?
   — Ich habe 'ne Vier in Englisch.
   — Ja, das ist wirklich nicht so gut! Der Herr Meier ist aber auch ganz schön schwer, nicht?

3. — Hallo!
   — Grüß dich! Wie geht's denn?
   — Oh, danke, ganz gut! Ich gehe am Wochenende in ein Rockkonzert. Darauf freue ich mich schon!

4. — Grüß dich!
   — Hallo!
   — Wie geht's denn so?
   — Hm, nicht schlecht, ich bin nur müde.

5. — Hallo! Wie geht's denn bei dir?
   — Danke, sehr gut!
   — Um 3 Uhr gehen Sabine, Dieter und ich ins Kino. Kommst du mit?
   — Na klar, danke!

### Activity 13, p. 148

1. — Du, Gudrun, willst du heute abend mit uns ins Kino gehen?
   — Mensch, schade. Danke für die Einladung, aber um Viertel nach sieben will ich Fernsehen schauen. Dann kommt eine Sendung über Elefanten in Afrika. Das brauch' ich halt für meine Erdkundeklasse am Mittwoch.

2. — Du Susanne, machst du was heute nachmittag?
   — Ja, um zwanzig nach drei ... hm ... ja, hab' ich meine Tennisstunde.

3. — Ich gehe jetzt ins Café Freizeit. Kommst du mit?
   — Nein, ich möcht' ja schon, aber ich kann nicht. Ich muß für Mathe lernen. Morgen um Viertel nach neun ist unsere Matheprüfung.

4. — Morgen, wie geht's? Du kommst ja heute schon so früh!
   — Ja, meine erste Stunde ist heute schon um Viertel vor acht. Deutsch bei Frau Stegel. Da muß man pünktlich sein.

5. — Du, die Eva und ich wollen am Samstag um neun bei Karstadt Klamotten anschauen. Willst du mitkommen?
   — Ich möchte schon mit, aber ich treffe um Viertel vor zwei Udo und Erika im Schwimmbad.

6. — Renate! Magda! Was macht ihr denn hier noch so spät? Es ist schon halb elf! Und morgen früh ist Schule.
   — Tut uns leid, Vati. Ist es zu laut? Diese Musik ist einfach Spitze!
   — Nein, nein. Zu laut ist es nicht ... aber es ist jetzt zu spät, Musik zu hören. Geht bitte ins Bett, hört ihr?

## Zweite Stufe

### Activity 16, p. 149

BEATE  Du, ich freue mich schon aufs Wochenende. Hast du heute auch Taschengeld bekommen?

SABINE  Ja, ein Glück, da können wir ja endlich mal wieder in die Stadt gehen. Was meinst du dazu?

BEATE  Ja klar doch, zuerst laß' uns ins Café gehen. Da können wir uns gut unterhalten und ...

SABINE  Du, ich weiß was, danach gehen wir ins Kino ...

BEATE  Gibt's denn gute Filme?

SABINE  Natürlich ... und ach ja, ich will auch zu Karstadt. Ich brauch' ein paar neue Klamotten für die Schule. Hast du Lust dazu?

BEATE  Okay! Wenn wir Zeit haben, können wir ja anschließend baden gehen. Das neue Schwimmbad soll ganz toll sein!

SABINE  Prima! Ich freue mich schon aufs Wochenende!

# Dritte Stufe

## Activity 27, p. 154

KATJA  Julia, was nimmst du?

JULIA  Ach, ich bestelle wie immer. Ich esse gern ein Stück Apfelkuchen und trinke einen Cappuccino dazu.

MICHAEL  Und du, Heiko? Was willst du? Auch Apfelkuchen?

HEIKO  Nein, keinen Kuchen für mich. Das ist zu süß. Ich möchte zuerst etwas trinken, ein Mineralwasser. Und dann esse ich lieber ein Wurstbrot. Vielleicht trinke ich einen Cappuccino zum Schluß.

JULIA  Und du, Katja?

KATJA  Hm! Ich habe einen Hunger kann ich dir sagen! Ich glaube, ich nehme eine Nudelsuppe, dann zwei Paar Wiener mit Senf, und ich trinke eine Limonade, ein großes Glas.

HEIKO  Und du, Michael? Was willst du nehmen?

MICHAEL  Ich habe Hunger auf eine Pizza, und dazu trinke ich dann eine Cola. Danach gibt's natürlich wie immer einen Eisbecher. Eis esse ich immer hier.

## Activity 31, p. 156

HEIKO  Hallo! Wir möchten zahlen!

MICHAEL  Ja schaut, es ist schon 4 Uhr. Wir müssen bald los!

KELLNER  Also für Sie ... ein Mineralwasser, drei Mark fünfzig; ein Wurstbrot, fünf Mark sechzig; einen Cappuccino, fünf Mark zwanzig. Das macht zusammen vierzehn Mark dreißig.

HEIKO  Fünfzehn Mark. Stimmt schon.

KELLNER  Danke. Und Sie ... einen Moment bitte ... ja, eine Nudelsuppe, vier Mark fünfzig; dazu kamen zwei Paar Wiener mit Senf, fünf Mark achtzig; und eine Limonade, drei Mark sechzig. Zusammen: dreizehn Mark neunzig.

KATJA  Vierzehn Mark. Stimmt so.

KELLNER  Ein Stück Apfelkuchen ist zwei Mark achtzig; ein Cappuccino fünf Mark zwanzig. Das macht zusammen genau acht Mark.

JULIA  Ja dann ... acht fünfzig, bitte.

KELLNER  Vielen Dank! Und Sie, eine Pizza, sechs Mark fünfzig; eine Cola, drei Mark und der Eisbecher sechs Mark achtzig. Alles zusammen: sechzehn Mark dreißig.

MICHAEL  Siebzehn Mark. Stimmt schon.

KELLNER  Vielen Dank. Auf Wiedersehen!

## Diktat, p. 157

You will hear Angelika talking to Thomas about his plans for the weekend. First listen to what they are saying, then write down their conversation.

ANGELIKA  Und, was machst du denn am Wochenende, Thomas?

THOMAS  Ich bin noch nicht ganz sicher. Ach, vielleicht gehe ich radfahren. Und du?

ANGELIKA  Ich möchte gern ins Kino. Willst du am Samstag nachmittag mitkommen? So um 4 Uhr?

THOMAS  Ja, das heißt ... nein, das geht leider nicht. Wir besuchen meine Großeltern.

ANGELIKA  Schade.

THOMAS  Du, um 20 Uhr spielt Udo Lindenberg, und es gibt noch Karten. Willst du ihn hören?

ANGELIKA  Ja prima. Also, bis später dann!

# Anwendung

## Activity 2, p. 160

1. Im Sommer reist Familie Bonsen gern an die Nordsee. Jedes Jahr bleiben sie für zwei Wochen im Hotel Hanseatik. Das hat sogar ein großes Schwimmbad. Die Familie ißt dort auch gern im Restaurant. Das Essen ist immer gut und auch preiswert.

2. Susanne und Michaela spielen gern Tennis und hören gern Musik. Sie haben beide viele Kassetten und CDs, aber am liebsten gehen sie doch in Konzerte. Im Juni gehen sie in ein Rockkonzert. Susanne geht auch manchmal mit ihren Eltern in die Symphonie.

3. Dieter und Lutz sind bei Lutz zu Hause. Sie spielen Karten, und Dieter gewinnt-wie immer!

4. Ute geht nicht gern in die Stadt. Das findet sie langweilig. Sie bleibt lieber zu Hause und übt auf ihrer Gitarre. Sie spielt schon seit drei Jahren und ist ziemlich gut.

5. Anja und Martina gehen am Samstag in die Stadt. Sie brauchen ein paar neue Klamotten für die Schule.

# Kapitel 6: Pläne Machen
## *Suggested Project*

**PROJECT**

*In this activity students will create an information guide to Schleswig-Holstein, the location of Chapters 4, 5, and 6. Begin this project before you start Chapter 6, allowing the students time for research and revision of their projects. This activity will take several days, so you may want to consider breaking it into smaller assignments and having it count as a major grade. Each project will be different.*

*This project is designed for students to do individually or in groups. Assign each group of students a topic or let them choose one.*

## MATERIALS

✂ **Students may need**
- *poster board*
- *glue*
- *scissors*
- *masking tape*

## SUGGESTED TOPICS

### Economy
natural resources; manufactured goods; important crops; importance of agriculture and industry

### Geography
a. a map of Schleswig-Holstein showing rivers, lakes, canals, important cities (with special attention to the **Landeshauptstadt**), and borders with other **Bundesländer** and countries
b. population: pictures depicting types of housing; dialects

### Culture
a. art, dances, folk music, **Trachten** for men and women
b. literature: biography and brief summaries of important works of Thomas Mann and

Theodor Storm (special attention should be paid to Storm's novel **Der Schimmelreiter**)
c. history: poster illustrating the history of Schleswig-Holstein
d. food: recipe booklet presenting specialties of the region. Students cook some of the dishes and bring them to class for everyone to taste.
e. a poster illustrating the history, importance, and meaning of the **Kieler Woche**

## SUGGESTED SEQUENCE

1. Students do research at a library (school, public, or university library) and look for information in atlases, almanacs, periodicals, world reference books, encyclopedias, etc. To provide the students with information, you may want to request brochures from the sources listed on pp. T38 and T39 of the *Teacher's Edition.*

2. Students begin their project by giving it a title and compiling their materials.

3. Students organize their notes and materials according to categories.

4. Students hand in a rough draft of their projects to get suggestions on improving them. Or have students exchange rough drafts with other students and give each other feedback.

5. Students finish their projects with an oral presentation and then turn in their final project.

## GRADING THE PROJECT

Give individual grades to students based upon their cooperation within their groups and an interim assessment of drafts. One final grade should be given to each student, based upon a holistic assessment of the finished information guide and the combination of individual and group work that went into it.

Suggested point distribution (total=100)

| | |
|---|---|
| Content | 40 |
| Oral presentation | 20 |
| Appearance | 10 |
| Correct usage (grammar, vocabulary) | 10 |
| Originality | 10 |
| Individual participation | 10 |

# Kapitel 6: Pläne machen
 *Games*

## BOARD RACE GAME

*This game gives students a fun way to practice writing numbers, time expressions, and other phrases.*

**Procedure** Depending on the class size, divide the class into two or more teams, appoint a score-keeper, and have one member of each team stand at the board with a piece of chalk. Read one of the situations, numbers, or times aloud (see examples below). Students then write the correct German phrase on the board. The team member who first writes the correct phrase or time expression on the board receives a point for his or her team. New team members should come to the board for each round. At the end of the time period, the team with the most points wins.

**Review numbers** Students must write out the number they hear. Example: you tell them 55 in German, and they write out the number **fünfund-fünfzig**.

**Review time expressions** You can review time by giving a time in German, for example 13:45, and having the students write out the time in words. (**dreizehn Uhr fünfundvierzig**) You can also review the new time expressions introduced in Chapter 6. For example, you can tell students in English to write half past nine in German, and they write **halb zehn**.

**Review phrases**
* *How would you ask someone what he or she wants to do?*
* *How would you tell someone that you want to go to a café?*
* *How would you ask someone what time it is?*
* *How would you tell someone that it is 1:30 P.M.?*
* *How would you ask someone what he or she wants to do on the weekend? on Saturday?*

## LOCATION GAME

*Playing the Location Game will help students develop a better knowledge of the geography of the German-speaking countries.*

**Procedure** Use a large map of German-speaking countries or use the overhead projector to project a map on the wall. Divide the class into two teams and have one member from each team come to the front of the class. Call out a place, and the first student to point out the location correctly wins a point. This student then challenges another student. The winner is the team that has scored the most points.

## GALGENMENSCHEN

*Students will enjoy reviewing spelling and vocabulary with this familiar game.*

**Procedure** Divide the class into two teams (A and B). Use the chalkboard or the overhead projector and draw two scaffolds. Write down the first and last letters of a word, leaving the correct number of blanks for the remaining letters. Possible categories are telling time, places to go, things to do, or ordering in a restaurant. (Look at the **Wortschatz** on p. 163 for specific words relating to **Kapitel 6.**) The first member of Team A gets a chance at choosing a letter. If the letter is correct, it is filled in, and the next person on that team continues. If that person is wrong, he or she starts the hanging process on his or her team's scaffold. Construct the **Galgenmenschen** in the following order: first draw a vertical line for the rope, a circle for the head, a line for the body, a line for each arm, and a line for each leg (you can add hands and feet if you want the game to last longer). The team that completes the **Galgenmenschen** first, loses.

# Kapitel 6: Pläne machen
## Lesson Plans, pages 140-163

# Using the Chapter Opener,
### pp. 140-141

## Motivating Activity

Ask students what they do with their friends when they go out. Where do they go out to eat? Have them look at the picture of the German students and the food the German teenagers are eating. Is it different from what Americans of the same age would eat?

## Teaching Suggestion

Ask your students to name the objects that are pictured on this page. (clock, watch, fork, napkin, dishes) Have them make suggestions about how these objects relate to the photos of the German teenagers.

## Thinking Critically

① **Drawing Inferences**  Have students focus on the picture of the **Teestubenhaus.** Can they guess what type of culinary establishment this might be? (tea room) What type of food and drinks would they expect to see served here? (See Culture Note on **Teestuben.**) What background music, might they hear? (relaxing music, such as classical)

① **Comparing and Contrasting**  Can students think of a restaurant in their area that would serve similar foods and have a similar type of atmosphere?

## Culture Note

① **Teestuben** are quaint and comfortable tea houses where people like to meet. Coffee, tea, soft drinks, pastries, ice cream, and other popular snacks are served there.

## Teaching Suggestion

① Ask students if they can recall the type of roof on this **Teestubenhaus** (**Reetdach**) from the Schleswig-Holstein location opener. Remind them of the location of this chapter and that the **Teestube** pictured on p. 140 is a typical representation of local architecture.

## Background Information

② In German-speaking countries (and most other European countries) young people on a date each pay for themselves.

## Thinking Critically

③ **Drawing Inferences**  Ask students about the photo of the clock. Given that the focus of this chapter is making plans, do they see any relationship among the three photos? Do they have any ideas about the German attitude toward time?

## Focusing on Outcomes

To get students to focus on the chapter objectives listed on p. 141, have them brainstorm about expressions in English needed to plan an outing with friends. What expressions would they need to arrange a place to go, a time to meet, etc.? Then have students preview the learning outcomes listed on p. 141. **NOTE:** Each of these outcomes is modeled in the video and evaluated in **Kann ich's wirklich?** on p. 162.

# Teaching Los geht's!
## pp. 142-144

### Resources for Los geht's!

- *Video Program* OR
  *Expanded Video Program,* Videocassette 2
- *Textbook Audiocassette* 3 B
- *Practice and Activity Book*

▶ **pages 142-143**

###  Video Synopsis

In this segment of the video, several friends (Julia, Katja, Heiko, and Michael) meet at **Café Freizeit** for a bite to eat. The student outcomes listed on p. 141 are modeled in the video: starting a conversation, telling time, talking about when you are going to do things, ordering food in a restaurant, talking about how something tastes, and paying the check.

### Motivating Activity

To help students focus on one of the functions modeled in the **Foto-Roman,** ask them when they ask the question *How are you?* and how they usually respond when someone asks them. Point out that **Wie geht's?** is not used by Germans when they have just met someone for the first time.

### Teaching Suggestions

- To lead the students into the text, do the pre-listening/prereading activity with them. Have students look for any visual clues that might help them figure out what the scene is about.

- Have students listen to the conversations while looking at the photos, or have them watch this segment of the video. Remind students that they do not need to understand every word. They should try to get the gist of what is happening in the story. Have them match visual clues with words or phrases that they read or hear.

###  Total Physical Response

Bring pictures of the various items on the menu (**Suppe, Käsebrot, Wurstbrot, Pizza,** etc.) and give students commands such as **Gib Mary die Nudelsuppe! Stell bitte die Pizza auf den Tisch!**

### For Individual Needs

**Visual Learners** You might want students to watch the video with the sound turned off to help them focus on the actions and the storyline before they have to focus on the language. Since it helps visual learners to see written text, you may want to have students read the **Foto-Roman** before playing the video with the sound on.

###  Culture Notes

- Americans visiting Germany are often surprised to learn that strangers commonly share the same table in restaurants. The fact that dogs are allowed in restaurants in Germany might be another surprise to students.

- Here are some places German-speaking students might eat with friends: **Eisdiele, Imbißstand, Pizzeria, Konditorei, Gaststätte.** Explain what each one is and ask where students would most like to eat and why.

### For Individual Needs

**Challenge** If you think your students are ready for it, ask some questions about the **Foto-Roman** in German such as **Wohin geht Julia? Was machen Julia und Katja? Wer sind die Freunde von Julia? Wer ist schon im Café? Wer hat Hunger und ißt viel? Wieviel muß Michael bezahlen? Wofür? Was hat er alles gegessen? Warum sagt Michael: „Es tut mir leid."? Was hat er gemacht?** Some students will be able to answer the questions in German, but a correct answer in English is also an indication that students have understood the text.

▶ **page 144**

### Teaching Suggestion

Ask students to work through Activities 1-5 with a partner. As they do, walk around the room and monitor their work.

### Closure

Remind students of the functions targeted in this chapter. Have them look at each outcome and try to find expressions in the **Foto-Roman** that carry out that function.

**LOS GEHT'S!**

# *Teaching Erste Stufe,*
## *pp. 145-148*

### Resources for Erste Stufe

*Practice and Activity Book*
*Chapter Resources,* Book 2
- Communicative Activity 6-1
- Additional Listening Activities 6-1, 6–2
- Student Response Form
- Realia 6-1
- Situation Card 6-1
- Teaching Transparency Master 6-1
- Quiz 6-1

*Audiocassette Program*
- *Textbook Audiocassette* 3 B
- *Additional Listening Activities, Audiocassette* 9 B
- *Assessment Items, Audiocassette* 7 B

▶ **page 145**

## *MOTIVATE*

### Teaching Suggestion
Ask students to think of some ways to start a conversation in English. Have pairs of students make a list of a few of their ideas and share them with the class.

## *TEACH*

### PRESENTATION: So sagt man das!
Have students look at the pictures in this function box. Ask them to identify who is responding positively and who negatively to the question **Wie geht's?** If you want to introduce the complete phrase **Wie geht es dir?/Wie geht es Ihnen?**, do it without going into an explanation of the dative case. Treat these phrases as lexical items.

## Building on Previous Skills

- Before doing Activity 8, review numbers with the following game. Divide the class into teams of ten students. Give each team member a card with a number from 0 to 9. (Students may have more than one card if you have an odd number of students.) Call out a number, for example **zweiunddreißig.** The students from each team holding cards 3 and 2 run to the front of the room and arrange themselves in the correct order. The first team to have a pair arranged correctly wins a point.

- Play *Tic-Tac-Toe* to review formal time before beginning Activity 8. Put a *Tic-Tac-Toe* grid on the chalkboard or on a transparency. Write a formal time in each square. Divide the class into two teams. The game is played like traditional *Tic-Tac-Toe,* but in order to place an X or an O in a specific box, a team member must say the time written in that box. The team which gets three in a row wins the round. Draw additional grids if desired.

| | | |
|---|---|---|
| 21.15 | 18.50 | 9.45 |
| 17.09 | 8.14 | 18.30 |
| 00.03 | 1.16 | 17.47 |

▶ **page 146**

## PRESENTATION: Wortschatz
Use clocks with moveable hands to present the **Wortschatz.** Place the hands on, before, and after the hour and tell students what time the clock says. Or have students bring or make their own clocks (see Teaching Suggestion, Chapter 4, p. 91J) and demonstrate to you that they understand times as you say them aloud.

## PRESENTATION: So sagt man das!

Using a transparency, write each question from the **So sagt man das!** box. Write the question words and phrases **wann, wie spät, wieviel Uhr,** and **um wieviel Uhr** in a different color or underline them in red. Ask students which question words they recognize. Have them use the words they recognize to try to infer the meaning of the whole question. **Wieviel Uhr** might be more difficult to guess, but using their knowledge of **wie** from **Wie alt bist du?** and **viel** from **Ich habe viel zu tun**, students might be able to understand **wieviel Uhr.** Cover up the answers to the questions and ask students to provide answers themselves using the **Wortschatz** box.

## For Additional Practice

Use a TV schedule to elicit program times, for example **Um wieviel Uhr beginnt** *Roseanne*? **Wann enden** *The Simpsons*? If you have a TV schedule from a German newspaper, use it to talk about time.

## Language Note

Remind students that there are often similarities between English and German that will help them. Point out to them that **vor** sounds similar to *before*.

## Teaching Suggestion

Have three students draw clocks on the board that depict time on the hour, after the hour, and before the hour as a reference for coming activities.

▶ *page 147*

## Thinking Critically

**11 Analyzing**  Ask students where one might see clocks like these. (See the following Culture Note.)

 ## Culture Note

Clocks like some of those pictured can be found on churches, towers, and town halls in European countries. You might want to tell students that the first mechanical clocks in Europe were invented by clergymen, for the purpose of performing their religious duties promptly and regularly. The first mechanical clocks were not designed to show the time, but rather to sound it. (The Middle English *clock* came from the Middle Dutch word for bell and is a cognate of the German **Glocke,** which means *bell.*) Jacopo de Dondi of Chioggi, Italy, is said to have invented the clock dial in 1344.

## Teaching Suggestion

**11**  Monitor pair work on this page by asking individual pairs to model one of the items for you as you move around the room.

 ## For Individual Needs

**Tactile Learners**  Have students use the clocks they created in Chapter 4 to practice the times in pairs. One student can say a time, the other student has to place the hands correctly.

 ## Multicultural Connection

Have students interview speakers of other languages to compare the German way of telling time with that of other cultures. Do other cultures (such as Spanish, French, Japanese) use both a formal and an informal time system? Have students try to find out how different cultures view time.

 ## For Individual Needs

**12 A Slower Pace**  Write each individual sentence on large cards. Have eight students each hold up a card. A ninth student tells them where to stand to put the sentences in the correct order.

## Reteaching: Telling time

- Show different times on your demonstration clock, and have students tell you what time you are showing.
- Show times on your clock and have students tell you what time it would be in 15 minutes, in half an hour, etc.

▶ page 148

## CLOSE

### 15 Teaching Suggestion

After completing Activity 15, ask questions based on the pictures in Activity 13. Examples: **Wann (um wieviel Uhr) geht Heiko zur Schule? Was macht Heiko um Viertel vor acht?**

### Focusing on Outcomes

Refer students back to the outcomes listed on p. 141. Students should recognize that they are now able to start a conversation, tell time, and talk about when they do things.

## ASSESS

- **Performance Assessment** Show students two cards: one with an activity (Example: **zur Schule gehen**), one with a time (Example: 7:45). Have them build sentences putting the two together: **Um Viertel vor acht gehe ich zur Schule.**
- Quiz 6-1, *Chapter Resources,* Book 2

LIBERTY IM MOTORAMA 21.00-3.00
Liberty
DISKOTHEK CAFÉ
Oldie Disco
Hits der 60er u. 70er Jahre

ZWEITE STUFE

# Teaching Zweite Stufe, pp. 149-153

**Resources for Zweite Stufe**

*Practice and Activity Book*
*Chapter Resources,* Book 2
- Communicative Activity 6-2
- Additional Listening Activities 6-3, 6-4
- Student Response Form
- Realia 6-2
- Situation Card 6-2
- Quiz 6-2

*Audiocassette Program*
- *Textbook Audiocassette* 3 A
- *Additional Listening Activities, Audiocassette* 9 B
- *Assessment Items, Audiocassette* 7 B

▶ page 149

## MOTIVATE

### Building on Previous Skills

Ask students in German about their favorite thing to do on a weekend. Students can do this activity in pairs. Suggest making use of expressions such as **Lieblings-**, **gern machen**, and sequencing words.

## TEACH

### PRESENTATION: Wortschatz

Present this vocabulary by making a transparency of the pictures without the captions. Number each picture. Write the captions in random order at the bottom of the transparency and assign each caption a letter. Ask students to read the captions silently and match each letter to its corresponding picture. The captions have many cognates and phrases that students will be able to recognize. Once students have matched the captions and the pictures correctly, read the six captions to the class.

### For Additional Practice

Ask students which of the six pictured activities they want to do and which ones they do not want to do.

## Teaching Suggestion

**17** Ask students to do this activity in writing. They should create six sentences using the word **und** to connect the sentence parts. Upon completion call on six students to read their sentences aloud.

▶ *page 150*

## PRESENTATION: So sagt man das!

Ask students to look at the sentences from Activity 17 and have them restate each of the six sentences using **möchte** instead of **wollen.** Then introduce the **So sagt man das!** function box and tell students that although **möchte** and **wollen** can be used interchangeably, **wollen** is somewhat more forceful and not quite as polite as **möchte.** Remind students not to confuse the German **will** with the English *will*. **Ich will** means *I want to*. It does not correspond to *I will* which expresses the future in English.

## PRESENTATION: Grammatik

Introduce modal auxiliary verbs or helping verbs. These verbs express ideas such as wish, obligation, ability and permission. Can students name some of these verbs in English? (want, may, should, must, can)

## Teaching Suggestion

**19** Have students work in pairs reading the roles of Julia and Sonja as they complete this conversation. Monitor students' work and then ask a pair to read the dialogue aloud for additional pronunciation practice.

▶ *page 151*

## Group Work

**20** Divide the class into small groups of 3-4 students. Assign one student in each group to be the writer. Each group tries to create as many correct sentences as possible in a set time. (Example: three minutes) Once the time is up, the writer comes to the board and lists the sentences his or her group created. As members of each group take turns reading their group's sentences, members of the other groups check for mistakes.

## PRESENTATION: Ein wenig Grammatik

Write the words from the two sentences in random order on the board. Ask students to rewrite the two sentences using correct word order. Then write out the possible sentences underneath the scrambled words as students read theirs aloud.

▶ *page 152*

## Cooperative Learning

Activities 23 and 24 can be completed as a cooperative learning activity. Divide the class into several groups of 3-4 students each. Each group should have a leader, a recorder, a reporter, and a checker. Within a given time, ask each group to read Monika's letter and then answer the questions that follow. As part of Activity 24 ask students to make a chart with **Freitag, Samstag,** and **Sonntag** on the top. Groups then read the letter a second time and complete the chart with the correct activities or suggestions for each of the days. Finally, groups work on a response to Monika's letter. Instruct students to decide what the content of their letter should be. Each group writes its response letter on a blank transparency, which the checker will proofread. After the groups have completed their work, call on the reporter of each group to display its transparency and read the response letter his or her group has composed. You may want to ask each group to put members' names on the written work and collect it for a possible grade.

## Group Work

**25** Divide the class into groups of three students. Ask them to create a short skit in which they discuss their busy schedules and finally reach an agreement on what to plan for the weekend.

▶ *page 153*

## PRESENTATION: Landeskunde

## Teaching Suggestion

Recycle vocabulary asking questions such as **Woher kommt Sandra?** and **Wo ist Hamburg?** Have students read the four paragraphs and make a list of what each person does in his or her free time.

ZWEITE STUFE

 ## Culture Note

Annika says that she is a **Pfadfinder. Pfadfinder** are the German equivalent of Boy Scouts and Girl Scouts.

## Language Notes

• Annika and Karsten, who are from Hamburg, might be familiar with **Plattdeutsch,** a dialect many northern Germans are trying to preserve. Here are some words in **Plattdeutsch** that students might recognize: **Grotvadder** (*grandfather*) and **Bookweeten-Pannkoken** (*buckwheat pancakes*). Ask students what other languages **Plattdeutsch** resembles. (English and Dutch)

• Sandra and Annika use the word **halt** in their interviews. This flavoring word is used frequently in casual conversation, especially in southern Germany.

 ## Culture Note

Germans have a variety of after-school activities that are organized differently from those in the United States. Students often pay monthly dues to belong to private clubs, such as photo or sewing clubs because these non-academic subjects are not offered at school.

## Group Work

Have students research and write reports about the three cities mentioned in the **Landeskunde.** You may want to request brochures from the sources listed on pp. T38 and 39 of the *Teacher's Edition.* Reports could include information about the region where each city is located and how the location affects recreational activities. Additional reports could be done on other cities. The reports should be in English. Give each group a section of the bulletin board or an area of the classroom to display pictures and materials about their city.

## Teacher Note

Mention to your students that the **Landeskunde** will also be included in Quiz 6-2 given at the end of the **Zweite Stufe.**

## Reteaching: Making plans

Put the sequencing words on the board in a column (**zuerst, dann, danach, zuletzt**). In a second column, write **will ich.** In a third column, make a list of activities learned in this and earlier chapters. Ask the class to create sentences to plan for a busy weekend.

## CLOSE

## Teaching Suggestion

Have students tell you at least two things they want to do this weekend using at least one sequencing word.

## Focusing on Outcomes

Refer students back to the learning outcomes listed on p. 141. They should recognize that they are now able to make plans.

## ASSESS

• **Performance Assessment** Make up envelopes with sentence strips ahead of time, using the sentences from Activity 20 on p. 151 or your own original sentences. Distribute the envelopes to students and ask them to use the pieces to form sentences using correct word order. Monitor students' work and ask several students to read their sentences aloud.

• Quiz 6-2, *Chapter Resources,* Book 2

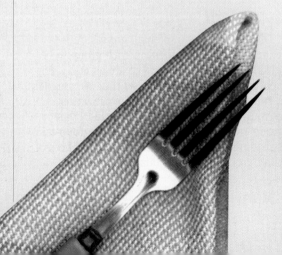

# *T*eaching Dritte Stufe,
## *pp. 154-157*

## Resources for Dritte Stufe

*Practice and Activity Book*
*Chapter Resources,* Book 2
- Additional Listening Activities 6-5, 6-6
- Student Response Form
- Realia 6-3
- Situation Card 6-3
- Teaching Transparency Master 6-2
- Quiz 6-3

*Audiocassette Program*
- *Textbook Audiocassette* 3 B
- *Additional Listening Activities, Audiocassette* 9 B
- *Assessment Items, Audiocassette* 7 B

▶ **page 154**

## *MOTIVATE*

### Teaching Suggestion
Ask students their favorite place to eat and what they like to order. What common expressions do they use in English when ordering food?

## *TEACH*

### Teaching Suggestion
**26** Look at the menu with your students. Which items do they recognize? Have them guess what the other dishes are. Explain the unfamiliar dishes if necessary. Are there any items students have never tried?

### Math Connection
Provide students with the current exchange rate and have them give you the approximate prices of several menu items in U.S. dollars. (Refer students back to Chapter 4, **Dritte Stufe**.)

### Thinking Critically
**Comparing and Contrasting**   Have students look at the menu again. Which items would they probably find on an American menu? Which ones would not likely appear?

##  Culture Note
Sandwiches (**Käsebrot, Wurstbrot**) are served open-faced. **Käsekuchen**, made with **Quark** (a soft, fresh cheese), is not as dense or quite as sweet as American cheesecake. In German cafés and restaurants you can order a cup of coffee or a little pot which contains about two cups. Tea is served in a heat-proof glass with a handle. There are no free refills on coffee or tea.

## Teaching Suggestion
**27** Ask students to write the students' names on a piece of paper after the first listening (Katja, Julia, Michael, Heiko). As students listen a second time they should write down what each of the four students is ordering. Let students listen a third time to check their answers.

## PRESENTATION: So sagt man das!
Model the expressions of this function box by addressing individual students using the questions the waiter would ask. Have students respond by reading the answers on the right side.

▶ **page 155**

## PRESENTATION: Wortschatz
Direct the question **Was nimmst du?** to a student who then answers with one of the expressions given in the **Wortschatz** box. The same student can then ask a classmate, **Und du Frank, was nimmst du?** Frank answers, and so on.

## For Additional Practice
After presenting the **Grammatik** box, recycle the expressions **gern** and **nicht gern** from Chapter 3. Ask students individual questions such as **Was ißt du gern?** or **Was ißt dein Vater nicht gern?** Students should keep their books open, using the **Wortschatz** and **Speisekarte** expressions to form their responses.

## Group Work
Put students in groups of three. Have the first student start with **Was ißt du gern?** The second student responds with **Ich esse (Pizza) gern.** Have the first student ask the third student **Was ißt er/sie gern?**, referring to the second student. The

**DRITTE STUFE**

# KAPITEL 6

**DRITTE STUFE**

third student answers **Er/Sie ißt Pizza gern.** Repeat until each student has practiced the first, second, and third person forms of **essen** and **nehmen**.

## ♜ Game
**29** Divide the class into two teams and have one member of Team A come to the board. Show the student the name of a food item. The student has to draw this item for his or her own group to guess. Set a time limit for the drawing. If students guess correctly, the team gets a point. If they cannot guess the word, the other team may guess and win the point if they guess correctly. Teams take turns. The team with the most points at the end of the game wins.

▶ *page 156*

## PRESENTATION: So sagt man das!
Using large index cards, write the expressions **Gut!, Lecker!, nicht so gut**, etc. from this function box on one side of the index cards and put tape on the other side. List items from the **Imbißkarte** on p. 154 on the chalkboard or a transparency. Ask students to rate the taste of each of the items from 1 to 5. Depending on the general opinion, you then attach an index card with an appropriate expression to the chalkboard next to each item. For example, you could ask, **Wie schmeckt das Eis?** If students respond with a 5, you might tape the index card with the expression **Sagenhaft!** next to the **Eisbecher.** After all food items have been labeled, go over the expressions and have students make up sentences. Example: **Der Eisbecher schmeckt sagenhaft!**

## ✺ For Individual Needs
**31** **A Slower Pace** To prepare students for the listening activity, have the class write down the students' names as they appear in order of the conversation: Heiko, Michael, Katja, Julia. During the first listening, have students write down the items the waiter lists for each teenager. As students listen a second time, have them write the prices for each food item, the total price, and the amount given to the waiter. Call on students to read out what they have written down.

▶ *page 157*

## 📁 Portfolio Assessment
**33** You might want to use this activity as an oral portfolio item for your students. See *Assessment Guide,* Chapter 6.

## Teaching Suggestion
**33** You might want to tell students that *to treat someone* or *to pay someone's way* is **jemanden einladen** in German.

## Thinking Critically
**Drawing Inferences** After reading **Ein wenig Landeskunde,** ask students why tipping is more important in America than in Germany. Why do they think Germans do not tip as much? (See following Culture Note.)

##  Culture Note
In the United States the minimum wage for waiters and waitresses is less than the minimum wage for other occupations. It is understood that they rely on tips to make up the difference. In German-speaking countries, waiters and waitresses are paid standard full salaries, so the tip is more a way to show appreciation for good service than a way of paying the waiter's or waitress' salary. The gratuity as well as a **Mehrwertsteuer** (*value-added tax*) are already included in the price of the meal.

## PRESENTATION: Aussprache
To help students distinguish between the two **ch** sounds, emphasize the differences between them. For the **ch** sound following **i** or **e**, tell students to exaggerate the pronunciation of the initial sound in the English word *huge.* For the **ch** sound following **a, o,** or **u,** have students imagine they are gargling without water. Then practice the different sounds using minimal pairs: **ich/ach, dich/doch, nicht/Nacht.**

## Teaching Suggestion
Ask students to number each sentence of the **Diktat** as they write down the script they hear. Once finished, ask a number of students to copy these sentences on the board. Call on these same students to read their sentences, and ask the rest of the class if the sentences need any corrections.

**139O** Dritte Stufe

## Reteaching: Ordering from a menu

On the day before you plan to do this activity, ask students to make menus for a restaurant they have just opened. On the day of the activity, set up the classroom as a café, using butcher paper tablecloths. Have students bring food, utensils, and their menus. Review essential words and phrases using props. A group of students can then play the roles of the wait staff and the rest will be patrons. Have students act out likely scenarios. Do not allow students to write out their conversations beforehand. The goal of this activity is to have students react as naturally and spontaneously as possible within the classroom setting.

## CLOSE

### Teaching Suggestion

Distribute a copy of the school menu and ask students for the names of items offered on given days. Supply the names of foods not learned in this unit. Ask students about their favorite foods and ask them to rate the foods by using the expressions they learned for describing tastes (p. 156).

## Focusing on Outcomes

Refer students back to the learning outcomes listed on p. 141. They should recognize that they are now able to order food and beverages, talk about how something tastes, and pay the check.

## ASSESS

• **Performance Assessment** Ask students to look back at the Imbißkarte on p. 154. Playing the role of the waiter, ask individual students what they would like to order. Have students "order" one or two items, ask them how each item tastes and then move on to the next student.

• Quiz 6-3, *Chapter Resources,* Book 2

### IMBISS-KARTE
### Café Freizeit
*Für den kleinen Hunger und Durst*

#### KLEINE SPEISEN

| | |
|---|---|
| NUDELSUPPE MIT BROT | DM 4,50 |
| KÄSEBROT | 5,20 |
| WURSTBROT | 5,10 |
| WIENER MIT SENF — 2 PAAR | 5,80 |
| PIZZA (15 CM) | |
| Nr. 1 mit Tomaten und Käse | 6,00 |
| Nr. 2 mit Wurst und Käse | 6,50 |
| Nr. 3 mit Wurst, Käse und Pilzen | 8,50 |

#### EIS

| | |
|---|---|
| FRUCHTEIS KUGEL | DM 1,10 |
| SAHNEEIS KUGEL | 1,30 |
| EISBECHER | 6,80 |

#### GETRÄNKE

| | |
|---|---|
| 1 TASSE KAFFEE | DM 4,30 |
| 1 KÄNNCHEN KAFFEE | 7,60 |
| 1 TASSE CAPPUCCINO | 5,20 |
| 1 GLAS TEE MIT ZITRONE | 3,20 |

#### ALKOHOLFREIE GETRÄNKE

| | | |
|---|---|---|
| MINERALWASSER | 0,5 l | DM 3,50 |
| LIMONADE, FANTA | 0,5 l | 3,60 |
| APFELSAFT | 0,2 l | 2,50 |
| COLA | 0,2 l | 3,00 |

#### KUCHEN

| | | |
|---|---|---|
| APFELKUCHEN | STÜCK | DM 2,80 |
| KÄSEKUCHEN | STÜCK | 3,00 |

# *Teaching Zum Lesen,*
## *pp. 158-159*

### Reading Strategy

The targeted strategy in this reading is using context to guess the meaning of a new or unknown word. The students will also be asked to skim for the gist, scan for specific information, answer questions to show comprehension, and transfer what they have learned.

## *PREREADING*

### Motivating Activity

Have students bring in the arts and entertainment section of the Sunday edition of a local newspaper. Looking at it together and discussing what information is found in this part of the paper will prepare students for the German entertainment ads in this reading.

### Teaching Suggestion

Have students look only at the bold print of the ads and tell you what activities come to mind. With whom would they go to the **Bahrenfelder Forsthaus?** to the **Crash** disco?

### Teacher Note

Activity 1 is a prereading activity.

## *READING*

###  For Individual Needs

**A Slower Pace**  Before working with all the ads on the page, group students and have them work with just one or two ads.

### Group Work

Divide students into groups. Have each group perform three tasks for each ad: find the name of the establishment(s), find the address(es), and make a list of the words students recognize. They can report their findings to the whole class.

### Skimming and Scanning

Remind students that most of the time when they read ads like these, they are looking either for the global picture (skimming) to get an idea about entertainment possibilities, or looking for specific information (scanning) such as the time a movie starts or the price of concert tickets. When students do activities 2b through 5, they will be using the strategies skimming and scanning.

###  For Individual Needs

**Challenge**  Ask students what the attraction of a **Tag und Nacht** restaurant is. What is the specialty of this particular restaurant?

### Language Notes

- Students may be curious about the abbreviations on the Lynyrd Skynyrd concert poster. **Vvk** = **Vorverkauf** (*advance ticket sales*); **Ak** = **Abendkasse** (*box office*); **Geb.** = **Gebühr** (*fee*)

- In the classical music ad, compositions are labeled as being in **Dur** (*major*) or **Moll** (*minor*) to indicate the key of the composition.

## *POST-READING*

### Teacher Note

Activities 6a, 6b, and 6c are post-reading tasks that will show whether students can apply what they have learned.

### Portfolio Assessment

**6c**  You might want to suggest this activity as a written portfolio item for your students. See *Assessment Guide,* Chapter 6

### Closure

After completing 6c, have students tell which activities in the reading they would like to do. They should use sequencing words and **wollen.**

# *U*sing Anwendung,
### *pp. 160-161*

## Teaching Suggestion

**1** As a whole class activity, use your clock to review time expressions from the **Wortschatz** box on p. 146 before beginning Activity 1.

 **For Individual Needs**

**2 A Slower Pace** Make the listening script available to students as they listen to the activity a second time.

**3 Visual Learners** Write four sentences describing the pictured activities in fragments on large cards. (Example: **Wir/ spielen/ Schach.**) Give each sentence to a group of students. Have them arrange themselves in individual sentences across the room. Then give four sequencing words (**zuerst, dann, danach, zuletzt**) to four other students. Each goes to one of the original groups. They should rearrange their word order to accomodate the sequencing words. Continue with the other sentences.

## Teaching Suggestion

You may want to have your students do another **Notizbuch** entry as a culminating task for this chapter. Ask them to write about activities they do with their friends on weekends.

# *K*ann ich's wirklich?
### *p. 162*

This page is intended to prepare students for the test. It is a brief checklist of the major points covered in the chapter. The students should be reminded that it is a checklist only and not necessarily everything that will appear on the test.

# *U*sing Wortschatz,
### *p. 163*

### Game

Play the *Board Race Game* to review time expressions and phrases. Play **Galgenmenschen** to review the remaining vocabulary. See p. 139F for procedures.

## Teaching Suggestion

Take a few minutes to have students quiz each other in pairs on the vocabulary words.

## Teacher Note

Give the **Kapitel 6** Chapter Test, *Chapter Resources,* Book 2.

**HAMBURG**
## KULINARISCHE HIGHLIGHTS

Jeden **Dienstag** lädt Don Diego Gonzales zur **Fiesta Mexicana:** Ein buntes Speazialitäten-Buffet und feurige Gitarrenklänge sorgen für einen stimmungsvollen mexikanischen Abend.

**Donnerstags** und **freitags** entführt Sie Neptun in sein Reich der sieben Meere: Genießen Sie sein lukullisches **Seafood-Buffet!**

# 6
# Pläne machen

① Wir wollen ins Café gehen, ein Eis essen.

**A**fter school and on the weekend, when you have finished your homework, there are a lot of things you can do. You can go to a movie, go shopping, or just hang out with your friends at your favorite café. If you were in Wedel and wanted to make plans, there are a number of things you would need to be able to say in German.

## In this chapter you will learn

- to start a conversation; to tell time and talk about when you do things
- to make plans
- to order food and beverages; to talk about how something tastes; to pay the check

## And you will

- listen to students making plans and ordering food and beverages
- read a story, a letter, a menu, and authentic German advertisements
- write about what you and your friends do and write an invitation
- find out how German students spend their free time

③ Wie spät ist es?

② Was bekommen Sie?

# Los geht's!

## Wollen wir ins Café gehen?

Look at the photos that accompany the story. Where are the scenes taking place? What are the people doing? What do you think will happen in the story?

Heiko

Julia

Katja      Michael

KAPITEL 6   Pläne machen

## 1 Was passiert hier?

1. do their homework, then go out for ice cream  2. join them
3. Café Freizeit  4. He spills soda on her T-Shirt. She says,
"Macht nichts. Es ist nur mein T-Shirt!"

Do you understand what is happening in the **Foto-Roman**? Check your comprehension by answering these questions. Don't be afraid to guess.

1. What plans have Julia and Katja made for the afternoon?
2. What is Heiko going to do?
3. Where do the three friends meet Michael?
4. Why does Michael apologize to Katja? How does Katja react?

## 2 Genauer lesen

Reread the conversations. Which words or phrases do the characters use to

1. ask how someone is doing
2. talk about time
3. name foods and drinks
4. tell a waiter they want to pay
5. apologize

1. Wie geht's denn?
2. Wie spät ist es?, Viertel nach drei, um halb fünf
3. Eis, Eisbecher, Pizza, Wurstbrot, Cappuccino, Cola
4. Ich möchte zahlen.
5. Es tut mir leid.

## 3 Was paßt zusammen?

Match each statement or question on the left with an appropriate response on the right.

1. Wie geht's denn?  b
2. Wohin gehst du?  e
3. Wie spät ist es jetzt?  d
4. Wer bekommt den Cappuccino?  a
5. Ich möchte zahlen.  c

a. Er ist für mich.
b. So lala.
c. Das macht zusammen vierzehn Mark zehn.
d. Viertel nach drei.
e. Zu Katja.

## 4 Was fehlt hier?

Based on the **Foto-Roman** that you've just read, complete each of the sentences below with an appropriate item from the list.

bekommt  Eis
möchte
Hausaufgaben
einen Eisbecher
Stimmt
zahlen  halb

Katja und Julia machen zuerst die ___1___. Dann wollen sie in ein Café gehen, ein ___2___ essen. Sie wollen so um ___3___ fünf gehen. Im Café fragt der Kellner: „Was ___4___ ihr?" Katja ___5___ einen Cappuccino. Julia sagt: „Ich bekomme ___6___, Fruchteis." Michael will gehen. Er sagt: „Ich möchte ___7___, bitte." Der Kellner sagt: „Vierzehn Mark zehn." Und Michael antwortet: „Fünfzehn Mark. ___8___ schon."

1. Hausaufgaben 2. Eis 3. halb 4. bekommt
5. möchte 6. einen Eisbecher 7. zahlen 8. Stimmt

| Café am Markt | | |
|---|---|---|
| Nudelsuppe | DM | 4,50 |
| Käsebrot | | 5,20 |
| Wurstbrot | | 5,60 |
| Wiener mit Senf | | 5,80 |
| Pizza | | 8,00 |
| Apfelkuchen | | 2,00 |
| Eis | | 1,10 |
| Mineralwasser | | 3,50 |
| Kaffee | | 4,20 |
| Cola | | 3,00 |

## 5 Und du?

Look at the menu from the **Café am Markt**. Which items are foods, and which are beverages? If you were with your friends at the **Café am Markt**, what would you order? Make a list, including the prices.

foods: **Nudelsuppe, Käsebrot, Wurstbrot, Wiener mit Senf, Pizza, Apfelkuchen, Eis**
drinks: **Mineralwasser, Kaffee, Cola**

*Starting a conversation; telling time and talking about when you do things*

## SO SAGT MAN DAS!

### Starting a conversation

If you want to find out how someone is doing, you ask:

**Wie geht's?**   *or*   **Wie geht's denn?**

The person might respond in one of these ways, depending on how he or she is doing.

| Sehr gut!<br>Prima! | Danke, gut!<br>Gut! | Danke, es geht.<br>So lala.<br>Nicht schlecht. | Nicht so gut.<br>Schlecht. | Sehr schlecht.<br>Miserabel! |
|---|---|---|---|---|
|  |  |  |  |  |
| Sven | Silke | Nadja | Kemal | Jörg |

## 6  Hör gut zu!   1. Kemal  2. Jörg  3. Silke  4. Nadja  5. Sven

You will hear several students respond to the question **Wie geht's?** As you listen, look at the faces in the box above and determine who is speaking.

## 7  Hallo! Wie geht's?

Greet several students around you and ask them how they are doing.

## 8  Was hast du um ... ?

Get together with your partner, greet him or her, and ask how he or she is doing. Then take turns asking each other what classes you have at the times shown below.

BEISPIEL   DU   **Was hast du um ... ?**

a. neun Uhr dreißig

b. acht Uhr

c. zehn Uhr zwanzig

d. elf Uhr dreißig

**Die Uhrzeit** You already know how to express time when referring to schedules: **um acht Uhr dreißig, um acht Uhr fünfundvierzig.** Now you will learn a more informal way of telling time.

neun Uhr

zehn vor zehn

zehn nach neun

**vor**

**nach**

Viertel vor zehn

Viertel nach neun

zwanzig vor zehn

zwanzig nach neun

halb zehn

---

## SO SAGT MAN DAS!

### Telling time and talking about when you do things

You might ask your friend:

**Wann gehst du ins Café?**
**Und um wieviel Uhr gehst
du schwimmen?**
**Wie spät ist es?**
**Wieviel Uhr ist es?**

The responses might be:

**Um halb fünf.**

**Um Viertel nach drei.**

**Es ist Viertel vor zwei.**

What specific information does each question ask for?

## 9 Wieviel Uhr ist es, bitte?

Using the clocks in the **WORTSCHATZ** box, take turns asking and telling your partner what time it is.

## 10 Was fehlt hier?

Katja is trying to find Heiko. His mom explains where he will be this afternoon. Complete what she says by filling in the blanks according to the times given. Use the words and phrases in the box to the right.

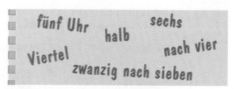

fünf Uhr    halb    sechs
Viertel    nach vier
zwanzig nach sieben

Um ===== drei (2.30) geht er ins Einkaufszentrum. Dann hat er um Viertel ===== (4.15) Fußballtraining. Danach geht er mit Michael um ===== (5.00) ins Schwimmbad. Um ===== vor ===== (5.45) gehen die zwei Jungen ins Café Freizeit. Und dann kommt Heiko um ===== (7.20) nach Hause.

halb; nach vier; fünf Uhr; Viertel ... sechs; zwanzig nach sieben

## 11  Wie spät ist es?

1. fünf vor sieben  2. halb drei  3. fünfundzwanzig nach zwei
4. fünfundzwanzig nach acht  5. halb zehn  6. halb zwölf

You are making plans to meet friends. Ask your partner what time it is. Take turns.

1.

2.

3.

4.

5.

6.

## 12  Wann macht Ulrike alles?

Work with a partner to reorder these statements into a chronological description of how Ulrike spends a typical Monday.

1. Jeden Montag um acht Uhr gehe ich zur Schule.

Und am Abend schaue ich Fernsehen.
8

Dann um halb elf, direkt nach der Pause, habe ich Bio.
3

Um Viertel nach neun habe ich Mathe.
2

Um drei Uhr oder um halb vier esse ich Kuchen oder vielleicht etwas Obst.
5

Und jeden Montag um vier Uhr gehe ich schwimmen.
6

Danach mache ich so um fünf Hausaufgaben.
7

Nach der Schule gehe ich nach Hause.
4

# 13 Hör gut zu!

Match what these students say with the illustrations below.

1. e  2. d  3. b  4. a  5. c  6. f

a. um 7.45: in die Schule gehen  b. um 9.15: Matheprüfung
c. um 1.45: schwimmen  d. um 3.20:
Tennis spielen  e. um 7.15:
Fernsehen schauen
f. um 10.30: Musik hören

# 14 Wann? Wer? Was?

Schau die Zeichnungen an!

1. Make a list of the times and corresponding activities shown in Activity 13.
2. Choosing your own activities, write six sentences stating what you do at the times shown above.

# 15 Um wieviel Uhr …?

Ask your partner at what time he or she does various activities or has certain classes.

## SPRACHTIP

Denn, mal, halt, and doch are words that you've seen a lot throughout this book. None of these words has a direct translation, but they are often used in everyday conversations to give emphasis to a question, command, or statement. For example, Wie sieht er denn aus? Sag mal, wann gehst du? Das hat halt nicht jeder. and Wir gehen doch um vier. Using these words in your conversations will help your German sound more natural.

*Making plans*

**Wohin gehen? Was machen?** Lies, was Katja und Julia planen! Julia sagt: „Katja und ich, wir wollen ..."

in ein Café gehen,
ein Eis essen

ins Schwimmbad gehen,
baden gehen

ins Kino gehen,
einen Film sehen

in eine Disko gehen,
tanzen und Musik hören

in die Stadt gehen,
Klamotten kaufen

ins Rockkonzert gehen,
Musik hören

**16 Hör gut zu!** For answers, see Interleaf, p. 139C.

You will hear two students talk about their plans for the weekend. List all of the places they want to go in the order you hear them mentioned.

**17 Was wollen wir machen?**

Wir wollen ...

ins Schwimmbad — gehen und ... — tanzen
ins Kino — Klamotten kaufen
in ein Café — Musik hören
in die Stadt — schwimmen
in eine Disko — einen Film sehen
ins Rockkonzert — ein Eis essen

**18 Für mein Notizbuch**

In your **Notizbuch** write some of the places you go and some of the things you do after school and on weekends. Look on page 321 for additional words you might want to use.

# SO SAGT MAN DAS!

## Making plans

You have been using the **möchte**-forms (*would like to*) to express your intentions:
**Er möchte Musik hören.** You can also use **wollen** (*to want to*).

Talking to someone:
**Heiko, was willst du machen?**

Talking about yourself:
**Ich will in ein Café gehen.**

Talking about someone:
**Wohin will Birte gehen?**

**Sie will ins Schwimmbad gehen.**

## Grammatik   The verb wollen

**Wollen** means *to want* or *to want* to do. The forms of this verb—and of other modal verbs — are different from those of regular verbs. Here are the forms:

Ich **will** ein Eis essen.
Du **willst** Musik hören.
Er/Sie **will** tanzen gehen.

Wir **wollen** Tennis spielen
Ihr **wollt** ins Kino gehen.
Sie (pl) }
Sie } **wollen** in eine Disko gehen.

What do you notice about the **ich** and **er/sie** forms?[1] Like the **möchte**-forms you learned in **Kapitel 3**, **wollen** is also a modal auxiliary verb. It is often used with another verb, although the second verb can be omitted if the meaning is obvious:

**Ich will ins Schwimmbad gehen.**
**Ich will ins Schwimmbad.**

Note the position of the verb **wollen** and the second verb, the infinitive.

## 19 Was willst du machen?

Julia and her friend Sonja are talking about their plans for the day. Complete their conversation with the correct forms of **wollen**.

JULIA   Was __1__ du heute machen?   willst
SONJA   Ich __2__ nach Hamburg fahren.   will
        Die Katja __3__ mitkommen.   will
JULIA   Und Michael? __4__ er auch mitkommen?   will
SONJA   Ich glaube, ja. Katja, Heiko und Michael
        __5__ alle mitkommen.   wollen
JULIA   Um wieviel Uhr __6__ ihr fahren?   wollt
SONJA   So um drei. Wir __7__ um sieben   wollen
        wieder zu Hause sein.

Fischmarkt in Hamburg

1. Though the pronouns are different, the verb forms are alike.

## 20 Sätze bauen

Wie viele Sätze kannst du bauen?

BEISPIEL **Katja will um vier Uhr ins Kino gehen.** *oder*
**Um vier Uhr will Katja ins Kino gehen.**

| | | | |
|---|---|---|---|
| ich<br>Katja<br>du<br>wir<br>ihr<br>die Jungen | wollen<br>willst<br>will<br>wollt | am Nachmittag<br>nach der Schule<br>um vier Uhr<br>von 3 bis 5 Uhr<br>am Abend | in ein Café gehen<br>ins Kino gehen<br>tanzen gehen<br>in die Stadt gehen<br>ins Konzert gehen<br>Musik hören |

## 21 Heikos Pläne für nächste Woche

1. Look at Heiko's plans for next week. Take turns saying what Heiko plans to do each day.
   BEISPIEL **Am Dienstag will er ins Kino gehen.**

2. Take turns asking each other when Heiko plans to do each of his activities.

## 22 Deine Pläne für nächste Woche

1. Write your own plans for the coming week on a calendar page. For each day write what you want to do and at what time you plan to do it.

2. Your partner will ask you about your plans. Tell him or her what you want to do and at what time. Then switch roles. Be prepared to share your partner's plans with the class.

| 26 Montag | Fußball 16 ³⁰<br>Schach mit Sven 19 ⁰⁰<br>Arbeitsgruppe Umwelt 20 ³⁰ |
|---|---|
| 27 Dienstag | Kino     14 ⁴⁵ |
| 28 Mittwoch | ? |
| 29 Donnerstag | schwimmen mit<br>Michael 17 ⁴⁵ |
| 30 Freitag | 16 ⁰⁰ - 18 ⁰⁰ zu Hause helfen |
| 31 Samstag | 13 ⁰⁰ Klavierstunde<br>Disko 19 ³⁰ |
| 1 Sonntag | 13 ³⁵ segeln<br>radfahren |

### Schon bekannt
### Ein wenig *Grammatik*

Monika could say of Katja:

**Katja will am Freitag in die Stadt gehen.** *or*
**Am Freitag will Katja in die Stadt gehen.**

You saw this type of word order before in **Kapitel 2**, when you learned about German word order:

**Wir spielen um 2 Uhr Fußball.**
**Um 2 Uhr spielen wir Fußball.**

What is the position of the conjugated verbs in the above sentences[1]?

1. The conjugated verb is in second position.

## 23 Monikas Pläne fürs Wochenende

Read the letter that Monika has written to Katja,
then answer the questions that follow.

Liebe Katja,

Es freut mich, daß Du am Donnerstag kommst.
Hier sind meine Pläne fürs Wochenende: Am
Freitag will ich mit Dir in die Stadt gehen —
zuerst ein paar Klamotten kaufen (ich brauche
Tennisschuhe!), dann etwas essen, danach ins
Kino gehen.

Samstag ist immer mein Sporttag. Am
Vormittag können wir radfahren, baden gehen
(wir haben ein prima Schwimmbad!), und später
am Abend will Vati für uns ein Grillfest
machen. Neun Klassenkameraden kommen!
Was willst Du am Sonntag machen? Willst Du
wieder in die Stadt fahren? In ein Museum
gehen? In ein Café gehen? Oder willst Du
faulenzen?
Mach's gut und bis bald.

Deine Monika

1. Why is Monika writing to Katja? How do you know?
2. When will Katja visit Monika?
3. How long will she stay? How do you know?

1. to tell her the weekend plans: **Hier sind meine Pläne fürs Wochenende.**
2. Thursday through Sunday
3. She arrives on Thursday and stays through Sunday: Monika mentions those days.

## 24 Monikas Pläne

List Monika's plans for Friday and Saturday and her suggestions for Sunday. Include all the words that indicate the sequence of the plans.

Am Freitag: **in die Stadt gehen**  Klamotten kaufen    am Samstag: radfahren
**Zuerst ...**                      etwas essen                     schwimmen
**Dann ...**                        ins Kino gehen                  ein Grillfest machen
                                                    am Sonntag: in die Stadt gehen
                                                                in ein Museum gehen
                                                                in ein Café gehen

## 25 Ihr macht Pläne

You and two of your friends are discussing your plans for the weekend. All of you are very busy, but you want to get together. Decide on several things you could do and places you could go together, then create a conversation discussing your plans.

# Was machst du in deiner Freizeit?

What do you think students in Germany like to do when they have time to spend with their friends? We have asked a number of students from different places this question, but before you read their responses, write down what you think they will say. Then read these interviews and compare your ideas with what they say.

### Sandra
*Stuttgart*

„Also, meine Freizeit verbringe ich am liebsten mit ein paar Freundinnen oder Freunden. Dann gehen wir abends in die Stadt Eis essen, oder wir setzen uns einfach in ein Café rein und reden. Aber am liebsten gehen wir halt tanzen."

### Annika
*Hamburg*

„Ich bin bei den Pfadfindern; da fährt man halt am Wochenende auf Fahrt, und ja, mit denen mach' ich auch hauptsächlich ziemlich viel, auch mal außerhalb, ins Kino gehen und so — und sonst spiel' ich noch Klavier."

### Marga
*Bietigheim*

„Während der Woche verabrede ich mich an sich nicht so oft, weil ich da ziemlich viel mit der Schule zu tun hab', Hausaufgaben und so. Aber sonst am Wochenende geh ich eben abends weg ins Kino oder in die Disko. Und sonst tanz' ich und einmal in der Woche spiele ich Flöte."

### Karsten
*Hamburg*

„Also, ich mach' als erstes natürlich Hausaufgaben und dann irgend etwas mit Sport, oder ich geh' in die Stadt einkaufen, oder meistens treff' ich mich mit meinen Freunden."

**A.** 1. Working with a partner, write beside each student's name where he or she likes to go and what he or she likes to do.
   2. Compare the lists you have prepared for the four German students. Which activities do they have in common?
   3. Discuss with your classmates which activities you and your friends like to do that are similar to those done by the students in Germany. Which are different?

**B.** Look at the list you made before you read the interviews. Does what you wrote match what the students say? If it is different, how? Where do your ideas about German students come from? How do you think students in Germany might describe a "typical" American student? Where might they get their ideas? Write a brief essay discussing these questions.

*Ordering food and beverages; talking about how something tastes; paying the check*

## 26 Im Café Freizeit

Read the menu of **Café Freizeit**, then list what you would order for yourself. Add up the cost of your snack. With a partner, compare your order and the amount each of you would spend.

27. Julia: Apfelkuchen, Cappuccino
Heiko: Mineralwasser, Wurstbrot, Cappuccino
Katja: eine Nudelsuppe, zwei Paar Wiener mit
Senf, eine Limonade
Michael: eine Pizza, eine Cola, einen Eisbecher

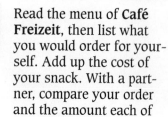

**IMBISS-KARTE**

*Café Freizeit*

*Für den kleinen Hunger und Durst*

### KLEINE SPEISEN

| | |
|---|---|
| NUDELSUPPE MIT BROT | DM 4,50 |
| KÄSEBROT | 5,20 |
| WURSTBROT | 5,10 |
| WIENER MIT SENF — 2 PAAR | 5,80 |
| PIZZA (15 CM) | |
| Nr. 1 mit Tomaten und Käse | 6,00 |
| Nr. 2 mit Wurst und Käse | 6,50 |
| Nr. 3 mit Wurst, Käse und Pilzen | 8,50 |

### EIS

| | |
|---|---|
| FRUCHTEIS KUGEL | DM 1,10 |
| SAHNEEIS KUGEL | 1,30 |
| EISBECHER | 6,80 |

### GETRÄNKE

| | | |
|---|---|---|
| 1 TASSE KAFFEE | DM | 4,30 |
| 1 KÄNNCHEN KAFFEE | | 7,60 |
| 1 TASSE CAPPUCCINO | | 5,20 |
| 1 GLAS TEE MIT ZITRONE | | 3,20 |

### ALKOHOLFREIE GETRÄNKE

| | | | |
|---|---|---|---|
| MINERALWASSER | 0,5 l | DM | 3,50 |
| LIMONADE, FANTA | 0,5 l | | 3,60 |
| APFELSAFT | 0,2 l | | 2,50 |
| COLA | 0,2 l | | 3,00 |

### KUCHEN

| | | | |
|---|---|---|---|
| APFELKUCHEN | STÜCK | DM | 2,80 |
| KÄSEKUCHEN | STÜCK | | 3,00 |

## 27 Hör gut zu!

You will hear four students saying what they want to eat and drink. Listen and decide what each one is ordering.

## SO SAGT MAN DAS!

### Ordering food and beverages

Here are some expressions you can use when you order something in a café or restaurant.

The waiter asks for your order:
**Was bekommen Sie?**
**Ja, bitte?**
**Was essen Sie?**
**Was möchten Sie?**
**Was trinken Sie?**

You order:
**Ich möchte ein Wurstbrot.**
**Ich möchte ein Stück Kuchen, bitte.**
**Einen Eisbecher, bitte!**
**Ich trinke einen Apfelsaft.**
**Ich bekomme einen Kaffee.**

You might ask your friend:
**Was nimmst du?**
**Was ißt du?**

Your friend might respond:
**Ich nehme ein Käsebrot.**
**Ich esse ein Eis.**

HEIKO: Was nimmst du?
MICHAEL: Ich nehme…

eine Nudelsuppe

ein Wurstbrot

ein Käsebrot

eine Pizza

ein Eis/
einen Eisbecher

ein Stück
Apfelkuchen

eine Tasse Kaffee

ein Glas Tee

## 28 Du hast Hunger!

Imagine that you are in **Café Freizeit**. You are very hungry and order a lot of food. Your partner plays the waiter, writing down everything you order, then tells the class what you have ordered. Switch roles.

BEISPIEL **Was bekommen Sie?**
DU **Ich esse … dann… und danach …**

## *G*rammatik   Stem-changing verbs

Remember the verb **nehmen** that you used in **Kapitel 5**? **Nehmen** has a change in the stem vowel of the **du**- and **er/sie** forms: **du nimmst, er/sie nimmt.** Another verb in this group is **essen** (*to eat*). Here are the forms of **essen**:

| | | | |
|---|---|---|---|
| Ich | **esse** ein Eis. | Wir | **essen** Pizza. |
| Du | **ißt** eine Nudelsuppe? | Ihr | **eßt** Apfelkuchen. |
| Sie/Er | **ißt** ein Wurstbrot. | Sie *(pl)* Sie | **essen** Obst. |

*LERNTRICK*

**Listening for gender cues.** It is important to listen not only for meaning, but also for other cues that may be helpful. If someone asks: **Nimmst du einen Apfelsaft?** the **einen** tells you that **Apfelsaft** is a masculine noun. You can have your response ready immediately:

**Ja, einen Apfelsaft, bitte.** *or*
**Ja, bitte! Der Apfelsaft ist wirklich gut.**

## 29 Was wollen alle essen?

Du hast großen Hunger! Schau auf die Speisekarte von Café Freizeit auf Seite 154.

a. Was ißt du?
b. Was ißt dein Partner? Frag ihn!

1. Both are masculine and in the accusative case.

## SO SAGT MAN DAS!

### Talking about how something tastes

If you want to ask how
something tastes, you ask:

**Wie schmeckt's?**

**Schmeckt's?**

Some possible responses are:

{ **Gut! Prima! Sagenhaft!**
**Die Pizza schmeckt lecker!** (*tasty, delicious*)
**Die Pizza schmeckt nicht.**

{ **Ja, gut!**
**Nein, nicht so gut.**
**Nicht besonders.** *Not especially.*

## 30 Wie schmeckt's?

1. Your partner was really hungry and ordered a lot to
   eat. Everything looks great! Ask him or her how the
   different dishes taste. (React to the foods ordered in
   Activity 29.)
2. The food doesn't taste very good. Ask your partner about different dishes that she or he has ordered. Then switch roles.

## SO SAGT MAN DAS!

### Paying the check

Calling the waiter's attention
Asking for the check
Totaling up the check
Telling the waiter to keep the change

**Hallo!**
**Hallo! Ich will/möchte zahlen.**
**Das macht (zusammen)...**
**Stimmt schon!**

## 31 Hör gut zu!

Heiko: 3,50 DM; 5,60 DM; 5,20 DM/14,30 DM; 15,00 DM
Katja: 4,50 DM; 5,80 DM; 3,60 DM/13,90 DM; 14,00 DM

After Heiko and his friends eat, the waiter brings them the check.
Listen as he adds up the bill, then write down each individual
price you hear, the total, and what they round it off to as a tip.

Julia: 2,80 DM; 5,20 DM/8,00 DM; 8,50 DM
Michael: 6,50 DM; 3,00 DM; 6,80 DM/16,30 DM; 17,00 DM

## 32 Du willst zahlen

You have finished your meal. Tell the waiter you want to pay.
Before you pay the check, the waiter mentions every item you
ordered and adds up the total. Role-play this situation with a
partner, using the orders below and the menu on page 154.
Be polite!

1. Nudelsuppe mit Brot, Mineralwasser
2. Tasse Cappuccino, Käsekuchen, Sahneeis
3. Wurstbrot, Cola, Tee mit Zitrone

*Café Freizeit*

geöffnet: Mo-Sa 10-10 Uhr
Sonntag: Ruhetag

6,—
5,60
3,50
3,00
———
18,10

## 33 Kommst du mit?

Get together with two other classmates and role-play the following situations.

1. Your German pen pal is visiting you while you are in Wedel. Treat him or her to dinner at **Café Freizeit**. Talk about what both of you want to eat and drink. Order for the two of you. A waiter will take the order.
2. The waiter brings the order but can't remember who ordered what. Help him out.
3. While you are eating, you comment to each other about how the food tastes.
4. Your friend wants to order something else. Call the waiter over and tell him what else you want.
5. It is time to pay. Call the waiter and ask for the check. The waiter will name everything you ordered and add up the bill. You pay and leave a tip.

## AUSSPRACHE

### Richtig aussprechen/richtig lesen

A. To practice these sounds pronounce after your teacher or after the recording the words and sentences in bold.

1. The letter combination **ch**: The consonant combination **ch** can be pronounced two different ways. When preceded by the vowels **i** and **e**, it sounds similar to the *h* in the English word *huge*. When preceded by the vowels **a**, **o** or **u**, it is produced farther back in the throat.
   **ich, Pech, dich / So ein Pech! Ich habe es nicht.**
   **ach, doch, Buch / Was macht Heiko am Wochenende? Spielt er Schach?**

2. The letter **r**: The German **r** sound does not exist in English. To produce this sound, put the tip of your tongue behind your lower front teeth. Then tip your head back and pretend that you are gargling.
   **rund, recht, Freizeit / Rolf, Rudi, und Rita gehen ins Café Freizeit.**

3. The letter combination **er**: At the end of a word the letter combination **er** sounds almost like a vowel. It is similar to the *u* in the English word *but*.
   **super, Lehrer, Bruder / Wo ist meine Schwester?**

## Richtig schreiben / Diktat

B. Write down the sentences that you hear.

# ZUM LESEN

## Wohin in Hamburg?

### LESETRICK

**Using context to guess meaning** When you run across a word you do not know, you can very often use the context (the surrounding words) to figure out the meaning of the word. You already use this strategy in your native language. For example, you may not know the English word *exacerbate*, but when you see it used in a sentence, you can make an intelligent guess about what it means. Look at this sentence: *A violent storm exacerbated the already-dangerous driving conditions.* If the driving conditions were already dangerous, what would a violent storm have done to them? You can guess that *exacerbate* means "to make worse."

People who live in Wedel often go into Hamburg for a day of entertainment.

1. What are the two main types of ads on these pages? food, music

2. a. Use context clues to guess the meaning of these German words. Match each word with its English equivalent.

   1) lädt    d          a) enjoy
   2) genießen  a        b) meeting
   3) Treffpunkt  b         place
   4) Bratkartoffel-      c) a dish of
      gerichte  e            ice cream
   5) Eisbecher  c        d) invites
                         e) fried potato

## HAMBURG
## KULINARISCHE HIGHLIGHTS

Jeden **Dienstag** lädt Don Diego Gonzales zur **Fiesta Mexicana:** Ein buntes Speazialitäten-Buffet und feurige Gitarrenklänge sorgen für einen stimmungsvollen mexikanischen Abend.

**Donnerstags** und **freitags** entführt Sie Neptun in sein Reich der sieben Meere: Genießen Sie sein lukullisches **Seafood-Buffet!**

**CRASH**
DISCOTEK

**FREITAG:**
**OLDIES bis 3 Uhr**

Täglich ab 20 Uhr   Montag Ruhetag

LIBERTY IM MOTORAMA 21.00-3.00

*Liberty*
DISKOTHEK CAFÉ

**Oldie Disco**
Hits der 60er u. 70er Jahre

Dienstag, 26. Januar
**Martha Argerich,** Klavier
**Guy Tourvton,** Trompete
**Württembergisches Kammerorchester Heilbronn**
Dirigent: **Jörg Faerber**
Haydn: Konzert für Klavier und Orchester D-Dur
Janáček: Suite für Streichorchester
Hindemith: Fünf Stücke für Streichorchester op. 44
Schostakowitsch: Konzert für Klavier, Trompete und
        Streichorchester op. 35

Dienstag, 25. Mai
**Murray Perahia,** Klavier
Mozart: Sonate F-Dur KV 332
Brahms: Rhapsodie h-Moll op. 79, Intermezzo es-Moll op. 118
        Capriccio h-Moll op. 76, Rhapsodie Es-Dur op. 119
Beethoven: Sonate B-Dur op. 106 (Hammerkavier)

b. Mexican, sea food, potato dishes, milk and ice cream
c. Don Diego Gonzales; Tuesday
d. Tag und Nacht Gestern & Heute Treff, Kaiser-Wilhelm-Straße 55
3a. Sporthalle (concerts) Discos (oldies)
b. Liberty, Crash; 9 pm - 3 am (6 hours)
c. Friday, April 16, 8 pm
   Friday, April 16, 8 pm
   no; concert postponed until September 10

---

Dienstag, 13.4. 20 Uhr, Sporthalle
Vvk: DM 40,– (+10% Vvk-Geb.) Ak: DM 45,–

## 13.4. LYNYRD SKYNYRD

special Guest: RED DEVILS

ACHTUNG! Konzert auf den 10.9 verlegt!
Karten behalten ihre Gültigkeit

................................................

Freitag, 16.4. 20 Uhr, Sporthalle
Vvk: DM 39,– (+10% Vvk-Geb.) Ak: DM 44,–
Mama Concert & Rau GmbH present:

## 16.4. BONNIE TYLER

Angel Heart-Tour

................................................

Freitag, 16.4. 20 Uhr, Sporthalle
Vvk: DM 48,– (+10% Vvk-Geb.) Ak: DM 55,–

## 16.4. PETER GABRIEL

US on Tour

................................................

---

# Milchbars

**IN 41%** **OUT 32%** Eis, Milch-Shakes und Banana-Split sind an heißen Tagen genau das Richtige zur Erfrischung. In kleineren und mittleren Städten ist die Milchbar auch heute noch der ideale Treffpunkt für die jungen Leute.

---

Tag u. Nacht

## deftige Bratkartoffelgerichte

Tag und Nacht warme Küche,
Frühstück zu jeder Zeit,
saftige Steaks,
das ganze Jahr Eisbergsalat,
tolle Eisbecher

## gestern & heute treff
Kaiser-Wilhelm-Straße 55

---

# Bahrenfelder Forsthaus

**Hamburger Küche und feine Spezialitäte**
Besondere Sonntagsmenüs
Restaurant, Romantischer Wintergarten, Café und Café-Terras
Von-Hutten-Str. 45 · 2000 Hamburg 50 · Telefon (0 40) 89 40

---

b. What kinds of foods are advertised here? Which restaurant ad interests you the most?
c. Where can you eat Mexican food? On what day?
d. Where can you get a "great Eisbecher"? Where is this place located?

3. a. Where can you hear music? What kinds of music can you hear?
   b. What are the names of the discos? How long is the **Liberty** open?
   c. When (day and time) can you see Bonnie Tyler? Peter Gabriel? Will Lynyrd Skynyrd fans get to hear them on 13.4? If not, why not?

4. What is the social purpose of the **Milchbar**? What word supports your opinion? meeting place for young people: **Treffpunkt**

5. Remembering the word you learned for "juice," find the word that means "juicy." **saftig**

6. Assume you and your family are in Wedel. You want to go to Hamburg for two or three days.
   a. To which places would you more likely go with your parents?
   b. To which places would you more likely go with your friends?
   c. Write a postcard to a friend telling of your plans for your weekend in Hamburg. Be sure to use sequencing words appropriately.

# ANWENDUNG

1. sieben Uhr zwanzig, zwanzig nach sieben
2. zwei Uhr dreißig, halb drei
3. drei Uhr fünfundvierzig, Viertel vor vier
4. zehn Uhr fünfzehn, Viertel nach zehn
5. elf Uhr fünfundfünfzig, fünf vor zwölf

**1** Express the times shown in as many different ways as you can.

**2** In each of the following reports an activity is mentioned. If the activity mentioned is shown in the photos below, match the activity with the appropriate photo.     1. c, f     2. e, b     3. Karten spielen: not pictured     4. a     5 h

a.

b.

c.

d.

e.

f.

g.

h.

**3** Look at the photos. Your partner will ask you what you want to do. Choose three activities from above and tell your partner which ones you want to do and at what time you want to do them. Then switch roles.

**4** You have a week off from school. What will you do? Jot down some plans in your calendar. Write down what you plan to do, when, and with whom. You need to study, too, so plan some time for that.

Hausaufgaben machen — Eis essen — ins Einkaufszentrum gehen — lesen — Tennis spielen — in ein Museum gehen — schwimmen — ins Kino gehen

**5** Just after you've made your plans, a friend calls to find out what you are doing during your week off and suggests doing something together. Decide what you want to do and when you want to do it. Consult your calendar.

**6** Write in German a conversation you might have had when you last ate a meal or a snack in a restaurant. Include ordering your food, some comments on how it tasted, and paying for it.

**7**

# R O L L E N S P I E L

Du bist mit einem Freund in Hamburg. Ihr habt Hunger und möchtet etwas essen.

You are in a hurry for the Peter Gabriel concert, so you decide to put dinner off until later and just grab a snack at an **Imbißstand**. You also don't want to spend very much money—each of you is limited to 10 marks.

**a.** Create a conversation in which you discuss the possibilities that are available, decide what each of you wants, and figure out how much it will cost.

**b.** One partner can then play the role of vendor, and you can order the food and drink that each of you decided upon. After you receive your food, pay for it.

Verkauf am Fenster

*Sensationell*

1/2 Hähnchen 3,20

| | |
|---|---|
| | 3,00 |
| Käsebrot | 2,90 |
| Wurstbrot | 6,60 |
| La Flute m. Schinken & Ananas | |
| Gr. Fladenbrot (Giros/Kochschinken/ | 8,40 |
| Schinken/Spießbraten) | 9,50 |
| Giros mit Krautsalat | gr. 4,00 |
| Currywurst, kl. 3,70 | 1,90 |
| Rostbratwurst | 1,90 |
| Bockwurst | 2,70 |
| Schokoladeneis | 2,70 |
| Vanilleeis | 2,80 |
| Fruchteis | |

| | Becher 0,3 | | 0,4 | |
|---|---|---|---|---|
| Cola | 0,3 | 1,50 | 0,4 | 1,90 |
| Milchshake | 0,3 | 1,80 | 0,4 | 2,20 |
| Apfelsaft | 0,3 | 1,80 | 0,4 | 2,40 |
| Orangensaft | 0,3 | 1,80 | 0,4 | 2,40 |
| Mineralwasser | | | | 1,95 |
| Fanta | 0,3 | 1,30 | 0,4 | 1,80 |

# KANN ICH'S WIRKLICH?

**Can you start a conversation? (p. 145)**

Answers will vary. **Guten Tag!/Tag! Wie geht's?**

**1** How would you greet a friend and ask how he or she is doing. If someone asks how you are doing, what could you say?
**Gut, danke!/Nicht schlecht!**

**Can you tell time? (p. 146)**

**2** How would you ask what time it is? Say the times shown below, using expressions you learned in this chapter.

| **1.** 1.00 | **2.** 11.30 | **3.** 9.50 | **4.** 2.15 | **5.** 7.55 |
|---|---|---|---|---|
| ein Uhr | halb zwölf | zehn vor zehn | viertel nach zwei | sieben Uhr |

**Can you talk about when you do things? (p. 146)**

**3** a. Using the time expressions above, say when you and your friends intend to **Wir wollen um ... Uhr ... gehen.**

**a.** go to the movies **ins Kino**     **c.** go to the swimming pool
**b.** go to a café **ins Café**                **ins Schwimmbad**

**4** How would you ask a friend when he intends to do the activities in Activity 3? **Wann willst du ...?**

**Can you make plans using wollen? (p. 150)**

**5** Say you intend to go to the following places and tell what you plan to do there. Establish a sequence: *first..., then...*

**a.** café
**b.** swimming pool
**c.** movies
**d.** department store
**e.** disco

a. Erst gehe ich ins Café, dann esse ich ein Eis.
b. Erst ... ins Schwimmbad, dann schwimmen.
c. Erst ... ins Kino, dann einen Film sehen.
d. ins Kaufhaus/Klamotten kaufen
e. in eine Disko/tanzen

**6** How would you say that the following people want to go to a concert?

**1.** Michael **will**     **3.** ihr **wollt**     **5.** Peter und
**2.** Silke **will**         **4.** wir **wollen**       Monika **wollen**

**Can you order food and beverages? (p. 154)**

**7** You are with some friends in a café. Order the following things for yourself.

**a.** (noodle) soup **Nudelsuppe**     **c.** a cheese sandwich **ein Käsebrot**
**b.** a glass of tea with lemon **ein Glas Tee mit Zitrone**

**8** Say that these people are going to eat the foods listed. Then say what you are going to eat (using **ich**). How would you ask your best friend what he or she is going to eat (using **du**)?

**a.** Michael - Käsekuchen **ißt**     **d.** Ahmet und ich - **essen**
**b.** Holger und Julia - **essen**          Wiener mit Senf
Apfelkuchen                                  **e.** Ich ... **esse**
**c.** Monika - Käsebrot **ißt**            **f.** Und du? Was ...? **ißt**

**Can you talk about how something tastes? (p. 156)**

**9** How would you ask a friend if his or her food tastes good? How might he or she respond? **Schmeckt's? Lecker, danke!**

**Can you pay the check? (p. 156)**

**10** Ask the waiter for the check, then tell him to keep the change.
**Ich möchte zahlen, bitte./Stimmt schon!**

**162** *hundertzweiundsechzig*                    KAPITEL 6    Pläne machen

## ERSTE STUFE

### STARTING A CONVERSATION

Wie geht's (denn)?  *How are you?*
Sehr gut!  *Very well!*
Prima!  *Great!*
Gut!  *Good/Well!*
Es geht.  *Okay.*
So lala.  *So-so.*

Schlecht.  *Bad(ly).*
Miserabel.  *Miserable.*

### TELLING TIME

Wie spät ist es?  *What time is it?*
Wieviel Uhr ist es?  *What time is it?*
Um wieviel Uhr ...?  *At what time...?*

Viertel nach  *a quarter after*
halb (eins, zwei, usw.)  *half past (twelve, one, etc.)*
Viertel vor ...  *a quarter to ...*
(zehn) vor ...  *(ten) till ...*
um (ein) Uhr ...  *at (one) o'clock*

## ZWEITE STUFE

### MAKING PLANS

Wohin?  *Where (to)?*
in ein Café/ins Café  *to a café*
ein Eis essen  *to eat ice cream*
in die Stadt gehen  *to go downtown*

ins Schwimmbad gehen  *to go to the (swimming) pool*
baden gehen  *to go swimming*
ins Kino gehen  *to go to the movies*
einen Film sehen  *to see a movie*

in eine Disko gehen  *to go to a disco*
tanzen gehen  *to go dancing*
ins Konzert gehen  *to go to a concert*
Musik hören  *to listen to music*
wollen  *to want*

## DRITTE STUFE

### ORDERING FOOD AND BEVERAGES

Was bekommen Sie?  *What will you have?*
Ich bekomme ...  *I'll have...*
eine Tasse Kaffee  *a cup of coffee*
ein Glas Tee  *a (glass) cup of tea*
  mit Zitrone  *with lemon*
eine Limo(nade)  *a lemon-flavored soda*
eine Nudelsuppe  *noodle soup*
  mit Brot  *with bread*
ein Käsebrot  *cheese sandwich*
einen Eisbecher  *a dish of ice cream*

ein Wurstbrot  *sandwich with cold cuts*
eine Pizza  *pizza*
Apfelkuchen  *apple cake*
ein Eis  *ice cream*
essen  *to eat*
er/sie ißt  *he/she eats*
nehmen  *to take*
er/sie nimmt  *he/she takes*

### TALKING ABOUT HOW FOOD TASTES

Wie schmeckt's?  *How does it taste?*

Schmeckt's?  *Does it taste good?*
Sagenhaft!  *Great!*
Lecker!  *Tasty! Delicious!*
Nicht besonders.  *Not really.*

### PAYING THE CHECK

Hallo! Ich möchte/will zahlen!  *The check please!*
Das macht (zusammen) ...  *That comes to....*
Stimmt (schon)!  *Keep the change.*

📼 **Location Opener**

# *München, pages 164-167*
### *Expanded Video Program*, Videocassette 3

## *U*sing the Photograph,
### pp. 164-165

### Background Information

With over one million inhabitants, Munich is the third largest city in Germany. It is a magnet to Germans and foreigners alike and is by far the most popular German city because of its many attractive features. Munich owes its origins to **Herzog Heinrich der Löwe,** Duke Henry the Lion, who built a bridge over the Isar river and established a customs station there in 1158. Munich draws business people to its fairs and trade shows, visitors to the annual **Oktoberfest,** athletes to its Olympic sport facilities, and tourists to its architecture as well as picturesque location at the foot of the Alps and the Alpine lakes.

Shown in the foreground of the picture is the **Pfarrkirche Heiliger Geist,** originally called **Spitalkirche.** Built between 1208 and 1397, the church was severely damaged during World War II and rebuilt shortly afterwards. It was recently remodeled, with work beginning in 1991.

## *U*sing the Almanac and Map,
### p.165

 The coat of arms of Bavaria shows the blue and white diamonds of the Wittelsbach dynasty that ruled the state from the Middle Ages until 1918.

### Teaching Suggestion

Ask students to research the name of the city **München** to determine its origin. The school library might have books such as *Names on the Globe* (G. R. Stewart) and *A Short History of German Place Names* (H. Davis) to help them with their research. (The name **München** comes from a small ninth century village that was close to a Benedictine monastery; **Mönche** (*monks*) → **München**.)

### Terms in the Almanac

- **Isar:** a tributary of the Danube that is 295 km (177 miles) long. The Isar generates enough energy to run several hydroelectric plants.

- **Maximilianeum:** built between 1857 and 1874, it is now the seat of the Bavarian **Landtag** and **Senat.**

- **Theatinerkirche:** a church famous for its baroque style. It dates back to 1663 when it was built to honor the birth of prince Max Emanuel, whose mother was of Italian descent.

- **Alte Pinakothek:** famous art gallery housing European paintings from the 14th to 18th centuries. It is considered one of the most impressive galleries in the world, with works by artists such as Dürer, Rembrandt, and Rubens.

- **Neue Pinakothek:** an art gallery holding 400 paintings and sculptures representing European art from the 18th to 20th centuries

- **Deutsches Museum:** the largest museum of science and technology in the world. It offers more than 15,000 exhibits.

- **Glyptothek:** gallery housing Greek and Roman antique marble sculptures

- **Schweinshaxe:** cured knuckle of pork cooked with junipers, bay leaves, greens and pork drippings. It is served with steamed sauerkraut.

- **Leberkäs:** made from liver, pork, egg, milk, flour and spices. It is served warm or cold on bread, often topped with mustard.

- **Weißwürste:** sausages made of veal, bacon, onions, lemon rind, parsley, herbs and spices.

### Using the Map

- Have students look at the map of Germany on p. 2 and name the countries that border Bavaria. (Czech Republic, Austria, and Switzerland) You may also want to use Map Transparency 1.

- Have students look at the map on p. 2 and name the **Bundesländer** that border Bavaria. (Baden-Württemberg, Hessen, Thüringen, Sachsen)

### Teaching Suggestion

Since Munich is known for its automobile industry, ask students if they know what the abbreviation BMW stands for. (**Bayerische Motoren Werke** = *Bavarian motorworks*)

## *I*nterpreting the Photo Essay, pp. 166-167

② **Lederhosen** originated in western Austria (Tyrol) and were introduced in Bavaria in 1800. As can be seen in the picture, the pants have suspenders with ornamental breastbands. Men usually wear a light-colored shirt with the **Lederhosen** as well as knee-high socks. A longer version of the **Lederhosen** comes below the knee and is worn on cool days.

- **Observing** Ask students if they can tell by looking at the picture or the word **Leder** what the **Lederhosen** are made of. (leather)

- **Drawing Inferences** Ask students when men might wear their **Lederhosen**. (Oktoberfest, dances, church festivals, holidays, etc.)

- The **Gamsbart** is from the long back mane of the chamois. The display of the **Gamsbart** on the hat is considered to be a trophy which once indicated that the man had killed a chamois.

③ The **Frauenkirche** (*church of our lady*) is the most distinguishing landmark of the Munich skyline. It was built between 1468 and 1488 in the late gothic style by Jörg v. Polling. Its onion-shaped towers stand 99 and 100 meters tall.

- **Teaching Suggestion** The many cafés in the foreground are part of the city's **Fußgängerzone**. Ask students if they can understand the meaning of the compound word **Fußgängerzone**. (*pedestrian zone*)

- **Comparing and Contrasting** Can students think of any pedestrian zones in U.S. cities? Why are they more common in the German-speaking countries than in the United States? (Designed to preserve older parts of towns where streets were very narrow and to encourage use of public transportation, **Fußgängerzonen** are very common in the German-speaking countries. Stores and restaurants can be found in the center of a city rather than in big malls, which are more of an American concept. Since parking is difficult, pedestrians have to leave their cars at parking garages or use public transportation for easier access to the city.)

- **Building on Previous Skills** Can students tell from the sign what is being served at this outdoor restaurant? (**Kaffee und Kuchen**)

④ **Culture Note** Traditionally, the first of May was celebrated with the **Maibaum** to signify the arrival of spring. It is a pole with a big wreath of green branches on the top. Long, colorful ribbons hang down from the wreath. Dances are performed around the pole. Each part of the pictured maypole depicts some historical or cultural aspect of life in Munich. The coat of arms of Munich at the bottom right of the pole bears the figure of a small, blue-clad monk, called **Münchner Kindl**, who symbolizes the city's origin as a village alongside a medieval monastery. The casks on the wagon represent the different local breweries, such as **Spatenbräu, Löwenbräu, Augustiner, Münchner Kindl, Paulaner, Hofbräu,** and **Franziskaner.** Next, two scenes from the famous **Oktoberfest** are shown. The scenes above depict barrel makers, **Schäffler,** performing their traditional dance. The dancing couple at the top wears the traditional costumes of Bavaria.

⑤ The old city hall was built from 1470 to 1475 by J.v. Halspach. The tower was completely destroyed during World War II and faithfully reconstructed in 1972.

- The **Mariensäule** (built in 1638) is a focal point of the **Marienplatz,** which is the center of the city. It is surrounded by numerous outdoor cafés and restaurants.

⑥ **Viktualien** is an old-fashioned word for groceries. The original market dates back as early as 1365 when a city ordinance allowed the butchers to sell their goods only at this location. Today the market vendors offer many specialties besides fresh produce and meats.

⑦ Flori, Markus, and Claudia are originally from Munich, but Flori's mother is American. Mara is from Croatia. She has been living in Munich for a number of years.

Komm mit nach

München!

# München

**Landeshauptstadt von Bayern**

**Einwohner:** 1,3 Millionen

**Fluß:** München liegt an der Isar

**Berühmte Gebäude:**
Frauenkirche, Rathaus, Maximilianeum, Theatinerkirche

**Museen:** Alte und Neue Pinakothek, Deutsches Museum, Glyptothek

**Industrien:** Elektrotechnik und Elektronik, Automobilindustrie, Brauereien, Verlage, Filmindustrie

**Bedeutende Münchner:** Josef von Fraunhofer (1787-1826, Physiker); Moritz von Schwind (1804-1871, Maler); Karl Valentin (1882-1948, Komiker); Annette Kolb (1870-1967, Schriftstellerin)

**Typische Gerichte:** Schweinshaxe, Leberkäs, Weißwürste

Foto ① Ein Blick über die Dächer von München

# München

*Munich is the capital of the state of Bavaria. Famous for its museums, theaters, and sports facilities (the city hosted the 1972 Olympic Games), Munich is also a center for automobile, computer, and aerospace industries.*

② Two men in **Lederhosen,** the traditional folk costume of **Oberbayern** *(Upper Bavaria).* The man on the right is also wearing a hat with a **Gamsbart** made from the hair of the chamois, an antelope-like animal living in the Alps.

③ A busy street in the center of **München** with a view of the twin towers of the **Frauenkirche.** In the foreground people enjoy a meal in a typical open-air café.

④ A maypole with figures showing scenes from everyday life. At the bottom you see the blue and white coat of arms of Bavaria and the **Münchner Kindl** symbolizing Munich.

**5** A view of the **Marienplatz** showing the **Mariensäule**, with the Old Town Hall in the background. This is part of the **Fußgängerzone** *(pedestrian zone)*.

**6** The **Viktualienmarkt** in the center of **München** offers a wide variety of fruits and vegetables. Many **Münchner** come here for their daily shopping.

*Chapters 7, 8, and 9 take place in Munich. The students in these chapters attend different schools. Flori goes to the **Einstein-Gymnasium,** Markus and Claudia attend the **Theodolinden-Gymnasium,** and Mara goes to the **Rudolf-Diesel Realschule.***

**7** Mara, Flori, Markus, and Claudia welcome you to Munich

# Kapitel 7: Zu Hause helfen *Chapter Overview*

| **Los geht's!** pp. 170-172 | Was mußt du machen? p. 170 | | | *Video Guide* |
|---|---|---|---|---|
| | **FUNCTIONS** | **GRAMMAR** | **CULTURE** | **RE-ENTRY** |
| **Erste Stufe** pp. 173-177 | •Extending and responding to an invitation, *p. 174* •Expressing obligations, *p. 174* | •The verb **müssen**, *p. 175* •The separable prefix verb **abräumen**, *p. 176* | Landeskunde: **Was tust du für die Umwelt?**, *p. 177* | •Separable-prefix verbs, *p. 176* (from **Kapitel 5**) •The verb **wollen**, *p. 174* (from **Kapitel 6**) •Vocabulary for free-time activities, *p. 175* (from **Kapitel 2** and **Kapitel 6**) |
| **Zweite Stufe** pp. 178-181 | •Talking about how often you have to do things, *p. 178* •Asking for and offering help and telling someone what to do, *p. 179* | •The verb **können**, *p. 179* •The accusative pronouns, *p. 180* | | •Time expressions, *p. 178* (from **Kapitel 1**) •Vocabulary for free-time activities, *p. 178* (from **Kapitel 2** and **Kapitel 6**) •Vocabulary for school supplies, *p. 181* (from **Kapitel 4**) |
| **Dritte Stufe** pp. 182-185 | Talking about the weather, *p. 183* | Using **morgen** to refer to the future, *p. 183* | •Weather map and weather report, *p. 182* •**Ein wenig Landeskunde:** Weather in German-speaking countries, *p. 184* | Using numbers in a new context, temperature, *p. 182* (from **Kapitel 1** and **Kapitel 3**) |
| **Aussprache** p. 185 | The short vowel **o**, the short vowel **u**, the letter **l**, the letter combination **th**, the letter combination **pf** | | | Diktat: *Textbook Audiocassette* 4 A |
| **Zum Lesen** pp. 186-187 | Wem hilfst du? Reading Strategy: Finding relationships between ideas | | | |
| **Review** pp. 188-191 | •Anwendung, *p. 188* •Kann ich's wirklich? *p. 190* •Wortschatz, *p. 191* | | | |
| **Assessment Options** | **Stufe Quizzes** •*Chapter Resources*, Book 3  Erste Stufe, Quiz 7-1  Zweite Stufe, Quiz 7-2  Dritte Stufe, Quiz 7-3 •*Assessment Items, Audiocassette* 8 A | | **Kapitel 7 Chapter Test** •*Chapter Resources*, Book 3 •*Assessment Guide*, Speaking Test •*Assessment Items, Audiocassette* 8 A  **Test Generator, Kapitel 7** | |

*Video Program* **OR**
*Expanded Video Program,* Videocassette 3

Textbook Audiocassette 4 A

| RESOURCES | RESOURCES |
|---|---|
| Print | Audiovisual |

*Textbook Audiocassette* 4 A

*Practice and Activity Book*
*Chapter Resources,* Book 3
- Communicative Activity 7-1
- Additional Listening Activities, 7-1, 7-2 . . . . . . . . . *Additional Listening Activities, Audiocassette* 10 A
- Student Response Form
- Realia 7-1
- Situation Card 7-1
- Teaching Transparency Master 7-1 . . . . . . . . . . . . . *Teaching Transparency* 7-1
- Quiz 7-1 . . . . . . . . . . . . . . . . . . . . . . . . . . . . *Assessment Items, Audiocassette* 8 A
*Video Guide.* . . . . . . . . . . . . . . . . . . . . . . . . . . . .*Video Program/Expanded Video Program,* Videocassette 3

*Textbook Audiocassette* 4 A

*Practice and Activity Book*
*Chapter Resources,* Book 3
- Communicative Activity 7-2
- Additional Listening Activity 7-3 . . . . . . . . . . . . . *Additional Listening Activities, Audiocassette* 10 A
- Additional Listening Activity 7-4 . . . . . . . . . . . . . *Additional Listening Activities, Audiocassette* 10 A
- Student Response Form
- Realia 7-2
- Situation Card 7-2
- Quiz 7-2 . . . . . . . . . . . . . . . . . . . . . . . . . . . . *Assessment Items, Audiocassette* 8 A

*Textbook Audiocassette* 4 A

*Practice and Activity Book*
*Chapter Resources,* Book 3
- Additional Listening Activity 7-5 . . . . . . . . . . . . . *Additional Listening Activities, Audiocassette* 10 A
- Additional Listening Activity 7-6 . . . . . . . . . . . . . *Additional Listening Activities, Audiocassette* 10 A
- Student Response Form
- Realia 7-3
- Situation Card 7-3
- Teaching Transparency Master 7-2 . . . . . . . . . . . . . *Teaching Transparency* 7-2
- Quiz 7-3 . . . . . . . . . . . . . . . . . . . . . . . . . . . . *Assessment Items, Audiocassette* 8 A

*Video Guide.* . . . . . . . . . . . . . . . . . . . . . . . . . . . .*Video Program/Expanded Video Program,* Videocassette 3

**Alternative Assessment**
- Performance Assessment, *Teacher's Edition*
  **Erste Stufe,** p. 167J
  **Zweite Stufe,** p. 167M
  **Dritte Stufe,** p. 167P
- Portfolio Assessment
  Written: **Zum Lesen,** Activity 10, *Pupil's Edition,* p. 187, *Assessment Guide*
  Oral: **Anwendung,** Activity 5, *Pupil's Edition,* p. 189, *Assessment Guide*
- **Notizbuch,** *Pupil's Edition,* p. 181; *Practice and Activity Book,* p. 151

**CHAPTER OVERVIEW**

# Kapitel 7: Zu Hause helfen
# *Textbook Listening Activities Scripts*

## Erste Stufe

### Activity 7, p. 174

PETER   Du, Jürgen, der Kinofilm fängt um 15 Uhr an. Gehen wir jetzt!

JÜRGEN   Spitze! Du, aber bevor wir gehen, muß ich noch meine Hausarbeit machen.

PETER   Kann ich dir dabei helfen?

JÜRGEN   Prima! Danke. Zuerst muß ich die Wohnzimmerfenster putzen. Das geht ganz schnell.

PETER   Und jetzt?

JÜRGEN   Gehen wir in mein Zimmer! Ich muß noch meine Klamotten aufräumen.

PETER   Was noch?

JÜRGEN   Ja, ... jetzt decken wir den Tisch fürs Abendbrot.

PETER   Wo sind denn die Teller?

JÜRGEN   Da oben im Schrank. Mensch, vielen Dank für deine Hilfe. Gehen wir!

PETER   Mußt du später auch noch helfen?

JÜRGEN   Ja, normalerweise räum' ich dann den Tisch auch abends ab. Und du?

PETER   Ja, ich helf' auch oft zu Hause.

JÜRGEN   Nach dem Abendbrot muß ich dann das Geschirr spülen. Machst du das auch?

PETER   Nee, wir haben eine Geschirrspülmaschine. Gott sei Dank!

### Activity 8, p. 174

1. — Hallo Mara! Wir wollen jetzt in die Eisdiele Rücker. Wir wollen mal wieder ein Eis essen gehen. Kommst du mit?
   — Ja, gern doch! Ich hol' schnell meine Tasche.

2. — Grüßt euch! Was habt ihr heute vor?
   — Ja eigentlich wollen wir ins Kino. Der neue Film mit Kevin Costner spielt in der Holtenauerstraße. Möchtest du ihn auch sehen?
   — Ja klar! Wann sollen wir uns denn treffen?

3. — Du, Claudia, ich brauche einen neuen Pulli für Monikas Fete am Samstag. Willst du mit ins Einkaufszentrum?
   — Nee, kann leider nicht. Donnerstags helf' ich immer meiner Oma zu Hause.

4. — Du, Robert, wir gehen jetzt Tennis spielen. Komm doch mit!
   — Schade, ich kann nicht. Ich habe heute Nachmittag meine Klavierstunde.
   — Na ja, vielleicht kannst du ja das nächste Mal mitspielen.

5. — He, willst du mit ins Café? Wir treffen da Lars und Frauke.
   — Hm ... weiß nicht. Ja doch! Ich muß nur später mit meiner Mutter einkaufen gehen.

## Zweite Stufe

### Activity 18, p. 179

Ja, also helfen muß ich ja schon zu Hause. Meine Schwester und ich teilen uns da halt die Arbeit. Am Samstag habe ich immer viel zu tun, denn da muß ich immer den Rasen mähen. Danach helf' ich meinem Vater, das Auto waschen. Aber das macht eigentlich Spaß. Ja und dann muß ich auch noch den Müll sortieren. Das ist ja auch irgendwie wichtig, find' ich. Na ja, Fenster putzen soll ich am Mittwoch, aber das tu' ich manchmal auch am Donnerstag. Es kommt ganz darauf an. Und in der Küche helf' ich nicht so gern, meine Schwester räumt immer den Tisch ab, und ich spül' dann das Geschirr. Das geht ja noch. Ja und mein Zimmer räum' ich nicht so gern auf, aber meine Mutter besteht darauf. Also das mache ich ein- oder zweimal in der Woche.

#### *Answers to Activity 18*

Samstag: Rasen mähen, Auto waschen, Müll sortieren; Mittwoch/Donnerstag: Fenster putzen; ein-oder zweimal in der Woche: Zimmer aufräumen

# Dritte Stufe
## Activity 26, p. 183

1. — Und nun die Wettervorhersage für Donnerstag, den 6. Januar. Das Wetter ist unverändert schlecht. Es wird bewölkt sein mit zeitweisen Regenschauern und Temperaturen um 10 Grad.
2. — Und hier die weiteren Wetteraussichten. Heute sehr heiß und schwül. Die Höchsttemperaturen werden bei 38 Grad liegen.
3. — Und jetzt das Wetter für morgen, den 28. Dezember. Die Tieftemperaturen der Nacht bringen einen leichten Schneefall und kaum Änderungen im Wetter. Es bleibt weiterhin kalt. Wir erwarten sonniges Wetter mit leichtem Wind aus dem Südwesten.
4. — Und nun zum Wetter: sonnig und warm. Am Nachmittag teilweise bewölkt mit Temperaturen um 20 Grad.

## Diktat, p. 185

You will hear about the chores that Ulli and Peter have to do before they can go to the concert tonight. First listen to what is said, then write down the text you hear.

Ulli und Peter gehen heute abend ins Rockkonzert. Zuerst müssen sie aber zu Hause etwas helfen. In der Küche gibt es viel zu tun. Ulli räumt den Tisch ab, und Peter spült das Geschirr auch gleich. Das Zimmer von Ulli ist wieder ziemlich schmutzig. Da hilft Peter schnell. Er räumt die Klamotten auf und macht das Bett. Zum Schluß saugt Ulli Staub im Haus, und der Peter sortiert den Müll. Jetzt ist es schon 19 Uhr, und das Konzert beginnt in einer Stunde.

# Anwendung
## Activity 1, p. 188

1. — Du, Silvia! Wir wollen ins Kino. Komm doch mit!
— Hm, ja gern. Was gibt's denn zu sehen?
— Den Film mit Wolf Schmidt, *Terror in den Alpen.*

2. — Sybille, kommst du mit zum Café Schulz, ein Eis essen?
— Schade, ich kann leider nicht. Ich muß Hausaufgaben machen. Ich habe zu viel zu tun. Und morgen habe ich auch noch Klavierstunde. Ich muß noch üben. Aber bestimmt das nächste Mal.

3. — Du, Claudia! Das Wetter ist toll. Gehen wir doch Tennis spielen!
— Nee, das geht nicht. Ich habe meiner Oma versprochen, den Rasen bei ihr zu mähen. Aber hab' vielen Dank für die Einladung.

4. — Kommst du heute abend zur Fete bei Markus? Das soll ganz stark werden. Mit gutem Essen und toller Musik.
— Ja, klar! Um 7 Uhr, ja? Was ziehst du denn dazu an?
— Nur Shorts und ein T-Shirt. Das ist schon fesch.

5. — Annette und ich wollen ins Einkaufszentrum gehen, weil ich eine neue Bluse für die Fete brauch'. Willst du mitkommen?
— Ich brauch' eigentlich ja auch neue Klamotten, aber heute kann ich wirklich nicht. Ich geh' nämlich um 3 Uhr schwimmen.

# Kapitel 7: Zu Hause helfen
## *Suggested Project*

*In this activity, students will create a world-wide weather map. After completing the **Dritte Stufe** of this chapter, each student can be assigned a city in a different part of the world for which he or she will prepare an oral and written weather report.*

## MATERIALS

✂ **Students may need**
- *large pieces of light-colored construction paper, poster board, or butcher paper*
- *markers*

## SUGGESTED CITIES

Berlin, Munich, Frankfurt, Rome, Paris, Madrid, Moscow, Stockholm, New York City, Miami, Mexico City, Vancouver, Anchorage, Amsterdam, Athens, Auckland, Cairo, Dublin, Geneva, Hong Kong, London, Nairobi, Seoul, Toronto, Seattle, New Orleans, Beijing, Belgrade, Lima, New Dehli, Lagos

## SUGGESTED SEQUENCE

1. Begin by asking several students to draw a large world map on construction paper.

2. Hang the completed map up on the wall.

3. Assign a city to each student and have the students label their cities on the map. Students should verify the location of the city in an atlas if necessary.

4. Have students check the weather section of a major newspaper for the weather conditions and forecasts of their assigned cities.

5. Have the class agree on symbols that reflect certain weather conditions. (Example: raindrops for rain)

6. Ask each student to prepare an oral and a written portion of the project. As the oral component, students should present the local weather conditions as a TV weather forecaster would do. Suggest that students begin their weather reports with **Guten Abend, liebe Zuschauer!** For a written exercise, students should write a complete weather report and forecast for their city.

Suggestion: Set a time limit of 1 to 2 minutes for the oral presentations.

## GRADING THE PROJECT:

Suggested point distribution (total=100 points)

| | |
|---|---|
| Oral Presentation | 50 |
| Written report | 50 |

## COMMUNITY LINK

You might want to encourage your students to present their projects to geography classes in their school or other schools in the area.

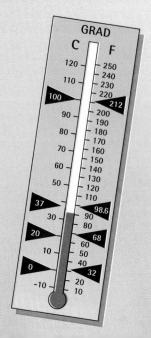

# Kapitel 7: Zu Hause helfen

# Games

## CHARADES

*This adaptation of the familiar party game is especially useful for helping kinesthetic learners review the vocabulary of household chores.*

**Materials**   You will need a set of index cards with a German phrase for a household chore written on each card. Example: **den Tisch abräumen**

**Procedure**   Divide the class into two teams. Have a member of Team A come to the front of the class. Show that student a chore that you have written on an index card. This student must then try to act out the chore to his or her team in 30 seconds. Members of the student's team may only ask **ja/nein** questions as they try to guess the chore. If the team cannot guess the chore within the set time, no point is given. Then Team B sends a member to the front to act out the next chore. The team with the most points wins.

## ZEICHENSPIEL

*This game will help tactile learners review the vocabulary listed on p. 191.*

**Materials**   You will need small index cards with the vocabulary from this chapter (chores, weather, months), a timer or stop watch, score card, pencils, and paper.

**Procedure**   Divide the class into groups of four and have each group arrange their chairs together. Two students make up a team competing against the other two students in their group. Hand each group several index cards that must be turned face down. Partners take turns as "artists" and "guessers." The artists in each pair pick up the top card and look at the vocabulary item. All artists begin to draw when you give the signal. The guessers try to guess the word or phrase their partners are drawing as quickly as possible. The partner who guesses correctly first wins a point for the pair. If time runs out before the word is identified by the partner, no point is scored. Players take turns drawing and guessing.

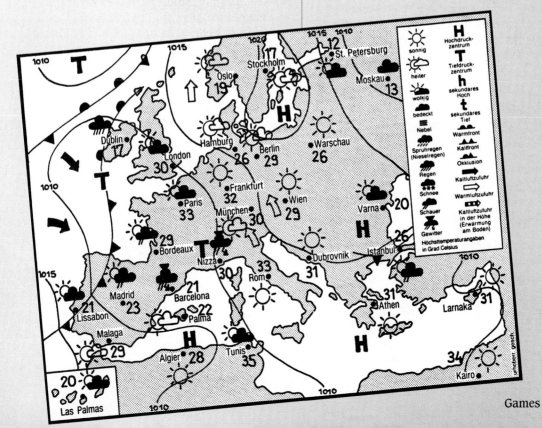

# Kapitel 7: Zu Hause helfen
## Lesson Plans, pages 168-191

## Using the Chapter Opener, pp. 168-169

### Motivating Activity

Ask students where they would like to go if they were planning a picnic with friends. What would they pack to eat and how would they get there?

### Background Information

① The **Englischer Garten** is a 364 **Hektar** park laid out by the landscape architect F.L. v. Schell from 1789 to 1795. It is 5 km long and 3 km wide. Famous artists come to this popular park to display their works, while other people come for walks and to ride their bikes.

### Math Connection

Have students calculate how many acres correspond to 364 **Hektar.** (1 **Hektar** = 2.471 acres; 364 **Hektar** = 899.44 acres)

### Thinking Critically

**Comparing and Contrasting** Can students think of any parks in the United States of similar popularity? (Examples: Central Park in New York City; Golden Gate Park in San Francisco; Forest Park in St. Louis)

### Building on Previous Skills

Ask students to come up with suggestions for activities that they could do in a large park such as the **Englischer Garten.** This should be done in German. Have students come to the board and write their ideas.

### Thinking Critically

② **Drawing Inferences** Ask students for an English translation of the phrase **Rasen mähen** based on the picture. Then have them determine which word is the noun and which is the verb. Students should explain their reasoning to the class. (Example: **Rasen** is capitalized so it must be a noun. **Mähen** is an unconjugated verb at the end of the sentence.)

### Thinking Critically

③ **Comparing and Contrasting** Begin by asking students what kinds of chores the girl still needs to do in her room. (make bed, pick up books, put up clothes) Then have students tell you what kinds of chores they most often have to do in their own rooms.

You might want to point out to students that in Germany, cannister-type vacuum cleaners are more common than upright vacuum cleaners.

### Building on Previous Skills

③ Ask students to name and describe in German all the objects they recognize in the room, using vocabulary from previous chapters. (Example: clothing, furniture)

### Focusing on Outcomes

To get students to focus on the chapter objectives listed on p. 169, ask them if there are certain chores that they regularly have to do around their house. Then have students preview the learning outcomes listed on p. 169. **NOTE:** Each of these outcomes is modeled in the video and evaluated in **Kann ich's wirklich?** on p. 190.

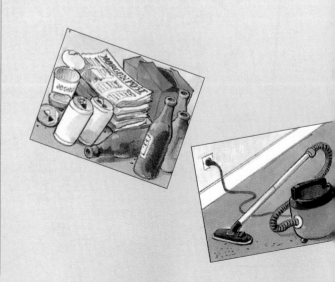

# *T*eaching Los geht's!
*pp. 170–172*

## Resources for Los geht's!

- *Video Program* **OR**
  *Expanded Video Program*
- *Textbook Audiocassette* 4 A
- *Practice and Activity Book*

▶ **pages 170–171**

### 📼 Video Synopsis

In this segment of the video, Mara, Flori, and Markus invite Claudia to go bike riding with them in the **Englischer Garten.** Claudia declines their invitation because she has to do some work at home. The friends end up helping Claudia with her chores. The student outcomes listed on p. 169 are modeled in the video: extending and responding to an invitation, expressing obligations, talking about how often you do things, asking for and offering help, telling someone what to do, and talking about the weather.

### Motivating Activity

As an advance organizer for the storyline of the **Foto-Roman,** ask students how they help out around the house. Do they have any chores they have to do today?

### Building on Previous Skills

Ask students to scan each picture and name the items they have learned in preceding units. (Examples: clothing items, furniture) Ask students to try to come up with at least two familiar words per picture.

### Teaching Suggestion

Point out the word **radeln** in the first picture and ask if students know the meaning of that verb. Tell them to use the pictures as a clue.

### Language Note

The word **radeln** is a dialect form for **radfahren** commonly used in southern Germany.

▶ **page 172**

### Teaching Suggestion

**1** Ask students to work in pairs as they answer Questions 1-6 in writing. Once the students are finished, go over their responses in class.

### ✦ For Individual Needs

**2 Visual Learners** Write the four phrases on the board and ask students to write the phrases they think belong underneath.

### ✦ For Individual Needs

**5 A Slower Pace** Begin by asking students to read the sentences quietly and to number them. Then have pairs of students read the sentences to each other, practicing pronunciation and intonation. Have a few volunteers read the whole sequence.

### Closure

Refer students back to the outcomes listed on p. 169, and ask students to list one German phrase or word from the **Foto-Roman** that they think would correspond with each function.

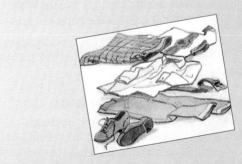

LOS GEHT'S!

# *T*eaching Erste Stufe,
## pp. 173-177

▶ *page 173*

## *MOTIVATE*

### Building on Previous Skills

Have students list at least three activities in German that they would like to do with a friend.

## *TEACH*

### Thinking Critically

**Drawing Inferences**  Ask students why the definite article in several picture captions is **den**. What can they infer about the noun in the phrase? (masculine)

▶ *page 174*

### PRESENTATION: So sagt man das!

Ask students if they can think of ways to extend an invitation to an event such as a concert using previously learned vocabulary. (**möchte**, time expressions) Can they think of ways to respond to an invitation? Make a list as students name expressions such as **Nein, danke! Ja, gern!** or **Ja, bitte!** Then go over the new expressions introduced in the **So sagt man das!** box.

▶ *page 175*

### Group Work

**9**  Brainstorm with students and make a list on the board of activities they have learned in preceding units.

### Teaching Suggestion

**11**  Have students make a list of a partner's chores and be able to tell the class what his or her chores are.

### PRESENTATION: Grammatik

Before introducing the verb **müssen**, ask students about the function of modal auxiliaries. Which one have they learned so far? (**wollen**)

###  For Individual Needs

**12  Challenge**  Ask four students to each describe one of the chores in the pictures.

▶ *page 176*

### PRESENTATION: Ein wenig Grammatik

After reading the grammar note with the class, give students some statements and questions containing separable prefix verbs. (Example: **Räumst du dein Zimmer auf?**) Students should respond using one of the modals learned so far: **mögen, wollen,** or **müssen**. (Example: **Ja, ich muß mein Zimmer aufräumen.**)

### Cooperative Learning

**16**  Begin by reading Markus' letter aloud to the class. Divide students into cooperative learning groups of three students each. Each group chooses a reader, a writer, and a checker for the assignment. To begin, the reader reads the **Brief** to his or her group again. Group members then answer questions 1-4, and the writer takes notes. The checker proofreads the answers, and the group proceeds with part b, collectively composing a response letter. After the groups have completed their assignments, ask several students to read their answers to questions 1-4, and if time permits, have students read a few letters aloud in class. At the end of the activity have members write their names on the assignment and turn it in for a grade.

## Language Note

Here are some German **Sprichwörter** that are appropriate for this **Stufe**.

- **Erst die Arbeit, dann das Vergnügen!** (*First work, then play!*)

- **Ohne Fleiß, kein Preis!** (*No pain, no gain!*)

## Reteaching: Separable prefix verbs

Prepare the following chart on a transparency. In the first column list sequencing words or time elements. In the second column list separable prefix verbs in the infinitive form. In a third column list subject pronouns. Finally, write examples of chores in the last column. Ask students to create meaningful sentences based on the chart. This can be done orally or in writing. In a second round, add modals.

Example: **Zuerst   abräumen   er   den Tisch**
**Montag   aufräumen   ich   das Zimmer**

##  PRESENTATION: Landeskunde

## Teaching Suggestions

- You might want to introduce the following phrases to help students better understand the video segment or listening script.

  **streng einhalten** *to adhere to*
  **den Müll vermeiden** *to skip garbage day*
  **wiederverwerten** *to recycle*
  **die Mehrwegflasche** *recyclable glass bottle*
  **das Putzmittel** *cleaning solution*

- After students have read the introductory paragraph above the pictures, ask them to close their books. While students watch the video segment or listen to the audiocassette, ask them to take notes of the expressions or phrases they are able to understand from each of the three interviews. Play the interviews several times. Then divide the board into three sections with the name of one of the three German teenagers written on the top of each section. Ask students to tell you the expressions they were able to understand and write them in each column. Then read the three interviews in the book and have students compare the phrases on the board with the actual readings.

##  Culture Note

In Germany, almost all glass bottles are returned to stores for deposit. They are called **Pfandflaschen,** and consumers get a deposit refund of 10-30 **Pfennig** per bottle. To reduce excessive packaging, consumers also have the right to refuse the packaging materials of purchased items at the check-out. The retailers must accept it and either reuse the packing or sort it for recycling.

##  Multicultural Connection

If possible, have students find information about other countries and how they deal with environmental issues such as the protection of water and soil, as well as the reduction of garbage, noise, and air pollution.

## Teacher Note

Mention to your students that the **Landeskunde** will also be included in Quiz 7-1 given at the end of the **Erste Stufe**.

## *CLOSE*

## TPR Total Physical Response

Ask all students to stand. Direct commands to individual students, asking them to perform imaginary chores around the classroom. Once the student has correctly completed the chore, he or she may be seated. Give commands such as **Gieß die Blumen!** or **Mach das Bett!**

## Focusing on Outcomes

Refer students back to the learning outcomes listed on p. 169. They should recognize that they are now able to extend and respond to an invitation and express obligations.

## *ASSESS*

- **Performance Assessment**   Extend invitations to individual students to sightsee in Munich. Students should decline each invitation, giving a reason (preferably a chore) why they cannot go.

- Quiz 7-1, *Chapter Resources,* Book 3

**ERSTE STUFE**

# *T*eaching Zweite Stufe,
*pp. 178-181*

## Resources for Zweite Stufe

*Practice and Activity Book*
*Chapter Resources,* Book 3
- Communicative Activity 7-2
- Additional Listening Activities 7-3, 7-4
- Student Response Form
- Realia 7-2
- Situation Card 7-2
- Quiz 7-2

*Audiocassette Program*
- *Textbook Audiocassette* 4 A
- *Additional Listening Activities,*
  *Audiocassette* 10 A
- *Assessment Items, Audiocassette* 8 A

▶ **page 178**

## *MOTIVATE*

### ♟ Game

Play the game "Charades." See page 167F for the procedure.

## *TEACH*

### ◈ For Individual Needs

**Kinesthetic Learners**  Before introducing the expressions of the **So sagt man das!** box, give a series of rapid commands which you have prepared ahead of time. Students are to carry out any command that applies to them. (Example: **Wenn du am Montag Müll sortierst, steh auf!**) To extend this activity and introduce **einmal, zweimal,** etc., model the action first and then ask students to follow your command. Example: **Schreib deinen Namen zweimal auf das Papier! Dreh dich einmal um!**

### PRESENTATION: So sagt man das!

Have students make a chart showing how many times they do certain chores in one month; one week. Then ask questions using the vocabulary the students learned in the **Erste Stufe.** Example: **Wer spült oft das Geschirr?**

## Teaching Suggestion

**17**  After having done this activity orally in class, you can assign it as homework and ask students to come up with a minimum of ten written sentences.

▶ **page 179**

## Teaching Suggestion

**18**  Provide each student with a blank, authentic copy of a page from a German calendar.

### PRESENTATION: So sagt man das!

Ask students how they would offer somebody help in English and how they would express their willingness to help. Make a list of the expressions students come up with. After introducing the German expressions, ask the class to compare the two.

### Group Work

**19**  Have students work in groups of three and write appropriate exchanges for the pictures. Set a time limit for this activity. When students have finished, call on several groups to read their conversations to the class.

▶ **page 180**

## Teaching Suggestion

**20**  Ask students to look at the title of this activity, **Peter macht ein Geschäft.** What do they think this conversation might be about? Put students in groups of three. Have the groups read the conver-

ZWEITE STUFE

sation aloud with a lot of expression. After they have practiced, have one or two groups read for the class.

## Building on Previous Skills

**20** After students have answered Questions 1-3, have them recall the accusative pronouns they have already learned. Provide sentences on a transparency in which students must replace the direct object with an accusative pronoun. Example: **Ich sauge für meine Mutter Staub. (sie); Sie kauft ein Buch für Michael. (ihn); Angela und Hermann besuchen Markus und Detlev. (sie)** Then proceed with Questions 4-6.

## PRESENTATION: Grammatik

Review the accusative pronouns introduced in **Kapitel 5 (ihn, sie, es)** by using them in sentences written on the board. Have students provide additional sentences orally. Next, introduce the four new accusative pronouns by using them in similar sentences written on the board. Help students infer the meaning of the new pronouns through demonstration and context. Example: **Hier ist dein Kuli. Der Kuli ist für dich.**

▶ *page 181*

## For Additional Practice

**21** Ask students to think of additional items that could be purchased at the **Schreibwarenladen** and create additional exchanges.

## Group Work

**22** This activity could be performed as a skit. Ask students to work in groups of three to prepare an outline for their skit. Encourage students to use props. They should bring these items the day you plan for them to act out their skit. If possible videotape the groups' performances.

## PRESENTATION: Und dann noch ...

Teach the pet vocabulary by holding up pictures (use children's books for pictures). Progress from **ja/nein** to either/or and finally to short-answer questions. Examples: **Ist das ein Vogel? Ist das eine Maus? Ist das ein Vogel oder eine Maus?**

## Teaching Suggestion

Animals make different sounds all over the world. The German dog, for example, says **wau, wau,** the bird says **piep, piep,** the rooster says **kikeriki** and the frog says **quak.** Ask students to give examples of animal sounds they learned when they were younger.

**ZWEITE STUFE**

###  Multicultural Connection

Have students ask friends from other countries about the sounds that animals make. You could also ask other foreign language teachers to help with the list. Then compare all the different sounds an animal can make around the world.

### Reteaching: Accusative pronouns

To prepare for this activity make sentence strips which include a direct object that can be replaced by an accusative pronoun. (Examples: **Daniel kauft ein Buch für Brigitte. Hier ist die Pizza für Jens und dich.**) Make one envelope per student and number each envelope. Each student receives a numbered envelope and begins by putting the sentence strips in the correct order. Then the student must rewrite the sentence on a sheet of paper, replacing the direct object with the appropriate accusative pronoun. When students are finished with their sentences, they put the strips back in the envelope and pass it to the next person. Remind students to number each sentence with the number that appears on the envelope. Have the sentences written on a transparency so that students can check their work at the end of this activity.

## *CLOSE*

###  Total Physical Response

Ask each student to perform a chore in the classroom before allowing him or her to leave the classroom. Example: **John, kannst du für mich bitte das Fenster zumachen? Robyn, kannst du für mich die Tafel saubermachen? Sylvia, kannst du für mich die Bücher einsammeln?**

### Focusing on Outcomes

Refer students back to the learning outcomes listed on p. 169. They should recognize that they are now able to talk about how often they have to do things, ask for and offer help, and tell someone what to do.

## *ASSESS*

- **Performance Assessment**  Conduct a survey addressing the functions introduced in this **Stufe.** Ask individual students questions related to chores around the house. Example: **Wie oft mußt du Staub saugen? Was machst du nicht gern zu Hause? Habt ihr Haustiere? Wie heißen sie?**

- Quiz 7-2, *Chapter Resources,* Book 3

ZWEITE STUFE

# Teaching Dritte Stufe,
## pp 182-185

### Resources for Dritte Stufe

*Practice and Activity Book*
*Chapter Resources,* Book 3
- Additional Listening Activities 7-5, 7-6
- Student Response Form
- Realia 7-3
- Situation Card 7-3
- Teaching Transparency Master 7-2
- Quiz 7-3

*Audiocassette Program*
- *Textbook Audiocassette* 4 A
- *Additional Listening Activities, Audiocassette* 10 A
- *Assessment Items, Audiocassette* 8 A

▶ *page 182*

## MOTIVATE
### Teaching Suggestion

Ask students in English about their favorite time of the year. What is the weather like during that time? What is their least favorite season and why? Have them think about the ways in which weather influences their activities.

## TEACH
### Background Information

The German physicist G.D. Fahrenheit (1686-1736) invented the Fahrenheit measurement of temperature which is used in the United States and in England. The other measurement, Celsius, is named after the Swedish astronomer and physicist Anders Celsius (1701-1744) and is used in most other European countries.

## Math Connection

Give students examples of temperatures reported from around the country. You could make a transparency from the weather report in a local newspaper. Ask students to convert Fahrenheit degrees into Celsius. (To convert Fahrenheit to Celsius, subtract 32, multiply by 5, and divide by 9. To convert Celsius into Fahrenheit, multiply by 9, divide by 5, and add 32.)

## Teaching Suggestion

You may want to give your students some additional weather vocabulary: **das Barometer; das Hoch; das Tief; das Thermometer; die Luftmasse** *(air mass);* **die Kaltfront/Warmfront; Wetter in Übersee; zeitweise** *(occasionally);* **wechselhaft** *(changing);* **unbeständig** *(unstable)*

## Language Notes

The German language has several proverbs related to weather. Here are some examples you can share with your class:

- **Wenn der Hahn kräht auf dem Mist, ändert sich das Wetter, oder es bleibt wie es ist!** *When the rooster crows on the dunghill, the weather changes, or it stays the same!*

- **Der April macht die Blumen, und der Mai hat den Dank dafür.** *April showers bring May flowers.*

## Thinking Critically

**Comparing and Contrasting** Ask students if they know of any English proverbs, sayings or expressions about the weather. (Example: It's raining cats and dogs.)

**DRITTE STUFE**

▶ *page 183*

## PRESENTATION: So sagt man das!

Teach the weather expressions using gestures (Examples: shivering, sweating), or simple drawings or photos. Describe the weather in such places as Alaska and Hawaii, or make general statements about typical weather during the four seasons.

## PRESENTATION: Ein wenig Grammatik

Ask students to name other time expressions they have learned that could refer to the near future. Example: **am Montag, am Wochenende, im Frühling.**

## For Additional Practice

Have the class keep a local weather chart for a week, with one person in charge of recording the weather conditions each day. After the data has been recorded each day, ask the students about the weather.

▶ *page 184*

## PRESENTATION: Wortschatz

To teach this vocabulary in context, ask students such questions as: **Wann ist Frühling?, St. Patrickstag?, Vatertag?, Muttertag?, St. Valentinstag?, Kolumbustag?**

## Group Work

**28** Ask students to work with a partner to put the sentences in order, and then practice reading the dialogue together. Monitor students' activity and make suggestions if necessary.

▶ *page 185*

## Teaching Suggestion

**29** Have students write the report as if they were going to read it over the radio. Suggest that students begin their reports with **Guten Abend, liebe Zuhörer!**

## PRESENTATION: Aussprache

To help students hear the difference between short and long **o**, contrast the sounds by using word pair: **Sohn/Sonne.** To help students hear the difference between long and short **u**, contrast the sounds by using word pair: **Du/dumm.** You might also want to point out to students that the letter combination **th** in German is always pronounced like the letter **t**.

## Teacher Note

Many northern Germans pronounce the letter combination **pf** as a simple **f**. For example, they pronounce the words **Pflaume** and **Pforte** as "flaume" and "forte".

## Teaching Suggestion

After students have written the sentences of the **Diktat,** ask them to exchange their papers with other students. Put up the script on the overhead projector, one sentence at a time. Have individual students read the sentences aloud and check the paper in front of them for errors. They should mark the errors and make corrections if necessary.

## Reteaching: Weather

Recycle the sports vocabulary from Chapter 2 and ask students which sports they would participate in during certain weather conditions. Example: **Was machst du, wenn es sonnig ist? Was machst du wenn es schneit?**

## CLOSE

### ♜ Game

For this game you will need a soft, light ball. Throw the ball to a student who must then say the first word of a series determined by you. For example, if the series were **Monate,** the student would say **Januar.** He or she then throws the ball to another student who must say the next word in that series, **Februar.** For an added twist, have any student who drops the ball stand up and repeat all the words that have been said up to that point. This is a great way to review seasons, months, numbers, or days of the week.

### Focusing on Outcomes

Refer students back to the learning outcomes listed on p. 169. Students should recognize that they are now able to talk about the weather.

## ASSESS

- **Performance Assessment** As students walk into the classroom, hand some of them small index cards with the following information: name of a city, current weather conditions, and temperature. Once the class gets underway, call on students to report their information in German.

- Quiz 7-3, *Chapter Resources,* Book 3

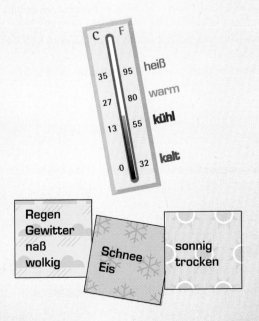

# Teaching Zum Lesen,
## pp. 186-187

### Reading Strategy

The targeted reading strategy is finding relationships between ideas. Students will also be asked to skim for the gist, scan for specific information, answer questions to show comprehension, and transfer what they have learned.

## PREREADING

### Motivating Activity

Go around the classroom and ask students whom they have helped this past week and in what way.

### Teaching Suggestion

Ask students what *conjunction* means (joining together), and how this part of speech can be used in a sentence. Can they give examples? Do students know what the word *subordinate* means? (not equal; a part that cannot stand by itself and depends on the rest of the sentence)

### Teacher Note

Activities 1-2 are prereading tasks.

## READING

### Skimming/Scanning

- Ask students to compare the written bold print of the three surveys. Do they notice anything? (repeated questions)

- Ask students to scan for expressions they recognize that refer to chores.

### Thinking Critically

**Observing** Have students look at the title of the article and the questions that are listed with the title. Can they point out the yes/no questions and also the questions that require a short answer? Ask students to make a list of the verbs in the questions. (**helfen, verdienen, anbieten, haben, bekommen**)

### Teaching Suggestion

As students orally list questions for Activity 4, write the interrogative pronouns they use on the board.

**ZUM LESEN**

ZUM LESEN

## Thinking Critically

**Drawing Inferences** Ask students to look at the question words listed on the board. Can they give general information as to what type of answer or content could be expected in response to each of the interrogatives? Example: **Wem (wer)?** → name; **Wann?** → time element; Verb in first position → yes/no answer

## Teaching Suggestion

Before reading Heiko's interview, you may want to introduce this additional vocabulary: **schimpfen** *to scold;* **aufdringlich** *pushy;* **Last abnehmen** *to remove a burden*

## Thinking Critically

• **Drawing Inferences** Can students tell why Heiko is not getting extra pay for doing chores? (Doing chores is expected.)

• **Analyzing** Ask students if they can understand from his last statement why Heiko likes to help others. What words were clues that helped them find the answer?

 ## Culture Note

Sven talks about giving **Nachhilfestunden**. Tutorials are often advertised on the bulletin board (**Anschlagebrett**) in the school lobby, on which students are allowed to put up notes. If a school has its own paper, **Nachhilfestunden** ads are also printed there.

 ## For Individual Needs

**Challenge** Ask students to write an ad advertising their offer to tutor in their best subject(s). They should list the subjects they can tutor, their hourly rate, and how they can be contacted. Students can also refer to the **Zum Lesen** section of Chapter 4 for examples.

## Teaching Suggestion

Introduce the new vocabulary from Tina's interview (**bügeln, putzen**) using props or dramatic demonstrations.

## *POST-READING*

## Teacher Note

Activities 9 and 10 are post-reading tasks that will show whether students can apply what they have learned.

 ## Portfolio Assessment

**10** You might want to suggest this activity as a written portfolio item for your students. See *Assessment Guide*, Chapter 7.

## Thinking Critically

**Comparing and Contrasting** Ask students to work with a partner and go back over the three surveys. Have them make a list of all the chores that Heiko, Sven, and Tina mentioned. Then have students number each chore by order of importance. Do American students seem to have attitudes toward helping similar to their German counterparts?

 ## Culture Note

Being an *au pair* is a very popular way for German students to study a foreign language after graduating from school. Being an *au pair* usually requires doing chores at the house in which you stay. Popular countries for *au pairs* are the United States, England, France, and Monaco.

## For Individual Needs

**Challenge** Ask students to research exchange programs in the United States. What is available to American students, and what is required of students who stay with a family? Do students know of anybody who has been an exchange student? Ask students why they would or would not like to be an *au pair* or an exchange student.

*Answers to Activity 7*

a. Heiko: mother; housework
Tina: family and friends; caring for children, helping sister with homework, housework
Sven: friends; helping with schoolwork

b. when he spends a long period of time not helping; yes; because of the phrase **sie haben recht**; it's an important thing to do.

c. helping her sister with her homework; day care center; to help others

d. He's good at these subjects; all nice people

# *U*sing Anwendung,
*p. 188-189*

## Teaching Suggestion

**1** As an advance organizer to the listening activity, ask students to list expressions they have learned for accepting and declining invitations. Tell them to listen for these in the activity.

## Thinking Critically

**4 Comparing and Contrasting** Ask students which of the western European cities shown has weather that most closely resembles that of their own area.

##  For Individual Needs

**Tactile Learners** Draw a large calendar on poster board for the month you plan to do this activity. Assign each student one day for which he or she is responsible for reporting the weather conditions. Students can draw simple pictures on the calendar to depict the weather for their assigned day. In addition, they should prepare a short oral report about the weather that day.

##  Portfolio Assessment

**5** You might want to use this activity as an oral portfolio item for your students. See *Assessment Guide*, Chapter 7.

# *K*ann ich's wirklich?
*p. 190*

This page is intended to prepare students for the test. It is a brief checklist of the major points covered in the chapter. The students should be reminded that it is a checklist only and not necessarily everything that will appear on the test.

# *U*sing Wortschatz,
*p. 191*

## Game

Play the game **Zeichenspiel** to review Chapter 7 vocabulary. See p. 167F for the procedure.

## Teaching Suggestion

Create scrambled versions of the vocabulary to be reviewed. For example, you could make a list of scrambled words using weather expressions or months. Each student gets a copy of the list and students then try to unscramble all the words. Example: **NESNO → SONNE**

## Teacher Note

Give the **Kapitel 7** Chapter Test, *Chapter Resources, Book 3*.

REVIEW

## März

| Mo | Di | Mi | Do | Fr | Sa | So |
|---|---|---|---|---|---|---|
| | 1 Staub saugen | 2 | 3 | 4 Müll sortieren | 5 Fenster putzen 4:00 Fußball spielen | 6 |
| 7 9:30 mit Michael ins Konzert | 8 Staub saugen | 9 3:30 Klavierunterricht 7:00 Volleyball | 10 | 11 9:00 Disko | 12 Rasen mähen 4:00 Fußball spielen | 13 |
| 14 8:30 Kino mit Sabine | 15 Staub saugen | 16 3:30 Klavierunterricht | 17 | 18 Müll sortieren | 19 Fenster putzen 4:00 Fußball spielen | 20 |
| 21 4:00 Schwimmen | 22 Staub saugen | 23 3:30 Klavierunterricht | 24 | 25 9:00 Disko | 26 Rasen mähen 4:00 Fußball spielen | 27 |
| 28 | 29 Staub saugen | 30 3:30 Klavierunterricht | 31 | | | |

# Zu Hause helfen

① Wir gehen in den Englischen Garten. Kommst du mit?

**W**hat is a typical Saturday like for teens in German-speaking countries? They get together with friends, make plans according to the weather, and help around the house. What do you do on Saturday? Do you see your friends? Do you also help with chores? If so, what do you do? What do you think German teens might do to help at home?

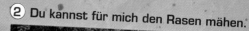
② Du kannst für mich den Rasen mähen.

## In this chapter you will learn

- to extend and respond to an invitation; to express obligations
- to talk about how often you have to do things; to ask for and to offer help and tell someone what to do
- to talk about the weather

## And you will

- listen to German weather reports
- read weather forecasts from a German newspaper
- make a list of the chores you have to do
- find out how teenagers in the German-speaking countries help around the house

③ Ich muß Staub saugen.

# Los geht's!

Claudia

Flori

Markus

Mara

## Was mußt du machen?

Look at the photos that accompany the story.
Who are the people pictured? What are they doing?
Where are they? What do you think they are talking about?
What do you suppose will happen in the story?

**①**

Wohin geht's?

Claudia, hallo!

In den Englischen Garten. Komm doch mit!

Das geht nicht. Ich muß zu Hause helfen.

Was mußt du denn tun, Claudia?

Schade, daß du nicht mitkommen kannst! Es ist heute so schönes Wetter zum Radeln.

Ich muß mein Zimmer aufräumen, den Müll sortieren, das ...

**②**

Ein Moment! Ich hab' eine Idee. Fahren wir alle zu Claudia und helfen ihr.

Prima Idee! — Ja, dann ist sie schnell fertig und kann mitkommen!

Das ist lieb von euch.

**BEI CLAUDIA**

**③**

Markus, du und der Flori, ihr könnt den Müll sortieren. Die Flaschen kommen hier rein, die Dosen kommen da rein.

Und die Zeitungen?

Die Zeitungen kommen in den Korb da.

## 1 Was passiert hier?

Do you understand what is happening in the **Foto-Roman**? Check your comprehension by answering these questions. Don't be afraid to guess.

1. Where do Claudia's three friends (Mara, Markus, and Flori) invite Claudia to go?
2. Does Claudia go along? Why or why not?
3. What does Flori suggest?
4. What are some things the friends do at Claudia's house?
5. Is the weather good enough for an outing in the park? What about tomorrow's weather?
6. At the end of the story, there is still a problem. What is it?

1. in den Englischen Garten        4. clean her room, sort garbage for recycling, vacuum
2. No, she has chores at home.      5. Yes, but it might rain tomorrow.
3. that they all help her           6. They have to search for Claudia's cat.

## 2 Genauer lesen

Reread the conversations. Which words or phrases do the characters use to

1. invite someone
   **Komm doch mit!**
2. express obligation
   **wir müssen, ich muß**
3. name chores
   **zu Hause helfen:
   das Zimmer aufräumen,
   den Müll sortieren, die
   Klamotten aufräumen, Staub saugen.**
4. describe the weather
   **Die Sonne scheint.
   Es bleibt schön.
   Morgen regnet es.**

## 3 Was ist richtig?

Choose the best answer to complete each of the following statements.

1. Claudia muß ═══. b
   **a.** in den Englischen Garten gehen      **b.** zu Hause helfen      **c.** radeln

2. Claudias Freunde wollen helfen. Das findet Claudia ═══. c
   **a.** furchtbar      **b.** nicht schlecht      **c.** lieb

3. Mara will ═══. c
   **a.** die Katze füttern      **b.** den Müll sortieren      **c.** Claudias Klamotten nicht aufräumen

4. Die Katze ist ═══. b
   **a.** schon im Haus      **b.** nicht zu Hause      **c.** im Englischen Garten

## 4 Was paßt zusammen?

Match each statement or question on the left with an appropriate response on the right.

1. Wohin geht's? c
2. Komm doch mit! a
3. Was mußt du tun? d
4. Du kannst den Müll sortieren. b
5. Was sagt der Wetterbericht? f
6. Ist die Katze wieder weg? e

**a.** Das geht nicht.
**b.** Gut! Mach' ich!
**c.** In den Englischen Garten.
**d.** Ich muß zu Hause helfen.
**e.** Ja. Wir müssen sie suchen.
**f.** Morgen regnet es.

## 5 Nacherzählen

Put the sentences in a logical order to make a brief summary of the **Foto-Roman**.

1. Mara, Markus und Flori wollen in den Englischen Garten gehen.

Dann wollen sie gehen, aber Micky ist weg.
5

Sie müssen zuerst die Katze suchen.
6

Sie müssen den Müll sortieren, das Zimmer aufräumen, Staub saugen und die Katze füttern.
4

Aber Claudia kommt nicht mit, denn sie muß zu Hause helfen.
2

Claudias Freunde wollen helfen.
3

*Extending and responding to an invitation; expressing
obligations*

## WORTSCHATZ

**Was mußt du zu Hause tun? — Ich muß ...**

mein Zimmer
aufräumen

das Bett machen

meine Klamotten
aufräumen

die Katze füttern

den Tisch decken

den Tisch abräumen

das Geschirr spülen

die Blumen gießen

den Müll sortieren

den Rasen mähen

Staub saugen

die Fenster putzen

## 6  Was muß Claudia tun?

Claudia needs to make a list of all the things she has to
do around the house. Help her out by completing each
of the items on the left with the appropriate verb from
the box.

1. das Zimmer
2. das Bett
3. den Rasen
4. die Katze
5. den Tisch
6. das Geschirr
7. den Müll
8. die Blumen

1. aufräumen
2. machen
3. mähen
4. füttern
5. decken
6. spülen
7. sortieren
8. gießen

spülen    aufräumen
füttern
machen    mähen
gießen
decken    sortieren

# 7 Hör gut zu!

Jürgen has a few chores to do before he and Peter can go to the movies. Listen to their conversation and put the illustrations below in the correct order.   b e a c d

a.          b.          c.          d.          e.

## SO SAGT MAN DAS!

### Extending and responding to an invitation

In **Kapitel 6** you learned to make plans. How would you invite someone to come along with you?

You might ask:

**Willst du in den Englischen Garten?** *or*

**Wir wollen in den Englischen Garten. Komm doch mit!** *or*

**Möchtest du mitkommen?**

Your friend might accept:

**Ja, gern!** *or*

**Toll! Ich komme gern mit.**

Or decline:

**Das geht nicht.** *or*

**Ich kann leider nicht.**

# 8 Hör gut zu!

1. **ein Eis essen** - accepts  2. **ins Kino** - accepts  3. **ins Einkaufszentrum** - declines
4. **Tennis spielen** - declines  5. **ins Café** - accepts

Listen to the conversations and decide if the person being invited is accepting or declining the invitation. What is each person being invited to do?

## SO SAGT MAN DAS!

### Expressing obligations

If you decline an invitation, you might want to explain your prior obligations.

You might say:

**Ich habe keine Zeit. Ich muß zu Hause helfen.**

Your friend might ask:

**Was mußt du denn tun?**

You might respond:

**Ich muß den Rasen mähen.**

What do you think the phrase **keine Zeit** means?[1]

1. *no time*

## 9 Kommst du mit?

Think of several places you would like to go and invite a classmate to come along. He or she will accept or decline and give a reason. Here are some suggestions to help you.

> ins Kino gehen    in ein Konzert gehen
> Tennis spielen    ein Eis essen
> in die Disko gehen    schwimmen gehen

## 10 Was ist los?

What would you tell this little boy to do instead of what he is doing? (Use **Du mußt ...** )

Answers may vary.
Examples: **Du mußt**

a. **die Blumen gießen!**    b. **die Katze füttern!**    c. **den Rasen mähen!**    d. **den Tisch decken!**    e. **das Bett machen!**

## 11 Ich muß zu Hause ...

Make a list in German of the things you do around the house, then take turns asking your classmates what they do and telling them what chores you do.

> *Grammatik*  The verb **müssen**
>
> The verb **müssen** expresses obligation and means that you *have to* or *must* do something. Here are the forms of **müssen**:
>
> Ich **muß** zu Hause helfen.        Wir **müssen** das Bett machen.
> Du **mußt** das Geschirr spülen.     Ihr **müßt** den Tisch decken.
> Er/Sie **muß** den Rasen mähen.   Sie(pl)/ Sie **müssen** auch helfen.
>
> **Müssen** is usually used with a second verb (an infinitive), although the second verb can be omitted if the meaning is obvious.

## 12 Was müssen alle tun?

Thomas has his friends over to help with spring-cleaning. Complete his sentences as he explains what everyone must do.

  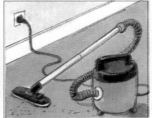 

1. Zuerst muß ich ...
**mein Zimmer/meine Klamotten aufräumen.**

2. Mara und ich, wir ...
**müssen den Müll sortieren.**

3. Du ...
**mußt Staub saugen.**

4. Und die Nikki ...
**muß die Fenster putzen.**

## 13 Was mußt du machen?

Using the list you made in Activity 11, you and your partner will take turns asking each other which chores you do around the house. As you talk, make a list of what your partner does. Compare lists to make sure you both understood everything correctly.

## 14 Und meine Familie

What are some of the things that your other family members have to do around the house? Share the information with your classmates.

## 15 Ich lade dich ein

**a.** First make a list of things you would like to do this afternoon and when you plan to do them.

**b.** Then invite your partner to do some of the activities on your list. Your partner will accept or decline and give a reason. Switch roles and let your partner invite you. Make a list of the things you agreed to do together and share your plans with the class.

a. 1. Roland
   2. ins Konzert

## 16 Ein Brief

**a.** Read Markus' letter to his friend Roland and answer the questions that follow.

  1. Wer kommt am Wochenende nach München?
  2. Was wollen Markus und Flori am Freitag machen?
  3. Was muß Markus am Samstag machen?
  4. Gefällt es Markus, daß er zu Hause helfen muß? Woher weißt du das?

**b.** If Markus were coming to visit you this weekend, what would the two of you do? Write him a letter inviting him to do whatever you have planned. Be sure to tell him any chores you have to do this weekend that might get in the way of your plans.

3. zu Hause helfen: den Rasen mähen, sein Zimmer aufräumen, die Blumen gießen, Staub saugen

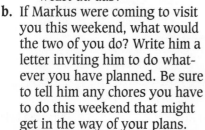

4. März 1994

Lieber Roland!

Mensch, das freut mich, daß Du am Wochenende hier in München bist!

Flori und ich wollen am Freitag ins Konzert. Die „Jungen Katzen" spielen! Toll, nicht! Willst Du auch mitkommen?

Am Samstag muß ich wie immer zu Hause helfen. Wie blöd! Ich muß den Rasen mähen, mein Zimmer aufräumen, die Blumen gießen und auch Staub saugen. Ach, das ist zu viel, nicht? Mußt Du auch zu Hause so viel tun?

Na ja, macht nichts. Am Sonntag hab' ich frei. Du, Flori und ich machen alles, was wir wollen.

Bis dann!
Dein Markus

4. Nein, er sagt, „Das ist zu viel."

# Was tust du für die Umwelt?

In both the old and new states, Germans today are very aware of the need to protect the environment. Young people all over Germany are involved in projects that range from recycling to cleaning up rivers and forests. We asked several students what they do for the environment, and here is what they told us.

LANDESKUNDE

**Marga,** *Bietigheim*
„Also bei uns zu Hause wird jeder Müll sortiert, eben in Plastik, Aluminium, Papier und so weiter. Das halten wir also ziemlich streng ein. Ja, und wenn schönes Wetter ist und es sich vermeiden läßt, mit dem Auto zu fahren, nehme ich lieber das Fahrrad."

**Fabian,** *Hamburg*
„Wir tun für die Umwelt, daß wir einmal Müll vermeiden, daß wir unser Altpapier wegbringen, Glas sammeln und möglichst auch Glas, was wiederverwertet werden kann, kaufen, also sprich Mehrwegflaschen, und daß wir halt möglichst wenig Putzmittel oder so sparsam brauchen."

**Elke,** *Berlin*
„Ich habe mit meinen Eltern angefangen, Flaschen zu sortieren und regelmäßig zum Container zu bringen. Der Müll wird meistens auch separat sortiert und dann, ja, einzeln weggebracht. Jetzt zähl' ich dazu, daß man mit dem Bus zur Schule fährt und nicht mit dem Auto."

A. 1. Write the names of the students interviewed, and beside each name, write what that student does for the environment. What things do they have in common?
2. Think about what you have learned about Germany. Do you think the environmental concerns of the Germans are the same as those of Americans? Why or why not?
3. Compare what you and your friends do for the environment with what these German students do. Is there anything you do that was not mentioned in these interviews?

B. a. Discuss with your classmates what you think the biggest environmental concerns in Germany and in the United States are.
b. Write in German your answer to the question **Was tust du für die Umwelt?**

*Talking about how often you have to do things; asking for and offering help and telling someone what to do*

## SO SAGT MAN DAS!

### Talking about how often you have to do things

You might want to ask a friend how often he or she has to do certain things, such as chores.

| You might ask: | Your friend might respond: |
|---|---|
| **Wie oft mußt du Staub saugen?** | **Einmal in der Woche.** |
| **Und wie oft mußt du den Tisch decken?** | **Jeden Tag.** |
| **Und wie oft mußt du den Rasen mähen?** | **Ungefähr zweimal im Monat.** |

Look at the words **einmal** and **zweimal**. What words do you recognize within each of these words?[1] What do you think the phrases **einmal in der Woche** and **zweimal im Monat** mean?[2] How would you say "three times a week"?[3] "Four times a month"?[4] What does the expression **jeden Tag** mean?[5] (*Hint: Look at the chore the speaker above does jeden Tag. How often would you do that task?*)

### WORTSCHATZ

**Wie oft ... ?**
einmal, zweimal, dreimal
... in der Woche
... im Monat
immer *always*
oft *often*
manchmal *sometimes*
nie *never*

## 17 Sätze bauen

Wie viele Sätze kannst du bauen? Wann und wie oft machst du das alles?

Example: **Im Herbst spiele ich einmal in der Woche Fußball.**

| | | | |
|---|---|---|---|
| Im Herbst | | | Karten |
| Im Frühling | | | Gitarre |
| Im Winter | | | Klavier |
| Im Sommer | spiele | | Geschirr |
| Am Montag | spüle | (ein)mal in der Woche | die Fenster |
| Am Wochen- | putze | (zwei)mal im Monat | ins Konzert |
| ende | gehe | ich nie | den Tisch |
| Nach der | decke | oft | Fußball |
| Schule | räume ... auf | manchmal | Basketball |
| Am Nachmittag | | immer | in eine Disko |
| Am Abend | | | mein Zimmer |

1. **ein(s)**, **zwei**  2. *once a week, twice a month*  3. **dreimal in der Woche**  4. **viermal im Monat**  5. *every day*

## 18 Hör gut zu!

Listen as Markus describes when and how often he does things. First make a calendar page for one week and then fill in a possible schedule for his activities.

**SO SAGT MAN DAS!**

### Asking for and offering help and telling someone what to do

If your friend has a lot to do, you might offer to help. Then he or she could explain what to do.

You might ask:
> **Was kann ich für dich tun?** *or*
> **Kann ich etwas für dich tun?**

Your friend might answer:
> **Ja, du kannst den Müll sortieren.** *or*
> **Willst du für mich Staub saugen?**

You agree:
> **Gut! Mach' ich!**

What are the English equivalents of the phrases **für dich** and **für mich**?[1]

Often, other elements besides the subject are placed at the beginning of a sentence to give them special emphasis. For example, if someone asks you: **Kannst du heute Volleyball spielen?**, you might respond: **Nein, heute muß ich zu Hause helfen, aber morgen kann ich sicher spielen.** The time expressions are placed first, because time is the most important issue in this conversation. By putting something other than the subject in first position, you not only add variety to your conversations but express yourself more exactly.

## 19 Du kannst für mich ...

Several people are offering to help their friends around the house. Create exchanges for the pictures below.

**BEISPIEL**

Können wir etwas für dich tun? Ja, ihr könnt den Rasen mähen. Danke!

### Ein wenig *G*rammatik

The words **kann** and **kannst** are forms of the verb **können**, a modal auxiliary verb. **Kann** is a cognate. What does it mean?[2] Here are the forms of **können**:

| | | | |
|---|---|---|---|
| ich | **kann** | wir | **können** |
| du | **kannst** | ihr | **könnt** |
| er/sie | **kann** | sie (pl)<br>Sie | **können** |

Kann ich etwas für dich tun? Ja, du kannst den Tisch abräumen.
Können wir etwas für dich tun? Ja, ihr könnt die Blumen gießen.
Können wir etwas für dich tun? Ja, ihr könnt den Müll sortieren.

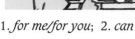

1. *for me/for you*; 2. *can*

## 20 Peter macht ein Geschäft

Katrin and her brother, Peter, are at home trying to get their chores done for the weekend. Read the conversation and answer the questions below.

KATRIN   Ach, ich hab' heute viel zu tun. He, du Peter! Kannst du etwas für mich tun?
PETER    Vielleicht.
KATRIN   Kannst du die Blumen gießen?
PETER    Ja, gern. Was kann ich noch für dich tun?
KATRIN   Müll sortieren?
PETER    Okay, aber das kostet fünf Mark. Danke!

*Ayla und Mario kommen vorbei.*

MARIO    Na, Katrin und Peter, was macht ihr? Können wir etwas für euch tun?
PETER    Sicher! Ihr könnt für uns die Blumen gießen und dann den Müll sortieren. Geht das?
MARIO    Klar. Wir helfen gern!

1. What does Katrin ask her brother Peter to do?
2. What kind of a deal does Peter make with Katrin?
3. How does Peter manage to get out of his end of the bargain?
4. Compare the following sentences from the conversations above: **Was kann ich noch für dich tun?** and **Können wir etwas für euch tun?** To whom do the pronouns **dich** and **euch** refer in the conversations?
5. Now compare these sentences: **Kannst du etwas für mich tun?** and **Du kannst für uns die Blumen gießen.** To whom do the pronouns **mich** and **uns** refer?
6. Which of these pronouns are used for talking to others? Which ones are used to talk about yourself?
7. What is the English equivalent for each of these pronouns?

1. water the flowers, sort the garbage
2. He asks for five marks.
3. He gets Ayla and Mario to do his work for him
4. Katrin; Katrin and Peter
5. Katrin; Katrin and Peter
6. **dich, euch; mich, uns**
7. you, you, me, us

---

## Grammatik   The accusative pronouns

In **Kapitel 5** you learned the accusative forms of the third person pronouns **er, sie, es,** and **sie** (pl). They are **ihn, sie, es,** and **sie**. The first and second person pronouns have these forms:

|  | *nominative* | *accusative* |  | *nominative* | *accusative* |
|---|---|---|---|---|---|
| *first* | ich | mich | *second* | du | dich |
| *person* | wir | uns | *person* | ihr | euch |

The accusative forms are used as direct objects, as in **Ich besuche dich morgen,** or as objects of prepositions, such as **für,** as in **Du kannst für mich den Müll sortieren.** To ask for whom someone is doing something, use **für wen: Für wen machst du das?**

## 21  Was kann ich für dich kaufen?

Mara is going to the **Schreibwarenladen** to buy a few things for herself. Before she leaves she asks some friends if she can buy anything for them. Create an exchange for each picture, telling what Mara would ask, and how the person or people pictured would respond.

BEISPIEL    MARA    **Kann ich etwas für dich kaufen?**

MARKUS    **Ja, bitte. Du kannst für mich einen Bleistift kaufen.**

1. für euch/für uns ein Heft kaufen
2. für dich/für mich einen Kuli kaufen
3. für euch/für uns ein Wörterbuch kaufen
4. für dich/für mich eine Kassette kaufen

## 22  Zu Hause helfen

Two of your friends are coming over to help you with your chores so that you can go swimming together. Before they arrive, make a list of six chores you have to do today. Then, with your partners, develop a conversation in which your friends offer to help and you discuss together who will do each of the chores. Be creative!

## 23  Arbeit suchen

You want to earn extra money doing odd jobs, so you need to place an ad in several public places. Include in your ad the following information: which chores you do, how often you can work, how much you charge, on which days of the week you are available, and how you can be reached.

**Und dann noch . . .**

der Vogel

die Maus

das Meer-
schweinchen

der Fisch

das Kaninchen

der Hamster

## 24  Für mein Notizbuch

Schreib, was du zu Hause alles machen mußt! Wann und wie oft machst du das? Was machst du gern? Was machst du nicht gern? Hast du ein Haustier? Wie heißt es? Wer füttert das Tier?

## Talking about the weather

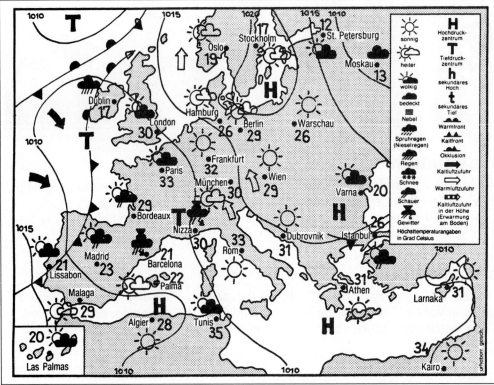

**Deutscher Wetterdienst Vorhersagekarte für 9. Juni 1993 12 Uhr (UTC)**

**Lage:** Am Rande einer Hochdruckzone über Osteuropa gelangt auch weiterhin Warmluft nach Deutschland.

**Vorhersage:** Am Mittwoch sonnig und trocken, dabei Temperaturanstieg auf 28 bis 32, im Nordosten auf Werte um 26 Grad. Nachts vielfach klar, Tiefstwerte um 16 Grad. Schwacher, tagsüber auflebender Wind aus unterschiedlichen Richtungen.

**Aussichten:** Am Donnerstag sonnig, im Tagesverlauf im Süden und Westen einzelne Gewitter, sehr warm. Am Freitag von Westen her aufkommende Bewölkung und nachfolgend Schauer und Gewitter, etwas kühler:

1. Europe
2. Temperatures, air pressure, wind, cloudiness, rain
4. St. Petersburg and Moscow; farther north
5. Barcelona, Nizza, Dublin
6. Frankfurt, Dubrovnik, Kairo
7. Thursday: **sonnig, sehr warm, einzelne Gewitter**
Friday: **aufkommende Bewölkung; Schaue Gewitter, etwas kühler**

## 25 Was sagt der Wetterbericht?

Answer the following questions about the weather map shown above.

1. What area of the world is this weather map for?
2. What kinds of information can you get from the map?
3. Look at the table of symbols and the words that go with them. Can you figure out what each word means?
4. Which cities are the coldest? What do you think the reason for this is?
5. Name three cities where you might need an umbrella.
6. Name three cities where you might do outdoor activities.
7. List the words in the weather forecast that describe the weather for Thursday and Friday.

**WORTSCHATZ**

### Das Wetter

3. **sonnig**=sunny; **heiter**=clear; **wolkig**=cloudy; **bedeckt**=overcast; **Nebel**=fog; **Sprühregen**=drizzle; **Regen**=rain; **Schnee**=snow; **Schauer**=shower; **Gewitter**=thunderstorm

# SO SAGT MAN DAS!

## Talking about the weather

For some plans you make with your friends, you might first need to know about the weather.

You could ask:

**Wie ist das Wetter heute?**

Or you might want to ask about tomorrow:

**Wie ist das Wetter morgen?**

Or you might want to ask for specific information:

**Regnet es heute?**
**Schneit es heute abend?**
**Wieviel Grad haben wir heute?**

What do you think the word **Grad** means?[1] Look at the response for a clue. When you tell someone the temperature, you might not know exactly what it is, so you say **ungefähr** ... What do you think **ungefähr** means?[2]

Some possible responses are:

**Heute regnet es.**
**Wolkig und kühl.**

**Sonnig, aber kalt.**

**Ich glaube schon.**
**Nein, es schneit nicht.**
**Ungefähr 10 Grad.**

### Ein wenig Grammatik

What do you notice about the verb that is used to ask and tell about the weather for tomorrow? The present tense is often used when referring to the near future. The meaning is made clear with words such as **morgen**. How would you invite a German friend to go to the movies tomorrow?[3]

## 26 Hör gut zu!

Listen to the weather reports from German radio. For each report determine which activity fits best with the weather described.

a.

b.

c.

d.

1. d      3. c
2. a      4. b

## 27 Wie ist das Wetter bei euch?

With your partner, discuss the weather where you live. Include the following topics in your discussion. For additional words, see page 323.

1. Wie ist das Wetter heute?
2. Wieviel Grad haben wir heute?
3. Und was sagt der Wetterbericht für morgen?
4. Wie ist das Wetter im Januar? Und im Juli?
5. Und im April? Und im Oktober?

1. *degree*  2. *approximately*  3. Ich gehe morgen ins Kino. Kommst du mit?

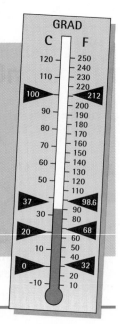

## EIN WENIG LANDESKUNDE

Weather in the German-speaking countries is extremely variable, depending on the latitude and seasons. These countries usually get a lot of rainfall. Summers are often rainy, and winters can be cold, especially in the Alps. As in other European countries, German-speaking countries use the Celsius system of measuring temperature, rather than the Fahrenheit system. Look at the thermometer. If it were 35°C would you need a jacket? If the temperature fell below 0°C would you expect rain or snow? What is a comfortable room temperature in Celsius? Look at the weather map on p. 182. If you were in Moscow, what kinds of clothes would you be wearing? In Athens?

## WORTSCHATZ

### Wie ist das Wetter im ...?

| | | | | | |
|---|---|---|---|---|---|
| Januar | März | Mai | Juli | September | November |
| Februar | April | Juni | August | Oktober | Dezember |

## 28 Gespräche

Put the following sentences in the correct order to form conversations based on the pictures below.

1. BRITTE    Hallo, Gupse! Gehen wir morgen schwimmen?

Toll! Also, bis morgen! ₅

Ja, klar. Aber was sagt der Wetterbericht? ₂

Gut! Dann gehen wir schwimmen. ₄

Morgen ist es sonnig und warm. ₃

1. HANNES    Tag, Jörg! Ich geh' ins Kino. Kommst du mit?

Gern! Du kannst für mich die Blumen gießen. ₄

Nein, ich kann nicht. Ich muß den Rasen mähen. ₂

Gut! Mach' ich! Aber schau mal, Hannes! Es regnet jetzt! ₅

Ach, dann gehen wir doch ins Kino! ₆

Brauchst du Hilfe, Jörg? ₃

## 29 Ein Wetterbericht für ...

Using the weather map on page 182, choose a city and write a weather report for that city. Describe what the weather is like there.

## 30 Pläne machen

With a partner, pretend that you are meeting tomorrow in the city that you chose for Activity 29. You would like to invite your friend to do something special that is appropriate for the expected weather. Create a conversation in which you invite your partner to do something. He or she will ask about the weather, and you say what you know about it. Your partner can either accept or decline the invitation. Then switch roles and create another conversation, using your partner's city.

## AUSSPRACHE

### Richtig aussprechen / Richtig lesen

A. To practice the following sounds, say the words and sentences below after your teacher or after the recording.

1. The letter **o:** In **Kapitel 3** you learned how to pronounce the letter **o** as a long vowel, as in **Oma.** However, when the letter **o** is followed by two or more consonants, it is pronounced as a short vowel, like the *o* in the English word *cot.*
   **wolkig, Sonne, Woche / Im Oktober ist es sonnig und trocken.**

2. The letter **u:** In **Kapitel 3** you learned how to pronounce the letter **u** as a long vowel, as in **super.** However, when the letter **u** is followed by two or more consonants, it is pronounced as a short vowel, like the *u* in the English word *put.*
   **uns, muß, putzen / Mutti, ich muß die Fenster putzen.**

3. The letter **l:** The letter **l** is pronounced like the *l* in the English word *million.* It is much more tense than the *l* sound in the English word *bill.*
   **Müll, kühl, April / Der Lehrer kann im Juli mit dem Müll helfen.**

4. The consonant combination **th:** The combination **th** within the same syllable is pronounced the same as the letter **t** in German.
   **Theater, Mathe, Theatinerkirche / Wie komme ich zur Theatinerkirche und zum Theater?**

5. The letter combination **pf:** The consonant combination **pf** sounds similiar to the *pf* combination in English, as in the word *cupful.* However, in German this letter combination often occurs at the beginning of a word and is pronounced as one sound.
   **Pfennig, Pfund, Kopfsalat / Zwei Pfund Pflaumen kosten neunundneunzig Pfennig.**

### Richtig schreiben/Diktat

B. Write down the words and sentences that you hear.

*Wem hilfst du?*

**Weißt du noch?** Using visual clues, such as illustrations or photos, will give you advance information about a text before you try to read it.

1. Before you try to read these three interviews, look at the title and at the photos. What do you expect the articles to be about? Answers will vary.
2. What do these three texts have in common? What kind of texts do you think they are? Teenagers helping people. interviews
3. You probably figured out that these articles have to do with young people helping others. Working in groups of three or four students, write as many German phrases as you can that have to do with offering to help people.
4. Read the interview questions. Even though you may not know all the words in each question, you can probably figure out what is being asked. With a partner, write what you think is being asked in each question. Whom do you help? And how do you help? Do you receive anything for your help? Are there people or special organizations that you would like to help? Why do you help other people?

# WEM

**Helfen Jugendliche ihren Eltern und Freunden? Verdienen sie dabei Taschengeld?**

# HILFST

**Oder bieten sie Hilfe freiwillig an? JUMA - Reporter Bernd hat sich umgehört.**

# DU?

*Hallo Heiko!*

**Wem hilfst du?** Ich helfe meiner Mutter.
**Und wobei hilfst du?** Ab und zu bei der Hausarbeit. Zum Beispiel helfe ich meiner Mutter beim Staubsaugen oder beim Wäscheaufhängen. Mein Zimmer räume ich allerdings seltener auf. Dazu habe ich meistens keine Lust. Und das Auto wäscht mein Vater lieber selbst. Dann wird es sauberer als bei mir.
**Bekommst du etwas für deine Hilfe?** Nein. Aber <u>wenn</u> ich längere Zeit nichts mache, schimpfen meine Eltern. Natürlich haben sie damit recht, <u>wenn</u> ich faul bin.
**Gibt es Menschen oder besondere Organisationen, denen du gerne helfen würdest?** Ich weiß jetzt nichts Spezielles. Aber ich weiß, wem ich nicht gerne helfen würde: aufdringlichen Freunden.
**Warum hilfst du anderen Menschen?** Ich finde wichtig, <u>daß</u> man anderen eine Last abnimmt. Außerdem ist Mithilfe eine nette Geste, über die sich wahrscheinlich jeder freut.

## Hallo Tina!

**Wem hilfst Du?** Meiner Familie, meinen Freunden und meinen Bekannten.

**Und wobei hilfst Du?** Ich passe auf Kinder auf oder helfe meiner Schwester bei den Hausaufgaben. Im Haushalt mache ich eigentlich alles: Spülen, Bügeln oder Putzen.

**Bekommst Du etwas für Deine Hilfe?** Ich helfe freiwillig, <u>obwohl</u> ich meiner Schwester die Hausaufgaben nicht so gerne erkläre. Meinen Eltern und Bekannten biete ich auch schon mal Hilfe an.

**Gibt es Menschen oder besondere Organisationen, denen Du gerne helfen würdest?** Ja. Ich möchte gerne einmal in einem Kinderhort mitarbeiten. Das ist bestimmt anstrengend, aber interessant.

**Warum hilfst du anderen Menschen?** Wichtig für mich ist es, Pflichten zu erfüllen. Anderen zu helfen, ist eine Pflicht.

## Hallo Sven

**Wem hilfst du?** Ich helfe meistens meinen Freunden.

**Und wobei hilfst du?** Eigentlich bei allem, was mit Schule zu tun hat. Meistens aber bei Hausaufgaben und Prüfungsvorbereitungen. Nachhilfestunden in Biologie oder Chemie gebe ich ziemlich regelmäßig, <u>weil</u> ich in diesen Fächern ganz gut bin.

**Bekommst du etwas für Deine Hilfe?** Ja, manchmal. Ich bessere mein Taschengeld mit Nachhilfe auf.

**Gibt es Menschen oder besondere Organisationen, denen du gerne helfen würdest?** Allen netten Leuten helfe ich gerne.

**Warum hilfst du anderen Menschen?** Es ist schön, <u>wenn</u> sie sich über Mithilfe freuen.

5. Scan the articles and list any subordinating conjunctions that you find. Using the information in the **Lesetrick,** determine what you expect each of the clauses introduced by these conjunctions to contain: a condition, a reason, a concession, an opinion, or a statement of fact. Write your guess beside the corresponding conjunction.

6. Read each clause that begins with a subordinating conjunction. Can you determine what the clause means? Now read the entire sentence. What does each sentence mean?

7. Now read the articles for the following information:
   a. Whom do these young people help? What are some of the things they do to help?
   b. When do Heiko's parents complain? Does Heiko think they have a right to complain? How do you know? What does Heiko say about "taking a burden from others"?
   c. What does Tina not like to do? Where does she want to work someday? What does she say is a "duty"?
   d. Why does Sven tutor other students in biology and chemistry? Whom does he like to help?

8. If you had been asked these questions by *Juma*, how would you have answered them?

9. Imagine that you will spend the next year as an exchange student with a German family. Write a letter to your host family and include an explanation of some of the chores you regularly do at home. Offer to do them for your German family while you are there.

5. **wenn** (condition)
   **daß** (statement of opinion)
   **weil** (reason)
   **obwohl** (concession)

7. Annos for rest of **Zum Lesen** in TE Interleaf pp. 167Q

**1** You will hear five students invite their friends to do something. Sometimes their friends accept, and sometimes they decline and give a reason. Listen to the exchanges and write the information you hear. Compare your notes with those of a classmate. The chart to the right will help you organize your information.

| invitation | accept/decline | reason |
|---|---|---|
| BEISPIEL schwimmen gehen | kommt nicht | muß Zimmer aufräumen |

1. Ins Kino gehen / kommt
2. Ins Café gehen / kommt nicht / muß Hausaufgaben machen
3. **Tennis spielen / kommt nicht / muß Rasen mähen**   4. **Fete bei Markus / kommt**   5. **ins Einkaufszentrum gehen / kommt nicht / geht schwimmen**

**2** Below is a page from Flori's calendar for the month of **März**. Take turns asking and telling your partner when and how often Flori does the activities. Now make your own calendar page. Fill in all the activities you do in a typical month. Describe to your partner the things you wrote on your calendar, and he or she will try to find out when and how often you do them. Then switch roles.

## März

| Mo | Di | Mi | Do | Fr | Sa | So |
|---|---|---|---|---|---|---|
|  | 1 Staub saugen | 2 | 3 | 4 Müll sortieren | 5 Fenster putzen 4:00 Fußball spielen | 6 |
| 7 9:30 mit Michael ins Konzert | 8 Staub saugen | 9 3:30 Klavier= unterricht 7:00 Volleyball | 10 | 11 9:00 Disko | 12 Rasen mähen 4:00 Fußball spielen | 13 |
| 14 8:30 Kino mit Sabine | 15 Staub saugen | 16 3:30 Klavier= unterricht | 17 | 18 Müll sortieren | 19 Fenster putzen 4:00 Fußball spielen | 20 |
| 21 4:00 Schwimmen | 22 Staub saugen | 23 3:30 Klavier= unterricht | 24 | 25 9:00 Disko | 26 Rasen mähen 4:00 Fußball spielen | 27 |
| 28 | 29 Staub saugen | 30 3:30 Klavier= unterricht | 31 |  |  |  |

**3** Ask your partner when and how often he or she does the activities shown in the photos below. Does he or she enjoy each activity? Then your partner will ask you the same questions.

a.

b.

c.

d.

f.

**4** Look at the weather map for Western Europe and answer the following questions in German.

1. Which cities are expecting rain?
2. In which cities could you probably go swimming?
3. Which city is expected to have the lowest temperature?
4. Which city will be the warmest?
5. What kinds of activities might you plan in **Berlin** for Monday, April 7?
6. Where might you go skiing?
7. Claudia is planning to drive to the **Zugspitze,** and then to have a picnic in the **Englischer Garten.** What would she say if she wanted to invite you? Would you accept or decline the invitation?

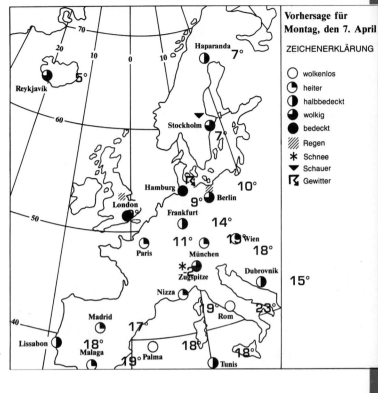

Vorhersage für Montag, den 7. April

ZEICHENERKLÄRUNG

○ wolkenlos
◖ heiter
◑ halbbedeckt
◕ wolkig
● bedeckt
▨ Regen
✳ Schnee
▼ Schauer
↯ Gewitter

**5** You and your friends are weather forecasters for the local TV station. Working in small groups, take turns reporting the local weather to your class every day for a week. Your report should include the forecast for the following day. Create a weather chart to use with your reports. On Friday, of course, you will want to sum up the week's weather. Always begin your **Wetterbericht** with: **Guten Tag, liebe Zuschauer!**

**6**

## R O L L E N S P I E L

It's raining today, so you are at home doing your chores. Your friends show up and offer to help. As you and your friends work around the house, you decide to invite your friends to go somewhere tomorrow. Great crashes of thunder turn your conversation to the weather for tomorrow. What will you do? Create a conversation with two other classmates. Be prepared to act it out in front of the class with props that will convey the idea of doing chores around the house.

1. **London und Berlin**
2. Answers may vary: **Rom, Malaga und Nizza.**
3. **Reykjavik (5 Grad)**
4. **Rom (23 Grad)**
5. Answers may vary: indoor activities
6. **(Auf der) Zugspitze**
7. Answers may vary. Example: **Nein, es ist zu kalt.**

**Can you extend and respond to an invitation? (p. 174)**

**1** How would you invite a friend to go    Willst du … / möchtest du …

  **a.** to a movie      **b.** to a café      **c.** shopping      **d.** swimming
  ins Kino gehen?        ins Café gehen?       einkaufen gehen?    schwimmen gehen?

**2** Accept or decline the following invitations. If you decline, give a reason why you can't go.    Answers may vary. Some possible answers:

  **a.** Wir gehen jetzt in eine Disko. Komm doch mit!
  **b.** Ich muß in die Stadt gehen. Möchtest du mitkommen?
  **c.** Wir spielen jetzt Tennis. Kannst du mitkommen?
  a. Das geht nicht. Ich muß zu Hause helfen.      b. Ja, gern!      c. Ich kann leider nicht. Ich muß

**Can you express obligation using müssen? (p. 174)**

**3** Say that the people below have to do the things indicated. Hausaufgaben machen.

  Bernd          Leyla          Pedro und Felipe          Karin

Bernd muß d
Rasen mähe
Leyla muß d
Blumen gieß
Pedro und Fe
müssen den
Tisch decke
Karin muß iℓ
Zimmer aufr
men.

**Can you talk about how often you have to do things? (p. 178)**

**4** How would you ask a classmate how often he or she has to

  **a.** wash the windows      **c.** clear the table      Wie oft mußt du …
  **b.** vacuum                **d.** do the dishes         a. die Fenster putzen? c. den Tisch abräi
                                                           b.Staub saugen?        d. das Geschirr s

**5** How would you tell a classmate how often you have to do each of the things above?    Answers may vary: zweimal in der Woche, dreimal in der Woche, jeden Tag

**Can you offer help and tell someone what to do using expressions with für? (p. 179)**

**6** How would you ask a classmate if you could help him or her? How would you ask two classmates?    Kann ich etwas für dich/für euch tun?

**7** Using **können**, explain to each of these people what they can do to help you:

  **a.** Sara: das Geschirr spülen
  **b.** Silke und Peter: das Zimmer aufräumen
  **c.** Markus: das Bett machen
  **d.** Claudia und Daniel: den Tisch decken

  a. Sara, du kannst das Geschirr spülen.
  b. Silke und Peter, ihr könnt das Zimmer aufräumen.
  c. Markus, du kannst das Bett machen.
  d. Claudia und Daniel, ihr könnt den Tisch decken.

**8** How might a friend respond if he or she agreed to do some chores for you?    Answers will vary: Ja, gern! or Gut, mach' ich!

**Can you talk about the weather? (p. 183)**

**9** How would you tell a classmate what the weather is like today? How would you tell him or her the weather forecast for tomorrow?
  Answers will vary: Heute ist es schön. Morgen regnet es/schneit es/wird es kühl.

**10** How would you tell someone new to your area what the weather is like in

  **a.** January      **c.** June      **e.** December
  **b.** March        **d.** October

  Answers will vary. Possible answers: Im Januar ist es kalt. Im März ist es kühl und windig.

## ERSTE STUFE

### EXTENDING AND RESPONDING TO INVITATIONS

**mitkommen** (sep)   *to come along*
**Komm doch mit!**   *Why don't you come along!*
**Ich kann leider nicht.**   *Sorry, I can't.*
**Das geht nicht.**   *That won't work.*

### EXPRESSING OBLIGATION

**tun**   *to do*
**helfen**   *to help*

**zu Hause helfen**   *to help at home*
**müssen**   *to have to*
**ich muß ...**   *I have to...*
   **mein Zimmer aufräumen**
   (sep)   *clean up my room*
   **Staub saugen**   *vacuum*
   **den Müll sortieren**   *sort the trash*
   **den Rasen mähen**   *mow the lawn*
   **die Katze füttern**   *feed the cat*
   **den Tisch decken**   *set the table*
   **den Tisch abräumen** (sep)   *clear the table*

**das Geschirr spülen**   *wash the dishes*
**die Blumen gießen**   *water the flowers*
**das Bett machen**   *make the bed*
**meine Klamotten aufräumen**   *pick up my clothes*
**die Fenster putzen**   *clean the windows*
**Ich habe keine Zeit.**   *I don't have time.*

---

## ZWEITE STUFE

### SAYING HOW OFTEN YOU HAVE TO DO THINGS

**Wie oft?**   *How often?*
**nie**   *never*
**manchmal**   *sometimes*
**oft**   *often*
**immer**   *always*
**einmal, zweimal, dreimal ...**   *once, twice, three times...*
  **in der Woche**   *a week*
  **im Monat**   *a month*

**jeden Tag**   *every day*

### ASKING FOR AND OFFERING HELP AND TELLING SOMEONE WHAT TO DO

**können**   *can, to be able to*
**Was kann ich für dich tun?**   *What can I do for you?*
**Kann ich etwas für dich tun?**   *Can I do something for you?*
**Du kannst ...**   *You can...*

**Gut! Mach' ich!**   *Okay! I'll do that!*
**für**   *for*
**Für wen?**   *For whom?*
**mich**   *me*
**dich**   *you*
**uns**   *us*
**euch**   *you* (pl)

### OTHER USEFUL WORDS AND EXPRESSIONS

**ungefähr**   *about, approximately*

---

## DRITTE STUFE

### TALKING ABOUT THE WEATHER

**Was sagt der Wetterbericht?**   *What does the weather report say?*
**Wie ist das Wetter?**   *How's the weather?*
**Es ist...**   *It is...*
  **heiß**   *hot*
  **warm**   *warm*
  **kühl**   *cool*
  **kalt**   *cold*
  **trocken**   *dry*
  **naß**   *wet*
  **sonnig**   *sunny*

**wolkig**   *cloudy*
**der Schnee**   *snow*
**Es schneit.**   *It's snowing.*
**der Regen**   *rain*
**Es regnet.**   *It's raining.*
**das Eis**   *ice*
**das Gewitter**   *thunder-storm*
**Die Sonne scheint.**   *The sun is shining.*
**heute**   *today*
**morgen**   *tomorrow*
**heute abend**   *this evening*
**Wieviel Grad haben wir?**   *What's the temperature?*
**der Grad**   *degree(s)*

**zwei Grad**   *two degrees*
**der Monat, -e**   *month*
**der Januar**   *January*
  **im Januar**   *in January*
  **Februar**   *February*
  **März**   *March*
  **April**   *April*
  **Mai**   *May*
  **Juni**   *June*
  **Juli**   *July*
  **August**   *August*
  **September**   *September*
  **Oktober**   *October*
  **November**   *November*
  **Dezember**   *December*

# Kapitel 8: Einkaufen gehen *Chapter Overview*

| **Los geht's!** pp. 194-196 | Alles für die Oma! p. 194 | | | *Video Guide* |
|---|---|---|---|---|
| | **FUNCTIONS** | **GRAMMAR** | **CULTURE** | **RE-ENTRY** |
| **Erste Stufe** pp. 197-201 | •Asking what you should do, p. 198 •Telling someone what to do, p. 199 | •The modal **sollen**, p. 199 •The **du**-commands, p. 200 | •**Ein wenig Landeskunde:** The German preference for small shops p. 198 •**Landeskunde: Was machst du für andere Leute?** p. 201 | •The **möchte**-forms, p. 198 (from **Kapitel 3**) •The modal **können**, p. 198 (from **Kapitel 7**) •Household chores vocabulary, p. 200 (from **Kapitel 7**) |
| **Zweite Stufe** pp. 202-204 | •Talking about quantities, p. 202 •Saying that you want something else, p. 203 | | **Ein wenig Landeskunde:** Weights and measures, p. 203 | •Numbers, p. 202 (from **Kapitel 3**) used in a new context, weights and measures •Expressing wishes when shopping, p. 203 (from **Kapitel 5**) |
| **Dritte Stufe** pp. 205-209 | •Giving reasons, p. 206 •Saying where you were and what you bought, p. 207 | •The conjunctions **weil** and **denn**, p. 206 •The past tense of **sein**, p. 207 | German advertisements, p. 205 | •Responding to invitations, p. 206 (from **Kapitel 7**) •Activity vocabulary, p. 206 (from **Kapitel 2**) •Household chores vocabulary, p. 208 (from **Kapitel 7**) •Sequencing words, p. 208 (from **Kapitel 4**) •Clothing vocabulary, p. 209 (from **Kapitel 5**) |
| **Aussprache** p. 209 | The short vowel **ü**, the short vowel **ö**, review diphthong **ei**, review vowel combination **ie**, review letter **z** | | | *Diktat:* *Textbook Audiocassette* 4 B |
| **Zum Lesen** pp. 210-211 | Richtig essen! Reading Strategy: Combining different strategies to guess the meaning of a text | | | |
| **Review** pp. 212-215 | •Anwendung, p. 212 •Kann ich's wirklich? p. 214 •Wortschatz, p. 215 | | | |

**Assessment Options**

**Stufe Quizzes**
•*Chapter Resources,* Book 3
  Erste Stufe, Quiz 8-1
  Zweite Stufe, Quiz 8-2
  Dritte Stufe, Quiz 8-3
•*Assessment Items, Audiocassette* 8 A

**Kapitel 8 Chapter Test**
•*Chapter Resources,* Book 3
•*Assessment Guide,* Speaking Test
•*Assessment Items, Audiocassette* 8 A

**Test Generator, Kapitel 8**

| | |
|---|---|
| *Video Program* **OR** *Expanded Video Program*, Videocassette 3 | Textbook Audiocassette 4 B |

| RESOURCES<br>Print | RESOURCES<br>AUDIOVISUAL |
|---|---|
| | *Textbook Audiocassette* 4 B |
| *Practice and Activity Book*<br>*Chapter Resources,* Book 3<br>•Communicative Activity 8-1<br>•Additional Listening Activities 8-1, 8-2 . . . . . . . . .<br>•Student Response Form<br>•Realia 8-1<br>•Situation Card 8-1<br>•Teaching Transparency Master 8-1 . . . . . . . . . . . . .<br>•Quiz 8-1 . . . . . . . . . . . . . . . . . . . . . . . . . . . . . . .<br>*Video Guide.* . . . . . . . . . . . . . . . . . . . . . . . . . . . . | <br><br><br>*Additional Listening Activities, Audiocassette* 8 A<br><br><br><br>*Teaching Transparency* 8-1<br>*Assessment Items, Audiocassette* 10 A<br>*Video Program/Expanded Video Program,* Videocassette 3 |
| | *Textbook Audiocassette* 4 B |
| *Practice and Activity Book*<br>*Chapter Resources,* Book 3<br>•Communicative Activity 8-2<br>•Additional Listening Activity 8-3 . . . . . . . . . . . . . .<br>•Additional Listening Activity 8-4 . . . . . . . . . . . . . .<br>•Student Response Form<br>•Realia 8-2<br>•Situation Card 8-2<br>•Quiz 8-2 . . . . . . . . . . . . . . . . . . . . . . . . . . . . . . . | <br><br><br>*Additional Listening Activities, Audiocassette* 8 A<br>*Additional Listening Activities, Audiocassette* 8 A<br><br><br><br>*Assessment Items, Audiocassette* 10 A |
| | *Textbook Audiocassette* 4 B |
| *Practice and Activity Book*<br>*Chapter Resources,* Book 3<br>•Additional Listening Activity 8-5 . . . . . . . . . . . . . .<br>•Additional Listening Activity 8-6 . . . . . . . . . . . . . .<br>•Student Response Form<br>•Realia 8-3<br>•Situation Card 8-3<br>•Teaching Transparency Master 8-2 . . . . . . . . . . . . .<br>•Quiz 8-3 . . . . . . . . . . . . . . . . . . . . . . . . . . . . . . . | <br><br>*Additional Listening Activities, Audiocassette* 8 A<br>*Additional Listening Activities, Audiocassette* 8 A<br><br><br><br>*Teaching Transparency* 8-2<br>*Assessment Items, Audiocassette* 10 A |

*Video Guide.* . . . . . . . . . . . . . . . . . . . . . . . . . . . . . . . . . . . . . *Video Program/Expanded Video Program,* Videocassette 3

**Alternative Assessment**

•Performance Assessment, *Teacher's Edition*
    **Erste Stufe,** p. 191K
    **Zweite Stufe,** p. 191M
    **Dritte Stufe,** p. 191P

•Portfolio Assessment
    Written: **Zum Lesen,** Activity 10, *Pupil's Edition,* p. 211, *Assessment Guide*
    Oral: **Anwendung,** Activity 3, *Pupil's Edition,* p. 212, *Assessment Guide*
•**Notizbuch,** *Pupil's Edition,* p. 204; *Practice* and *Activity Book,* p. 152

# Kapitel 8: Einkaufen gehen
# *Textbook Listening Activities Scripts*

## *Erste Stufe*
### Activity 6, *p. 198*

CLAUDIA  So Flori, was brauchen wir denn für heute abend? Wann kommen Sabine und Udo?

FLORI  Sie kommen gegen 6 Uhr. Erst essen wir zusammen Abendbrot, dann schauen wir uns die zwei Videos an. Wohin gehen wir zuerst?

CLAUDIA  Ja also, fangen wir doch beim Metzger an. Der ist gleich um die Ecke.

FLORI  Was brauchen wir denn da?

CLAUDIA  Hm, etwas Hackfleisch und auch Aufschnitt.

FLORI  Und Udo ißt gern Wurst. Also auch Wurst kaufen für ihn und für mich, ja ... ich esse Bratwurst sehr gern.

CLAUDIA  Na und dazu brauchen wir ja frisches Brot. Danach gehen wir dann zur Bäckerei und holen Brot. Was meinst du?

FLORI  Klar und meine Mutter braucht noch Semmeln. Die hole ich dann auch gleich.

CLAUDIA  Die neue Bäckerei hat immer frische Brezeln. Da will ich eine für mich kaufen.

FLORI  Nee, Brezeln mag ich nicht. Die sind mir zu salzig.

CLAUDIA  Wirklich?... Du, wir dürfen nicht vergessen, zum Supermarkt zu gehen.

FLORI  Wieso? Was brauchen wir denn da?

CLAUDIA  Butter fürs Brot und ... na Milch zum Trinken.

FLORI  Oh ja, natürlich. Und zum Schluß müssen wir dann noch beim Obst- und Gemüseladen vorbei.

CLAUDIA  Wieso?

FLORI  Äpfel kaufen, damit wir Bratäpfel backen können als Nachtisch. Das schmeckt so lecker!

CLAUDIA  Also, dann los! Wir haben viel zu tun.

### Activity 11, *p. 200*

OMI  Na, ist ja schön, daß ihr alle hier seid. Flori, kannst du bitte zuerst den Tisch decken?

FLORI  Okay Omi! Wie können wir dir sonst noch helfen?

OMI  Na, da laß mal sehen. Ja, bitte Flori, hol doch danach etwas Limo und Mineralwasser aus dem Keller!

FLORI  Klar doch, mach, ich schon.

MARKUS  Mara und ich können auch helfen.

OMI  Das ist ja nett. Hm, Moment. Also, Markus, geh bitte zum Supermarkt und hol zwei Pfund Tomaten! Hier sind 10 Mark. Das soll reichen. Und du, Mara, vielleicht kannst du zum Bäcker gehen und ein Dutzend Semmeln holen. Hier sind 5 Mark für dich!

MARA  Soll ich sonst noch etwas beim Bäcker kaufen?

OMI  Tja, zum Kaffeetrinken brauchen wir ja noch etwas. Dann kauf mal einen kleinen Kuchen! Hier sind noch mal 10 Mark.

MARA  Oh nein, ich brauche das Geld nicht. Das bezahl' ich schon.

OMI  Doch, doch! Nimm das Geld! Das ist schon gut so. Beeilt euch! Bis später!

## *Zweite Stufe*
### Activity 14, *p. 202*

VERKÄUFER  Was darf es sein, bitte?

KUNDE  Ja, ich hätte gern Tomaten.

VERKÄUFER  Wieviel denn?

KUNDE  Hm, ... ja lassen Sie mal sehen. Also, ein Pfund bitte. Das soll reichen.

VERKÄUFER  Sonst noch etwas?

KUNDE  Ja bitte zwei Pfund Äpfel, die dort. Und das ist dann alles.

VERKÄUFER  Also, ein halbes Kilo Tomaten, zwei Pfund Äpfel, das macht 8,90. Vielen Dank. Wer ist der Nächste, bitte?

KUNDIN  Ja, bitte, ein Kilo Kartoffeln, und haben Sie auch frische Trauben?

VERKÄUFER  Ja, unsere Trauben kommen täglich frisch. Hier, probieren Sie mal!

KUNDIN  Oh, sehr lecker, dann nehme ich ein Viertel Pfund, nein, lieber ein halbes Pfund.

VERKÄUFER  So, ein Kilo Kartoffeln, ein halbes Pfund Trauben, das macht 10,50 zusammen. Sonst nocht etwas?

### Activity 16, *p. 203*

1. — Was darf's denn heute sein?
   — Ich möchte bitte 500 g Hackfleisch.
   — 500 g Hackfleisch. Sonst noch etwas?
   — Ja, noch 200 g Aufschnitt. Das ist alles.

2. — Guten Tag, Frau Motz!
   — Guten Tag, Frau Schmidt!
   — Und was bekommen Sie denn heute?
   — Es ist fast Viertel vor sieben.

3. — Und wie kann ich Ihnen helfen, bitte?
   — Ja, bitte einen Liter Milch. Hier ist meine Flasche.
   — Haben Sie sonst noch einen Wunsch?
   — Ja, dann auch noch zehn Eier, aber braune, bitte.

4. — Was brauchen Sie heute?
   — Ich brauche heute Äpfel. Zwei Pfund, bitte.
   — Sonst noch etwas? Unsere Tomaten sind heute sehr frisch, gerade gekommen.
   — Na ja gut. Dann geben sie mir mal das Brot. Wieviel macht das zusammen?

5. — Ein Liter Milch, 250 g Butter, 100 g Käse. Ist das alles heute?
   — Ja, das soll's sein. Danke schön.

## *D*ritte Stufe
### Activity 21, *p. 206*

1. MARA Hallo! Hier ist die Mara. Ich bin jetzt leider nicht zu Hause. Bitte, hinterlassen Sie mir eine kurze Nachricht, und ich rufe so bald wie möglich zurück. Danke!

(Beep of answering machine)

MARKUS Hallo Mara! Hier ist der Markus. Tut mir leid, aber ich kann zu deiner Fete nicht kommen, weil ich am Samstag abend mit Heiko ins Kino gehe. Wir haben die Karten schon gekauft. Also, bis bald!

CLAUDIA Du Mara. Ich bin's ... Claudia. Hab Dank für die Einladung. Leider kann ich nicht kommen, denn ich habe viele Hausaufgaben. Tschüs!

FLORI Ja hier ist Flori. Mara, klar komm' ich. Kann ich den Udo mitbringen? Laß mich's wissen. Du kennst ja meine Nummer.

CHRISTIAN Christian hier. Ja, Mara, danke für die Einladung. Ich würde ja gern kommen, aber ich muß da zu Hause helfen. Nächstes Mal komme ich aber bestimmt.

STEFAN Servus, Mara. Ich bin's, Stefan. Ja, wann fängt denn die Fete an, und soll ich etwas mitbringen? Sag Bescheid! Bis dann!

BARBARA Hallo Mara, hier Barbara. Super! Find' ich ja toll, daß du 'ne Fete am Wochenende hast. Ich komme so gegen sieben und bring' ein paar neue CDs. Bis dann!

BRIGITTE Grüß dich Mara! Habe gerade deine Einladung bekommen. Leider habe ich eine Chemieprüfung am Montag und muß noch jede Menge lernen. Schade! Ach ja, ich bin's ... Brigitte. Tschau!

### Activity 24, *p. 208*

1. CLAUDIA Du, Mara, was machst du denn heute?
   MARA Hm, zuerst geh' ich ins Einkaufszentrum, so ein paar Klamotten kaufen. Danach geht's nach Hause, um Hausaufgaben zu machen.
2. CLAUDIA Mensch du, Flori! Wo warst du denn heute morgen? Ich hab' versucht, dich anzurufen.
   FLORI Ich war beim Bäcker. Da hab' ich Brot für meine Oma gekauft. Und im Musikhaus Walter war ich auch kurz. Hab' die neue CD von Peter Maffay gekauft. Total stark!
3. CLAUDIA He, Markus, Ich geh' jetzt ins Eiscafé, ein Spaghettieis essen. Komm doch mit!
   MARKUS Kann leider nicht. Um 3 Uhr kommt Stefan. Wir lernen Chemie.
4. CLAUDIA Grüß dich, Heike, Tag, Marianne! Ich bin gestern vorbeigekommen, aber ihr wart ja nicht zu Hause. Wo wart ihr denn?
   HEIKE Gestern? Was haben wir denn gestern gemacht? Ach ja, wir waren im Kino. Wir haben den neuen Film aus Italien gesehen. Der war aber blöd.

5. CLAUDIA Und du, Ahmet, wo warst du gestern, so um vier? Ich bin vorbeigekommen, und keiner war da.
   AHMET Tja, ich war im Supermarkt. Meine Mutter hat mir die Einkaufsliste für die ganze Woche gegeben. Das hat vielleicht lange gedauert. Nächste Woche ist meine Schwester aber dran.
6. CLAUDIA Hi, Andreas! Ich geh' am Nachmittag in den Schreibwarenladen. Brauchst du etwas, das ich dir mitbringen kann?
   ANDREAS Oh ja! Morgen ist die Mathearbeit! Da brauche ich noch ein paar Bleistifte. Du, vielen Dank, Claudia!

### Diktat, *p. 209*

You will hear about the different foods and drinks Mara's friends plan to bring to her party. First listen to what is said, then write down what you hear.

Am Samstag hat Mara eine Fete, und sie hat viele Freunde eingeladen. Alle Freunde bringen etwas zu Essen mit. Die Sabine geht zum Bäcker und kauft frischen Kuchen, und der Stefan holt beim Metzger drei Hähnchen für den Grill. Brigitte geht zum Supermarkt und kauft Gemüse und auch etwas Obst. Und der Ahmet will wieder die Getränke mitbringen. Wenn jeder etwas hilft, hat Mara nicht so viel Arbeit.

## *A*nwendung
### Activity 1, *p. 212*

MUTTER Du, Flori, kannst du bitte für mich einkaufen gehen? Die Omi kommt gleich. Und ich habe keine Zeit dafür.

FLORI Ja klar, Mutti. Mach' ich schon. Hast du den Einkaufszettel fertig?

MUTTER Noch nicht ganz, Moment mal! Was brauche ich denn da alles? Tomaten ... Also, ein Kilo, das soll wohl reichen. Und zwei Pfund Kartoffeln. Was noch? Ich will später noch einen Apfelkuchen backen, dazu brauche ich zwei Kilo Äpfel, ein Pfund Butter und, hmm, haben wir noch Eier? Ach, nein, Eier haben wir nicht. Also, auch zehn Eier.

FLORI Ist das denn alles, Mutti?

MUTTER Moment, ich glaub' nicht. Morgen ist Sonntag. Hm, dann brauchen wir ja auch einen Liter Orangensaft, ein bißchen Käse, ja, 200 g, Emmentaler am liebsten. Aber nur wenn er im Sonderangebot ist. Klar?

FLORI Ja, ich werd' schon sehen. Ist das alles Mutti?

MUTTER Oh ja, ich hab' fast vergessen. Ich hab' keinen Kaffee mehr, und Brot haben wir auch nicht genug. Kauf bitte noch ein Pfund Kaffee, den milden und ein Brot. Das ist jetzt aber wirklich alles. Hier ist das Geld. Das soll ausreichen.

FLORI Tschüs, Mutti! Bis später!

# Kapitel 8: Einkaufen gehen
## *Suggested Project*

*In this activity students will prepare a poster promoting a balanced diet. This project should be started after students have completed the* **Zum Lesen** *section of this chapter. This project can be done individually or in groups of three students, in which case each student would be responsible for featuring one of the meals—breakfast, lunch, or dinner.*

## MATERIALS

✂ **Students may need**
- *1 poster board per group*
- *health and food magazines*
- *scissors*
- *glue*
- *mail-order catalogs that feature food*
- *pens and markers*
- *grocery advertisements*

## SUGGESTED SEQUENCE

1. Decide whether to do this project as individual or group work, depending on your class size and time allotment for this activity.

2. Have students look for pictures to illustrate a nutritional meal. If students are not able to find a picture of a certain food item but would like to include it in their project, encourage them to draw the item.

3. Once a selection of items has been gathered, students should make an outline of the information and materials they will include on their poster.

4. Students must label each food with its German name, and indicate quantities per serving. Example: **100 Gramm Kartoffeln**

5. Suggest that students review the quantity expressions from the **Zweite Stufe.** They could also ask the health teacher or check their health textbook for guidelines for appropriate serving sizes and daily totals of the different food groups.

6. Students in each group must proofread each other's features before putting the final descriptions on the poster.

9. Each group presents its poster.

## GRADING THE PROJECT

Since the outcome of the poster is based on group cooperation and effort, one grade should be given to all members of the group based on the following criteria.

Suggested point distribution (total=100)

| | |
|---|---|
| Appearance and neatness | 25 |
| Accurate descriptions/ correct language usage | 50 |
| Oral presentation | 25 |

Im Obst- und Gemüseladen
Frisch

Tomaten 1 kg 4,80

Kartoffeln 1 kg 1,98

Salat St. -,99

Trauben 1 kg 4,98

Äpfel 1 kg 3,20

# Kapitel 8: Einkaufen gehen

# ♖ *Games*

## AUSREDEN FINDEN

*This game will help students review giving excuses and reasons using* **weil** *clauses.*

**Materials**  Each student needs a sheet of paper and a pen.

**Procedure**  Before the game gets underway, each student writes a question that begins with the interrogative pronoun **Warum.** They should write this question close to the top of the paper. Example: **Warum gehst du heute nicht ins Kino?** Once all students have written their sentences, they should fold the paper so that the question is covered up. Then each student passes his or her paper to the next person. Each student should write a statement below the fold without looking at the question. This statement should begin with the conjunction **weil.** (Example: **Weil ich kein Geld habe.**) At this point, each paper should have two phrases—one question and one statement. Ask students to pass all papers to the front and shuffle them. Next, divide the class into two teams and redistribute the papers so that each team member has a piece of paper. Members of each team then take turns reading the question and responses, which tend to be quite humorous. As each student reads the phrases on his or her sheet of paper, he or she must also translate the sentences. If the translation is correct, that student scores a point for his or her team.

## WAS IST HIER FALSCH?

*With this game, students are able to review vocabulary and parts of speech.*

**Materials**  You will need one index card for each student and the **Wortschatz** to be reviewed.

**Procedure**  Begin by asking each student to write down four words on his or her index card. Three of the four words should belong to a group, one of the words should not belong. (Example: **Milch, Brot, Schuhe, Apfel)** The groups can be based on meaning or part of speech. When students have finished, collect all the cards and shuffle them. Divide the class into two teams and give each person on both teams one index card. The first person on Team A asks the first person on Team B: **Was ist falsch hier?** and reads the four words on his or her index card. If the person on Team B answers correctly by pointing out the wrong word, he or she scores a point for the team. Teams alternate asking the questions until all cards have been read, thus giving every student a chance to talk. The team with the most points at the end of the game wins.

# Kapitel 8: Einkaufen gehen
## Lesson Plans, pages 192-215

## Using the Chapter Opener,
### pp. 192-193

### Motivating Activity

Prepare two typical shopping lists, one that could have been written by an American parent in English and one written by a German parent in German. Have the same items on both lists, but on the German one, quantities should be more specific and generally smaller. Put both lists on a transparency or a handout and ask students to compare the two lists, writing down the differences they notice about the German list. Example: smaller quantities purchased, quantities expressed in grams

### Thinking Critically

**Drawing Inferences** Ask students to think about what the German list reveals about food storage and shopping habits in German-speaking countries. (shop for food more often than Americans; refrigerators are smaller; like fresh foods: meats, cold cuts, fruit and vegetables; prefer to shop in specialty shops rather than supermarkets)

### Teaching Suggestion

① Ask students if they can tell from the picture how much the tomatoes (**Eiertomaten=** *plum tomatoes*) cost and in what quantities they are sold. (DM 7,80/kg)

###  Multicultural Connection

① Have students try to determine from the picture where the tomatoes come from. (Italy) Can students think of produce items that are imported to the United States? Ask them to name some examples.

### Background Information

② In German-speaking countries it is customary for guests to offer a small bouquet of flowers to the hostess. Fresh flowers are often purchased at the open-air market, such as the one pictured.

### Teaching Suggestion

Ask students if it is also typical to offer a small gift to a host or hostess in the United States. What might be an appropriate gift for an American host or hostess? (Examples: flowers, candy)

###  Multicultural Connection

Do similar customs exist in other countries around the world? Have students conduct a survey with students or adults of other nationalities. Also have students ask other foreign language teachers. Ask students to share their information with the class.

### Building on Previous Skills

③ Do students recall two open-air markets from preceding units? (in Wedel **am Rathausplatz** and the **Vitualienmarkt** in Munich)

### Teaching Suggestion

Ask students if they ever go shopping for their parents. Can they recall what they bought the last time they shopped for somebody? Did they know what to look for and where to find it? Do their parents prefer certain stores and brands?

###  Culture Note

German parents routinely send their older children shopping for them. The children know what their parents usually buy, and the local merchants often do, too. Much shopping is done in specialty stores and open-air markets.

### Focusing on Outcomes

Have students preview the learning outcomes listed on p. 193. Which of the functions listed could be used in the Chapter Opener photos? (Examples: talking about quantities, saying what you bought) **NOTE:** Each of these outcomes is modeled in the video and evaluated in **Kann ich's wirklich?** on p. 214.

# Teaching Los geht's!
## pp. 194-196

### Resources for Los geht's!

- *Video Program* OR
  *Expanded Video Program,*
- *Textbook Audiocassette* 4 B
- *Practice and Activity Book*

▶ **pages 194-195**

 ## Video Synopsis

In this segment of the video, Flori visits his grandmother, who has cooked one of his favorite dishes, **Kaiserschmarren.** After lunch, Flori's grandmother gives him a shopping list and some money to go grocery shopping for her. After going to several specialty stores for his errands, Flori comes back to his grandmother's house but discovers that he has lost the wallet she had given him.

## Motivating Activity

To help students prepare for the content and functions modeled in the pictures, ask them to imagine that they will be in charge of getting the groceries for the next two to three days at their home. What would they need to get, and where would they go? Have them make a list and tell them to be as specific as possible.

## Language Note

**Kaiserschmarren,** mentioned in frame 1, is a sweet omelet made of eggs, sugar, raisins, flour, rum, and milk, then scrambled with a fork to make bite-size pieces.

## Culture Note

Many people in German-speaking countries eat sweet dishes such as **Kaiserschmarren** as a main dish.

## Teaching Suggestion

After students have viewed or read the **Foto-Roman,** put the phrase **Floris Einkaufszettel** on the board. Based on the content of the story, ask students to work with a partner and write down the items and quantities that should be on the list. Call on several students to write the different items on the board.

▶ **page 196**

 ## For Individual Needs

**2 Challenge** After students have completed Activity 2, ask them to find all the phrases in which the speaker has abbreviated a sentence and implied part of it.

Examples: **(Du kochst) Kaiserschmarren?**
**(Das ist) super!**
**(Haben sie) sonst noch einen Wunsch?**

**3 Challenge** Have students use vocabulary from preceding chapters to try to name one additional item that can also be purchased at each of the four stores.

**4 Challenge** After students have completed Activity 4, ask them to replace one part of each of the sentences on the left (not the subject) in such a way that the reason given on the right still fits. Example: **Omi gibt Flori *Geld*, denn er geht für sie einkaufen.**

**5 Visual Learners** Have the eight sentences written on sentence strips before starting this activity. Have students work with a partner to figure out the correct sequence of the sentences in Activity 5. Then give one sentence strip to each of eight pairs of students and have them arrange themselves in the correct order. Have one student help oversee the activity. Ask students to read the sentences aloud.

## Closure

Before this activity, you will need to prepare copies of each of the seven frames from the **Foto-Roman** in which several words have been removed (whited out) from the dialogue. Write the words that have been removed from the text in random order on the board or on a transparency. Divide the class into seven groups and assign one **Foto-Roman** frame to each group. Ask students to close their books and complete each conversation within a set amount of time, using the words on the board as an aid. When all groups are finished, ask students to check their answers against the story in the book.

**LOS GEHT'S!**

## ERSTE STUFE

# Teaching Erste Stufe,
## pp. 197-201

### Resources for Erste Stufe

*Practice and Activity Book*
*Chapter Resources,* Book 3
- Communicative Activity 8-1
- Additional Listening Activities 8-1, 8-2
- Student Response Form
- Realia 8-1
- Situation Card 8-1
- Teaching Transparency Master 8-1
- Quiz 8-1
*Audiocassette Program*
- Textbook Audiocassette 4 B
- *Additional Listening Activities,*
  *Audiocassette* 10 A
- *Assessment Items, Audiocassette* 8 A

▶ *page 197*

## MOTIVATE

### Teaching Suggestion

Ask students to brainstorm to create a list of some foods they believe to be of German origin. Make a list on the board. Here are some examples: hamburger, strudel, muesli (Swiss), pretzel, sauerkraut, selzer, zwieback, frankfurter, marzipan (from Lübeck), wiener.

### Thinking Critically

**Drawing Inferences** Can students tell by looking at the word what **Zwieback** might mean? (**zweimal backen** = *twice baked*)

## TEACH

### PRESENTATION: Wortschatz

Look through your local grocery ads and cut out items representative of the vocabulary in this **Wortschatz** box. Tape the pictures on construction paper (you might want to laminate these for future activities). Using these as visual aids, introduce the vocabulary by naming the items, then using **ja/nein** questions, continuing with either/or questions, and finally building up to short-answer questions.

## For Additional Practice

- Have students identify all the compound nouns in the ads. (Examples: **Hackfleisch, Bratwurst**)
- Have students identify the cognates in the ads and practice the pronunciation of these words. (Examples: **Salat, Apfel, Tomaten**)

 ## Culture Notes

- In Germany, eggs are typically sold in cartons of ten, rather than twelve as in the United States.
- You might want to point out to students the difference between a **Torte** and a **Kuchen**. **Torte** and **Kuchen** are both cakes. However, the word **Torte** is used for more elaborate cakes with several layers, creamy icing, and decorations. **Kuchen** tend to be less fancy than **Torten** and often look like coffee cake or even fruit pies (**Apfelkuchen**).

▶ *page 198*

## For Additional Practice

**6** Ask students if they can think of any other items they could buy at each store.

## Teaching Suggestion

**7** Provide students with the current exchange rate and ask them to compare prices using the information on how to use the exchange rate from Chapter 4.

## PRESENTATION: So sagt man das!

Prepare a three-column chart on the board, a transparency, or a handout for students. In the left-hand column write questions: **Was soll ich für dich tun? Wo soll ich ... kaufen? Wo soll ich ... holen?**
In the second column write the "was" answers: **einkaufen gehen, Brot kaufen, Brot holen, Fleisch holen, Tomaten kaufen.**
In the third column write the "wo" answers: **beim Bäcker, beim Metzger, im Supermarkt, im Gemüseladen.**
Ask the questions and have students answer using one of the entries in columns 2 or 3:
**Was soll ich für dich tun?**
**Du kannst für mich Brot holen.**
After students have practiced with you, have them practice in pairs. Then have them answer the questions in the **So sagt man das!** box.

▶ *page 199*

## PRESENTATION: Grammatik

Review with students the verbs **möchte, wollen, müssen,** and **können.** Then practice the forms of **sollen** by asking questions and having students answer them. Write on the board the three questions: **Was soll ich ...? Was soll er ...? Was sollen wir ...?** Have students quickly answer, using the expressions in the function box as a guide: **Du sollst ..., Er soll ..., Ihr sollt ...** After they have practiced the forms in this way, have them answer the discovery questions in the function box.

## Teaching Suggestion

**9** This activity could be done first as an oral exercise in class and then, for additional practice, assigned as written homework.

## For Additional Practice

**9** Instead of questions, have students form statements, first with the subject in first position (**Ihr sollt das Hackfleisch beim Metzger holen.**), and then with the object in first position. (**Das Hackfleisch sollt ihr beim Metzger kaufen.**).

## PRESENTATION: So sagt man das!

Begin by having each student ask you the question: **Was soll ich für Sie tun?** Using the vocabulary of this **Stufe** (**Wortschatz** and verbs such as **einkaufen, holen, gehen, helfen, aufmachen, zumachen, bringen**), address commands to several students in response to their questions.

▶ *page 200*

## PRESENTATION: Grammatik

Write several command forms on the board (Examples: **geh, zeig, gib, such, lauf, iß, nimm**) Then call on individual students to use one of the verbs on the board to command another student in class to do something. When all listed verbs have been used, ask the students what the infinitive of each verb is and which form of address they used to form the commands. (**du-**form) Ask students if they see how the **du-**command form differs from the regular **du-**form of a verb. (minus **st**)

 **Total Physical Response**

To review the **du-**command forms, have students prepare a list of three to five commands that can be carried out in class. Each student will then give his or her commands to individual students. (Example: **Mary, nimm mein Buch!**)

 **For Individual Needs**

**11** **Auditory Learners** Have students listen to the activity a second time, focusing on the amount of the money Markus and Mara are given for their trips to the store. (DM 10, DM 15)

## For Additional Practice

**12** Ask students to tell you in German which of the pictured chores their parents usually have to remind them to do.

▶ *page 201*

## PRESENTATION: Landeskunde

## Teaching Suggestions

- Take a survey of your students in which you have them list the things they do most often to help other people. Write the small jobs and chores on the board and determine what things the class does most often to help others.

- You may want to introduce the following vocabulary to help students with the video segment and the readings.

  **die Rechtschreibung**  *spelling and punctuation*
  **die Kinderkirche**  *Sunday school*
  **unregelmäßig**  *irregular*

## Culture Note

In the German-speaking countries high school students, like Silvana, often offer tutorials (**Nachhilfe**) in their strongest subjects. Tutoring younger students is a good way for teenagers to earn extra spending money.

## Teaching Suggestion

Ask students to read Sandra's interview and point out the word **grad'.** Can students guess its meaning within the context of the sentences? Is the word necessary to understand the sentence in which it is being used?

## Teacher Note

Mention to your class that the **Landeskunde** will also be included in Quiz 8-1 given at the end of the **Erste Stufe**.

## Reteaching: Stores and grocery items

Make a list of stores and all the items that can be found in each store. List the items in random order on one side of the board and list the names of the stores on the other side. Ask students to come to the board and draw lines correctly matching each store with its merchandise.

## CLOSE

### Game

Play the game *Memory* to review the food vocabulary introduced in this **Stufe**. See Chapter 2, p. 39F for the procedure.

## Focusing on Outcomes

Refer students back to the learning outcomes listed on p. 193. Students should recognize that they are now able to ask what they should do and to tell someone what to do.

## ASSESS

• **Performance Assessment**   Have the following information listed on a transparency you have prepared ahead of time. List four different kinds of stores and at least three items per store.

| Metzger | Bäcker | Obst- und Gemüseladen | Schreibwar-enladen |
|---------|--------|------------------------|---------------------|
| Wurst | Kuchen | Äpfel | Kuli |

Show the transparency to the class for one minute as you go over the words and review the vocabulary. Then turn off the overhead and call on students to list as many items as they can remember.

• Quiz 8-1, *Chapter Resources*, Book 3

# Teaching Zweite Stufe, pp. 202-204

**Resources for Zweite Stufe**

*Practice and Activity Book*
*Chapter Resources,* Book 3
- Communicative Activity 8-2
- Additional Listening Activities 8-3, 8-4
- Student Response Form
- Realia 8-2
- Situation Card 8-2
- Quiz 8-2

*Audiocassette Program*
- *Textbook Audiocassette* 4 B
- *Additional Listening Activities, Audiocassette* 10 A
- *Assessment Items, Audiocassette* 8 A

▶ page 202

## MOTIVATE

### Teaching Suggestion

Bring empty cereal boxes, flour bags, cans of food, etc, and ask students to look at the labels. Have them write the quantities on the chalkboard.

## TEACH

### PRESENTATION: Wortschatz

Try to get a scale with grams on it from the science department and have students bring different foods in different amounts. Ask them to guess how much each food item weighs using German (metric) measurements. Then measure each item and state the weight in German.

### Math Connection

Have some items on hand which do not show metric measures. Ask students to convert the U.S. measurements into German measurements using the **Wortschatz** information.

### Language Note

In spoken German, the word **Kilo** is used more frequently than **Kilogramm.**

### Background Information

Here are some additional conversions students might want to use as they try to compare the weights of different foods.

1 **Gramm** (**g**) = 0.035 ounces
1 **Pfund** (**Pfd.**) = 1.1 pounds
1 **Kilogramm** (**kg**) = 2.2 pounds
1 **Liter** (**l**) = 2.11 pints; 1.06 quarts
**3,78 Liter** = 1 gallon

### Teaching Suggestion

Have students look back at frame 5 of the **Foto-Roman** (where Flori is at the butcher's). Ask students how and what Flori orders. Then have students turn to p. 197 and, with a partner, read the names and quantities of the items pictured. Example: **1 Kilo Hackfleisch**

▶ page 203

### PRESENTATION: So sagt man das!

Ask students to look at frames 5 and 6 of the **Foto-Roman.** Can students infer the meaning of the vendor's lines (**Sonst noch einen Wunsch? Sonst noch etwas?**) from Flori's responses?

### For Individual Needs

**16 A Slower Pace** Have students listen a second time and determine in which stores the conversations take place. (1. **Metzger** 2. can't be determined 3. **Supermarkt** 4. **Obst- und Gemüseladen** 5. **Supermarkt**)

▶ page 204

### Group Work

**17** Ask students to prepare a skit based on this activity. They should use props such as a vendor's apron, money, receipts, toy cash registers, shopping bags, and plastic food props. Assign students into groups of three to prepare their skits. Monitor students' progress and make suggestions if needed. When the skits have been completed and rehearsed, students should act out their story. If possible record each group's performance on audio or video tape.

## Language Note

**17** Point out to students that the abbreviation **cm** in the pizza recipe stands for **Zentimeter**.

## Math Connection

**17** Have students find out the conversion ratio of centimeters to inches, and then determine how big the pizza crust for this recipe should be. (1 inch = 2.54 centimeters; the pizza crust should be about 12.5 inches in diameter.)

## Teacher Note

**17** Students might want to know that **gitterförmig** means *criss-crossed* in this context.

## Building on Previous Skills

**17** The pizza needs to be baked at **250 Grad**. Using the conversion formula for Celsius to Fahrenheit degrees given in the Math Connection on p. 167N of Chapter 7, have students determine how much **250 Grad** would be in Fahrenheit degrees. (482° F)

##  Culture Notes

- **17** **Quark** is a soft, fresh cheese often used in the preparation of **Käsekuchen**, dips, or eaten as a spread as is the case for the **Pikanter Quark** in the recipe. Since **Quark** might not be readily available in the United States, tell students that they can substitute ricotta cheese, or smooth cottage cheese.

- **Joule** is a unit used to indicate the amount of energy in food. The term was introduced because it is more precise than the word **Kalorien**. It is named after the English physicist James Prescott Joule (1818-1889). This term is often used in German recipes along with the word **Kalorien**, although most Germans use "**Kalorien**" in everyday speech.

## Teaching Suggestion

**18** Once the ads are completed, display them on your bulletin boards and incorporate them into vocabulary review whenever possible.

## Reteaching: Vocabulary and word order

Write out various sentences from the activities of this **Stufe** and the **Foto-Roman** on sentence strips. Cut the sentences apart and put them into numbered envelopes. Have students practice word order by putting the words into the correct order. Have students work individually or in pairs. When students are finished, call on several volunteers to read their sentences aloud to the class.

## CLOSE

### Teaching Suggestion

Have students working in pairs come up with as many food items as possible for a given topic in 30-45 seconds. (Examples: **Frühstück, Fete, Abendessen, Mittagessen, Oktoberfest**) Students should write all their words down. Monitor work, and ask students to read the food items they have listed when you call time.

### Focusing on Outcomes

Refer students back to the learning outcomes listed on p. 193. They should recognize that they are now able to talk about quantities and to say that they want something else.

## ASSESS

- **Performance Assessment** Divide the class into groups of three. Each group should have a writer, a checker, and a reporter. Tell groups that they are responsible for making a grocery list and a menu for an upcoming party they are giving together. Give each group a number of friends to invite. Each group will decide what foods to serve at the party. They also need to determine the quantities for each item to be purchased. The writer then makes out the shopping list as well as an outline for the menu. The checker proofreads the assignment, and the reporter tells the class the **Einkaufsliste** and menu for the upcoming event.

- Quiz 8-2 *Chapter Resources,* Book 3

# Teaching Dritte Stufe,
## pp. 205-209

### Resources for Dritte Stufe

*Practice and Activity Book*
*Chapter Resources,* Book 3
- Additional Listening Activities 8-5, 8-6
- Student Response Form
- Realia 8-3
- Situation Card 8-3
- Teaching Transparency Master 8-2
- Quiz 8-3

*Audiocassette Program*
- *Textbook Audiocassette* 4 B
- *Additional Listening Activities,
  Audiocassette* 10 A
- *Assessment Items, Audiocassette* 8 A

▶ **page 205**

## MOTIVATE

### Teaching Suggestion

As a warm-up activity at the beginning of class, ask students to find out what a partner had for breakfast or lunch that day. Students should be able to report what they found out to the class.

## TEACH

###  For Individual Needs

**20  A Slower Pace**  Ask students to scan each ad for words or expressions they recognize. On the board write down what students recognize in each ad. Paraphrase the words or parts of sentences that students do not understand.

▶ **page 206**

### PRESENTATION: So sagt man das!

Ask students to come up with an excuse for not doing their homework. Example: **Ich höre jetzt Musik.** Write some of the students' answers on the board, underlining the verbs in each sentence. Then write the sentence **Ich kann meine Hausaufgaben nicht machen** and connect it with the students' sentences, using **weil** or **denn.** Example: **Ich kann meine Hausaufgaben nicht machen, weil ich jetzt Musik höre.**

### Teaching Suggestion

Suggest that students add **denn** and **weil** to their list of connectors.

### Thinking Critically

**Drawing Inferences**  Ask students what type of function the words **denn** and **weil** fulfill in a sentence. (They join clauses.) What can students tell from the examples about the word order in the following subordinate clause? (**weil ich keine Zeit habe**)

|  | Subject | Direct object | Conjugated verb |
|---|---|---|---|
| weil | ich | keine Zeit | habe |

### Language Note

Mention to students that in German a comma must be used between a main clause and a subordinate clause.

### For Additional Practice

**21**  After students have completed the activity, have them tell which people cannot come and the reasons they give. Students must use complete sentences including clauses with either **weil** or **denn.**

### Teaching Suggestion

**22**  Ask students to do this activity orally with a partner and later assign it as written homework. Have students come up with at least five pairs of sentences.

▶ **page 207**

###  Cooperative Learning

**23**  Begin by dividing students into groups of three. Each group should have a writer, a discussion leader, and a reporter. Set a time limit of approximately 5 minutes for this activity. Ask each group to follow the example and discuss each of the four statements. Once they come to an agreement, they should write down their opinion following the example. When students are finished, ask each group reporter to share his or her group's discussion outcomes with the rest of the class.

DRITTE STUFE

## PRESENTATION: So sagt man das!

Ask students how they would ask a friend in English about his or her activities during the past weekend. Record the different forms students would use. Underline the verbs in these sentences. Example: What did you do last weekend? What were you doing last weekend? Tell students that the German language also has several ways of expressing the past tense.

### Teacher Note

The conversational past tense of **kaufen** in the **So sagt man das!** box is introduced here as a lexical item only. As few grammar explanations as possible should be given at this stage. The conversational past tense is introduced as a grammar item in Chapter 3 of Level 2.

## PRESENTATION: Wortschatz

Use a current calendar to introduce the **Wortschatz** by giving examples of each new expression as you point to the day. Example: **Vorgestern war Montag. Gestern war Dienstag.**

## PRESENTATION: Grammatik

In Chapter 1 students learned the present tense forms of **sein.** Review these forms with students before introducing the past tense of **sein.**

▶ *page 208*

 **For Individual Needs**

**24  A Slower Pace**  Before students listen to the tape, ask them what types of markers they need to listen for in order to distinguish between present and past tenses. (verbs and adverbs) Note some of their examples on the board.

### For Additional Practice

**25**  Ask students to go over Flori's and Mara's lists again and have them tell you what the two teenagers did at certain times using 24-hour time.

### Teaching Suggestion

**26**  For reading practice, ask students to read the brief dialogues in pairs. Students should switch roles for additional practice.

▶ *page 209*

 **Culture Note**

**27**  **Langer Samstag** is the first Saturday of every month, and stores remain open until 6 P.M. or **18.00 Uhr.** This is also the case for all Saturdays in the month of December, to give holiday shoppers extra time for shopping. Otherwise all stores close at 2 P.M. on Saturdays.

### Language Note

**Schaufensterbummeln** (from **bummeln** - *to stroll*) is very popular in all of the German-speaking countries. People often go window shopping on Sunday afternoons, when stores are closed.

## PRESENTATION: Aussprache

Point out to students that the short vowels **ö** and **ü** are articulated with less muscular exertion than the long **ö** and **ü.** Have students compare the following words:
**Wörter** vs. **Größe**
**hübsch** vs. **Gemüse**

### Teaching Suggestion

After students finish the **Diktat,** have several students write their sentences on the board. Ask the class to check the sentences for possible errors as you go over the **Diktat.**

*„Für mich gibt's zum Braten nichts Besseres, denn Butaris und der feine Buttergeschmack sind einfach unschlagbar."*

**Butaris**®
BUTTERSCHMALZ
*Zum Braten, Backen, Kochen und Fritieren*
soft
250 g

## Reteaching: Past tense of sein

Prepare a transparency or handout with four columns listing the following expressions from this **Stufe.**

| | | | |
|---|---|---|---|
| vorgestern | war | ich | im Kino |
| gestern | warst | du | im Café |
| gestern abend | wart | Michael | im Englischen Garten |
| | waren | ihr | |
| heute morgen | | wir | auf dem Land |
| | | | bei meinen Freunden |
| heute nachmittag | | | |
| letztes Wochenende | | | |

Ask four students to create as many sentences as possible using expressions from all four columns.

## CLOSE

### Teaching Suggestion

Provide students with the following **Lückensatz** which each one of them should try to complete in a creative or interesting way.
**Vorgestern war ich nicht in der Schule, denn ...**
Point out that students should use the past tense of **sein.** Have four or five students read their sentences to the class.

### Focusing on Outcomes

Refer students back to the learning outcomes listed on p. 193. They should recognize that they are now able to give reasons and to say where they were and what they bought.

## ASSESS

- **Performance Assessment**  Ask students to tell you what they bought the last time they went shopping. They should use the expression **habe ... gekauft.**

- Quiz 8-3 *Chapter Resources,* Book 3

## Teaching Zum Lesen, pp. 210-211

### Reading Strategy

The targeted strategy in this reading is combining different strategies to understand a text. Students should learn about this strategy before beginning Question 3.

## PREREADING

### Motivating Activity

Ask students to list foods that they consider to be healthful from all major food groups. This should be done in German. Then take a survey asking students which of these foods they like and dislike.

### Teacher Note

Activities 1 and 2 are prereading tasks.

## READING

### Teaching Suggestion

**5**  Before students scan the texts for the German words, ask them to look for parts of words they recognize from preceding units. Example: **Tag** in the word **alltäglich**

### Thinking Critically

**Analyzing**  Ask students where they might find these types of ads.

### Language Note

**Man ist, was man ißt** is the original German saying that is used in one of the **Müller Brot** ads. It can be compared to the English saying *You are what you eat.*

### Thinking Critically

- **Comparing and Contrasting**  Can students think of American proverbs or sayings that involve foods? See if they can guess the English equivalent of this German saying: **Liebe geht durch den Magen.** (*The best way to a man's heart is through his stomach.*)

- **Analyzing**  Ask students if they can tell by looking at the products who the manufacturers are. (**Müller, Almenrausch, Leerdammer**)

**DRITTE STUFE**

## Health Connection

Ask students to name the major food groups of a balanced diet. How does the ad **Der Mensch ist, wie er ißt** tie into those requirements? From a nutritional point of view how important are the products featured in the readings?

 ## For Individual Needs

**A Slower Pace** Ask students to make a list of words that they already know or believe might be cognates. Examples: **Fitneß, Marathon, Vitamine, Mineralstoffe, Tag, Mahlzeit, Fett**

## Teaching Suggestion

Ask students to look at the **Müller Brot** ad to see the different varieties of bread **Müller Brot** has to offer. (**Isartaler, Zwergerl, Sonne, 4 Korn plus**)

## Thinking Critically

**Drawing Inferences** Before reading the **Müller Brot Hotline** ad, ask students for reasons why there might be such hotlines. Who would call for information? (people concerned about what they eat and the nutritional value of products)

 ## For Individual Needs

**Challenge** Ask students to think of one question they might ask if they called the **Müller Brot Hotline.**

## Thinking Critically

**Comparing and Contrasting** After looking at the cheese ads, ask students to think of similar products in the United States that advertise their low fat content? Why is it so important to consumers that cheeses be light?

## POST-READING

### Teacher Note

Activity 10 is a post-reading task that will show whether students can transfer what they have learned.

 ### Portfolio Assessment

**10** You might want to use this activity as a written portfolio item for your students. See *Assessment Guide,* Chapter 8.

### Closure

Ask students which bread and cheese shown in the advertisements they would pick to serve as a snack if they had friends over to their house.

# Using Anwendung,
### pp. 212-213

### Teaching Suggestion

**1** Have students listen to the activity twice. During the first listening, students should write down only what Flori is supposed to get. During the second listening, have students add the needed quantities next to each item.

 ### Portfolio Assessment

**3** You might want to use this activity as an oral portfolio item for your students. See *Assessment Guide,* Chapter 8.

### For Additional Practice

Ask students to compile a list of a minimum of eight foods they like and dislike using the phrases listed in the box next to Activity 3. Remind students to use the conjunctions **weil** and **denn** in their descriptions.

## Thinking Critically

**Comparing and Contrasting** Ask students to contrast the meals typically prepared in the United States with those in Germany. Also ask them to compare the times of day the meals are served. Example: The main meal in Germany is served at noon as **Mittagessen** whereas the main meal in the United States is usually served around 6 P.M. for dinner.

##  Multicultural Connection

Foods and food preferences differ among nationalities and cultures. Have students conduct a survey of students of other nationalities to determine their eating habits. What do typical meals consist of? Include other foreign language teachers in the survey to tell about meals of other countries. Have students share their findings with the class.

## Teaching Suggestion

**5** Ask students to read their letters aloud in class. As an option, you might ask students to come up with at least one question based on their own letter that they could ask to check other students' comprehension.

**6** Since students always enjoy food days, ask students to bring the actual ingredients for the recipe they have chosen. These should be recipes with little preparation involved. At the end of the dialogues, ask students to prepare their recipe or dish. The different dishes can then be served to the class. Students should be responsible for bringing plates, napkins, and plastic utensils to prepare and serve their dishes.

## *K*ann ich's wirklich?
*p. 214*

This page is intended to prepare students for the test. It is a brief checklist of the major points covered in the chapter. The students should be reminded that it is a checklist only and not necessarily everything that will appear on the test.

## *U*sing Wortschatz,
*p. 215*

### Teaching Suggestion

Practice giving vocabulary definitions in German. Describe an item without saying the word. For example: **Banane: es ist Obst, und es ist lang und gelb. Pfund: es hat 500 Gramm.** Have students try to guess the word you describe. As an alternative, have students take turns describing food items and have the rest of the class guess what the word is.

### Game

- Play the game **Ausreden finden** with the vocabulary of this chapter. See p. 191F for the procedure.

- Play the game **Was ist hier falsch?** See p. 191F for the procedure.

### Teacher Note

Give the **Kapitel 8** Chapter Test, *Chapter Resources,* Book 3.

# Einkaufen gehen

① Ein Kilo Tomaten, bitte.

**O**ne way that teenagers in German-speaking countries help out is by shopping for groceries. Do you sometimes go grocery shopping for your family? If you are in a German-speaking country and want to go shopping for groceries, there are a number of expressions that you need to know.

② Ich hab' ein paar Blumen gekauft.

## In this chapter you will learn

- to ask what you should do; to tell someone what to do
- to talk about quantities; to say that you want something else
- to give reasons; to say where you were and what you bought

## And you will

- listen to customers ordering groceries in different stores
- read food ads and recipes
- write a shopping list
- find out how people in German-speaking countries do their shopping

Hasen Futter ...mh!!

③ Möchten Sie noch etwas?

Knackige Kirschen

# Los geht's!

Flori     Omi

 **Alles für die Oma!**

Look at the photos that accompany the story.
Who are the people pictured? What are they doing?
Where are they? What do you think they are talking about?
What do you suppose will happen in the story?

❶

| | |
|---|---|
| FLORI | Hallo, Omi! |
| OMI | Hallo, Flori! |
| FLORI | Hm, Omi, was kochst du denn? Es riecht so gut! Kaiserschmarren? Super! |
| OMI | Den ißt du doch so gern! |
| FLORI | Und wie! |

❷

| | |
|---|---|
| FLORI | Hm, Omi, der Kaiserschmarren war gut! Wie immer! |
| OMI | Wirklich? Nicht zu süß? |
| FLORI | Nein, überhaupt nicht. Er war gerade richtig! |
| OMI | Na, das freut mich! |

❸

| | |
|---|---|
| FLORI | Und was soll ich heute für dich einkaufen? |
| OMI | Hier ist der Einkaufszettel. |
| FLORI | Wo soll ich denn die Tomaten kaufen? |
| OMI | Die kannst du im Supermarkt kaufen. Dort sind sie nicht so teuer. |
| FLORI | Und das Brot? Kann ich es auch gleich da kaufen? |
| OMI | Hol das Brot lieber beim Bäcker! Dort ist es immer frisch und schmeckt besser. |

**OMI** Hier sind hundert Mark. Verlier das Geld nicht!
**FLORI** Keine Sorge, Omi! Ich pass' schon auf!

**FLORI** Hm ... ein Pfund Hackfleisch, bitte!
**VERKÄUFERIN** Hast du noch einen Wunsch, bitte?
**FLORI** Dann noch hundert Gramm Aufschnitt.
**VERKÄUFERIN** Sonst noch einen Wunsch?
**FLORI** Nein, danke! Das ist alles.

**VERKÄUFERIN** Bitte schön?
**FLORI** So ein Brot, bitte!
**VERKÄUFERIN** Sonst noch etwas?
**FLORI** Jetzt bekomme ich noch zwei Semmeln.
**VERKÄUFERIN** Macht fünf Mark und achtzig, bitte!
**FLORI** Einen Moment! Dann noch bitte so eine
Brezenstange für mich!
**VERKÄUFERIN** Alles, dann? Sechs Mark vierzig dann, bitte!

**FLORI** So, Omi, hier bin ich wieder. Hier sind noch ein
paar Blumen für dich!
**OMI** Das ist aber nett!
**FLORI** So, jetzt packen wir erst mal aus! Die Eier, die
Butter ... Tja, wo ist denn das Portemonnaie?
**OMI** Wo warst du denn zuletzt?
**FLORI** Einen Moment, Omi, ich bin gleich wieder da!
Tschau!

# 1 Was passiert hier?

Do you understand what is happening in the story? Check your comprehension by answering these questions. Don't be afraid to guess.

1. What does Flori do when he first arrives at his grandmother's house?
2. What does Flori offer to do for his grandmother?
3. Why does she give him money? What else does she give him for his errand?
4. What types of stores does Flori go to?
5. Why do you think Flori rushes out of his grandmother's house at the end of the story?

1. greets her, asks what she is cooking, eats **Kaiserschmarren**
2. go shopping
3. so that he can go shopping; a shopping list
4. supermarket, butcher, bakery.
5. He can't find his wallet.

# 2 Genauer lesen

Reread the conversations. Which words or phrases do the characters use to

1. express satisfaction or praise
2. refer to different kinds of stores
3. name foods
4. express quantities in weight
5. ask if someone wants more

1. Super, freut mich
2. Supermarkt, Bäcker
3. Kaiserschmarren, Tomaten, Brot, Hackfleisch, Aufschnitt, Semmeln, Brezenstange, Butter, Eier
4. Ein Pfund, hundert Gramm
5. Sonst noch einen Wunsch? Sonst noch etwas?

# 3 Wo war Flori?

Flori went to several different stores when he was shopping for his grandmother. In which of the places listed might he have made these statements?

1. Ein Pfund Hackfleisch, bitte!  b
2. Jetzt bekomme ich noch zwei Semmeln.  a
3. Ein Kilo Tomaten, bitte!  d
4. Ich möchte bitte ein paar Rosen.  c

a. beim Bäcker
b. beim Metzger
c. im Blumengeschäft
d. im Supermarkt

# 4 Was paßt zusammen?

You can use the word **denn** (*since, for, because*) to show the relationship between two sentences that express an action and the reason for that action: **Hol das Brot beim Bäcker, denn dort ist es immer frisch**! Connect the following pairs of sentences in this way to logically explain some of the actions in the story.

1. Es riecht sehr gut bei Omi  e
2. Flori kauft Tomaten im Supermarkt  c
3. Flori kauft Brot beim Bäcker  b
4. Omi gibt Flori einen Einkaufszettel  a
5. Flori geht schnell weg  d

a. er geht für sie einkaufen.
b. dort ist es immer frisch.
c. dort sind sie nicht so teuer.
d. er kann das Portemonnaie nicht finden.
e. sie kocht Kaiserschmarren.

# 5 Nacherzählen

Put the sentences in logical order to make a brief summary of the story.

1. Zuerst kocht die Großmutter Kaiserschmarren für den Flori.

Dann gibt sie Flori auch das Geld. 4

Dann fragt Flori die Großmutter, was er für sie einkaufen soll. 2

Zuletzt kauft er auch Blumen für die Großmutter. 6

Die Tomaten kauft er im Supermarkt, das Brot beim Bäcker und das Hackfleisch beim Metzger. 5

Sie gibt Flori den Einkaufszettel. 3

Nach dem Einkaufen kommt Flori wieder zurück. 7

Aber er kann das Portemonnaie nicht finden und geht es suchen. 8

*Asking what you should do; telling someone what to do*

### Einkaufen gehen

Look at the ads below. What type of store is represented by each ad? What other things could you buy at each store?

*Beim Bäcker Motz*

Semmel
Stück -,30

Brot
1 kg 3,40

Brezeln
Stück -,55

Torte
Stück 2,40

## BEIM METZGER SEIBT

Hackfleisch
1 kg
5,98

Hähnchen
7,95

Aufschnitt
100 g 1,19

Bratwurst
100 g 1,29

Im Obst-
und Gemüseladen
Frisch

Tomaten
1 kg 4,80

Kartoffeln
1 kg 1,98

Äpfel
1 kg 3,20

Salat
St. -,99

Trauben
1 kg 4,98

# IM SUPERMARKT KRAUS

Kleefeld
H
fettarme
Milch
1,5 %
1 Liter

Milch
l 2,20

Eier
10 St.
2,20

IDEE
KAFFEE

Kaffee
1 Pfd.
7,49

Süßrahm-
Butter
Deutsche Markenbutter

Butter
250 g
2,20

Fisch      100 g 1,69

WARBURGER
ZUCKER
FEIN

Zucker
1 kg 4,20

Käse
100 g
1,39

Goldstaub
Mehl
TYPE 405

Mehl
500 g
Beutel
2,80

## LEBENSMITTEL • GANZ PREISWERT!

Although there are many large, modern supermarkets in Germany, many people still shop in small specialty stores or at the open-air markets in the center of town. Many Germans shop frequently, buying just what they need for one or two days. Refrigerators are generally much smaller than in the United States, and people prefer to buy things fresh.

## 6 Hör gut zu!

Im Supermarkt: Milch, Butter
Beim Metzger: Hackfleisch, Aufschnitt, Wurst, Bratwurst
Beim Bäcker: Semmeln, Brot, Brezeln

Flori and Claudia are at a café discussing their plans for the day. They decide to do their shopping together. Make lists of the things they are going to buy at each of the following kinds of stores.

im Supermarkt  beim Bäcker
beim Metzger  im Obst- und Gemüseladen

Im Obst- und Gemüseladen: Äpfel

Milch  Kuchen  Wurst
Hackfleisch  Aufschnitt
Brot  Äpfel
Fisch  Bratwurst
Butter  Semmeln  Brezeln

## 7 Was möchtest du kaufen?

Look again at the ads on page 197 and decide what you would like to buy at each store. Make an **Einkaufszettel** using the stores listed in Activity 6 as heads, then add up the prices. How do the prices compare with what you would spend at home?

## 8 Was möchte dein Partner?

Working with your grocery list from Activity 7, ask your partner what items he or she would like to buy. Take notes. Then switch roles. Be prepared to report to the class what your partner said.

BEISPIEL  DU  **Beim Bäcker möchte er/sie ...**

---

## SO SAGT MAN DAS!

### Asking what you should do

If you were going to help a friend or relative run errands, you would first ask what you should do:

The responses might be:

**Was soll ich für dich tun?**
**Wo soll ich das Brot kaufen?**
**Soll ich das Fleisch im Supermarkt holen?**

**Und die Tomaten? Wo soll ich sie kaufen?**

**Du kannst für mich einkaufen gehen.**
**Beim Bäcker.**

**Nein, du holst das besser beim Metzger.**

**Im Gemüseladen, bitte.**

What do you think the word **soll** means? In the sentences with **soll** and **kannst** what happens to the word order? Where is the main verb?

## Grammatik The verb sollen

**Sollen** is used to express what you *should* or *are supposed to* do. Which verbs do you already know that are similar to **sollen**? In what ways are they similar? Here are the forms of **sollen**:

Ich **soll** nach Hause gehen.          Wir **sollen** zum Blumengeschäft.

Du **sollst** nach Hause gehen.          Ihr **sollt** zum Supermarkt gehen.

Er/sie **soll** zum Bäcker.          Sie (pl)/Sie **sollen** zum Metzger gehen.

## 9 Sätze bauen!

Wie viele Fragen kannst du bauen? (Be sure to match the food items with the correct store.)

| Sollen<br>Sollt<br>Sollst<br>Soll | ich<br>wir<br>er<br>ihr<br>du<br>Flori und<br>Claudia | | | holen?<br>kaufen? |

Examples:
**Soll ich die Wurst beim Metzger holen? Soll er die Semmeln beim Bäcker kaufen?**

## 10 Wo soll ich ... kaufen?

You are an exchange student living in Germany. Your host mother has asked you to go shopping for her and has given you the grocery list. Using the list to the right, take turns with your partner asking and answering where you should buy the various items.

> Wurst
> Käse
> Brot
> Äpfel
> Semmeln
> Salat
> Mineralwasser
> Zucker
> Aufschnitt

## SO SAGT MAN DAS!

### Telling someone what to do

You have learned one way to tell someone what he or she can do to help you using **können**. Here are some other ways to express the same thing:

Someone might ask:          The response might be:

**Was soll ich für dich tun?**          **Geh bitte einkaufen!** *or*

**Tomaten und Milch holen, bitte!**

What would be the English equivalent of the first response?[1] Look at the second response. Why do you think only a phrase is used here?[2]

1. *Go shopping, please.* 2. The command form **geh** is understood.

Markus: zum Supermarkt gehen und Tomaten holen
Mara: zum Bäcker gehen und Semmeln und einen Kuchen holen
Flori: den Tisch decken, Limo und Mineralwasser holen

## 11   Hör gut zu!

Flori's grandmother is preparing lunch on Saturday for him and his friends, Markus and Mara. She needs help and tells everyone what to do. Listen and decide what each person is supposed to do. Under each of their names (Markus, Mara, Flori) list their tasks.

## 12   Alles ist in Unordnung!

Answers will vary. Examples:
Putz die Fenster! Spül das Geschirr!

Frank has been really busy with school and has neglected his household chores for quite a while. Look at the illustration below and take turns with your classmates saying what you think Frank's parents would tell him to do in order to get things cleaned up.

## 13   Eine Fete

You are having a party and two friends are helping you get ready. You've already gone shopping but have forgotten some of the things you need. Get together with two other classmates and, using your lists from Activity 7, each of you chooses six things you still need to buy. First you are the host, and your partners will ask what they can do to help. Tell each person to buy three items and where to buy them. Then switch roles so that each person plays the host once.

# Was machst du für andere Leute?

LANDESKUNDE

How do you think students in German-speaking countries help others? We asked several students whom they help and in what ways they help them. Before you read, try to guess what they might say.

**Silvana,** *Berlin*
„Zweimal in der Woche gebe ich Nachhilfe, und hab' ich einen kleinen Schüler. Der ist in der dritten Klasse, und dem geb' ich Nachhilfe in Rechtschreibung und Lesen und Mathematik."

**Brigitte,** *Bietigheim*
„Also, ich hab' mit Kindern zu tun. Ich hab' mal Kinderkirche sonntags, und da beschäftigt man sich mit kleinen Kindern und spielt mit denen, und das mach' ich aber unregelmäßig. Also ich habe das schon lange Zeit nicht mehr gemacht."

**Sandra,** *Stuttgart*
„Bei uns in der Nachbarschaft gibt's grad' ältere Leute. Und unter uns wohnt eine Frau, die ... für die mach' ich manchmal kleine Einkäufe oder geh' einfach nur hin und rede mit ihr, damit sie halt nicht grad' so allein ist, und besuch' sie einfach oder bring' ihr halt mal was rüber, wenn wir zum Beispiel Obst aus dem Garten haben."

**Iwan,** *Bietigheim*
„Also meistens da helf' ich zum Beispiel meinem Bruder irgendwie, wenn er irgendwelche Probleme in der Schule hat. Und wenn ich bei meiner Oma bin, dann helf' ich auch meiner Oma."

**A.** 1. Write each student's name. Then write whom each student helps.
2. The people whom the students help fall into two groups. What are they? With a partner, make a chart for these two groups and list the ways in which the students help each one. two groups; young children, older people
3. Now make a list of the people you help and how you help them. Ask your partner what he or she does to help others: **Was machst du für andere Leute?** Then switch roles.

**B.** With your classmates, discuss some of the ways you help other people. Do you do any of the same things the German students do? What is your impression: Do people help others more in Germany than in the United States? What are your reasons for deciding one way or the other? When you have finished your discussion, write a brief essay explaining your answers.

*Talking about quantities; saying you want something else*

### Und wieviel?

wiegen ungefähr
1 Kilo (kg)
= 1000 Gramm (g)
= (*2.2 lb.*)

wiegen ungefähr
1/2 (ein halbes) Kilo
= 500 Gramm
= 1 (deutsches)
Pfund (Pfd.)

wiegen ungefähr
100 Gramm

1 Liter (l) ist
ein bißchen mehr
als *1 quart*
= (*1.057 quarts*)

2 Pfund = 1 Kilo = 1000 Gramm

Das amerikanische
Pfund hat nur 453 g.

Das deutsche
Pfund hat 500 g.

## SO SAGT MAN DAS!

### Talking about quantities

When shopping for groceries in Germany, you will need to know how much to ask for using weights. For example, at the butcher's the salesperson might ask you:

You might respond:

**Was bekommen Sie?**          **Aufschnitt und Hackfleisch, bitte.**
**Wieviel Hackfleisch?**        **500 Gramm Hackfleisch.**
**Und wieviel Aufschnitt?**     **100 Gramm, bitte!**

## 14 Hör gut zu!

Tomaten - ein Pfund          Kartoffeln - ein Kilo
Äpfel - zwei Pfund           Trauben - 1/2 Pfund

You are standing in line at the **Gemüseladen** and overhear other customers asking the salesperson for specific amounts of certain items. First, listen to the conversations and write down what the customers are asking for. Then listen again and decide how much of each item they want.

Look back at the ads on page 197 and find the abbreviations that are used to describe quantities. What do they stand for? How many different units of measurement are listed? How does this compare with measures in the United States? In German-speaking countries, the metric system is used for weights and measures. At the open-air markets, and in many specialty stores, such as the bakery and the butcher shop, you will have to ask the salesperson for certain foods rather than serve yourself. You will need to be able to tell the vendor how much of each item you would like.

## 15 Was bekommen Sie?

You are in a store using the shopping list on the right. Your partner, the salesperson, asks what you need, and you respond using at least four items from the list and the quantities indicated. Then switch roles.

| | |
|---|---|
| VERKÄUFER | **Was ...?** |
| DU | **Ich brauche ...** |
| VERKÄUFER | **Wieviel?** |
| DU | **...** |

1 kg Tomaten
250 g Kaffee
250 g Butter
1 l Milch
100 g Käse
200 g Aufschnitt
500 g Hackfleisch

## SO SAGT MAN DAS!

### Saying that you want something else

In **Kapitel 5** you learned how to tell a salesperson what you would like. You will also need to know how to tell him or her if you need something else.

The salesperson might ask:
**Sonst noch etwas?**
*or*
**Was bekommen Sie noch?**
*or*
**Haben Sie noch einen Wunsch?**

You might respond:
**Ja, ich brauche noch ein Kilo Kartoffeln.**
**Ich bekomme noch sechs Semmeln.**
**Nein, danke.** *or*
**Danke, das ist alles.**

In several of the questions and answers, the word **noch** appears. Can you guess what it means?

## 16 Hör gut zu!

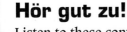

Listen to these conversations in various food stores and determine whether the response in each case is logical or not.

1. logisch
2. unlogisch
3. logisch
4. unlogisch
5. logisch

| | logisch | unlogisch |
|---|---|---|
| 1 | | |
| 2 | | |

## 17 Noch einen Wunsch?

You are trying out new recipes tonight, and you still need to buy several things. Make shopping lists for the two recipes below. Then get together with two other classmates. One will play the salesperson at the supermarket, and the other will be another customer shopping for the second recipe. The salesperson will ask the customers what and how much they need and if they need something else.

### Salami-Riesenpizza

Pizzateig (32 cm ⌀) für 2 Personen mit 4–6 Eßlöffeln Tomatenstückchen belegen. 125 g Pizzakäse in Streifen schneiden, gitterförmig darüber legen.

10–12 Scheiben Salami und 6–8 blättrig geschnittene Champignons auf der Pizza verteilen.

Mit 1/2 Teelöffel Pizzagewürz bestreuen und bei 250 Grad 14 Minuten im Ofen backen.

### Pikanter Quark

Zutaten:

250 g Quark
- etwa 4 Eßlöffel Sahne
- etwa 4 Eßlöffel Milch
- 1 Knoblauchzehe
- 1 Teelöffel Kümmel
- Salz

Insgesamt etwa 2370 Joule/565 Kalorien

## 18 Das Angebot der Woche

Pick a specific kind of food store and make your own ad. Either cut pictures from a newspaper or draw your own pictures. You may want to refer to page 197 for a model. Below are some additional grocery items you may want to include. Remember to include prices per unit (**Kilo**, **Gramm**, **Pfund**, or **Liter**).

**Und dann noch . . .**

| | |
|---|---|
| Bananen | Joghurt |
| Erdnußbutter *peanut butter* | Ananas *pineapple* |
| Marmelade *jam, jelly* | Birnen *pears* |
| Erdbeeren *strawberries* | Melonen |
| Apfelstrudel | Müsli |

**LERNTRICK**

When you are learning a lot of new words, group them together in meaningful categories: group baked goods under **die Bäckerei**, meat items under **die Metzgerei**, etc. Putting the words in context will help you recall them more easily.

## 19 Für mein Notizbuch

Schreib in dein Notizbuch, wo du gern einkaufst! Was kaufst du? Was kaufst du gern? Was ist dein Lieblingsgericht (*favorite dish*)? Welches Essen schmeckt dir und welches Essen schmeckt dir nicht?

*Giving reasons; saying where you were and what you bought*

SPAR supermarkt

*D*ie elegante Fassade fällt auf, weil sie frei von jeglichen Preisplakaten ist.

„Für mich gibt's zum Braten nichts Besseres, denn Butaris und der feine Buttergeschmack sind einfach unschlagbar."

Milch veredelt den Geschmack und ist gut für Ihr Wohlbefinden, denn Milch bringt erst die Wirkung des Koffeins in Einklang!

**Butaris** ®
BUTTERSCHMALZ
*Zum Braten, Backen, Kochen und Fritieren* soft 250 g

1 A supermarket, milk, shortening. Milk is supposed to improve the taste of coffee and harmonize the effect of caffein. **Butaris** is ideal for frying because of its buttery taste. SPAR Supermarket has an elegant look because the display window is not covered with price posters and signs.

2. **Weil** and **denn** mean "because." They express the reason for something.

3. In a **weil** clause the verb is in final position, in a **denn** clause it is in second position.

## 20 Warum?

Look at the ads above and answer the following questions.

1. Using the reading strategies you have learned so far, try to get the gist of each ad. What is each ad promoting? What reason does each ad give to persuade you to buy the product or to shop at a particular store?

2. Identify the words **weil** and **denn**. What do they mean? How do you know?

3. In the **SPAR Supermarkt** ad, what is the position of the verb in a clause that starts with **weil**? How does this compare with clauses starting with **denn**?

# SO SAGT MAN DAS!

## Giving reasons

In **Kapitel 7** you learned how to make an excuse and express obligation using **müssen: Claudia kommt nicht mit. Sie muß zu Hause helfen.** You can also do this with expressions beginning with **weil** or **denn**.

A friend might ask you:

**Kannst du für mich einkaufen gehen?**

You might respond giving a reason:

**Es geht nicht, denn ich mache die Hausaufgaben.** *or*
**Ich kann jetzt nicht (gehen), weil ich die Hausaufgaben mache.**

## 21 Hör gut zu!

Claudia/nein/macht Hausaufgaben/
Flori/ja/
Christian/nein/muß zu Hause helfen/

Mara is having a party on the weekend. Listen to the messages left on her answering machine and take down the following information: the name of the person who called, if that person is coming to the party, and if not, the reason why not.

Stefan/ja/
Barbara/ja/
Brigitte/nein/lernt für die Prüfung

| wer | ja oder nein? | warum (nicht)? |
|---|---|---|
| BEISPIEL Markus | nein | geht ins Kino |

### Ein wenig *G*rammatik

**Denn** and **weil** are called *conjunctions*. Using them will help your German sound more natural. Both words begin clauses that give reasons for something (for example, why you can or can't do something). Clauses beginning with **denn** have the regular word order pattern, that is, the conjugated verb is in second position. However, in clauses that begin with **weil**, the conjugated verb is in final position.

## 22 Pläne fürs Wochenende

Using the cues in the left hand column or other activities, tell your classmates the things you can do this weekend. Then identify the activities you cannot do and give a reason from the right hand column using **weil**. Pay attention to word order!

Answers will vary. Examples:
Ich kann nicht Baseball spielen, weil ich zu Hause helfe.

BEISPIEL    DU    **Am Wochenende kann ich ins Kino gehen.**
**Am Wochenende kann ich nicht ins Konzert gehen, weil ich keine Zeit habe.**

Am Wochenende

**Was?**
Baseball spielen
ins Kino gehen
tanzen gehen
Klamotten kaufen
wandern
ins Café gehen
Freunde besuchen
Volleyball spielen
Pizza essen
?

weil

**Warum?**
ich habe keine Zeit
ich habe kein Geld
ich muß zu Hause helfen
ich mähe den Rasen
ich putze die Fenster
ich lerne für die (Mathe)prüfung
ich mache Hausaufgaben
die Großeltern besuchen uns
?

## 23 Bist du damit einverstanden? *Do you agree?*

Look at the following statements. Agree or disagree and give a reason why. First write your answers, then discuss your opinions with your classmates.

BEISPIEL **Ich bin damit einverstanden, weil/denn ...**
**Ich bin nicht damit einverstanden, weil/denn ...**

1. Jugendliche sollen das ganze Jahr in die Schule gehen.
2. Jugendliche sollen nicht Auto fahren, bevor sie 18 sind.
3. Wir sollen mehr Geld für die Umwelt (*environment*) ausgeben.
4. Jugendliche müssen vor 10 Uhr abends zu Hause sein.

## SO SAGT MAN DAS!

### Saying where you were and what you bought

If a friend wants to find out where you were or what you bought, he or she might ask:

You might respond:

**Wo warst du heute morgen?**

**Zuerst war ich
beim Bäcker und dann beim Metzger.
Danach war ich im Supermarkt und
zuletzt war ich im Kaufhaus.**

**Und was hast du beim
Bäcker gekauft?**
**Wo warst du gestern?**

**Ich habe Brot gekauft.**
**Ich war zu Hause.**

What do the phrases **ich war** and **du warst** mean? What are their English equivalents? What other words or expressions in these sentences indicate the past?

## WORTSCHATZ

gestern *yesterday*
vorgestern *day before yesterday*
gestern abend *yesterday evening*

heute morgen *this morning*
heute nachmittag *this afternoon*
letztes Wochenende *last weekend*

## Grammatik   The past tense of sein

**War** and **warst** are past tense forms of the verb **sein** (*to be*) and are used to talk about the past. Look at the following sentences.

Ich **war** heute beim Metzger.
Du **warst** gestern im Supermarkt.
Er/Sie **war** am Montag beim Bäcker.

Wir **waren** gestern zu Hause.
Ihr **wart** im Kino.
Sie (pl)/Sie **waren** letzte Woche
in der Stadt.

What are the English equivalents of these sentences?

## 24 Hör gut zu!

Listen to the following exchanges as Claudia talks with her friends. For each conversation, decide if the person Claudia is talking to has already done the activity mentioned or plans to do it in the future. 1. plans to do 2. already done 3. plans to do 4. already done 5. already done 6. plans to do

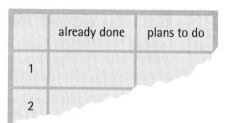

| | already done | plans to do |
|---|---|---|
| 1 | | |
| 2 | | |

## 25 Wo waren Flori und Mara heute?

Look at the pages out of Mara's and Flori's lists of things to do. Your partner will ask you where Flori was during the day. Use his schedule to answer your partner's questions. Then switch roles and ask your partner about Mara's day. Remember to use **zuerst**, **dann**, **danach**, and **zuletzt** to organize your answers.

Mara
10:00 Supermarkt für Mutti
12:00 mit Markus im Café essen
13:00 ins Einkaufszentrum gehen, Klamotten kaufen
14:30 Zimmer aufräumen

Flori
9:30 Brot und Äpfel für die Omi kaufen
13:00 zu Hause Mittag essen
13:30 Omis Fenster putzen
15:00 Kaufhaus, Fußball kaufen

## 26 Wer hat was gemacht?

Claudia has been trying to make plans with her friends, but she has had a hard time getting hold of anyone. Match each exchange with one of the illustrations below. 1. a 2. c 3. d 4. b

a.

b.

c.

d.

**1. CLAUDIA** Sag mal, Petra, wo warst du denn heute morgen?

**PETRA** Ich war in der Stadt. Zuerst war ich beim Bäcker, dann im Obstladen. Heute abend essen meine Tante und mein Onkel bei uns.

**2. CLAUDIA** Und wo war denn die Michaela? Weißt du das? Sie war auch nicht zu Hause.

**PETRA** Na, sie war im Eiscafé mit Gabi und Susanne. Die drei essen immer nur Joghurteis! Ingo hat sie später in der Disko gesehen.

**3. CLAUDIA** Tag, Oma! Wo warst du denn heute morgen? Ich bin vorbeigekommen, und du warst nicht da.

**OMA** Die Tante Dorle war da, und wir haben im Café am Markt zu Mittag gegessen. Ach, Kind, das Essen war köstlich!

**4. CLAUDIA** Hallo, ihr zwei! Wo wart ihr am Samstag abend?

**HEIKE** Robert und ich, wir waren im Kino — im neuen Cinedom. Mensch, das war echt toll! Wir haben den Film *Cape Fear* gesehen. Unheimlich spannend!

## 27 Einkaufsbummel

Your partner just got back from shopping **am langen Samstag.** Your partner will decide on three items that he or she bought at each of the stores pictured. Ask your partner what he or she bought at each store. Switch roles, and be prepared to tell the class about your **Einkaufsbummel.**

## Richtig aussprechen / Richtig lesen

**A.** To practice or review the following sounds, say the words and sentences below after your teacher or after the recording.

1. The letters **ü** and **ö**: In **Kapitel 1** you learned how to pronounce the letters **ü** and **ö** as long vowels, as in **Tschüs** and **Hör**. However, when the letters **ü** and **ö** are followed by two or more consonants, they are pronounced as short vowels.
**müssen, Stück, Würste / Wir müssen fünf Stück Kuchen holen.**
**können, köstlich, Wörterbuch / Könnt ihr für mich ein Wörterbuch kaufen?**

2. The letter combinations **ei** and **ie**: The letter combination **ei** is pronounced like the *i* in the English word *mine*. The combination **ie** is pronounced like the *e* in the English word *me*.
**Bäckerei, Eier, Fleisch / Kauf das Fleisch in der Metzgerei!**
**wieder, wieviel, lieber / Wieviel bekommen Sie? Vier Stück?**

3. The letter **z**: In **Kapitel 2** you learned that the letter **z** is always pronounced like the *ts* sound in the English word *hits,* although in German, this sound often occurs at the beginning of a word.
**Zeit, zahlen, ziehen / Ich habe keine Zeit, in den Zoo zu gehen.**

## Richtig schreiben / Diktat

**B.** Write down the sentences that you hear.

*Richtig essen!*

**LESETRICK**
**Combine the strategies that you have learned** As you learn to read German, keep in mind that you will use many different reading strategies at the same time. You will combine them in different ways, depending on the type of text you are trying to read. You will probably go through several steps every time you read new material: you may start by looking at visual clues, then skim to get the gist, scan for specific information, and finally read the text for comprehension.

1. Before you read these ads, think about what foods you like to eat. Which of the food items you eat on a regular basis are really good for you?

2. Compare your weekly diet to a partner's and try to figure out together what percentage of your diet is carbohydrate, fat, and protein.

3. Look at the illustrations in the ads, then try to figure out the meaning of the boldfaced titles and subtitles. Judging from what you learned from these two sources, what do you think these ads are about? b
   a. snack foods
   b. healthful foods
   c. ways to make sandwiches

4. You have figured out the general topic of these articles. Now skim the ads to get the gist. What information are these ads trying to get across to you?

These foods taste good and are good for you.

**MÜLLER BROT**

**HOTLINE**
Armin Roßmeier
08165/79345

## Das Thema im Juli:
**Die herzhaften Fünf – Original Mühlbacher Bauernbrote**

Nur wenige Brote verdienen den Namen Bauernbrot. Was darf rein, was nicht? Der bekannte Ernährungsexperte und Fernsehkoch Armin Roßmeier sagt Ihnen alles, was Sie schon immer über Brot wissen wollten: Rufen Sie Ihn an. Jeden ersten Mittwoch im Monat:
7. Juli, 4. August, 1. September

*Das haben Sie jetzt davon.*

Alle wollen Leerdammer, nur:

Manche mögen's leicht. Na gut.

Dann nehmen manche jetzt eben den

Leerdammer Light. Und wer's nicht

leicht nimmt, läßt sich den

Leerdammer so schmecken wie bisher.

**LEERDAMMER Light** 15%

**LEERDAMMER**

## GOURMETS GENIESSEN PUR.

### DER LEICHTE
### Almenrausch
WEICHKÄSE
NEU
150 g ℮ · Fettstufe · Nur 20% Fett

**SAHNIGER GESCHMACK AUF DIE LEICHTE ART.**
Der Leichte Almenrausch. Eine Weichkäse-Spezialität mit dem sahnig-milden Geschmack, den Gourmets noch pur zu genießen verstehen. Almenrausch gibt es auch extrasahnig als de Luxe und mit feinem Knoblauch.

### GUTER GESCHMACK AUS TRADITION.

## Der Mensch ist, wie er ißt.

Körperliche Fitness und Leistungsvermögen beruhen in erster Linie auf einer ausgewogenen Ernährung. Das gilt für den Spitzensport ebenso wie für den alltäglichen Lebens-„Marathon".

Wir alle benötigen bestimmte Mengen an Kohlehydraten, Proteinen, Vitaminen und Mineralstoffen, um gesund und in Form zu bleiben.

Wichtigste Voraussetzung für Leistungsvermögen und körperliche Fitness ist die richtige Kombination der drei Hauptnahrungsgruppen.

**Als Faustregel für den Wochendurchschnitt gilt:** 50 % Kohlehydrate, 30 % Fett und 20 % Eiweiß sind ideal für 100 %iges Wohlbefinden.

**Auf das Frühstück kommt es an.**

Besonders wichtig ist es, wie Sie den Tag beginnen: Das „richtige" Frühstück ist die wichtigste Mahlzeit des Tages. Dafür serviert Ihnen Müller-Brot auf den folgenden Seiten wertvolle Tips: Gesunden Appetit!

**Beispielhafte Fitmacher für den Start in den Tag:**

## Die Vollkorn-Spezialitäten von Müller-Brot – Fitness, die man essen kann.

---

5. Based on your knowledge of German, match these compound words with the most logical English equivalent.

> **Weißt du noch?** Remember that knowing the meaning of root words can help you guess the meaning of many compound words.

1. Mahlzeit  e
2. Fernsehkoch  d
3. alltäglich  a
4. Ernährungs-experte  f
5. Vollkornbrot  c
6. der Weich-käse  b

a. daily
b. soft cheese
c. whole-grain bread
d. television chef
e. meal
f. nutrition expert

Wohlbefinden

6. Read the ad for **Vollkornbrot**. Which word in the ad means "well-being"? According to the ad, in order to have 100% physical well-being, what is the percentage of carbohydrates you should eat on the average in a week? What is the percentage of fat? And what is the percentage of protein?   50% 30% 20%   7. breakfast

7. According to the ad, what is the most important meal of the day?

8. What is the name of the person who has the hotline? When can you call him? What kind of information would he give you?

9. Scan the articles for the following information.
   a. Who can enjoy **Almenrausch** soft cheese?   Gourmets
   b. What kind of **Leerdammer** do some people want to eat?   light
   c. What company advertises itself as a whole-grain specialist?   Müller-Brot

10. You are an exchange student in Germany. You and your friends are opening up a student-run snack stand at school, and you plan to have plenty of healthful snacks. Write an article for the school newspaper describing the foods you will offer at your stand.

8. **Armin Roßmeier;** first Wednesday of the month: July 7, August 4, September 1.

# **A**NWENDUNG

| | |
|---|---|
| 1 Kilo Tomaten | 1 Brot |
| 2 Pfd. Kartoffeln | 200 g Käse |
| 2 Kilo Äpfel | 1 Pfd. Kaffee |
| 1 Pfd. Butter | 1 Liter Orangensaft |
| 10 Eier | |

**1** Flori's mother would like him to go shopping for her. Listen as she tells him what to get, and make a shopping list for Flori. Be sure to include the amounts she needs.

**2** You and a friend are about to go grocery shopping. You have only 25 marks and want to get the most for your money. **Kaufmarkt** always has great daily specials. Look at the ads on the right and tell your partner eight things you want to buy and how much of each you are buying. Your partner will make a list and add up the cost for you. When finished, switch roles.

**3** Could you convince someone to buy a specific product? Bring in pictures of several food or clothing items from a magazine, or use props, and create a commercial to convince your classmates to buy one or more of the products. Use statements with **denn** and **weil** to persuade them. Then present your commercial to the class. Here are some phrases that might be helpful:

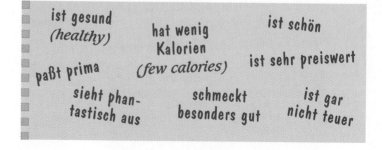

**4** You and two of your friends work with a local charity organization that helps people who have a hard time doing things around the house. Your team has been assigned three different people to help today. As leader of the team, it is your job to go over each list with each volunteer and tell that person what to do. When you have finished, switch roles, so that each person on the team is the leader once.

Frau Meyer:
Fenster putzen
Müll sortieren
½ Pfd. Kaffee kaufen
Staub saugen
5 Semmeln kaufen
375 g Wurst kaufen

Herr Schmidt:
Wohnzimmer aufräumen
500 g Aufschnitt kaufen
250 g Butter kaufen
Müll sortieren
400 g Hackfleisch
holen
Blumen gießen

Frau Heppner:
Blumen gießen
1 Kilo Kartoffeln kaufen
Staub saugen
Fisch holen
Rasen mähen
1 Pfd. Tomaten kaufen

**5** A relative sent you 100 marks for your birthday. Write a letter thanking him or her for the money and describing what you bought with it.

Liebe(r) ═══!

Herzlichen Dank für das
Geburtstagsgeschenk. Ich habe …

Dein(e) …

**6**

# R O L L E N S P I E L

Get together with a classmate and role-play the following scenes.

**a.** You and a friend are preparing lunch. Read the recipe for **Obstsalat** and tell your friend what you need, where to get it, and how much you need based on the recipe. Your friend will make a shopping list.

**b.** With your list in hand, go to the store to get what you need. Your partner plays the salesperson and will ask what you need, how much, and if you need anything else.

## OBSTSALAT

1 Apfel, 2 Bananen, 1 Birne,
1 Kiwi, 150 g Trauben (blau),
1 Orange, 2 EL Zitronensaft,
3 EL Honig, 2 EL Rosinen,
2 EL Walnußkerne, gehackt

Zubereitung: 20 Minuten

185 Kalorien

# KANN ICH'S WIRKLICH?

Was soll ich für dich tun?
a. Du kannst für mich Brot beim Bäcker kaufen.
b. Du kannst für mich Hackfleisch beim Metzger kaufen.
c. Du kannst für mich Milch im Supermarkt kaufen.
d. Du kannst für mich Äpfel im Obstladen kaufen.

**Can you ask someone what you should do using sollen?** (p. 198)

**1** How would you ask someone what you should do for him or her? How might he or she answer using the following items?

a. bread: at the baker's   c. milk: at the supermarket
b. ground meat: at the butcher's   d. apples: at the produce store

a. Hol das Brot ...
b. Kauf das Fleisch
c. Kauf die Milch ...
d. Kauf die Äpfel ...

**Can you tell someone what to do using a du-command?** (p. 199)

**2** How would you tell someone where to buy the food items above?

**3** How would you tell a friend to

a. Mäh den Rasen!   c. Räum das Zimmer auf!
b. Kauf 500 g Tomaten!   d. Kauf sechs Äpfel!

a. mow the lawn   c. clean the room
b. buy 500 grams of tomatoes   d. get 6 apples

**Can you ask for specific quantities?** (p. 202)

**4** How would you tell a salesperson you need the following things?

a. 500 Gramm Hackfleisch   d. 1 Pfd. Tomaten
b. Brot   e. 2 Kilo Kartoffeln
c. 1 Liter Milch

a. 500g Hackfleisch, bitte!
b. Ein Brot, bitte!
c. Einen Liter Milch, bitte!
d. Ein Pfund Tomaten, bitte.
e. Zwei Kilo Kartoffeln, bitte.

**Can you say that you want something else?** (p. 203)

**5** How would a salesperson ask you if you wanted something else? How would you respond using the following items?

5. Sonst noch etwas? or Was bekommen Sie noc
or Noch einen Wunsch?

a. 10 Semmeln   b. 100 Gramm Aufschnitt   c. 200 Gramm Käse

a. Ich bekomme noch zehn Semmeln.   b. Ich brauche noch 100 Gramm Aufschnitt.   c. Ich bekomme n
200 Gramm Kä

**Can you give reasons using denn and weil?** (p. 206)

**6** How would you say that you can't do each of the following and give a reason why not?

Answers will vary. Examples: Ich kann nicht ins Kino gehen, denn ich habe kein Geld. ..., weil ich zu Hause helfe

a. go to a movie   b. go shopping   c. go to a café

**Can you say where you were (using sein) and what you bought?** (p. 207)

**7** How would you ask someone where he or she was yesterday? How would you ask two friends? Can you say where you were using the following cues?

a. at the baker's in the morning   c. at the butcher's yesterday morning
b. at the supermarket yesterday   d. at home this afternoon

**8** How would you ask your friend what he or she bought? How would you say that you bought the following items?

a. bread   c. a sweater   e. pants
b. a shirt   d. cheese

7. Wo warst du gestern? Wo wart ihr gestern?
a. Ich war am Morgen beim Bäcker.
b. Ich war gestern im Supermarkt.
c. Ich war gestern morgen beim Metzger.
d. Ich war heute Nachmittag zu Hause.

8. Was hast du gekauft?
a. Ich habe Brot gekauft.
b. Ich habe das (ein) Hemd gekauft.
c. ... den (einen) Pulli
d. ... den Käse
e. ... die (eine) Hose

## ERSTE STUFE
### ASKING WHAT YOU SHOULD DO; TELLING SOMEONE WHAT TO DO

sollen    *should, to be supposed to*
einkaufen gehen    *to go shopping*
einkaufen (sep)    *to shop*
holen    *to get, fetch*
das Angebot der Woche    *weekly special*
der Laden, ¨    *store*
die Lebensmittel (pl)    *groceries*
die Bäckerei, -en    *bakery*
 beim Bäcker    *at the baker's*
das Brot, -e    *bread*
die Semmel, -n*    *roll*
die Brezel, -n    *pretzel*
die Torte, -n    *layer cake*

die Metzgerei, -en    *butcher shop*
 beim Metzger    *at the butcher's*
das Fleisch    *meat*
das Hackfleisch    *ground meat (mixture of beef and pork)*
die Wurst, ¨e    *sausage*
der Aufschnitt    *cold cuts*
das Hähnchen,-    *chicken*
der Obst- und Gemüseladen, ¨    *fresh produce store*
 im Obst- und Gemüseladen    *at the produce store*
 das Obst    *fruit*
 die Traube, -n    *grape*
 der Apfel, ¨    *apple*
 das Gemüse    *vegetables*
 die Kartoffel, -n    *potato*

die Tomate, -n    *tomato*
der Salat, -e    *lettuce*
der Supermarkt, ¨e    *supermarket*
 im Supermarkt    *at the supermarket*
die Milch    *milk*
die Butter    *butter*
der Käse    *cheese*
das Ei, -er    *egg*
der Kaffee    *coffee*
der Zucker    *sugar*
das Mehl    *flour*
der Fisch, -e    *fish*

### OTHER USEFUL WORDS
besser    *better*
frisch    *fresh*

---

## ZWEITE STUFE
### TALKING ABOUT QUANTITIES

Wieviel?    *How much?*
wiegen    *to weigh*
das Pfund    *pound*
das Gramm    *gram*
das Kilo    *kilogram*

der Liter    *liter*
ein bißchen mehr    *a little more*

### SAYING YOU WANT SOMETHING ELSE
Sonst noch etwas?    *Anything else?*

Haben Sie noch einen Wunsch?    *Would you like anything else?*
Ich brauche noch ...    *I also need...*
Das ist alles.    *That's all.*

### OTHER USEFUL WORDS
ungefähr    *about, approximately*

---

## DRITTE STUFE
### GIVING REASONS
denn    *because, for*
weil    *because*

### SAYING WHERE YOU WERE AND WHAT YOU BOUGHT
war    *was (see p. 207)*
Wo warst du?    *Where were you?*
Ich war beim Bäcker.    *I was at the baker's.*

Was hast du gekauft?    *What did you buy?*
Ich habe Brot gekauft.    *I bought bread.*

### TIME EXPRESSIONS
heute morgen    *this morning*
heute nachmittag    *this afternoon*
gestern    *yesterday*
gestern abend    *yesterday evening*

vorgestern    *day before yesterday*
letztes Wochenende    *last weekend*
letzte Woche    *last week*

*In northern Germany these are called **Brötchen**, and in Baden-Württemberg and in other areas in southern Germany they are called **Wecken**.

# Kapitel 9: Amerikaner in München *Chapter Overview*

| Los geht's! pp. 218-220 | München besuchen, p. 218 | | | *Video Guide* |
|---|---|---|---|---|
| | **FUNCTIONS** | **GRAMMAR** | **CULTURE** | **RE-ENTRY** |
| **Erste Stufe** pp. 221-224 | Talking about where something is located, *p. 222* | The verb **wissen**, and dependent clauses with **wo**, *p. 222* | •**Ein wenig Landeskunde:** The German **Innenstadt**, *p. 221* <br> •**Landeskunde: Was ißt du gern?** *p. 224* | Vocabulary, types of stores, *p. 223* (from **Kapitel 8**) |
| **Zweite Stufe** pp. 225-228 | Asking for and giving directions, *p. 226* | •The verbs **fahren** and **gehen**, *p. 227* <br> •The formal commands with **Sie**, *p. 227* | Map of a German neighborhood, *p. 225* | •Vocabulary, types of stores, *p. 226* (from **Kapitel 8**) <br> •Preposition **zu**, p. 226 (from **Kapitel 1**) <br> •**Du**-commands, *p. 227* (from **Kapitel 8**) |
| **Dritte Stufe** pp. 229-233 | •Talking about what there is to eat and drink, *p. 229* <br> •Saying you do or don't want more, *p. 230* <br> •Expressing opinions, *p. 232* | •The phrase **es gibt**, *p. 229* <br> •Using **noch ein**, *p. 230* <br> •Using **kein**, *p. 231* <br> •The conjunction **daß**, *p. 232* | •**Imbißstube** menu, *p. 229* <br> •**Ein wenig Landeskunde: Leberkäs**, *p. 229* | •Food items vocabulary, *p. 230* (from **Kapitel 8**) <br> •The accusative case of indefinite articles, *p. 230* (from **Kapitel 5**) <br> •Saying you want something else, *p. 230* (from **Kapitel 8**) <br> •Verb **möchte**, *p. 230* (from **Kapitel**) <br> •Expressing opinions, *p. 232* (from **Kapitel 2**) <br> •Subordinate-clause word order, *p. 232* (from **Kapitel 8**) |
| **Aussprache** p. 233 | Review long vowels **ü** and **ö**, review letters **s**, **ss**, and **ß** | | | **Diktat:** *Textbook Audiocassette* 5 A |
| **Zum Lesen** pp. 234-235 | **Ein Bummel durch München** <br> Reading Strategy: Reading for a purpose | | | |
| **Review** pp. 236-239 | •**Anwendung**, *p. 236* <br> •**Kann ich's wirklich?** *p. 238* <br> •**Wortschatz**, *p. 239* | | | |
| **Assessment Options** | **Stufe Quizzes** <br> •*Chapter Resources*, Book 3 <br>    **Erste Stufe**, Quiz 9-1 <br>    **Zweite Stufe**, Quiz 9-2 <br>    **Dritte Stufe**, Quiz 9-3 <br> •*Assessment Items, Audiocassette* 8 A | | **Kapitel 9 Chapter Test** <br> •*Chapter Resources*, Book 3 <br> •*Assessment Guide*, Speaking Test <br> •*Assessment Items, Audiocassette* 8 A <br><br> **Test Generator, Kapitel 9** | |

Video Program **OR**
Expanded Video Program, Videocassette 3

Textbook Audiocassette 5 A

| RESOURCES Print | RESOURCES Audiovisual |
|---|---|

Textbook Audiocassette 5 A

Practice and Activity Book
Chapter Resources, Book 3
 • Communicative Activity 9-1
 • Additional Listening Activity 9-1 . . . . . . . . . . . . . . Additional Listening Activities, Audiocassette 10 A
 • Additional Listening Activity 9-2 . . . . . . . . . . . . . . Additional Listening Activities, Audiocassette 10 A
 • Student Response Form
 • Realia 9-1
 • Situation Card 9-1
 • Quiz 9-1 . . . . . . . . . . . . . . . . . . . . . . . . . . . . Assessment Items, Audiocassette 8 A
Video Guide. . . . . . . . . . . . . . . . . . . . . . . . . . . . . Video Program/Expanded Video Program, Videocassette 3

Textbook Audiocassette 5 A

Practice and Activity Book
Chapter Resources, Book 3
 • Communicative Activity 9-2
 • Additional Listening Activity 9-3 . . . . . . . . . . . . . . Additional Listening Activities, Audiocassette 10 A
 • Additional Listening Activity 9-4 . . . . . . . . . . . . . . Additional Listening Activities, Audiocassette 10 A
 • Student Response Form
 • Realia 9-2
 • Situation Card 9-2
 • Quiz 9-2 . . . . . . . . . . . . . . . . . . . . . . . . . . . . Assessment Items, Audiocassette 8 A

Textbook Audiocassette 5 A

Practice and Activity Book
Chapter Resources, Book 3
 • Additional Listening Activity 9-5 . . . . . . . . . . . . . . Additional Listening Activities, Audiocassette 10 A
 • Additional Listening Activity 9-6 . . . . . . . . . . . . . . Additional Listening Activities, Audiocassette 10 A
 • Student Response Form
 • Realia 9-3
 • Situation Card 9-3
 • Teaching Transparency Master 9-2 . . . . . . . . . . . . . Teaching Transparency 9-2
 • Quiz 9-3 . . . . . . . . . . . . . . . . . . . . . . . . . . . . Assessment Items, Audiocassette 8 A

Video Guide. . . . . . . . . . . . . . . . . . . . . . . . . . . . . Video Program/Expanded Video Program, Videocassette 3

**Alternative Assessment**
 • Performance Assessment, Teacher's Edition
   **Erste Stufe**, p. 215J
   **Zweite Stufe**, p. 215M
   **Dritte Stufe**, p. 215P
 • Portfolio Assessment
   Written: **Anwendung**, Activity 4, Pupil's Edition, p. 237, Assessment Guide
   Oral: **Anwendung**, Activity 5, Pupil's Edition, p. 237, Assessment Guide
 • **Notizbuch,** Pupil's Edition, p. 228; Practice and Activity Book, p. 153

# Kapitel 9: Amerikaner in München
## Textbook Listening Activities Scripts

## Erste Stufe
### Activity 6, *p. 222*

TOURIST  Entschuldigen Sie bitte ... Hallo, können Sie mir helfen?
MÜNCHNER  Ich?... Ja, selbstverständlich.
TOURIST  Ich kenne München nicht so gut, und ich suche das Hotel International.
MÜNCHNER  Ja, da lassen Sie mich mal nachdenken. Ja also, das Hotel International ... Ich glaube, das ist in der Brienner Straße.
TOURIST  Und wie finde ich eine Post? Ich brauche nämlich Briefmarken.
MÜNCHNER  Ja ... mal sehen. Na, vom Hotel gehen Sie rechts in die Brienner Straße und dann fünf Straßen weiter, dann biegen sie links in die Ludwigstraße ab und gehen weiter geradeaus bis Sie zur Schönfeldstraße kommen. Da ist die Post ... in der Schönfeldstraße.
TOURIST  Und wo kann man hier Geld umtauschen?
MÜNCHNER  Ja, sicher in einer Bank.
TOURIST  Und wo find' ich die?
MÜNCHNER  Ah, muß mal nachdenken. Ich glaube, es gibt eine Bank am Marienplatz neben dem Rathaus.
TOURIST  Und wo finde ich die U-Bahnstation?
MÜNCHNER  Ganz einfach. Die U-Bahnstation ist direkt am Karlstor, in der Schwanthalerstraße.
TOURIST  Ja, ich möchte auch gern das Stadtmuseum besuchen. Wie komm' ich denn dahin?
MÜNCHNER  Ja, das finden Sie ganz leicht. Das ist nämlich gleich neben der Post in der Schönfeldstraße.
TOURIST  Ja, ich muß natürlich auch in den Englischen Garten. Wie komme ich denn dahin?
MÜNCHNER  Ja also, der Garten ist so 100 Meter südlich vom Odeonsplatz.
TOURIST  Und zum Schluß möchte ich noch schnell wissen, wo die Frauenkirche ist.
MÜNCHNER  Ja, die können Sie von hier sehen. Schauen Sie mal da drüben. Da ist sie, in der Neuhauser-Kaufingerstraße.
TOURIST  Haben Sie recht vielen Dank!
MÜNCHNER  Gern geschehen! Viel Spaß noch in München!

## Zweite Stufe
### Activity 12, *p. 226*

STUDENT  Entschuldigen Sie bitte! Könnten Sie mir bitte helfen?
FUSSGÄNGER  Selbstverständlich.
STUDENT  Wie komme ich am besten zum Obst- und Gemüseladen von hier?
FUSSGÄNGER  Da gehen Sie hier von der Guardinistraße, bis Sie in die Ehrwalder Straße kommen. An der Ehrwalder Straße sehen Sie rechts die Mittenwalder Straße. Da gehen Sie dann nach rechts und sehen den Obst- und Gemüseladen auf der linken Seite.
STUDENT  Und wo liegt bitte das große Einkaufszentrum?
FUSSGÄNGER  Ja, also ganz einfach. Hier vom Metzger gehen Sie in die Neufriedenheimer Straße, bis Sie zum Hans-Grässel-Weg kommen. Da gehen Sie nach rechts, und das Einkaufszentrum ist auf der rechten Seite, gleich nach der Rheinsteinstraße.
STUDENT  Die Bäckerei hier im Ort ... wo kann ich sie finden?
FUSSGÄNGER  Ja, wie gesagt, von hier gehen Sie auf der Guardinistraße, bis Sie zur Werdenfelsstraße kommen. Da gehen Sie rechts. Die Bäckerei sehen Sie nach der zweiten Straße auf der rechten Seite.
STUDENT  Vielen Dank!
FUSSGÄNGER  Gern geschehen! Auf Wiedersehen!

### Activity 15, *p. 227*

AUSKUNFT  Guten Tag! Wie kann ich Ihnen behilflich sein?
FREUND  Ja, hallo. Können Sie mir bitte sagen, wie ich am besten von hier aus zum Viktualienmarkt komme?
AUSKUNFT  Ja also, da schauen Sie mal hier auf den Stadtplan. Hier sind wir ... und da ist der Viktualienmarkt. Da gehen Sie also die Bayerstraße entlang bis Sie zum Karlsplatz kommen. Dann gehen Sie über den Karlsplatz in die Neuhauserstraße. An der linken Seite sehen Sie die Frauenkirche. Gehen Sie geradeaus zum Marienplatz und dann rechts in die Prälat-Zistl-Straße. Dann kurz geradeaus und nach der nächsten Kreuzung sehen Sie den Viktualienmarkt auf der linken Seite.
FREUND  Hoffentlich kann ich mir das alles merken. Vielen Dank!
AUSKUNFT  Gern geschehen! Auf Wiedersehen!

# Dritte Stufe

## Activity 21, *p. 230*

MARKUS So, Mara, möchtest du noch eine Semmel? Die schmecken gut, nicht?

MARA Stimmt! Nein, keine Semmel mehr für mich, aber ich möchte noch einen Saft. Ich habe Durst.

MARKUS Klar ... bin gleich wieder da. Und du Silvia! Schmeckt das Hähnchen?

SILVIA Lecker!

MARKUS Und kann ich dir noch eine Limo holen?

SILVIA Nee, danke. Ich habe wirklich genug gegessen und getrunken.

MARKUS He, Thomas, tolle Fete, was? Kann ich dir noch eine Bretzel holen und auch noch etwas Saft?

THOMAS Klar, 'ne Bretzel mit Senf. He du, wo ist denn die Mara?

MARKUS Die steht da drüben, ... mit Silvia. Du Flori, wie geht's, wie steht's? Noch 'nen Leberkäs?

FLORI Nee, danke. Ich habe schon genug.

MARKUS Aber kann ich dir das Glas mit Mineralwasser auffüllen?

FLORI Ja, danke dir!

MARKUS Na, Claudia, wie geht's dir? Bist du schon satt, oder möchtest du noch etwas?

CLAUDIA Du, die Weißwurst schmeckt lecker. Ich möchte noch eine und auch noch ein Glas Limo bitte. Danke, Markus. Das ist nett von dir.

FRANK Du, Markus ... der Salat schmeckt echt gut.

MARKUS Ja, die Tomaten sind aus unserem Garten. Willst du noch mehr davon, Frank? Auch noch etwas mehr Apfelsaft?

FRANK Nee, nichts mehr, danke! Du, Markus, die Fete ist wirklich toll!

## Activity 27, *p. 233*

1. Ja also, ich heiße Christoph Nolte, und ich bin 12. Unsere Katze heißt Jupp so wie mein Vater. Ich mag Katzen am liebsten. Ich finde, daß sie nicht so viel Arbeit machen wie andere Tiere. Jupp hat manchmal sogar lebende Mäuse mit nach Hause gebracht. Die mußten wir dann natürlich schnell einfangen. Aber das passiert jetzt nur noch selten. Besonders toll ist es, wenn Jupp auf der Lauer liegt und Vögel im Garten beobachtet.

2. Ich heiße Birgit und wohne in Regensburg. Ich bin jetzt 14 Jahre alt. Mein Hobby ist Tanzen, und mein Lieblingstanz ist Rock 'n Roll. Meine Tanzpartnerin heißt Katarina. Ich finde es OK, daß in Deutschland zwei Mädchen miteinander tanzen dürfen. In einigen Ländern ist das ja nicht erlaubt. Darum dürfen wir nicht an Wettbewerben im Ausland teilnehmen. Das finde ich total blöd! Später möchte ich schon gern Tanzlehrerin werden.

3. Ich heiße Nils und bin 19. Ein guter Freund muß zu mir halten, mit mir durch dick und dünn gehen. Mit einem Mädchen geht das nicht so gut. Mit meinen Freunden kann ich meistens über alles reden, mit meiner Freundin nicht immer. Meine Freunde verstehen meine Probleme. Vielleicht liegt das auch nur daran, daß ich meine Freundin noch nicht so lange kenne. Kann sein. Ich glaube aber, daß es leichter ist, eine Freundin zu finden als einen guten Freund.

4. Ich heiße Alex, und ich bin 16 Jahre alt. Ich trage ausschließlich Schwarz. Ich find' das total stark. Hosen, Hemden, Stiefel, alles ist bei mir schwarz. Ich ändere das nie. Und andere Sachen habe ich nicht viel. Ich glaube, daß die Mode, die man trägt etwas über einen aussagt.

## Diktat, *p. 233*

You will hear Thomas and Silvie talking about what they did last weekend. First listen to what they are saying. Then write down their conversation.

THOMAS Grüß dich, Silvie!

SILVIE Tag, Thomas!

THOMAS Wo warst du denn am Wochenende?

SILVIE Ich war im Münchener Stadtzentrum und habe ein bißchen eingekauft.

THOMAS Hast du sonst was gemacht?

SILVIE Oh, ja. Ich war auch im Kino, und am Samstag habe ich das Deutsche Museum besucht. Das ist total interessant. Was hast du gemacht?

THOMAS Ich war zu Hause. Ich habe nur Fernsehen geschaut und auch gelesen. Das war langweilig.

SILVIE Du, ich muß jetzt weiter, Thomas. Also, bis später!

THOMAS Tchüs! Ich rufe dich diese Woche an, dann können wir ja etwas machen.

# Anwendung

## Activity 1, *p. 236*

Heute waren wir den ganzen Tag in München. Das war echt super! München ist eine tolle Stadt. Da gibt es so viel zu sehen und zu tun. Die Mara und der Markus sind mit uns einkaufen gegangen. Zuerst waren wir bei Dallmayr, da haben wir Weißwürste gekauft. Und ja, dann waren wir im Kaufhaus Ludwig Beck. Das ist ziemlich groß. Da haben wir ein paar CDs und etwas Schmuck gekauft. Das war gerade im Sonderangebot. Na, und zum Schluß waren wir dann noch in einem Fotogeschäft, denn die Mara wollte sich noch ein neues Fotoalbum kaufen. Danach sind wir mit der Straßenbahn nach Hause gefahren. Das war ein toller Tag!

# Kapitel 9: Amerikaner in München
## *Suggested Project*

*In this activity, students will compile and design an extended guide to their own town, city, or area written completely in German. It should be started after completion of the* **Zum Lesen** *section of this chapter. The project should be divided equally among students to facilitate completion of all parts of the guide. Divide students into 6 groups.*

## MATERIALS

✄ **Students may need**

- *Large piece of construction paper or posterboard, which will display all 6 projects*
- *glue or masking tape*
- *scissors*
- *markers*

## SUGGESTED OUTLINE

The guide should include

- a detailed map of the area, including landmarks, labeled streets, and noteworthy sights;
- places of interest, including background information and descriptions (this can be completed by two groups, each describing a minimum of five places);
- food and drink, including popular restaurants and what is served there;
- lodging, including the types of accommodations available, location, and cost;
- other important information that would be useful to visitors.

## SUGGESTED SEQUENCE

1. Assign students to groups, dividing them equally according to the number of project parts.

2. Once groups have been assigned, have students look over the possible topics. They might want to choose their topic depending on their strength in certain areas. For example, students with artistic abilities might want to work on designing a detailed map.

3. Groups begin gathering materials for their topics by making a list of possible resources. Make suggestions for such resources. (Examples: chamber of commerce, tourist information center, school or public library, local historical foundations)

4. Once groups have compiled their information, they make an outline of their projects. This outline should be shown to you for suggestions and approval.

5. Students begin their final drafts using all gathered information and materials.

6. Allow class time for all groups to give a short presentation of their parts of the guide.

7. Upon completion of all parts of the guide, students attach and display their project on the construction paper or poster board.

8. Display the guide on your bulletin board in your classroom, in the foreign language area, or a hallway in your school.

## GRADING THE PROJECT

Since the outcome of each section of the guide is based upon group cooperation and effort, one grade should be given to all members of each group based on the following criteria:

Suggested point distribution (total=100)

| | |
|---|---|
| Appearance/originality | 25 |
| Completion of assignment requirements | 25 |
| Correct language usage | 25 |
| Oral presentation | 25 |

PROJECT

# Kapitel 9: Amerikaner in München

# Games

## WAS BEDEUTET DIESES ZEICHEN?

*Playing this game will help your students review the vocabulary of city buildings and landmarks.*

**Procedure**   In preparation for this game, have a set of ten large index cards that you have numbered and labeled with the symbols used in this chapter to represent buildings or landmarks in a city. Divide students into groups of two or three, depending on your class size. Give each group a sheet of paper that is numbered from 1 to 10. Begin by calling out the number of the first card and then hold the card so that all students will be able to see it. Students will have ten seconds to decide what the symbol stands for. The writer of the group then records the word, including the article. You may want to give bonus points to students who can use the words correctly in a sentence. After you have shown all ten cards, put up a transparency with the correct words. The group with the most correct locations wins.

## KETTENSPIEL

*This game is a good vocabulary review for auditory learners.*

Begin the game by making the following statement: **Wenn ich in München bin, besuche ich das Deutsche Museum.** The next student repeats your sentence and adds another place or activity he or she would do when visiting Munich. The game continues with each student repeating all locations and/or activities that have been named up to his or her turn.

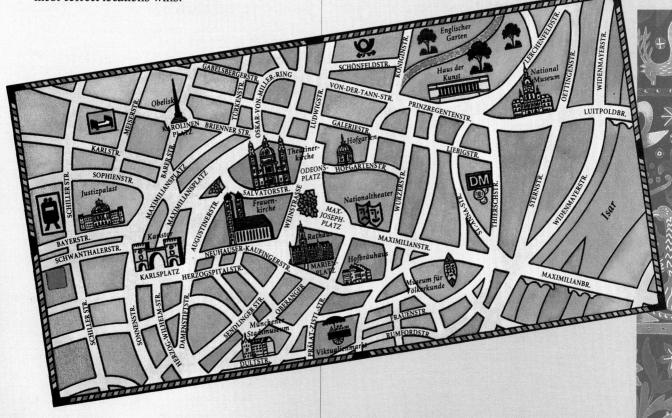

# Kapitel 9: Amerikaner in München
## *Lesson Plans, pages 216-239*

## *U*sing the Chapter Opener, *pp. 216-217*

### Motivating Activity

Ask students how they would give directions to their homes in English using the school as the starting point. Students should imagine that these directions are for a new student who is not too familiar with the area yet. They should be as specific as possible and include some landmarks, signs, etc.

### Background Information

① The **Marienplatz** did not get its present name until 1855. Originally this location was simply called **Marktplatz**. The name was temporarily changed to **Kornmarkt**, then **Schrannenplatz**. (**Schranne** is an old word meaning *baker's* or *butcher's stall*.)

### Building on Previous Skills

① Can students recall the building in this picture from Picture 5 of the photo essay on p. 167? (**Altes Rathaus** located at the **Marienplatz**)

### Thinking Critically

② **Drawing Inferences** Can students tell what kind of vendor stand this is? Have students name the products offered. How much do the juices cost and in what quantities are they served? (**0,2 Liter** = 7 oz; about one cup) What are the ingredients of the special **Kiwi-Flip?** (Kiwi, Banane und Orange)

② **Comparing and Contrasting** Ask students where they would be able to find such juices in the United States. Examples: healthfood stores, delicatessens

### Building on Previous Skills

② Ask students which of these juices they would like to try and what German phrases they would use to order one of these beverages.

### Background Information

③ These students are standing at an **Imbißstube** or **Schnellimbiß,** which is a snack stand where one can expect to find a variety of sausages and beverages, all at reasonable prices. Patrons eat and drink (usually standing) at a nearby counter where they also find the condiments.

### Thinking Critically

③ **Drawing Inferences** Ask students if they can infer the meaning of **hausgemachter Fleischspieß.** (*homemade spit-roasted meat*) Do students remember **Semmel** and **Breze** from preceding units?

### Focusing on Outcomes

Ask students to look at the objectives for this chapter listed on p. 217. Which of these functions would be useful for each of the pictures? **NOTE:** Each of these outcomes is modeled in the video and evaluated in **Kann ich's wirklich?** on p. 238.

# *T*eaching Los geht's!
## *pp. 218-220.*

> **Resources for Los geht's!**
> - *Video Program* **OR** *Expanded Video Program,*
> - *Textbook Audiocassette* 5 A
> - *Practice and Activity Book*

▶ **pages 218-219**

## 📼 Video Synopsis

In this segment of the video, Mara and Markus are having some juice at a juice bar when some American students ask them for directions to the **Marienplatz.** They run into each other again at an **Imbißstube** later in the day. Markus and Mara talk the Americans into trying a Bavarian specialty, **Leberkäs,** and then decide to show them around Munich. The student outcomes listed on p. 217 are modeled in the video: talking about where something is located, asking for and giving directions, talking about what there is to eat and drink, saying you do or don't want more, and expressing opinions.

## Motivating Activity

Ask students how they would prepare for a sightseeing tour in a city such as Munich. What items might they want to bring along? Have students make suggestions. Examples: maps, dictionary, coins for using public transportation

## Teaching Suggestions

- Let students scan each pictured dialogue for any cognates or previously learned phrases and expressions. Then have students watch the video segment of this **Foto-Roman.** What additional words or phrases helped them follow the storyline?

- In the Chapter Opener, students saw a picture of a **Saftstand** on p. 217. Do they remember what is sold there?

## Language Note

The term **Pommes frites,** which means *French fries,* was borrowed from the French language by the Germans.

▶ **page 220**

##  For Individual Needs

**2 A Slower Pace** Begin this activity by having students work in pairs, concentrating on pronunciation as they reread the conversations on pp. 218-219. Monitor their work and make pronunciation corrections as appropriate. Then, while students are working on Activity 2, write the numbers 1 through 5 on the board. Afterwards, have students write their answers on the board. Go over the phrases with the class.

**2 Challenge** Instead of rereading the conversations on pp. 218-219, have students listen for the words and phrases indicated in sentences 1 through 5 while watching the video or listening to the audiotape.

**4 Challenge** Have students think of a different response to each of the questions and expressions given on the left. Example: **Was macht ihr hier? Wir sind aus Amerika und wollen München sehen.**

**5 Visual Learners** Make enlarged copies of the sentences from this activity and cut them into sentence strips ahead of time. Make one set per student or pair of students, depending on your class size. Put these strips into numbered envelopes. Ask students to arrange the sentence strips in the correct order on their desks. Once all students have finished, ask several volunteers to read the summary of the story.

## Closure

Have students go back to the Location Opener on pp. 164-167. Ask students what they would like to do and see if they had the chance to visit Munich.

LOS GEHT'S!

## Teaching Erste Stufe, pp. 221-224

### Resources for Erste Stufe

*Practice and Activity Book*
*Chapter Resources,* Book 3
- Communicative Activity 9-1
- Additional Listening Activities 9-1, 9-2
- Student Response Form
- Realia 9-1
- Situation Card 9-1
- Quiz 9-1

*Audiocassette Program*
- *Textbook Audiocassette* 5 A
- *Additional Listening Activities, Audiocassette* 10 A
- *Assessment Items, Audiocassette* 8 A

▶ **page 221**

## MOTIVATE

### Teaching Suggestion
Brainstorm with students phrases they might need to know in order to ask for and understand directions in an unfamiliar city.

## TEACH

### Teaching Suggestion
Have students familiarize themselves with the map of Munich while scanning for cognates. (Examples: **Nationaltheater, Englischer Garten**) Also have students go back to the Location Opener on pp. 164-167 and find some of the locations pictured on the map on p. 221.

### PRESENTATION: Wortschatz
Ask students to find each of the places listed in the **Wortschatz** box on the map of Munich. Point out that many of these words for places do not appear by themselves on the map but are part of proper names. Examples: **Theatinerkirche, Viktualienmarkt**)

### Thinking Critically
**Drawing Inferences**  Ask students to think of symbols that could replace some of these places in town. Have them describe or draw them. Ask students for reasons why symbols are helpful and to whom they are helpful. Might there be other places where signs without words might be helpful? Examples: women's and men's restrooms, gas stations, banks that exchange currency.

## Background Information
German post offices also perform some banking functions that the U.S. postal service does not. Many Germans keep a postal savings account, which is convenient for travelers because it can be drawn on in different **Bundesländer** and countries.

## Teaching Suggestion
After reading **Ein wenig Landeskunde**, ask students whether they can recall seeing a **Fußgängerzone** in the location opener. (**am Marienplatz**) What can pedestrians typically find in a pedestrian zone, and why is it so popular? (outdoor cafés, shops, restaurants, relaxed atmosphere)

▶ **page 222**

### PRESENTATION: So sagt man das!
Ask students what they usually say in English when they approach strangers to ask for information. (Excuse me.) What form of address would they expect to use in German when asking a stranger where something is located. (**Sie**-form)

### PRESENTATION: Grammatik
Review with students the word order changes that occur in phrases beginning with the conjunctions **denn** or **weil**. Do they recall the type of clause that the conjunctions introduce? (dependent, meaning that it cannot stand by itself without the main clause of the sentence) Explain that **wissen** is often used to introduce a dependent clause that begins with an interrogative such as **wo**. In this case, the verb in the dependent clause is in the final position.

▶ **page 223**

### ✦ For Individual Needs
**7 A Slower Pace**  Ask students to do this activity in writing. Students may refer back to the **Grammatik** box on p. 222 to complete this task if necessary. Call on several students to read their statements aloud.

## Group Work

**8** Suggest that students expand this activity by performing a skit. Students should begin by making a brief outline and making note of any props that might be appropriate. They could perform this skit the following day or when time permits. This could also be done for extra credit.

## Cooperative Learning

**10** Divide the class into groups of three students each for this activity. Each group will need an "artist," a reader, and a demonstrator. Students will need construction paper, permanent markers, masking tape, and rulers. Set a time limit for this activity during which students should work together on the list of important places. The artist of the group draws the map as the other two students help to label the places. Finally, have students write out directions to at least three places that a visitor would enjoy seeing. Have each group come up to the front and tape its map to the board. The reader of the group reads the directions out loud as the demonstrator traces the directions with a ruler.

▶ *page 224*

## PRESENTATION: Landeskunde

### Teaching Suggestion

Take a survey of the class asking students to list the German foods they have tried before. Which ones did they like or dislike?

### Background Information

Here are a few descriptions of some of the specialities mentioned by the German teenagers: **Berliner Currywurst** is sausage that is browned and then cut lengthwise. Curry, pepper, and paprika are then sprinkled on top. **Scholle** is flounder. **Maultaschen** are triangular shaped dough pockets filled with spinach, bacon, onion, egg, herbs, and spices and cooked in broth. **Schnitzel** is cutlet, either pork (**Schweineschnitzel**) or veal (**Kalbsschnitzel**).

### History Connection

German immigrants in several different areas of the United States have tried to preserve their language and many culinary specialties. Ask students about such areas and have them research a few

foods that are well known within those particular areas. (Example: The Pennsylvania Germans in eastern Pennsylvania—referred to as the Pennsylvania Dutch—have a specialty called *shoofly pie.*)

##  Multicultural Connection

Ask students to interview foreign exchange students or people from other countries about their countries' culinary specialities. Have students report their findings to class.

### Teacher Note

Mention to your students that the **Landeskunde** will also be included in Quiz 9-1 given at the end of the **Erste Stufe.**

### Reteaching: Landmark vocabulary

On a transparency, list several places and landmarks in your town or area with which students should be familiar. Then have students ask each other: **Weißt du, wo ... ist?** The other student responds either with **Ja** or **Nein** and a complete sentence. Examples: **Ja, ich weiß, wo ... ist. Nein, es tut mir leid. Das weiß ich nicht.**

## *CLOSE*

### Game

Play the game **Was bedeutet dieses Zeichen?** See p. 215F for the procedure.

### Focusing on Outcomes

Refer students back to the learning outcomes listed on p. 217. Students should recognize that they are now able to talk about where something is located.

## *ASSESS*

• **Performance Assessment** Make a list of landmarks and locations in your town or city using the **Wortschatz** expressions of this **Stufe.** (Examples: **Kirche, Rathaus**) Ask students to tell the location of each item in German.

• Quiz 9-1, *Chapter Resources,* Book 3

# Teaching Zweite Stufe,
## p. 225-228

### Resources for Zweite Stufe

*Practice and Activity Book*
*Chapter Resources,* Book 3
- Communicative Activity 9-2
- Additional Listening Activities 9-3, 9-4
- Student Response Form
- Realia 9-2
- Situation Card 9-2
- Teaching Transparency Master 9-1
- Quiz 9-2

*Audiocassette Program*
- *Textbook Audiocassette* 5 A
- *Additional Listening Activities, Audiocassette* 10 A
- *Assessment Items, Audiocassette* 8 A

▶ *page 225*

## MOTIVATE

### Teaching Suggestion

Ask students to give you the simplest directions possible from your school to another place with which they are familiar. Have them be as specific as possible.

## TEACH

### PRESENTATION: Wortschatz

Teach the three basic directions first, using the appropriate symbols on the board or a transparency: **nach rechts, nach links, geradeaus.** Then teach **bis zum (zur) ... dann ...,** using the names of streets and symbols for landmarks. Finally, introduce **die nächste (erste, zweite) Straße nach (links, rechts)**, using a simplified street map.

###  Total Physical Response

Practice the expressions in the vocabulary box by first modeling and then asking individual students to follow your directions as they move around the classroom. Students could also perform certain tasks which would be additional practice of some familiar vocabulary and expressions. Example: directions to the door: **Angela, steh auf und geh zwei Schritte geradeaus! Jetzt bitte einmal links, mach die Tür auf! Danke!**

▶ *page 226*

## ❖ For Individual Needs

**13** **A Slower Pace** Make this activity into guided oral production. Choose students randomly to give directions in stages. For example, you could have one student give the first directions, then call on another student to continue, then another until the destination is reached. Then begin again. Always have students start at the place where the previous student left off.

### PRESENTATION: So sagt man das!

Introduce **Wie komme ich ...** as an alternate way of asking for directions. Prepare a transparency with several requests for directions written out both ways. (Example: **Verzeihung! Wissen Sie, wo das Rathaus ist? Verzeihung! Wie komme ich zum Rathaus?**) Be sure to vary the subject pronouns so all forms of **kommen** are practiced. Then practice responses with **gehen** and **fahren** plus the specific directions introduced in the **Wortschatz.** Finally, using a simple street map, have students give you directions to certain key places indicated.

► *page 227*

## PRESENTATION: Ein wenig Grammatik

Have students practice the use of **fahren** vs. **gehen** by providing cue cards with picture cues (a man walking, a bus, the **U-Bahn** symbol, etc.) or verbal cues (**mit dem Bus, zu Fuß,** etc.). Students should make up sentences based on the cues. Examples: **Er geht zu Fuß. Sie fährt mit dem Bus.**

## PRESENTATION: Grammatik

Before introducing the **Sie**-commands, review the **du**-command forms by asking students to give random commands to each other using the vocabulary of this chapter. Then ask students to write the verb form of their commands on the board. Now use the same commands but address the students formally, using their last names. (Example: **Fräulein Osborn, gehen Sie bitte ...!**) Then address two students formally and give them a series of commands. (Example: **Herr Walter und Herr Borau, stehen Sie bitte auf und gehen Sie ...!**) Make sure students recognize the change in verb form and the addition of the personal pronoun.

## Teaching Suggestion

**16** Have students work with a partner as they take turns reading and following the directions. Monitor students' work and offer suggestions in pronunciation if needed.

► *page 228*

## For Additional Practice

**18** To review the conjunctions **weil** and **denn** from Chapter 8, ask students to include a reason why they would like to see a certain landmark. Students can work this into the skit by asking: **Warum wollen Sie das sehen?**

## Reteaching: Giving directions

Tell students that the new student in school is not sure how to get from German class to the office, the band hall, the school nurse, the math class, or the gymnasium. Ask students to write out directions in German to help the new student find his or her way around.

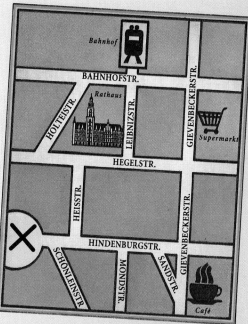

## CLOSE

### Teaching Suggestion

Blindfold one student as the rest of the class (one student at a time) gives that student careful directions around the classroom. Have the blindfolded student guess where he or she is at the end.

### Focusing on Outcomes

Refer students back to the learning outcomes listed on p. 217. Students should recognize that they are now able to ask for and give directions.

## ASSESS

• **Performance Assessment** Prepare a set of index cards with a location from Transparency 9-1 written on each. Have two students, A and B, come to the front of the room and draw a card each. Student A's location is the starting point, and student B must guide him or her to Location B. Have Student A go to the overhead projector and trace with his or her finger the oral directions given by Student B. Once Student A reaches Location B, have another student (C) come to the front and select a location. Repeat the activity with student A calling directions. Continue bringing up students and changing roles until all students have given and followed directions.

• Quiz 9-2, *Chapter Resources,* Book 3

IMBiẞ STUBE
am Rathaus

Leberkäs mit Senf 4,00
   mit Semmel 4,50
Hähnchen vom Grill 6,00
Gyros 4,50
   mit Salat 7,50
Weißwurst 3,80
Volkornsemmel -,50

Brezel 1,00
Käsebrot 3,20
Milch 2,00
Mineralwasser 1,00
Apfelsaft 2,4
Tee, Glas 2,5

Hobby

Ich heiße Eva Hörster und bin am 17.10.74 in München geboren. Ich

laufe mit den Rollschuhen auf der Straße oder auf der Rollschuhbahn. Meine Eltern finden es gut, daß ich Sport treibe. Sie begleiten mich immer zum Training und Langlauf. Ich hoffe, daß Rollschuhlaufen eine olympische Sportart wird. Das Foto ist nach meinem ersten Pokalsieg aufgenommen worden.

Viele Grüße,
Eva Hörster, München

# *T*eaching Dritte Stufe, *pp. 229-233*

▶ **page 229**

## *MOTIVATE*

### Teaching Suggestion

Ask students to recall some of the Bavarian food specialties from the Munich Location Opener on pp. 164-167 and the Chapter 9 **Foto-Roman** on pp. 218-219. What seems different and unusual to them? Which of these regional specialities would they like to try?

## *TEACH*

### PRESENTATION: So sagt man das!

Ask students to look back at Picture 7 of the **Foto-Roman** and name the expressions that the German teenagers use to show their American friends what they've ordered from the **Imbißstube.**

### Language Note

Mention to students that Germans have several words to refer to rolls. For example, in southern Bavaria people use the word **Semmel,** in Baden-Württemberg they use the word **Wecken,** in the Berlin area, **Schrippe,** and in northern Germany, **Brötchen.** And there are often local terms for rolls and bread.

## Thinking Critically

**Comparing and Contrasting** Can students think of food items that have different names in different parts of the United States? Examples: soda, soda pop, pop, soft drink

**Comparing and Contrasting** Ask students to name some specialties popular in their area. Do they know of foods that are associated with a city or region in the United States? Examples: New York: bagels; New Orleans: beignets, Cajun-style food; Philadelphia: cheesesteak sandwiches; Texas: chili

## ▪ Multicultural Connection

To expand this comparison beyond the United States, ask students whether they know of specialties of other countries. Have students make a list.

## For Additional Practice

Ask students about the foods and beverages available at school using **es gibt.** (Example: **Was gibt's in der Schule zu essen?**) Have students answer with the phrase **Es gibt ...**

▶ **page 230**

## PRESENTATION: So sagt man das!

Ask students for the different ways they would respond to a friend when he or she offers more food or drink at his or her home. Can students make suggestions in German as to how to express these statements? Write the expressions on the board or on a transparency as students name them. Then introduce the responses from the **So sagt man das!** box. Practice the different yes-and-no responses by offering individual students something else to eat or drink and cueing a positive response with a nod and a negative response with a shake of the head.

**For Individual Needs**

**21 Visual Learners** Make the transcript from this activity available to students after they have listened to it once. Students could use the script to complete the chart.

▶ *page 231*

## PRESENTATION: Grammatik

Begin by asking students to negate a sentence such as **Ich gehe morgen ins Kino.** → **Ich gehe morgen nicht ins Kino.** Then put the following sentences on a transparency, one in the affirmative and one in the negative: **Ich kaufe einen Taschenrechner. Ich kaufe keinen Taschenrechner.** Can students infer the difference between the two negated sentences? (**Nicht** negates a verb and means *not,* whereas **kein** negates a noun and means *no* or *none*.) Point out to students that **kein** used before a noun takes the same endings as other **ein**-words.

## Teaching Suggestion

**23** Start this activity by having students think of as many things as they can that they don't like to eat or drink. List them on the board with their articles. Then give students the following three phrases to complete:

Ich esse kein _____.
Ich esse keine _____.
Ich esse keinen _____.

## Building on Previous Skills

**24** In Chapter 8 students were introduced to the adverb **noch.** Ask students what **noch** refers to in sentences such as **Was bekommen Sie noch?** or **Ich brauche noch eine Semmel.** (refers to the items they buy) Tell students that in conjunction with **ein** (**noch ein**) **noch** means *one more* or *another*.

▶ *page 232*

## Teaching Suggestion

**26** You might ask students to report (in third person) what Eva says in her letter. Example: **Sie kommt aus _____.**

## PRESENTATION: So sagt man das!

Hand each student an index card with the name of a food item, a sport, a leisure activity, etc. accompanied by a verb in the infinitive. (Example: **Tennis spielen**) Then go around the class and ask several students to express their opinion about the phrase listed on their card. You might want to begin by expressing your own opinion about a sport you do or do not like. Next, use one of the opinions stated in the **So sagt man das!** function box and write it on the board. (Example: **Ich finde Tennis langweilig.**) Then rewrite the statement using **daß.** (Example: **Ich finde, daß Tennis langweilig ist.**) Ask students to compare the two statements on the board, inferring the meaning of **daß.** Then you could ask some students to restate the opinion they already expressed about the phrase written on their index card, this time using **daß** in their statement.

## PRESENTATION: Grammatik

Write these two sentences on a transparency: **Ich will essen, weil ich Hunger habe. Ich glaube, daß du auch Hunger hast.** Have students compare these two sentences, especially the word order in the dependent clauses.

## Language Note

Daß-clauses, like all dependent clauses, are always separated from their preceding phrases by a comma.

▶ *page 233*

 **For Individual Needs**

**27 Challenge** As students listen a second time, have them make note of any additional information in each caller's topics or opinions.

## For Additional Practice

**28** After completing the activity, conduct a survey of your students. Repeat the statements and ask students to raise their hands if they agree or disagree with the statements. (Example: **Wer glaubt hier, daß ...? Hebt die Hand, wenn ihr glaubt, daß, ...**) Then call on individual students and ask them to state their opinion using a **daß**-clause.

## Reteaching: Daß-clauses

Use sentence strips to write out various sentences which include the conjunction **daß** as well as phrases that state opinions. Prepare enough envelopes so that each student or group has one. Give students a time limit in which to reconstruct each statement. Have students pass the envelope to the next student or group after they have finished with it.

## PRESENTATION: Aussprache

An explanation of these sounds can be found in Chapters 1 and 3 of the *Pupil's Edition*.

## CLOSE

### Teaching Suggestion

As a closing activity, hand each student an index card with the name of a Munich landmark written on it. Have students tell the class where they are going and what they expect to see or do there based on the landmark written on their cards.

### Focusing on Outcomes

Refer students back to the learning outcomes listed on p. 217. Students should recognize that they are now able to say they do or don't want more and to express opinions.

## ASSESS

- **Performance Assessment** Make a town out of the classroom. Use rows as streets. You can label them with opened-up folders with street names on them and also by laying signs on the floor. Make signs indicating different places in the city. (Examples: **Kirche, Postamt**) Have students hold signs in different parts of the room. Then call on students randomly to role-play a situation. A student can ask for directions to a certain place. That student follows directions given by classmates as he or she moves around the make-believe city.

- Quiz 9-3, *Chapter Resources,* Book 3

DRITTE STUFE

ZUM LESEN

# Teaching Zum Lesen,
## pp. 234-235

## Reading Strategy

The targeted reading strategy in this chapter is reading for a purpose. Students should learn about this strategy before doing Question 2. As in previous chapters, students will also be asked to skim for the gist, answer questions to show comprehension, and transfer what they have learned.

## PREREADING

### Motivating Activity

Before doing Activity 1, ask students how they would plan a trip to a foreign country, such as Germany. What type of information would they look for? Where would they get information? What preparations would they make?

### Teaching Suggestion

After doing Activity 1, have students look at sample travel guides of places such as New York City, Boston, Portland, or have them bring travel guides their family might have used in the past. Then do Activity 2.

### Teacher Note

Activities 1–3 are prereading activities.

## READING

### Thinking Critically

**Drawing Inferences** Can students infer the meaning of abbreviations such as **S-Bahn** and **U-Bahn**? (**Schnellbahn/Untergrundbahn**) Why is the abbreviation **U-/S-Bahn** followed by the word **Marienplatz**? (to tell tourists the station at which they need to get on or off) What does that suggest about how visitors are encouraged to tour the city?

 ### Culture Note

If tourists fall ill in Germany, they might find immediate help at an **Apotheke** (*pharmacy*). The local phone book will direct customers to the one or two pharmacies that are open all night. In pharmacies in major cities, the personnel also speak several languages. You can check to see if your language is spoken in the pharmacy by checking the

nationality flags that represent the languages spoken. These flags are usually posted on the door.

## Background Information

You might want to let your students know that Munich is one of the leading cities that host trade fairs, exhibitions, and conventions. It ranks sixth in exhibition space among all German cities.

## POST-READING

### Teacher Note

Activity 9 is a post-reading task that will show whether students can apply what they have learned.

### Group Work

Ask students to work in groups of two or three. Have them choose one of the months suggested in Activity 9 for their visit to Munich. The group must agree and rank the sights of its choice and also make a brief statement telling why the group members chose the activities planned.

### Closure

Ask students to name at least two new facts about Munich from the excerpts of the tour guide that they did not hear or see in the preceding chapters about Munich.

*Answers to Activity 1*
c. a travel guide

*Answers to Activity 2*
skim to gather general information; scan to find specific information

*Answers to Activity 3*
Essen und Trinken: Cafés, Restaurants, Stehimbisse, Konditorien; Einkaufen: Sportmode, Geschenkwaren, Kaufhäuser, Fotogeschäfte; Sehenswertes: Deutsches Museum, Alte Pinakothek, Peterskirche, Englischer Garten

*Answers to Activity 4*
Essen und Trinken: Dallmayr; Einkaufen: Dallmayr, Ludwig Beck; Sehenswertes: Englischer Garten, Olympiapark, Peterskirche

*Answers to Activity 5*
fine foods: Dallmayr; fashionable clothes: Ludwig Beck

*Answers to Activity 6*
a. **Faschingsball** (**Chrysanthemenball, Magno-lienball, Madameball, Filmball, Presseball**); b. **Englischer Garten;** c. **Internationale Ludwigs-Apotheke** or **Von Mendel'sche Apotheke;** d. **Dall-mayr**

*Answers to Activity 7*
take the **Isar-Floßfahrt;** you must plan ahead be-cause the trips are booked well in advance; **Ter-mine sind schon lange im voraus gebucht.**

*Answers to Activity 8*
over nine hundred years old; the four bells and the city; 1972; 52 meters; ruins from World War II

# Using Anwendung,
## pp. 236-237

###  For Individual Needs

**1 Challenge** Have students give a reason why they would like to see the local landmarks that the American students saw. Students should use **weil** or **denn** in their answers.

### Thinking Critically

**2 Drawing Inferences** Can students think of other locations that a foreign visitor would need to know about? Examples: **Jugendherberge, Pension, Flughafen, Polizei, Konsulat**

###  Portfolio Assessment

**4** You might want to use this activity as a written portfolio item for your students. See *Assessment Guide,* Chapter 9.

###  Portfolio Assessment

**5** You might want to use this activity as an oral portfolio item for your students. See *Assessment Guide*, Chapter 9.

## Teaching Suggestion
**6** Ask students to refer to the **Foto-Roman** on p. 219 for some foods typically found at an **Imbißstube** and the prices asked for such foods.

# Kann ich's wirklich?
## p. 238

This page is intended to prepare students for the test. It is a brief checklist of the major points covered in the chapter. The students should be reminded that it is a checklist only and not necessarily everything that will appear on the test.

# Using Wortschatz,
## p. 239

###  Game
Play the game **Kettenspiel.** See p. 215F for the procedure.

### Teacher Note
Give the **Kapitel 9** Chapter Test, *Chapter Resources, Book 3.*

*Feuchtfröhliche Gaudi ohnegleichen: Isarfloßfahrten*

# Amerikaner in München

① Entschuldigung! Wissen Sie, wo das alte Rathaus ist?

It's not always easy to find your way around in a new city, and you might have to ask for directions. In this chapter you will meet some American students who are visiting Munich. How do they find their way around? What do they think of Munich? What would you like to do if you were visiting Munich?

**In this chapter you will learn**

- to talk about where something is located
- to ask for and give directions
- to talk about what there is to eat and drink; to say you do or don't want more; to express opinions

**And you will**

- listen to people ask for and give directions
- read about Munich and locate places on a map of Munich
- write a postcard giving directions
- find out about famous places in Munich

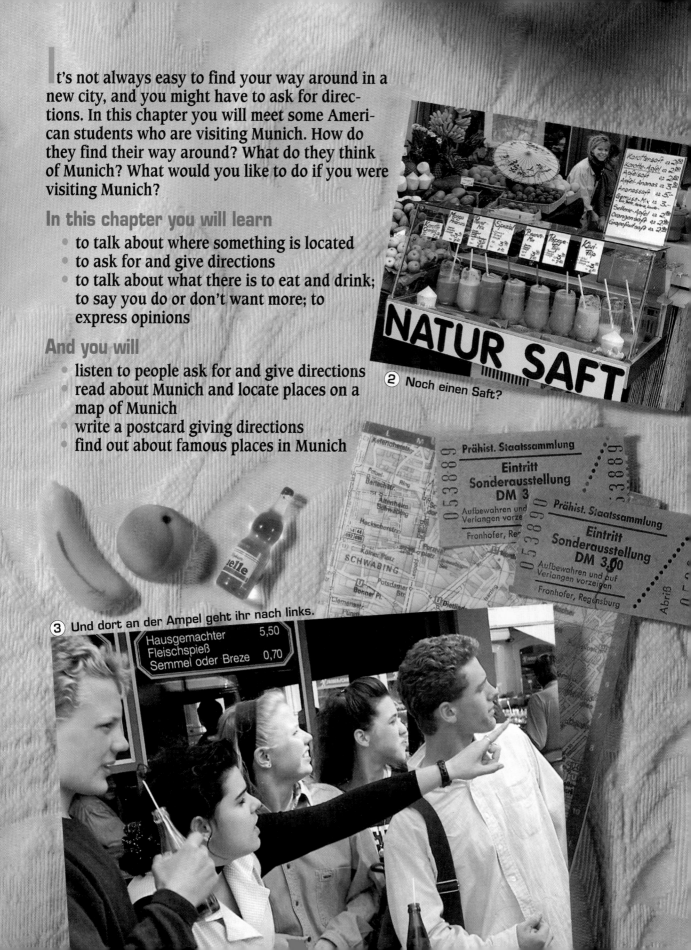

② Noch einen Saft?

③ Und dort an der Ampel geht ihr nach links.

Hausgemachter
Fleischspieß          5,50
Semmel oder Breze   0,70

# Los geht's!

## München besuchen

Look at the photos that accompany the story.
Who are the people pictured? What are they doing?
Where are they? What do you think they are talking about?
What do you suppose will happen in the story?

**Amerikaner**   **Markus**   **Mara**

**❶** Die Säfte hier sind doch wirklich Spitze!

Ja, und vor allem gesund!

**❷** Entschuldigung!

Ja?

Wie kommen wir zum Marienplatz?

Ganz einfach! Da geht ihr geradeaus bis zur Ampel und dann nach rechts.

**❸** Das stimmt doch gar nicht! An der Ampel nach links!

Klar, nach links! Da kommt ihr direkt zum Marienplatz.

Ah, vielen Dank!

Bitte, gern geschehen.

**❹** Ihr seid Amerikaner, nicht?

Ja, wir sind aus Wisconsin.

Wirklich? Was macht ihr hier?

Ja ... wir wohnen in Rosenheim, und heute besuchen wir München.

## 1 Was passiert hier?

Do you understand what is happening in the **Foto-Roman**? Check your comprehension by answering these questions. Don't be afraid to guess.

1. Where are Mara and Markus at the beginning of the story? What are they doing?
2. Who approaches Mara and Markus? What kind of information do these people need?
3. What does Markus recommend to eat? Why do you think he recommends this?
4. What do Markus and Mara decide to do at the end of the story?

1. at a snack bar, drinking juice
2. American students; how to get to Marienplatz

3. **Leberkäs**, because it is a typical Bavarian
4. give the American students a tour of the

## 2 Genauer lesen

Reread the conversations. Which words or phrases do the characters use to

1. start conversations or get someone's attention
2. end conversations
3. name foods and drinks
4. ask for and give directions
5. ask if someone would like more of something

1. Entschuldigung; Hallo.
2. Gern geschehen!; Na dann, viel Spaß.

3. Säfte, Bratwurst, Weißwurst, Leberkäs
4. Wie kommen wir zum ...? geradeaus/ bis zur/nach rechts/nach links
5. Noch etwas?

## 3 Stimmt oder stimmt nicht?

Are these statements right or wrong? Answer each one with either **stimmt** or **stimmt nicht**. If a statement is incorrect, try to state it correctly.

1. Zuerst trinken Markus und Mara Kaffee.
2. Der Amerikaner möchte zum Marienplatz gehen.
3. Mara und Markus besuchen Amerika.
4. Dann wollen der Amerikaner und seine Freunde etwas essen, denn sie haben Hunger.
5. Aber Markus ißt Leberkäs nicht gern.
6. Leberkäs ist eine bayrische Spezialität.
7. Dann wollen Markus und Mara den Amerikanern die Stadt München zeigen.

1. Stimmt nicht. Sie trinken Säfte.
2. Stimmt.
3. Stimmt nicht. Sie sind in München.
4. Stimmt.
5. Stimmt nicht. Er ißt Leberkäs gern.
6. Stimmt.
7. Stimmt.

## 4 Was paßt zusammen?

Match each statement or question on the left with an appropriate response on the right.

1. Wie kommen wir zum Marienplatz?
2. Vielen Dank!
3. Was macht ihr hier?
4. Was eßt ihr hier?
5. Ißt du noch eine Bratwurst?
6. Schmeckt's?

1. c
2. b
3. a
4. e
5. f
6. d

a. Wir besuchen die Stadt München.
b. Gern geschehen!
c. Ihr müßt an der Ampel nach links.
d. Ja, wirklich gut!
e. Hier gibt's Leberkäs und Weißwurst.
f. Nein, danke! Ich habe genug.

## 5 Nacherzählen

Put the sentences in a logical order to make a brief summary of the **Foto-Roman**.

1. Am Saftstand trinken Mara und Markus einen Saft.

5 Dann probiert er den Leberkäs.

4 Später wollen der Junge und seine Freunde wissen, was Mara und Markus essen.

3 Er wohnt in Rosenheim und besucht heute München.

6 Danach zeigen Mara und Markus den Amerikanern München.

2 Ein Junge kommt vorbei und möchte wissen, wie er zum Marienplatz kommt.

*Talking about where something is located*

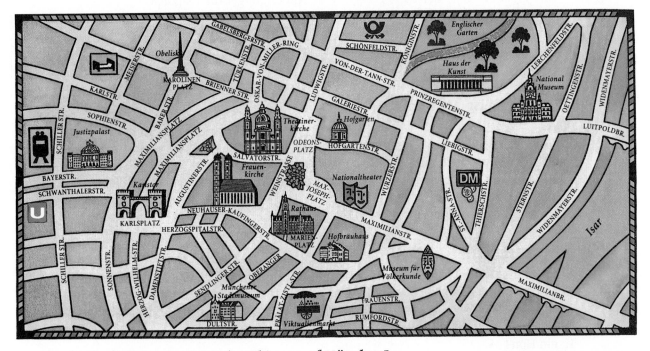

What kinds of places are pictured on this map of **München**? What do you think a **Kirche** is? And the **Rathaus**? How many museums can you find? And parks? Judging by the types of buildings on this map, what part of the city do you think this is?

## WORTSCHATZ

### In der Innenstadt    Wo ist ... ?

das
Hotel

die
Kirche

das
Rathaus

der
Marktplatz

die
Bank

die
Post

das
Museum

der
Bahnhof

das
Theater

der
Garten

die
U-Bahn-
station

### EIN WENIG LANDESKUNDE

Many cities in Germany were originally built around the **Markt-platz,** with the **Rathaus** and the main **Kirche,** nearby. A wall surrounded the city and offered protection to the inhabitants. In a number of cities, parts of the original city wall are still standing around the **Innenstadt** (*downtown*). In many cities the main streets are closed to traffic and are designated as a **Fußgängerzone** (*pedestrian zone*).

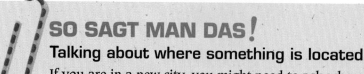

### Talking about where something is located

If you are in a new city, you might need to ask where things are located.

You might ask a passer-by:

**Verzeihung! Wissen Sie, wo das Rathaus ist?**
**Und wo ist das Karlstor?**
**Entschuldigung! Weißt du, wo der Bahnhof ist?**
**Und wo ist hier ein Café?**

You might get the responses:

**In der Innenstadt am Marienplatz.**
**In der Neuhauser Straße.**

**Es tut mir leid. Das weiß ich nicht.**
**Keine Ahnung! Ich bin nicht von hier.**

What is the position of the second verb in questions that begin with **wissen** and **weißt**? Which expression might you use to ask someone older than yourself? To ask a person your own age? Which responses were probably made by someone who does not live in Munich?

## 6 Hör gut zu!

At the tourist information center in **München** you overhear a conversation between an American tourist and someone who doesn't know the city very well. Using the map on page 221, decide whether the information the tourist is given for each of the places listed below is correct or incorrect.

1. ein Hotel          correct
2. die Post           correct
3. eine Bank          incorrect
4. eine U-Bahnstation correct
5. das Stadtmuseum    incorrect
6. der Englische Garten incorrect
7. die Frauenkirche   correct

## *Grammatik*   The verb **wissen**

The verb **wissen** means *to know* (a fact, information, etc.). Here are the forms:

Ich **weiß** nicht, wo es ist.
Du **weißt** es, ja?
Er/Sie **weiß**, wo es ist.

Wir **wissen**, wo die Kirche ist.
Ihr **wißt** das auch.
Sie (pl) / Sie **wissen** es nicht.

Look at the sentences below.

Wo ist das Museum?
Weißt du, wo das Museum **ist**?

Ich weiß nicht.
Ich weiß nicht, wo das Museum **ist**.

What is the position of the verbs in the clauses introduced by **wo**? Used in this way, **wo** introduces a dependent clause. The verb is in final position.

## 7 Wer weiß, wo es ist?

Ich weiß, wo das Rathaus ist. Vater und ich wissen, wo die Frauenkirche ist. Ali weiß, wo die Post ist.

Mara und ihre Familie fahren heute in die Innenstadt. Sie möchten sich viel ansehen und sie müssen auch viel einkaufen *(to shop)*. Wissen sie, wo alles ist? Ergänze Maras Aussagen mit der richtigen Form von **wissen**!

Du weißt, wo der Hofgarten ist. Ihr wißt, wo die Bank ist. Leyla und Jasmin wissen, wo das Theater ist.

BEISPIEL **Mutti weiß, wo das Theater ist.**

1. Ich ...   2. Vater und ich ...   3. Ali ...   4. Du ...   5. Ihr ...   6. Leyla und Jasmin ...

## 8 Amerikaner treffen Engländer in München

A group of American students is lost in **München**. Several students in the group ask passers-by how to get to various places. However, they have mistakenly asked a group of British tourists, who themselves are lost. Create possible exchanges using the correct form of **wissen**. Watch out for the position of the second verb.   Answers will vary.

Wissen Sie, wo die Post ist? / Nein, es tut mir leid.

Wißt ihr, wo der Bahnhof ist?/ Keine Ahnung.

Weißt du, wo der Marktplatz ist? Nein, ich weiß nicht.

Wissen Sie, wo die U-Bahnstation ist? / Nein ...

## 9 Entschuldigung! Wissen Sie, wo ...?

You are in **München** and have lost your travel guide. You need to ask where certain landmarks are located. Using the map on page 221, choose five places you would like to see. Make a list. Get together with two other classmates, one of whom will be a passer-by about 50 years old, the other a person your own age. Ask them where the places of interest on your list are located. Then switch roles.

## 10 Wie sieht deine Stadt aus?

A German exchange student coming to your school needs to know how to get around in your town. With your partner sketch a map of your neighborhood or downtown area. Make a list of important places. What would the student enjoy seeing? Where could he or she buy food and clothing? Label all the streets and important places on your map and share it with the class. Turn to page 323 for additional vocabulary.

## Was ißt du gern?

We asked some people in the German-speaking countries to tell us about what kinds of foods they like to eat. Before you read what they said, make a list of some of the things you would consider "German specialties."

LANDESKUNDE

Schweineschnitzel

Kaiserschmarren

Würstchen

**Melina,**
*Bietigheim*

„Ich esse am liebsten so Eis, vor allem Erdbeereis oder so, mit Früchten drin. Und so ... von Gerichten mag ich ja Schnitzel oder Linseneintopf. Ja, trinken mag ich eigentlich so mehr Cola oder so Apfelsaft."

**Rosi,**
*Berlin*

„Ach, ich esse auch gern Süß-speisen, also Kaiserschmarren als österreichisches [Gericht] oder Eierkuchen — ja, also eigentlich alles mögliche!"

**Uli,**
*München*

„Dafür lieb' ich Würstchen, jeglicher Art, besonders die Berliner Currywürstchen, die es hier in München leider nicht so oft gibt. Ja und das ist so das, was ich gern esse."

### Here are a few other German specialties

Scholle, Hamburg

Maultaschen, Baden-Württemberg

**A. 1.** Write the people's names and list the German specialties each likes to eat. Are there any foods mentioned that are not German specialties?

1. yes; ice cream

**2.** Look at the list you made before reading and discuss the following questions with your classmates. Did your guesses differ from what the people said? If so, how? Where did you get your ideas about German specialties? What do you think people in German-speaking countries would name as American specialties? Where do you think they get their ideas?

**B.** Write a letter in German to one of the people interviewed telling her about the local spe-cialties you like to eat. The person may not know what they are, so it might be a good idea to describe the foods in as much detail as you can.

*Asking for and giving directions*

## 11 Den Weg zeigen

Below is a map of Mittersendling, a neighborhood in Munich. Start at the **U-Bahnstation** and follow the directions given in the **Wortschatz** box. Where do you end up when you follow these directions?   die Bäckerei

**Gehen Sie ...**

nach rechts

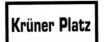

bis zum Krüner Platz

dann geradeaus

bis zur Ampel, dann nach rechts

dann die erste (zweite, dritte) Straße nach rechts

die nächste Straße nach links

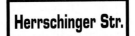

bis zur Herrschinger Str.

und wieder nach rechts.

dann geradeaus. Da ist ...

## 12 Hör gut zu! 1. Yes   2. No-**Jugendclub**   3. Yes

An American exchange student is trying to find the produce store, shopping center, and the bakery in Mittersendling. He is standing in front of the butcher's asking a passer-by for directions. Listen to their conversation several times and determine whether the directions given will take him where he wants to go or not. If not, where do they lead him?

## 13 Du gehst nach links, dann nach ...

Possible answers in TE
Interleaf, p. 215C

Zeig den Weg zu den folgenden Orten (*places*) in Mittersendling! Fang beim Hotel an! Tausche die Rolle mit deinen Klassenkameraden aus!

a. vom Hotel bis zur Post
b. von der Post bis zum Supermarkt
c. von der Bank bis zum Hotel

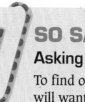

## SO SAGT MAN DAS!

### Asking for and giving directions

To find out where things are located, you will want to be able to ask for directions.

You might ask a passer-by:

> **Verzeihung! Wie komme ich zum Hotel am Bahnhof?**

> **Und wie kommt man\* zur Bäckerei? Entschuldigung! Wie kommen wir zum Einkaufszentrum?**

> **Und wie kommen wir zur U-Bahnstation?**

The responses might be:

> **Gehen Sie geradeaus bis zur Alpseestraße, dann nach links! Die nächste Straße nach rechts.**

> **Fahren Sie geradeaus bis zur Ampel, dann nach links!**

> **Sie fahren hier nach rechts, dann die zweite Straße wieder nach rechts.**

What do you think the words **zum** and **zur** mean?[1] Why is there a difference and what does it depend on?[2] In two of the responses, the verb is in first position. Can you figure out why?

1. *to the*  2. It depends on the noun that follows: masculine/neuter nouns > **zu dem (zum)**; feminine nouns > **zu der (zur)**.

\***man** means *one, you* (in general), *people*; it is used with the **er/sie**-form of the verb: **man geht, man fährt.**

**226**   *zweihundertsechsundzwanzig*      KAPITEL 9   Amerikaner in München

## 14 Wie kommt man dahin?

You are at the post office in Mittersendling and have several things to do today. You still have to buy rolls, exchange money, buy a T-shirt, and then meet your friends at the youth center. Choose two things to do and ask your partner how to get from place to place, using the map on page 225. Then switch roles.

> zum Einkaufszentrum     zur Bank
>
> zur Bäckerei     zum Jugendclub

### Ein wenig *Grammatik*

In the **So sagt man das!** box on page 226 both **gehen** and **fahren** are used. How is **fahren** different in meaning from **gehen**? **Fahren** is used whenever someone is using a vehicle to go somewhere, such as **ein Auto, ein Bus,** or **ein Fahrrad**. **Fahren** has a stem-vowel change in the **du-** and **er/sie**-forms: **Du fährst mit dem Bus, und sie fährt mit dem Auto.** However, with **du**-commands, the umlaut is not used: **Fahr jetzt nach Hause!**

---

## *Grammatik*    The formal commands with **Sie**

In **Kapitel 8** you learned how to use commands with people you know well: **Kauf ein Kilo Kartoffeln, bitte!** In this chapter you have seen how you would give a command to a person whom you do not know well and who is older than yourself. Look at the following sentences:

     **Fahren Sie nach links!**      **Gehen Sie geradeaus!**

What do you notice about the word order in formal commands.[1] How would you give a command to someone your own age using **fahren** and **gehen**?[2] To two strangers older than yourself?[3]

---

## 15 Hör gut zu!

a. At the information counter at the main train station in Munich, a friend of yours is asking how to get to the **Viktualienmarkt**. Listen to the directions given several times and jot down some notes as you listen.

b. Check your notes with the map on page 221. Did you understand the directions correctly?

c. Now use your notes to explain in your own words to another friend how he or she can get to the **Viktualienmarkt**.    Answers will vary.

---

## 16 Wie kommt man zum Jugendclub?

Dein Freund kommt am Samstag mit der U-Bahn und möchte dich im Jugendclub treffen (*to meet*). Schau auf den Stadtplan auf Seite 225 und schreib die Postkarte fertig! Beschreib den Weg von der U-Bahnstation bis zum Jugendclub!

nach links in die Neufriedenheimerstraße, dann gerade-aus; dann rechts in den Hans-Grässel-Weg; geradeaus

> Hallo ▓▓▓!
> Schön, daß Du kommst! Ich bin um
> 14 Uhr im Jugendclub. Von der
> U-Bahnstation gehst du ▓▓▓
>      Bis bald,
>      Dein(e) ▓▓▓

---

1. The verb is in first position and is always followed by **Sie**.   2. **Fahr/Geh ... !**   3. **Fahren/Gehen Sie ... !**

## 17 Wohin?

b. Theatinerkirche

Your friend wants you to see some famous places in Munich and has left behind a set of directions from the **Bahnhof** to somewhere in Munich. However, he forgot to tell you what you will see. Read his directions and use the map of Munich (page 221) to find out where they lead. Match the destination with one of the photos.

a.

b.

c.

Also, du kommst aus dem Bahnhof, gehst über die Straße und dann in Richtung Karlsplatz. Du gehst durchs Karlstor, und hier kommst du in die Neuhauser und Kaufingerstraße. Die führen zum Marienplatz. Am Marienplatz mußt du links in die Weinstraße einbiegen. Geh jetzt immer geradeaus, bis du zum Odeonsplatz kommst. Auf der linken Seite ist ein großes Gebäude. Da bin ich!

## 18 Also, fahren Sie ...

Role-play the following situation with two classmates. One of you will be a German student at the **Rathaus** where several people ask you for directions. Another will be an American high school teacher sightseeing in Munich by car, and the third classmate will be a young student from Los Angeles on a bike. Each tourist will think of two places he or she wants to see in downtown **München** and will ask you for directions. Use the map on page 221 to help them. Then switch roles.

BEISPIEL     **Wie komme ich ...?**

zum Hofbräuhaus     zum Haus der Kunst
zum Münchner Stadtmuseum
zum Karlstor          zum Hofgarten
zum Nationalmuseum
zum Bahnhof     zum Englischen Garten
zur Theatinerkirche
zum Nationaltheater     zur Frauenkirche

## 19 Für mein Notizbuch

Ein deutscher Austauschschüler möchte dich besuchen. Beschreib in deinem Notizbuch den Weg von deiner Schule bis zu deinem Haus! Fährst du mit dem Bus oder vielleicht mit der U-Bahn? Das kannst du auch beschreiben.

BEISPIEL     **Du gehst ...**          *oder*
            **Du fährst mit dem Bus/der U-Bahn Nummer ... bis ..., dann ...**

*Talking about what there is to eat and drink; saying you do or don't want more; expressing opinions*

## SO SAGT MAN DAS!

### Talking about what there is to eat and drink

If you go to a restaurant for the first time, you might ask your friend or a waiter what there is to eat or drink.

You might ask:

**Was gibt es hier zu essen?**

**Und zu trinken?**

The response might be:

**Es gibt Leberkäs, Vollkornsemmeln, Weißwurst ...**

**Cola, Apfelsaft und auch Mineralwasser.**

What do you think the expressions **Was gibt es?** and **Es gibt ...** mean?

### Ein wenig *G*rammatik

The phrase **es gibt** (*there is, there are*) is a fixed expression that stays the same despite the number of objects referred to. In the example **Gibt es hier in der Nähe einen Supermarkt?** is **Supermarkt** in the nominative or accusative case? How can you tell? What can you say about noun phrases following **es gibt?**[1]

**IMBIß STUBE** *am Rathaus*

Leberkäs mit Senf 4,00
mit Semmel 4,50
Hähnchen vom Grill 6,00
4,50
Gyros mit Salat 7,50
Weißwurst 3,80
Volkornsemmel -,50

Brezel 1,00
Käsebrot 3,20
Milch 2,00
Mineralwasser 1,00
Apfelsaft 2,40
Tee, Glas 2,50

## EIN WENIG LANDESKUNDE

**Leberkäs** is a Bavarian specialty of ground beef or pork liver, pork, and spices. Most people eat it with a **Semmel** or **Brezel** and sweet mustard. How would you tell a German friend about specialties available in your area?

### 20 Was gibt es hier zu essen und zu trinken?

Du kannst dich nicht entscheiden (*to decide*), was du in der **Imbißstube am Rathaus** bestellen möchtest. Frag deinen Partner, was es zu essen und zu trinken gibt! Sag deinem Partner, was du möchtest! Tauscht dann die Rollen aus!

1. Noun phrases that follow **es gibt** are always in the accusative case.

### Saying you do or don't want more

In **Kapitel 8** you learned how to ask if someone wants something else when shopping. When eating at a café or at your friend's house, you may also be asked what else you would like.

The host or your friend might ask:

**Möchtest du noch etwas?**

You might respond:

**Ja, bitte, ich nehme noch eine Brezel.** *or*
**Nein, danke! Ich habe keinen Hunger mehr.** *or*
**Nein, danke! Ich habe genug.** *or*
**Danke, nichts mehr für mich.**

**Möchtest du noch einen Saft?**

**Ja, bitte. Noch einen Saft.** *or*
**Nein, danke, keinen Saft mehr.**

**Noch eine Semmel?**

**Ja, gern!**

What do you think the phrases **noch einen Saft** and **keinen Saft mehr** mean?[1]
What subject and verb might be understood in the question **Noch eine Semmel?**[2]

## 21 Hör gut zu!

Markus is having a **Grillfest**. His friends have just finished eating, and he asks them if they want more. Listen to the conversations and decide what each person had to eat or drink. Then listen again and determine whether each person wanted more or not.

|  | Mara | Silvia | Thomas | Flori | Claudia | Frank |
|---|---|---|---|---|---|---|
| zu essen | Semmel | Hähn-chen | Brezel | Leber-käs | Weiß-wurst | Salat |
| zu trinken | Saft | Limo | Saft | Mineral-wasser | Limo | Apfel-saft |
| noch mehr? | ja | nein | ja | ja | ja | nein |

## 22 Logisch oder unlogisch?

Sind die folgenden Aussagen logisch oder unlogisch? Wenn sie unlogisch sind, ändere die Aussagen, damit sie logisch sind!

1. Ja, bitte, ich möchte noch einen Leberkäs. Ich habe keinen Hunger.
2. Nein, danke! Nichts mehr für mich. Ich möchte noch eine Weißwurst.
3. Ja, ich habe Hunger. Ich möchte noch eine Semmel.
4. Ja, bitte, ich trinke noch einen Saft. Ich habe Apfelsaft gern.
5. Ich habe noch Hunger. Ich nehme noch ein Käsebrot.
6. Ja, bitte, noch eine Tasse Tee. Ich trinke Tee nicht gern. 1. Unlogisch. „Ich habe Hunger." 2. Unlogisch. „Ich möchte keine Weißwurst mehr." 3. Logisch 4. Logisch 5. Logisch 6. Unlogisch. „Ich trinke Tee gern."

In **Kapitel 5** you learned about the indefinite article **ein** (*a, an*). If the noun is a subject, **ein** is used with masculine and neuter nouns, and **eine** with feminine nouns. When the noun following **ein** is used as a direct object, the masculine form is **einen**. The possessive pronouns **mein, dein, sein,** and **ihr** also have these same endings.

When **noch** precedes the indefinite article **ein**, it has the meaning of *another*.

1. *another juice, no more juice* 2. **Möchtest du**

## *Grammatik*  Negation of indefinite articles with **kein**

You have already learned some expressions using **kein: Ich habe keinen Hunger. Ich habe keine Zeit.** What does **kein** mean?[1] What do you notice about the endings that **kein** takes?[2] **Kein** is used to negate a noun, rather than an entire statement. Often when people say that they want more, they say **Ja, noch ein (Käsebrot).** If they don't want more, they simply say: **Keinen (Kaffee) mehr, danke.**

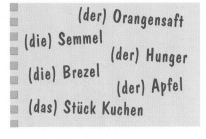

(der) Blumenkohl *(cauliflower)*

(der) Rosenkohl *(Brussel sprouts)*

(die) Zwiebel *(onion)*

(die) Milch  (der) Spinat *(spinach)*

(der) Haferbrei *(oatmeal)*

(die) Leber *(liver)*

(die) Wurst

## 23  **Was ißt oder trinkst du überhaupt nicht?**

Are there some things that you refuse to eat or drink? Take turns asking and telling your classmates about these things, using **kein** in your answers. For example, **Ich trinke keine Limo.** Use the box for ideas or turn to page 321 for additional words.

Answers will vary. Examples:  **Ich esse keine Zwiebeln. Ich esse keinen Spinat.**

## 24  **Noch etwas?**

Nach der Schule sind einige Freunde bei Mara zu Hause und essen etwas. Ergänze das Gespräch mit den Wörtern im Kasten und der richtigen Form von **kein** und **noch ein**!

1. noch einen Apfel
2. keinen Orangensaft
3. noch ein Stück Kuchen
4. keine Semmel
5. keinen Hunger
6. noch eine Brezel

| | |
|---|---|
| MARA | Wer möchte noch was trinken oder essen? Du, Flori, möchtest du __1__ ? |
| FLORI | Ja, gern, Äpfel esse ich sehr gern. |
| MARA | Und mehr Orangensaft? |
| FLORI | Nein danke. __2__ mehr. |
| MARA | Und du Claudia, du hast nur ein Stück Kuchen gegessen. Möchtest du noch etwas? |
| CLAUDIA | Ja, __3__ bitte und auch ein Mineralwasser. |
| MARA | Und Markus? Willst du auch noch eine Semmel? |
| MARKUS | Nein, __4__ mehr. Danke! Ich habe __5__ . |
| MARA | Und du, Rolf? Hast du noch Hunger? |
| ROLF | Ja, ein bißchen. Ich hab' nur eine Brezel gegessen. Ich möchte __6__ . Brezeln esse ich immer gern! |
| CLAUDIA | Das weiß ich! |

(der) Orangensaft

(die) Semmel

(der) Hunger

(die) Brezel

(der) Apfel

(das) Stück Kuchen

L E R N T R I C K

## 25  **Möchtest du noch ein ...?**

Du hast jetzt ein Grillfest. Es gibt noch viel zu essen und zu trinken. Frag deinen Partner, ob er noch etwas haben möchte! Dein Partner sagt ja (mit **noch ein**) oder nein (mit **kein ... mehr**). Dann tauscht ihr die Rollen aus!

Take note of words that are similar and follow the same grammatical patterns. For example, **ein** and **kein** look and sound alike and have the same endings before nouns. Can you think of other words you have learned that look and sound like **ein** and **kein**?[3]

1. *not, not any,* or *no*  2. **Kein** has the same endings as **ein.**  3. **mein, dein,** and **sein.**

a.: 1. Munich  2. October 17, 1974  3. skating  4. Her parents support her.  5. She hopes that skating will become an Olympic sport.

## 26  Ein Leserbrief

Lies diesen Brief an die Zeitschrift **Jugend** und beantworte die Fragen!

**a.** 1. Woher kommt Eva?
   2. Wann ist sie geboren?
   3. Welches Hobby hat Eva?
   4. Wie finden die Eltern Evas Hobby?
   5. Was hofft Eva? (**hoffen** *to hope*)

**b.** Find the two sentences in which the word **daß** is used. What is Eva trying to express in these sentences? What is the English equivalent of **daß**? What is the position of the verb in the clauses that begin with **daß**?

b.: **Daß** introduces clause that tells what her parents find good and what she (Eva) believes. **Daß**=*that*. verb-at end of clause

*Hobby*

Ich heiße Eva Hörster und bin am 17.10.74 in München geboren. Ich laufe mit den Rollschuhen auf der Straße oder auf der Rollschuhbahn. Meine Eltern finden es gut, daß ich Sport treibe. Sie begleiten mich immer zum Training und Langlauf. Ich hoffe, daß Rollschuhlaufen eine olympische Sportart wird. Das Foto ist nach meinem ersten Pokalsieg aufgenommen worden.

Viele Grüße,
Eva Hörster, München

## SO SAGT MAN DAS!

### Expressing opinions

In **Kapitel 2** you learned to express opinions such as: **Ich finde Tennis super!** You can also use a **daß**-clause to elaborate on your opinions.

Your friend might ask:

**Wie findest du München?**

You might respond:

**Super! Ich finde es toll, daß es hier so viele Parks und Museen gibt. Und ich glaube, daß die Leute sehr freundlich sind. Aber ich finde es schlecht, daß das Essen so teuer ist.**

What are the different phrases that begin the sentences expressing opinions? What is the subject in each **daß**-clause? What opinion is being expressed in each sentence?

## *G*rammatik  The conjunction **daß**

Look again at the responses in the **So sagt man das!** box. Name the verbs in the **daß**-clauses.[1] What is the position of these verbs?[2] The conjunction **daß** often begins clauses that express opinions: **Ich finde, daß** .... **Ich glaube, daß** .... In clauses that begin with **daß**, the conjugated verb is at the end of the clause.

München **ist** sehr schön.
Ich glaube, daß München [  ] sehr schön **ist**.

What other conjunction do you know that affects the word order in the same way?[3]

1. **gibt, sind, ist**  2. at the end of the clause  3. **weil**

## 27 Hör gut zu!

Christoph-12-Katze; Birgit-14-Tanzen; Nils-19-Freunde; Alex-16-Mode

You're listening to a radio talk show as several teenagers call in to give their opinion on different topics. Listen to the four call-ins and for each one write the name and the age of the person calling and the general topic on which he or she is expressing an opinion.

## 28 Was sagst du dazu?

Sag deinen Klassenkameraden, was du glaubst!

BEISPIEL     **Die Münchner sind sehr freundlich.**
DU    **Ich glaube, daß die Münchner sehr freundlich sind.** *oder*
       **Ich glaube nicht, daß die Münchner sehr freundlich sind.**

1. Kinokarten sind zu teuer.
2. Politik ist interessant.
3. Hausaufgaben machen Spaß.

4. Fernsehen macht klug *(smart)*.
5. Schüler sind faul *(lazy)*.
6. Pizzaessen ist gesund *(healthy)*.

## 29 Wie findest du …?

Write down at least two opinions about three of the topics on the right. Then, work with your partner and ask each other about some of the topics.

BEISPIEL      DU    **Wie findest du …**
         PARTNER    **Ich glaube, daß …**

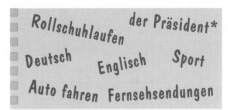

Rollschuhlaufen   der Präsident*
Deutsch   Englisch   Sport
Auto fahren   Fernsehsendungen

## AUSSPRACHE

### Richtig aussprechen / Richtig lesen

**A.** To practice the following sounds, say the words and sentences below after your teacher or after the recording.

1. The long vowels **ü** and **ö**: In **Kapitel 1** you learned how to pronounce the letters **ü** and **ö** as long vowels.

   **führen, für, spülen / Kannst für mich das Geschirr spülen?**
   **blöd, hören, Österreich / Ich höre gern Rock, aber Disko finde ich blöd.**

2. The letters **s, ss,** and **ß**: At the beginning of a syllable the letter **s** is pronounced much like the *z* in the English word *zebra*. However, if it is followed by the letters **t** or **p**, it sounds like the *sh* combination in the English word *shine*. In the middle or at the end of a syllable, the letter **s** is pronounced the same as the *s* in the English word *post;* the letters **ß** and **ss** are always pronounced this way as well.

   **Senf, super, Semmel / Sonja will eine Wurst mit Senf und eine Semmel.**
   **Straße, Innenstadt, Spaß / Wo ist die Spatzenstraße? In der Innenstadt?**
   **Wurst, besser, Imbiß / Die Wurst ist besser in der Imbißstube hier rechts.**

### Richtig schreiben / Diktat

**B.** Write down the sentences that you hear.

---

*****Der Präsident** belongs to a small group of nouns (called *weak nouns*) that add **-n** or **-en** in the accusative case: **Ich kenne den Präsidenten.** Some other nouns in this group are: **der Name (den Namen), der Junge (den Jungen),** and **der Herr (den Herrn).**

## Ein Bummel durch München

| | Durchschnittstemperaturen in °C | | Sonnenstunden pro Tag | Regentage |
|---|---|---|---|---|
| | Tag | Nacht | | |
| | | | 1,8 | 11 |
| Januar | 1,4 | -5,6 | 2,9 | 10 |
| Februar | 3,4 | -5,1 | 3,9 | 9 |
| März | 8,7 | -1,5 | 5,4 | 10 |
| April | 13,5 | 2,8 | 6,0 | 12 |
| Mai | 18,0 | 6,6 | 7,5 | 14 |
| Juni | 21,3 | 10,0 | 7,8 | 13 |
| Juli | 23,2 | 12,1 | 6,7 | 12 |
| August | 22,7 | 11,4 | 6,0 | 10 |
| September | 19,6 | 8,4 | 4,5 | 9 |
| Oktober | 13,3 | 3,7 | 1,9 | 9 |
| November | 6,6 | 0,1 | 1,2 | 10 |
| Dezember | 2,3 | -3,8 | | |

Quelle: Deutscher Wetterdienst, Offenbach

1. These articles are from a book called **Merian live! München**. What kind of book do you think it is?
   a. a history book
   b. a book about parks and gardens
   c. a travel guide

2. When you read a travel guide, you generally have one of two specific purposes: to gather general information about what is going on, or to find specific information about an event — cost, time, date, etc. In which case would you skim to get the gist, and in which case would you scan for specific information?

3. How is information in a travel guide organized? Group the places listed below under one of these three general headings: **Essen und Trinken, Einkaufen, Sehenswertes.**

**Sportmode, Deutsches Museum, Cafés, Restaurants, Geschenkwaren, Alte Pinakothek, Peterskirche, Stehimbisse, Kaufhäuser, Englischer Garten, Konditoreien, Fotogeschäfte**

Answers on p. 215Q.

### Lebensmittel

**Dallmayr**
In den heiligen Hallen der Gaumenfreuden wird sogar der Kauf einer banalen Kiwi zum gastronomischen Ereignis. Münchens ältestes Feinkosthaus ist nicht zuletzt seines aromatischen Kaffees wegen weit über die Grenzen der Stadt hinaus bekannt geworden.
2 Dienerstr. 14/15
U-/S-Bahn: Marienplatz

Januar
**Fasching**
Die »närrische Saison« beginnt in München mit dem 7. Januar und endet in der Nacht zwischen Faschingsdienstag und Aschermittwoch. In diesen Wochen quillt das städtische Veranstaltungsprogramm über von Faschingsbällen aller Art – exklusiven und volkstümlichen, intimen und massenhaften.

Als gesellschaftliche Höhepunkte der Faschingssaison gelten der Chrysanthemenball, Magnolienball, Madameball, Filmball und Presseball. Die phantasievollsten oder auch aufwendigsten Kostüme und Dekorationen sind beim Karneval in Rio im Bayerischen Hof, bei den Festen der Damischen Ritter, den Weißen Festen und der Vorstadthochzeit zu sehen.

Seiner Tradition nach findet der Münchner Fasching im Saal statt, nicht auf der Straße wie etwa der Rheinische Karneval. Nur während der drei letzten Faschingstage – von Sonntag bis Dienstag – tummelt sich das närrische Volk auch im Freien, vor allem in der Fußgängerzone, am Marienplatz und auf dem Viktualienmarkt, wo am Faschingsdienstag ab 6 Uhr in der Früh die Marktfrauen tanzen.

**Englischer Garten**
Münchens vielgeliebte »grüne Lunge« – etwa 5 km lang, bis zu 1 km breit und mit einer Gesamtausdehnung von nahezu 4 km². Entstanden ist der Englische Garten aus einer Anregung des unter Kurfürst Karl Theodor amtierenden Ministers Benjamin Thompson (später Graf Rumford), einen Volkspark in der Art der englischen Landschaftsgärten in den Isarauen anzulegen. 1789 begannen die Arbeiten am Park, die ab 1804 vom Gartenarchitekten Ludwig von Sckell geleitet wurden. Am auffälligsten unter den Bauten im Park sind der Chinesische Turm (1790), nach der Zerstörung im Krieg1952 originalgetreu wiederaufgebaut, der Monopteros, ein klassizistischer Rundtempel nach einem Entwurf Leo von Klenzes im Auftrag Ludwigs I. (1837/38), das Japanische Teehaus, das Mitsuo Nomura 1972 anläßlich der Olympischen Spiele in München als Geschenk Japans an die Olympia-Stadt erbaut hat. Hinzu kommt der künstlich angelegte Kleinhesseloher See mit drei kleinen Inseln, einem Bootsverleih und dem Seehaus (Restaurant und Biergarten).

Zugänge zum Park gibt es am Haus der Kunst, an der Veterinärstraße (Nähe Universität), Gunezrhainerstraße (Nähe Münchner Freiheit), am Seehaus (Ausfahrt Mittlerer Ring) sowie an der Tivolistraße (Nähe Max-Joseph-Brücke). (→ Spaziergänge)

## Olympiapark

Auf dem ehemaligen Oberwiesenfeld wurde für die XX. Olympischen Spiele 1972 von der Architektengemeinschaft Günter Behnisch und Partner dieser Park entworfen.

Der 52 m hohe Olympiaberg wurde auf zusammengetragenen Ruinentrümmern des Zweiten Weltkrieges angelegt und mit voralpiner Vegetation begrünt.

Als weitere Sportstätten gibt es das Eissportstadion, die Schwimmhalle (»Europas schönstes Garten-Hallenbad«) und das Radstadion. Die Olympiahalle selbst dient auch Kongressen, Ausstellungen und Konzerten.

## Kaufhäuser

### Ludwig Beck

Eine Münchner Institution. Auf vier Stockwerken gibt es vom Lodenmantel bis zum Gaultier-Jäckchen vor allem Mode zu kaufen; man findet aber auch den passenden Schmuck dazu, Tisch- und Bettwäsche, originelles Küchenzubehör, eine riesige Jazz-Auswahl auf CD – sowie Münchens netteste Verkäufer! Für das leibliche Wohl empfehlen sich drei Restaurants, darunter eine Sushi-Bar.
Marienplatz 11
U-/S-Bahn: Marienplatz

## Medizinische Versorgung

Bitte wenden Sie sich an den Hotelportier.

### Auskunft dienstbereiter Apotheken:
Tel. 59 44 75

### Große Apotheken im Zentrum:
Internationale Ludwigs-Apotheke
Neuhauser Str. 8
Von Mendel'sche Apotheke
(große Abteilung für homöopathische Medikamente)
40 Leopoldstr. 58

## Peterskirche, St. Peter

Erste und lange Zeit einzige Pfarrkirche der Stadt, deren erster Bau (erste Hälfte 11. Jh.) älter als die Stadt selbst ist. In der Folgezeit erlebte das Gotteshaus zahlreiche Erweiterungen und Modernisierungen in den Stilen der Gotik, der Renaissance und des Barock. Die Bombenzerstörungen der Jahre 1944/45 waren so schwer, daß man die Kirche beinahe gänzlich gesprengt hätte.

Der Turm »Alter Peter« ist – neben den Türmen der Frauenkirche – das Wahrzeichen der Stadt geblieben. 302 hölzerne Stufen führen an den vier Glocken vorbei zur Aussichtsgalerie.

## DER BESONDERE TIP

**Isar-Floßfahrt** Floßfahrten auf der Isar zwischen Wolfratshausen und München sind eine bei Alt und Jung sehr beliebte »Gaudi«. Die Fahrt selbst dauert etwa sieben Stunden; eine Mittagspause wird an Land eingelegt. Zu einer Floßfahrt kann man sich freilich nicht spontan entschließen: Die meisten Termine sind (von Firmen, Vereinen, Freundeskreisen) schon lange im voraus gebucht. Einzelpassagiere wenden sich an das Amtliche Bayerische Reisebüro (ABR), das sich ein Kontingent für »Individualisten« zu sichern pflegt.

...chtfröhliche Gaudi ohnegleichen: Isarfloßfahrten

4. What general types of information appear in these texts? Which excerpts can you classify, using the categories you developed in Activity 3?

5. What are the names of some places to go shopping for fine foods? For fashionable clothes?

6. Where would you go in these situations?
   a. It's the middle of January and you want to go dancing.
   b. You want to go for a long relaxing walk.
   c. You have a sore throat and you need throat lozenges.
   d. You have been invited to someone's home and you want to buy a special coffee for them.

7. If you had a whole day free and wanted to do something out of the ordinary, what special tip does the guidebook give? Could you do it on the spur of the moment, or do you have to plan ahead? How do you know?

8. Read the excerpts **Peterskirche, St. Peter** and **Olympiapark** and see if you can answer these questions. How old is the **Peterskirche**? What would you see if you climbed the steps of the **Alter Peter**? When was the **Olympiapark** built? How high is the mountain in the **Olympiapark**, and what is it made out of?

9. You are going to be in Munich for a day in June. Plan what you would do. How will the weather chart help you in making your plans? What can you do in June that you could not have done in January? What could you have done in January that you cannot do in June?

in January: **Fasching** parties; in June: **Isar-Floßfahrt**

# ANWENDUNG

**1** Listen to some American students tell their friends back in Rosenheim about their day in **München** with Mara and Markus. Make a list of where they were and what they bought. Dallmayr-Weißwürste; Ludwig Beck-CDs, Schmuck; Fotogeschäft-Fotoalbum

**2** You work at the information desk in the train station, and several people need your help. Take turns with your partner asking for and giving the requested information. Use the cues below to formulate your questions. Different people want to know:

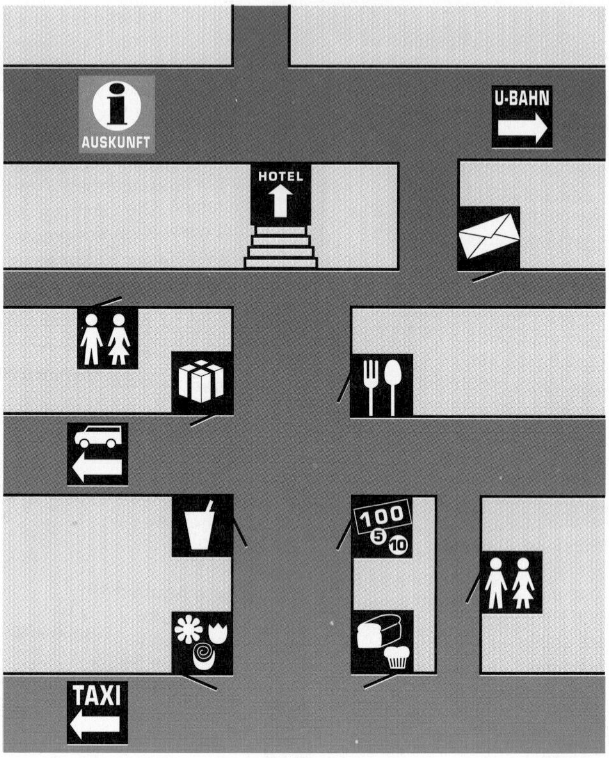

where a bank is

where the post office is

where a restaurant is

if there is a hotel here

if there's a subway station here

where to buy flowers

**3** Lies die Postkarte rechts und beantworte die folgenden Fragen!

a. Wie findet Jörg die Stadt München? Was sagt er?

b. Warum ißt er soviel Leberkäs und so viele Weißwürste?

c. Was besichtigt (besichtigen: *to sightsee*) Jörg in München?

a. unheimlich stark
b. weil sie sagenhaft gut sind
c. die Frauenkirche, das Rathaus

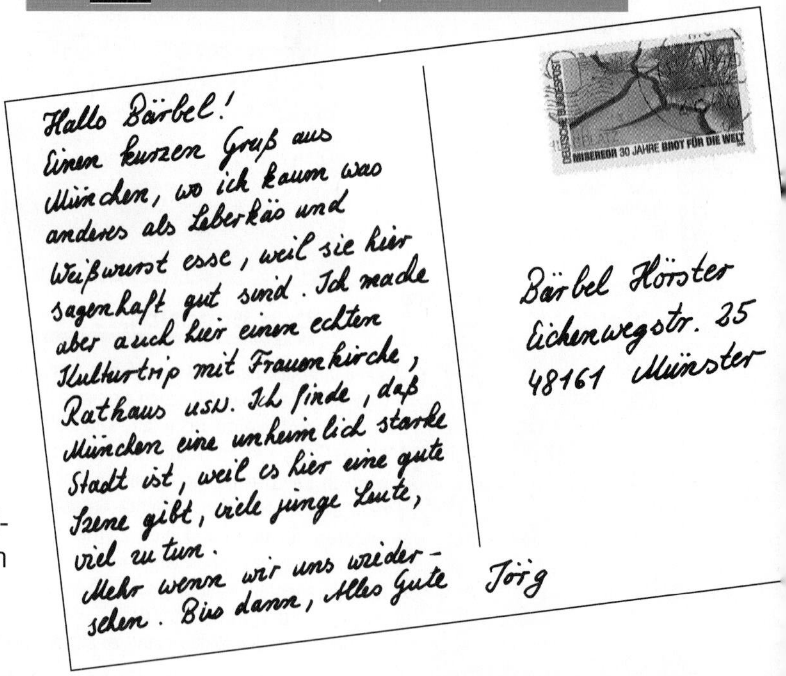

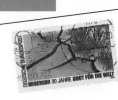

Hallo Bärbel!
Einen kurzen Gruß aus
München, wo ich kaum was
anderes als Leberkäs und
Weißwurst esse, weil sie hier
sagenhaft gut sind. Ich mache
aber auch hier einen echten
Kulturtrip mit Frauenkirche,
Rathaus usw. Ich finde, daß
München eine unheimlich starke
Stadt ist, weil es hier eine gute
Szene gibt, viele junge Leute,
viel zu tun.
Mehr wenn wir uns wieder-
sehen. Bis dann, Alles Gute   Jörg

Bärbel Hörster
Eichenwegstr. 25
48161 Münster

**4** In this chapter you have learned a lot about Munich. Write a postcard either to your parents or to a friend giving your opinions about the city or write a postcard about some other place you have visited. Use the postcard on page 236 as a model for your salutation and closing.

**5** You have learned your way around Mittersendling but your visiting American friend has not. Your friend will tell you three things he or she needs to do or buy. Tell your friend where he or she needs to go (bakery, butcher shop, etc.) and how to get there. Decide together on a starting point and use the map on page 225. Then switch roles.

DU **Ich brauche ...** *oder* **Ich muß ... kaufen.**
PARTNER **Also, du mußt zum/zur ... gehen?**
**Geh ...!**

**6**

## R O L L E N S P I E L

Get together with two other classmates and role-play the following scene.

Design a menu for an **Imbißstube** and write it on a piece of paper or poster board. Then, with three other classmates, develop a conversation at the snack stand that is based on the following situation.

**a.** You are discussing with your friends what's available at the stand. Then each of you orders something. Ask what it costs and pay the person behind the counter. Be polite!

**b.** As you enjoy the food, discuss how the food tastes and if someone wants more or not. If so, order more. Discuss with your friends some of your opinions about the city of Munich, which you are visiting today.

**Wissen Sie, wo ... ist?**
**Weißt du, wo ... ist?**

**Can you talk about where something is located? (p.222)**

**1** How would you ask an older passerby where the following places are using **wissen**? How would you ask someone who is your own age? How would you answer?

a. Frauenkirche (... Straße) — in der
b. Rathaus (Marienplatz) — am
c. Museum (Maximilianstraße) — in der

**Can you ask for and give directions? (p. 226)**

**2** How would you ask for directions from the **X**-mark to the following places?

a. zum Bahnhof — a. Wie komme ich zum Bahnhof?
b. zum Theater — b. zum Theater?
c. zum Marktplatz — c. zum Marktplatz?
d. zur Bank — d. zur Bank?

**3** How would you tell an older person to get to the following places using the command forms? Someone your own age? Use the **X**-mark as the starting point.

a. Hindenburgstr.-geradeaus; Heisstr.-links; Hegelstr.-rechts; Leibnizstr.-links

By vehicle:
a. to the train station
b. to the town hall

On foot:
a. to the supermarket
b. to the café

**Can you talk about what there is to eat and drink? (p. 229)**

**4** How would you ask what there is to eat? And to drink? How would you tell someone what there is to eat or drink, using the items below?

a. Leberkäs
b. whole wheat rolls
c. apple juice
d. tea
e. salad
f. grilled chicken

4. Was gibt es zu essen? Zu trinken? Es gibt a. Leberkäs. b. Vollkornsemmeln c. Apfelsaft d. Tee e. Salat f. Hähnchen

**Can you ask or tell someone that you do or don't want more? (p. 230)**

**5** How would you ask someone if he or she wants more? How would you tell someone that you want more of the items below or that you don't want more, using **noch ein** and **kein ... mehr**?

Möchtest du noch etwas?
a. Ja bitte, noch ein Stück Kuchen. Nein danke, keinen Kuchen mehr.
b. Ja bitte, noch eine Semmel. Nein danke, keine Semmel mehr.

a. piece of cake
b. roll
c. mineral water
d. ice-cream

c. Ja bitte, noch ein Mineralwasser. Nein danke, kein Mineralwasser mehr. d. Ja bitte, noch ein Eis. Nein danke, kein Eis mehr.

**Can you express opinions using daß-clauses? (p. 232)**

**6** a. How would you give your opinion about the following statement. How would you agree with it? And disagree?

**Autofahren ist gefährlich.**

Answers will vary. Examples: Ich finde, daß Autofahren gefährlich ist. Ich finde nicht, daß Autofahren gefährlich ist.

b. State your opinions about school in general. Write at least two sentences using **daß**-clauses.

## ERSTE STUFE
### IN DER INNENSTADT

die Stadt, ¨e   *city*
das Rathaus, ¨er   *city hall*
der Marktplatz, ¨e   *market square*
die Post   *post office*
der Bahnhof, ¨e   *railroad station*
die Bank, -en   *bank*

die Kirche, -n   *church*
das Hotel, -s   *hotel*
der Garten, ¨   *garden*
das Museum, die Museen   *museum*
das Theater, -   *theater*
die U-Bahnstation, -en   *subway station*

### TALKING ABOUT WHERE SOMETHING IS LOCATED

die Straße, -n   *street*
am ... platz   *on ... Square*
wissen   *to know (a fact, information, etc.)*
Entschuldigung! }
Verzeihung! }   *Excuse me!*
Es tut mir leid.   *I'm sorry.*
Keine Ahnung!   *I have no idea!*

---

## ZWEITE STUFE
### ASKING FOR AND GIVING DIRECTIONS

Wie komme ich zum (zur) ...   *How do I get to ...*
nach links   *to the left*
nach rechts   *to the right*
geradeaus   *straight ahead*
bis zur Ampel   *until you get to the traffic light*

bis zur ... Straße   *until you get to ... Street*
bis zum ... Platz   *until you get to ... Square*
die nächste Straße   *the next street*
die erste (zweite, dritte, vierte) Straße   *the first (second, third, fourth) street*

wieder   *again*
fahren   *to go somewhere, ride, drive (using a vehicle)*
er/sie fährt   *he/she drives is driving/is going*
Vielen Dank!   *Thank you very much!*
Gern geschehen!   *My pleasure!*

---

## DRITTE STUFE
### TALKING ABOUT WHAT THERE IS TO EAT AND DRINK

die Imbißstube, -n   *snack bar*
der Leberkäs   *Bavarian specialty* See p. 229.
   mit Senf   *with mustard*
die Weißwurst, ¨e   *Southern German sausage specialty* See p. 229.
die Vollkornsemmel, -n   *whole wheat roll*
das Gyros   *gyros*

### SAYING YOU DO OR DON'T WANT MORE

Ich möchte noch ein(e)(en) ...   *I'd like another ...*
Ich möchte kein(e)(en) ... mehr.   *I don't want another .../anymore*
noch ein(e) (en)   *more, another one*
genug   *enough*
kein   *no, none, not any*
kein (en)... mehr   *no more ...*
Nichts mehr, danke!   *No more, nothing else, ... thanks!*

### EXPRESSING OPINIONS

daß   *that*
Ich finde, daß ...   *I think that...*
Ich finde es gut/schlecht, daß ...   *I think it's good/ bad that...*
die Leute (pl)   *people*

**Location Opener**

# Baden-Württemberg, pages 240–243
## Expanded Video Program, Videocassette 4

## $\mathcal{U}$sing the Photograph,
### pp. 240-241

### Background Information

- The building pictured is **das alte Schloß** in **Meersburg am Bodensee.** At the center of this elongated castle is the **Dagobert-Turm** which was built at the end of the 12th century. In 1803, Freiherr Joseph von Laßberg bought the castle from the state, which had planned to tear it down. Von Laßberg kept his collection of art, sculpture, and antiques in this castle. His sister-in-law, the poet Annette von Droste-Hülshoff lived here from 1841 until she died in 1848.

- Known as the **Schwäbisches Meer,** Lake Constance, or **Bodensee,** is the largest inland body of water that Germany has any claim to. The lake encompasses 538 square kilometers and is up to 252 meters deep in some places. The Romans established the first harbor and wharf in Lintavia, which is known today as Lindau. Until the 17th century, only military ships used the lake. Later, commercial ships transported goods across the lake. Today, one of the most modern fleets of ships in Europe travels this lake, and it is operated jointly by Germany, Switzerland, and Austria. In addition to such historic seaports as Lindau, Konstanz, and Friedrichshafen, the lake has two beautiful islands, Reichenau and Mainau, which are popular tourist spots.

### Teaching Suggestion

Have students locate Lake Constance on a map. Ask them to name the two other countries with which Germany shares this lake. (Switzerland and Austria)

### Math Connection

To get an idea of the size of Lake Constance, ask students to convert 538 square kilometers into square miles. (1 square km = 0.386 square miles)

## $\mathcal{U}$sing the Almanac and Map,
### p. 241

The three striding lions on the Baden-Württemberg shield date back to the 12th century, when the Swabian ruler Duke Philipp was crowned German king. Up until then (1198), Swabian kings had used a single standing lion as their crest. When a public referendum created the Federal State of Baden-Württemberg in 1951, crests were selected from the old Duchy of Swabia, which had once represented all of what is now southwest Germany. The symbol selected for the Swabian coat of arms was that of the ruling Staufer Family and shows three lions on a golden shield.

### Background Information

Baden-Württemberg is the third largest **Bundesland** in Germany. In 1951 a public referendum created this Bundesland from the three smaller provinces of Baden, Württemberg-Hohenzollern, and Württemberg-Baden. Most people who have never heard of Baden-Württemberg are at least familiar with the **Schwarzwald** (*Black Forest*) which is located in the southwestern part of the state.

### 🌐 Culture Notes

- The Black Forest received its name because the density of the towering fir trees makes the forest appear almost black and very frightening. Even the Romans avoided it when possible. They rarely ventured into the gloomy forest unless drawn by the many refreshing springs.

- Stuttgart, the capital of Baden-Württemberg, is also called **Stadt des guten Sterns** as it has the highest per capita income of all German cities. It is home to over 500 businesses, several universities, and Germany's largest wine-growing community. The most important companies located in the city are Daimler-Benz, Porsche, and Bosch.

## Terms in the Almanac

- **Donau:** at 2,850 km, the second longest river in Europe. It originates in the Black Forest and ends in the Black Sea. In English, it is known as the Danube.

- **Rhein:** the third longest river in Europe at 1,320 km, 867 km of which run through Germany. It originates in the Swiss Alps and ends in the North Sea in Holland. The drive along the **Rhein** is known for its endless vineyards, fairy tale castles, and fortresses.

- **Karlsruhe:** the seat of the **Bundesverfassungsgericht** (*Federal Constitutional Court*), and the **Bundesgerichtshof** (*Federal Court of Justice*)

- **Heidelberg:** home of the oldest university in Germany. The university was founded in 1386.

- **Spätzle**: small dumplings made by dropping bits of dough into boiling salt water

- **Schwarzwälder Kirschtorte:** most famous product of Baden-Württemberg. It is a delicate chocolate cake layered with sour cherries, cherry liquor, shavings of dark chocolate, red currant jelly, and whipped cream. (See Photo 2 on p. 269 of the *Pupil's Edition*.)

- **Maultaschen:** triangular shaped dough pockets filled with spinach, bacon, onion, egg, herbs, and spices cooked in broth

## Using the Map

- Have students look at the map of Germany on p. 2 and name the countries and **Bundesländer** that border on Baden-Württemberg. (France; Switzerland; Bavaria; Hessen; Rheinland-Pfalz) You may also want to use Map Transparency 1.

- Looking at the map on p. 2, ask students which two **Bundesländer** are larger than Baden-Württemberg. (Bayern, Niedersachsen**)**

 **Culture Note**

According to the **Lorelei** legend, a beautiful blond mermaid sat on a cliff overlooking the **Rhein.** With her beauty and her song, she often distracted the crewmen of ships and caused many shipwrecks.

## *Interpreting the Photo Essay, pp. 242-243*

②  St. Märgen is a popular vacation spot in the Black Forest. Mills like this one were used to crush or grind materials such as grains and wood.

- **Drawing Inferences**  Ask students what natural resource was used to operate this particular mill. (water)

③  Small villages such as this arose in the 12th and 13th centuries. Farmers, charcoal burners, and woodcutters cleared the forest and used its natural resources for their livelihood.

④  With a population of only 9,700, Besigheim is a typical Swabian town. It has an old bridge spanning the Enz river that dates back to 1581.

⑤  Construction of this city hall dates back to 1507. It was completed in 1783. The **Rathaus** is used for official functions and festivities such as weddings. The detailed facade of the building reflects different aspects of the city's history.

⑥  The witch on the broomstick is called a **Küchenhexe,** a good witch who brings good luck. She is believed to keep the fire in the stove burning, help dough rise, and protect the house in general.

⑦  These students all live in the Bietigheim-Bissingen area and attend the **Ellental Gymnasium** in Bietigheim. They are Andreas (top row), Martin (middle row left), Sabine (middle row center), Sandra (middle row right), Thomas (front row left), and Nicole (front row right).

Komm mit nach

# Baden-Württemberg!

# Baden-Württemberg

**Einwohner:** 9 300 000

**Fläche:** 36 000 Quadratkilometer (13 896 Quadratmeilen), etwa halb so groß wie Südkarolina

**Landeshauptstadt:** Stuttgart (570 000 Einwohner)

**Große Städte:** Mannheim, Karlsruhe, Freiburg, Heilbronn, Heidelberg, Pforzheim

**Flüsse:** Donau, Rhein, Neckar, Jagst, Kocher

**Seen:** Bodensee

**Berge:** Feldberg (1493 Meter hoch), Belchen (1414 Meter hoch)

**Industrien:** Maschinenbau, Automobilindustrie, Elektrotechnik, Chemie, Feinmechanik, Optik

**Beliebte Gerichte:** Spätzle, Schwarzwälder Kirschtorte, Maultaschen, Schinken

**Foto ①:** Das Alte Schloß in Meersburg am Bodensee

# Baden-Württemberg

*The southwestern German state of Baden-Württemberg is known both for its charming landscapes and for its high-tech industries. The **Schwarzwald** (Black Forest) with its traditional farmhouses is one of Germany's most popular tourist regions. The area around Stuttgart, the state capital, is home to major automobile and electronics firms, as well as hundreds of highly specialized small companies producing textiles, watches, and optical iinstruments.*

③ A typical village in the Black Forest

② The **Hexenloch Mühle** in St. Märgen in the Black Forest.

④ The picturesque town of Besigheim on the river Enz

⑤ The City Hall (**Rathaus**) in Bietigheim, built in 1507

*The remaining chapters (10, 11, and 12) are set in Bietigheim-Bissingen, a town near Stuttgart. This historic town on the River Enz still has many old half-timbered houses. Among its inhabitants are the teenagers in these three chapters, who attend the* **Ellental Gymnasium.**

⑥ A typical house facade along the witches' walk (**Hexenwegle**) in Bietigheim

⑦ Martin, Andreas, Thomas, Sabine, Sandra, and Nicole invite you to join them in Bietigheim.

# Kapitel 10: Kino und Konzerte *Chapter Overview*

| **Los geht's!** pp. 246-248 | Wie verbringt ihr eure Freizeit? p. 246 | | | *Video Guide* |
|---|---|---|---|---|
| | **FUNCTIONS** | **GRAMMAR** | **CULTURE** | **RE-ENTRY** |
| **Erste Stufe** pp. 249-252 | •Expressing likes and dislikes, p. 250 •Expressing familiarity, p. 252 | •The verb **mögen**, p. 250 •The verb **kennen**, p. 252 | •**Ein wenig Landeskunde:** The German movie-rating system, p. 251 •**Ein wenig Landeskunde:** A German pop chart, p. 251 | •Expressing likes and dislikes, p. 250 (from **Kapitel 2**) •The verb **wissen**, p. 252 (from **Kapitel 7**) •Talking about when you do things, p. 252 (from **Kapitel 2**) •Talking about how often you do things, p. 252 (from **Kapitel 7**) |
| **Zweite Stufe** pp. 253-257 | Expressing preferences and favorites, p. 253 | •Using **lieber** and **am liebsten** with **haben**, p. 253 •The stem-changing verb **sehen**, p. 253 | •Movie ads, p. 255 •**Landeskunde:** Welche kulturellen Veranstaltungen besuchst du? p. 257 | •The stem-changing verb **aussehen** p. 253 (from **Kapitel 5**) •Activity vocabulary, p. 254 (from **Kapitel 2** and **Kapitel 6**) •**Können**, p. 254 (from **Kapitel 7**) •Expressing opinions, p. 256 (from **Kapitel 2**) •Giving reasons, p. 256 (**Kapitel 8**) •Describing people, p. 256 (from **Kapitel 8**) |
| **Dritte Stufe** pp. 258-261 | Talking about what you did in your free time, p. 260 | •The phrase **sprechen über**, p. 259 •The stem-changing verbs **lesen** and **sprechen**, p. 259 | •Upcoming events poster, p. 258 •Best-seller lists, p. 258 •Video-hits list, p. 258 •Popular German novels, p. 259 | •The stem-changing verbs **nehmen** and **essen**, p. 259 from (**Kapitel 5** and **Kapitel 6**) •Giving reasons, p. 259 (from **Kapitel 8**) •Talking about when you do things p. 260 (from **Kapitel 2**) •The verb **sein** (past tense), p. 260 (from **Kapitel 8**) |
| **Aussprache** p. 261 | Review short vowel **o**, review long vowel **o**, review short vowel **u**, review long vowel **u**, review combination **ch** | | | Diktat: *Textbook Audiocassette 5 B* |
| **Zum Lesen** pp. 262-263 | **Was sagen die Kritiker?** Reading Strategy: Looking for cognates and recognizing false cognates | | | |
| **Review** pp. 264-267 | •Anwendung, p. 264 •Kann ich's wirklich? p. 266 •Wortschatz, p. 267 | | | |

**Assessment Options**

**Stufe Quizzes**
•*Chapter Resources*, Book 4
  Erste Stufe, Quiz 10-1
  Zweite Stufe, Quiz 10-2
  Dritte Stufe, Quiz 10-3
•*Assessment Items, Audiocassette* 10 B

**Chapter Test Kapitel 10**
•*Chapter Resources*, Book 4
•*Assessment Guide*, Speaking Test
•*Assessment Items, Audiocassette* 10 B

**Test Generator, Kapitel 10**

| | |
|---|---|
| *Video Program* **OR** *Expanded Video Program,* Videocassette 4 | Textbook Audiocassette 5 B |

| RESOURCES Print | RESOURCES Audiovisual |
|---|---|

Textbook Audiocassette 5 B

*Practice and Activity Book*
*Chapter Resources,* Book 4
- Communicative Activity 10-1
- Additional Listening Activity 10-1 . . . . . . . . . . . . . *Additional Listening Activities, Audiocassette* 10 B
- Additional Listening Activity 10-2 . . . . . . . . . . . . . *Additional Listening Activities, Audiocassette* 10 B
- Student Response Form
- Realia 10-1
- Situation Card 10-1
- Teaching Transparency Master 10-1 . . . . . . . . . . . . . *Teaching Transparency* 10-1
- Quiz 10-1 . . . . . . . . . . . . . . . . . . . . . . . . . . . . . . . *Assessment Items, Audiocassette* 8 B

Textbook Audiocassette 5 B

*Practice and Activity Book*
*Chapter Resources,* Book 4
- Communicative Activity 10-2
- Additional Listening Activity 10-3 . . . . . . . . . . . . . *Additional Listening Activities, Audiocassette* 10 B
- Additional Listening Activity 10-4 . . . . . . . . . . . . . *Additional Listening Activities, Audiocassette* 10 B
- Student Response Form
- Realia 10-2
- Situation Card 10-2
- Quiz 10-2 . . . . . . . . . . . . . . . . . . . . . . . . . . . . . . . *Assessment Items, Audiocassette* 8 B
*Video Guide.* . . . . . . . . . . . . . . . . . . . . . . . . . . . . . . *Video Program/Expanded Video Program,* Videocassette 4

Textbook Audiocassette 5 B

*Practice and Activity Book*
*Chapter Resources,* Book 4
- Additional Listening Activity 10-5 . . . . . . . . . . . . . *Additional Listening Activities, Audiocassette* 10 B
- Additional Listening Activity 10-6 . . . . . . . . . . . . . *Additional Listening Activities, Audiocassette* 10 B
- Student Response Form
- Realia 10-3
- Situation Card 10-3
- Teaching Transparency Master 10-2 . . . . . . . . . . . . . *Teaching Transparency* 10-2
- Quiz 10-3 . . . . . . . . . . . . . . . . . . . . . . . . . . . . . . . *Assessment Items, Audiocassette* 8 B

*Video Guide.* . . . . . . . . . . . . . . . . . . . . . . . . . . . . . . *Video Program/Expanded Video Program,* Videocassette 4

**Alternative Assessment**
- Performance Assessment, *Teacher's Edition*
  **Erste Stufe,** p. 243J
  **Zweite Stufe,** p. 243M
  **Dritte Stufe,** p. 243P

- Portfolio Assessment
  Written: **Anwendung,** Activity 3, *Pupil's Edition,* p. 264, *Assessment Guide*
  Oral: **Dritte Stufe,** Activity 24, *Pupil's Edition,* p. 260, *Assessment Guide*
- **Notizbuch,** *Pupil's Edition,* p. 261; *Practice and Activity Book,* p. 154

# Kapitel 10: Kino und Konzerte
# *Textbook Listening Activities Scripts*

## Erste Stufe
### Activity 7, p. 250

ERWIN  Ja also, ich bin der Erwin, und ich geh' schon gern mal ins Kino. Meistens ja mit meinem Freund Udo, denn wir mögen beide die gleichen Filme ... besonders ja Komödien, die halt lustig sind und einen zum Lachen bringen. Die finden wir am besten. Dagegen aber mag ich Kriegsfilme überhaupt nicht. Zu brutal and deprimierend. Da kann man sich nicht entspannen.

DAVID  Ich heiße David und ah ... ich sehe Kinofilme unwahrscheinlich gern. Welche? Tja ... eine ganze Reihe, aber doch am liebsten Fantasyfilme, so wie zum Beispiel *Die unendliche Geschichte.* Die finde ich Spitze. Ich mag auch andere Filme, aber ich sehe mir nie Western an, die finde ich nämlich langweilig und auch ein bißchen albern.

JUDITH  Guten Tag! Ich bin Judith, und meine beste Freundin und ich gehen regelmäßig ins Kino, meistens am Wochenende. Welche Filme bevorzuge ich? Na, James Bond Filme zum Beispiel ... also Abenteuerfilme. Die sind immer spannend und interessant. Was ich so gar nicht mag sind Krimis. Die sind oft zu brutal. Ich finde sie furchtbar blöd.

AYSHA  Hin und wieder geh' ich auch ins Kino, aber meistens mit Freunden. Ach ja, ich heiße Aysha. Wenn ich ins Kino gehe, schau' ich mir nur Liebesfilme an — so wie *Ghost.* Das ist so romantisch, nicht wahr? Solche Filme sehe ich mir oft mehrmals an. Was ich an Filmarten nicht besonders gern sehe sind Science-fiction-Filme. Sowas interessiert mich nämlich überhaupt nicht.

### Activity 11, p. 252

1. — Kennst du schon den neuesten Film mit Arnold Schwarzenegger?
   — Meinst du den *Terminator 2®?*
   — Ja klar! Hast du den Film auch schon gesehen?
   — Ja, fand ich echt stark! Seine Filme sind immer spannend.

2. — Am Freitag war ich mit Rolf im Konzert. Die *Toten Hosen* haben gespielt. Kennst du die?
   — Welche Lieder haben sie gespielt?
   — Die von der neuen CD!
   — Die sind total gut. Die CD habe ich gerade letzte Woche gekauft.

3. — Am liebsten höre ich eigentlich Disko. Kennst du das neue Lied *Hals über Kopf?*

— Und wer singt das denn?
— Na, die Nicki!
— Noch nie von ihr gehört!

4. — Ich wollte heute nachmittag mal wieder ins Kino. Da im Cinedom läuft gerade *Dead Again.* Schon davon gehört?
   — Ja, sicher doch! Ich hab' ihn schon vor zwei Wochen mit Flori gesehen. Der war echt toll. Aber ich seh mir den gern noch mal mit dir an!

## Zweite Stufe
### Activity 13, p. 253

1. Grüß Gott! Ich heiße Marianne. Also Filme sehe ich gern, aber nicht alle Arten davon. Im Fernsehen seh' ich abends gern Krimis. Die find' ich doch schon gut ... sind immer ganz interessant. Wenn ich aber ins Kino gehe, sehe ich lieber Western. Aber Horrorfilme, die mag ich ja überhaupt nicht ... zu gruselig für mich. Und am liebsten sehe ich Abenteuerfilme, weil sie eben so spannend sind.

2. Ich bin der Stefan. Was ich gern sehe? Tja ... Komödien mag ich gern, weil sie unterhaltend sind. Neulich war ich mit meiner Freundin im Kino und habe einen Liebesfilm gesehen. Schrecklich! Die mag ich also wirklich nicht ... zu schmalzig. Da sehe ich schon lieber Fantasyfilme, die sind wenigstens ganz phantasievoll. Am liebsten sehe ich natürlich Science-fiction-Filme. Die sind total stark. Wenn's die im Kino gibt, bin ich immer in der ersten Spielwoche da.

## Dritte Stufe
### Activity 26, p. 260

1. — Ich war im Konzert. Das war echt toll!
   — Ja? Wer hat denn dieses Mal gespielt?

2. — Susanne und ich haben am Samstag einige Klamotten gekauft. Das hat Spaß gemacht!
   — Find' ich toll! Wie war der Film denn?

3. — Hab' mir drei neue Krimis in der Buchhandlung gekauft.
   — Und ... wie hat dir die CD gefallen? Starke Musik, nicht?

4. — Ich habe heute das Buch *Jurassic Park®* gekauft. Hast du es schon gelesen?

— Nein, aber ich habe den Film letzte Woche gesehen.

5. — Wir haben zuerst das Museum besucht, danach eine Schiffahrt auf dem Bodensee gemacht.
— Ja, das höre ich auch gern. Aber Rockmusik höre ich am liebsten.

## Diktat, p. 261

You will hear a description of what Thomas and his friend Martin, and Sandra and her friend Sabine like to do in their free time. First listen to the description, then write down what you hear.

Am Wochenende haben Thomas und Martin viel gemacht. Zuerst haben sie gekegelt, und Thomas hat dabei gewonnen. Sie gehen auch gern ins Kino, und so haben sie einen Abenteuerfilm gesehen. Er war sehr spannend. Sandra und Sabine haben andere Interessen. Sie sind lieber zu Hause und hören neue Kassetten oder CDs. Natürlich diskutieren sie viel, über Musik, Filme, Stars und so. Und wenn das Wetter schlecht ist, spielen sie Brettspiele oder auch Karten.

## Anwendung
### Activity 1, p. 264

INTERVIEWER  Grüß dich! Wir schreiben einen Artikel über Freizeit, was Jugendliche so machen. Wie heißt du denn?
PETRA  Ich heiße Petra.
INTERVIEWER  So, Petra, wenn du mit deinen Freunden ausgehst, wohin geht ihr?
PETRA  Tja, wir gehen meistens in die Innenstadt.
INTERVIEWER  Und was macht ihr da?
PETRA  Wir gehen oft ins Kino und sehen uns einen Film an.
INTERVIEWER  Wann geht ihr denn ins Kino?
PETRA  Jeden Montag nach dem Abendbrot.
INTERVIEWER  Soso. Also abends.
PETRA  Ja, wir haben immer Spaß dabei.
INTERVIEWER  Vielen Dank, Petra! Nun sag mal, wer ist der Junge da drüben?
PETRA  Das ist der Rudi. Soll ich ihn mal holen?
INTERVIEWER  Ja, bitte!
PETRA  Du, Rudi, komm mal her!
RUDI  Ja, was gibt's?
PETRA  Die Leute möchten dich auch mal fragen, wie du deine Freizeit verbringst. Geht das?

RUDI  Ja, gern. Was wollen Sie wissen?
INTERVIEWER  Wohin gehst du, wenn du ausgehst, und mit wem gehst du aus?
RUDI  Ich geh' mit meinen Freunden aus, und tja ... wir gehen gern ins Konzert, um gute Musik zu hören.
INTERVIEWER  Wann macht ihr das denn und wie oft?
RUDI  Wir machen das meistens sonntags. Und wenn wir genug Taschengeld haben, gehen wir sogar zweimal im Monat.
INTERVIEWER  Vielen Dank, Rudi!
RUDI  Gern geschehen.
INTERVIEWER  Grüß dich! Dürfte ich dir ein paar Fragen stellen?
MAX  Na sicher!
INTERVIEWER  Könntest du dich vorstellen und uns sagen, was du in deiner Freizeit machst?
MAX  Ja also, ich bin der Max, und ja ... meine Freizeit verbringe ich gern mit meinem Freund, dem Otto. Wir sind dann meistens bei ihm zu Hause. Der hat nämlich eine total starke Stereoanlage. Da hören wir uns nachmittags seine CDs an.
INTERVIEWER  Macht ihr das jeden Tag?
MAX  Nee, das nicht. Aber mindestens einmal in der Woche.
INTERVIEWER  Dank' dir, Max! Könntest du uns das Mädchen da drüben mal vorstellen?
MAX  Ja, das da ist die Renate. Einen Augenblick mal!
INTERVIEWER  Guten Tag! Renate?
RENATE  Ja, ich heiße Renate.
INTERVIEWER  Wir wollten dir auch einige Fragen stellen für unsere Umfrage. Geht das?
RENATE  Ja, warum nicht?
INTERVIEWER  Was machst du gern in deiner Freizeit, und wann und wie oft hast du Zeit dafür?
RENATE  Ich gehe nicht so gern aus, denn so viele freie Zeit habe ich nicht ... Da bleib' ich schon lieber mal zu Hause.
INTERVIEWER  Und was machst du da?
RENATE  Am liebsten lese ich Bücher und ...
INTERVIEWER  Entschuldigung ... und wann machst du das?
RENATE  Lesen? ... Ja, manchmal abends, wenn ich mit den Hausaufgaben fertig bin. Ich wünschte, ich hätte mehr Zeit dafür.
INTERVIEWER  Ja, also hab' recht vielen Dank, Renate.
RENATE  Ja, bitte. Tschüs!

# Kapitel 10: Kino und Konzerte
## *Suggested Project*

*In this project, each student will create a* **Flugblatt** *(flyer) and an oral presentation reviewing a movie, book, or concert. These will be put up on a* **Litfaßsäule** *(kiosk) that students can make together. Start this project after completing the* **Zum Lesen** *activities.*

## MATERIALS

✂ **Students may need**
- *paper*
- *sources for written assignment*
- *pens*
- *sturdy cardboard paper that can be rolled into the shape of a* Litfaßsäule

## SUGGESTED TOPICS

**Book Review**
title and author; brief summary; short review explaining why the student did or did not like the book and whether he or she would recommend it to others; where it can be purchased and for what approximate price

**Movie Review**
title, director, and important actors and actresses; brief summary; short review explaining why the student did or did not like the film and whether he or she would recommend it to others; where it is showing

**Music Review**
name of music group, group members, and concert; brief summary; review explaining why the student did or did not like the concert and whether he or she would recommend it to others; where tickets were available and ticket price

## SUGGESTED SEQUENCE

1. Students choose a topic and make an outline showing how they plan to organize their flyer.
2. Students prepare the written assignment.
3. As an oral component, students should also prepare a brief (1 minute) statement about their flyer. Students should not read directly from the flyer; instead, they should use index cards on which a few phrases are written to give their oral report.
4. Students show their flyers and give their oral presentations.
5. Students display their flyers on the **Litfaßsäule** in the classroom or foreign language department.

## GRADING THE PROJECT

Suggested point distribution (total = 100)

| | |
|---|---|
| Originality and design | 30 |
| Written assignment | 40 |
| Oral presentation | 30 |

 **Culture Note**

**Litfaßsäulen** were named after Ernst Litfaß, a printer from Berlin who created this type of pillar in 1854.

**K-PUR TAGESTIP**

**The Romeos**

Nicht aus dem New Yorker Italo-Distrikt, sondern aus Bremen und Oldenburg kommen die Mitglieder der Band. Weniger banal die Musik der Jungs. Bei einer großen Plattenfirma unter Vertrag gelten sie als vielleicht eines der größten Talente der deutschen Popszene.

**29.4. Marquee, 21:00 Uhr**

# Kapitel 10: Kino und Konzerte
## ♜ *Games*

## WER BIN ICH?

*This game will be useful at the end of the* **Zweite Stufe** *to review nouns, adjectives, and expressions learned in previous chapters.*

**Procedure** To prepare for this game, make each student one index card on which you have written the name of a famous musician or actor students are likely to know. As students enter the classroom, hand each of them one of the cards and ask them not to show the card to anyone else. Choose a student to come to the front of the class. The rest of the class asks yes/no questions one at a time to find out who the mystery person is. Examples of possible questions are **Ist es eine Frau? Ist es ein Mann? Spielt er/sie in Filmen? Spielt er/sie in Horrorfilmen? In Liebesfilmen? Spielt er/sie Musik? Spielt er/sie Rock and Roll? Spielt er/sie schmalzige Musik?** The student who guesses the name on the card wins a point. The student with the most points at the end of the game is the winner.

## KÖNNT IHR MEIN WORT ERRATEN?

*In this game, students will be challenged to test their recall of previously learned vocabulary.*

**Procedure** For this game you will need the letters from a Scrabble® game, or small pieces of cardboard with the letters of the alphabet written on them. Put the letters in a small box or hat. Call one student to the front of the class and have him or her pull ten letters from the box or hat. He or she has 30 seconds to make a word using as many of the ten letters as possible. The teacher checks the word to make sure it exists and is spelled correctly. Then the student writes the ten letters randomly on the blackboard, and the rest of the class tries to guess the word that he or she has made.

## WAS BEGINNT MIT ...?

*This game will help students review the vocabulary they have learned so far in a fun, fast-paced way.*

**Procedure** Begin by dividing the class into groups of three or four students, depending on the size of your class. Choose a word from the **Wortschatz** you want to review and write it on the chalkboard. (Example: A B E N T E U E R F I L M) Each group writes that word on a sheet of paper, spacing the letters across the page. Each group must come up with as many German words as they can that begin with each letter of the word. Emphasize before the game begins that each word can only be used once, and proper names are not allowed. The group with the most correct words at the end of a specified time limit wins. To make this game more challenging, you could specify a topic ahead of time and require that all words be related to that topic.

| A | B | E | N | T | E | U | E | R | F | I | L | M |
|---|---|---|---|---|---|---|---|---|---|---|---|---|
| P | A | L | A | A | S | N | I | O | A | N | E | U |
| F | N | T | U | N | S | T | S | L | H | N | S | S |
| E | A | E | N | T | E | E | | L | R | E | E | I |
| L | N | R | | E | N | N | | S | E | N | N | K |
| | E | N | | | | | | C | N | S | | |
| | | | | | | | | H | | T | | |
| | | | | | | | | U | | A | | |
| | | | | | | | | H | | D | | |
| | | | | | | | | | | T | | |

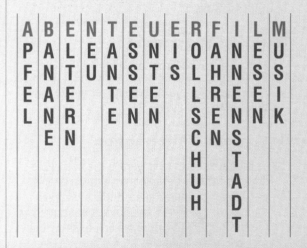

# Kapitel 10: Kino und Konzerte
## Lesson Plans, pages 244-267

## Using the Chapter Opener, pp. 244-245

### Motivating Activity

Ask students if they know of any popular music groups, actors, or actresses from any other countries. Who are they and where are they from?

### Background Information

① German teenagers enjoy all types of music, including music by American, British, and French artists. Young people buy music at stores very similar to those in the United States.

###  Culture Note

① It is common for shopkeepers in German-speaking countries to display some of their merchandise on racks placed in front of their stores. This is a way of attracting the attention of passers-by.

### Teaching Suggestion

① Ask students to look at the photo and determine where the shop might be located. (along a **Fußgängerzone**) Do students recognize any of the CDs on display?

### Background Information

② This photo shows teenagers at the box office of a movie theater. German movie theaters operate differently than American theaters, even though they look similar. Moviegoers can enter the theater up to 30 minutes before showtime to watch advertisements. Refreshments are limited and generally cannot be purchased at a concession stand. Vendors use the 30 minutes prior to showtime to walk through the aisles selling ice cream, candy, and drinks.

### Thinking Critically

② **Observing** Have students look at the advertisement between the boy and the girl in this picture. Can they tell what is being advertised? The brand name of the products? The names of the individual products? (ice cream; **Langnese; Cornetto Nuß, Cornetto Erdbeer, Calippo Fizz**)

###  Multicultural Connection

Ask students if they have ever watched a movie with subtitles. If so, which movies, and what languages were spoken in them?

### Building on Previous Skills

③ Based on the summer movie schedule shown, can students make a general statement as to how dates are written in German? Ask students in which order the month and day appear. Can they remember where the year would go? What is the accompanying punctuation? (day. month. year; these elements are separated with periods)

### Focusing on Outcomes

Ask students how they usually decide what movies to see. Do they read movie reviews or watch previews on TV? Do they rely on their friends' opinions? What type of films do they prefer? Have students preview the learning outcomes on p. 245. **NOTE:** Each of these outcomes is modeled in the video and evaluated in **Kann ich's wirklich?** on p. 266.

Mittwoch, 19. 5.
20.00 Uhr
Olympia Bissingen

Donnerstag, 20. 5.
20.00 Uhr
Delta Bietigheim

The Wall
mit Bob Geldof,
Pink Floyd
Regie: Alan Parker

Der Boss der Familie ist
der mit der großen Schnauze

Ein Hund namens
Beethoven

14.00/16.00/18.00/20.00   Fr./Sa. auch

# Teaching Los geht's!
*pp. 246-248*

**Resources for Los geht's!**

- *Video Program* **OR**
  *Expanded Video Program,* Videocassette 4
- *Textbook Audiocassette* 5 B
- *Practice and Activity Book*

▶ **pages 246-247**

##  Video Synopsis

This segment of the video is an interview in which five friends (Thomas, Sandra, Martin, Nicole, and Sabine) are asked what they like to do in their free time. The student outcomes listed on p. 245 are modeled in the video: expressing likes and dislikes, expressing familiarity, expressing preferences and favorites, and talking about what you did in your free time.

## Motivating Activity

Take a survey of class members. Ask students about the last movie they saw. When did they go and what did they see?

## Teaching Suggestions

- Before reading **Wie verbringt ihr eure Freizeit?** remind students of the many reading strategies they have learned so far. (using visual clues to determine meaning; scanning for specific information; using root words; using cognates to infer meaning; using what you already know; using context to determine meaning; finding relationships between ideas; identifying key words and expressions)
- To introduce students to the text, do the prereading activity at the top of p. 246 with the class. Then have students look for visual clues, cognates, or previously learned words, phrases, or expressions to help them figure out what each monologue is about.

## Culture Note

Remind students that German teenagers get out of school early in the afternoon (around 1:00). That explains the many activities they have time for in the afternoon after they've completed their homework.

▶ **page 248**

## For Individual Needs

**1 A Slower Pace** To ensure comprehension of the text, go through the frames individually, eliciting responses to each of the three questions from students.

**4 Visual Learners** Write the six phrases on the chalkboard and ask students to write appropriate expressions under each phrase. Each category should have several examples. Review all expressions with the class.

## Teaching Suggestion

**5** This activity could be assigned for homework. Students could begin in class by making an outline and then complete the final draft at home.

## Closure

Refer students back to the learning outcomes listed on p. 245 and ask them to list one German phrase from the **Foto-Roman** that would fulfill each function.

**LOS GEHT'S!**

# ERSTE STUFE

## Teaching Erste Stufe, pp. 249-252

### Resources for Erste Stufe

*Practice and Activity Book*
*Chapter Resources,* Book 4
- Communicative Activity 10-1
- Additional Listening Activities 10-1, 10-2
- Student Response Form
- Realia 10-1
- Situation Card 10-1
- Teaching Transparency Master 10-1
- Quiz 10-1

*Audiocassette Program*
- *Textbook Audiocassette* 5 B
- *Additional Listening Activities, Audiocassette* 10 B
- *Assessment Items, Audiocassette* 8 B

▶ *page 249*

## MOTIVATE

 ### Game

Ask one player to leave the classroom while the rest of the class chooses the name of a movie. Have the player from outside return and stand in front of the class. He or she begins by asking questions that will eventually lead him or her to identify the film. Example: **Ist der Film alt oder neu? Wer spielt in dem Film?** Have several students take turns guessing.

## TEACH

### Culture Note

American movies and movie stars are well known and popular in German-speaking countries. Some German-speaking actors have also become popular stars in America: Marlene Dietrich, Curd Jürgens, Gert Fröbe, Arnold Schwarzenegger.

### PRESENTATION: Wortschatz

The items in this vocabulary box provide students with the vocabulary to talk about different kinds of movies. After introducing the vocabulary, have students name some current films and have others say what kinds of films they are.

▶ *page 250*

### PRESENTATION: So sagt man das!

Before presenting the function box, brainstorm with students the ways they have already learned to express likes and dislikes. Take some already familiar expressions with **gern haben** or **gefallen** and substitute **mögen** orally. Then have students look at the examples in the function box and ask them what they mean. Focus on **mag** and **magst**. Make up other examples.

###  Total Physical Response

Have students stand up at their desks. Give a series of quick commands based on the **So sagt man das!** box, using verbs such as **heben, klatschen, applaudieren, buhen, hinsetzen.** Examples: **Wenn du Rockmusik magst, applaudiere! Wenn du klassische Musik magst, heb deine linke Hand!**

### For Individual Needs

**7 Challenge** Ask students to comment on the interviews of the German teenagers. Using their notes from this listening activity and the expressions in the **Wortschatz** box to the right of Activity 7, have several students each make one statement about the movies the German teenagers talked about.

### PRESENTATION: Grammatik

Ask students to point out changes they observed in the conjugation of the verb **mögen**. What other verbs have they learned that follow a similar pattern? (**können, sollen, wollen, müssen**) Have students read the sample sentences in the grammar box. Then, have them make their own sentences using the **Wortschatz** box. Have one student call out a pronoun and another student finish the sentence.

▶ *page 251*

### PRESENTATION: Ein wenig Landeskunde

Ask students why they think rating guidelines have been established in the United States. Have them compare the ratings systems in Germany and in the United States.

## Teaching Suggestion

**9** Have students take turns going to the front of the class and conducting a survey about the most popular kind of movie. Students would ask: **Was für Filme mag (Carlos) besonders gern?** Have them create an ongoing chart on the board.

(Cathy) mag ...   (Joe) mag ...

▶ *page 252*

## Teaching Suggestion

**10a** To make this activity more enjoyable, have students pretend to be reporters from a teen magazine interviewing teenagers about their taste in music.

### ✦ For Individual Needs

**10b** **Auditory Learners** Have several students stand up and read the report about their partner to the rest of the class. In addition, each student should come up with two questions about his or her report. After reading his or her report, each student should ask questions to check classmates' comprehension.

## PRESENTATION: Ein wenig Grammatik

Prepare several sentences on a transparency illustrating the difference between **kennen** and **wissen.** (Examples: **Ich kenne den Film Dracula. Ich weiß, wo er jetzt spielt. Ich kenne München sehr gut. Ich weiß, wie man zum Marienplatz kommt.**) Ask students if they can see the difference in the way the two verbs are used. Next, give students several sentences for which they must supply the correct verb: **kennen** or **wissen.** Examples: _____ du, wer die Schauspielerin ist? _____ du die Schauspielerin?

## For Additional Practice

**12** Have each pair add several other examples and pose the same questions to other students in the class.

## Reteaching: The verb mögen

Prepare a chart like the following example on a transparency. Give students a set amount of time to come up with as many sentences as they can. Have students read their sentences aloud and ask the rest of the class to listen for correct usage.

| Subject | Verb | Object | Adverbs |
|---|---|---|---|
| **Sie** (formal) | **mögen** | Heavy Metal | nicht |
| **Michael** | | Actionfilme | gern |
| **Wir** | | Liebesfilme | besonders |
| **Du** | | Horrorfilme | gern |
| **Ihr** | | Jazz | furchtbar |
| **Ich** | | klassische | gern |
| **Sie** (sing.) | | Musik | überhaupt |
| **Anna und** | | Opern | nicht gern |
| **Christian** | | Rock and Roll | |

## *CLOSE*

### Teaching Suggestion

To prepare for this activity, cut out several movie ads with large pictures from your local newspaper. Hold up one picture from a movie ad and ask students in German what kind of film it is. (Example: **Was für ein Film ist das?**) Students must reply in a complete German sentence. (Example: **Das ist ein Liebesfilm.**) To expand the activity, write the following adjectives on the board along with their accompanying numbers. Then, ask students to rate the film.

1. furchtbar!
2. blöd!
3. ziemlich gut
4. sehr gut!
5. Klasse!

### Focusing on Outcomes

Refer students back to the learning outcomes listed on p. 245. Students should recognize that they are now able to express likes and dislikes.

## *ASSESS*

- **Performance Assessment** Ask students to give a description and a short critique of the last movie they saw in a movie theater or on video.
- Quiz 10-1, *Chapter Resources*, Book 4

ERSTE STUFE

## ZWEITE STUFE

# *T*eaching Zweite Stufe,
### *pp. 253-257*

**Resources for Zweite Stufe**

*Practice and Activity Book*
*Chapter Resources,* Book 4
- Communicative Activity 10-2
- Additional Listening Activities 10-3, 10-4
- Student Response Form
- Realia 10-2
- Situation Card 10-2
- Quiz 10-2

*Audiocassette Program*
- *Textbook Audiocassette* 5 B
- *Additional Listening Activities, Audiocassette* 10 B
- *Assessment Items, Audiocassette* 8 B

▶ *page 253*

## *MOTIVATE*

### Teaching Suggestion

As a warm-up for the activities in this **Stufe,** put the following incomplete statement on the board and ask students to think about how they would complete it. Example: **Ich sehe gern ...**

## *TEACH*

### PRESENTATION: So sagt man das!

Remind students that they learned to express preferences when they talked about sports and hobbies in Chapter 2. To refresh their memories, ask students several questions about their preferences. (Examples: **Was spielst du besonders gern? Was machst du nicht so gern? Was kaufst du lieber, Karten für Fußball oder Tennis? Was spielst du am liebsten?**) Then introduce the new functions, asking students what they like to see: **Was siehst du gern? Was siehst du lieber? Was siehst du am liebsten?**

### PRESENTATION: Ein wenig Grammatik

Review the forms of **sehen** by asking someone a question and then asking the class what that person said. (Example: **David, was für Filme siehst du gern? Was für Filme sieht David gern?**) Use this opportunity to review other verbs that have a

stem-vowel change from **e → i: essen, geben,** and **nehmen.** Again, use question/answer practice and directed dialogue to elicit the critical forms.

 **For Individual Needs**

**13 Challenge** Have students listen to the activity a third time. They should listen for one word or phrase that would justify Marianne or Stefan's likes or dislikes. (Examples: **langweilig, schmalzig, lustig**) Then ask follow-up questions to elicit these from students. Example: **Warum sieht Stefan nicht gern Liebesfilme?**

▶ *page 254*

 **For Individual Needs**

**14 A Slower Pace** Before doing Activity 14, help students understand the idea of **lieber** with some structured practice. Hold up two cards at a time with words or pictures on them. (Examples: **Actionfilme; Horrorfilme**) Ask individual students: **Was siehst du lieber? Was spielst du lieber? Was ißt du lieber?**

### For Additional Practice

**15** Ask students to use the same information, this time describing the likes and dislikes of their best friend, brother, or sister. This could be assigned for homework.

**For Individual Needs**

**16 Auditory Learners** After students have completed Part B of this activity, collect all paragraphs. Read the paragraphs to the class and have them guess which paragraph best describes each student.

▶ page 255

 ## Cooperative Learning

**17** Divide the class into groups of three or four, depending on the size of your class. Group members choose a reader, a recorder, and a reporter. Students then work through questions 1-8 within a specific amount of time. Once the groups have completed their assignments, call on the reporters of each group to present their answers.

▶ page 256

## PRESENTATION: Wortschatz

Use these new adjectives in context and have students guess their meanings. (Examples: **James Bond Filme sind sehr spannend. Filme mit John Candy sind lustig. Filme mit Stallone oder Schwarzenegger sind meistens brutal.**) Be sure to help students with the pronunciation of the new adjectives, concentrating especially on the cognates.

## Teaching Suggestion

**20** After students have completed their descriptive paragraphs, divide the class into two teams. Teams take turns asking yes/no questions to guess who the mystery person is.

▶ page 257

## PRESENTATION: Landeskunde

• Ask students to name the last cultural event they attended. When was it, where did it take place and with whom did they go?

• You might want to introduce the following expressions to help students understand the interviews with the four German teenagers.
**die Ausstellung** *exhibition, display*
**witzig** *funny, comical*
**die Vergünstigung** *discount*
**verabreden** *to make plans to meet someone*
**dafür sein** *to be in favor of, to advocate*

## Background Information

Teachers in Germany try to incorporate cultural events or field trips into their curriculum whenever possible. If students read a play by Bertolt Brecht, for example, the class will try to see it on stage as well. History classes often attend documentary films at movie theaters, and classes frequently visit museums.

## Music and Theater Connection

Provide students with the Arts and Entertainment section of a local newspaper or that of a major city nearby. Ask students to categorize upcoming events (plays, shows, concerts, ballets, exhibitions, etc.) and to determine which event in each category they would most like to attend.

## Thinking Critically

**Comparing and Contrasting** German students grow up learning about German-speaking composers such as Mozart, Beethoven, Bach, and Händel. Ask students if they know any American composers. (Examples: Ellen Zwilich, Aaron Copeland, Leonard Bernstein, John Williams, John Phillip Sousa, George Gershwin, Amy Beach)

 ## Multicultural Connection

Ask students to interview foreign exchange students, other foreign language teachers, or anybody else they know from a different country as to what cultural events teenagers there typically attend. Have students report their findings in class.

## Teacher Note

Mention to your students that the **Landeskunde** will also be included in Quiz 10-2 given at the end of the **Zweite Stufe.**

## Reteaching: Expressing preferences and favorites

Put the following groups of incomplete sentences on the board and let students complete the statements in a meaningful way.
Ich sehe _____ gern, aber _____ sehe ich lieber. Am liebsten sehe ich _____.
Ich höre _____ gern, aber ich höre _____ lieber. Am liebsten höre ich _____.
In der Schule habe ich _____ gern. _____ habe ich lieber. Am liebsten habe ich _____. Ja, mein Lieblingsfach ist _____.

## CLOSE

### ♜ Game
Play the game **Wer bin ich?** See p. 243F for the procedure.

### Focusing on Outcomes
Refer students back to the learning outcomes listed on p. 245. They should recognize that they are now able to express preferences and favorites.

## ASSESS

- **Performance Assessment** Write a list of current movies or popular songs on the board. Ask individual students to give one reason why someone should or should not see a particular movie or listen to a specific song.

- Quiz 10-2, *Chapter Resources,* Book 4

### Hanns-Martin-Schleyer-Halle

Sonntag, 1. März
**Peter Maffay**

Montag, 2. März
**Joe Cocker**

Sonntag, 8. März
**Musikantenstadl**

Samstag, 14. März
**Udo Jürgens**

Sonntag, 15. März
**Placido Domingo und Julia Migenes**

Samstag, 28. März
**Schöller Oldie Night**

---

**Vor und nach der Vorstellung!**

*Der Treff • für Leute von heute!*

**WÜRTTEMBERGER-STUBEN**
- Dieter Franke -

70174 Stuttgart 10, Schloßstraße 33 (bei der Liederhalle) ☎ 0711/29 03 14
Täglich von 11-24 Uhr geöffnet. **Küche bis 24 Uhr.**

### VIDEO-HITS FILM-VERLEIH
ERMITTELT VON VIPP VIDEO

1 Kevin— Allein zu Haus (Fox Video)
2 Der Feind in meinem Bett (Fox Video)
3 Arielle, die Meerjungfrau (Walt Disney)
4 Pappa ante Portas (Warner)
5 Flatliners (RCA/Columbia)
6 Highlander 2 (Highlight)
7 Das Rußlandhaus (Cannon/VMP)
8 Ghost (CIC)
9 Aus Mangel an Beweisen (Warner)
10 Deadly Revenge (Warner)

### Belletristik

1. Antonia Byatt: Besessen
Insel, 48 Mark (Vorwoche: 1)
2. Rosamunde Pilcher: Die Muschelsucher
Wunderlich, 42 Mark (3)
3. Donna Tartt: Die geheime Geschichte
Goldmann, 44 Mark (-)
4. John Grisham: Die Akte
Hoffmann und Campe, 44 Mark (6)
5. Gabriel García Márquez Zwölf Geschichten aus der Fremde
Kiepenheuer & Witsch, 36 Mark (8)
6. Eva Heller: Der Mann, der's wert ist
Droemer, 38 Mark (2)
7. Mel Gilden: Heißkalte Liebe
vgs, 25 Mark (-)
8. Barbara Wood Das Paradies
Krüger, 49,80 Mark (7)
9. Noah Gordon: Der Schamane
Droemer, 44 Mark (9)
10. Harry Mulisch: Die Entdeckung des Himmels
Hanser, 49,80 Mark (-)

Quelle: R. Stuart GmbH

### Sachbuch

1. Michael Baigent/Richard Leigh: Verschlußsache Jesus
Droemer, 39,80 Mark (Vorwoche: 2)
2. Carmen Thomas: Ein besonderer Saft
vgs, 24,80 Mark (1)
3. Günther Ogger: Nieten in Nadelstreifen
Droemer, 38 Mark (3)
4. Peter Kelder: Die Fünf "Tibeter"
Integral, 19 Mark (6)
5. Helmut Schmidt: Handeln für Deutschland
Rowohlt, 34 Mark (4)
6. Al Gore: Wege zum Gleichgewicht
S. Fischer, 39,80 (7)
7. Robert Eisenman/Michael Wise: Jesus und die Urchristen
C. Bertelsmann, 39,80 Mark (5)
8. Paul Kennedy: In Vorbereitung auf das 21. Jahrhundert
S. Fischer, 48 Mark (9)
9. Dale Carnegie: Sorge dich nicht - lebe!
Scherz, 42 Mark (8)
10. Rut Brandt: Freundesland
Hoffman und Campe, 35 Mark (-)

Quelle: R. Stuart GmbH

# Teaching Dritte Stufe,
## pp. 258-261

### Resources for Dritte Stufe

*Practice and Activity Book*
*Chapter Resources,* Book 4
- Additional Listening Activities 10-5, 10-6
- Student Response Form
- Realia 10-3
- Situation Card 10-3
- Teaching Transparency Master 10-2
- Quiz 10-3

*Audiocassette Program*
- *Textbook Audiocassette* 5 B
- *Additional Listening Activities, Audiocassette* 10 B
- *Assessment Items, Audiocassette* 8 B

▶ *page 258*

## MOTIVATE

### Teaching Suggestion

Go around the class and ask students what they have recently read for pleasure. What was the name of the book, magazine, or article? Who was the author? Why did they choose that particular reading material?

## TEACH

### Teaching Suggestion

**21** Have students work with partners for this activity. After students have completed their assignments, have three or four of them write their answers to each of the five questions on the board. Go over the responses with the class.

▶ *page 259*

## PRESENTATION: Wortschatz

To introduce the new vocabulary, bring an example of each vocabulary item and teach the types of books by holding up each book for all students to see. Tell them what type of book it is, as well as its title and the author's name. In addition, you might want to ask students if they know the book, using **kennen,** and whether or not they like that kind of book.

## PRESENTATION: Grammatik

Read the examples from the **Grammatik** box aloud to students. Have individual students repeat the sentences. Ask individual students questions using **lesen** and **sprechen.** (Example: **Liest du oft Sachbücher?**) Vary the subject form of the questions (**du, ihr, Sie, er, sie, sie** *pl*), and have students respond using the correct verb form. Then, have students take turns asking each other these questions.

## PRESENTATION: Ein wenig Grammatik

On a transparency, prepare the question **Worüber sprecht ihr?** and three sample answers: **Wir sprechen über den Film/Mode/die Umwelt.** Use these sentences to demonstrate to students the use of the accusative case following the preposition **über.** Have pairs of students brainstorm other topics they could use to complete the statement **Wir sprechen über....**

### Teaching Suggestion

After introducing **sprechen,** ask students if they can recall similar verbs they have previously learned. (**sagen**)

▶ *page 260*

##  Portfolio Assessment

**24** You might want to use this activity as an oral portfolio item for your students. See *Assessment Guide,* Chapter 10.

## PRESENTATION: So sagt man das!

In Chapter 8, students learned the simple past tense of the verb **sein**. Review the different forms by asking students personalized questions such as **Wo warst du gestern abend?** Then ask students to name some of the adverbs they have learned for expressing past time. (Examples: **gestern, vorgestern**) See Chapter 8 for a complete list. Finally, ask students to recall the meaning of the sentence **Was hast du gestern beim Bäcker gekauft?** Then introduce the items from the **So sagt man das!** function box on p. 260. Have students find the four new past tense verb forms (**gemacht, gelesen, gesehen, gesprochen**). Ask students to look at the word order in the sentences that use the conversational past. Where is the past participle? Students should see that the auxiliary **haben** is always in the second position (before or after the subject) while the past participle is in the last position.

 **For Individual Needs**

**26 Challenge** After students have completed the activity, play the tape again and ask students to listen for the word or phrase that did not make sense.

▶ *page 261*

## Teaching Suggestions

**27** Ask several students to create a few sentences orally, then assign the activity as written homework.

**28** This works well as a warm-up activity after a weekend. Put the activity on the board before the students enter the classroom. Have students work on the activity in pairs at the beginning of class.

## PRESENTATION: Aussprache

An explanation of these sounds can be found in Chapters 3, 6, and 7 of the *Pupil's Edition*.

## Reteaching: The verb lesen

Using the verb **lesen**, ask students about their reading preferences. (Examples: **Was liest du gern? Was lest ihr gern?**) Have them tell you what they enjoyed reading last week, something interesting they are reading today, and what they have to read for tomorrow. (**Was hast du letzte Woche gelesen? Was liest du heute? Was liest du morgen?**)

## CLOSE

### ♜ Game

Begin this **Kettenspiel** by making the following statement: **Letzten Sommer war ich in Hollywood und habe drei Fernsehstars gesehen.** Have the next student repeat your statement and add his or her own phrase, using one of the past tense phrases he or she has learned. See how many phrases students can remember.

### Focusing on Outcomes

Refer students back to the learning outcomes listed on p. 245. Students should recognize that they are now able to talk about what they did in their free time.

## ASSESS

- **Performance Assessment** Have students prepare a list of statements in the present tense using the verbs **machen, sprechen, sehen,** and **lesen.** Ask individual students to repeat each statement and then change it to the conversational past. Then have students tell you about a movie they saw yesterday, a book they read last week, a topic they are talking about today, and another book they'll read tomorrow.

- Quiz 10-3, *Chapter Resources,* Book 4

FREITAG, 9. JULI 1993

## DER MIT DEM WOLF TANZT

USA 1990, 180 Minuten, CinemaScope, Dolby-Stereo;
Ein Film von Kevin Costner.
Mit Kevin Costner, Mary MacDowell und anderen.

*V*om Bürgerkrieg und militärischem Drill desillusioniert , läßt sich Lieutenant John J. Dunbar, ein Offizier der Nordstaaten im äußersten Westen, am Rand der Zivilisation, im Sioux-Gebiet nieder. In einem abgelegenen Blockhaus bezieht er Stellung und knüpft behutsamen Kontakt mit den Indianern, deren Kultur er langsam zu begreifen und zu schätzen lernt. Er nimmt ihre Sitten und Gebräuche an, und sie beginnen, ihn als einer der ihren zu akzeptieren. Sie geben ihm den Namen "der mit dem Wolf tanzt". Doch die scheinbare Idylle findet ein jähes Ende, als eine Einheit der US-Kavallerie anrückt, die den verschollen geglaubten Dunbar aufspüren soll.

ZUM LESEN

## *T*eaching Zum Lesen,
*p. 262-263*

### Reading Strategy

The targeted reading strategy in this chapter is recognizing cognates and false cognates from context. Students should learn about this strategy before doing Question 2. Students will also be asked to skim for the gist, scan for specific information, answer questions to show comprehension, and transfer what they have learned.

## *PREREADING*

### Motivating Activity

Go around the classroom and ask several students to tell the class about the last movie they saw in a theater or on video. Ask them to give a brief, simple summary in German.

### Teaching Suggestion

Remind students that many of the words they have learned so far were easy to understand because they were similar to English. Tell students that words that appear similar across languages and have the same meaning are called cognates. False cognates, on the other hand, appear similar but have different meanings. Learning to use context clues to determine whether a word is a cognate or a false cognate will help students improve their reading ability.

### Teacher Note

Activities 1-2 are prereading activities.

## *READING*

### Teaching Suggestion

On the chalkboard or a transparency, make a chart divided into three parts: cognates, false cognates, familiar words and phrases. As students skim and scan for answers to activities 3 through 5, note their comments in the appropriate place on the chart.

### Thinking Critically

**Observing**   Ask students to scan the ads to find out which of the films will be shown in English. *(Groundhog Day)* How did they know? (The title is given in English first.) Some students may also be able to infer the meaning of **Englische Original-fassung** at the bottom of the ad. This is addressed in Activity 7a.

### Thinking Critically

• **Drawing Inferences**   Can students think of reasons why *Groundhog Day* would be shown in English while *Jurassic Park*® is dubbed in German? (It might be more cost-effective to show some films with subtitles and forego the cost of dubbing a film. Or it might be that a large percentage of the population is more interested in the original version than in the dubbed version.)

• **Analyzing**   Ask students to determine the German word for movie director. (**Regie, Regisseur**) Point out to students that these words have been borrowed from French.

### Cooperative Learning

**7** Assign small groups of students to do 7a, 7b, and 7c as a cooperative learning activity within a set amount of time. Each group member should have a specific task as part of this activity, i.e, reader, recorder, reporter. Call on two or three groups to share their answers with the class.

## POST-READING

### Teacher Note

Activity 8 is a post-reading activity that will show whether students can transfer what they have learned.

### Closure

Divide the class into two groups and ask each group to come up with the pros and cons of video rental. Divide the chalkboard in half and write students' arguments **für** or **gegen** on each side. Remind students to use conjunctions such as **denn, weil, und,** and **aber** in their discussion.

## Using Anwendung,
### pp. 264-265

### ✦ For Individual Needs

**1 Challenge** After students have completed the chart, ask them which of the two students interviewed they would most like to spend their free time with and why. Questions and answers should be in German.

### ■ Portfolio Assessment

**3** You might want to use this activity as a written portfolio item for your students. See *Assessment Guide,* Chapter 10.

### Teaching Suggestion

**4** You might want to obtain a copy of *Kino* by Nena. Then make a mini-lesson out of this activity. Begin by giving the students an introduction to the content of the song so that students know what to listen for. Then have students listen to the song. Ask students what words or phrases they recognized and understood after the first listening. During the second listening, ask them to write down the words they hear and recognize. Finally, prepare a script of the lyrics (see p. 264 of the *Pupil's Edition*) by removing numerous key words or phrases. Have students try to fill them in as they listen to the song a third time. If you are unable to get a copy of the cassette or CD *99 Luftballons* that contains *Kino,* read the lyrics aloud, then proceed with the mini-lesson.

### Teaching Suggestion

**7** Remind students to include connectors and conjunctions in this writing assignment.

## Kann ich's wirklich?
### p. 266

This page is intended to prepare students for the test. It is a brief checklist of the major points covered in the chapter. The students should be reminded that it is a checklist only and not necessarily everything that will appear on the test.

## Using Wortschatz,
### p. 267

### Teaching Suggestion

Give the vocabulary definitions in German whenever possible to help build vocabulary through the study of synonyms.

### ♜ Game

- Play the game **Was beginnt mit ...?** See p. 243F for the procedure.

- Play the game **Könnt ihr mein Wort erraten?** See p. 243F for the procedure.

### Teacher Note

Give the **Kapitel 10** Chapter Test, *Chapter Resources,* Book 4.

# Kino und Konzerte

**1** Ich mag am liebsten klassische Musik.

**T**eenagers in German-speaking countries like to do things together. Sometimes they go to movies and concerts. Groups of students often go to someone's house and watch a video or just sit around and talk. Does this sound like you and your friends? Do you go out together—or stay at home and watch videos, listen to music, and talk? When you get together with your friends, there are a lot of things you'll want to be able to talk about.

## In this unit you will learn

- to express likes and dislikes;
  to express familiarity
- to express preferences and favorites
- to talk about what you did in your free time

## And you will

- listen to a popular German song
- read reviews of films, music, and books
- write about your favorite music group, singer, or movie star
- find out what kind of movies, music, and books students in German-speaking countries enjoy

**Sommer-Programm im August**

**Dienstags 22.⁰⁰ ➤ ➤ ➤ KINO**

Monty Python:
2 Folgen Flying Circus
+ Die wunderbare Welt
der Schwerkraft

3.8.  Beatles Night
Yellow Submarine + Help
10.8. Die Kleinen Stolche
17.8. Das siebte Zeichen
24.8. Cyrano de Bergerac
31.8. Zeit des Erwachens

③ Hast du „Monty Python" gesehen?

② Actionfilme sehe ich furchtbar gern.

# Los geht's!

## *Wie verbringt ihr eure Freizeit?*

Look at the above title and the photos that accompany these interviews. What are the people in the photos doing? What clues in the photos help you determine what the students might be talking about?

### THOMAS

Wir sind eine Clique, drei Jungen und drei Mädchen, und — na ja — wir machen viel zusammen, besonders Sport. Wir joggen zusammen, wir fahren Rad, einmal im Monat gehen wir kegeln. Aber sonst hat jeder auch seine eigenen Interessen. Ich zum Beispiel gehe oft in Konzerte. Rockkonzerte höre ich am liebsten.

### SANDRA

Ab und zu gehe ich auch in ein Rockkonzert. Aber die Karten sind so furchtbar teuer und, ehrlich gesagt, höre ich lieber Country. Die Clique kommt manchmal zu mir, und jeder bringt eine Kassette oder eine CD. Wir hören dann Musik und spielen Karten oder Brettspiele.

## MARTIN

Ich muß sagen, ich mag Rock überhaupt nicht. Ich mag auch die meisten Country Sänger nicht. Ich mag am liebsten klassische Musik, Brahms, Ravel und so. Ich gehe sehr gern ins Konzert und auch in die Oper.

## NICOLE

Was ich am liebsten mache? Ganz einfach! Ich geh' am liebsten ins Kino. Fantasyfilme und Komödien sind meine Lieblingsfilme. Was ich nicht mag? Ich hasse Actionfilme. Die sind meistens so brutal. Mein Lieblingsfilm ist und bleibt *Kevin — Allein zu Haus,* und meine Lieblingsschauspieler sind Joe Pesci und Whoopi Goldberg.

## SABINE

Ja, unsere Clique ist toll. Es stimmt, wir sind viel unterwegs, sehen viel. Wir kommen aber oft zusammen und diskutieren über Filme, Musik, Stars und so. Ich selbst bin auch gern zu Hause. Ich lese furchtbar gern. Ich habe viele Bücher.

## 1 Was passiert hier?

Do you understand what the students are talking about in the interviews? Check your comprehension by answering the following questions. Don't be afraid to guess.

1. What is the main idea of each of the five interviews?
2. What is each student's main interest or interests?
3. Which of the students mention something they don't like? What do they mention?

1. The students' interests and how they spend their free time.
2. Thomas—sports; rock music; Sandra—Country and Western; games, especially cards or board games; Martin—classical music, concerts, opera; Nicole—movies; Sabine—books, talking with friends.
3. Martin—rock music, country music; Nicole—action films.

## 2 Mix und Match: Interessen

Match each students name with his or her interests or with the interests and activities of that student's **Clique**.

1. Thomas  b    **a.** klassische Musik hören und in Konzerte und in die Oper gehen
2. Sandra  d    **b.** joggen, radfahren, kegeln
3. Martin  a    **c.** über Filme, Musik, Stars usw. diskutieren, Bücher lesen
4. Nicole  e    **d.** Musik hören, Karten und Brettspiele spielen
5. Sabine  c    **e.** ins Kino gehen, besonders Fantasyfilme und Komödien sehen

## 3 Erzähl weiter!

Which of the students might have made each of these statements in his or her interview?

1. Heute abend, zum Beispiel, gehe ich ins Beethovenkonzert.   Martin
2. Mein Lieblingsbuch ist *Die unendliche Geschichte*.   Sabine
3. Und ich habe alle Filme mit Steve Martin gesehen.   Nicole
4. Meine Freunde hören auch gern Country.   Sandra
5. Ach ja! Wir segeln auch gern.   Thomas

## 4 Genauer lesen

Reread the interviews. Which words or phrases do the students use to

1. name sports    1. joggen, fahren Rad, kegeln
2. name different kinds of music    2. Rock, Country, klassische Musik
3. name other free time activities    3. Karten spielen, Brettspiele spielen, diskutieren, lesen
4. name different kinds of films    4. Actionfilme, Fantasyfilme, Komödien
5. express likes and dislikes    5. lieber, mag ... überhaupt nicht, hasse
6. say that something is their favorite    6. Lieblings-..., am liebsten

Frühkonzert in einer Halle auf dem Hamburger Fischmarkt

## 5 Und du?

Now write your own interview. First choose the interview that most closely describes the free time activities you like to do. Then rewrite the interview, replacing any information with your own particular interests.

*Expressing likes and dislikes; expressing familiarity*

## WORTSCHATZ

SANDRA  Wie verbringst du deine Freizeit?

MARTIN  Ich gehe gern mit Freunden ins Kino und sehe ...

Actionfilme — Der Terminator 2

Horrorfilme — Dracula

Krimis — Eine Frage der Ehre

Abenteuerfilme — Indiana Jones–und der letzte Kreuzzug

Liebesfilme — Entscheidung aus Liebe

Kriegsfilme — Das Boot

Komödien — Kevin - Allein in New York

Westerns — Zwölf Uhr mittags

Science-fiction-Filme — Star Trek 6 - Das unbekannte Land

## 6 Welche Filme erkennst du? *Which films do you recognize?*

Welche Filme auf Seite 249 erkennst du? Wie heißen sie auf deutsch? Was bedeuten Wörter wie, zum Beispiel, Horrorfilme oder Krimis? Wie heißen diese Filmarten auf englisch?

### SO SAGT MAN DAS!
#### Expressing likes and dislikes

You have learned several ways of expressing likes and dislikes, using **gern** and **nicht gern** with various verbs, and using the verb **gefallen**. Another way to express what you like or don't like is with the present tense of the verb **mögen**.

You might ask:

**Was für Musik magst du?**
**Und Filme?**
**Magst du auch Abenteuerfilme?**

**Magst du Kevin Costner?**

The responses might be:

**Ich mag Rock und auch Jazz.**
**Horrorfilme mag ich sehr gern.**
**Ja, furchtbar gern!** *or*
**Nein, überhaupt nicht.**
**Ja, ich mag ihn besonders gern.**

What do you think the phrase **Was für ...** means?[1]

## 7 Hör gut zu!

Erwin: mag Komödien, mag Kriegsfilme nicht
David: mag Fantasyfilme, mag Westerns nicht

Listen to the following interviews about the kinds of movies these German teenagers enjoy seeing. For each interview, write the name of the person being interviewed. Then, beside each name, write the kinds of movies the person likes and does not like.

Judith: mag Abenteuerfilme, mag Krimis nicht
Aysha: mag Liebesfilme, mag Science-fiction-Filme nicht

## 8 Und was magst du?

You can use **mögen** to talk about anything you like or do not like. Ask your classmates how much they like or don't like some forms of entertainment and some of the entertainers listed in the box.

### WORTSCHATZ

You can use these expressions to talk about how much you like or don't like someone or something.

furchtbar gern
besonders gern
sehr gern
gern

nicht gern
gar nicht gern
überhaupt nicht gern

Westerns    Jazz    Horrorfilme
Madonna    Andy Garcia    Krimis
Eddie Murphy    Klaviermusik

### *Grammatik*  The verb **mögen**

The verb **mögen** (*to like, care for*) has the following forms.

Ich **mag** Filme gern.
Du **magst** auch Jazz, nicht?
Er/Sie **mag** Krimis nicht.

Wir **mögen** Horrorfilme.
Ihr **mögt** aber Krimis, nicht?
Sie/Sie(pl) **mögen** Westerns.

1. *what kind of...*

| Alba<br>252 25 45<br>Central | 3/5/7/9    Ab 12 Jahren    E/d/f<br>**LITTLE MAN TATE —**     4. Woche<br>**Das Wunderkind Tate**    Jodie Foster<br>Bewegendes Regiedebut mit D. Wiest, Harry<br>Connick jr. erobert im Sturm die Herzen der<br>Presse und des Publikums . . . |
|---|---|
| **Capitol 2**<br>251 37 00<br>beim Central | 2.45/4.45/6/6.45/8/45   Fr/Sa 22.45   E/d/f<br>**THE ADDAMS FAMILY**     Ab 12 J.<br>Verrückt sein ist relativ<br>. . . um das Unglück abzuwenden, muß der Clan<br>schon seine ganze morbide Raffinesse ausspielen. |
| **Radium**<br>251 18 07<br>Mühlengasse<br>7 | 3/5/7/9   7.Woche   Letzte Tage   Tun/d/f<br>**DAS VERLORENE HALSBAND DER TAUBE**<br>**— VON DER LIEBE UND DEN LIEBENDEN**<br>Nacer Khemirs traumhaft schöner Märchenfilm<br>über die Liebe     Ab 9 Jahren |

Judging by the excerpt of movie listings from Germany to the left, from which country do you think most foreign films come? Think about how movies are rated in the U.S. Then scan the movie listing and see if you can find the rating system used in Germany. *(Hint: Look for something that has to do with age.)* How is it different from the one in the U.S.? How much does admission for one person cost in Germany? As you discovered, American movies are very popular in German-speaking countries. Most movies are dubbed into German; however, larger cities usually have at least one movie theater that shows foreign movies with the original sound track.

## 9   Eine Umfrage

a. Ask your partner what kinds of movies he or she likes and does not like. Then ask what kinds of movies he or she especially likes. Switch roles.

b. Working with your classmates, conduct a survey about the most popular kinds of movies (**Abenteuerfilme, Krimis usw.**). Take turns going to the front of the room and asking someone **Was für Filme mag (Susan) besonders gern?** Write the answers you get in an ongoing chart on the chalkboard. When everyone has been asked, discuss together which types of movies are most popular.

BEISPIEL    **(Cathy) mag ... besonders gern.**

Herbert Grönemeyer

### WORTSCHATZ

| | |
|---|---|
| Rock and Roll | Jazz |
| Heavy Metal | Disko |
| klassische Musik | Oper |
| Country | |

**DEUTSCHE Bestseller**
*Ermittelt von Media-Control*

### SINGLES

**1** *What's up* — 4 Non Blondes
(1) 8. Wo.

**2** *Life* — Haddaway
(2) 7. Wo.

**3** *Living on my own* — Freddie Mercury
(6) 3. Wo.

**4** *Runaway Train* — Soul Asylum
(5) 5. Wo.

**5** *Keep on dancing!* — D.J. Bobo
(7) 2. Wo.

**6** *Somebody dance . . .* — D.J. Bobo
(4) 11. Wo.

**7** *Mr. Vain* — Culture Beat
(3) 17. Wo.

**8** *Falling in Love . . .* — UB 40
(8) 13. Wo.

**9** *Happy Nation* — Ace of Base
(9) 5. Wo.

**10** *Two Princes* — Spin Doctors
(10) 11. Wo.

Looking at the pop chart from *Bravo* magazine, what can you say about popular music among teenagers in Germany? Where does most of it come from? There are many well-known German singers, such as Herbert Grönemeyer, Marius Müller-Westernhagen and Ina Deter. Much of it comes from the United States.

## 10 Ein Interview

a. Create a list of questions to ask your partner about his or her taste in music. Be sure to obtain the following information: name, age, what kind of music the person likes or dislikes, how much he or she likes or dislikes the music mentioned; if he or she goes to concerts, when, and how often. Take notes using a chart like the one below. Then switch roles.

| wer? | wie alt? | was für Musik? | gern/ nicht gern? | Konzerte? | wie oft/ wann? |
|------|----------|----------------|-------------------|-----------|----------------|
|      |          |                |                   |           |                |

b. Schreib einen Bericht über deinen Partner! Verwende dabei die Information aus dem Interview oben (*above*)!

### SO SAGT MAN DAS!

#### Expressing familiarity

You may want to find out if your friend is familiar with the films, songs, and groups that you like. You might ask:

**Kennst du den Film *Das Rußlandhaus?***

Your friend might respond positively:

**Ja, sicher!** *or*
**Ja, klar!**

Or negatively:

**Nein, den Film kenne ich nicht** *or*
**Nein, überhaupt nicht.**

1. familiar   2. familiar   3. not familiar   4. familiar

## 11 Hör gut zu!

Listen to some students talking about movies and music with their friends. For each exchange decide whether the person they are speaking to is or is not familiar with the groups, songs or films mentioned.

## 12 Kennst du die neuste Gruppe aus Amerika?

List three lesser known films, songs, or groups that you like (for example, local musicians). Ask your partner if he or she is familiar with them. If not, he or she will ask questions to find out what kind of movie/music you are talking about. Describe it to your partner. Then switch roles.

### Schon bekannt
### Ein wenig *G*rammatik

In **Kapitel 7** you learned the verb **wissen** (*to know a fact, information*). The verb **kennen** means *to know* as in *to be acquainted or familiar with* someone or something:

**Ja, ich kenne Udo Lindenberg. Kennst du das Lied „Sonderzug nach Pankow"?**

The forms of **kennen** are regular in the present tense.

## *Expressing preferences and favorites*

### SO SAGT MAN DAS!

#### Expressing preferences and favorites

When discussing music groups and movies, your friend might ask you about your preferences and favorites.

He or she might ask:

**Siehst du gern Horrorfilme?**

**Siehst du lieber Abenteuerfilme oder Science-fiction-Filme?**

**Und du, Gabi? Was siehst du am liebsten?**

What is the idea expressed by **gern**, **lieber**, and **am liebsten**?[1] What other way can you express that something is your favorite?[2]

You might respond:

**Ja, aber Krimis sehe ich lieber. Und am liebsten sehe ich Westerns.**

**Lieber Science-fiction-Filme. Aber am liebsten sehe ich Liebesfilme.**

**Am liebsten sehe ich Komödien.**

### Ein wenig *Grammatik*

The words **lieber** and **am liebsten** express preferences and favorites. They are used with **haben** and other verbs in the same way **gern** is used.

> **Ich sehe gern Actionfilme, aber ich sehe Komödien lieber. Am liebsten sehe ich Krimis.**

## 13 Hör gut zu!

**a.** Listen to two students tell you what they like and don't like, what they prefer, and what they like most of all. Make a chart like the one below and fill in the information.

|  | likes | doesn't like | prefers | likes most of all |
|---|---|---|---|---|
| Marianne | Krimis | Horror-filme | Western | Abenteuer-filme |
| Stefan | Komödien | Liebes-filme | Fantasy-filme | Science-fiction-Filme |

**b.** Using the chart you've just completed, take turns with your classmates reporting back in your own words the information from Marianne's and Stefan's interviews.

1. *like; prefer; like best of all*  2. **Lieblings-**

### Ein wenig *Grammatik*

In **Kapitel 5** you learned that the verb **aussehen** *(to look, appear)* is irregular in the **du-** and **er/sie-** forms. The verb **sehen** *(to see),* of course, follows this same pattern:

> **Siehst du gern Horrorfilme?**
> **Er sieht Abenteuerfilme am liebsten.**

How would you answer the question **Siehst du gern Horrorfilme?**

## 14 Was wollen wir tun?

Du willst heute abend mit deinem Partner etwas tun. Du wählst etwas von der linken Seite aus, dein Partner von der rechten. Er sagt dir, was er lieber tun möchte. Dann tauscht die Rollen aus!

DU **Wir können ...**
PARTNER **Ich möchte lieber ...**

## 15 Und was hast du lieber oder am liebsten?

Stell Fragen an einen Klassenkameraden! Dann beantworte die Fragen selbst *(yourself)*! Verwende die Wörter im Kasten *(in the box)* unten mit verschiedenen *(different)* Verben!

Frag deinen Partner:

a. Was hast du oder was machst du gern?
b. Was hast du oder was machst du nicht gern? Was hast du oder was machst du lieber?
c. Was hast du oder was machst du am liebsten?

Western    Country and Western    Kuchen    Pizza    Heavy Metal    Basketball
Rock'n Roll    Fußball    Kaffee    Tennis    schwimmen    Mathe    Klavier    Cola
Oper    Horrorfilme    Karten    Schach
Technik    Gitarre    kegeln    Apfelsaft    sammeln    angeln    Jazz

## 16 Und du? Wie steht's mit dir?

a. Create a chart in German similar to the one you used in Activity 13 and fill in the following information about yourself: the music you like, prefer, or like the best, and the music you do not like at all. Then get together with your partner and ask him or her questions in order to find out the same information. Take notes using your chart. Then switch roles. Use the chart to help you organize your answers.

b. You must introduce your partner at the next German club meeting, where the topic of the afternoon is music. Use the notes you took on your partner's preferences and favorites in music and write a paragraph introducing him or her and describing his or her interests in music.

# 17

# Das Kinoprogramm

Look at the ads below and answer the questions that follow.

Mittwoch, 7. 7.
20.00 Uhr
Olympia Bissingen

**Der mit dem Wolf tanzt**
mit Kevin Costner,
Mary McDonell
Regie: Kevin Costner

Donnerstag, 8. 7.
20.00 Uhr
Delta Bietigheim

Mittwoch, 19. 5.
20.00 Uhr
Olympia Bissingen

**The Wall**
mit Bob Geldof,
Pink Floyd
Regie: Alan Parker

Donnerstag, 20. 5.
20.00 Uhr
Delta Bietigheim

☎ **55 75 40**

| 16.00 | MY GIRL — Meine erste Liebe | 20. Wo./ab 6 J. |
| 18.00 | VATER DER BRAUT | |
| 20.15 | mit Steve Martin | 7. Wo./ab 6 J. |
| 22.30 | DER GEFALLEN, DIE UHR & DER SEHR GROSSE FISCH | 5. Wo./ab 16 J. |
| | mit Bob Hoskins, Jeff Goldblum „Eine sehr schöne Komödie" | tz 100% |

„Peppige Dialoge, feinsinniger Humor und jede Menge skurriler Typen." *Cinema*

**MEIN VETTER WINNIE**

Eine Gerichtskomödie v. Jonathan Lynn
mit Oscar-Preisträger Joe Pesci

Schwanthalerstr. 3
Tel. 55 57 54 - ab 6 J.

14.45, 17.30, 20.15, Fr./Sa. a. 23.00

Der Boss der Familie ist der mit der großen Schnauze

**Ein Hund namens Beethoven**

14.00/16.00/18.00/20.00     Fr./Sa. auch 22.00

| DO 27.05. | 21.30 | Filmkritikers Liebling |
| FR 28.05. | | |
| SA 29.05. | | |
| SO 30.05. | | |
| MO 31.05. | | |
| DI 1.06. | | |
| MI 2.06. | USA 1991 | |

**Thelma & Louise**

von Ridley Scott, mit
Geena Davis, Susan Sarandon
und Harvey Keitel

„DIE LUSTIGSTE KOMÖDIE AUS DEUTSCHLAND SEIT ÜBER 10 JAHREN"

*Hollywood Reporter*

13. Wo.

GÖTZ GEORGE • UWE OCHSENKNECHT

▼**SCHTONK!**
DER FILM ZUM BUCH VOM FÜHRER

**RIO-PALAST**
Rosenheimer Platz, Tel. 48 69 79
18.15, 20.30, Di./Mi. auch 16.00

**NEUES REX**
Agricolastraße 16, Tel. 56 25 00
Täglich 20.30 Uhr

---

1. What kind of ads are these?
2. Which films do you recognize? Using the pictures and cognates as cues, try to guess what the English titles are for all the different movies listed.
3. What specific kinds of information can you find in these ads?
4. At what times on Friday can you see the movie *Ein Hund namens Beethoven*?
5. What telephone number do you need to call to find out what day *Vater der Braut* is showing? Figure out how long *Vater der Braut* has been showing.
6. Is the movie *Schtonk* showing in more than one movie theater? If so, what are the addresses of the theaters?
7. Look at the listing for *Der mit dem Wolf tanzt*. What does **Regie** mean?
8. How would you describe these movies using the movie categories you learned on page 249 (for example, **Horrorfilme**)?

movie ads
[Answers will vary]
day and time of showing, names of actors, age rating, how many weeks the film has been showing, critics' comments
14:00, 16:00, 18:00, 20:00, 22:00
55 75 40; seven weeks
Yes: Rio-Palast, Rosenheimer Platz and Neues Rex, Agricolastr. 16.
director or directed by
[Answers will vary]

## LERNTRICK

In the expression **am liebsten**, the part of the word that expresses the superlative (= most of all) is the suffix **-sten**. Watching for this suffix will frequently help you understand the meaning of new words. In the ad for *Schtonk* you see the phrase: **die lustigste Komödie**. **Lustig** means *funny*. What is the ad saying about the film *Schtonk?* What kind of film are you talking about if you say **der traurigste Film**? **der brutalste Film**? You will learn more about the superlative forms later.

## 18 Wie findest du ...?

From the films listed on page 255, choose three that you've already seen or three other movies. Write them on a piece of paper and give it to your partner. He or she will do the same. Now ask your partner his or her opinion of the movies on the list. Then switch roles. Use **weil**-clauses and the adjectives below to express why you do or don't like the movie.

BEISPIEL  PARTNER  **Wie findest du den Film** *Vater der Braut*?

DU  **Den Film mag ich gar nicht, weil er zu doof ist.**

---

### WORTSCHATZ

**Gut!**

phantasievoll
lustig
spannend
sensationell

**Schlecht!**

grausam
zu brutal
zu schmalzig (*corny, mushy*)
dumm
zu traurig
doof (*stupid*)

Don't forget these words that you already know:

*Spitze  toll  langweilig*
*interessant  blöd  prima*

Komödien sind lustig.

Horrorfilme sind grausam, aber Krimis sind spannend.

Liebesfilme können traurig oder oft sehr schmalzig sein.

---

## 19 Welchen Film sehen wir heute abend?

You and your partner are using the movie listings on page 255 to select a movie to see tonight. Discuss the types of movies each of you prefers, then make a suggestion and see if your partner agrees. Once you agree on a movie, decide on a time. Share your plans with your classmates.

## 20 Rate mal!

a. Write a paragraph describing your favorite film or rock star using the new vocabulary and phrases you've learned in this chapter. Refer to your favorite star as **mein Lieblingsstar** or **mein(e) Lieblingssänger(in)**. Here are some questions you will want to answer in your paragraph.

1. Woher kommt er/sie?
2. Wie sieht er/sie aus?
3. Was für Filme macht er/sie? (Was für Lieder singt er/sie?)
4. Was ist sein/ihr neuster Film? (Was ist sein/ihr neustes Lied?)

b. Now read your description to the class. Your classmates will take turns asking questions and guessing who the mystery person is.

---

# Welche kulturellen Veranstaltungen besuchst du?

We asked several teenagers in the German-speaking countries what cultural events they usually go to for entertainment. What do you think they might have said? Before you read the interviews, make a list of the types of cultural events that you think German-speaking teenagers might find interesting.

**Silvana,** *Berlin*

„Also, kulturelle Veranstaltungen ... geh' ich manchmal ins Ballett mit meiner Mutter, also uns interessiert das Ballett: *Schwannensee* war ich schon, *Nußknacker* von Tschaikowsky, und ab und zu gehen wir mit der Schule ins Museum oder zu irgendwelchen Ausstellungen, aber eigentlich nicht so oft."

**Silke,** *Hamburg*

„Ich geh' auch gern ins Theater, ich kuck' mir auch mal Shakespeare an oder so und auch mal so witzige Theaterstücke, und ich geh' auch sehr gern ins Museum. Und es gab da hier vor kurzem die Picasso-Ausstellung, und die war auch ganz gut."

**Tim,** *Berlin*

„Also, ich versuch's so oft wie möglich—bei jeder Chance—in ein Theater oder in eine Oper zu gehen, sobald ich günstig Karten bekomme, das heißt über die Schule krieg' ich Vergünstigung, oder daß meine Eltern mich halt einladen oder was sponsern, daß ich dann ins Theater gehe."

**Rosi,** *Berlin*

„Ich geh' nicht oft zu kulturellen Veranstaltungen, weil ... meine Eltern wollen mich da immer mitnehmen, aber ich hab' dann andere Sachen vor, dann bin ich verabredet und hab' keine Lust. Aber meine Eltern sind schon dafür, daß ich dahin gehen würde."

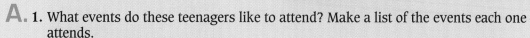

**A.**
1. What events do these teenagers like to attend? Make a list of the events each one attends.
2. With your partner, write answers for the following questions. Are all of these teenagers interested in cultural events? If not, what reasons are given for not going to the events? What does the person say? Now look at Tim's interview. What do you think might keep Tim from attending a play or an opera?
3. Compare the list you made before reading the text with what the teenagers actually said. Do teenagers in the German-speaking countries like the same types of cultural events as teenagers where you live? What are some of the differences? Do you think teenagers in the German-speaking countries are more or less interested in cultural events than teenagers where you live? Why do you think this is so? Discuss these answers with your classmates and then write a brief essay in German about the topic.

**B.** What would you say if you were interviewed about the kinds of cultural events you like? Write your answer in German giving reasons for why you do or don't like particular events.

## Talking about what you did in your free time

## 21 Was machen die Jugendlichen in ihrer Freizeit?

Sieh dir die Anzeigen (*ads*) zur Freizeitplanung an!

1. Was für Anzeigen siehst du hier?
2. Welche Bücher, Filme oder Stars kennst du schon? Mach eine Liste!
3. Lies die Buchtitel auf den Bestsellerlisten! Was bedeuten „Sachbuch" und „Belletristik"?
4. Wenn du Konzerte magst, welche Anzeige interessiert dich? Wann ist das Konzert von Udo Jürgens? Wo ist es?
5. Welche Videohits kennst du schon? Was kannst du im allgemeinen (*in general*) über den deutschen Videomarkt sagen?

1. ads for concerts, videos, and books
2. Answers will vary.
3. non-fiction, fiction
4. the concert schedule on the left; Saturday, March 14 in the Hans-Martin-Schleyer-Halle
5. Answers will vary. American movies are very popular

JOACHIM  Was liest du?
UTE  Oh, ich lese viel, zum
Beispiel ...

**Sachbücher**

**Romane**
  **Krimis**
  **Gruselromane**
  **Liebesromane**
  **Fantasyromane**
  **Science-fiction-**
    **Romane**
**Hobbybücher**

**Zeitungen**

JOACHIM  Und worüber sprichst du
mit deinen Freunden?
UTE  Wir sprechen oft über ...
**Politik, Mode, die Umwelt**

**Zeitschriften**

## 22  Was liest du?

Beantworte die folgenden Fragen mit deinen
Klassenkameraden!

1. Liest du gern? Wenn nicht, warum nicht?
2. Was liest du am liebsten?
3. Was ist dein Lieblingsbuch? Was für ein
   Buch ist das?
4. Worüber sprichst du mit deinen Freunden?

### Ein wenig *G*rammatik

The phrase **sprechen über** means *to
talk about* or *discuss*. When you use
a sentence with **sprechen über,** the
noun phrase following the preposition **über** is in the accusative case:

**Wir sprechen über den Film**
*Mein Vetter Vinny.*

When you want to find out what
topic people are talking about, you
use **worüber** to begin your sentence:

**Worüber sprecht ihr?**

### *G*rammatik  Stem changing verbs

You have learned some verbs that have stem-vowel
changes, such as **nehmen** and **essen**. Here are two
more: **lesen** *(to read)* and **sprechen** *(to speak)*.

| | | | | |
|---|---|---|---|---|
| Ich | **lese** gern Romane. | | Ich | **spreche** gern über Politik. |
| Du | **liest** oft Sachbücher. | | Du | **sprichst** über Mode. |
| Er/Sie | **liest** gern Krimis. | | Er/Sie | **spricht** Deutsch. |

| | | | | |
|---|---|---|---|---|
| Wir | **lesen** Gruselromane. | | Wir | **sprechen** über die Umwelt. |
| Ihr | **lest** Liebesromane. | | Ihr | **sprecht** über Politik. |
| Sie (pl) / Sie } | **lesen** Zeitschriften. | | Sie (pl) / Sie } | **sprechen** Spanish? |

Where does the stem-vowel change occur?[1]  What are the changes in each verb?[2]

1. **du**- and **er/sie**-forms  2. **lesen:** e>ie; **sprechen:** e>i

## 23 Was fehlt hier?

Complete the following interview of Nicole and her friends by choosing the correct word from the choices given.

REPORTER  Was für Bücher __1__ du am liebsten? (lese, sprecht, liest)

NICOLE  Tja, normalerweise __2__ ich Fantasybücher oder Krimis. (lesen, lest, lese)

REPORTER  __3__ du auch die Zeitung? (liest, sprechen, lesen)

NICOLE  Na klar! Aber Zeitschriften __4__ ich lieber. (lese, sprecht, spricht)

REPORTER  Und worüber __5__ du mit deinen Freunden? (spreche, lesen, sprichst)

NICOLE  Hm ... normalerweise __6__ wir über Klamotten oder über einen Film aber manchmal auch halt über Politik oder die Umwelt. (sprechen, lesen, spreche)

REPORTER  Und ihr zwei, was __7__ ihr am liebsten? (sprechen, lest, lesen)

MONIKA  Ganz einfach! Wir beiden haben Gruselromane furchtbar gern. Wir __8__ sie immer! (sprechen, liest, lesen)

## 24 In einer Buchhandlung

You are the salesperson in a bookstore and your partner is a customer. Using the clues below, ask questions to find out what type of book to recommend. Make your recommendation, then switch roles.

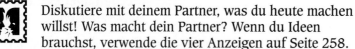

Was für Bücher ...?  Was für Interessen ...?
Worüber sprechen Sie ...?  Lieblingsbuch?

## 25 Was machst du heute abend?

Diskutiere mit deinem Partner, was du heute machen willst! Was macht dein Partner? Wenn du Ideen brauchst, verwende die vier Anzeigen auf Seite 258.

## SO SAGT MAN DAS!

### Talking about what you did in your free time

To find out what someone did last weekend you ask:

**Was hast du am Wochenende gemacht?**

The response might be:

**Am Samstag war ich im Herbert Grönemeyer Konzert. Und ich war am Sonntag zu Hause. Am Nachmittag habe ich gelesen, und am Abend habe ich mit Thomas und Martin das Video „Der mit dem Wolf tanzt" gesehen. Danach haben wir über den Film gesprochen.**

## 26 Hör gut zu!

1. logisch  2. unlogisch  3. unlogisch  4. logisch  5. unlogisch

Schüler erzählen, was sie letztes Wochenende gemacht haben. Sind die Antworten zu jedem Gespräch logisch oder unlogisch?

## 27 Sätze bauen

Answers will vary. Possible answers:
*Ich war zu Hause und habe das Video* Ghost *gesehen.*

Was hast du letztes Wochenende gemacht? Wie viele Sätze kannst du bauen?

Ich war ...

im Konzert
im Kino
zu Hause
bei meinen
Freunden

und ich/wir habe(n) ...

den Film ...
die Gruppe ...
das Buch ...
das Video ...
über (die
Hausaufgaben)

gemacht
gesprochen
gesehen
gelesen

## 28 Hat es Spaß gemacht? *Was it fun?*

Was hast du am Wochenende gemacht? Mach eine Liste! Dann frag deinen Partner, was er gemacht hat! Danach tauscht ihr die Rollen aus!

## 29 Für mein Notizbuch

Beschreib in deinem Notizbuch dein Lieblingswochenende! Wo warst du? Was hast du alles gemacht? Was hast du gesehen, gelesen oder gekauft?

## auAUSSPRACHE

## Richtig aussprechen / Richtig lesen

A. To review the following sounds, say the sentences below after your teacher or after the recording.

1. The long and short **o**: The long **o** sounds similar to the long *o* in the English word *toe.* When the letter **o** is followed by two or more consonants (except when followed directly by **h**), it is pronounced as a short vowel, as in the English word *top.*
   **Wo wohnt die Monika? In der Bodenstraße?**
   **Mein Onkel Otto kommt oft in der Woche zu Besuch.**

2. The long and short **u**: The long **u** is pronounced much like the vowel sound in the English word *do.* However, when the letter **u** is followed by two or more consonants, it is pronounced as a short vowel like the *u* in the English word *put.*
   **Ich find' die Musik super. Du auch, Uwe?**
   **Ulrike mag die Gruppe „Untergrund" furchtbar gern. Und ihr?**

3. The letter combination **ch**: When the consonant combination **ch** follows the vowels **e, i, ä, ö,** and **ü,** it is pronounced like the *h* in the English word *huge.* Following the vowels **a, o,** and **u,** it is pronounced further back in the throat.
   **So ein Pech! Ich möchte gern mit Michaela ins Kino, aber ich kann nicht.**
   **Jochen geht doch lieber nach Hause und liest ein Buch und macht Hausaufgaben.**

## Richtig schreiben / Diktat

B. Write down the sentences that you hear.

*Was sagen die Kritiker?*

## LESETRICK

**Watch for false cognates** Remember to look for cognates as individual words as well as in compound words to help you determine meanings. Occasionally, you will encounter false cognates (words that look alike in both languages but have totally different meanings). Context clues can sometimes help you recognize false cognates. (A good example of a false cognate is the English word *gift*. You will find the same word in German (**Gift**), but you would hardly want to give it to someone you care about: it means *poison!*)

1. Write the English equivalents for the following cognates:
   a. **exklusiven** exclusive
   b. **militärischem** military
   c. **desillusioniert** disillusioned
   d. **Radio-Meteorologe** meteorologist
   e. **zynische** cynical

2. You already know a couple of false cognates. Try to determine (from the choices given) what the false cognates in the following sentences might mean.
   a. Wenn du wissen möchtest, welche Themen in Deutschland **aktuell** sind, mußt du eine deutsche Zeitung lesen.
      1. *actual*  2. *out of date*
      3. *current*
   b. Wer einmal diesen Krimi zu lesen begonnen hat, kann **die Lektüre** nicht unterbrechen, weil das Buch so spannend ist.
      1. *lecture*  2. *lesson*  3. *reading*

3. a. With a partner, write down all the cognates you can find in

## Groundhog Day
### (UND TÄGLICH GRÜSST DAS MURMELTIER)

Phil ist ein Ekel. Doch eines Tages wird der zynische und oberflächliche Radio-Metereologe verzaubert: Die Zeit steht still. Wieder und wieder muß er den von ihm so gehaßten GROUNDHOG DAY, ein Frühlingsfest, in den skurrilsten und wahnwitzigsten Situationen erleben, bis aus ihm endlich ein liebenswerter Mensch geworden ist.

GROUNDHOG DAY von Harold Ramis, mit Bill Murray, Andie MacDowell, Chris Elliott, Stephen Tobolowski u.a.
Englische Originalfassung          103 Min.

## MTV NEWS

• Chris Isaak (»Blue Hotel« und »Wicked Game«) hat sich die Arbeit zu seinem neuen Video leicht gemacht. Er engagierte den Kameramann von Regisseur Bertolucci und überließ ihm die ganze Arbeit.

• Bruce Springsteen macht seinen europäischen Fans ein ganz großes Kompliment: Sie unterstützen ihn mehr als die amerikanischen!

## NEU

### John Grisham • Die Firma

Etwas ist faul an der exklusiven Kanzlei, bei der Mitch McDeere arbeitet. Der hochbegabte junge Anwalt wird auf Schritt und Tritt beschattet, er ist umgeben von tödlichen Gefahren. Als er dann noch vom FBI unter Druck gesetzt wird, erweist sich der Traumjob endgültig als Alptraum ...

Roman. 544 Seiten.
Gebunden mit Schutzumschlag.

Nr. 02001 6
Club-Preis **34.**90

### The Romeos

Nicht aus dem New Yorker Italo-Distrikt, sondern aus Bremen und Oldenburg kommen die Mitglieder der Band. Weniger banal die Musik der Jungs. Bei einer großen Plattenfirma unter Vertrag gelten sie als vielleicht eines der größten Talente der deutschen Popszene.

**29.4. Marquee, 21:00 Uhr**

## JURASSIC PARK™

Spielbergs spektakulärster Film seit Jahren. Gen-Ingenieure haben für einen Freizeitpark Dinosaurier zum Leben erweckt. Eines Tages wird aus dem Spiel mit der Vorzeit blutiger Ernst...

Mit: Sam Neill, Laura Dern, Richard Attenborough
Regie: Stephen Spielberg
Verleih: UIP

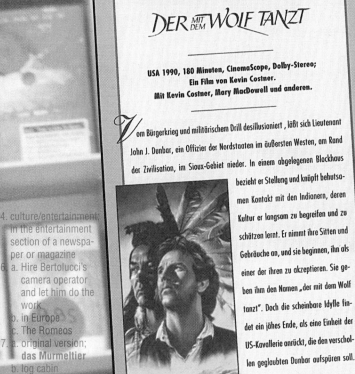

### FREITAG, 9. JULI 1993

## DER MIT DEM WOLF TANZT

USA 1990, 180 Minuten, CinemaScope, Dolby-Stereo;
Ein Film von Kevin Costner.
Mit Kevin Costner, Mary MacDowell und anderen.

Vom Bürgerkrieg und militärischem Drill desillusioniert, läßt sich Lieutenant John J. Dunbar, ein Offizier der Nordstaaten im äußersten Westen, am Rand der Zivilisation, im Sioux-Gebiet nieder. In einem abgelegenen Blockhaus bezieht er Stellung und knüpft behutsamen Kontakt mit den Indianern, deren Kultur er langsam zu begreifen und zu schätzen lernt. Er nimmt ihre Sitten und Gebräuche an, und sie beginnen, ihn als einer der ihren zu akzeptieren. Sie geben ihm den Namen „der mit dem Wolf tanzt". Doch die scheinbare Idylle findet ein jähes Ende, als eine Einheit der US-Kavallerie anrückt, die den verschollen geglaubten Dunbar aufspüren soll.

these selections. Include those cognates that are in compound words, even if part of the compound is not a cognate.

b. List any false cognates that you find. Were you able to figure out the meaning? If so, how?

4. What do these reading selections have in common? Where do you think you might find them?

5. How many of the selections mention something or someone you are familiar with? How does being familiar with the topics help you read the selections?

Answers will vary.

6. Read the articles and see if you can figure out
   a. what Chris Isaak did to ease the difficulties in making his new video
   b. where Bruce Springsteen thinks he has more fans: in Europe or in America
   c. the name of the group regarded as one of the most talented on the German pop scene

7. In groups of two to four, read the articles about the movies and the book, then answer these questions. Be prepared to share your findings with the class.
   a. What do you think **Original-fassung** means at the end of the article on *Groundhog Day*? What is the German word for groundhog?
   b. What do you think the word **Bürgerkrieg** means in the article on *Der mit dem Wolf tanzt*?
   c. What do you think **Traumjob** means in the article on *Die Firma*? Knowing the story, what do you think then that **Alptraum** means?

8. Your German pen pal wants to know what movies or books you have seen or read recently and would recommend. Write a two or three sentence response in German, recommending one movie or book that you like.

4. culture/entertainment; in the entertainment section of a newspaper or magazine
6. a. Hire Bertolucci's camera operator and let him do the work.
   b. in Europe
   c. The Romeos
7. a. original version; **das Murmeltier**
   b. log cabin
   c. dream job/nightmare

# ANWENDUNG

Petra/ins Kino/einen Film sehen/abends/jeden Montag
Rudi/ins Konzert/Musik hören/sonntags/zweimal im Monat
Max/zu Otto/CDs hören/nachmittags/einmal in der Woche
Renate/zu Hause/Bücher lesen/abends/manchmal

**1** You will hear two students talk about how they spend their free time. Make a chart like the one here and fill in the information for each student as you listen.

| Name | wohin? | was? | wann? | wie oft? |
|---|---|---|---|---|
| 1 | | | | |
| 2 | | | | |

**2** Now interview two classmates, asking them where they go and what they do in their free time, and when and how often they do these things. Continue the above chart, filling in the appropriate information for your classmates. Then switch roles.

**3** **a.** Choose a film or concert that you have recently seen and design a movie or concert poster for it in German.

**b.** Using your movie or concert poster, tell the class what kind of concert or film it is, when you saw it, and why you liked it or didn't like it.

**4** Read the transcript of the song to the right and answer the following questions about it.

1. sitting in movie theater
2. midnight
3. adventure/love/comedy
4. monster (horror)
5. attitude changes from "Alles klar" to „Nichts ist klar."

**1.** What is the person doing in the song?

**2.** What time of day is it?

**3.** What types of films is the singer watching in the first stanza? Make a list of all the film stars you recognizein this stanza.

**4.** What type of movie is the singer watching in the last two stanzas? How do you know?

**5.** How does the singer's attitude change from the beginning of the song to the end? What phrases let you know? How do you think she feels at the end?

## „Kino"  99 Luftballons -

Jeden Abend um die gleiche Zeit
vor der Kasse für den Film bereit
Sternenglanz aus Hollywood
Bogart mit Trenchcoat und Hut
Alles klar!
Möchte seh'n 'nen Film mit Marylin,
oder lieber mit James Dean
Ich warte auf das Happy End
Arm in Arm mit Cary Grant
Alles klar!

*Um Mitternacht sitz' ich im Kino,*
*Um Mitternacht läuft das Spätprogramm*
*Um Mitternacht sitz' ich im Kino,*

Ich seh' mir alles an
In der Reihe eins bis zehn
kann man leichenblasse Leute seh'n
Hinter mir im Hochparkett
findet man die Monster nett
Alles klar!

Durch die Nacht der langen Messer geistern Zombies, Menschenfresser
Im Kino ist der Teufel los
Ich hab's gewußt, was mach' ich bloß?
Nichts ist klar!

*Um Mitternacht sitz' ich im Kino, usw.*
*Um Mitternacht sitz' ich im Kino,*
*Ich seh' mir alles an.*

**5** Working in pairs, write the lyrics to a song expressing your feelings about "the movies" or about a specific movie you have seen.

**6** Write down the nine different kinds of films you learned on page 249, each on a separate slip of paper, and put them into a container. The class will divide up into two teams. Partners from each team will take turns drawing a movie type and acting that movie type out in front of the class. The two teams will take turns guessing what kind of movie it is. *Answers will vary.*

a.

b.

c.

d.

**7** Look at the illustrations on the right, and write a story to go along with them. Your **Bildergeschichte** (*picture story*) should include something about each picture.

**8**

R O L L E N S P I E L

Get together with two or three other classmates and create an original scene for one of the following situations. Role-play your scene in front of the class.

a. You are in front of a movie theater and want to see a film. Talk about the different movies and say which ones you like, dislike, and strongly dislike, and which one(s) you have already seen. Then decide together which movie you will see.

b. You and your friends are at the video store to rent (**ausleihen**) a movie. Talk about what kinds of movies each of you likes and decide on a movie everyone will enjoy. Don't forget to mention any movies you have already seen.

# KANN ICH'S WIRKLICH?

Can you express likes and dislikes using **mögen**? (p. 250)

**1** How would you ask a friend what type of movie he or she likes? How might he or she respond? Was für Filme magst du? Ich mag …

**2** How would you say that

   **a.** Thomas likes horror films a lot    a. Thomas mag Horrorfilme sehr gern.

   **b.** Julia really doesn't like rock music at all    b. Julia mag Rockmusik überhaupt nicht.

   **c.** Sabine and Nicole like fantasy films   c. Sabine und Nicole mögen Fantasy-filme.

   **d.** We don't care for romance movies    d. Wir mögen Liebesfilme nicht.

Can you express familiarity using **kennen**? (p. 252)

**3** How would a friend ask if you are familiar with

   **a.** the movie *Rocky 4*    a. Kennst du den Film Rocky IV?

   **b.** the singer Ina Deter    b. Kennst du die Sängerin Ina Deter?

   **c.** the group R.E.M.    c. Kennst du die Gruppe R.E.M.?

   **d.** the film star Clint Eastwood    d. Kennst du den Filmstar Clint Eastwood?

**4** How would you respond to each of your friend's questions? Answers will vary.

Can you express preferences and favorites? (p. 253)

**5** How would you tell a friend what type of movies you like to see, what type of movies you prefer, and what type of movies you like best of all? Ich sehe gern … ich sehe lieber … am liebsten sehe ich …

**6** How would you say that

    a. Martin mag Abenteuerfilme, aber Liebesfilme sieht er lieber.

   **a.** Martin likes adventure movies, but prefers movies about romance.

   **b.** Sandra likes horror films best of all    b. Sandra sieht am liebsten Horrorfilme.

   **c.** Sabine doesn't like to read magazines and prefers to read newspapers
    c. Sabine liest nicht gern Zeitschriften; sie liest lieber Zeitungen.

Can you talk about what you did in your free time? (p. 260)

**7** How would you ask a friend what he or she did on the weekend? How would your friend respond if he or she

   **a.** saw the movie *Jurassic Park* on Saturday evening

   **b.** read a newspaper on Sunday

   **c.** saw the movie *Sister Act* on video on Friday evening

   **d.** read the book *Hunt for Red October* on Saturday

   **e.** was at the Billy Joel concert on Friday evening

   **f.** bought clothes and talked about fashion with his or her friends

**8** Write a short paragraph describing what you saw, read, or talked about with your friends last weekend.

Answers will vary.

7. Was hast du am Wochenende gemacht?
a. Am Samstag abend habe ich den Film *Jurassic Park* gesehen.
b. Am Sonntag habe ich eine Zeitung gelesen.
c. Am Freitag abend habe ich das Video *Sister Act* gesehen.
d. Am Samstag habe ich das Buch *The Hunt for Red October* gelesen.
e. Am Freitag abend war ich im Billy Joel-Konzert.
f. Ich habe Klamotten gekauft und mit meinen Freunden über Mode gesprochen.

## ERSTE STUFE
### EXPRESSING LIKES AND DISLIKES

**verbringen**   *to spend (time)*
**mögen**   *to like, care for*
**Was für Filme magst du gern?**
   *What kind of movies do you like?*
**der Film, -e**   *movie*
   **der Abenteuerfilm, -e**   *adventure movie*
   **der Actionfilm, -e**   *action movie*
   **der Horrorfilm, -e**   *horror movie*
   **die Komödie, -n**   *comedy*
   **der Kriegsfilm, -e**   *war movie*

**der Krimi, -s**   *detective movie, crime drama*
**der Liebesfilm, -e**   *romance*
**der Science-fiction-Film,**   *science fiction movie*
**der Western, -**   *western (movie)*
**Was für Musik hörst du gern?**
   *What kind of music do you like?*
**klassische Musik**   *classical music*
**die Oper, -n**   *opera*

### EXPRESSING FAMILIARITY

**kennen**   *to know, be familiar or acquainted with*

**der Schauspieler, -**   *actor*
**die Schauspielerin, -nen**   *actress*
**der Sänger, -**   *singer (male)*
**die Sängerin, -nen**   *singer (female)*
**die Gruppe, -n**   *group*

### DEGREES OF LIKING AND DISLIKING

**besonders gern**   *especially like*
**furchtbar gern**   *like a lot*
**gar nicht gern**   *not like at all*
**überhaupt nicht gern**   *strongly dislike*

---

## ZWEITE STUFE
### EXPRESSING PREFERENCES AND FAVORITIES

**lieber (mögen)**   *prefer*
**am liebsten (mögen)**   *like most of all*
**sehen**   *to see*
   **er/sie sieht**   *he/she sees*

**phantasievoll**   *imaginative*
**spannend**   *exciting, thrilling*
**sensationell**   *sensational*
**lustig**   *funny*
**zu**   *too*
   **grausam**   *cruel*

**dumm**   *dumb, stupid*
**brutal**   *brutal, violent*
**schmalzig**   *corny, mushy*
**traurig**   *sad*
**doof**   *dumb*

---

## DRITTE STUFE
### TALKING ABOUT WHAT YOU DID IN YOUR FREE TIME

**Was hast du am Wochenende gemacht?**   *What did you do on the weekend?*
**lesen**   *to read*
   **er/sie liest**   *he/she reads*
**Was hast du gelesen?**   *What did you read?*
**das Buch, ¨er**   *book*

**der Roman, -e**   *novel*
**der Gruselroman, -e**   *horror novel*
**der Liebesroman -e**   *love story*
**das Sachbuch, ¨er**   *nonfiction book*
**die Zeitung, -en**   *newspaper*
**die Zeitschrift, -en**   *magazine*
**das Hobbybuch, ¨er**   *hobby book*
**sprechen über**   *to talk about*

**er/sie spricht über ...**   *he/she talks about ...*
**Worüber habt ihr gesprochen?**
   *What did you (pl) talk about?*
**die Politik**   *politics*
**die Mode**   *fashion*
**die Umwelt**   *environment*
**Was hast du gesehen?**   *What did you see?*
**das Video, -s**   *video (cassette)*

# Kapitel 11: Der Geburtstag *Chapter Overview*

| Los geht's! pp. 270-272 | Der Geburtstag, p. 270 | | | *Video Guide* |
|---|---|---|---|---|
| | **FUNCTIONS** | **GRAMMAR** | **CULTURE** | **RE-ENTRY** Print |
| **Erste Stufe** pp. 273-276 | Using the telephone in Germany, *p. 274* | | **Ein wenig Landeskunde:** Using the telephone, *p. 275* | • Numbers 0-20, *p. 275* (from **Vorschau** and **Kapitel 1**) <br> • Time and days of the week, *p. 275* (from **Kapitel 6**) |
| **Zweite Stufe** pp. 277-280 | • Inviting someone to a party and accepting or declining, *p. 277* <br> • Talking about birthdays and expressing good wishes, *p. 278* | | • **Ein wenig Landeskunde:** Saints' days, *p. 279* <br> • Good luck symbols, *p. 279* <br> • **Was schenkst du zum Geburtstag?** *p. 280* | • Numbers *p. 278* (from **Vorschau, Kapitel 1,** and **Kapitel 3**) <br> • Months, *p. 278* (from **Kapitel 7**) |
| **Dritte Stufe** pp. 281-285 | Discussing gift ideas, *p. 282* | • Introduction to the dative case, *p. 283* <br> • Word order in dative case, *p. 284* | • German gift ideas, *p. 281* <br> • Magazine article, *p. 282* | • Accusative case, *p. 283* (from **Kapitel 5**) <br> • Family members, *p. 284* (from **Kapitel 3**) |
| **Aussprache** p. 285 | Review the sounds **r** and **er**, review the vowel **a**, review the diphthongs **eu, äu,** and **au**. | | | **Diktat:** *Textbook Audiocassette* 6 A |
| **Zum Lesen** pp. 286-287 | **Billig einkaufen gehen** Reading Strategy: Reading for understanding of ideas, not of isolated words | | | |
| **Review** pp. 288-291 | • Anwendung, *p. 288* <br> • Kann ich's wirklich? *p. 290* <br> • Wortschatz, *p. 291* | | | |
| **Assessment Options** | **Stufe Quizzes** <br> • *Chapter Resources,* Book 4 <br>    Erste Stufe, Quiz 11-1 <br>    Zweite Stufe, Quiz 11-2 <br>    Dritte Stufe, Quiz 11-3 <br> • *Assessment Items, Audiocassette* 8 B | | **Kapitel 11 Chapter Test** <br> • *Chapter Resources,* Book 4 <br> • *Assessment Guide,* Speaking Test <br> • *Assessment Items, Audiocassette* 10 B <br><br> **Test Generator, Kapitel 11** | |

| *Video Program* **OR** *Expanded Video Program*, Videocassette 4 | Textbook Audiocassette 6 A |

**RESOURCES**
Audiovisual
**RESOURCES**

*Textbook Audiocassette* 6 A

*Practice and Activity Book*
*Chapter Resources*, Book 4
- Communicative Activity 11-1
- Additional Listening Activity 11-1 . . . . . . . . . . . . . *Additional Listening Activities, Audiocassette* 10 B
- Additional Listening Activity 11-2 . . . . . . . . . . . . . *Additional Listening Activities, Audiocassette* 10 B
- Student Response Form
- Realia 11-1
- Situation Card 11-1
- Quiz 11-1 . . . . . . . . . . . . . . . . . . . . . . . . . . . . . *Assessment Items, Audiocassette* 8 B

*Textbook Audiocassette* 6 A

*Practice and Activity Book*
*Chapter Resources*, Book 4
- Communicative Activity 11-2
- Additional Listening Activities 11-3, 11-4 . . . . . . . . *Additional Listening Activities, Audiocassette* 10 B
- Student Response Form
- Realia 11-2
- Situation Card 11-2
- Teaching Transparency Master 11-1 . . . . . . . . . . . . *Teaching Transparency* 11-1
- Quiz 11-2 . . . . . . . . . . . . . . . . . . . . . . . . . . . . . *Assessment Items, Audiocassette* 8 B
*Video Guide* . . . . . . . . . . . . . . . . . . . . . . . . . . . . . . *Video Program/Expanded Video Program*, Videocassette 4

*Textbook Audiocassette* 6 A

*Practice and Activity Book*
*Chapter Resources*, Book 4
- Additional Listening Activity 11-5 . . . . . . . . . . . . . *Additional Listening Activities, Audiocassette* 10 B
- Additional Listening Activity 11-6 . . . . . . . . . . . . . *Additional Listening Activities, Audiocassette* 10 B
- Student Response Form
- Realia 11-3
- Situation Card 11-3
- Teaching Transparency Master 11-2 . . . . . . . . . . . . *Teaching Transparency* 11-2
- Quiz 11-3 . . . . . . . . . . . . . . . . . . . . . . . . . . . . . *Assessment Items, Audiocassette* 8 B

*Video Guide* . . . . . . . . . . . . . . . . . . . . . . . . . . . . . . *Video Program/Expanded Video Program*, Videocassette 4

**Alternative Assessment**
- Performance Assessment, *Teacher's Edition*
  **Erste Stufe**, p. 267J
  **Zweite Stufe**, p. 267M
  **Dritte Stufe**, p. 267O
- Portfolio Assessment
  Written: **Zweite Stufe**, Activity 16, *Pupil's Edition*, p. 277, *Assessment Guide*
  Oral: **Erste Stufe**, Activity 9, *Pupil's Edition*, p. 275, *Assessment Guide*
- **Notizbuch**, *Pupil's Edition*, p. 278; *Practice and Activity Book*, p. 155

# Kapitel 11: Der Geburtstag
# *Textbook Listening Activities Scripts*

## *E*rste Stufe

### Activity 7, *p. 274*

1. — Rezeption hier. Einen Moment bitte!... Wie kann ich Ihnen behilflich sein?
   — Ja ... ich bin in 319, und mein Fernseher scheint nicht richtig zu funktionieren.
   — Das tut mir leid. Ich werde sofort jemanden schicken. Sie sagten 319, nicht?
   — Ja, stimmt. Wird das lange dauern?
   — Nein, in den nächsten fünf Minuten kommt jemand bei Ihnen vorbei.

2. — ... Ja, was meinst du? Was sollen wir denn alles mitnehmen?
   — Vielleicht zwei Flaschen Limo, einige Wurstbrote und etwas Obst. Hast du darauf Hunger?
   — Klar! Prima! Ich bringe die Decke.
   — Also, bis später. Wir treffen uns so gegen 12 Uhr unter der alten Eiche.
   — Ich freu' mich schon. Tschüs!

3. — Ja, guten Tag! Ich möchte mich gern nach Ihren Reparaturpreisen erkundigen.
   — Ja, das kommt natürlich auf die Reparatur an. Könnten Sie etwas genauer sein?
   — Ja. Mein Fahrrad braucht unbedingt neue Speichen. Die jetzigen sind alle schon ziemlich verrostet.
   — Ja, das ist einfach und dauert auch nicht lange. Pro Speiche kostet das DM 1,00 einschließlich Arbeitslohn.
   — Könnte ich mein Rad morgen vormittag abliefern?
   — Sicher, und ihr Name bitte?
   — Klaus ... Klaus Schmidt.

4. — Guten Morgen! Unser Motto hier bei Autowinkel: Wir kommen schnell und fahren sicher. Womit kann ich Ihnen heute helfen?
   — Ich möchte gern ein Taxi für 8 Uhr 30 bestellen.
   — Und ihre Addresse, bitte?
   — Holtenauerstraße 54.
   — Und wohin darf es sein?
   — Ja, zum Hauptbahnhof. Mein Zug fährt um 9 Uhr 12 ab. Kann man das schaffen?
   — Aber natürlich, mein Herr ... das Taxi ist schon auf dem Weg. Vielen Dank und nicht vergessen: Wir kommen schnell und fahren sicher. Auf Wiederhören!

### Activity 12, *p. 276*

— Hier bei Hansen.
— Ja, Ludwig Ottman hier. Könnt' ich bitte mit Ditmar oder Ursel sprechen?
— Das tut mir leid, aber die sind zur Zeit nicht zu Hause.
— Mensch, schade! Ich wollte dem Ditmar ..., na macht nichts. Darf ich bitte eine Nachricht hinterlassen?
— Natürlich. Einen Moment, ich hole nur schnell einen Bleistift und das Gesprächs-Notizbuch ... ja, so hier hab' ich's. Ja bitte? Wie war noch gleich Ihr Name?
— Ludwig ... Ludwig Ottman. Ich bin ein Verwandter der Familie. Bin gerade umgezogen, am besten gebe ich gleich meine neue Adresse und Telefonnummer, ja? Also, ich wohne jetzt in der Neubaustraße 9, das ist in Marktbreit.
— Und was ist die Postleitzahl bitte?
— Na, da muß ich schnell mal nachdenken. Ach ja ... Die ist 97413.
— Und die Telefonnummer?
— Ja, die Vorwahl hier ist, hm ... 09331 und dann anschließend 1367.
— Das hab' ich nicht ganz mitgekriegt. Könnten Sie das noch mal wiederholen?
— Also 09331 und dann 1367. Alles klar?

— Ja ... danke.
— Ich rufe an, weil wir meinem Vater, also dem Onkel Michael, eine Geburtstagsparty geben, und dazu wollen wir ja den Ditmar und die Ursel einladen. Die Feier soll am 2. Juni stattfinden, in Nürnberg, wo er ja auch wohnt. Die Feier beginnt so um 17 Uhr im Hotel Löwe. Das ist leicht zu finden auf der Straßenkarte. Die Adresse ist Rosenthal 8. Alles mitbekommen?
— Ja, ich glaub' schon. Danke.
— OK, dann noch vielen Dank. Also auf Wiederhören!
— Auf Wiederhören!

## *Z*weite Stufe

### Activity 19, *p. 278*

ANJA   Du, sag mal Bernd, wann hast du eigentlich Geburtstag?
BERND   Wieso willst du das wissen?
ANJA   Nur so, für mein Adreßbuch.
BERND   Mein Geburtstag ist am 22. Mai.
ANJA   Und wie steht's mit dir, Maja?
MAJA   Mein Geburtstag war im Winter, am 4. Februar.
ANJA   Ach ja, stimmt. Wir sind ja alle an dem Tag ins Kino gegangen. Das war toll! He, du Benjamin! Wann ist denn dein Geburtstag? Ich kann mich daran nicht mehr erinnern.
BENJAMIN   Im Frühling, so wie du.
ANJA   Wann war das noch gleich?
BENJAMIN   Am 28. März.
ANJA   Katrin, dein Geburtstag war aber noch nicht. Das weiß ich bestimmt.  Ist der nicht bald?
KATRIN   Ja, am 14. August. Ich ruf' dich dann an und lad' dich zu meiner Fete ein.
ANJA   Mensch, toll! Danke ... Und den Mario muß ich auch noch fragen, denn seinen Geburtstag weiß ich auch nicht. Mario, wann hast du eigentlich Geburtstag?
MARIO   Im Winter, also am 29. Dezember ... gleich nach Weihnachten.
ANJA   Prima, jetzt habe ich alle Geburtstage, die mir in meinem Buch fehlten.

### Activity 21, *p. 279*

1. — Ich muß noch schnell zum Schreibwarengeschäft.
   — Wieso denn?
   — Ich habe ganz vergessen, für Sonntag eine Karte zu kaufen. Was machst du denn für deine Mutter?
   — Ich mache immer selber eine Karte, und dann mache ich meistens Frühstück und kaufe ihr einen schönen Blumenstrauß.
   — Gute Idee!

2. — Die haben hier ja eine große Auswahl an Karten.
   — Prima! Ich will meiner Freundin und ihrer Familie eine Karte kaufen.
   — Und wofür ist die Karte?
   — Na, die feiern doch Chanukka im Dezember.
   — Stimmt ja ...

3. — Dieses Jahr haben wir viel Besuch über die Feiertage. Dann muß ich meiner Mutter immer viel helfen. Und wie ist das bei euch?
   — Genauso, nur fahren wir dieses Jahr zu meiner Oma nach Bayern. Da trifft sich dann unsere ganze Familie. Da bleiben wir drei Tage, bis zum 27. Dezember.

4. — Der Rolf wird sich bestimmt freuen. Die CD wollte er immer schon haben.
   — Die fand ich im Musikhaus Schlemmer. Hoffentlich kauft ihm nicht noch einer das gleiche Geschenk!
   — Ach, bestimmt nicht. Du, wie alt wird Rolf eigentlich?
   — Hm ... 16.

# Dritte Stufe

## Activity 25, *p. 282*

— Interkulturelle Beratung und Information ... Fräulein Kaldenkirchen am Apparat. Womit kann ich Ihnen behilflich sein?

— Ja, also ich hoffe, daß Sie mir aushelfen können. Diesen Sommer besuche ich verschiedene Länder in Europa, und während meines Aufenthaltes übernachte ich bei Gastfamilien. Nur weiß ich eben nicht so ganz, was ich denn jeder Familie mitbringen soll ... was da so üblich ist, wissen Sie das?

— Natürlich. Dazu sind wir da. Sagen sie mir doch, wohin ihre Reisen gehen, und ich kann Ihnen ja einige Ratschläge geben.

— Also, meine erste Gastfamilie besuche ich in Frankreich.

— Für Frankreich gibt es eine Anzahl von akzeptablen Geschenken, aber am sichersten sind Getränke.

— Oh, das ist eine gute Idee. Und anschließend besuche ich eine Familie in Italien. Was schlagen Sie dafür vor?

— Italien. Ja, es ist eigentlich allgemein bekannt, daß die Italiener gern Blumen bei einem Besuch erhalten.

— Wirklich?

— Ja, aber sie müssen frisch sein.

— Klar, das kann ich machen ... und dann reise ich auch für einen kurzen Aufenthalt nach Spanien. Was soll ich der Familie mitbringen?

— Ja, das kommt ganz darauf an. Ich würde da ebenfalls Getränke vorschlagen.

— Interessant. Zum Schluß besuche ich dann noch Österreich. Darauf freue ich mich schon sehr. Was kann ich der Gastfamilie mitbringen?

— Das ist einfach. Die Österreicher lieben Schokolade. Also, eine Schachtel Pralinen wäre da ein sehr passendes Geschenk.

— Ja, vielen Dank für Ihre Hilfe! Ich habe mir das alles aufgeschrieben.

— Kann ich Ihnen sonst noch behilflich sein?

— Nein, vielen Dank! Auf Wiederhören!

— Auf Wiederhören!

## Activity 26, *p. 283*

Also, du kannst deinem Opa eine CD kaufen. Der hört doch gern klassische Musik, nicht wahr? Und deiner Oma kannst du ein gutes Buch schenken—die Verkäuferin kann uns dabei helfen, ein passendes Buch zu finden. Deinem Vater—hmmm—vielleicht einen Kalender? So was finden wir bestimmt in der Buchhandlung. Anschließend im Kaufhof kaufen wir deiner Mutter ein schönes Parfüm. So was mag meine Mutter immer gern als Geschenk. Sollen wir deinem Freund Otto ein Poster von den „Toten Hosen" geben? Und der Martina? Ihr können wir Schmuck holen—einen Ring oder eine Armbanduhr vielleicht? Schmuck ist immer ein gutes Geschenk, find' ich. Na, gehen wir los! Wir haben noch viel zu tun, wenn wir das alles heute kaufen wollen.

## Diktat, *p. 285*

You will hear about different items Gerd and Frauke would like to buy their mother for her birthday. First listen to what is said, then write down what you hear.

Gerd und Frauke wollen heute im Kaufhof einkaufen gehen, denn ihre Mutter hat am Donnerstag Geburtstag. Sie sehen verschiedene Sachen. Gerd findet eine schicke Armbanduhr, aber die kostet zu viel. Frauke sieht eine flotte Bluse, leider weiß sie die Größe von ihrer Mutter nicht genau. Schließlich finden sie eine Kette, die ihrer Mutter bestimmt gefallen wird. Schmuck paßt ja zu vielen Sachen. Und zum Schluß gehen Gerd und Frauke noch beim Blumengeschäft vorbei und kaufen einen frischen Blumenstrauß.

# Anwendung

## Activity 1, *p. 288*

| | |
|---|---|
| HELENE | Du Volker, bevor wir heute abend ins Kino gehen, muß ich noch zwei Geburtstagsgeschenke kaufen. Kommst du mit? |
| VOLKER | Gute Idee! Ich muß auch zwei Geschenke kaufen. Wollen wir zu Hertie gehen? |
| HELENE | Ja, klar! Zuerst brauche ich ein passendes Geschenk für den Ulf. |
| VOLKER | Na, der hört doch gern Musik. |
| HELENE | Dann kauf' ich ihm halt eine CD von seiner Lieblingsgruppe. |
| VOLKER | Das findet er sicher stark. |
| HELENE | Und was suchst du? |
| VOLKER | Ja, die Sonja hat übermorgen Geburtstag. In der Schreibwarenabteilung gibt es verschiedene Kalender. Da werde ich schon einen für sie finden. |
| HELENE | Ach ja, und dann hat Ute in zwei Wochen Geburtstag. Die ist ein Bücherwurm. Ich will ihr ein neues Taschenbuch kaufen. Was meinst du? |
| VOLKER | Prima, Tja, eigentlich sollte ich Rolf auch schon sein Geschenk kaufen, obwohl er erst in drei Wochen Geburtstag feiert. |
| HELENE | Hast du schon irgendwelche Ideen? |
| VOLKER | Eigentlich doch. Er sitzt viel an seinem Computer. Vielleicht ein neues Programm? |
| HELENE | Wie wär's mit einem neuen Videospiel? |
| VOLKER | Mensch toll! Ein Videospiel- das finde ich toll! Also kaufen wir die Sachen, und dann gehen wir anschließend ins Kino. |

## Activity 3, *p. 289*

| | |
|---|---|
| PHILIPP | Glaubst du, Bernhard weiß, daß wir eine Überraschungsparty für ihn planen? |
| GABRIELE | Bestimmt nicht. Du, wir haben aber viel zu tun. Wie wollen wir da am besten anfangen? |
| PHILIPP | Wo hast du die Gästeliste? Oh, hier liegt sie. Am besten schicken wir die Einladungen heute ab. Hier ist mein Adreßbuch. |
| GABRIELE | Und ich habe Briefmarken mitgebracht, dann können wir später zur Post gehen und die Einladungen abschicken. Anschließend laß' uns ins Einkaufszentrum gehen. Da können wir nach einem Geschenk für Bernhard gucken. |
| PHILIPP | Prima! Wieviel Geld hast du denn? |
| GABRIELE | So rund DM 20,00. Und du? |
| PHILIPP | Ungefähr DM 25,00. Da läßt sich schon was finden. |
| GABRIELE | Am Tag der Party komm bitte schon früher, damit du mir helfen kannst! |
| PHILIPP | Was gibt's da noch zu tun? |
| GABRIELE | Na, Mensch, wir müssen ein wenig aufräumen, Staub saugen, die Fenster putzen und so was alles. |
| PHILIPP | Hausarbeit mag ich eigentlich nicht so gern. |
| GABRIELE | Muß aber sein, und danach bereiten wir das Essen vor. |
| PHILIPP | Chips 'n' Dip schmeckt prima. Das mache ich. |
| GABRIELE | Ich mach' auch einen Tomatensalat und backe einen Kuchen. |
| PHILIPP | Vergiß nicht, daß wir Getränke brauchen! Limo und Cola, was meinst du? |
| GABRIELE | Klar! Also ich hoffe, daß Bernhard überrascht sein wird! |
| PHILIPP | Bestimmt! Das wird eine tolle Party! |

# Kapitel 11: Der Geburtstag
## *Suggested Project*

*In this activity students will design a personality collage describing themselves. The project could be called* **Darf ich mich vorstellen?** *The project will help review previously learned vocabulary such as descriptive adjectives, leisure activities, hobbies, and dates. It should be written in and presented in German.*

## MATERIALS

✂ **Students may need**
- *personal pictures*
- *old magazines*
- *poster board*
- *5 x 7 index cards*
- *scissors*
- *glue*
- *markers*

## SITUATION

Have students imagine that a group of German-speaking students is visiting their school and attending a meeting of the German Club. As sponsor of the German Club, you have asked each of them to introduce themselves to the visitors by giving a presentation. They should describe themselves and tell a little about their interests and hobbies. When they make their presentations, you might want to designate some of the students to be the visitors and ask them to listen closely and find the American students whose interests and hobbies are most compatible with their own.

## SUGGESTED ITEMS TO INCLUDE IN PRESENTATION

- pictures from their childhood
- pictures of friends and family
- a picture of their home
- birth certificate or something showing important dates
- items that represent something they have done that is important to them (Examples: report cards, medals, certificates)

- pictures of themselves doing activities they are interested in (Examples: ice skating, playing football) or of others doing those activities
- objects or pictures of objects or things that mean a lot to them (Examples: a pet, a car, a certain book)

## SUGGESTED SEQUENCE

1. Announce the title and content of the project and brainstorm with students to help develop ideas about what could be used as part of the collage. (See above list.)

2. After students have had the opportunity to gather materials, ask them to arrange and begin to paste the pictures they have chosen on the poster board.

3. Ask students to provide a brief label for each picture (Example: **Mein erster Geburtstag, 15. Mai 1978**)

4. After students make the labels, ask them to write a short description of each picture or illustration on a 5 x 7 index card.

5. After projects are completed, have students present their collages, show the pictures, and talk about themselves. **Note:** At this point students are encouraged not to read from the cards, but rather to present each illustration spontaneously.

6. Once each student has made his or her presentation, you may want to display the projects in the classroom until the end of the school year.

## GRADING THE PROJECT

Since this project will be written and presented in German, you may want to divide the 50 points for the written work into categories such as choice of vocabulary, correct use of grammar, etc.

Suggested point distribution (total = 100 points)

| | |
|---|---|
| Written work (labels and description) | 50 |
| Poster (originality and appearance) | 25 |
| Oral presentation | 25 |

# Kapitel 11: Der Geburtstag
## ♜ *Games*

## KATEGORIENLISTE

*This game will help students use the chapter vocabulary and review expressions from previous chapters.*

**Procedure** Divide the class into two groups and have all students stand up. Have the following categories written on the board or a transparency: **Feiertage; Geschenkideen; Partygerichte; Freizeitideen.** Begin by asking the first student from Team A to name a German word or phrase that belongs to one of these categories. Alternate teams and write down the words as students name them. A student who cannot think of a new word or makes a mistake must sit down. The team who has the most students still standing at the end of a predetermined time period wins.

## PASSWORD

*This game is especially good for helping visual learners acquire new vocabulary words.*

**Preparation** Make a set of 4 × 6 inch index cards based on the **Wortschatz** for this chapter. On one side of each card write a German vocabulary item, and write its English equivalent on the other side. Make at least ten cards for every pair of students.

**Procedure** Have students sit facing each other in pairs. Give each pair an equal number of index cards. Then give students five to ten minutes to learn or review the vocabulary. One partner gives a word in English and the other responds with the German equivalent. After the review period, have the pairs go through their set of words in a specific amount of time. Example: ten words in twenty seconds. You can also vary this game by using German synonyms rather than English equivalents.

GAMES

# Kapitel 11: Der Geburtstag
## *Lesson Plans, pages 268-291*

## *U*sing the Chapter Opener,
### pp. 268-269

### Motivating Activity

Ask your students what special occasions they celebrate in their families. How do they celebrate? What presents do they give? Do they know the birthdays and anniversaries of family members and close friends?

### Background Information

Young people in the German-speaking countries are very aware of birthdays, anniversaries, and other special occasions. They know this not only for immediate family members, but very often for extended family and closest friends. Young people are usually expected to attend family celebrations. This is possible because, for the most part, families still live close to each other.

### Teaching Suggestion

① Ask students what type of store this is. (**Trödelladen**) Why would the students in the photograph be shopping at a **Trödelladen**? (It's an excellent place to find unusual gifts at good prices.) Ask students if they exchange gifts on certain occasions with friends or relatives. If so, what kinds of presents do they give, and where do they like to shop for those types of gifts?

### Thinking Critically

**Drawing Inferences**   When German students shop for small gifts, the emphasis is on *small.* Teenagers in Germany often cannot afford to buy expensive gifts. Ask students if they know the reason. (In general, German teenagers do not have part-time jobs to make extra money. The job market is so regulated that it is against the law to hire people who have not had training in the position they're about to enter. Salespeople, for example, undergo formal apprenticeship programs. Therefore, teenagers rely on their allowances or money earned through doing small jobs like paper routes for money to spend.)

### Building on Previous Skills

Ask students to come up with ideas for inexpensive gift items for a friend. This should be done in German. Write some of the ideas on the board.

### Background Information

② This picture shows a **Schwarzwälder Kirschtorte,** a T-shirt with the German composer Johannes Brahms (1833-1897), and a cassette of Falco, a popular Austrian singer from Vienna.

### Teaching Suggestion

Ask students for what occasions they buy greeting cards. Ask them what they say in English to express congratulations and good wishes on special occasions. List the expressions on the board. Then tell students that the phrases underneath Picture 2 and on the card next to Picture 3 are ways to express birthday wishes in German.

###  Culture Note

It is customary to send cards for special occasions in Germany, but not to the extent that it is in the United States. Children and young people are expected to sign birthday cards and letters sent to relatives.

###  Culture Note

③ German teenagers tend to talk on the phone less than American teenagers do. One reason is that there is a charge for local calls. For example, one unit (**eine Einheit**) is equal to 8 minutes. Each **Einheit** costs 23 **Pfennig.**

### Teaching Suggestion

Take a survey, asking students how much time they spend on the phone talking to friends and whether they have their own phones.

### Focusing on Outcomes

To get students to focus on the chapter objectives listed on p. 269, ask them how they would organize a surprise party for their best friend. What steps would be involved? Then preview the learning outcomes listed on p. 269. **NOTE:** Each of these outcomes is modeled in the video and evaluated in **Kann ich's wirklich?** on p. 290.

# Teaching Los geht's!
## pp. 270-272

---
### Resources for Los geht's!
---

- *Video Program* **OR**
  *Expanded Video Program,* Videocassette 4
- *Textbook Audiocassette* 6 A
- *Practice and Activity Book*

▶ **pages 270-271**

###  Video Synopsis

In this segment of the video, Nicole calls Sabine to invite her to the birthday party she is organizing for Martin. Later, Sabine and Nicole go shopping and discuss what they should give Martin for his birthday. Finally, Nicole discovers that she has planned the party for the wrong date. The student outcomes listed on p. 269 are modeled in the video: using the telephone in Germany, inviting someone to a party and accepting or declining, talking about birthdays and expressing good wishes, and discussing gift ideas.

### Motivating Activity

Ask students how they would divide the work of organizing a party in order to dispute the following statement: **Eingeladen werden ist schön, aber einladen ist zu viel Arbeit.**

### Thinking Critically

**Analyzing**   After students have watched the video, ask them to look at the first frame of the **Foto-Roman.** What can students say about phone etiquette based on this frame? How do Germans identify themselves on the phone?

###  Culture Note

When Germans answer the phone, they normally state their family name. Children in the house give their first and last name. A caller always identifies himself or herself immediately along with an appropriate greeting for the time of day.

### Thinking Critically

**Comparing and Contrasting**   Ask students how they typically answer the phone and how the caller identifies himself or herself.

▶ **page 272**

###  For Individual Needs

**1 Challenge**   After students have seen the video or listened to the audiocassette, use these four questions to check for comprehension. Do this orally. If you feel some students are insecure about answering the questions, have them look at the text.

### Group Work

**2** Ask students to work with a partner as they read the conversations from pp. 270-271 aloud. Monitor students' pronunciation and intonation and make suggestions when needed. Next, put the five language functions on the board, elicit the appropriate words and phrases from students and have them write them underneath.

### For Individual Needs

**3 A Slower Pace**   Ask students to do this activity in writing as they refer to the **Foto-Roman** to complete the statements. When finished, call on several students to read their sentences.

### Thinking Critically

**4 Analyzing**   After students have completed this activity, ask them to read through it again and underline or make note of all the connectors, conjunctions and adverbs that tie the summary together.

### Closure

Refer students back to the outcomes listed on p. 269 and ask them to list one German phrase or word from the **Foto-Roman** that they think corresponds to each of the functions.

**LOS GEHT'S!**

Los geht's!   **267H**

# Teaching Erste Stufe,
## pp. 273-276

### Resources for Erste Stufe

*Practice and Activity Book*
*Chapter Resources,* Book 4
- Communicative Activity 11-1
- Additional Listening Activities 11-1, 11-2
- Student Response Form
- Realia 11-1
- Situation Card 11-1
- Quiz 11-1

*Audiocassette Program*
- *Textbook Audiocassette* 6 A
- *Additional Listening Activities, Audiocassette* 10 B
- *Assessment Items, Audiocassette* 8 B

▶ **page 273**

## MOTIVATE

### Teaching Suggestion

Ask students to imagine that they are in a phone booth trying to call someone. Have them tell you step-by-step how they make the call, up until the point when the person answers the phone. Tell students that at the end of the **Erste Stufe** they will be able to do this in German.

## TEACH

### Thinking Critically

**6 Observing** Ask students if they can tell where this phone booth is located. (**München, Kemptener-Allgäuer Str.**)

 **Total Physical Response**

Demonstrate the expressions of the **Wortschatz** box using a telephone as a prop. Act out each of the actions with the phone and model the appropriate expression. After going over the expressions several times, hand the phone to a student and give him or her instructions based on the expressions just introduced. Example: **Jesse, nimm bitte den Hörer ab! Danke. Gib Robert das Telefon!**

### Building on Previous Skills

Have students practice giving their phone number, including area code, in German.

 **Culture Note**

Students have already learned that many Germans keep a savings account at their local post office. While the German Federal Post Office no longer administers the telephone network (that is done by a branch of the post office called **Telekom**), it still offers services such as local and long distance calling, transferring of money into bank accounts, sending telegrams, and distribution of mail. Because of its satellite equipment, it also functions as a transmission facility for several television stations. Though the new telephone booths are gray and red, most postal vehicles and buildings are easily recognized by their trademark color: bright yellow.

## Thinking Critically

**Comparing and Contrasting** Have students compare the functions of the German and U.S. postal systems.

## Multicultural Connection

Have students ask students from other countries and students taking other foreign languages about the phone service in their country or the country (countries) they are studying. What is the trademark color? Have them describe public phone booths.

▶ **page 274**

## PRESENTATION: So sagt man das!

Ask students to look back at the **Foto-Roman** and have them find some of the expressions introduced in the **So sagt man das!** box. How were the expressions used in the context of the **Foto-Roman**?

## Thinking Critically

**Comparing and Contrasting** Ask students how they learned to say *goodbye* in Ch. 1. Why do they think **Auf Wiederhören!** is used instead of **Auf Wiedersehen!** when people talk on the phone?

## Teaching Suggestion

Ask students to name some ways they might end a conversation in English. Put these expressions on the board. Then mention to students that Germans also have several different ways of ending a phone conversation depending on the situation (formal vs. informal) and time of day. However, you might

want to point out that the expressions **Auf Wiederhören!** and **Wiederhören!** are acceptable regardless of formality or time of day.

▶ *page 275*

###  Portfolio Assessment

**9** You might want to use this activity as an oral portfolio item for your students. See *Assessment Guide,* Chapter 11.

###  Culture Note

The cost of having and using a phone is much higher in Germany than it is in the United States. As mentioned before, even local calls cost a fee. When the monthly bill arrives at a German home, it is not itemized. Only the number of **Einheiten** used during a monthly billing period appears on the bill. Bills are itemized only at the request of customers for an additional cost.

▶ *page 276*

###  Culture Note

Germans have an advertisement similar to "Reach out and touch someone" to encourage the use of phones. In Germany, you will see stickers inside phone booths which say **Ruf doch mal an!** This can be translated loosely as *Go ahead and call!*

### Reteaching: Using the telephone

Prepare a text in which you give step-by-step instructions on how to use the phone. Leave out key words and phrases. This can be done on a transparency, or you can provide a copy for each student. Also provide the students with a random-order list of the missing words and phrases. Ask students to read the directions and fill in the missing words from the list provided.

## *CLOSE*

### Teaching Suggestion

As students walk into the class, hand every other student an index card that you have prepared ahead of time. Once class gets underway, ask students with a card to find a partner who does not have one. Each pair of students will then make up a phone conversation that is based on the following situation. The student with the card is calling

the other student around dinner time and is trying to sell him or her the item written on the card. The student answering the phone is annoyed by the time of the call and is trying to get rid of the caller. Ask students to be as creative as possible. Suggestions for the cards: encyclopedias, dictionaries, tickets to the opera, newspaper or magazine subscriptions, vacuum cleaners

### Focusing on Outcomes

Refer students back to the outcomes listed on p. 269. They should recognize that they are now able to use the telephone in Germany.

## *ASSESS*

- **Performance Assessment** This activity should be conducted with students individually, if time allows. Ask individual students to dramatize the following situations in mini-skits: You (the student) call a friend at home. You find out that he or she is not home so you give your name and phone number. Ask when your friend will be back and leave a message. Say you would like your call returned before 9:00 P.M. if possible.

- Quiz 11-1, *Chapter Resources,* Book 4

## ZWEITE STUFE

# *T*eaching Zweite Stufe,
## *pp. 277-280*

### Resources for Zweite Stufe

*Practice and Activity Book*
*Chapter Resources,* Book 4
- Communicative Activity 11-2
- Additional Listening Activities 11-3, 11-4
- Student Response Form
- Realia 11-2
- Situation Card 11-2
- Teaching Transparency Master 11-1
- Quiz 11-2

*Audiocassette Program*
- *Textbook Audiocassette* 6 A
- *Additional Listening Activities,*
  *Audiocassette* 10 B
- *Assessment Items, Audiocassette* 8 B

▶ **page 277**

## *MOTIVATE*

### Teaching Suggestion

Ask students how they are usually invited to a party. Do they get a written or oral invitation? What kind of information are they typically given when they are invited to a party?

## *TEACH*

### PRESENTATION: So sagt man das!

Brainstorm with students some different expressions they would use to invite someone to a party in German. Write students' ideas and suggestions on the board. Can they also think of ways to accept and decline? Compare the expressions in the **So sagt man das!** box to the expressions the students came up with.

 **Portfolio Assessment**

**16** You might want to use this activity as a written portfolio item for your students. See *Assessment Guide,* Chapter 11.

▶ **page 278**

### Building on Previous Skills

Review the months by asking questions such as **In welchem Monat ist dein Geburtstag? Weihnachten? Muttertag? Schulanfang?**

### PRESENTATION: So sagt man das!

Write the question **Wann hast du Geburtstag?** on the board. (Make sure that all students understand the word **Geburtstag.**) Answer the question for yourself and write your answer on the board, writing out the number and all the endings: **Ich habe am dreiundzwanzigsten März Geburtstag.** Write two or three other birthdates on the board. Ask **Wann hast du Geburtstag?** and call on volunteers to answer. Then have students imagine that one or several of them have their birthday today. Walk around the room and say: **Ach, Carmelita! Du hast heute Geburtstag? Herzlichen Glückwunsch!** or **Alles Gute zum Geburtstag, Carmelita!** Now have students look at the function box.

### PRESENTATION: Wortschatz

First introduce the ordinal numbers introduced in the **Wortschatz** box. Then, holding up a calendar large enough for students to see, tell students about certain days using the expressions from the **So sagt man das!** box. Examples: **Heute ist Freitag, der erste Mai. Hier ist mein Geburtstag. Der ist am einundzwanzigsten Oktober.**

### Thinking Critically

**Comparing and Contrasting**  Have students observe the endings of the ordinal numbers and the differences in spelling when compared to cardinal numbers.

 **For Individual Needs**

**19** **Auditory Learners**  After students have completed this activity, personalize it by using students' own birthdays. Using a list of students' birthdays, ask students to identify themselves when they hear their birthday called. Example: **Wer hat am zweiten August Geburtstag?** Possible student replies: **Das ist mein Geburtstag.** or **Ich habe am zweiten August Geburtstag.**

▶ *page 279*

##  Culture Note

Mention to students that many German calendars list Saints' Days, and most people are aware of theirs, even if they don't always celebrate it.

## Thinking Critically

**Analyzing** Ask students if they can determine the meaning of the statement below the **Namenstage** in July. (**Gratulieren Sie mit Blumen!** = *Congratulate with flowers!*)

## PRESENTATION: Wortschatz

Teach the names of the holidays in the vocabulary box and tie the names in with your classroom calendar by pointing out the month and date of each of the holidays.

##  Multicultural Connection

Ask students from other countries to share holidays that might be different and unusual to American students. Students could get information about other countries' holidays from exchange students, other foreign language teachers, students taking other foreign languages, or the library.

## Thinking Critically

**22 Comparing and Contrasting** Here students are introduced to some of the good luck symbols in German. Are they the same in the United States? Can students think of some symbols they know of for good luck? For those who do not believe in good luck symbols, Germans have a saying: **Jeder ist seines Glückes Schmied.**

## Teaching Suggestion

**22** Ask each student to make this card for the special occasion in the near future. You might want to provide students with colored paper, glue, scissors, and pens.

▶ *page 280*

## PRESENTATION: Landeskunde

• Ask each student to name one gift they really liked that they have received as a birthday present from a friend or family member.

• You might want to introduce the following additional vocabulary to help students understand the four interviews:
**Ähnliches** (colloq) *something similar*
**die Kleinigkeit** *a little something*
**bemalt** *painted*

• Begin the **Landeskunde** page by having students do the prereading activity. Then either play the audiocassette or have students watch the interviews on the video. Divide the class into four groups and have each group work with one of the interviews and figure out 1. how that person celebrates birthdays, 2. to whom that person gives presents, and 3. what kinds of presents that person gives. Have each group share this information with the rest of the class, using as much German as possible. Do Questions 2, 3, and 4 together in class. Have students work in pairs on Question B; then discuss it together.

## Thinking Critically

**Synthesizing** Books are popular gifts in German-speaking countries. However, the prices of hardbound and paperback books are generally much higher in Germany than they are in the United States. Can students think of a reason for this? (See following Background Information.)

## Background Information

In the United States publishers deal with a much larger market and can offer a lower price than can publishers in the smaller German market. In addition, the international market for English books is far greater than that for German books. Finally, the production cost of books is higher in Germany because of the higher cost of labor and raw materials.

**ZWEITE STUFE**

## Teaching Suggestion

**A1** Ask students to review Eva's statement about giving **Gutscheine** (*gift certificates*). Why does she like giving them instead of gifts? Ask students to agree or disagree.

## Teacher Note

Mention to your students that the **Landeskunde** will also be included in Quiz 11-2 given at the end of the **Zweite Stufe**.

## Reteaching: Expressing good wishes

Name several different holidays and occasions in German and ask students to give an appropriate expression of good wishes.

## CLOSE

### ♜ Game

Play the game **Kategorienliste.** See p. 267F for the procedure.

## Focusing on Outcomes

Refer students back to the learning outcomes listed on p. 269. Students should recognize that they are now able to invite someone to a party and accept or decline, talk about birthdays, and express good wishes.

## ASSESS

- **Performance Assessment**   Go around the class and ask individual students questions to which they have to respond by giving specific days, dates, and months. Vary questions. Example: **Sam, wann feiern wir dieses Jahr Thanksgiving?**
  **Welches Datum haben wir heute?**
  **Welches Datum war gestern?**

- Quiz 11-2, *Chapter Resources,* Book 4

Namenstag im Juli

10. Erich/Erika
13. Margarete
15. Heinrich
24. Christine
25. Jakob
26. Anne Marie
29. Martha

Gratulieren Sie mit Blumen!

Fröhliche Weihnachten!

Zum Muttertag!

Alles Gute!

# *T*eaching Dritte Stufe,
## pp. 281-285

### Resources for Dritte Stufe

*Practice and Activity Book*
*Chapter Resources,* Book 4
- Additional Listening Activities 11-5, 11-6
- Student Response Form
- Realia 11-3
- Situation Card 11-3
- Teaching Transparency Master 11-2
- Quiz 11-3

*Audiocassette Program*
- *Textbook Audiocassette* 6 A
- *Additional Listening Activities, Audiocassette* 10 B
- *Assessment Items, Audiocassette* 8 B

▶ page 281

## *MOTIVATE*

### Teaching Suggestions

Ask students what kind of gifts they typically buy for a friend's birthday. Students should do this in German. For words they don't know, encourage students to give a description of the gift.

## *TEACH*

###  Cooperative Learning

**23** Begin by reading the *Juma* excerpt with the class. Then ask students to work in groups of three and assign each student a specific task (reader, writer, reporter). The reader reads the excerpt as well as Questions 1-4 aloud. The members of each group then work together to answer the questions as the writer takes notes for the group. Set a time limit for the activity, and encourage students to converse in German as they try to answer Question 4. Once groups have completed their assignment, call on the reporters from different groups to give their answers to the questions.

### PRESENTATION: Wortschatz

Have the items from the vocabulary box on hand, or bring pictures of the items you are not able to bring. Use the items to introduce the new words. Work especially with the pronunciation of the cog-

nates in which the stress in the German word is on a different syllable than the stress in the English word. (Examples: **Kalénder Pralínen, Parfüm**)

▶ page 282

## PRESENTATION: So sagt man das!

Ask students if they can think of synonyms of the verb **schenken** that they have learned in preceding units. (**geben, mitbringen.**)

### Multicultural Connection

**25** Ask students to find out what gifts would be appropriate for a host or hostess in other countries.

▶ page 283

## PRESENTATION: Grammatik

Put several sentences on the board and ask students to come to the front and label the parts of the sentences. (Example: **Michael gibt seinem Bruder das Geld. Tina schenkt ihrer Mutter einen Blumenstrauß.**) Help students recognize the indirect objects in the sentences. Remind students of the article changes that occur in the accusative, then let students discover the dative changes through further examples using nouns that clearly show a change. Examples:

**Sein Vater hat Geburtstag.**
**Er schenkt seinem Vater ein Buch.**
(sein → seinem)

**Meine Kusine besucht uns jetzt.**
**Ich schenke meiner Kusine eine neue CD.**
(meine → meiner)

**Das Kind hat Geburtstag.**
**Ilse schenkt dem Kind ein Buch.** (das → dem)

You might want to underline the articles in a different color to emphasize the difference between the nominative and the dative case.

###  For Individual Needs

**26 Challenge** After students have completed the listening activity, ask students to use the notes they took to comment on the gift suggestion. Would the recipient like the gift or prefer something else? Students should use expressions for describing likes, dislikes, preferences, and opinions in their statements.

▶ *page 284*

### ◆ For Individual Needs

**27 A Slower Pace** To give students the opportunity to work individually on word order and dative case, assign this activity to be done in writing in class. Set a time limit, then ask several students to put their sentences on the board. Go over each sentence with the class and make necessary corrections.

### For Additional Practice

**28** Ask students to add a specific occasion to each statement. Example: **Was schenkst du deinem Bruder zu Weihnachten?**

**30** Ask students who finish this activity early to change the occasion from birthday to another occasion and make another list.

▶ *page 285*

### For Additional Practice

**31** Ask students if they can think of at least two more souvenirs that would be typical for each of the five countries. Help students to name them in German.

### Teaching Suggestion

**32** This activity could be assigned as written homework. Remind students to use the conversational past in their letters to describe what they did on their trip.

### PRESENTATION: Aussprache

Have those students who feel comfortable doing so demonstrate the guttural **r** in class. Students have used all of these sounds a great deal by this time and should be able to find a number of words containing them. Divide students into pairs and assign each pair one of the three targeted sounds. Have them find as many words as they can that contain those sounds, then use those words in sentences. Their sentences should be in context and should, when read together, present either a coherent paragraph or a conversation. (Encourage humor and creativity.) Have as many pairs as time permits read their sentences to the class. After they have done the **Diktat,** have them exchange papers and make corrections.

### Reteaching: Dative case endings and word order

Prepare the following chart on a transparency or have a copy for each student. Ask students to create as many sentences as possible.

| names of class members | geben kaufen schenken | seiner Schwester seinem Opa ihrer Tante names of class members | eine Brille ein Schloß einen Mercedes other silly gift ideas |
|---|---|---|---|

### *CLOSE*

### Teaching Suggestion

Divide the class into two groups and have each group argue for and against **Geschenkegeben.** Each group should find several arguments (in German) to support its point of view. Divide the chalkboard in half and write down students' arguments.

### Focusing on Outcomes

Refer students back to the outcomes listed on p. 269. Students should recognize that they are now able to discuss gift ideas.

### *ASSESS*

- **Performance Assessment** As students enter the class, give each one an index card with the name of a famous person written on it. Once class gets underway, ask students what they would give that person on his or her birthday.

- Quiz 11-3, *Chapter Resources,* Book 4

Schweiz (in der Schweiz)

Spanien

DRITTE STUFE

# *T*eaching Zum Lesen,
*pp. 286-287*

## Reading Strategy

The targeted strategy in this reading is reading for understanding of ideas, not isolated words. Students will also be asked to skim for the gist, scan for specific information, answer questions to show comprehension, and transfer what they have learned.

## *PREREADING*

### Motivating Activity

Ask students if they have ever heard their grandparents or parents refer to the "good ol' days" when everything was cheaper and they could, for example, buy a soda for a nickel. What types of comparisons can students recall? Ask them to name a few.

### Teaching Suggestion

Ask students how they choose to read a particular article or story when they pick up a magazine or newspaper. What makes them decide to read a certain text? Do they skim a newspaper for interesting headlines or look for eye-catching features in the table of contents of a magazine? People generally do not begin reading without having some idea of what they are about to read. Point out to students that whether they read for pleasure or information, they always have some expectation or ideas about the materials they are about to read.

### Building on Previous Skills

**1** Write the different gift items students come up with on the board. Then ask students to categorize them according to where these items could be purchased. Examples: **Schreibwarenladen, Musikgeschäft, Kaufhaus, Supermarkt**

### Teacher Note

Activities 1-4 are prereading tasks.

## *READING*

### Thinking Critically

**Drawing Inferences**   Ask students where they might find a reading selection similar to this one in American magazines. Can they think of magazines where such texts could appear? (Examples: *Seventeen, US*)

### Teaching Suggestions

- Ask students to name any words or phrases that stand out. Which ones are they familiar with and which ones are they curious about? Make two separate lists on the chalkboard and ask students to write down words or phrases in either category.

- Before reading Stefan's article, you may want to introduce this additional vocabulary: **zufrieden** *satisfied, content;* **nützlich** *useful;* **Filzschreiber** *felt-tipped pen;* **der Betrag** *the amount;* **auswandern** *emigrate.*

### Background Information

You might want to remind students that the price shown on an item for sale reflects the total purchase price. **Mehrwertsteuer** (*value added tax*) is always included in the labeled price.

###  For Individual Needs

**A Slower Pace**   Stefan's article is divided into three parts. Ask students to give the main idea for each of those parts.

### Teaching Suggestion

Before reading Ben's article, you may want to introduce the following additional vocabulary: **vergleichen** *to compare;* **die Auswahl** *selection;* **der Unterschied** *difference;* **die Werbung** *advertisement;* **sparen** *to save;* **das Tauchen** *scuba diving.*

###  For Individual Needs

**Visual Learners**   Divide the board in half and put the name Stefan on one side, and Ben on the other. Ask students to list the items each boy purchased and how much each item cost. Then ask students where they would buy these same items in the United States. Example: **Wo kaufst du ... ? Wo kann man ... billig kaufen?**

**ZUM LESEN**

## Thinking Critically

**Drawing Inferences** Ask students to compare Stefan's and Ben's thoughts about what they would do if they had a lot of money. (Stefan: **Tierschutz- und Umweltorganisationen**; Ben: **Schutz der Weltmeere**) Can students make a general statement about German teenagers and their interests and concerns for the environment? (Remind students of the teenagers in Chapter 7 who sorted garbage to have it recycled.)

## 🌐 Culture Note

For highly industrialized countries, protecting the environment is extremely important. Many German children are introduced to environmental awareness activities as early as the seventh or the eighth grade. For example, they are taught in their **Erdkunde** classes how they can help recycle paper products, bottles, or aluminium cans.

## POST-READING

## Thinking Critically

**Comparing and Contrasting** Ask students to work with a partner and make a list of possible gift ideas they feel are representative or typical of their town, area, or state.

## Closure

Ask students what gifts they think are typical of the German-speaking countries. If they were traveling to one of the German-speaking countries, what kinds of small gifts would they plan to bring back for friends and family members in the United States?

*Answers to Activity 7*

a. **Schreibwarengeschäft**; sketchpad, colored pencils, pencil sharpener, eraser, birthday card; 10.04 marks

b. 50 marks; candy, CDs, small gifts; school supplies

c. emigrate to Australia or the United States

*Answers to Activity 8*

a. supermarket; things for everyday use

b. school supplies and clothes; CDs, small gifts

c. scuba gear; protection of the oceans and the environment

# Using Anwendung,
*pp. 288-289*

## ◆ For Individual Needs

**1 A Slower Pace** Tell students that they will hear the tape twice. As they listen the first time, they should try to listen only for the answer to **wer.** As they listen the second time, students should listen for the answers to **wem** and **was.**

**3 Challenge** Once students have put the drawings in order, ask them to give specific details about what the teenagers need to do. What do they need to write on the invitations? What kind of presents should they buy, and where? What do they plan to serve at the party? What specific chores need to be done to have the house look nice?

**5 Tactile Learners** As students design and create their invitations, they may want to think of a theme for the party, and make this a part of the invitation. Provide students with materials such as colored construction paper, scissors, glue, rulers, and old magazines. Since this could be a time-consuming activity, you might want students to finish their invitations at home and bring them to class the following day.

**6 Challenge** Ask students to write about little presents and gifts that they gave their teachers in elementary school. What did they give and what was the occasion? Students should use the conversational past.

## Teaching Suggestion

**7** Set a specific time limit for students to prepare the role-playing. Once all groups have their assignments, they should make an outline detailing the content and sequence of their commercial. They should also make note of the props they plan to use. Students may want to share their outline with you for suggestions and answers to questions they might have. On the day of the performances, plan to video- or audiotape the performances if possible.

# Kann ich's wirklich?
*p. 290*

This page is intended to prepare students for the test. It is a brief checklist of the major points covered in the chapter. The students should be reminded that it is a checklist only and not necessarily everything that will appear on the test.

# Using Wortschatz,
*p. 291*

## Teaching Suggestions

• Give vocabulary definitions in German and have students try to guess the word or expression.

• Divide students into small groups and assign each group a **Stufe.** Have them write short skits using the words in that **Stufe** and present their skits to the class.

## ♜ Game

Play the game *Password.* See p. 267F for the procedure.

## Teacher Note

Give the **Kapitel 11** Chapter Test, *Chapter Resources,* Book 4.

**1** Was schenkst du deiner Kusine zu Weihnachten?

**B**irthdays and holidays are important events in German-speaking countries. Teenagers in those countries often plan birthday parties for themselves or their friends. They spend time making invitations, calling their friends, and buying or making presents and cards. How are birthdays and holidays celebrated where you live? What do you give and receive as presents? What are some things you say when you plan and celebrate these special events?

## In this chapter you will learn

- to use the telephone in Germany
- to invite someone to a party and to accept or decline; to talk about birthdays and express good wishes
- to discuss gift ideas

## And you will

- listen to authentic German phone conversations
- read a birthday invitation
- write a telephone message
- find out what teenagers in German-speaking countries give as gifts; learn to make a call from a German phone booth

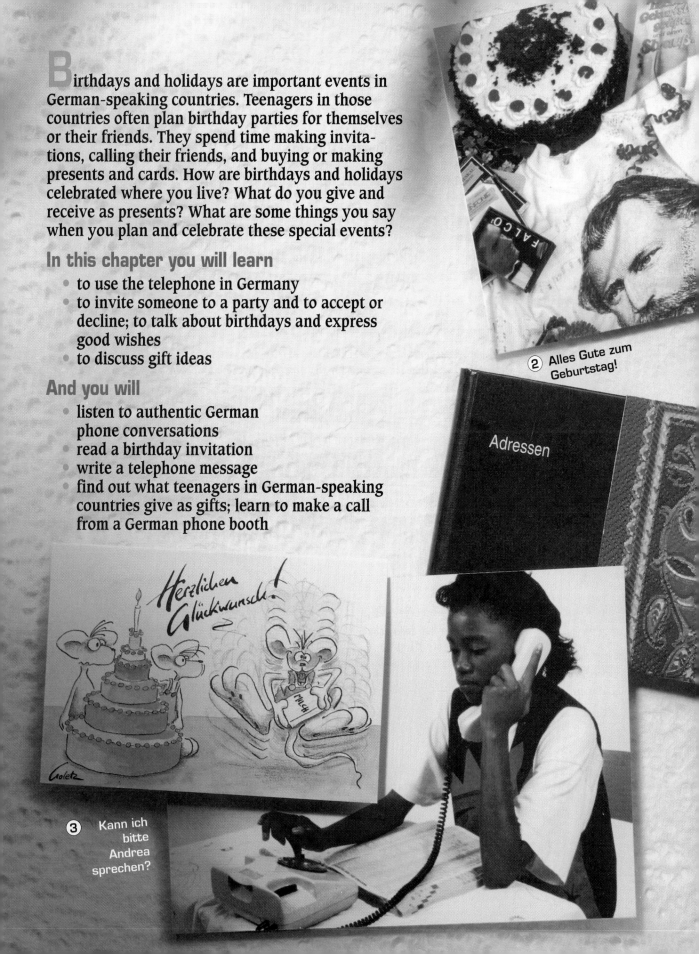

② Alles Gute zum Geburtstag!

Herzlichen Glückwunsch!

③ Kann ich bitte Andrea sprechen?

# Los geht's!

Sabine

Nicole

## Geschenke aussuchen

Look at the photos that accompany the story.
What are the girls doing in each picture? Where are they?
What do you think they are talking about?

**1**

Kroll.

Guten Tag, Frau Kroll! Hier ist die Nicole. Ist die Sabine da?

Nein, Sabine ist mit ihrem Vater weg. Kann ich ihr etwas sagen?

Ja, hm ... sagen Sie ihr bitte, daß der Martin am Samstag Geburtstag hat! Und ich möchte für ihn eine Fete organisieren.

Na, prima! Ich sag es Sabine. Tschüs!

Wiederhören, Frau Kroll!

**2**

Was schenkst du dem Martin?

Kein Problem! Ich kaufe ihm eine Kassette.

Aber er hat doch schon so viele Kassetten.

Na und?

Warum kaufst du ihm keine CD?

Er hat doch keinen CD-Player.

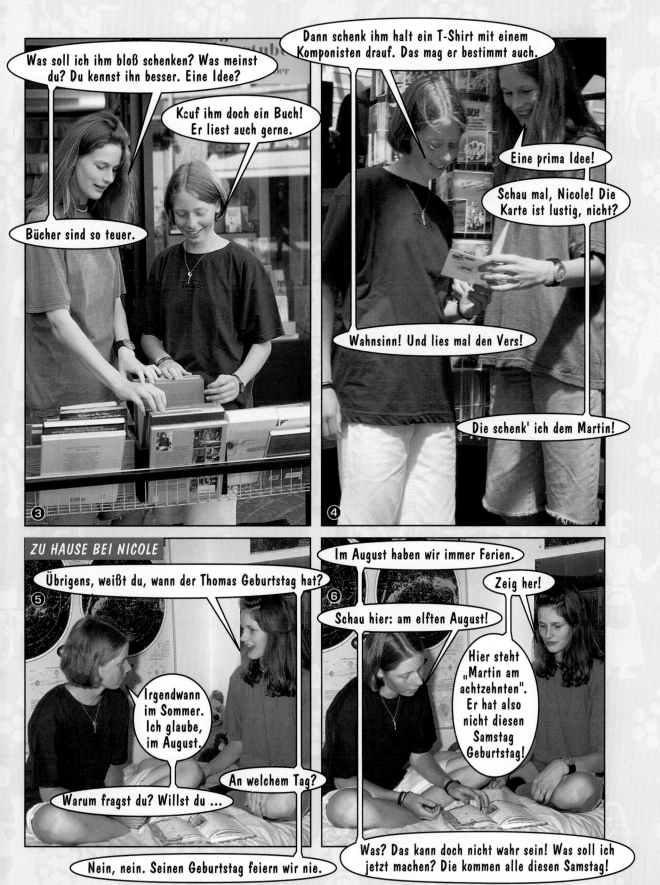

## 1 Was passiert hier?

Do you understand what is happening in the **Foto-Roman**? Check your comprehension by answering these questions. Don't be afraid to guess.

1. Why does Nicole call Sabine? *She wants to organize a birthday party for Martin.*
2. What do they discuss when they get together later? *what gifts to give him*
3. What suggestions does Nicole make to Sabine? Which one does Sabine like the best? *book, T-Shirt Sabine thinks Thomas will like the T-Shirt best.*
4. What does Sabine discover when she looks up Thomas's birthday? What is Nicole's predicament? *that Martin's birthday is also in the summer—and not Saturday. She has already invited people.*

## 2 Genauer lesen

Reread the conversations. Which words or phrases do the characters use to
*Hier ... (name); Tag; Wiederhören*

1. begin and end a phone conversation
2. name gift ideas *Kassetten, CD; Buch; T-Shirt*
3. ask for advice and opinions
   *Was meinst du? Eine Idee?*
4. say when someone's birthday is *... hat am 18. Geburts... .. hat am Samstag ...*
5. express disbelief *Was!* *... hat im Sommer ...*
   *Das kann doch nicht wahr sein!*

## 3 Was ist richtig?

Complete each statement with the best possible answer based on the **Foto-Roman**.

1. Nicole ruft Sabine an. Sie will ihr sagen, ▬▬▬. b
   a. daß sie eine Kassette gekauft hat
   b. daß sie für Martin eine Party geben will
   c. daß sie mit Martin ausgeht
2. Nicole kauft dem Martin keine CD, ▬▬▬. b
   a. weil er so viele Kassetten hat
   b. weil er keinen CD-Player hat
   c. weil er gern liest
3. Sabine schenkt Martin auch ▬▬▬ zum Geburtstag. c
   a. eine CD   b. ein Buch   c. eine Karte

4. Nicole und Sabine feiern nie den Geburtstag von Thomas, ▬▬▬. b
   a. weil sie Martin eine Karte schenken möchten
   b. weil alle im August Ferien haben
   c. weil Martin am 18. Geburtstag hat
5. Am Ende weiß Nicole nicht, was sie tun soll, ▬▬▬. a
   a. denn Martin hat am 18. Geburtstag, nicht diesen Samstag
   b. denn Thomas gibt Martin ein Buch
   c. denn sie hat Ferien

## 4 Nacherzählen

Put the sentences in logical order to make a brief summary of the **Foto-Roman**.

1. Nicole ruft Sabine an. Sie möchte über Martins Geburtstag sprechen.

5 Aber Sabine weiß nicht genau, was sie Martin kaufen soll.

7 Sabine findet, daß das T-Shirt die beste Idee ist.

Aber die Sabine ist 2 nicht zu Hause.

4 Nicole will Martin eine Kassette kaufen.

9 Am Ende sieht Sabine in ihrem Adreßbuch, daß Martin am 18. Geburtstag hat.

6 Dann hat Nicole eine Idee: vielleicht ein Buch oder ein T-Shirt.

Später sprechen die zwei Mädchen über 3 Martins Geschenk.

Danach findet Sabine eine tolle Geburtstagskarte für Martin. 8

## 5 Und du?

Was möchtest du zum Geburtstag? Mach eine Liste! Dann frag deinen Partner, was er zum Geburtstag haben möchte!

## Using the telephone in Germany

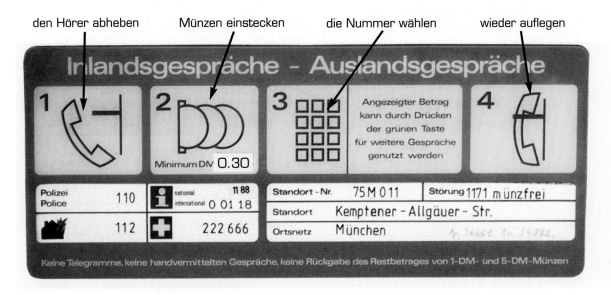

den Hörer abheben    Münzen einstecken    die Nummer wählen    wieder auflegen

**Inlandsgespräche – Auslandsgespräche**

**1**

**2**
Minimum DM **0.30**

**3**
Angezeigter Betrag kann durch Drücken der grünen Taste für weitere Gespräche genutzt werden

**4**

| | | | |
|---|---|---|---|
| Polizei Police | 110 | national **11 88** / international **0 01 18** | |
| 🔥 | 112 | ✚ | 222 666 |

| | | | |
|---|---|---|---|
| Standort - Nr. | 75 M 0 11 | Störung 1171 münzfrei | |
| Standort | Kemptener - Allgäuer - Str. | | |
| Ortsnetz | München | *Ap. 36661  An. 54872* | |

Keine Telegramme, keine handvermittelten Gespräche, keine Rückgabe des Restbetrages von 1-DM- und 5-DM-Münzen

## 6 In der Telefonzelle

Answer the following questions based on the information given above.

1. What kind of information is this? Where would you expect to find it? *1. directions on using a phone; in a phone booth*
2. What is the minimum amount of money you need to make a local call? *2. 0.30 DM*
3. What number could you call to find out someone else's number in Germany? *3. 1188*
4. Where on the directions can you find information about what services the public phone does not provide? *4. at the bottom*
5. Which emergency numbers are provided? *5. 110-police; 112-fire; 222-666-hospital*
6. How would you tell a German exchange student (in German) how to use a phone booth in the United States? Use the four steps pictured above. *Answers may vary.*

## WORTSCHATZ

### Telefonieren ist nicht schwer!

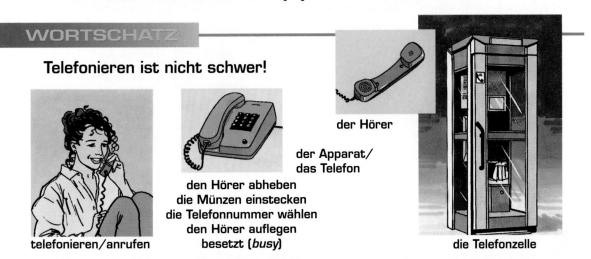

der Hörer

der Apparat/
das Telefon

den Hörer abheben
die Münzen einstecken
die Telefonnummer wählen
den Hörer auflegen
besetzt (*busy*)

telefonieren/anrufen

die Telefonzelle

## SO SAGT MAN DAS!

### Using the telephone in Germany

Here are some phrases you will need to know in order to talk on the phone in German:

| | |
|---|---|
| The person who answers says his or her name: | **Kroll.** *or* **Hier Kroll.** |
| The person calling says who he or she is: | **Hier ist die Nicole.** |
| The person calling asks to speak to someone: | **Ich möchte bitte Sabine sprechen.** *or* **Kann ich bitte Sabine sprechen?** |
| The person who answered says: | **Einen Moment, bitte.** |
| After the person comes to the phone, he or she might say: | **Tag! Hier ist die Sabine.** |
| The conversation may end with: | **Wiederhören!** *or* **Auf Wiederhören!** *or* **Tschüs!** |

How are these phrases different from the ones you use when talking on the phone?

## 7 Hör gut zu!   1. c  2. b  3. d  4. a

Listen to four telephone conversations and match each one with an appropriate illustration.

a.

c.

b.

d.

## 8 Tag! Hier ist ...

Get together with a classmate and practice "calling" a friend on the telephone. Your partner will be the parent of the friend you are calling. Use the expressions you have learned so far. Then practice saying good-bye. When you are finished, switch roles.

## 9 Willst du einen Film sehen?

"Call" your partner on the phone and ask if he or she wants to go to a movie tonight. Discuss what you want to see and what kinds of movies you like. Use the cues in the boxes below for help.

**person answering**

> Was für Filme magst du?
>
> Ja, prima!          Tschüs!
>
> Hier ist ...    Tag ...!

**person calling**

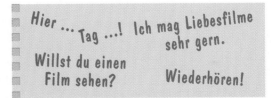

> Hier ... Tag ...! Ich mag Liebesfilme sehr gern.
>
> Willst du einen Film sehen?
>
> Wiederhören!

## 10 Ich möchte bitte ... sprechen

Answers may vary. For examples, see TE Interleaf for Chapter 11.

You worked in the office at the youth center today, and a lot of people called in and left messages for their friends. Work with a partner to create the telephone conversations you would have as you attempt to pass along the messages to the appropriate people. Take turns playing the role of the office worker.

1. Call Stefan (who is not at home; you reach his mother) and let him know that Petra wants to play tennis tomorrow at 4 P.M.
2. Call Ulrike and remind her that the biology class on Tuesday is at 9 A.M instead of (**anstatt**) at 10 A.M.
3. Call Holger and tell him that soccer practice is at 3 P.M. on Tuesday.
4. Monika is not home yet, but you need to let her know that Ulla called and wants to go shopping with her on Saturday morning at 9 A.M.

### EIN WENIG LANDESKUNDE

It's easy to make a phone call in Germany from a private phone or from a phone booth. Local numbers usually have four to seven digits depending on the size of the town or city. Long distance calls (**Ferngespräche**) require an area code (**Vorwahlnummer**), such as 089 or 030. When you want to call Germany from the United States you must first dial 01149, then the **Vorwahlnummer** without the zero, and then the number. If you want to call the United States from one of the German-speaking countries, you must first dial 001 and then the area code and number. How would you tell a German exchange student to reach you by phone after he or she returns to Germany?

## Gesprächs-Notiz

| Gesprächs-Notiz | | uhrzeit | | | | |
|---|---|---|---|---|---|---|
| | | 7 \| 8 \| 9 \|10 \| 11 \|12 | | | | |
| | | tag | | | | |
| mit _____ | | | 19 | | | |
| | | 13 \|14\| 15\| 16\| 17 \|18 | | | | |
| ○ Straße _____ | | | | | | |
| Ort _____ | | | | | | |
| Vorwahl _____ | Ruf _____ | | | | | |
| Betreff: _____ | | | | | | |

Unterschrift: _____

○

## 11 Gesprächs-Notiz

Answer the following questions.

1. What do you think the page on the left is used for? Which words are the clues for your answer? To record phone messages; **Gespräch / Notiz**
2. Where would you record the date and time? **Tag / Uhrzeit**
3. Where would you record the information about the person who called? What specific information is asked for in this section?
4. Where would you write the message? **Betreff:**
5. Where would you sign the page if you took the call? **Unterschrift**

3. Beside **mit**, name of person who called. Other information: address (**Straße, Ort**), area code (**Vorwahl**), and telephone number (**Ruf**).

12. Uhrzeit: **9**; Tag: **3.5.94** mit: **Ludwig Ottmann**;
Straße: **Neubaustr. 9**; Ort: **97413 Marktbreit**
Vorwahl: **09331**, Ruf: **1367** Betreff:

Geburtstagsparty für
Onkel Michael-2. Juni, um 17 Uhr in
Nürnberg, Hotel Löwe,Rosenthal 8

## 12 Hör gut zu!

At your host family's home in Germany, someone calls while one of the family members is out. Make a German phone message page like the one pictured above. Then take down all the information asked for on the **Gesprächs-Notiz**. For the actual message, just write down a few notes. What phrase did the person answering the phone use at the beginning of the conversation? What is its English equivalent? phrase: **Hier bei ...**
means: **... residence**

## 13 Zum Schreiben

Using your notes from Activity 12, rewrite the message in neat sentences so that it can be easily understood by the person receiving it. Then switch papers with a partner and check whether your partner wrote his or her message correctly.

## 14 Ruf mal an!

Decide on a free time activity that you would like to do with your partner. Call your partner and invite him or her to come along. Then switch roles. Here are a few possibilities:

**Ich habe am Samstag eine Party. Kannst du kommen?**
**Ich möchte heute in die Stadt fahren. Kommst du mit?**

*Inviting someone to a party and accepting or declining; talking about birthdays and expressing good wishes*

## 15 Eine Einladung

Schau die Einladung an und beantworte die folgenden Fragen!

1. Wer schickt die Einladung? Nicole
2. Für wen ist die Fete? Warum?
3. Wann ist die Fete? An welchem Tag? Um wieviel Uhr?
4. Wo ist die Fete? Martin-Luther-Str. 8
5. Welche Nummer kannst du anrufen, um Information zu bekommen? 07142-6376
6. Was mußt du tun, um zu sagen, ob (*whether*) du kommen kannst?
   Ruf Nicole an.

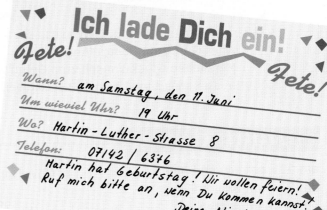

**Fete!** **Ich lade Dich ein!** **Fete!**

Wann? am Samstag, den 11. Juni
Um wieviel Uhr? 19 Uhr
Wo? Martin-Luther-Strasse 8
Telefon: 07142 / 6376

Martin hat Geburtstag! Wir wollen feiern!
Ruf mich bitte an, wenn Du kommen kannst.
Deine Nicole

2. Martin / Geburtstag
3. Am Samstag, den 11. Juni, um 19 Uhr

## SO SAGT MAN DAS!

### Inviting someone to a party and accepting or declining

You invite a friend:

> **Ich habe am Samstag eine Party.**
> **Ich lade dich ein.**
> **Kannst du kommen?**

Your friend might respond:

> **Ja, gern!** *or*
> **Aber sicher!** *or*
> **Natürlich!** *or*
> **Leider kann ich nicht.**

Which response would you use if you already had a previous engagement?[1]

## 16 Zum Schreiben

Schreib eine Einladung! Was für eine Fete ist das? An welchem Tag ist die Fete? Um wieviel Uhr beginnt sie? Wo ist sie? Wenn man nicht kommen kann, soll man anrufen?

## 17 Ich möchte dich einladen!

You are having a party and want to invite several of your friends. "Call" two other classmates and invite each of them to the party. They will ask you for information about the party and then tell you whether they can come. If not, they should give you a reason. You should respond appropriately. End your conversation, then switch roles so that each person takes a turn extending the invitations.

1. **Leider kann ich nicht.**

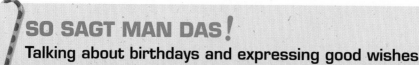

## SO SAGT MAN DAS!

### Talking about birthdays and expressing good wishes

If you want to find out when a friend has his or her birthday,

you ask:

**Wann hast du Geburtstag?**

Your friend might respond:

**Ich habe am 28. Oktober\* Geburtstag.** *or*
**Am 28. Oktober.**

There are a number of things you can say to express good wishes:

**Alles Gute zum Geburtstag!**
**Herzlichen Glückwunsch zum Geburtstag!**

\*Read as: **am achtundzwanzigsten Oktober.**

---

## WORTSCHATZ

am 1. = am ersten (Juli)
am 2. = am zweiten
am 3. = am dritten
am 4. = am vierten
am 5. = am fünften
am 6. = am sechsten
am 7. = am siebten
am 8. = am achten
am 9. = am neunten
am 10. = am zehnten
am 11. = am elften
     usw.
am 20. = am zwanzigsten
am 21. = am einundzwanzigsten
     usw.

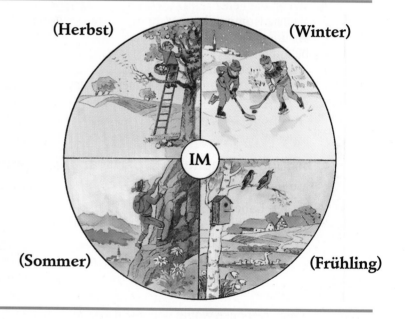

(Herbst)   (Winter)   IM   (Sommer)   (Frühling)

---

## 18 Geburtstagskette

One person in the class begins the chain by asking another: **Wann hast du Geburtstag?**
That person answers and asks someone else. Continue until everyone has been asked.

## 19 Hör gut zu!

Das Schuljahr ist bald zu Ende. Anja will wissen, wer im Sommer Geburtstag hat. Sie fragt
ihre Klassenkameraden und schreibt dann die Geburtstage in ihr Adreßbuch. Schreib,
wann Anjas Freunde Geburtstag haben!

1. Bernd    2. Maja    3. Benjamin    4. Katrin    5. Mario
22. Mai     4. Februar    28. März     14. August    29. Dezember

## 20 Für mein Notizbuch

Schreib, wann du Geburtstag hast! Welches Geschenk hast du am liebsten? Schreib auch,
wann deine Eltern, deine Geschwister und deine Freunde Geburtstag haben!

## EIN WENIG LANDESKUNDE

Birthdays are important occasions in German-speaking countries and are usually celebrated with family and friends. In some areas of Germany (primarily in the strongly Catholic areas) and in Austria, the **Namenstag**, or Saint's Day, is also celebrated. Children in these areas are named after certain saints, such as **Johannes, Josef**, and **Maria**. There is a saint's day for each day of the year. Anyone named for a saint also celebrates on the day that honors that saint. The **Namenstag** celebration is similar to a birthday celebration, with a party, gifts, and flowers for the honoree.

### Namenstag im Juli

10. Erich/Erika
13. Margarete
15. Heinrich
24. Christine
25. Jakob
26. Anne Marie
29. Martha

**Gratulieren Sie mit Blumen!**

## WORTSCHATZ

### Feiertage

**Weihnachten:**
Fröhliche Weihnachten!

**Chanukka:**
Frohes Chanukka-Fest!

**Ostern:**
Frohe Ostern!

**Vatertag:**
Alles Gute zum Vatertag!

**Muttertag:**
Alles Gute zum Muttertag!

1. Muttertag  2. Chanukka

## 21 Hör gut zu!

You will hear four conversations about four different holidays. Match each conversation to the most appropriate card.

3. Weihnachten  4. Geburtstag

## 22 Eine Geburtstagskarte

Design a German birthday card or a card for another special occasion to send to a friend or family member. Below are some common German good luck symbols.

**Schornsteinfeger**

**Glücksschwein**

**Glücksklee**

**Hufeisen**

**Marienkäfer**

## Was schenkst du zum Geburtstag?

We asked several teenagers what they usually give as birthday presents. Before you read the interviews, write what you give your friends and relatives for their birthdays.

### Melanie, *Hamburg*

„Ich geh' mit Freunden essen, oder lade sie zu mir ein. Und dann sitzen wir zusammen und unterhalten uns nett oder Ähnliches, … ansonsten gar nichts weiter. Bei Familienmitgliedern ist es ähnlich, da feiern wir auch in der Familie. Und schenken tu' ich dann meiner Schwester zum Beispiel, die hört ziemlich gerne Musik, und der schenk' ich dann Kassetten oder CDs oder Ähnliches. Und ansonsten eben schenk' ich Bücher oder eben andere Kleinigkeiten, für die sich die Freunde oder Familienmitglieder interessieren."

### Eva, *Berlin*

„Eigentlich hass' ich Geburtstage, weil ich nie weiß, was ich schenken soll. Es ist irgendwie immer dasselbe, Bücher oder Kassetten oder CDs. Und naja, dann sucht man sich immer was aus. Meistens verschenkt man Gutscheine, weil … da kann man nichts falsch machen."

### Rosi, *Berlin*

„Also wenn ich auf Geburtstage gehe von Freunden oder Freundinnen, die ich gut kenne, dann geb' ich auch mal mehr Geld aus. Dann kriegen sie schon persönliche Geschenke, wo sie sich auch darüber freuen. Und wenn ich auf Geburtstage gehe von Leuten, die ich nicht so gut kenne, dann nehme ich nur Kleinigkeiten mit. Aber ich nehm' eigentlich immer was mit, wenn ich auf Geburtstage gehe."

### Jutta, *Hamburg*

„Ich hab' einen kleinen Bruder, und er ist elf, und der spielt unheimlich gern mit Lego,™ und dem schenk' ich dann was zum Spielen oder eine Musikkassette. Und wenn ich bei Freunden eingeladen bin, meistens was Selbstgemachtes, ein bemaltes T-Shirt, ja auch eine Musikkassette, ein Buch oder ein gemaltes Bild."

cassettes (sister, brother); CDs, books

**A. 1.** Make a list of the gifts these teenagers give as birthday presents and to whom they give them. What do you think **Gutscheine** might be? *Hint: they are available for many different things, such as cassettes, CDs, and books.* Gutschein (gift certificate)

**2.** Rosi has two categories of people she buys gifts for. What are they? What are some of the differences in the types of gifts she buys for each one? good friends/acquaintances; less money on acquaintances

**3.** Why does Eva not care much for birthdays? Do you agree or disagree with her? hard to find right present

**4.** Of the four people interviewed, who do you think puts the most thought and time into giving just the right gift? What statements support your answer? Answer will vary.

**B.** Use the list you made earlier to write an answer to the questions **Was schenkst du zum Geburtstag, und wem schenkst du das?** Share your answers with your classmates and decide which of the interviews above most closely resembles your own. Are there any differences in the things teenagers give as gifts in the German-speaking countries and in the United States? If so, what are they and why do you think this is so? If not, why not?

Geschenkladen=gift shop

2. no-too expensive   3. a candle; possibly candy   4. Answers will vary.

## 23  Im Geschenkladen

Here is an excerpt from an article in the teen magazine *Juma.* Look at the photo and read the caption. Then answer the questions that follow.

1. Using the photo as a cue, what do you think a **Geschenkladen** is? What do you think the topic of this article is?   giving/finding present
2. Reread the caption. Do you think Martina is finding a lot of things she could buy? Why or why not?
3. What gift does Martina decide to buy for her friend? Do you think she buys anything else? If so, what?
4. Was für Geschenke schenkst du Verwandten (*relatives*) und Freunden? Wo kaufst du gewöhnlich Geschenke? Zehn Mark sind ungefähr sechs Dollar. Was kannst du für sechs Dollar kaufen?

Martina, 14, will ihrer Freundin etwas zum Namenstag schenken. Im Geschenkladen sucht sie lange nach einer Kleinigkeit. Die meisten Sachen kosten mehr als 10 Mark. Martina entscheidet sich für eine Kerze. Dann geht sie in ein Süßwarengeschäft.

## WORTSCHATZ

**Geschenkideen**   Bärbel: Was schenkst du Jutta zum Geburtstag?
Berndt: Ich weiß noch nicht. Vielleicht ...

eine
Armbanduhr

Pralinen

einen Blumen-
strauß

einen
Kalender

ein Poster

eine CD

Parfüm

Schmuck

Was schenkst du zu verschiedenen Feiertagen, z. B. zu Muttertag?

# SO SAGT MAN DAS!

## Discussing gift ideas

When talking about birthdays and holidays with friends, you'll also want to be able to discuss gift ideas.

You might ask your friend:

**Schenkst du deinem Vater einen Kalender zum Geburtstag?**

**Und was schenkst du deiner Mutter zum Muttertag?**

**Kauf ihr doch ein Buch!**

**Wem schenkst du den Blumenstrauß?**

Your friend might respond:

**Nein, ich schenke ihm wahrscheinlich eine CD, weil er doch Musik so gern hört.**

**Ich weiß noch nicht. Hast du eine Idee?**

**Prima Idee! Das mach' ich!**

**Der Nicole schenke ich den Strauß.**

Can you find the subject and the verb in each of these sentences? What is the item being given (the direct object) in the first question?[1] Who is the person receiving the gift (the indirect object)?[2] In the first response, you see the word **ihm**. To whom does it refer?[3] To whom does the word **ihr** refer in the sentence **Kauf ihr doch ein Buch!**?[4]

1. Interkulturelle Beratung und Information; Information über Gastgeschenke im Ausland

## 24 Was soll man schenken?

Mechtild Kaldenkirchen and Gothild Thomas of Essen offer a unique information service. Read the article on the right, then answer these questions.

1. Wie heißt der Informationsservice von Mechtild und Gothild? Was für Information können sie uns geben? Gib ein oder zwei Beispiele!
2. Was muß man machen, um die Information zu bekommen? anrufen
3. Wie sagt man den letzten Satz auf Englisch?
Other countries, other customs (When in Rome ...)

## 25 Hör gut zu!

You call **Interkulturelle Beratung und Information** to find out the proper gifts for families you'll visit on your trip to France, Italy, Spain and Austria. On a separate piece of paper, write the gift(s) they advise you to give in each country: **Frankreich, Italien, Spanien,** and **Österreich.**

Frankreich: Getränke; Italien: Blumen; Spanien: Getränke; Österreich: Pralinen

1. **einen Kalender** 2. **deinem Vater** 3. **ihm = Vater** 4. **ihr = Mutter**

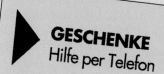

**GESCHENKE**
Hilfe per Telefon

Was bringt man als Gast einer Familie in Frankreich mit — Blumen, Pralinen oder Getränke? Wer viel reist, hat solche Probleme öfter. Helfen kann ein Bürgertelefon in Essen. Mechtild Kaldenkirchen und Gothild Thomas leiten die „Interkulturelle Beratung und Information": Sie informieren Anrufer aber nicht nur über Gastgeschenke im Ausland. Man kann nämlich auch erfahren, wie man sich im Ausland richtig benimmt. Denn eines ist ja allgemein bekannt: andere Länder, andere Sitten.

# *Grammatik*   Introduction to the dative case

You have learned that the subject of a sentence is in the nominative case and that the direct object is in the accusative case. A third case, the dative case, is used for indirect objects, which express the idea of "to someone" or "for someone." Look at the following sentences:

Robert, was schenkst du
   **deinem Opa**?
Und was schenkst du
   **deiner Oma**?

Ich schenke **ihm** einen
   Taschenrechner.
Ich schenke **ihr** ein Buch.

How would you say each of the above sentences in English?[1] Look at the photos for cues. You have already seen several examples of the dative case with definite articles after prepositions: **mit dem Bus, mit der U-Bahn.** Definite articles may also be used with proper names in the dative case:

Was kaufst du **dem Martin**?
Gibst du **der Sandra** das Geld?

Ich kaufe **ihm** ein T-Shirt.
Ja, ich gebe **ihr** morgen das Geld.

To ask the question "To whom ...?" or "For whom ...?" you use the dative form "**Wem ...?**"

**Wem** schenkst du die Blumen?     *To whom are you giving the flowers?*

**Dative Case**

masculine ⎫
neuter    ⎬ **dem, ihm, deinem, meinem**
feminine  ⎭ **der, ihr, deiner, meiner**

What pattern do you notice in the formation of the dative case? Make a chart of the definite articles, pronouns for *he* and *she*, and the posessive **mein** for all the cases you have learned so far. What patterns do you notice?

Opa-eine CD; Oma-ein Buch; Vater-einen Kalender; Mutti-das Parfüm; Otto-ein Poster; Martina-Schmuck

# 26  Hör gut zu!

You're visiting Germany during the holiday season and would like to send something to your friends and family members. You ask your German friend for gift ideas. Your friend makes suggestions for specific family members and friends. Write down which gift he suggests for each person.

1. *Robert, what are you giving your grandfather? I'm giving him a calculator. And what are you giving your grandmother? I'm giving her a book.*

## 27 Sätze bauen

Put the following sentence elements in the correct order to say what you and others are planning to give as presents at an upcoming party.

1. kaufe
eine Bluse
Ich
meiner Oma

2. eine CD
Peter
schenken
Wir

3. meinem Onkel
Ich
Pralinen
schenke

4. Und ich
ihm
schenke
auch ein Buch

5. Sie
dem Opa
kauft
einen Kalender

6. schenken
ein Buch über Musik
Wir
meiner Mutter

### Grammatik

Notice the word order when you use the dative case. The indirect object (dative case) comes before the direct object (accusative case):

**Ich schenke meiner Mutter ein Buch.**
**Ich schenke ihr ein Buch.**

## 28 Was schenkst du ...?

Take turns with your classmates asking and telling who is getting which gift. Practice replacing the noun phrases with the appropriate pronoun in the response. Use the drawings below as cues.

BEISPIEL            DU  **Was schenkst du deinem Bruder?**
MITSCHÜLER  **Ich schenke ihm einen Kuli.**

dein Bruder

dein Vater          deine Kusine          deine Oma          deine Lehrerin          dein Onkel          deine Schwester

## 29 Memory-Spiel

Wem schenkst du ein Buch?

BEISPIEL            DU  **Ich schenke meiner**
**Mutter ein Buch.**

MITSCHÜLER  **Ich schenke meiner**
**Mutter und meinem**
**Freund ein Buch. usw.**

## 30 Eine Geschenkliste

Make a list of what you would like to buy for three of your friends or family members for their birthdays. Give your partner a list with just the names of the people receiving gifts. Your partner will ask you what you plan to give them. Respond according to your list. Then switch roles. Jot down your partner's answers, then compare lists to see if you understood everything.

### LERNTRICK

When you use indirect objects in your conversations, they must be in the dative case. It helps to remember that the dative forms for masculine and neuter articles and pronouns always end in -m: **dem, ihm, meinem, deinem.** The dative forms for feminine articles and pronouns always end with -r: **der, ihr, meiner, deiner.**

## 31 Deine Europareise

**a.** You're going to Europe! Decide which three countries you would like to visit. On a card write down the countries you choose, the souvenir you would buy from each, and the name of the person to whom you would like to give each souvenir.

Italien

Schuhe    ein Halstuch

Deutschland

einen Pulli   eine Kerze

Schweiz (in der Schweiz)

Pralinen     eine
            Armbanduhr

Spanien

einen      Kastagnetten
Fächer

**b.** Get together with two other classmates. Tell your partners what you will buy in each country. Your partners will take turns asking whom the souvenirs are for: **Wem schenkst du ein Buch?** Share this information with your partners. Then switch roles.

Österreich

ein Sachbuch   eine CD
über           von Mozart
Musik

## 32 Ein Brief aus Europa

Schreib einem Freund oder deiner Familie einen Brief über deine Europareise! Schreib, wo du warst, was du gekauft hast und wem du die Andenken (*souvenirs*) schenkst! Benutze deine Information von Übung 31!

## AUSSPRACHE

### Richtig aussprechen

**A.** To review the following sounds, say the sentences below after your teacher or after the recording.

1. The letters **r** and **er**: The letter **r** is pronounced by placing the tip of the tongue behind your lower front teeth and then tipping the head back and pretending to gargle. The combination **er** at the end of a syllable or word is pronounced like the *a* in the English word *sofa*.
   **Ich schenke meinem Bruder Rolf und seiner Frau ein Radio.**
   **Und ich schenke meiner Mutter Bücher und einen Kalender.**

2. The letter **a**: The letter **a** is pronounced much like the *a* sound in the word *father*.
   **Kaufst du dem Vater Schokolade zum Vatertag?**

3. The diphthongs **eu**, **äu**, and **au**: The vowel combinations **eu** and **äu** sound similiar to the *oy* sound in the English word *toy*. The diphthong **au** is pronounced like the *ow* sound in the English word *how*.
   **Heute war der Verkäufer am Telefon ganz unfreundlich.**
   **Ich kaufe der Claudia einen Blumenstrauß.**

## Richtig schreiben / Diktat

**B.** Write down the sentences that you hear.

## Was gibt's heute noch für 10 Mark?

*Im Supermarkt läuft Ben durch die Regalreihen und vergleicht Preise. Viele Dinge nimmt er Zuerst aus dem Regal und stellt sie wieder zurück, nachdem er den Preis gelesen hat. Er kauft Orangensaft und Cola.*

ch möchte etwas Sinnvolles kaufen. Etwas, das ich auch brauchen kann." Stefan lebt in der kleinen Stadt Schwalmtal nahe der niederländischen Grenze. Dort gibt es nicht viele Läden. Darum entscheidet er sich für ein kleines Schreibwarengeschäft am Marktplatz. Dort kauft er einen Zeichenblock, zwei Buntstifte, einen Anspitzer, ein Radiergummi und eine Geburtstagskarte. Die Geburtstagskarte ist das teuerste Teil seines Einkaufs: 3,50 Mark. Insgesamt hat er 10,04 Mark ausgegeben. Vier Pfennig zuviel! „Es ist fast unmöglich, für genau 10 Mark einzukaufen."

Stefan ist mit seinem Einkauf zufrieden. „Nur die Geburtstagskarte fand ich ganz schön teuer. Aber insgesamt konnte ich doch einige nützliche Dinge kaufen. Einen dicken Filzschreiber für 2,80 Mark fand ich übertrieben teuer. Den habe ich nicht gekauft."

Stefan bekommt 50 Mark Taschengeld im Monat. Den Betrag findet er „in Ordnung", obwohl das Geld selten reicht. In den Ferien verdient Stefan etwas dazu. „Dann räume ich in einem Lebensmittelgeschäft Ware in Regale ein." Von seinem Taschengeld kauft Stefan Süßigkeiten, Musik-CDs, kleine Geschenke wie Notizbücher oder Stifte und Pflanzen. Schulsachen muß er nicht kaufen. „Die bezahlen meine Eltern." Sein größter Wunsch: „Wenn ich viel Geld hätte, würde ich nach Australien oder Amerika auswandern. Und wenn ich Geld zu verschenken hätte, würden es Tierschutz- und Umweltorganisationen bekommen."

gifts you can buy for 10 marks or under

1. You are invited to a party and need to bring a gift. What can you buy for $5.00?

2. A foreign exchange student is also invited to the party. Where would you suggest that person should go to buy a gift for $5.00? What would you suggest might be a good gift for the foreign exchange student to buy?

3. Look at the title, the pictures, and the captions. Without actually reading the texts, what would you say is the type of reading selection on these pages? Are they ads, postcards, poems, or articles?  articles

4. Judging by the title, what kind of information do you expect to find in these selections?

5. Read the article about Stefan through without

Stefans Freund Ben wohnt in der Kleinstadt Brüggen. Er entscheidet sich für den Einkauf in einem Supermarkt. „Wenn man nur 10 Mark zur Verfügung hat, bekommt man in einem Supermarkt wahrscheinlich die meisten Dinge. Außerdem gibt es in Supermärkten viele nützliche Sachen, die man für das tägliche Leben braucht." Im Supermarkt geht Ben durch die Regalreihen und vergleicht Preise. Die Auswahl fällt ihm schwer. Manche Dinge stellt er wieder ins Regal zurück. Ben bekommt für 10,10 Mark eine Zahnbürste, eine Flasche Orangensaft, eine Dose Cola, einen Sport-Drink und einen Lippenpflege-Stift. Der Lippenpflege-Stift ist teuer. Er kostet 2,69 Mark. Ben glaubt, daß er gut eingekauft hat. „Ich habe mehr bekommen, als ich dachte. Einen Riesen-Unterschied gab es allerdings bei den Preisen für Getränkedosen. Das Marken-Getränk aus der Werbung kostete 1,99 Mark. Die Dose Cola war dagegen spottbillig: nur 49 Pfennig. Ben bekommt pro Woche 8 Mark Taschengeld. Ihm reicht der Betrag. „Ich kann sogar ein bißchen Geld sparen, denn Schulsachen oder Kleidung muß ich nicht bezahlen. Diese Dinge kaufen meine Eltern." Von seinem Taschengeld kauft Ben ab und zu eine Compact Disc für sich oder ein kleines Geschenk, zum Beispiel ein Taschenbuch, für seine Freunde. Was würde Ben mit viel Geld machen? „Ich würde sofort eine Taucherausrüstung kaufen. Tauchen ist mein Hobby. Und wenn ich Geld verschenken könnte, dann würde ich es zum Schutz der Weltmeere und zum Schutz der Umwelt einsetzen."

*Stefan wird im Schreibwarengeschäft von der Verkäuferin beraten. Sie zeigt ihm verschiedene Dinge und nennt ihm die Preise. Stefan braucht einige Zeit, bis er möglichst viele Sachen für zehn Mark gekauft hat.*

stopping to ask about words you don't know. Then summarize the article in two or three sentences.

6. Read the article about Ben through without stopping to ask about words you don't know. Then summarize the article in two or three sentences. In both articles, notice how much you can understand without knowing every word!

7. Read the article about Stefan again and try to answer these questions.
   a. What kind of store did Stefan shop in? What did he buy? What was his total bill?
   b. How much is Stefan's allowance per month? What does he buy with that money? What do his parents buy for him?
   c. What would Stefan do if he had a lot of money?

8. Read the article about Ben again and try to answer these questions.
   a. Where does Ben think he can find the largest selection of useful items for 10 marks? How does he define "useful"?
   b. What do Ben's parents buy for him? For what does he use his own money?
   c. If Ben had a lot of money, what would he buy? To what cause would he give?

9. You are planning a trip to a German-speaking country in the summer and are going to stay with a family. Write a short note asking them what small items you might bring them.

Answers to these questions appear on page 267Q of the TE Interleaf.

# ANWENDUNG

**1** Listen to Helene and Volker's conversation about what they are buying their friends as birthday presents. Write down who's giving what to whom as a present.

| | wer | wem | was |
|---|---|---|---|
| 1 | Helene | dem Ulf | eine CD |
| 2 | Volker | der Sonja | einen Kalender |

**2** Drei Schüler sprechen darüber, was sie am liebsten zum Geburtstag bekommen möchten und warum.

3. Helene/der Ute/ein Buch

**a.** Read the interviews and decide what each of the three teenagers would like to have and why. Write down the information.

| 4. Volker | dem Ralf | ein Videospiel |

### Ingo, 17

„Du fragst, was ich am liebsten zum Geburtstag haben möchte? — Ganz einfach! Du weißt doch, daß ich gern lese. Du kannst mir also ein Buch kaufen, vielleicht etwas über gefährdete Tiere in Afrika, oder — ich hab' da noch eine Idee. Du kannst mir zum Geburtstag ein Karl-May-Buch schenken, denn seine Bücher sind wieder ganz populär. Und ich lese Karl May furchtbar gern."

ein Buch
über gefährdete Tiere in Afrika oder
von Karl May (Er liest gern.)

### Margot, 16

„Ja, am liebsten möchte ich irgend etwas, was mit Musik zu tun hat. Eine prima Kassette, Mathias Reim vielleicht, oder eine CD. Du weißt, ich höre auch klassische Musik gern. Und unter den Klassikern gibt es eine wirklich große Auswahl, zum Beispiel etwas von … nein, ich hab's: die schönsten Arien aus den populärsten Opern. Das ist etwas für mich!"

eine Kassette-Mathias Reim-oder eine CD (Sie mag Musik.)

### Clarissa, 16

„Du kannst mir eine große Freude machen und mir eine Karte zum nächsten Rockkonzert schenken. Die „Toten Hosen" kommen nächsten Monat hierher, und die möchte ich unbedingt hören. Natürlich sind die Karten furchtbar teuer, ich weiß. Aber du kannst dich vielleicht mit zwei andern Leuten zusammentun, und ihr könnt mir gemeinsam eine Karte kaufen. Dann ist es für jeden nicht so teuer."

Karte für Rockkonzert (Sie möchte „Die Toten Hosen" hören.)

**b.** Now let your partner interview you to find out what you would like to have and why. Based on your answers, he or she will write an interview similar to the ones above. Then switch roles and interview your partner.

**3** Gabriele and Philipp are making plans for Bernhard's birthday. What do they plan to do first? First look at the pictures and decide what Gabriele and Philipp are doing in each one. Then listen to their conversation and put the following drawings in the correct order.   b, d, a, c

a.

b.

c.

d.

**4 a.** Get together with two or three classmates and plan an end-of-school party. Decide where and when it will take place.

**b.** Within your group, tell each other the things you'll need for the party. Use the words in the box for ideas. Create a list of at least six things you need, then each of you volunteer to take care of certain things on the list.

Getränke  CDs  Kassetten
Tassen  Kuchen oder Kekse
Obst- und Gemüseteller
Chips 'n Dip  Ballons

**5** Write an invitation to the party you planned in Activity 4. First, everyone will write his or her name on a piece of paper and put it in a box. Then each student will draw a name and send his or her invitation to that person. Use a lot of color on your invitation and remember to include all the necessary information.

**6** Ihr möchtet der Lehrerin/dem Lehrer etwas schenken. Macht eine Liste von Geschenkideen! Dann sprecht darüber, was ihr schenken möchtet. Fragt alle in der Gruppe, was sie schenken wollen. Wie sind ihre Ideen? Toll oder blöd?

**7**

## R O L L E N S P I E L

Get together with two or three classmates and role-play the following situation:

Each group picks one type of store you have learned about so far, (**Metzgerei, Modegeschäft, Schreibwarenladen . . .** ). Write it on a card, and put the cards in a box. One person from each group draws a card from the box. Your group has just been hired by the store you drew to write some commercials to help boost sales for the holidays. Write a commercial to convince people to buy the items at your store as gifts. Suggest people in the family to give the gifts to. (You will have to be pretty persuasive in order to convince people to buy gifts at a **Metzgerei!**) Bring in props and perform your commercial in front of the class.

# KANN ICH'S WIRKLICH?

**Can you use the telephone in Germany? (p. 274)**

**1** If you were calling someone in Germany, how would you

   **a.** say who you are   Tag, hier ist …

   **b.** ask to speak to someone   Kann ich bitte … sprechen?

   **c.** say hello to the person you wanted to speak with   Tag, …

   **d.** say goodbye   Auf Wiederhören!

**2** If you were answering the phone in Germany, how would you

   **a.** identify yourself        **b.** ask the caller to wait a minute
     Hier ist … (last name)          Einen Moment, bitte.

**3** How would you tell someone how to use a public telephone to make a call? (Use **zuerst, dann, danach,** and **zuletzt.**)   Zuerst hebst du den Hörer ab. Dann steckst du die Münzen ein. Danach wählst du die Nummer. Zuletzt legst du wieder auf.

**Can you invite someone to a party and accept or decline? (p. 277)**

**4** How would a friend invite you to his or her birthday party on Saturday evening at 8:00?   Ich habe am Samstag um 8 Uhr eine Geburtstagsparty. Ich lade dich ein!

**5** How would you respond if

   **a.** you can come   Ja, gern!

   **b.** you can't come because a relative is coming to visit   Leider kann ich nicht, (meine Kusine) kommt zu Besuch.

   **c.** you can't come because you are going to a concert   … weil ich ins Konzert gehe.

   **d.** you can't come because you have to do your homework   … denn ich muß Hausaufgaben machen.

**Can you talk about birthdays and express good wishes? (p. 278)**

**6** How would you ask a friend when he or she has a birthday?   Wann hast du Geburtstag?

**7** How would your friend respond if he or she has a birthday on

   **a.** May 29     **b.** March 9     **c.** February 16     **d.** July 7
   am 29. Mai     am 9. März     am 16. Februar     am 7. Juli

**8** How would you express good wishes for the following occasions?

   **a.** birthday        **b.** Christmas        **c.** Hanukkah
   Alles Gute zum Geburtstag!   Frohe/Fröhliche Weihnachten!   Frohes/Fröhliches Chanukka-Fest!

**Can you discuss gift ideas? (p. 282)**

**9** How would you ask a friend what he or she is getting another friend for his or her birthday? How might your friend respond?   Was schenkst du
    Ich schenke ihm/ihr … dem/der … zum Geburtstag?

**10** How would you tell a friend that you are going to give these items to various relatives for their birthdays?   Answers will vary.

  a.              b.             c.             d.
  **mein Vater**       **meine Tante**      **meine Oma**      **mein Bruder**

## ERSTE STUFE

### USING THE TELEPHONE IN GERMANY

**telefonieren**   *to call on the phone*
**anrufen (sep)**   *to call*
**der Apparat, -e**   *telephone*
**das Telefon, -e**   *telephone*
**der Hörer, -**   *receiver*
**die Telefonzelle -n**
   *telephone booth*

**die Telefonnummer, -n**   *telephone number*
**Münzen einstecken (sep)**   *to insert coins*
**abheben (sep)**   *to pick up (the phone)*
**auflegen (sep)**   *to hang up (the phone)*
**die Nummer wählen**   *to dial the number*

**besetzt**   *busy*
**Einen Moment, bitte!**   *Just a minute, please.*
**Hier (ist) ...**   *This is ...*
**Hier bei ...**   *The ... residence*
**Kann ich bitte ... spechen?**   *Can I please speak to...?*
**Auf Wiederhören!**   *Goodbye!*
**Wiederhören!**   *Bye!*

## ZWEITE STUFE

### INVITING SOMEONE TO A PARTY

**einladen (sep)**   *to invite*
   **er/sie lädt ... ein**   *he/she invites*

### ACCEPTING OR DECLINING

**Natürlich!**   *Certainly!*

### TALKING ABOUT BIRTHDAYS AND EXPRESSING GOOD WISHES

**der Geburtstag, -e**   *birthday*

**Ich habe am ... Geburtstag.**   *My birthday is on...*
**Wann hast du Geburtstag?**   *When is your birthday?*
**am ersten (1.), zweiten (2.), dritten (3.), usw.**   *on the first, second, third, etc....*
**Alles Gute zum Geburtstag!**   *Happy Birthday!*
**Herzlichen Glückwunsch zum Geburtstag!**   *Best wishes on your birthday!*

**der Feiertag, -e**   *holiday*
   **Weihnachten**   *Christmas*
   **Fröhliche Weihnachten!**   *Merry Christmas!*
   **Chanukka**   *Hanukkah*
   **Frohes Chanukka-Fest!**   *Happy Hanukkah!*
   **Ostern**   *Easter*
   **Frohe Ostern!**   *Happy Easter!*
   **der Muttertag**   *Mother's Day*
   **Alles Gute zum Muttertag!**   *Happy Mother's Day!*
   **der Vatertag**   *Father's Day*
   **Alles Gute zum Vatertag!**   *Happy Father's Day!*

## DRITTE STUFE

### DISCUSSING GIFT IDEAS

**schenken**   *to give (a gift)*
**geben**   *to give*
   **er/sie gibt**   *he/she gives*
**die Geschenkidee, -n**   *gift idea*
**das Geschenk, -e**   *gift*
   **die Praline, -n**   *fancy chocolate*
   **die Armbanduhr, -en**   *(wrist) watch*
   **der Kalender, -**   *calendar*
   **der Blumenstrauß, ¨-e**   *bouquet of flowers*

**das Poster, -**   *poster*
**die CD, -s**   *compact disc*
**das Parfüm, -e**   *perfume*
**der Schmuck**   *jewelry*
**deinem Vater**   *to/for your father*
**meinem Vater**   *to/for my father*
**deiner Mutter**   *to/for your mother*
**meiner Mutter**   *to/for my mother*

### PRONOUNS, DATIVE CASE

**ihm**   *to/for him*
**ihr**   *to/for her*

### ARTICLES, DATIVE CASE

**dem**   *the* (masc.)
**der**   *the* (fem.)

### OTHER USEFUL WORDS

**wahrscheinlich**   *probably*
**vielleicht**   *maybe*
**verschieden**   *different*

# Kapitel 12:
# Die Fete  Wiederholungskapitel *Chapter Overview*

| Los geht's!<br>pp. 294-296 | Die Geburtstagsfete, p. 294 | | Video Guide |
|---|---|---|---|
| | **REVIEW OF FUNCTIONS** | **REVIEW OF GRAMMAR** | **CULTURE** |
| **Erste Stufe**<br>pp. 297-301 | •Offering help and explaining what to do, p. 297<br>•Asking where something is located and giving directions, p. 299 | •the verb **können**; the preposition **für**; accusative pronouns; and **du**-commands, p. 297<br>•the verb **wissen** and word order in clauses following **wissen**, p. 300 | •**Ein wenig Landeskunde: Spätzle** and **Apfelküchle**, p. 298<br>•**Landeskunde: Mußt du zu Hause helfen?** p. 301 |
| **Zweite Stufe**<br>pp. 302-305 | •Making plans and inviting someone to come along, p. 302<br>•Talking about clothing, p. 304<br>•Discussing gift ideas, p. 305 | •the verbs **wollen** and **müssen**; word order, p. 302<br>•nominative and accusative pronouns; definite and indefinite articles, p. 305<br>•dative endings, p. 305 | •**Polo mit Eskimorolle**, p. 303<br>•German gift ideas, p. 305 |
| **Dritte Stufe**<br>pp. 306-309 | •Describing people and places, p. 306<br>•Saying what you would like and whether you do or don't want more, p. 308<br>•Talking about what you did, p. 309 | •the nominative pronouns **er, sie, es**, and **sie** pl; possessive pronouns, p. 306<br>•the **möchte**-forms; **noch ein** and **kein ... mehr**, p. 308 | •Photos from furniture ads, p. 307<br>•Menu from an **Imbißstube**, p. 308 |
| **Aussprache**<br>p. 309 | review letters **w**, **v**, and **j**; review short vowels **ä** and **e**; review long vowels **ä** and **e** | | Diktat:<br>*Textbook Audiocassette* 6 B |
| **Zum Lesen**<br>pp. 310-311 | Mahlzeit!<br>Reading Strategy: Combining reading strategies (Using visual clues, cognates, and context to determine meaning) | | |
| **Review**<br>pp. 312-315 | •Anwendung, *p. 312*<br>•Kann ich's wirklich? *p. 314*<br>•Wortschatz, *p. 315* | | |
| **Assessment Options**<br><br>Final Exam,<br>*Assessment Guide Audiocassette* 8 B | **Stufe Quizzes**<br>•*Chapter Resources*, Book 4<br>   **Erste Stufe**, Quiz 12-1<br>   **Zweite Stufe**, Quiz 12-2<br>   **Dritte Stufe**, Quiz 12-3<br>•*Assessment Items, Audiocassette* 6 B | | **Kapitel 12 Chapter Test**<br>•*Chapter Resources*, Book 4<br>•*Assessment Guide*, Speaking Test<br>•*Assessment Items, Audiocassette* 6 B<br><br>**Test Generator, Kapitel 12** |

*Video Program* **OR**
*Expanded Video Program,* Videocassette 4

Textbook Audiocassette 6 B

| RESOURCES Print | RESOURCES Audiovisual |
|---|---|

*Textbook Audiocassette* 6 B

*Practice and Activity Book*
*Chapter Resources,* Book 4
  •Communicative Activity 12-1
  •Additional Listening Activities 12-1, 12-2 . . . . . . . . *Additional Listening Activities, Audiocassette* 10 B
  •Student Response Form
  •Realia 12-1
  •Situation Card 12-1
  •Teaching Transparency Master 12-1 . . . . . . . . . . . . *Teaching Transparency* 12-1
  •Quiz 12-1 . . . . . . . . . . . . . . . . . . . . . . . . . . . . . . . *Assessment Items, Audiocassette* 8 B
*Video Guide.* . . . . . . . . . . . . . . . . . . . . . . . . . . . . . . . *Video Program/Expanded Video Program,* Videocassette 4

*Textbook Audiocassette* 6 B

*Practice and Activity Book*
*Chapter Resources,* Book 4
  •Communicative Activity 12-2
  •Additional Listening Activity 12-3 . . . . . . . . . . . . . *Additional Listening Activities, Audiocassette* 10 B
  •Additional Listening Activity 12-4 . . . . . . . . . . . . . *Additional Listening Activities, Audiocassette* 10 B
  •Student Response Form
  •Realia 12-2
  •Situation Card 12-2
  •Quiz 12-2 . . . . . . . . . . . . . . . . . . . . . . . . . . . . . . . *Assessment Items, Audiocassette* 8 B

*Textbook Audiocassette* 6 B

*Practice and Activity Book*
*Chapter Resources,* Book 4
  •Additional Listening Activity 12-5 . . . . . . . . . . . . . *Additional Listening Activities, Audiocassette* 10 B
  •Additional Listening Activity 12-6 . . . . . . . . . . . . . *Additional Listening Activities, Audiocassette* 10 B
  •Student Response Form
  •Realia 12-3
  •Situation Card 12-3
  •Teaching Transparency Master 12-2 . . . . . . . . . . . . *Teaching Transparency* 12-2
  •Quiz 12-3 . . . . . . . . . . . . . . . . . . . . . . . . . . . . . . . *Assessment Items, Audiocassette* 8 B

*Video Guide.* . . . . . . . . . . . . . . . . . . . . . . . . . . . . . . . *Video Program/Expanded Video Program,* Videocassette 4

**Alternative Assessment**
•Performance Assessment,
*Teacher's Edition*
  **Erste Stufe,** p. 291K
  **Zweite Stufe,** p. 291M
  **Dritte Stufe,** p. 291O

•Portfolio Assessment
  Written: **Anwendung,** Activity 2, *Pupil's Edition,* p. 312,
  *Assessment Guide*
  Oral: **Erste Stufe,** Activity 6b, *Pupil's Edition,* p. 297, *Assessment Guide*
•**Notizbuch,** *Pupil's Edition,* p. 307; *Practice and Activity Book,* p. 156

# Kapitel 12: Die Fete
# *Textbook Listening Activities Scripts*

## *Erste Stufe*
### Activity 5, *p. 297*

THOMAS  Das wird ja eine tolle Fete, was, Nicole?

NICOLE  Bestimmt, aber ihr müßt mir wirklich ein wenig dabei helfen. Ich kann das alles gar nicht alleine schaffen.

THOMAS  Mensch, sicher ... sag' mir, wie ich dir helfen kann.

NICOLE  Thomas, am besten sortier erst mal den Müll. Da ist diesmal eine Menge. Die Tüten findest du in der Abstellkammer. Anschließend könntest du den Rasen mähen.

THOMAS  Und wo ist der Rasenmäher?

NICOLE  In der Garage. Und du, Andreas, sei nicht so faul! Zeitung lesen gibt es hier nicht. Hier sind saubere Tücher und Putzmittel.

ANDREAS  Und was soll ich damit?

NICOLE  Was wohl? Fenster putzen! Und wenn du damit fertig bist, sei so lieb und saug Staub hier oben!

SABINE  Ich bin ja auch noch hier. Wie kann ich dir helfen, Nicole?

NICOLE  Sabine, du kannst zuerst den Tisch decken, du weißt ja, wo das Geschirr und das Besteck bei uns sind.

SABINE  Sonst noch was? Soll ich in der Küche helfen?

NICOLE  Nee, Sabine, du kannst lieber das Geschirr spülen. Das ist wohl alles. Ach, Moment mal! Mir fehlen einige Sachen fürs Essen. Anschließend kannst du ja diese Sachen im Supermarkt kaufen, geht das?

SABINE  Ja, sicher!

THOMAS  Bin fertig! Ah ... jetzt ruh' ich mich mal aus.

NICOLE  Ja, also wenn du so schnell fertig bist, Thomas, dann räum dieses Zimmer etwas auf. Dann ist alles getan.

THOMAS  So ein Pech!

### Activity 9, *p. 300*

SABINE  Du wohnst gar nicht so weit von mir, Laubenweg 17, ja? Also von euch geht das am einfachsten, wenn du nach rechts auf dem Laubenweg bis zur Königstraße gehst. Bei der Kreuzung an der Königstraße gehst du dann nach rechts, und kurz danach gehst du in die erste Straße links. Auf der rechten Seite kannst du die Post sehen. Du bist dann auf der Wengertgasse und bleibst darauf, bis du zur Pfarrgasse kommst. Geh nach links in die Pfarrgasse bis zur Gartenstraße. Dort wohne ich an der Ecke. Du brauchst nur zu klingeln. Vergiß nicht, Sonntag um 12 Uhr!

NICOLE  Ich hatte ganz vergessen, daß du ja noch nie bei mir warst. Also, ich glaub', von euerem Haus, ... geh am besten links auf dem Laubenweg, bis du zur Ursulinergasse kommst. Da gehst du dann in die erste Straße rechts, also in die Ursulinergasse, und bleibst darauf, bis du das Schild von der Rosmaringasse siehst. Da gehst du in die erste Straße rechts, also in die Rosmaringasse, bis zur Herzog-Ernst-Straße. Du gehst links in die Herzog-Ernst Straße und dann geradeaus bis zur Marktstraße. Da wohne ich. Wir wohnen im Erdgeschoß. Die Tür ist unten auf. Alles verstanden? Und die Fete fängt so um halb acht an. Bis dann!

## *Zweite Stufe*
### Activity 12, *p. 303*

PETER  Grüß Gott! Mein Name ist Peter Ludwig. Freizeit hab' ich ja nicht sehr viel, mit Hausaufgaben nach der Schule, dann noch die ganze Hausarbeit, da will ich schon ausspannen. Meinem Freund Guido geht das genauso. Wir treffen uns meistens bei mir zu Hause, und spielen Schach oder andere Brettspiele. Dabei hören wir immer Musik. Und der Guido hat eine tolle Stereoanlage. Da bringe ich auch mal meine CDs, wenn wir uns bei ihm zu Hause treffen.

SANDRA  Ich bin die Sandra. Ich komme aus München, aber jetzt wohne ich in Stuttgart. Das ist mir noch alles ein bißchen neu, aber es ist auch gleichzeitig sehr interessant. Wenn das Wetter gut ist, nehm' ich meistens mein Rad und fahr' in der Altstadt herum. Ja, und manchmal geh' ich dann auch ins Kino, aber allein macht das ja nicht immer so viel Spaß. Neulich war ich auf dem Stuttgarter Fernsehturm. Der befindet sich auf dem Bopser. Von der oberen Aussichtsplattform konnte man die ganze Stadt sehen, das war echt toll.

FRANZ  Ich heiße Franz Stifter, und in meiner Freizeit bin ich oft mit meinen Freunden unterwegs. Was wir so tun? Tja ... kommt ganz darauf an. Meistens treffen wir uns im Jugendzentrum. Die Leute da brauchen manchmal unsere Hilfe. Dann helfen wir halt mit Ausflügen für die Kinder. Die gehen dann in Parks oder im Winter Schlittschuh laufen. Einmal haben wir sogar den Tierpark besucht. Das hat natürlich Spaß gemacht.

JUDITH  Mein Name ist Judith Heinemann, und ich wohne auch hier in der Nähe. Ich interessier' mich hauptsächlich für Sport. Schon als ich

klein war. Zuerst habe ich Gymnastik gemacht, aber das war irgendwie langweilig. Dann habe ich mit Tennis angefangen. Und das mache ich am liebsten. Ich trainiere drei- manchmal auch viermal pro Woche. Das mache ich immer nachmittags, wenn ich mit meinen Hausaufgaben fertig bin.

## Activity 15, *p. 304*

1. — Bei Biedermeyers gibt es diese Woche wieder mal tolle Sonderangebote.
   — Wirklich? Stand das in der Zeitung?
   — Ja, gestern. Und ich brauche unbedingt neue Fußballschuhe. Eigentlich brauche ich auch ein paar Socken. Meine haben alle Löcher vorne.
   — Wir können ja mal hingehen. Ich möchte sehen, ob sie eine Badehose in meiner Größe haben.
2. — Die jungen Leute sind ja wie wild in den Laden Lassofänger gestürmt.
   — Ja, also die Ware dort finde ich schrecklich, und du, Irma?
   — Na, Jeans mag ich schon anziehen, aber diese Cowboystiefel, die sehen doch unmöglich aus, findest du nicht?
   — Du hast recht. Ich habe einen anderen Geschmack.
3. — Für die Fete am Samstag bei Rudi möchte ich mir bei Zimmermanns gern eine neue Bluse und vielleicht einen schwarzen Rock kaufen. Die haben fesche Sachen und gute Preise.
   — Da habe ich mir neulich dieses Kleid gekauft. Wie findest du es?
   — Es steht dir wirklich ausgezeichnet.
4. — Bist du schon in das neue Geschäft neben Neckermann gegangen? Wie heißt das noch gleich?
   — Du meinst Walters. Die haben schicke Hosen ... und ganz tolle Anzüge. Die sind aber auch ganz schön teuer. Die haben italienische Hemden und Schuhe. Also, für die Disko kannst du da eine Menge Sachen finden.
   — Tja, dafür reicht mein Taschengeld nicht ganz aus.

## *D*ritte Stufe
### Diktat, *p. 309*

You will hear about the clothes Veronika would like to buy to go to Andreas' party. First listen to what is said, then write down what you hear.

Für Werners Fete am 18. Juni will sich Bärbel einige neue Klamotten kaufen. Sie hat vom neuen Modegeschäft Zimmermanns gehört und hofft, da vielleicht einen Rock und eine neue Bluse zu finden. Sie hat nämlich in der Zeitung gelesen, daß es in dem Geschäft zur Zeit gute Sonderangebote gibt. Ihre Freundinnen Julia und Bettina waren gerade gestern in dem Geschäft und haben schicke

Hosen und T-Shirts für die Fete gefunden. Wenn Bärbel bei Zimmermanns nichts findet, will sie ins große Einkaufszentrum fahren, denn da gibt es noch viele andere Boutiquen.

## *A*nwendung
### Activity 1, *p. 312*

1. — Mensch, der Kartoffelsalat war ja ganz schön salzig, findest du nicht?
   — Nee, mir hat der eigentlich ganz gut geschmeckt. Ich habe auch die belegten Brötchen gegessen. Die waren sehr gut. Vielleicht solltest du die mal probieren.
   — Nein, danke! Jetzt will ich nichts mehr.
2. — Bayern München liegt jetzt an der Tabellenspitze, nach dem Spiel am letzten Wochenende. Hast du das im Fernsehen gesehen?
   — Ja, die haben wirklich ausgezeichnet gespielt, und der Kopfschuß von Matthäus war ja einmalig, was?
   — Ja, klar! Wollen wir wetten, die gewinnen den Pokal diese Saison?
   — Ganz sicher!
3. — Was, du hast noch Karten dafür bekommen? Ich dachte, die sind schon alle ausverkauft. Mit wem gehst du denn ins Konzert?
   — Mit der Sandra. Ihre Lieblingsgruppe spielt nämlich. Sie hat alle CDs von denen. Kannst du das glauben?
4. — ... und wie hast du *Drei Männer und ein Baby* gefunden?
   — Ach, das war doch blöd. Da seh' ich schon lieber Abenteuerfilme. Das nächste Mal suche ich den Film aus.
   — Wieso? Wer hat denn den Film ausgesucht?
   — Na, die Ute, und die mag solche Filme unwahrscheinlich gern.
5. — Was hat der Scholz dir denn gestern gegeben?
   — Eine drei.
   — Das geht ja noch.
   — Wieso, was hast du bekommen?
   — 'ne vier. Das wird meinen Eltern nicht besonders gefallen. Da muß ich dieses Wochenende sicher zu Hause bleiben und Mathe lernen, damit meine Noten besser werden.

# Kapitel 12: Die Fete
## *Suggested Project*

*In this project students will create a poster displaying a nutritious five-day menu they have planned for the school cafeteria.*

## MATERIALS

✄ **Students may need**
- *large poster board*
- *grocery advertisement flyers*
- *food magazines*
- *scissors*
- *glue or tape*
- *markers*

## ORGANIZATION

Students' menus should include the following information:

Days of the week and corresponding dates
Prices for each item
Nutritional information
German Day (offering a variety of German specialties)

## SUGGESTED SEQUENCE

1. Students get into groups of three or four students, depending on the class size.

2. All groups discuss and make outlines of what they plan to include on their menus (pizza, hamburgers, and hot dogs are NOT allowed). Caution students that each day's meal should be nutritionally balanced and include all food groups.

3. Students write a complete lunch menu for five days, including the information outlined above.

4. Students display their menu on poster board.

5. Groups present their menus to the rest of the class in short oral presentations.

6. The class votes via secret ballot for the best menu.

7. Ballots are counted, and the winner is announced.

## GRADING THE PROJECT

Suggested point distribution (total=100 points)

| | |
|---|---|
| Appearance | 20 |
| Accuracy of written language | 20 |
| Creativity of ideas | 20 |
| Oral presentation | 40 |

## COMMUNITY LINK

If there are any German **Vereine** in your community or neighboring areas, you might want to suggest that students organize **einen Kulturabend** or **eine Fete** with them.

PROJECT

# Kapitel 12: Die Fete

## *Games*

## WORTFAMILIEN

*This game will help students review vocabulary from the whole book.*

**Procedure**  For this activity, prepare a list of vocabulary items that are related to a particular category. (Examples: **eine Fete, die Stadt, zu Hause helfen, Schule**) Have students work with a partner or in a small group. Announce the first category to the class and give students two minutes to write down as many related words as they can think of. Then have each group write its words on the chalkboard. Go through each list and verify that the words belong to the right category and that they are spelled correctly. The group with the most correct words wins.

## SCAVENGER HUNT

*This game can be used to review vocabulary and culture notes that have been introduced throughout the book in the almanacs, location openers, chapter openers, and* **Landeskunde** *entries.*

**Procedure**  In preparation for this game, go through the chapters and compile a list of questions and cues that you feel will help students review the material. This list will become the "Scavenger List." Give a copy of the list to each group. Determine a time limit in which students can use the book and their notes to answer the questions. The group that has the most correct answers when time is up wins.

**Suggestions for Scavenger Questions**

1. __ heißt die Hauptstadt von Bayern?
2. Hier fanden 1972 die Olympischen Spiele statt.
3. __ ist das deutsche Wort für *pedestrian zone*.
4. __ sind zwei Getränke.
5. Die Familie sitzt am __ und ißt zu Mittag.
6. __ ist der Bruder von meinem Vater.
7. __ ist ein Spezialgeschäft für Fleischwaren.
8. Hier fand die Potsdamer Konferenz statt.
9. __ ist ein Monat im Herbst.
10. __ sind zwei Sachen, die man im Obst- und Gemüseladen kaufen kann.

# Kapitel 12: Die Fete
## *Lesson Plans, pages 292-315*

## Using the Chapter Opener, pp. 292-293

### Motivating Activity

Play the game *What's in the Bag?* to reinforce previously learned vocabulary. Have several small objects in a bag and tell your students that these items all have something to do with a party or **Fete**. Students try to guess what these objects might be. Examples: **Einladung, Kassette, Kerze**

### For Individual Needs

**Challenge**  To reinforce the vocabulary for describing furniture and where people live, ask students to tell you where they would like to give a party. Would they rather have it in their house, backyard, or basement? What furniture would they need?

### Building on Previous Skills

① Ask students to describe what the German teenagers are wearing.

### Thinking Critically

① **Comparing and Contrasting**  Ask students what they would wear if they were invited to a backyard BBQ during the summer. Would their clothes look different from the ones students in Pictures 1 and 2 are wearing?

### Building on Previous Skills

② The students in this picture are being served **Bratwurst**. What other types of German sausage have students learned about in previous chapters? (**Frankfurter** and **Weißwurst**)

### Teaching Suggestion

③ You might want to introduce the following vocabulary for this photo: **die Schüssel** (*bowl*); **die Zwiebel** (*onion*); **die Petersilie** (*parsley*)

### Culture Note

③ This picture shows **Tomatensalat**, a very popular side dish in Germany. Also popular is **Gurkensalat** (*cucumber salad*) with lemon and parsley dressing.

### Thinking Critically

**Comparing and Contrasting**  Ask students if they think American students in general eat as much salad and fruit as German students do.

### Building on Previous Skills

Ask students to list the ingredients of their favorite salad in German.

### For Individual Needs

**Challenge**  Can students give simple instructions in German for the preparation of their favorite salad? Remind students to use connectors in their directions.

### Teaching Suggestion

Ask each student to take out a piece of paper and write down in German one thing people typically talk about at a party. Put all the pieces in a bag and have several students pull one out and read it to the class. Divide the class into groups of four or five students, and have each group prepare a short skit based on one of the topics.

### Focusing on Outcomes

To get students to focus on the chapter objectives listed on p. 293, ask students to discuss what is involved in preparing a party and what is involved in preparing to go to a party. Then have students preview the learning outcomes listed on p. 293. NOTE: Each of these outcomes is modeled in the video and evaluated in **Kann ich's wirklich?** on p. 314.

# Teaching Los geht's!
*pp. 294-296*

## Resources for Los geht's!
- *Video Program* **OR**
  *Expanded Video Program,* Videocassette 4
- *Textbook Audiocassette* 6 B
- *Practice and Activity Book*

▶ **pages 294-295**

### 📼 Video Synopsis

In this segment of the video, Nicole and her friends prepare for and hold a party to celebrate Martin's birthday. The student outcomes listed on p. 293 are modeled in the video: offering help and explaining what to do, asking where something is located and giving directions, making plans and inviting someone to come along, talking about clothing, discussing gift ideas, describing people and places, saying what you would like and whether you do or don't want more, and talking about what you did.

### Motivating Activity

As an advance organizer for the story line of the **Foto-Roman,** ask students how they would help a friend get ready for a party. What things need to get done before the guests arrive?

### Teaching Suggestion

After students have read and watched or listened to the **Foto-Roman,** ask them if they can tell by looking at frame 5 what **Bowle** is. (*punch*)

### Background Information

In southern Germany, **Bowle** is served at parties of all kinds. It is made with fresh, canned, or frozen fruit, such as apples, oranges, strawberries, raspberries, peaches, or cherries. Fruit juice is added to cover the fruit and then the mixture is refrigerated. Cloves are also added, but they are removed before the **Bowle** is served.

### Language Note

What is known as **Bowle** in southern Germany is often referred to as **Punsch** in the northern parts of the country.

▶ **page 296**

### Teaching Suggestions

- Ask students to work with a partner as they answer Questions 1-4 in writing.

**1** Students should find one phrase or statement from the **Foto-Roman** that supports each of their answers.

### ✛ For Individual Needs

**2 Challenge** Ask students to find one additional description for each person that has not been mentioned before.

### Thinking Critically

**3 Analyzing** Once students have put the sentences in order, ask them to point out the connectors (adverbs of time). You may want to write them in order on the chalkboard.

### ✛ For Individual Needs

**3 Challenge** Ask students to summarize each picture by giving it an original title.

### Closure

Play the video of the **Foto-Roman** one last time, but without sound. Have students take turns playing the roles of the German teenagers, making up the lines as well as they can.

LOS GEHT'S!

*T*eaching Erste Stufe,
*pp. 297-301*

### Resources for Erste Stufe

*Practice and Activity Book*
*Chapter Resources,* Book 4
- Communicative Activity 12-1
- Additional Listening Activities 12-1, 12-2
- Student Response Form
- Realia 12-1
- Situation Card 12-1
- Teaching Transparency Master 12-1
- Quiz 12-1

*Audiocassette Program*
- *Textbook Audiocassette* 6 B
- *Additional Listening Activities, Audiocassette* 10 B
- *Assessment Items, Audiocassette* 8 B

▶ *page 297*

## MOTIVATE

### Teaching Suggestion
Have the following skeletal script on the board or a transparency as students walk into the classroom. As a warm-up activity, ask students to copy the script and to complete it. Students can then read their short paragraphs aloud. **Die beste Party war ___. Sie war so gut, weil ___. Die ___ und ___ schmeckten einfach Klasse! Wir haben viel ___ und ___. Wir haben die Musik von ___ und ___ gehört und dazu getanzt.**

## TEACH

### PRESENTATION: So sagt man das!
Ask students to work with a partner and imagine the following situation. One of them has won a bet, and now the other has to do all the chores around the house. The winner has to tell the loser of the bet what needs to be done. Students take turns using the expressions from the **So sagt man das!** box and those learned in preceding units (especially Chapter 7).

 **For Individual Needs**

5 **Challenge** After students have completed this activity, ask them if anyone at home has ever made them an **Arbeitsliste**. What are some typical things they get asked to do?

### 📁 Portfolio Assessment

6b You might want to use this activity as an oral portfolio item for your students. See *Assessment Guide,* Chapter 12.

▶ *page 298*

## Building on Previous Skills
Ask students to look at the recipes and give definitions of the abbreviations **g**, **l**, and **EL**. (**Gramm, Liter, Eßlöffel**)

## Math Connection
7 Have students make all possible conversions from metric to U.S. measurements. You may need to remind students that 1 **Gramm** equals 0.035 ounces and that 1 **Liter** equals 1.056 quarts.

7 Ask students to determine how each recipe could be doubled to serve eight people.

## Teaching Suggestion
7 You may want to introduce the following new vocabulary from the two recipes: **das Mehl** (*flour*); **verdünnen** (*dilute*); **das Spatzenbrett** (*a board on which Spätzle are made and cut*); **der Emmentaler** (*a type of mild cheese*).

**Käsespätzle**
Für 4 Personen

400 g Mehl
2 Eier
etwas Salz
1/8 - 1/4 l Wasser
(oder Milch verdünnt)
1 EL Öl
200 g Emmentaler
4 Zwiebeln
50 g Butter
1 Spatzenbrett

ERSTE STUFE

**Apfelküchle**
Für 4 Portionen

200 g Mehl
3 Eier
1/4 l Milch
1 Prise Salz
4 möglichst säuerliche Äpfel (groß)
1 Zitrone
1 EL Zucker
1 EL Zimt
Butterschmalz zum Ausbacken

## Language Note

Ask students to look at the words **Spätzle** and **Apfelküchle**. Knowing that these are both words used in southern regional dialects, can students draw a general conclusion about regional language usage as they note the endings of both words? Have students guess how people in northern Germany would spell and say **Apfelküchle**. (**Apfelkuchen**)

## PRESENTATION: Wortschatz

Bring the items from this vocabulary box to class if possible. Introduce the vocabulary to the class.

###  Total Physical Response

Give students commands using the objects you brought to class to introduce the new vocabulary. Example: **Peter, gib Mary zwei Sachen, die in einen Salat gehören! Susy, gib Uwe bitte das Salz!**

## Teaching Suggestion

**8** Before students begin with this activity, review the vocabulary for rooms in a house and furniture using pictures or eliciting words by giving oral descriptions.

▶ page 299

## Language Note

The ending -**gasse** means *alley* and -**weg** means *path* or *way*.

## Thinking Critically

- **Drawing Inferences**   Ask students to look up the following words in a German or bilingual dictionary: **Schuster, Pfarrer, Laube, Mühle.** Then ask students what type of businesses were or might still be found on streets with these words as part of their names. What does the street name reveal about the street? Example: **Laubenweg** (*covered arbor*)

- **Analyzing**   Have students determine what the words **Rupp, Bischof, Vogt,** and **Schellmann** refer to. (the names of business owners)

▶ page 300

## Thinking Critically

**9   Comparing and Contrasting**   After students have completed the listening portion of this activity, you might want to ask them what foods would probably be served at Nicole's party on Saturday evening and compare it to what would be served at Sabine's house on Sunday afternoon. Would students in the United States serve similar foods for both occasions if they had friends over? If not, what would they serve? This discussion should be done in the target language.

## Language Note

**11**   Ask students to take a closer look at the milk. How much of the carton inscription can they understand or guess? (Examples: <u>Kleefeld</u> = *clover* field; **fettarm** = *lowfat;* **1,5% fett** = 1.5% *fat*) Point out that in Germany milk can be purchased in this type of carton, and it doesn't have to be refrigerated until after it is opened.

ERSTE STUFE

**ERSTE STUFE**

▶ *page 301*

 **PRESENTATION: Landeskunde**

- Begin by asking students to compare chores that need to be done in a house versus chores that need to be done in an apartment. (This activity should be conducted in German.)

- You might want to introduce this additional vocabulary to help students with the four interviews:
  **Mülleimer** *trash can*
  **zusammenlegen** *to fold*
  **anfallen** here: *to come up*
  **teilweise** *on and off, occasionally*

 **Culture Note**

In Silvana's interview, students heard that she hangs, takes down, and folds the laundry. In the German-speaking countries, **Wäscheleinen** (*clotheslines*) are a common sight on apartment balconies and in backyards. Not all German households have dryers; even if they do they are very compact, so hanging laundry is often necessary. Many people don't use dryers in an attempt to save energy, since oil, gas, and electricity costs are much higher in Germany than in the United States.

**Background Information**

In his interview, Gerd mentions that he often buys **Getränke**. German families tend to buy their **Limo** and **Brause** (*soft drinks*) at a **Getränke**-shop rather than at the grocery store because they can buy bottles by the case instead of individually. They pay a deposit for the bottles and the plastic case. This deposit is refunded upon return or applied toward the next purchase.

**Teacher Note**

Mention to your students that the **Landeskunde** will also be included in Quiz 12-1 given at the end of the **Erste Stufe**.

*CLOSE*

**Game**

Play the game **Wortfamilien.** See p. 291F for the procedure.

**Focusing on Outcomes**

Refer students back to the learning outcomes on p. 293. Students should recognize that they are now able to offer help, explain what to do, ask where something is located, and give directions.

*ASSESS*

- **Performance Assessment** Ask students to give directions or describe the path they take from their bedroom to the refrigerator in the kitchen for a midnight snack. Ask them to describe what they would choose for their midnight snack.

- Ask students to describe in German the steps they would take to make pancakes. You might want to put the following vocabulary words on the board: **das Mehl, die Milch, die Eier, das Öl, das Salz, die Butter.**

- Quiz 12-1, *Chapter Resources,* Book 4

## *Teaching Zweite Stufe,*
### *pp. 302-305*

▶ *page 302*

## *MOTIVATE*
### Teaching Suggestion
Ask students to copy the following incomplete statement and complete it as they see fit. **Das Leben in** (insert name of your town or city) **ist ___ und auch ___. Man kann hier ___.** Then ask students to read what they have written.

## *TEACH*
### PRESENTATION: So sagt man das!
Ask students to imagine that they are calling a friend to invite him or her to come along on an errand. Have them practice the expressions from this **So sagt man das!** box and from previous chapters (especially Chapter 11) to extend the invitation, and to accept or decline, giving a reason.

### PRESENTATION: Wortschatz
As you read through the new phrases, practice the difficult words: **be-sich-ti-gen, Schlitt-schuh-laufen, Brett-spiel.** Follow up with question and answer practice, providing students a context to guide their responses. Examples: **Es ist Winter. Die Sonne scheint. Was willst du heute tun? Du bist neu in dieser Stadt. Was möchtest du tun?**

### Teaching Suggestion
After you have introduced the vocabulary from the **Wortschatz** box, ask students specifically why they would want to do each of these activities. Make a list of suggestions on the board.

▶ *page 303*

### For Additional Practice
**13** Ask students to indicate which of the activities listed on the **Anschlagbrett im Jugendzentrum** they absolutely would not do. Have them give a reason using **weil** or **denn**. Remind students of the word order in dependent clauses.

▶ *page 304*

### PRESENTATION: So sagt man das!
Bring clothes of different sizes and styles to the classroom. Have two students come to the front. Ask the first student to put on clothes that you know are too long or too large. This student must ask his or her partner questions such as **Wie paßt der Pulli?** The partner answers with phrases such as **Er paßt überhaupt nicht** or **Er ist zu lang.**

### ◆ For Individual Needs
**15 Challenge** After having completed the listening portion of this activity, ask several students in which of the four stores they would like to shop and what they would buy there.

### PRESENTATION: Wortschatz
Bring articles of clothing that feature the characteristics of the **Wortschatz** box. Show these items as you introduce the new vocabulary.

###  Culture Note
*C & A* is a large clothing department store chain in Germany. Other popular stores for clothing are *Karstadt, Kaufhof,* and *Hertie.*

ZWEITE STUFE

## Math Connection

Provide students with the current exchange rate and ask them to convert the prices of the items in the *C & A* ad to U.S. dollars. Then ask students to comment on the prices using expressions such as **preiswert, günstig, billig,** and **teuer.**

▶ *page 305*

## Teaching Suggestion

**16** Since this activity involves extra time, you could assign it as homework for extra credit.

## PRESENTATION: So sagt man das!/Grammatik

Put the four German sentences from the **So sagt man das!** box on the chalkboard. Call four students to the board and have each label the sentence parts to review the nominative, accusative, and dative cases. Use different colored chalk for each case.

## Reteaching: Sentence building

Compile a list of sentences from this **Stufe**, write them on paper, and cut them into sentence strips. Place each of the sentence strips in an envelope and number them. Distribute the envelopes to pairs of students, who then try to put their sentence in correct order. Pairs should write down their sentence twice, once exactly as it appears on the paper, and a second time, substituting appropriate pronouns for each noun. Students then pass their envelopes to the next group and continue with the activity until each pair has solved each sentence puzzle, or until time is up. Go over all the sentences with the class. This activity is good for tactile and visual learners.

## *CLOSE*

### ♜ Game

Write the different activities from the **Tafel** on p. 303 on small pieces of paper and put them into a bag. Have a student come to the front of the class and pull a piece of paper from the bag. He or she then acts out the activity as the rest of the class tries to guess the activity. The student who guesses the activity first gets to act out the next one.

## Focusing on Outcomes

Refer students back to the outcomes listed on p. 293. Students should recognize that they are now able to make plans and invite someone to come along, talk about clothing, and discuss gift ideas.

## *ASSESS*

- **Performance Assessment** Put the following expressions on the board: **ins Kino gehen; ins Theater gehen; Schlittschuh laufen gehen; zu einer Fete gehen; die Stadt besichtigen.** Then ask students to describe what they would wear for each of these activities.
- Quiz 12-2, *Chapter Resources,* Book 4

# *T*eaching Dritte Stufe,
## *pp. 306-309*

▶ *page 306*

## *MOTIVATE*

### ♜ Game
Divide the class into two groups to play *Tic-Tac-Toe.* Fill the nine squares of the *Tic-Tac-Toe* grid with nine infinitives of irregular verbs, such as **lesen, sehen, haben, sprechen, sein, fahren, nehmen,** and **essen.** Alternating between teams, have team members form sentences in the present tense using the verbs indicated in order to get an X or an O in a square. The first team to get three in a row wins. Encourage students to change pronouns or proper nouns frequently so that different verb forms must be used.

## *TEACH*

### PRESENTATION: So sagt man das!
Prepare a description of a room to read out loud to the class. The room should have typical furniture and other items reflecting the vocabulary learned in earlier chapters. Ask students to take out a blank sheet of paper. As you read the description, students should try to visualize it and make a rough sketch of the room on their paper, indicating the items mentioned.

## Teaching Suggestion
19 Remind students to include physical attributes as well as personality features in their descriptions.

▶ *page 307*

## PRESENTATION: Wortschatz
Use pictures from decorating magazines, catalogs, and newspapers to introduce the items in this **Wortschatz** box.

## Thinking Critically
**Comparing and Contrasting**   From what students have learned so far, what are their impressions of how Germans furnish their homes? What similarities and differences between the United States and Germany can they think of?

## ◆ For Individual Needs
**Challenge**   To reinforce the new vocabulary, write a definition or description for each word. Ask students to guess the object or adjective that is defined or described.

**DRITTE STUFE**

**DRITTE STUFE**

▶ *page 308*

## PRESENTATION: So sagt man das!

Ask students to work with a partner as they use the expressions from this **So sagt man das!** box to role-play the following situation: two students are going to Student A's house after school. They are hungry and thirsty and ready to raid the refrigerator. They should create a brief dialogue talking about what they want to eat. They should try to use the expressions from this function box.

## PRESENTATION: Ein wenig Grammatik

Make a long list of foods and beverages the students know in German. Try to bring the actual items, props, or pictures of each to class. Offer each student a second helping of one of the items and have them respond with **Ja, bitte, noch ein(e, en)** ... or **Nein, danke, kein(e, en)** ... **mehr.**

▶ *page 309*

## PRESENTATION: So sagt man das!

Ask students to recall some adverbs which can express events that have already taken place. (Examples: **gestern, vorgestern, letzte Woche, letzten Monat**) Then ask students to use one of those adverbs and tell about something they have done in the recent past.

## PRESENTATION: Aussprache

After students have listened to the recording of these sounds and sentences, have them do the dictation. Have them exchange papers and correct each other's sentences. Then ask students, working in pairs, to find as many words as they can that contain these sounds. Using the words they find, have then try to think of funny sentences, such as tongue twisters, using the words. Ask for volunteers to read the sentences to the class.

## Reteaching: Talking about what you did

Ask students to review the Baden-Württemberg Location Opener on pp. 240-243 and write a fictional postcard detailing what they saw and did on an imaginary trip there.

## CLOSE

### Teaching Suggestion

Show a picture that students can describe. For example, show a picture of some teenagers sitting in a living room, watching TV, and munching on snacks. Have students describe the people, the room, and the snacks.

### Focusing on Outcomes

Refer students back to the learning outcomes listed on p. 293. Students should recognize that they are now able to describe people and places, say what they would like and whether they do or don't want more, and talk about what they did.

## ASSESS

- **Performance Assessment**   Give each student a piece of paper on which you have written the name of a book, movie, TV show, or an item which could have been bought. (Examples: *Star Wars*®, ***Ein Hund namens Beethoven***, *The Cosby Show*, **ein Pulli, eine Stereoanlage**) Then ask students individually what they did at some point in the past. (Example: **Kim, was hast du gestern abend gemacht?**) The students should respond based on the information on their cards. For example, a student with the card **"ein Pulli"** would respond **Ich habe einen Pulli gekauft.** Next, ask each student a follow-up question leading him or her to describe the item (book, film, show) in some way. Example: **Wie sieht dein Pulli aus?** or **Wie war der Film?**
- Quiz 12-3, *Chapter Resources,* Book 4

# Teaching Zum Lesen,
## pp. 310–311

## Reading Strategy

The targeted strategies in this reading are the combined use of visual clues, cognates, and context to determine meaning. Students should review these strategies before doing Questions 1-3. As in previous chapters, students will also be asked to skim for the gist, scan for specific information, answer questions to show comprehension, and transfer what they have learned.

## PREREADING

## Motivating Activity

Ask students when they last prepared or helped prepare a dish. What was it and what were some of the ingredients?

## Teaching Suggestion

Bring pictures of recipes from magazines and show them to your class. Ask students to guess what ingredients go into each dish based only on the picture.

## Home Economics Connection

Ask students to list measurements that are commonly used in the directions of a recipe. (Examples: teaspoon, tablespoon, cup)

## Teacher Note

Activities 1, 2, and 3 are prereading tasks.

## READING

## Skimming and Scanning

Ask students to look at the names of the recipes and have them guess at what meal they might be served in Germany. (**Kartoffelsalat**: dinner—Germans generally don't have a warm meal at night; **gefüllte Eier**: appetizer; **Mandelkuchen**: afternoon coffee break)

## Building on Previous Skills

Ask students to make a list of the measurement abbreviations that are used in the recipes and what they stand for. (**Pfd.: Pfund; g: Gramm**) You may want to remind students that solids are measured by weight and liquids by volume, in contrast to recipes in the United States, where most ingredients are measured by volume only.

##  Culture Note

In the German-speaking countries, baking powder is mostly sold in individual packages. Although the recipe for **Mandelkuchen** printed here calls for a teaspoon of baking powder, it is more common for recipes to call for **ein Päckchen Backpulver.**

## Geography Connection

The recipe for **Mandelkuchen** calls for almonds. Almonds are grown in two areas of Germany, Westphalia and the Upper Rhine region. Ask students to locate those two areas on a map.

## Thinking Critically

**6 Comparing and Contrasting** Provide students with a copy of a recipe for a typical American potato salad. Ask students to compare the American recipe to the German recipe. How do they differ? (Germans generally do not make **Kartoffelsalat** with mayonnaise.)

KARTOFFELSALAT MIT SPECK

ZUM LESEN

**ZUM LESEN**

### Teaching Suggestion

**9** Remind students that temperatures in Celsius can be converted to Fahrenheit by multiplying the number (here 175) by 9, dividing by 5, and adding 32 (=347). Emphasize to students that learning the conversion formula is a way to help them learn to relate Celsius temperatures to their own experiences. Their goal should be <u>not</u> to convert, but rather to "feel" the differences and make accurate approximations.

### Teaching Suggestion

To teach some of the ingredients in the recipes, bring them to class and display them on a table in front of the class. Introduce each item by holding up the item and naming it.

###  For Individual Needs

**Tactile Learners**   As you discuss each recipe, ask several students to group or arrange the ingredients by recipe.

### Background Information

**10** **Gefüllte Eier** are eaten as an appetizer throughout Germany, but the filling may vary, depending on the region. In northern Germany, for example, diced crabmeat and dill make a popular filling.

###  Cooperative Learning

Put students in groups of four. Ask them to choose a discussion leader, a recorder, a proofreader, and an announcer. Give students a specific amount of time in which to complete Activities 4-10. Monitor group work as you walk around, helping students if necessary. At the end of the activity call on each group announcer to read his or her group's results. You can decide whether on not to collect their work for a grade at the end of the activity.

## POST-READING

### Teacher Note

Activity 11 is a post-reading task that will show whether students can apply what they have learned.

### Teaching Suggestion

**11** Ask students to act out this situation with a partner. Encourage students to use props and not to read from a prepared script.

### Closure

Ask students to prepare one of the three recipes and bring them to class for a food day. Make sure students take the size of the class into account and prepare enough for everyone to try.

**MANDELKUCHEN**

### GEFÜLLTE EIER

Hartgekochte Eier, nach Bedarf — Butter — Salz — feingehackte Kräuter (Thymian, Majoran, Basilikum, Estragon)

Die Eier halbieren, die Dotter herausnehmen und in einer Schüssel mit der Butter, dem Salz und den feingehackten Kräutern gut verrühren. Die Masse wieder in die Eihälften füllen.

# Using Anwendung,
*pp. 312-313*

## Teaching Suggestions

**1** As an advance organizer for the listening activity, ask students to list at least three vocabulary words or phrases that are associated with each of the five topics.

**2** If students want to keep the identity of their favorite person anonymous, they can use a fictitious name.

### ◼ Portfolio Assessment

**2** You might want to use this activity as a written portfolio item for your students. See Assessment Guide, Chapter 12.

### ◆ For Individual Needs

**5 Tactile Learners** Once students have decided what they are going to see in Stuttgart, ask them to design a maze to trace their excursion route. After students have completed the mazes, they can exchange them with another student. They then try to trace each other's excursions and name the final destination of their partner's trip.

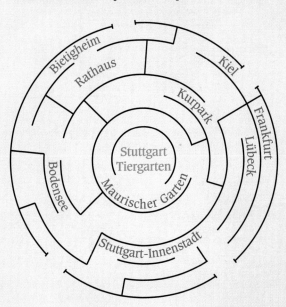

# Kann ich's wirklich?
*p. 314*

This page is intended to prepare students for the test. It is a brief checklist of the major points covered in the chapter. The students should be reminded that it is a checklist only and not necessarily everything that will appear on the test.

# Teaching Wortschatz,
*p. 315*

## Teaching Suggestions

- Ask students to make a list of ingredients for a typical salad.

- Show students some photos or ads from furniture catalogs or magazines featuring the vocabulary of the **Dritte Stufe.** Ask students to work with a partner to write down as many of the items in the pictures as they can recall. Students then read their lists aloud in class.

### ♜ Game
Play the game *Scavenger Hunt*. See p. 291F for the procedure.

# 12
# Die Fete

① So, was möchtet ihr trinken?

Teenagers in German-speaking countries like to get together and have parties with their friends. A lot of work goes into getting ready for a party, but sometimes the preparation is half the fun. What do you do to prepare for a party? Do you buy new clothes? Clean your house? Buy or cook special foods? If you are in a German-speaking country and want to prepare for a party, there are many things you will need to discuss.

## In this chapter you will

- offer help and explain what to do; ask where something is located and give directions
- make plans and invite someone to come along; talk about clothing; discuss gift ideas
- describe people and places; say what you would like and whether you do or don't want more; talk about what you did

## And you will

- listen to conversations at a party
- read some German recipes
- write a description of your kitchen and living room
- find out what people in German-speaking countries do to get ready for parties

② Es gibt noch viel Bratwurst.

③ Der Tomatensalat sieht lecker aus!

# Los geht's!

## Die Geberststagsfete

Look at the pictures that accompany the story.
What big event is taking place in the story?
What preparations are being made for this event?
Who is helping?

 Nicole    Andreas    Thomas    Sabine

 Mutter    Vater    Martin

---

①

**Nicoles Freunde sind da. Sie wollen ihr helfen.**

ANDREAS   So, Nicole, was können wir für dich tun?

NICOLE   Zuerst muß ich einkaufen gehen. Wer will mitkommen? Ich muß zum Supermarkt.

ANDREAS   Wir beide können ja mit den Rädern fahren.

NICOLE   Lieb von dir! Aber wir müssen so viel einkaufen. Die Mutti fährt uns mit dem Auto hin. — Aber du kannst mitkommen, wenn du willst.

ANDREAS   Klar!

---

②

THOMAS   Und was mache ich?

NICOLE   Thomas, du kannst dem Vati im Garten helfen, und dann müssen wir noch das Gemüse waschen.

ANDREAS   Okay! Wir können das ja machen, wenn wir zurückkommen.

---

③

**Nicole und Andreas kommen vom Einkaufen zurück.**

VATER   Was habt ihr mitgebracht? Oh, die Bratwurst sieht gut aus! Hm ... ganz frisch. Und, was habt ihr sonst noch?

NICOLE   Wir haben noch Eier, Mehl, Zucker ... Andreas und ich, wir backen dann einen Kuchen.

VATER   Schön!

④

Die Fete beginnt. Martin kommt.

**NICOLE** Vati! Das ist Martin!

**VATER** Hallo, Martin! Herzlich willkommen bei uns!

**MARTIN** Guten Tag! Vielen Dank für die Einladung!

**VATER** Schon gut! Wir freuen uns, wenn wir einmal im Jahr Nicoles Freunde zu uns einladen können. — Was willst du trinken? — Andreas, willst du Martin etwas zu trinken geben? Ich muß zum Grill.

⑤

**ANDREAS** Okay, Martin, was möchtest du denn haben?

**NICOLE** Die Bowle schmeckt gut.

**MARTIN** Gut! Dann probier' ich die Bowle.

**ANDREAS** Prost!

**MARTIN** — Hm, die ist wirklich gut!

⑥

**MUTTER** So, wer möchte was? Es gibt Kartoffelsalat, Krautsalat, Gurkensalat, Tomatensalat ... Thomas? Möchtest du Kartoffelsalat?

**THOMAS** Ja, bitte! — Die Wurstbrote sehen auch ganz lecker aus!

**MUTTER** Nimm doch gleich zwei! — Und eine Brezel!

**THOMAS** Okay. — Wo ist denn der Kuchen?

**MUTTER** Pst! Der Kuchen kommt erst nachher.

**THOMAS** Ach so!

⑦

Happy birthday to you ...

Was für eine Überraschung! Vielen, vielen Dank!

Andenken - Souvenir
aus Berlin
die Geschenkidee
Tel.:(030) 345 93 98

# 1 Was passiert hier?

Do you understand what is happening in the story? Check your comprehension by answering these questions. Don't be afraid to guess. *1. helping with preparations for a birthday party / help with shopping and in the kitchen; help father in the garden.*

1. Why are Nicole's friends at her house? What does Nicole tell them they can do to help?
2. Why does Nicole need **Eier, Mehl,** and **Zucker?** *to bake a cake.*
3. Why does Nicole's mother tell Thomas to keep his voice down? *It is supposed to be a surprise.*
4. What do you think might happen next in the story? *Answers may vary.*

# 2 Welche Beschreibung paßt zu welcher Person?

Match each person from the story with the most appropriate description.

1. Martin  c
2. Thomas  b
3. Nicole  d
4. Andreas  a
5. Nicoles Vater  e

a. geht mit Nicole einkaufen.
b. hilft Nicoles Vater im Garten und fragt Nicole, wo der Kuchen ist.
c. bekommt heute einen Geburtstagskuchen.
d. lädt ihre Freunde zur Fete ein, geht einkaufen und bäckt den Kuchen.
e. findet es super, daß Nicoles Freunde kommen, steht am Grill und grillt die Bratwurst.

# 3 Nacherzählen

Put the sentences in logical order to make a brief summary of the story.

1. Andreas, Sabine und Thomas kommen vorbei, um Nicole zu helfen.

5 Andreas gibt Martin etwas zu trinken.

2 Zuerst gehen Andreas und Nicole zum Supermarkt, und Thomas hilft Nicoles Vater im Garten.

4 Als letzter kommt der Martin.

3 Später am Nachmittag kommen die Gäste.

6 Es gibt Bowle zu trinken, und es gibt viel zu essen: Kartoffelsalat, Tomatensalat, Krautsalat, Gurkensalat und Bratwurst.

7 Nach dem Essen bringen Nicole und Thomas den Geburtstagskuchen, und die Freunde singen „Happy Birthday!"

# 4 Und ihr?

Du und dein Partner habt heute abend eine Fete. Was gibt's zu essen? Und zu trinken? Macht eine Liste! Schreibt alles auf, was ihr braucht! Dein Partner sagt dir, was er bringt, dann sagst du ihm, was du bringst. Dann besprich mit deinem Partner, wen ihr eingeladen habt und wer kommt!

BEISPIEL   PARTNER   Ich bringe ... mit. Was bringst du?
                DU   Ich bringe ...
           PARTNER   Und wen lädst du ein?
                DU   Ich lade ... ein.

*Offering help and explaining what to do; asking where something is located and giving directions*

## SO SAGT MAN DAS!

*Schon bekannt*

### Offering help and explaining what to do

You are having a party! Your friends come over to help you get things ready.
A friend might ask:

**Kann ich etwas für dich tun?**

*or*

**Was kann ich für dich tun?**

You could respond:

**Du kannst für mich das Geschirr spülen.**

**Geh bitte einkaufen! Hol ein Pfund Bratwurst und 10 Semmeln! Kauf die Bratwurst beim Metzger und die Semmeln beim Bäcker!**

Thomas: **Müll sortieren, Rasen mähen, Zimmer aufräumen**
Andreas: **Staub saugen, Fenster putzen**

## 5 Hör gut zu!

Nicole hat viel zu tun, denn sie muß alles für die Fete vorbereiten. Schau ihre Arbeitsliste an! Hör dir das Gescpräch gut an und schreib auf, was jede Person macht, um Nicole zu helfen!

Sabine: **Tisch decken, Geschirr spülen, Einkaufen gehen**

*Arbeitsliste für die Fete*
*Müll sortieren*
*Rasen mähen*
*Staub saugen*
*Fenster putzen*
*Zimmer aufräumen*
*Tisch decken*
*Geschirr spülen*
*Einkaufen gehen — Tomaten, Brot, Semmeln, Bratwurst, Hackfleisch, Eier, Mehl, Zucker, Äpfel, Orangen, Kartoffeln, Mineralwasser, Cola kaufen*

### Schon bekannt
### Ein wenig *G*rammatik

The preposition **für** is always followed by an accusative case form:
**Kannst du für mich 200 Gramm Aufschnitt kaufen?** See page 329 to review the accusative pronouns. To review **du**-commands, see page 333. If you need to review the forms of **können**, see page 332.

## 6 Du hast eine Fete!

a. Heute abend hast du eine Fete für eine Freundin. Schreib einen Einkaufszettel und eine Arbeitsliste!
b. Dein Partner fragt dich, wie er dir helfen kann. Sag ihm, was er für dich kaufen und machen kann! Sag deinem Partner auch, wo er die Lebensmittel kaufen soll! Dann tauscht ihr die Rollen aus!

**Spätzle** and **Apfelküchle** are specialties of Baden-Württemberg. **Spätzle** ("little sparrow" in the local dialect) are thick, round noodles made by spreading dough onto a board, then cutting it into small strips or pieces, and dropping them into boiling water.

**Apfelküchle** is a dessert made of apple slices dipped in a pancake batter and fried. The apples are then sprinkled with sugar and cinnamon. **Apfelküchle** is often served with vanilla sauce or vanilla ice cream.

### Apfelküchle
Für 4 Portionen

200 g Mehl
3 Eier
1/4 l Milch
1 Prise Salz
4 möglichst säuerliche Äpfel (groß)
1 Zitrone
1 EL Zucker
1 EL Zimt
Butterschmalz zum Ausbacken

### Käsespätzle
Für 4 Personen

400 g Mehl
2 Eier
etwas Salz
1/8 - 1/4 l Wasser
(oder Milch verdünnt)
1 EL Öl
200 g Emmentaler
4 Zwiebeln
50 g Butter
1 Spatzenbrett

## 7  Soll ich backen oder kochen?

Some friends are coming over for dinner. You and your partner are planning to make **Apfelküchle** and **Spätzle**, two popular southern German dishes. Each of you pick one recipe. Tell your partner what to buy for your recipe and how much. Then switch roles.

WORTSCHATZ

(die) Zwiebel    (die) Zitrone

(das) Öl

das Salz
der Zimt *cinnamon*
das Butterschmalz *shortening*

## 8  Am nächsten Tag

What a party! You and your friends had a great time last night, but now it's time to clean up the mess. You also promised your parents that you would do some other things around the house. Look at the picture of the house on the right and tell your partner what he or she can do to help. Then switch roles.

Answers may vary. Some examples **Du kannst den Müll sortieren. Du kannst Staub saugen.**

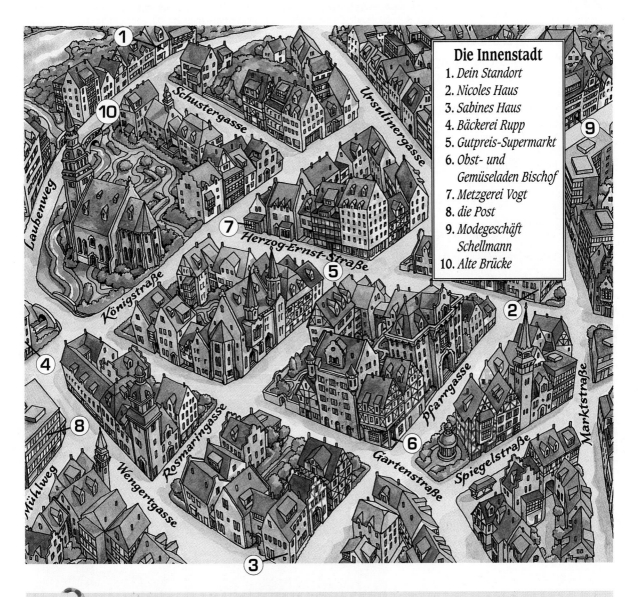

### Die Innenstadt
1. *Dein Standort*
2. *Nicoles Haus*
3. *Sabines Haus*
4. *Bäckerei Rupp*
5. *Gutpreis-Supermarkt*
6. *Obst- und Gemüseladen Bischof*
7. *Metzgerei Vogt*
8. *die Post*
9. *Modegeschäft Schellmann*
10. *Alte Brücke*

## SO SAGT MAN DAS!

### Asking where something is located and giving directions

If your friend asks you to pick up a few things at the butcher shop, you might first have to ask someone:

**Weißt du, wo die Metzgerei ist?**

The response might be:

**In der Herzog-Ernst-Straße.**

After you leave the house, you realize that you don't know how to get to **Herzog-Ernst-Straße**.

You ask a passer-by:

**Entschuldigung! Wie komme ich zur Metzgerei?**

The response might be:

**Gehen Sie geradeaus bis zur Schustergasse, dann nach rechts, dann die nächste Straße nach links.**

Sabine: nach rechts in den Laubenweg bis zur Königstr., dann nach rechts und die erste Straße links. Geh bis zur Gartenstr. Dort ist mein Haus. Nicole: Nach links und die erste Straße rechts bis zur Rosmaringasse. Dann rechts und die erste Straße links (Herzog-Ernst-Str.) bis zur Marktstraße. Da wohne ich.

## 9 Hör gut zu!

Following Nicole's party on Saturday, Sabine has invited everyone over on Sunday afternoon for a little get-together. Listen as both Sabine and Nicole give directions over the phone from where you are (**dein Standort**) to their houses. Write each set of instructions so that you know how to get to both parties. Check your directions on the map to see if you got them right.

die nächste Straße nach ...    nach links

nach rechts     an der Ampel nach ...

bis zum ...platz    bis zur ...straße

geradeaus

die (erste, zweite... ) Straße nach...

> ### Schon bekannt
> ### Ein wenig Grammatik
>
> See pages 335 and 330 to review the forms of **wissen** and word order following **wissen**. To review formal commands, see page 333.

## 10 Wie komm' ich zurück?

1. Nach rechts in die Herzog-Ernst.-Str. bis zur Königstr. Dann links und die erste Straße rechts.   2. Nach links in die Pfarrgasse. Die zweite Straße rechts. Dann links und die erste Straße rechts.

You are at the **Bäckerei Rupp** and your partner is at Nicole's house. Tell your partner how to get to the bakery. Then switch roles: Now you're at Sabine's house, and your partner will give you directions to the **Modegeschäft Schellman**.

## 11 Ihr habt Hunger

Du und deine Partnerin, ihr seid bei Sabine. Ihr habt Hunger. Wähl zwei von den folgenden Lebensmitteln aus und erzähl deiner Partnerin, wo sie die kaufen kann und wie sie dahin kommt. Schau auf den Stadtplan auf Seite 299!

LERNTRICK

When you are learning or reviewing vocabulary, remember to use the word or phrase in a sentence or conversation that gives it meaning. For example, when trying to learn the phrase **zur Bäckerei**, use it in an imaginary conversation:

— **Wie komme ich zur Bäckerei? Ich muß Brot kaufen.**
— **Die nächste Straße nach links.**

# Mußt du zu Hause helfen?

You've already discovered how German students like to spend their free time, and you know that they enjoy planning and going to parties. However, life isn't all fun! Often before they go out or meet with their friends, they have to help around the house. What chores do you think German students have to do? Make a list of chores that the following German students might mention. Then read the interviews.

### Heide,
*Berlin*

„Ich muß zweimal in der Woche die Toilette saubermachen, und dann ab und zu halt den Geschirrspüler ausräumen oder die Küche wischen und halt mein Zimmer aufräumen."

### Monika,
*Berlin*

„Also, ich muß fast jeden Tag den Mülleimer runter-bringen und ab und zu mal Waschmaschine an, Waschmaschine aus, Wäsche aufhängen ... Dann ab und zu Staub saugen, wischen—also wir haben in der Küche so Fliesen *(tiles)* und—aber meistens, wenn meine Eltern keine Zeit dazu haben. Abwaschen muß ich nicht, also, wir haben einen Geschirrspüler."

### Silvana,
*Berlin*

„Zu Hause helf' ich meistens so beim Ab-waschen, Spülma-schine ausräumen, oder die Wäsche aufhängen oder abnehmen, zusammen-legen, immer so, was anfällt."

### Gerd,
*Bietigheim*

„Ich saug' halt ab und zu Staub, räum' die Spülma-schine aus, bring' den Müll raus, hol' halt teilweise Getränke und so, mäh' manchmal den Rasen — kommt ganz darauf an."

Some chores in common: **Wäsche aufhängen; Spülmaschine ausräumen; Staub saugen; Müll raustragen**

**A.** 1. Make a list of the chores that are mentioned by each of the students. Do they have chores in common? How do the chores they mention compare to those you listed before reading the interviews?

2. Which of these students do the same kinds of things that you do at home? Answers will vary.

3. Which of the chores mentioned do you like or dislike? Give a reason in English.

**B.** You and your friends probably have chores to do at home. Make a list in German, indicat-ing what you have to do and for whom, and report it to your class. Keep track of which chores your classmates do. How do the chores that American students do at home compare to those of German students? Write a brief essay in which you discuss this question point-ing out the differences and similarities.

*Making plans and inviting someone to come along; talking about clothing; discussing gift ideas*

## SO SAGT MAN DAS!

*Schon bekannt*

### Making plans and inviting someone to come along

There are many times when you will want to make plans with your friends and invite them to go places with you.

You could say:

**Ich will um halb drei ins Einkaufszentrum gehen, Klamotten kaufen. Willst du mitkommen?** *or* **Kommst du mit?**

Your friend might accept:

**Ja gern!** *or*
**Super! Ich komme gern mit!**

Or decline and give a reason:

**Das geht leider nicht, denn ich muß am Nachmittag die Hausaufgaben machen.**

## WORTSCHATZ

THOMAS **Wohin willst du gehen? Was willst du tun?**
SABINE **Ich will ...**

die Stadt besichtigen

in den Park gehen

in den Zoo gehen

Schlittschuh laufen

joggen

ein Brettspiel spielen

### Schon bekannt
### Ein wenig Grammatik

See page 332 to review the forms of **wollen** and **müssen**. In German the conjugated verb in a main clause of a statement is always in second position. If there is a second verb, it is at the end of the sentence or clause and is in the infinitive. To review German word order, see page 330.

## 12 Hör gut zu!

A youth magazine recently interviewed four teens in the German-speaking countries about what they like to do in their free time. Match each person interviewed with the activity below that best fits that person's interests.

1. ... in den Zoo gehen
2. ... jeden Tag joggen
3. ... Brettspiele spielen, z. b., Monopoly®
4. ... die Altstadt besichtigen

## 13 Jugendzentrum in Bietigheim

Du und dein Partner, ihr seid Austauschschüler in der Stadt Bietigheim. Heute besucht ihr das Jugendzentrum. Schaut auf die Tafel, dann wählt vier Tätigkeiten, die ihr zwei gern macht, und sagt, wann ihr diese Tätigkeiten machen könnt.

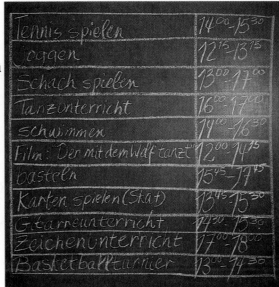

| | |
|---|---|
| Tennis spielen | 14⁰⁰-15³⁰ |
| Joggen | 12¹⁵-13¹⁵ |
| Schach spielen | 13⁰⁰-17⁰⁰ |
| Tanzunterricht | 16⁰⁰-17⁰⁰ |
| Schwimmen | 14⁰⁰-16³⁰ |
| Film: „Der mit dem Wolf tanzt" | 12⁰⁰-14¹⁵ |
| Basteln | 15⁴⁵-17¹⁵ |
| Karten spielen (Skat) | 13⁴⁵-15³⁰ |
| Gitarrenunterricht | 14⁰⁰-15³⁰ |
| Zeichenunterricht | 17⁰⁰-18⁰⁰ |
| Basketballturnier | 13⁰⁰-14³⁰ |

Answers may vary.

## 14 Willst du mitkommen?

a. Schau die Fotos an und lies den Text! Dann beantworte die Fragen!

1. Was spielen die Jungen hier?  Polo
2. Wo spielen sie?  im Wasser
3. Warum nennt (to name) man den Sport „Polo mit Eskimorolle"?  Weil sie oft eine Eskimorolle machen.
4. Glaubst du, daß dieser Sport Spaß macht?  Answers may vary.
5. Möchtest du „Polo mit Eskimorolle" spielen? Warum oder warum nicht?

b. Hast du Freizeitinteressen, die so ungewöhnlich sind, wie „Polo mit Eskimorolle"? Mach eine Liste mit drei Aktivitäten, die du gern machst, und lad dazu deinen Partner ein! Tauscht dann die Rollen aus!

*Kein Sport für Wasserscheue: Manchmal muß man mit dem Kopf ins Wasser. In der Fachsprache heißt das „Eskimorolle".*

*Wo ist der Ball? Besonders geschickte Spieler führen ihn mit ihrem Paddel unter Wasser.*

*Wo ist das Tor? Der Ball muß zwei Meter über dem Wasser in einen Korb.*

# SO SAGT MAN DAS!

*Schon bekannt*

## Talking about clothing

You might have the following conversation with the salesperson in a clothing store:

**VERKÄUFERIN:**
Haben Sie einen Wunsch?

**DU:**
Ich brauche einen Pulli, in Gelb, bitte!
Oh, und ich suche auch ein T-Shirt.
Der Pulli dort drüben sieht sehr fesch aus. Ich probiere ihn mal an.

Wie paßt er? Nicht zu lang oder zu eng?

Nein, überhaupt nicht. Er paßt prima, und er gefällt mir.

Ja, er sieht phantastisch aus.

Wirklich?

Wirklich!

Ja, das finde ich auch. Ich nehme ihn.

---

## 15 Hör gut zu! 1 d., 2 a., 3 c., 4 b.

Heute gibt es viele neue Modegeschäfte in Bietigheim. Leute in einem Eiscafé sprechen über diese Geschäfte. Welches Gespräch paßt zu welchem Schaufenster?

a.

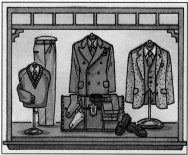

b.

c.

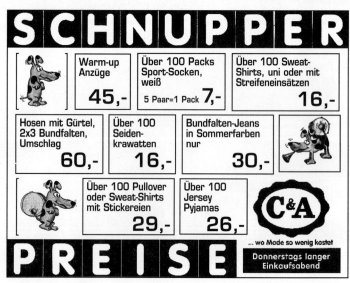

d.

### WORTSCHATZ

aus Seide    *made of silk*
aus Baumwolle    *made of cotton*
aus Leder    *made of leather*
gestreift    *striped*
gepunktet    *polka-dotted*

---

## 16 Du hast einen Laden

Make a window display for a clothing store. Either draw the items of clothing or cut pictures out of magazines and newspapers, then add price tags to your items. Name your store and write an advertisement for it. Look at the C & A ad on page 304 for ideas.

To review the nominative and accusative pronouns, see page 329. To review the definite and indefinite articles in the nominative and accusative cases, see pages 326–327.

**Schon bekannt**
*Ein wenig* **𝒢rammatik**

## 17 Was bekommen Sie?

You are looking for one of the items to the right in a clothing store. Your partner is the salesclerk. Find out if his or her store has the exact item you want. Find out the cost and where the item is located in the store. Then switch roles.

## SO SAGT MAN DAS!

*Schon bekannt*

### Discussing gift ideas

In **Kapitel 11** you learned to talk about giving gifts on special occasions.

A friend might ask:

> **Was schenkst du deinem Bruder zum Geburtstag?**
>
> **Und was schenkst du deiner Kusine zu Weihnachten?**

You might respond:

> **Ich schenke ihm eine Armbanduhr.**
>
> **Ich schenke ihr ein Buch.**

## 18 Besondere Geschenke

Unten sind ein paar typische Geschenke aus Deutschland und der Schweiz. Schau dir die Geschenke an. Dann erzähl deinem Partner, wem du sie schenkst (z.B. dem Vater, der Mutter). Dann erzählt dir dein Partner, wem er was schenkt.

**die Kuckucksuhr**

**der Krug**

**das Poster**

**ein Stück von der Berliner Mauer**

**die Armbanduhr**

**Schon bekannt**
*Ein wenig* **𝒢rammatik**

Do you remember the dative pronouns **ihm** (*to him*) and **ihr** (*to her*) and the definite articles **dem** and **der**? Don't forget the dative endings for **dein** and **mein**.

| *masculine* | *feminine* |
|---|---|
| dein- ⎱ em | dein- ⎱ er |
| mein- ⎰ | mein- ⎰ |

*Describing people and places; saying what you would like and whether you do or don't want more; talking about what you did*

## SO SAGT MAN DAS!

*Schon bekannt*

### Describing people and places

You will probably meet people at parties who will ask you about yourself, your friends, and your family.

Someone might ask:

**Woher kommst du, Lisa?**
**Und wo wohnst du jetzt?**

**Ist das deine Schwester?**

**Und was machst du in deiner Freizeit?**
**Wer ist denn Michael?**
**Wie sieht er aus?**

You might respond:

**Aus Kalifornien.**
**Ich wohne jetzt in Berlin, in der Schönleinstraße.**
**Ja, das ist meine Schwester. Sie heißt Jennifer.**

**Ich spiele oft Schach mit Michael.**
**Mein Freund.**
**Er hat lange, braune Haare und grüne Augen und er hat eine Brille.**

You'll also want to be able to describe places, like your own room:

**Mein Zimmer, das ist wirklich toll! Die Möbel sind echt schön, das Bett sogar ganz neu, ja und auch der Schreibtisch. Dann habe ich auch eine Couch. Die Farbe, na ja, das Grün ist nicht sehr schön, aber sonst ist die Couch wirklich sehr bequem.**

### Schon bekannt
### Ein wenig *G*rammatik

When you refer to people and places, you will use the nominative pronouns **er, sie, es,** and **sie** (pl), for example, **Das ist mein Vater. Er heißt Gerd.** To review these pronouns, look at page 329. To review possessives like **mein** and **dein,** see page 327.

## 19 Berühmte Leute

Cut out magazine photos of two famous people and bring them to class. Place the photos in a container. Each student will take out a photo. Describe the person in the photo you picked with as much detail as possible so that your partner can guess who it is. Switch roles.

## 20 Auf einer Fete

Dein Freund hat eine Fete, und du bist eingeladen. Du möchtest auf der Fete andere Leute kennenlernen (*meet*). Mach eine Liste mit acht Fragen, z.B. **Wo wohnst du? Was machst du in deiner Freizeit?** Frag deine Partnerin, und schreib ihre Antworten auf! Dann tauscht ihr die Rollen aus.

## 21 **Deine Partnerin vorstellen** *Introducing your partner*

Heute tagt (*meets*) der Deutsch-Club. Du mußt deine Partnerin vorstellen. Erzähl der Klasse alles, was du über deine Partnerin weißt! (Verwende Information von Übung 20.)

### Welche Möbel habt ihr im Wohnzimmer?

**Wir haben ...**
> ein Sofa
> einen Tisch
>> aus Holz
>> aus Kunststoff
> eine Lampe

**einen Teppich**      **einen Sessel**

> rund
> eckig *(with corners)*
> modern

**Und in der Küche gibt es ...**
> einen Eßtisch

**einen Kühlschrank**      **einen Herd**

**einen Ofen**      **ein Spülbecken**

## 22 **Beschreib den Raum!**

Beschreib deinem Partner die Möbel im Wohnzimmer! Frag ihn, wie er die Möbel findet! Sag ihm, wie du die Möbel findest! Jetzt beschreibt dein Partner die Möbel in der Küche.

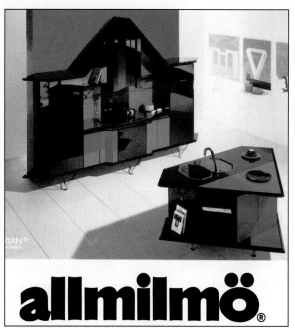

**allmilmö**®

## 23 **Für mein Notizbuch**

Beschreib dein Wohnzimmer und deine Küche! Was für Möbel gibt es da? Wie sehen diese Möbel aus? Du kannst auch eine Skizze machen.

# SO SAGT MAN DAS!

**Saying what you would like and whether you do or don't want more**

When eating at a friend's house, you may be asked by your host:

Was möchtest du trinken?

You could respond:

Ich möchte eine Limo, bitte!

Later your host might ask if you want more of something:

Möchtest du noch etwas?
Und noch eine Semmel?

Ja, bitte! Noch einen Saft.
Nein, danke! Keine Semmel mehr.

---

### Schon bekannt
### Ein wenig *G*rammatik

To review the **möchte** forms, see page 332. To review the use of **kein ... mehr,** see page 327.

## 24 Auf einer Geburtstagsfete

Spiel mit zwei oder drei Klassenkameraden die folgende Szene vor der Klasse: Ihr seid auf einer Geburtstagsfete. Ein Schüler spielt den Gastgeber (*host*). Er fragt die Gäste, was sie essen und trinken möchten. Später sagen die Gäste, wie das Essen schmeckt. Dann fragt der Gastgeber, wer noch etwas möchte.

## 25 Eine Imbißstube in Bietigheim

Du besichtigst heute mit zwei Klassenkameraden die Stadt Bietigheim. Ihr habt Hunger und wollt etwas essen. Schaut auf die Speisekarte und schreibt ein Gespräch! Was gibt es zu essen? Was bestellt ihr? Was kostet das Essen? Wie schmeckt das Essen? Wollt ihr noch mehr?

## SO SAGT MAN DAS!

*Schon bekannt*

### Talking about what you did

You will often want to describe to friends or family what you did in the past, for example, last week or over the weekend.

A friend might ask:

**Was hast du am Wochenende gemacht?**

Your response might be:

**Am Samstag war ich in der Innenstadt. Zuerst habe ich Klamotten gekauft, dann war ich im Supermarkt, danach im Eiscafé mit Andreas, und zuletzt bei Andreas zu Hause. Am Sonntag war ich die ganze Zeit zu Hause. Am Nachmittag habe ich gelesen, und am Abend habe ich ein Video gesehen. Danach haben Antje, Jörg und ich über Filme und Musik gesprochen.**

## 26 Hast du ein schönes Wochenende gehabt?

Frag deine Partnerin, was sie am Wochenende gemacht hat! Dann fragt dich deine Partnerin. Verwende die Vorschläge (*suggestions*) hier rechts.

Wo warst du am
Wochenende?
im Kaufhaus
beim Bäcker
zu Hause
bei Freunden
in der Stadt
im Konzert

Was hast du
gemacht?
gekauft?
gelesen?
gesehen?
Worüber habt
ihr gesprochen?

## AUSSPRACHE

## Richtig aussprechen / Richtig lesen

A. To review the following sounds, say the sentences below after your teacher or after the recording.

1. The letter w: The letter w is always pronounced like the *v* in the English word *vent*.
**Weißt du, wann Werners Geburtstag ist? Am Mittwoch?**

2. The letter v: The letter v sounds like the *f* in the English word *fence*.
**Volker hat viele Fische und findet immer mehr.**

3. The letter j: The letter j is pronounced the same as the *y* in the English word *you*.
**Die Julia besucht Jens im Juli, nicht Juni.**

4. The letters ä and e: The letters ä and e are pronounced as short vowels when followed by two consonants. When followed by one consonant or the letter h the ä and e are usually pronounced as long vowels.
**Ich finde den Sessel häßlich. Er gefällt mir nicht.**
**Peter kauft Käse. Das Mädchen mäht den Rasen.**

## Richtig schreiben / Diktat

B. Write down the sentences that you hear.

# ZUM LESEN

*Mahlzeit!*

## LESETRICKS

**Combining reading strategies** You can often derive the main idea of a text by looking at visual clues and format, and then searching for cognates and words you already know. In trying to figure out the meaning of unknown words, look at the context in which they occur. Often the surrounding text will give you clues about the meaning of the unknown word.

recipes

1. Judging by their form, what kinds of texts are these? What kinds of expressions do you expect to find in them? List in English the words and expressions you would find in typical recipes at home.

2. Recalling what you know about cognates and compound words, what do the following words mean in English?

   **gefüllte Eier**  deviled eggs
   **Kartoffelsalat**  potato salad
   **Mandelkuchen**  almond cake
      (**Mandeln**=*almonds*)

3. Since German recipes often use infinitives in the directions, you need to look at the end of the sentences to determine what to do with the ingredients. Make an educated guess about the meaning of the verbs in these phrases.

## KARTOFFELSALAT MIT SPECK

1 Pfd. gekochte Kartoffeln —50 g Speck — 1 Zwiebel — 3 Eßlöffel Essig — Salz — Pfeffer — 4 Eßlöffel Brühe

Kartoffeln in Scheiben schneiden. Warmhalten. Etwas Speck in kleine Würfel schneiden und mit feingehackter Zwiebel anrösten. Essig dazugeben und die Kartoffeln und den Speck mit Salz und Pfeffer abschmecken. Die heiße Fleischbrühe dazugeben.

## GEFÜLLTE EIER

| | |
|---|---|
| 1. mit Salz und Pfeffer **abschmecken** b | a. *take out* |
| 2. die Eier **halbieren** d | b. *season* |
| 3. die Dotter **herausnehmen** a | c. *brown lightly* |
| 4. Essig **dazugeben** f | d. *halve* |
| 5. Speck in kleine Würfel **schneiden** e | e. *cut* |
| 6. mit feingehackter Zwiebel **anrösten** c | f. *add* |

## MANDELKUCHEN

150 g Butter oder Margarine — 200 g Zucker — 1 Päckchen Vanillin-Zucker — 5 Eier — 3 Tropfen Bittermandelöl — 100 g Weizenmehl — 50 g Maisstärke — 1 Teelöffel Backpulver

Aus den Zutaten einen Rührteig bereiten, dann 150 g Mandeln, gemahlen und 150 g Schokoladenstücke unterheben und alles in eine gefettete Kastenform füllen.
Bei 175 Grad etwa 60-70 Minuten backen.

## MANDELKUCHEN

## GEFÜLLTE EIER

Hartgekochte Eier, nach Bedarf — Butter — Salz — feingehackte Kräuter (Thymian, Majoran, Basilikum, Estragon)

Die Eier halbieren, die Dotter herausnehmen und in einer Schüssel mit der Butter, dem Salz und den feingehackten Kräutern gut verrühren. Die Masse wieder in die Eihälften füllen.

---

in grams rather than cups

4. Scan the lists of ingredients. How are most of the ingredients measured? How does that compare to recipes in the United States?

5. What ingredients will you need to make the deviled eggs? What do you think **Kräuter** means? *(Hint: look at the words in parentheses that follow.)*

6. What ingredients will you need to make **Kartoffelsalat**? How does this differ from the way you would make potato salad?

7. What steps will you need to follow to make the **Kartoffelsalat**?

8. What ingredients will you need to make the **Mandelkuchen**? What do you think **Bittermandelöl** is?

9. What cooking temperature is given for the cake? The baking temperature for electric ovens is 175°. This number is much lower than the usual temperature needed for baking cakes. How can you explain this? (Remember what you learned in **Kapitel 7** about how temperature is measured in German-speaking countries.)

10. What are the steps in making deviled eggs?

11. Assume you are in Germany, and you have been asked to bring your favorite food to a party, along with the recipe. Choose something that is not too complicated to make and write out the recipe.

---

5. eggs, butter, salt, chopped herbs; Herbs
6. potatoes, bacon, onion, vinegar, salt, pepper, broth
7. Slice potatoes. Brown bacon and onions. Add vinegar, salt, pepper, potatoes and broth.
8. butter or margarine, sugar, vanilla sugar, eggs, almond flavor, flour, cornstarch, baking powder, almonds, chocolate chips
9. given in centigrade
10. Cut eggs in half, take out yolks and mix them with other ingredients. Fill eggs with yolk mixture.

**1** You will hear five different conversations taking place at Martin's party. Listen and decide which of the five topics below belongs with which conversation.

**a.** Filme      **b.** Musik      **c.** Essen      **d.** Sport      **e.** Schule

a-4; b-3; c-1; d-2; e-5

**2** Wer ist deine Lieblingsperson? Schreib alles über deine Lieblingsperson in dein Notizbuch. Wer ist diese Person? Wie alt ist sie? Wo wohnt sie? Wie sieht diese Person aus? Was macht diese Person in der Freizeit? Was für Interessen hat sie?

**3** **a.** Use the illustrations below to plan a weekend in Bietigheim and perhaps a trip to the nearby city of Stuttgart. First use the captions as clues to decide which activity is shown in each photo. Then write in German three activities that look interesting.

Im Restaurant

Musikpavillon im Kurpark Bad Cannstatt

Maurischer Garten in der Wilhelma

Königstraße: Stuttgarter Innenstadt

Badepark Ellental — das Freizeitvergnügen im Sommer

Schlittschuhlaufen in der Eissporthalle

Das große Reitturnier

**b.** Get together with a partner and invite him or her to come with you. Your partner will want to know exactly when you're going. Then he or she will accept, or decline and give a reason, for example: **Nein, danke! Ich schwimme nicht gern.** or **Ich kann nicht. Ich muß noch aufräumen.**

**c.** After you have agreed on at least three things to do together, write the activities and next to each, write a time expression telling when or in what order you will do them. Share your plans with the class.

**4** Du gehst bald zu einem Familientreffen (*family reunion*). Du willst den Verwandten etwas schenken. Was schenkst du ihnen? Zum Beispiel, was schenkst du deinem Onkel? Und deiner Kusine? Erzähl es deinem Partner! Danach sagt er dir, was er schenkt.

**5** You are taking a day trip to Stuttgart and would like to visit some interesting places. Go to the information center and find out how to get to the following places. Your partner will give you directions at the information counter.

Nach rechts und der rechts in Schillerstr. erste Straße hts und geaus bis zur nie Str. und t rechts.

**1.** ins Theater in der Altstadt
**2.** zum Rathaus
**3.** zum Alten Schloß
**4.** zur tri-bühne

2. Links herunter. Die fünfte Straße links, dann geradeaus. Rechts in die Eberhardstr., dann noch mal rechts.  3. Links herunter. Danach die vierte Straße links. Dann rechts in die Marktstr. und die erste Straße links.  4. Nach rechts und wieder rechts in die Schillerstr. Die erste Straße rechts und immer geradeaus bis zur Torstr., dann rechts.

Universität
Keplerstr.
Friedrichstr.
Lautenschlagerstr.
Schillerstr.
Mittl.-Schloßgarten
Stadtgarten
Schellingstr.
Th.-Heuss-Str.
Kronenstr.
Ober.-Schloßgarten
Domk. St. Eberhard
Bolzstr.
Post
Königsbau
Staatstheater
1
Kernerstr.
16
Kienestr.
Büchsenstr.
Stiftskirche
Schloß-pl.
Neues Schloß
Staatsgalerie
K.-Adenauer-Str.
19
Altes Schloß
Kronprinzstr.
Königstr.
Nadlerstr.
Marktstr.
Dorotheenstr.
Rathaus
Marktpl.
Marktstr.
Planie Str.
4
Torstr.
18
20
2
Leonhards-pl.
Hauptstätter Str.
Eberhardstr.
Hohenheimer Str.
Olgastr.
11

1 Staatstheater Stuttgart
2 Altes Schauspielhaus
3 Komödie im Marquardt
4 Theater der Altstadt
5 Renitenz-Theater
6 Wilhelma-Theater
7 Varieté-Theater Stuttgart
8 Theater im Westen
9 Theaterhaus Stuttgart
10 Die Rampe
11 tri-bühne

## 6  R O L L E N S P I E L

Everyone writes the name of the store that he or she created in Activity 16 on page 305 on a slip of paper and puts it into a small box. Draw out five stores. The people whose stores were chosen will line up at the front of the class with their store windows and play the **Verkäufer.** Bring in old clothing for the customers to try on. The rest of the class will divide into pairs and take turns visiting the stores on the **Einkaufsstraße.** When you are finished, draw more store names and continue your shopping spree. Remember to ask the salesperson about color and price. Try the clothes on and discuss the fit. Comment on your friend's clothing when he or she tries something on.

# KANN ICH'S WIRKLICH?

Can you offer help and explain what to do? (p. 297)

**1** How would you offer to help a classmate do some chores around the house? *Kann ich etwas für dich tun? Was kann ich für dich tun?*

**2** How would he or she respond if he or she needed you to

  **a.** pick up clothes     **c.** go to the store

  **b.** clean the windows   **d.** buy some tomatoes

*a. Du kannst für mich die Klamotten aufräumen.*
*b. Du kannst für mich die Fenster putzen.*
*c. Du kannst für mich einkaufen gehen.*
*d. Du kannst für mich Tomaten kaufen.*

Can you ask directions and say where something is located? (p. 299)

**3** How would you tell a classmate how to get to school from your house? How would you tell him or her where your school is located?

Can you make plans and invite someone to come along? (p. 302)

**4** How would your friend invite you to go to a concert at 8:30 on Saturday evening? How would you respond if

*Answers may vary. Some examples:*   *Kommst du mit?*

  **a.** you accept   *Ich will um halb neun ins Konzert gehen.*   *Ja, gern! / Das geht leider nicht; denn ich*

  **b.** you decline because you're going to a movie at 8:00   *gehe um 8 Uhr ins Kino.*

Can you talk about clothes in a clothing store? (p. 304)

**5** Write a conversation you would have with a salesperson in a clothing store. Talk about particular items of clothing, price, color, fit, and make some comments about how the clothing looks on you. *Answers will vary.*

Can you discuss gift ideas? (p. 305)

**6** How would you tell a classmate what you plan to give two family members for their birthdays?

*Answers will vary. Some examples: Ich schenke meinem Bruder eine CD. Ich schenke meiner Mutter ein Buch.*

Can you describe people and places? (p. 306)

**7** How would you describe your partner: how he or she looks, his or her interests, and where he or she lives? *Answers will vary.*

**8** How would you describe your living room and your kitchen? *Answers will vary.*

Can you say what you would like and that you do or don't want more? (p. 307)

**9** How would you say that you do or don't want more of the following items?

*a. Ich möchte noch eine Semmel. Nein danke! Keine Semmel mehr.*
*b. Ich möchte noch einen Apfel. Nein danke! Keinen Apfel mehr.*

  **a.** eine Semmel     **c.** ein Apfelsaft

  **b.** ein Apfel       **d.** ein Käsebrot

*c. Ich möchte noch einen Apfelsaft. Nein danke! Keinen Apfelsaft mehr.*
*d. Ich möchte noch ein Käsebrot. Nein danke! Kein Käsebrot mehr.*

Can you talk about what you did? (p. 309)

**10** How would a friend ask you what you did last weekend? How would you respond telling where you were, what you bought, what movies you saw, or what books you read?

*Answers may vary. Examples: Was hast du am Wochenende gemacht?*
*Ich war in der Innenstadt. Ich habe Bücher gekauft. Am Sonntag habe ich „Jurassic Park"*
*gesehen. Am Abend habe ich „Neuromancer" gelesen.*

## ERSTE STUFE
### INGREDIENTS FOR A RECIPE

**das Salz**   *salt*
**das Öl**   *oil*
**die Zwiebel, -n**   *onion*

**die Zitrone, -n**   *lemon*
**der Zimt**   *cinnamon*
**das Butterschmalz**   *shortening*

---

## ZWEITE STUFE

### MAKING PLANS

**die Stadt besichtigen**
  *to visit the city*
**in den Park gehen**
  *to go to the park*
**in den Zoo gehen**
  *to go to the zoo*
**Schlittschuh laufen**   *ice skate*
**joggen**   *to jog*
**ein Brettspiel spielen**   *to play a
  board game*

### TALKING ABOUT CLOTHING

**aus Seide**   *made of silk*
**aus Baumwolle**   *made of cotton*
**aus Leder**   *made of leather*
**gestreift**   *striped*
**gepunktet**   *polka-dotted*

---

## DRITTE STUFE
### DESCRIBING PLACES

**im Wohnzimmer**   *in the living
  room*
  **das Sofa, -s**   *sofa*
  **der Tisch, -e**   *table*
    **aus Holz**   *made of wood*
    **aus Kunststoff**
      *made of plastic*

**die Lampe, -n**   *lamp*
**der Teppich, -e**   *carpet*
**der Sessel, -**   *armchair*
**die Küche, -n**   *kitchen*
  **in der Küche**   *in the kitchen*
**der Eßtisch, -e**   *dining table*
**der Kühlschrank, ¨e**
  *refrigerator*

**der Herd, -e**   *stove*
**der Ofen, ¨**   *oven*
**das Spülbecken, -**   *sink*
**rund**   *round*
**eckig**   *with corners*
**modern**   *modern*

# SUMMARY OF FUNCTIONS

*Functions* are probably best defined as the ways in which you use a language for specific purposes. When you find yourself in specific situations, such as in a restaurant, in a grocery store, or at school, you will want to communicate with those around you. In order to do that, you have to "function" in the language so that you can be understood: you place an order, make a purchase, or talk about your class schedule.

Such functions form the core of this book. They are easily identified by the boxes in each chapter that are labeled SO SAGT MAN DAS! These functions are the building blocks you need to become a speaker of German. All the other features in the chapter—the grammar, the vocabulary, even the culture notes—are there to support the functions you are learning.

Here is a list of the functions presented in this book and the German expressions you will need in order to communicate in a wide range of situations. Following each function is the chapter and page number where it was introduced.

## SOCIALIZING

**Saying hello**   Ch. 1, p. 21

Guten Morgen!
Guten Tag!
Morgen!
Tag!      ⎤ *shortened forms*
Hallo!
Grüß dich!  ⎦ *informal*

**Saying goodbye**   Ch. 1, p. 21

Auf Wiedersehen!
Wiedersehen!   *shortened form*
Tschüs!
Tschau!   ⎤ *informal*
Bis dann!  ⎦

**Offering something to eat and drink**   Ch. 3, p. 70

Was möchtest du trinken?
Was möchte *(name)* trinken?
Was möchtet ihr essen?

**Responding to an offer**   Ch. 3, p. 70

Ich möchte *(beverage)* trinken.
Er/Sie möchte im Moment gar nichts.
Wir möchten *(food/beverage)*, bitte.

**Saying please**   Ch. 3, p. 72

Bitte!

**Saying thank you**   Ch. 3, p. 72

Danke!
Danke schön!
Danke sehr!

**Saying you're welcome**   Ch. 3, p. 72

Bitte!
Bitte schön!
Bitte sehr!

**Giving compliments**   Ch. 5, p. 127

Der/Die/Das *(thing)* sieht *(adjective)* aus!
Der/Die/Das *(thing)* gefällt mir.

**Responding to compliments**   Ch. 5, p. 127

Ehrlich?
Wirklich?
Nicht zu *(adjective)*?
Meinst du?

**Starting a conversation**   Ch. 6, p. 145

Wie geht's?
Wie geht's denn?   ⎤ *Asking how someone is doing*

Sehr gut!
Prima!
Danke, gut!
Gut!
Danke, es geht.
So lala.       *Responding to* **Wie geht's?**
Nicht schlecht.
Nicht so gut.
Schlecht.
Sehr schlecht.
Miserabel.

**Making plans**   Ch. 6, p. 150

Was willst du machen?      Ich will *(activity)*.
Wohin will *(person)* gehen?   Er/Sie will in(s) *(place)* gehen.

**Ordering food and beverages**   Ch. 6, p. 154

| | |
|---|---|
| Was bekommen Sie? Ja, bitte? | Ich bekomme *(food/beverage)*. |
| Was essen Sie? | Ein(e)(n) *(food)*, bitte. |
| Was möchten Sie? | Ich möchte *(food/beverage)*, bitte. |
| Was trinken Sie? | Ich trinke *(beverage)*. |
| Was nimmst du? | Ich nehme *(food/beverage)*. |
| Was ißt du? | Ich esse *(food)*. |

### Talking about how something tastes
Ch. 6, p. 156

| Wie schmeckt's? | Gut! |
| | Prima! |
| | Sagenhaft! |
| | Der/die/das *(food/beverage)* schmeckt lecker! |
| | Der/die/das *(food/beverage)* schmeckt nicht. |
| Schmeckt's? | Ja, gut! |
| | Nein, nicht so gut. |
| | Nicht besonders. |

### Paying the check   Ch. 6, p. 156

Hallo!
Ich will/möchte zahlen.
Das macht (zusammen) *(total)*.
Stimmt schon!

### Extending an invitation   Ch. 7, p. 174;
Ch. 11, p. 277

Willst du *(activity)*?
Wir wollen *(activity)*. Komm doch mit!
Möchtest du mitkommen?
Ich habe am *(day/date)* eine Party. Ich lade dich ein.
 Kannst du kommen?

### Responding to an invitation   Ch. 7, p. 174;
Ch. 11, p. 277

| Ja, gern! | |
| Toll! Ich komme gern mit. | |
| Aber sicher! | *accepting* |
| Natürlich! | |
| Das geht nicht. | |
| Ich kann leider nicht. | *declining* |

### Expressing obligations   Ch. 7, p. 175

Ich habe keine Zeit. Ich muß *(activity)*.

### Offering help   Ch. 7, p. 179

| Was kann ich für dich tun? | |
| Kann ich etwas für dich tun? | *asking* |
| Brauchst du Hilfe? | |
| Gut! Mach' ich! | *agreeing* |

### Asking what you should do   Ch. 8, p. 198

| Was soll ich für dich tun? | Du kannst für mich *(chore)*. |
| Wo soll ich *(thing/things)* kaufen? | Beim (Metzger/Bäcker). In der/Im *(store)*. |
| Soll ich *(thing/things)* in der/im *(store)* kaufen? | Nein, das kannst du besser in der/im *(store)* kaufen. |

### Telling someone what to do   Ch. 8, p. 199

Geh bitte *(action)*!
*(Thing/Things)* holen, bitte!

### Getting someone's attention   Ch. 9, p. 222

Verzeihung!
Entschuldigung!

### Offering more   Ch. 9, p. 230

Möchtest du noch etwas?
Möchtest du noch ein(e)(n) *(food/beverage)*?
Noch ein(e)(n) *(food/beverage)*?

### Saying you want more   Ch. 9, p. 230

Ja, bitte. Ich nehme noch ein(e)(n) *(food/beverage)*.
Ja, bitte. Noch ein(e)(n) *(food/beverage)*.
Ja, gern.

### Saying you don't want more   Ch. 9, p. 230

Nein, danke! Ich habe keinen Hunger mehr.
Nein, danke! Ich habe genug.
Danke, nichts mehr für mich.
Nein, danke, kein(e)(n) *(food/beverage)* mehr.

### Using the telephone   Ch. 11, p. 274

| Hier *(name)*. | |
| Hier ist *(name)*. | |
| Ich möchte bitte *(name)* sprechen. | *starting a conversation* |
| Kann ich bitte *(name)* sprechen? | |
| Tag! Hier ist *(name)*. | |
| Wiederhören! | |
| Auf Wiederhören! | *ending a conversation* |
| Tschüs! | |

### Talking about birthdays   Ch. 11, p. 278

| Wann hast du Geburtstag? | Ich habe am *(date)* Geburtstag. |
| | Am *(date)*. |

### Expressing good wishes   Ch. 11, p. 278

Alles Gute zu(m)(r) *(occasion)*!
Herzlichen Glückwunsch zu(m)(r) *(occasion)*!

## EXCHANGING INFORMATION

### Asking someone his or her name and giving yours   Ch. 1, p. 22

| Wie heißt du? | Ich heiße *(name)*. |
| Heißt du *(name)*? | Ja, ich heiße *(name)*. |

### Asking and giving someone else's name
Ch. 1, p. 22

| Wie heißt der Junge? | Der Junge heißt *(name)*. |
| Heißt der Junge *(name)*? | Ja, er heißt *(name)*. |
| Wie heißt das Mädchen? | Das Mädchen heißt *(name)*. |
| Heißt das Mädchen *(name)*? | Nein, sie heißt *(name)*. |

### Asking and telling who someone is   Ch. 1, p. 23

Wer ist das?     Das ist der/die *(name)*.

### Asking someone his or her age and giving yours   Ch. 1, p. 25

Wie alt bist du?     Ich bin *(number)* Jahre alt.
                     Ich bin *(number)*.
                     *(Number)*.
Bist du schon *(number)*?     Nein, ich bin *(number)*.

### Asking and giving someone else's age   Ch. 1, p. 25

Wie alt ist der Peter?     Er ist *(number)*.
Und die Monika? Ist
  sie auch *(number)*?     Ja, sie ist auch *(number)*.

### Asking someone where he or she is from and telling where you are from   Ch. 1, p. 28

Woher kommst du?     Ich komme aus *(place)*.
Woher bist du?     Ich bin aus *(place)*.
Bist du aus *(place)*?     Nein, ich bin aus *(place)*.

### Asking and telling where someone else is from   Ch. 1, p. 28

Woher ist *(person)*?     Er/sie ist aus *(place)*.
Kommt *(person)* aus
  *(place)*?     Nein, sie kommt aus *(place)*.

### Talking about how someone gets to school   Ch. 1, p. 31

Wie kommst
  du zur Schule?     Ich komme mit der/dem *(mode of transportation)*.

Kommt Ahmet zu
  Fuß zur Schule?     Nein, er kommt auch mit der/dem *(mode of transportation)*.
Wie kommt
  Ayla zur Schule?     Sie kommt mit der/dem *(mode of transportation)*.

### Talking about interests   Ch. 2, p. 46

Was machst du in
  deiner Freizeit?     Ich *(activity)*.
Spielst du *(sport/
  instrument/game)*?     Ja, ich spiele *(sport/ instrument/game)*.
                     Nein, *(sport/instrument/ game)* spiele ich nicht.
Was macht *(name)*?     Er/Sie spielt *(sport/ instrument/game)*.

### Saying when you do various activities   Ch. 2, p. 53

Was machst du nach
  der Schule?     Am Nachmittag *(activity)*.
                 Am Abend *(activity)*.
Und am Wochenende?     Am Wochenende *(activity)*.
Was machst du im
  Sommer?     Im Sommer *(activity)*.

### Talking about where you and others live   Ch. 3, p. 69

Wo wohnst du?     Ich wohne in *(place)*.
                  In *(place)*.
Wo wohnt der/die *(name)*?     Er/Sie wohnt in *(place)*.
                  In *(place)*.

### Describing a room   Ch. 3, p. 75

Der/Die/Das *(thing)* ist alt.
Der/Die/Das *(thing)* ist kaputt.
Der/Die/Das *(thing)* ist klein, aber ganz bequem.
Ist *(thing)* neu?     Ja, er/sie/es ist neu.

### Talking about family members   Ch. 3, p. 78

Ist das dein(e)
  *(family member)*?     Ja, das ist mein(e)
                     *(family member)*.

Und dein(e) *(family
  member)*? Wie heißt er/sie?     Er/Sie heißt *(name)*.
Wo wohnen deine *(family
  members)*?     In *(place)*.

### Describing people   Ch. 3, p. 80

Wie sieht *(person)* aus?     Er/sie hat *(color)* Haare und *(color)* Augen.

### Talking about class schedules   Ch. 4, p. 98

Welche Fächer hast du?     Ich habe *(classes)*.
Was hast du am *(day)*?     *(Classes)*.
Was hat die Katja am *(day)*?     Sie hat *(classes)*.
Welche Fächer habt ihr?     Wir haben *(classes)*.
Was habt ihr nach der Pause?     Wir haben *(classes)*.
Und was habt ihr am Samstag?     Wir haben frei!

### Using a schedule to talk about time   Ch. 4, p. 99

Wann hast du *(class)*?     Um *(hour)* Uhr *(minutes)*.
Was hast du um
  *(hour)* Uhr?     *(Class)*.
Was hast du von
  *(time)* bis *(time)*?     Ich habe *(class)*.

### Sequencing events   Ch. 4, p. 101

Welche Fächer
  hast du am *(day)*?     Zuerst hab' ich *(class)*, dann *(class)*, danach *(class)*, und zuletzt *(class)*.

### Talking about prices   Ch. 4, p. 107

Was kostet *(thing)*?     Er/sie kostet nur *(price)*.
Was kosten *(things)*?     Sie kosten *(price)*.
Das ist (ziemlich) teuer!
Das ist (sehr) billig!
Das ist (sehr) preiswert!

### Pointing things out   Ch. 4, p. 108

Wo sind die *(things)*?     Schauen Sie!
                     Dort!
                     Sie sind dort drüben!
                     Sie sind da hinten.
                     Sie sind da vorn.

## Expressing wishes when shopping   Ch. 5, p. 122

| | |
|---|---|
| Was möchten Sie? | Ich möchte ein(e)(n) (thing) sehen, bitte. |
| | Ich brauche ein(e)(n) (thing). |
| Was bekommen Sie? | Ein(e)(n) (thing), bitte. |
| Haben Sie einen Wunsch? | Ich suche ein(e)(n) (thing). |

## Describing how clothes fit   Ch. 5, p. 125

Es paßt prima.
Es paßt nicht.

## Talking about trying on clothes   Ch. 5, p. 131

Ich probiere den/die/das (item of clothing) an.
Ich ziehe den/die/das (item of clothing) an.

| If you buy it: | If you don't: |
|---|---|
| Ich nehme es. | Ich nehme es nicht. |
| Ich kaufe es. | Ich kaufe es nicht. |

## Telling time   Ch. 6, p. 146

| | |
|---|---|
| Wie spät ist es jetzt? | Es ist (time). |
| Wieviel Uhr ist es? | Es ist (time). |

## Talking about when you do things   Ch. 6, p. 146

| | |
|---|---|
| Wann gehst du (activity)? | Um (time). |
| Um wieviel Uhr (action) du? | Um (time). |
| Und du? Wann (action) du? | Um (time). |

## Talking about how often you do things   Ch. 7, p. 178

| | |
|---|---|
| Wie oft (action) du? | (Einmal) in der Woche. |
| Und wie oft mußt du (action)? | Jeden Tag. |
| | Ungefähr (zweimal) im Monat. |

## Explaining what to do   Ch. 7, p. 179

Du kannst für mich (action).

## Talking about the weather   Ch. 7, p. 183

| | |
|---|---|
| Wie ist das Wetter heute? | Heute regnet es. |
| | Wolkig und kühl. |
| Wie ist das Wetter morgen? | Sonnig, aber kalt. |
| Regnet es heute? | Ich glaube schon. |
| Schneit es am Abend? | Nein, es schneit nicht. |
| Wieviel Grad haben wir heute? | Ungefähr 10 Grad. |

## Talking about quantities   Ch. 8, p. 202

| | |
|---|---|
| Wieviel (food item) bekommen Sie? | 500 Gramm (food item). |
| | 100 Gramm, bitte. |

## Asking if someone wants anything else   Ch. 8, p. 203

Sonst noch etwas?
Was bekommen Sie noch?
Haben Sie noch einen Wunsch?

## Saying you want something else   Ch. 8, p. 203

Ich brauche noch ein(e)(n) (food/beverage/thing).
Ich bekomme noch ein(e)(n) (food/beverage/thing).

## Telling someone you don't need anything else   Ch. 8, p. 203

Nein, danke.
Danke, das ist alles.

## Giving a reason   Ch. 8, p. 206

Jetzt kann ich nicht, weil ich (reason).
Es geht nicht, denn ich (reason).

## Saying where you were   Ch. 8, p. 207

| | |
|---|---|
| Wo warst du heute morgen? | Ich war (place). |
| Wo warst du gestern? | Ich war (place). |

## Saying what you bought   Ch. 8, p. 207

| | |
|---|---|
| Was hast du gekauft? | Ich habe (thing) gekauft. |

## Talking about where something is located   Ch. 9, p. 222

| | |
|---|---|
| Verzeihung, wissen Sie, wo der/die/das (place) ist? | In der Innenstadt. Am (place name). In der (street name). |
| Wo ist der/die/das (place)? | Es tut mir leid. Das weiß ich nicht. |
| Entschuldigung! Weißt du, wo der/die/das (place) ist? | Keine Ahnung! Ich bin nicht von hier. |

## Asking for directions   Ch. 9, p. 226

Wie komme ich zu(m)(r) (place)?
Wie kommt man zu(m)(r) (place)?

## Giving directions   Ch. 9, p. 226

Gehen Sie geradeaus bis zu(m)(r) (place).
Nach rechts/links.
Hier rechts/links.

## Talking about what there is to eat and drink   Ch. 9, p. 229

| | |
|---|---|
| Was gibt es hier zu essen? | Es gibt (foods). |
| Und zu trinken? | Es gibt (beverage) und auch (beverage). |

## Talking about what you did in your free time   Ch. 10, p. 260

| | |
|---|---|
| Was hast du (time phrase) gemacht? | Ich habe (person/thing) gesehen. (book, magazine, etc.) gelesen. mit (person) über (subject) gesprochen. |

## Discussing gift ideas, Ch. 11, p. 282

Schenkst du *(person)*
ein(e)(n) *(thing)*
zu(m)(r) *(occasion)*?   Nein, ich schenke ihm/ihr
ein(e)(n) *(thing)*.

Was schenkst du *(person)*
zu(m)(r) *(occasion)*?   Ich weiß noch nicht. Hast
du eine Idee?

Wem schenkst du
den/die/das *(thing)*?   Ich schenke *(person)*
den/die/das *(thing)*.

# EXPRESSING ATTITUDES AND OPINIONS

## Asking for an opinion   Ch. 2, p. 55; Ch. 9, p. 232

Wie findest du *(thing/activity/place)*?

## Expressing your opinion   Ch. 2, p. 55; Ch. 9, p. 232

Ich finde *(thing/activity/place)* langweilig.
*(Thing/Activity/Place)* ist Spitze!
*(Activity)* macht Spaß!
Ich finde es toll, daß ...
Ich glaube, daß ...

## Agreeing   Ch. 2, p. 56

Ich auch!
Das finde ich auch!
Stimmt!

## Disagreeing   Ch. 2, p. 56

Ich nicht!
Das finde ich nicht!
Stimmt nicht!

## Commenting on clothes   Ch. 5, p. 125

Wie findest du den/die/
das *(clothing item)*?   Ich finde ihn/sie/es
*(adjective)*.
Er/Sie/Es gefällt mir (nicht).

## Expressing uncertainty, not knowing   Ch. 5, p. 125; Ch. 9, p. 222

Ich bin nicht sicher.
Ich weiß nicht.
Keine Ahnung!

## Expressing regret   Ch. 9, p. 222

Es tut mir leid.

# EXPRESSING FEELINGS AND EMOTIONS

## Asking about likes and dislikes   Ch. 2, p. 48; Ch. 4, p. 102; Ch. 10, p. 250

Was *(action)* du gern?
*(Action)* du gern?
Magst du *(things/activities)*?
Was für *(things/activities)* magst du?

## Expressing likes   Ch. 2, p. 48; Ch. 4, p. 102; Ch. 10, p. 250

Ich *(action)* gern.
Ich mag *(things/activities)*.
*(Thing/Activities)* mag ich (sehr/furchtbar) gern.

## Expressing dislikes   Ch. 2, p. 48; Ch. 10, p. 250

Ich *(action)* nicht so gern.
Ich mag *(things/action)* (überhaupt) nicht.

## Talking about favorites   Ch. 4, p. 102

Was ist dein
Lieblings*(category)*?   Mein Lieblings*(category)*
ist *(thing)*.

## Responding to good news   Ch. 4, p. 104

Toll!
Das ist prima!
Nicht schlecht.

## Responding to bad news   Ch. 4, p. 104

Schade!
So ein Pech!
So ein Mist!
Das ist sehr schlecht!

## Expressing familiarity   Ch. 10, p. 252

Kennst du
*(person/place/thing)*?   Ja, sicher!
Ja, klar! or
Nein, den/die/das kenne
ich nicht.
Nein, überhaupt nicht.

## Expressing preferences and favorites   Ch. 10, p. 253

(Siehst) du gern ...?   Ja, aber ... (sehe) ich lieber.
Und am liebsten (sehe) ich ...

(Siehst) du lieber
... oder ...?   Lieber ... Aber am liebsten
(sehe) ich ...

Was (siehst) du
am liebsten?   Am liebsten (sehe) ich ...

# ADDITIONAL VOCABULARY

This list includes additional vocabulary that you may want to use to personalize activities. If you can't find the words you need here, try the German–English and English–German vocabulary sections beginning on page 340.

## SPORT UND INTERESSEN
### (SPORTS AND INTERESTS)

angeln  *to fish*
Baseball spielen  *to play baseball*
Brettspiele spielen  *to play board games*
fotografieren  *to take photographs*
Gewichte heben  *lift weights*
Handball spielen  *to play handball*
joggen  *to jog*
kochen  *to cook*
malen  *to paint*
Münzen sammeln  *to collect coins*
nähen  *to sew*
radfahren  *to ride a bike*
reiten  *to ride (a horse)*
Rollschuh fahren  *to roller skate*
segeln  *to sail*
Skateboard fahren  *to ride a skateboard*
Ski laufen  *to (snow) ski*
stricken  *to knit*
Tischtennis spielen  *to play table tennis*
Videospiele spielen  *to play video games*

## INSTRUMENTE
### (INSTRUMENTS)

die Blockflöte, -n  *recorder*
das Cello (Violoncello), -s  *cello*
die Flöte, -n  *flute*
die Geige, -n  *violin*
die Harfe, -n  *harp*
die Klarinette, -n  *clarinet*
der Kontrabaß, (pl) Kontrabässe  *double bass*
die Mandoline, -n  *mandolin*
die Mundharmonika, -s  *harmonica*
die Oboe, -n  *oboe*
die Posaune, -n  *trombone*
das Saxophon, -e  *saxophone*
das Schlagzeug, -e  *drums*
die Trompete, -n  *trumpet*
die Tuba, (pl) Tuben  *tuba*

## GETRÄNKE  (BEVERAGES)

die Limo, -  *lemon-flavored drink*
ein Glas Milch  *a glass of milk*
ein Glas Tee  *a glass of tea*
eine Tasse, -n Kaffee  *a cup of coffee*

## SPEISEN  (FOODS)

die Ananas, -  *pineapple*
der Apfelstrudel, -  *apple strudel*
die Banane, -n  *banana*
die Birne, -n  *pear*
der Chip, -s  *potato chip*
der Eintopf  *stew*
die Erdbeere, -n  *strawberry*
die Erdnußbutter  *peanut butter*
das Gebäck  *baked goods*
die Gurke, -n  *cucumber*
die Himbeere, -n  *raspberry*
der Joghurt, -  *yogurt*
die Karotte, -n  *carrot*
die Marmelade, -n  *jam, jelly*
die Mayonnaise  *mayonaise*
die Melone, -n  *melon*
das Müsli  *muesli (cereal)*
die Nuß, (pl) Nüsse  *nut*
die Orange, -n  *orange*
das Plätzchen, -  *cookie*
die Pommes frites (pl)  *french fries*
der Spinat  *spinach*
die Zwiebel, -n  *onion*

## MÖBEL *(FURNITURE)*

das Bild, -er *picture*
der Computer, - *computer*
die Lampe, -n *lamp*
der Sessel, - *armchair*
das Sofa, -s *sofa*
der Teppich, -e *carpet, rug*
der Tisch, -e *table*
der Vorhang, ¨e *curtain*

## KLEIDUNGSSTÜCKE *(CLOTHING)*

der Anzug, ¨e *suit*
der Badeanzug, ¨e *swimsuit*
der Blazer, - *blazer*
das Halstuch, ¨er *scarf*
der Handschuh, -e *glove*
der Hut, ¨e *hat*
die Krawatte, -n *tie*
der Mantel, ¨ *coat*
die Mütze, -n *cap*
die Sandalen (pl) *sandals*
der Schal, -s *shawl*
die Strumpfhose, -n *panty hose*
die Weste, -n *vest*

## FAMILIE *(FAMILY)*

der Halbbruder, ¨ *half brother*
die Halbschwester, -n *half sister*
der Stiefbruder, ¨ *stepbrother*
die Stiefmutter, ¨ *stepmother*
die Stiefschwester, -n *stepsister*
der Stiefvater, ¨ *stepfather*

## FARBEN *(COLORS)*

beige *beige*
bunt *colorful*
gepunktet *polka-dotted*
gestreift *striped*
golden *gold*
lila *purple*
orange *orange*
rosa *pink*
silbern *silver*
türkis *turquoise*

## FÄCHER *(SCHOOL SUBJECTS)*

Algebra *algebra*
Band *band*
Chemie *chemistry*
Chor *chorus*
Französisch *French*
Hauswirtschaft *home economics*
Informatik *computer science*
Italienisch *Italian*
Japanisch *Japanese*
Orchester *orchestra*
Russisch *Russian*
Spanisch *Spanish*
Sozialkunde *social studies*
Werken *shop*
Wirtschaftskunde *economics*

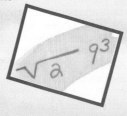

## HAUSARBEIT *(HOUSEWORK)*

das Auto polieren *to polish the car*
das Auto waschen *to wash the car*
den Fußboden kehren *to sweep the floor*
den Müll wegtragen *to take out the trash*
putzen *to clean*
Staub wischen *to dust*
saubermachen *to clean*
die Wäsche waschen *to do the laundry*
    trocknen *to dry*
    aufhängen *to hang*
    legen *to fold*
    bügeln *to iron*
    einräumen *to put away*

ADDITIONAL VOCABULARY

## HAUSTIERE    (PETS)

die Eidechse, -n  *lizard*
der Fisch, -e  *fish*
der Frosch, ¨e  *frog*
der Hamster, -  *hamster*
der Hase, -n  *hare*
der Kanarienvogel, ¨  *canary*
die Maus, ¨e  *mouse*
das Meerschweinchen, -  *guinea pig*
der Papagei, -en  *parrot*
das Pferd, -e  *horse*
die Schildkröte, -n  *turtle*
die Schlange, -n  *snake*
das Schwein, -e  *pig*
der Vogel, ¨  *bird*

## WETTER    (WEATHER)

feucht  *damp*
gewittrig  *stormy*
halbbedeckt  *partly cloudy*
heiter  *bright*
kühl  *cool*
neblig  *foggy*
nieslig  *drizzly*
trüb  *murky*
windig  *windy*

## IN DER STADT
(PLACES AROUND TOWN)

die Brücke, -n  *bridge*
die Bücherei, -en  *library*
der Flughafen, (pl) Flughäfen  *airport*
das Fremdenverkehrsamt, (pl) Fremdenverkehrsämter
    *tourist office*
der Frisiersalon, -s  *beauty shop*
das Krankenhaus, (pl) Krankenhäuser  *hospital*
der Park, -s  *park*
die Polizei  *police
    station*
der Zoo, -s  *zoo*

## ZUM DISKUTIEREN
(TOPICS TO DISCUSS)

die Armut  *poverty*
die Gesundheit  *health*
der Präsident  *the president*
die Politik  *politics*
die Reklame  *advertising*
die Umwelt  *the environment*
das Verbrechen  *crime*
der Wehrdienst  *military service*
der Zivildienst  *alternate service*

## GESCHENKIDEEN
(GIFT IDEAS)

das Bild, -er  *picture*
die Kette, -n  *chain*
der Ohrring, -e  *earring*
die Puppe, -n  *doll*
das Puppenhaus, ¨er  *dollhouse*
der Ring, -e  *ring*
... aus Silber  *made of silver*
... aus Gold  *made of gold*
die Schokolade  *chocolate*
das Spielzeug, -e  *toy*

# ERDKUNDE  (GEOGRAPHY)

Here are some terms you will find on German-language maps:

## LÄNDER  (STATES)

Most of the states in the United States (**die Vereinigten Staaten**) have the same spelling in German that they have in English. Listed below are those states that have a different spelling.

| | |
|---|---|
| Kalifornien | *California* |
| Neumexiko | *New Mexico* |
| Nordkarolina | *North Carolina* |
| Norddakota | *North Dakota* |
| Südkarolina | *South Carolina* |
| Süddakota | *South Dakota* |

## STAATEN  (COUNTRIES)

| | |
|---|---|
| Ägypten | *Egypt* |
| Argentinien | *Argentina* |
| Brasilien | *Brazil* |
| Indien | *India* |
| Indonesien | *Indonesia* |
| Kanada | *Canada* |
| Mexiko | *Mexico* |
| Rußland | *Russia* |
| die Vereinigten Staaten | *The United States* |

## KONTINENTE  (CONTINENTS)

| | |
|---|---|
| Afrika | *Africa* |
| die Antarktik | *Antarctica* |
| Asien | *Asia* |
| Australien | *Australia* |
| Europa | *Europe* |
| Nordamerika | *North America* |
| Südamerika | *South America* |

## MEERE  (BODIES OF WATER)

| | |
|---|---|
| der Atlantik | *the Atlantic* |
| der Golf von Mexiko | *the Gulf of Mexico* |
| der Indische Ozean | *the Indian Ocean* |
| das Mittelmeer | *the Mediterranean* |
| der Pazifik | *the Pacific* |
| das Rote Meer | *the Red Sea* |
| das Schwarze Meer | *the Black Sea* |

## GEOGRAPHICAL TERMS

| | |
|---|---|
| der Breitengrad | *latitude* |
| die Ebene, -n | *plain* |
| der Fluß, (pl) Flüsse | *river* |
| das ... Gebirge | *the ... mountains* |
| die Grenze, -n | *border* |
| die Hauptstadt, ¨e | *capital* |
| der Kontinent, -e | *continent* |
| das Land, ¨er | *state* |
| der Längengrad | *longitude* |
| das Meer, -e | *ocean, sea* |
| der Nordpol | *the North Pole* |
| der See, -n | *lake* |
| der Staat, -en | *country* |
| der Südpol | *the South Pole* |
| das Tal, ¨er | *valley* |

# DEUTSCHE NAMEN *(GERMAN NAMES)*

Some German names are listed in the **Vorschau,** but here are some additional ones that you will
hear when you visit a German-speaking country.

## MÄDCHEN *(GIRLS)*

| | | |
|---|---|---|
| Andrea | Gabriele (Gabi) | Marta |
| Angela, Angelika | Gertrud (Trudi(e)) | Martina |
| Anja | Gisela | Meike |
| Anna | Grete | Michaela |
| Anneliese | Gudrun | Monika |
| Annette | Hannelore | Nicole |
| Antje | Heidi/Heidemarie | Petra |
| Barbara | Heike | Regina |
| Bärbel | Helga | Renate |
| Beate | Hilde | Roswitha |
| Birgit | Hildegard | Rotraud |
| Brigitte | Ilse | Sabine |
| Britta | Ina | Sara |
| Christa | Inge | Silke |
| Christiane | Ingrid | Simone |
| Christine | Irmgard | Stephanie |
| Claudia | Jennifer | Susanne |
| Connie | Julie | Silvia |
| Cordula | Jutta | Tanja |
| Dorothea | Karin | Ulrike (Uli) |
| Dorothee | Katharina | Ursel |
| Elfriede | Katja | Ursula (Uschi) |
| Elisabeth (Lisa) | Katrin | Ute |
| Elke | Kirstin | Veronika |
| Erika | Liselotte (Lotte) | Waltraud |
| Eva | Marie | |

## JUNGEN *(BOYS)*

| | | |
|---|---|---|
| Alexander | Hans-Georg | Martin |
| Andreas | Hans-Jürgen | Mathias |
| Axel | Hartmut | Max |
| Bernd(t) | Hauke | Michael |
| Bernhard | Heinrich | Norbert |
| Bruno | Heinz | Otto |
| Christian | Heinz-Dieter | Patrick |
| Christoph | Helmar | Paul |
| Daniel | Helmut | Peter |
| Detlev(f) | Ingo | Philipp |
| Dieter | Jan | Rainer (Reiner) |
| Dietmar | Jens | Ralf |
| Dirk | Joachim | Reinhard |
| Eberhard | Jochen | Reinhold |
| Erik | Johann | Rolf |
| Felix | Johannes | Rudi |
| Frank | Jörg | Rüdiger |
| Franz | Josef | Rudolf |
| Friedrich | Jürgen | Sebastian |
| Fritz | Karl | Stefan (Stephan) |
| Georg | Karl-Heinz | Thomas |
| Gerd | Klaus | Udo |
| Gerhard | Konrad | Ulf |
| Gottfried | Kurt | Ulrich (Uli) |
| Gregor | Lars | Uwe |
| Günter | Lothar | Volker |
| Gustav(f) | Lutz | Werner |
| Hannes | Manfred | Wilhelm (Willi) |
| Hans | Markus | Wolfgang |

# GRAMMAR SUMMARY
## NOUNS AND THEIR MODIFIERS

In German, nouns (words that name a person, place, or thing) are grouped into three classes or genders: masculine, feminine, and neuter. All nouns, both persons and objects, fall into one of these groups. There are words used with nouns that signal the class of the noun. One of these is the definite article. In English there is one definite article: *the*. In German, there are three, one for each class: **der, die,** and **das**.

### THE DEFINITE ARTICLE

#### SUMMARY OF DEFINITE ARTICLES

|  | NOMINATIVE | ACCUSATIVE | DATIVE |
|---|---|---|---|
| *Masculine* | der | den | dem |
| *Feminine* | die | die | der |
| *Neuter* | das | das | dem |
| *Plural* | die | die | den |

When the definite article is combined with a noun, a noun phrase is formed. Noun phrases that are used as subjects are in the nominative case. Nouns that are used as direct objects or the objects of certain prepositions (such as **für**) are in the accusative case. Nouns that are indirect objects, the objects of certain prepositions (such as **mit, bei**), or the objects of special verbs that you will learn about in Level 2, are in the dative case. Below is a summary of the definite articles combined with nouns to form noun phrases.

#### SUMMARY OF NOUN PHRASES

|  | NOMINATIVE | ACCUSATIVE | DATIVE |
|---|---|---|---|
| *Masculine* | der Vater<br>der Ball | den Vater<br>den Ball | dem Vater<br>dem Ball |
| *Feminine* | die Mutter<br>die Kassette | die Mutter<br>die Kassette | der Mutter<br>der Kassette |
| *Neuter* | das Mädchen<br>das Haus | das Mädchen<br>das Haus | dem Mädchen<br>dem Haus |

# THE INDEFINITE ARTICLE

Another type of word that is used with nouns is the *indefinite article:* **ein, eine, ein** in German, *a, an* in English. There is no plural form of **ein**.

## SUMMARY OF INDEFINITE ARTICLES

|  | NOMINATIVE | ACCUSATIVE | DATIVE |
|---|---|---|---|
| *Masculine* | ein | einen | einem |
| *Feminine* | eine | eine | einer |
| *Neuter* | ein | ein | einem |
| *Plural* | — | — | — |

# THE NEGATING WORD KEIN

The word **kein** is also used with nouns and means *no, not,* or *not any*. Unlike the **ein**-words, **kein** has a plural form.

|  | NOMINATIVE | ACCUSATIVE | DATIVE |
|---|---|---|---|
| *Masculine* | kein | keinen | keinem |
| *Feminine* | keine | keine | keiner |
| *Neuter* | kein | kein | keinem |
| *Plural* | keine | keine | keinen |

# THE POSSESSIVES

These words also modify nouns and tell you *whose* object or person is being referred to (*my* car, *his* book, *her* mother). These words have the same endings as **kein**.

## SUMMARY OF POSSESSIVES

|  | BEFORE MASCULINE NOUNS | | | BEFORE FEMININE NOUNS | | BEFORE NEUTER NOUNS | | BEFORE PLURAL NOUNS | |
|---|---|---|---|---|---|---|---|---|---|
|  | NOM | ACC | DAT | NOM & ACC | DAT | NOM & ACC | DAT | NOM & ACC | DAT |
| *my* | mein | meinen | meinem | meine | meiner | mein | meinem | meine | meinen |
| *your* | dein | deinen | deinem | deine | deiner | dein | deinem | deine | deinen |
| *his* | sein | seinen | seinem | seine | seiner | sein | seinem | seine | seinen |
| *her* | ihr | ihren | ihrem | ihre | ihrer | ihr | ihrem | ihre | ihren |

Other possessive adjectives that you will learn more about in Level 2 are

| | |
|---|---|
| unser | *our* |
| euer | *your* (informal, plural) |
| ihr | *their* |
| Ihr | *your* (formal) |

# NOUN PLURALS

Noun class and plural forms are not always predictable. Therefore, you must learn each noun together with its article (**der, die, das**) and with its plural form. As you learn more nouns, however, you will discover certain patterns. Although there are always exceptions to these patterns, you may find them helpful in remembering the plural forms of many nouns.

Most German nouns form their plurals in one of two ways: some nouns add endings in the plural; some add endings and/or change the sound of the stem vowel in the plural, indicating the sound change with the umlaut (¨). Only the vowels **a, o, u,** and the diphthong **au** can take the umlaut. If a noun has an umlaut in the singular, it keeps the umlaut in the plural. Most German nouns fit into one of the following five plural groups.

1. Nouns that do not have any ending in the plural. Sometimes they take an umlaut.
   **NOTE:** There are only two feminine nouns in this group: **die Mutter** and **die Tochter.**

   | | | |
   |---|---|---|
   | der Bruder, die Brüder | der Schüler, die Schüler | das Fräulein, die Fräulein |
   | der Lehrer, die Lehrer | der Vater, die Väter | das Mädchen, die Mädchen |
   | der Onkel, die Onkel | die Mutter, die Mütter | das Poster, die Poster |
   | der Mantel, die Mäntel | die Tochter, die Töchter | das Zimmer, die Zimmer |

2. Nouns that add the ending **-e** in the plural. Sometimes they also take an umlaut.
   **NOTE:** There are many one-syllable words in this group.

   | | | |
   |---|---|---|
   | der Bleistift, die Bleistifte | der Sohn, die Söhne | das Jahr, die Jahre |
   | der Freund, die Freunde | die Stadt, die Städte | das Spiel, die Spiele |
   | der Paß, die Pässe | | |

3. Nouns that add the ending **-er** in the plural. Whenever possible, they take an umlaut, i.e., when the noun contains the vowels **a, o,** or **u,** or the diphthong **au**. **NOTE:** There are no feminine nouns in this group. There are many one-syllable words in this group.

   | | |
   |---|---|
   | das Buch, die Bücher | das Haus, die Häuser |
   | das Fach, die Fächer | das Land, die Länder |

4. Nouns that add the ending **-en** or **-n** in the plural. These nouns never add an umlaut.
   **NOTE:** There are many feminine nouns in this group.

   | | | |
   |---|---|---|
   | der Herr, die Herren | die Klasse, die Klassen | die Tante, die Tanten |
   | der Junge, die Jungen | die Karte, die Karten | die Wohnung, die Wohnungen |
   | die Briefmarke, die Briefmarken | der Name, die Namen | die Zahl, die Zahlen |
   | die Familie, die Familien | der Vetter, die Vettern | die Zeitung, die Zeitungen |
   | die Farbe, die Farben | die Küche, die Küchen | |
   | die Frau, die Frauen | die Schwester, die Schwestern | |

   Feminine nouns ending in **-in** add the ending **-nen** in the plural.

   | | |
   |---|---|
   | die Freundin, die Freundinnen | die Verkäuferin, die Verkäuferinnen |
   | die Lehrerin, die Lehrerinnen | |

5. Nouns that add the ending **-s** in the plural. These nouns never add an umlaut. **NOTE:** There are many words of foreign origin in this group.

   | | |
   |---|---|
   | der Kuli, die Kulis | das Auto, die Autos |
   | die Kamera, die Kameras | das Hobby, die Hobbys |

## SUMMARY OF PLURAL ENDINGS

| Group | 1 | 2 | 3 | 4 | 5 |
|---|---|---|---|---|---|
| Ending: | - | -e | -er | -(e)n | -s |
| Umlaut: | sometimes | sometimes | always | never | never |

# PRONOUNS

## PERSONAL PRONOUNS

|  | | NOMINATIVE | ACCUSATIVE | DATIVE |
|---|---|---|---|---|
| Singular | | | | |
| 1st person | | ich | mich | mir |
| 2nd person | | du | dich | dir |
| | *m.* | er | ihn | ihm |
| 3rd person | *f.* | sie | sie | ihr |
| | *n.* | es | es | ihm |
| Plural | | | | |
| 1st person | | wir | uns | uns |
| 2nd person | | ihr | euch | euch |
| 3rd person | | sie | sie | ihnen |
| *you* (formal, sing. & pl.) | | Sie | Sie | Ihnen |

## DEFINITE ARTICLES AS DEMONSTRATIVE PRONOUNS

The definite articles can be used as demonstrative pronouns, giving more emphasis to the sentences than the personal pronouns **er, sie, es**. Note that these demonstrative pronouns have the same forms as the definite articles:

**Wer bekommt *den* Cappuccino? *Der* ist für mich.**

|  | NOMINATIVE | ACCUSATIVE |
|---|---|---|
| *Masculine* | der | den |
| *Feminine* | die | die |
| *Neuter* | das | das |
| *Plural* | die | die |

# INTERROGATIVES

## INTERROGATIVE PRONOUNS

|  | PEOPLE | | THINGS | |
|---|---|---|---|---|
| *Nominative* | wer? | *who?* | was? | *what?* |
| *Accusative* | wen? | *whom?* | was? | *what?* |
| *Dative* | wem? | *to, for whom?* | | |

# OTHER INTERROGATIVES

| | | | | | |
|---|---|---|---|---|---|
| **wann?** | *when?* | **wie viele?** | *how many?* | **welche?** | *which?* |
| **warum?** | *why?* | **wo?** | *where?* | **was für (ein)?** | *what kind of (a)?* |
| **wie?** | *how?* | **woher?** | *from where?* | **(eine)** | |
| **wieviel?** | *how much? how many?* | **wohin?** | *to where?* | **(einen)** | |

# WORD ORDER

## POSITION OF VERBS IN A SENTENCE

| | |
|---|---|
| *The conjugated verb is in* **first** *position in:* | **yes/no** *questions (questions that do not begin with an interrogative)*<br>**Trinkst du Kaffee?**<br>**Spielst du Tennis?**<br>**Möchtest du ins Konzert gehen?**<br><br>*both formal and informal commands*<br>**Kommen Sie bitte um 2 Uhr!**<br>**Geh doch mit ins Kino!** |
| *The conjugated verb is in* **second** *position in:* | *statements with normal word order*<br>**Wir spielen heute Volleyball.**<br>*statements with inverted word order*<br>**Heute spielen wir Volleyball.**<br><br>*questions that begin with an interrogative*<br>**Wohin gehst du?**<br>**Woher kommst du?**<br>**Was macht er?** |
| *The conjugated verb is in* **second** *position and the infinitive or past participle is* **final** *in:* | *statements with modals*<br>**Ich möchte heute ins Kino fahren.**<br>*statements in conversational past*<br>**Ich habe das Buch gelesen.** |
| *The conjugated verb is in* **final** *position in:* | *clauses following the verb* **wissen**<br>**Ich weiß, wo das Hotel ist.**<br>*clauses that begin with* **weil** *or* **daß**<br>**Ich gehe nicht ins Kino, weil ich kein Geld habe.**<br>**Ich glaube, daß er Rockmusik gern hört.** |

**NOTE:** In Level 2 you will learn more about word order in clauses with modals and verbs with separable prefixes:

Ich komme morgen nicht, weil ich zu Hause helfen muß.
Ich weiß nicht, wer heute morgen angerufen hat.

## POSITION OF NICHT IN A SENTENCE

| To negate the entire sentence, as close to end of sentence as possible: | Er fragt seinen Vater | nicht. | |
|---|---|---|---|
| Before a separable prefix: | Ich rufe ihn | nicht | an. |
| Before any part of a sentence you want to negate, contrast, or emphasize: | Er kommt | nicht | heute. (Er kommt morgen.) |
| Before part of a sentence that answers the questions **wo?** | Ich wohne | nicht | in Berlin. |

# VERBS

## PRESENT TENSE VERB FORMS

| | | REGULAR | -eln VERBS | STEM ENDING WITH t/d | STEM ENDING WITH s/ß |
|---|---|---|---|---|---|
| INFINITIVES | | spiel -en | bastel -n | find -en | heiß -en |
| PRONOUNS | | stem + ending | stem + ending | stem + ending | stem + ending |
| *I* | ich | spiel -e | bastl -e | find -e | heiß -e |
| *you* | du | spiel -st | bastel -st | find -est | heiß -t |
| *he* *she* *it* | er sie es | spiel -t | bastel -t | find -et | heiß -t |
| *we* | wir | spiel -en | bastel -n | find -en | heiß -en |
| *you* (plural) | ihr | spiel -t | bastel -t | find -et | heiß -t |
| *they* | sie | spiel -en | bastel -n | find -en | heiß -en |
| *you* (formal) | Sie | spiel -en | bastel -n | find -en | heiß -en |

**NOTE:** There are important differences between the verbs in the above chart:

1. Verbs ending in -**eln** (**basteln, segeln**) drop the **e** of the ending -**eln** in the **ich**-form: **ich bastle, ich segle** and add only -**n** in the **wir**-, **sie**-, and **Sie**-forms. These forms are always identical with the infinitive: **basteln, wir basteln, sie basteln, Sie basteln.**

2. Verbs with a stem ending in **d** or **t**, such as **finden**, add an **e** before the ending in the **du**-form (**du findest**) and the **er**- and **ihr**-forms (**er findet, ihr findet**).

3. All verbs with stems ending in an **s**-sound (**heißen**) add only -**t** in the **du**-form: **du heißt.**

# VERBS WITH A STEM-VOWEL CHANGE

There are a number of verbs in German that change their stem vowel in the **du-** and **er/sie-** forms. A few verbs, such as **nehmen** (*to take*), have a change in the consonant as well. You cannot predict these verbs, so it is best to learn each one individually. They are usually irregular only in the **du-** and **er/sie-** forms.

|          | e → i | | | e → ie | | a → ä | |
|----------|-------|------|--------|------|------|--------|----------|
|          | essen | geben | nehmen | lesen | sehen | fahren | einladen |
| *ich*    | esse  | gebe  | nehme  | lese  | sehe  | fahre  | lade ein |
| *du*     | ißt   | gibst | nimmst | liest | siehst| fährst | lädst ein|
| *er, sie*| ißt   | gibt  | nimmt  | liest | sieht | fährt  | lädt ein |
| *wir*    | essen | geben | nehmen | lesen | sehen | fahren | laden ein|
| *ihr*    | eßt   | gebt  | nehmt  | lest  | seht  | fahrt  | ladet ein|
| *sie*    | essen | geben | nehmen | lesen | sehen | fahren | laden ein|
| *Sie*    | essen | geben | nehmen | lesen | sehen | fahren | laden ein|

# SOME IMPORTANT IRREGULAR VERBS: HABEN, SEIN, WISSEN

|          | haben | sein | wissen |
|----------|-------|------|--------|
| *ich*    | habe  | bin  | weiß   |
| *du*     | hast  | bist | weißt  |
| *er, sie*| hat   | ist  | weiß   |
| *wir*    | haben | sind | wissen |
| *ihr*    | habt  | seid | wißt   |
| *sie*    | haben | sind | wissen |
| *Sie*    | haben | sind | wissen |

# MODAL (AUXILIARY) VERBS

The verbs **können, müssen, sollen, wollen, mögen** (and the **möchte-**forms) are usually used with an infinitive at the end of the sentence. If the meaning of that infinitive is clear, it can be left out: **Du mußt sofort nach Hause!** (**Gehen** is understood and omitted.)

|          | können  | müssen | sollen | wollen | mögen | möchte   |
|----------|---------|--------|--------|--------|-------|----------|
| *ich*    | kann    | muß    | soll   | will   | mag   | möchte   |
| *du*     | kannst  | mußt   | sollst | willst | magst | möchtest |
| *er, sie*| kann    | muß    | soll   | will   | mag   | möchte   |
| *wir*    | können  | müssen | sollen | wollen | mögen | möchten  |
| *ihr*    | könnt   | müßt   | sollt  | wollt  | mögt  | möchtet  |
| *sie*    | können  | müssen | sollen | wollen | mögen | möchten  |
| *Sie*    | können  | müssen | sollen | wollen | mögen | möchten  |

# VERBS WITH SEPARABLE PREFIXES

Some verbs have separable prefixes: prefixes that separate from the conjugated verbs and are moved to the end of the sentence.

| | INFINITIVE: aussehen |
|---|---|
| ich sehe ... aus | Ich sehe heute aber sehr schick aus! |
| du siehst ... aus | Du siehst heute sehr fesch aus! |
| er/sie/es sieht ... aus | Sieht sie immer so modern aus? |
| | Sieht dein Zimmer immer so unordentlich aus? |
| wir sehen ... aus | Wir sehen heute sehr lustig aus. |
| ihr seht ... aus | Ihr seht alle so traurig aus. |
| sie sehen ... aus | Sie sehen sehr schön aus. |
| Sie sehen ... aus | Sie sehen immer so ernst aus. |

Here are the separable-prefix verbs you learned in Level 1.

| | | |
|---|---|---|
| abheben | anziehen | einkaufen |
| abräumen | auflegen | einladen |
| anprobieren | ausgehen | einstecken |
| anrufen | aussehen | mitkommen |

# COMMAND FORMS

| *Regular Verbs* | gehen | kommen |
|---|---|---|
| Persons you address with **du** (singular) with **Sie** (sing & pl) | Geh! Gehen Sie! | Komm! Kommen Sie! |

| *Separable-prefix Verbs* | mitkommen | anrufen | einladen | anziehen | ausgehen |
|---|---|---|---|---|---|
| | Komm mit! Kommen Sie mit! | Ruf an! Rufen Sie an! | Lad ein! Laden Sie ein! | Zieh an! Ziehen Sie an! | Geh aus! Gehen Sie aus! |

| *Stem-changing Verbs* | essen | nehmen | geben | sehen | fahren |
|---|---|---|---|---|---|
| | Iß! Essen Sie! | Nimm! Nehmen Sie! | Gib! Geben Sie! | Sieh! Sehen Sie! | Fahr! Fahren Sie! |

**NOTE:** The vowel changes **e → i** and **e → ie** are maintained in the **du**-form of the command. The umlaut vowel change **a → ä** does not occur in the command form.

# EXPRESSING FUTURE TIME

You can use the present tense with a time expression to talk about events that will take place in the future:

**Wir fahren morgen nach Berlin.**

**Am Wochenende besuche ich meine Großeltern.**

# PAST TENSE VERB FORMS

In this book, you learned the following verbs to express past time:

| WEAK VERBS | | STRONG VERBS | |
|---|---|---|---|
| PRESENT TENSE FORM | PAST TENSE FORM | PRESENT TENSE FORM | PAST TENSE FORM |
| Er macht das. Sie kauft das. | Er hat das gemacht. Sie hat das gekauft. | Er spricht oft. Sie sieht das nicht. Du liest gern. | Er hat oft gesprochen. Sie hat das nicht gesehen. Du hast gern gelesen. |

In addition you learned the simple past form of the verb **sein**:

### THE SIMPLE PAST OF SEIN

| | |
|---|---|
| *ich* | war |
| *du* | warst |
| *er, sie* | war |
| *wir* | waren |
| *ihr* | wart |
| *sie* | waren |
| *Sie* (formal) | waren |

# THE CONVERSATIONAL PAST

In Level 2 you will learn more about how to express past events. In general, German verbs are divided into two groups: weak verbs and strong verbs. Weak verbs usually follow a regular pattern, as do the English verb forms *play, played, has played*. In German, weak verbs add a **ge-** and a **-t** to the verb stem to form the past participle. Strong verbs usually have irregularities, like the English verb forms *run, ran, has run* and *go, went, has gone*. Look at the past tense verb forms chart above and compare the present tense forms of the verbs on the left with the past tense forms on the right. As a rule of thumb, verbs that are irregular (stem-changing verbs) in the present tense are irregular, or strong, in the past tense.

In Level 1 you have learned that **haben** is used as the helping verb with the past participle. In Level 2 you will also learn some verbs that use **sein** as their helping verb, such as the verb **gehen** in the following example:

**Ich gehe oft ins Kino.    Ich bin gestern ins Kino gegangen.**

# PRINCIPAL PARTS OF THE VERBS PRESENTED IN LEVEL 1*

This list includes all verbs included in the **Wortschatz** sections of this textbook. Both strong and weak verbs, including verbs with separable prefixes, stem-vowel changes, and other irregularities are listed. Though most of the verbs in this list form the conversational past with **haben**, a few of the verbs you have learned take **sein** in the present perfect tense. You will work with these verbs and learn more about them in Level 2.

## STRONG VERBS

| INFINITIVE | PRESENT (stem vowel change and/or seperable prefix) | PAST PARTICIPLE | MEANING |
|---|---|---|---|
| abheben | hebt ab | abgehoben | to lift (the receiver) |
| anrufen | ruft an | angerufen | to call up |
| anziehen | zieht an | angezogen | to put on (clothes) |
| aussehen | sieht aus | ausgesehen | to look, appear |
| bekommen | bekommt | bekommen | to get, receive |
| einladen | lädt ein | eingeladen | to invite |
| essen | ißt | gegessen | to eat |
| fahren | fährt | (ist) gefahren | to drive, ride |
| finden | findet | gefunden | to find |
| geben | gibt | gegeben | to give |
| gefallen | gefällt | gefallen | to like, be pleasing to |
| gehen | geht | (ist) gegangen | to go |
| gießen | gießt | gegossen | to pour; to water |
| haben | hat | gehabt | to have |
| heißen | heißt | geheißen | to be called |
| helfen | hilft | geholfen | to help |
| kommen | kommt | (ist) gekommen | to come |
| lesen | liest | gelesen | to read |
| nehmen | nimmt | genommen | to take |
| scheinen | scheint | geschienen | to shine |
| schreiben | schreibt | geschrieben | to write |
| schwimmen | schwimmt | (ist) geschwommen | to swim |
| sehen | sieht | gesehen | to see |
| sein | ist | (ist) gewesen | to be |
| sprechen | spricht | gesprochen | to speak |
| trinken | trinkt | getrunken | to drink |
| tun | tut | getan | to do |
| wissen | weiß | gewußt | to know |

*The past participles in this chart are for reference only. Most of them will be taught in Level 2.

| | | | |
|---|---|---|---|
| abräumen | räumt ab | abgeräumt | *to clear away* |
| anprobieren | probiert an | anprobiert | *to try on* |
| auflegen | legt auf | aufgelegt | *to hang up (receiver)* |
| aufräumen | räumt auf | aufgeräumt | *to pick up/clean room* |
| basteln | bastelt | gebastelt | *to do arts and crafts* |
| besichtigen | besichtigt | besichtigt | *to sight see* |
| besuchen | besucht | besucht | *to visit* |
| brauchen | braucht | gebraucht | *to need* |
| decken | deckt | gedeckt | *to set (the table)* |
| füttern | füttert | gefüttert | *to feed* |
| einkaufen | kauft ein | eingekauft | *to shop* |
| einstecken | steckt ein | eingesteckt | *to insert (coin)* |
| glauben | glaubt | geglaubt | *to believe* |
| holen | holt | geholt | *to get* |
| hören | hört | gehört | *to hear* |
| kaufen | kauft | gekauft | *to buy* |
| kennen | kennt | *gekannt | *to know* |
| kosten | kostet | gekostet | *to cost* |
| machen | macht | gemacht | *to do or make* |
| mähen | mäht | gemäht | *to mow* |
| meinen | meint | gemeint | *to think, be of the opinion* |
| passen | paßt | gepaßt | *to fit* |
| putzen | putzt | geputzt | *to clean* |
| regnen | regnet | geregnet | *to rain* |
| sagen | sagt | gesagt | *to say* |
| sammeln | sammelt | gesammelt | *to collect* |
| schauen | schaut | geschaut | *to look (at)* |
| schenken | schenkt | geschenkt | *to give (a gift)* |
| schmecken | schmeckt | geschmeckt | *to taste* |
| sortieren | sortiert | sortiert | *to sort* |
| spielen | spielt | gespielt | *to play* |
| spülen | spült | gespült | *to wash dishes* |
| suchen | sucht | gesucht | *to look for* |
| tanzen | tanzt | getanzt | *to dance* |
| telefonieren | telefoniert | telefoniert | *to call (on the phone)* |
| verbringen | verbringt | *verbracht | *to spend time* |
| wählen | wählt | gewählt | *to dial* |
| wandern | wandert | (ist) gewandert | *to hike* |
| wohnen | wohnt | gewohnt | *to live* |
| zahlen | zahlt | gezahlt | *to pay* |
| zeichnen | zeichnet | gezeichnet | *to draw* |

*Although weak, these verbs have a vowel change in the past participle.

# GUIDE TO PRONUNCIATION FEATURES

Learning to pronounce new and different sounds can be one of the most challenging aspects of learning a new language. You must first learn to hear new sounds. Then you have to learn to use your tongue, lips, jaw, and facial muscles in new ways to produce the sounds. Pronunciation can also be a very important aspect of learning a language; poor pronunciation can often interfere with communication. Although it is not necessary to learn to speak "like a native," it is important that you learn to make the sounds in order to communicate clearly and effectively.

The pronunciation features treated in this book are intended to be as helpful as possible. The descriptions of the German sound system used throughout this book focus on spelling and how different letters or letter combinations are usually pronounced. The **Aussprache** sections are meant to familiarize you with the German sound system, to help you recognize individual sounds when they occur, and to enable you to "sound out" new words and pronounce them correctly. Luckily, in German there is a much closer relationship between spelling and pronunciation than there is in English. There are, of course, exceptions, and for the most conspicuous ones, we have provided examples to remind you that these pronunciation rules are usually true, but not always.

Whenever possible, a familiar sound in an English word is compared to the German sound being introduced. All German sounds are designated by bold faced print, and all English sounds are designated by italics. For sounds not occurring in English, we have provided brief descriptions of how to produce the sounds. In general, German vowels require more tension in the facial muscles and less movement of the tongue than English. The vowels usually do not glide, which means the sounds are more pure or continuous.

The thought of learning a whole new sound system might be intimidating at first, but practice will be your key to success. Here are some hints that might make learning pronunciation seem a little easier:

**Don't be afraid to guess the pronunciation of an unfamiliar German word!**
In general, German words are pronounced just like they are written. By looking at the spelling of a German word you can often guess the pronunciation. Regardless of whether you are dealing with a short word, like **Katze,** or a much longer word, such as **Donaudampfschiffahrtsgesellschaftskapitän**, you should be able to sound out the word using the spelling as a guide.

**Don't be afraid to make pronunciation mistakes!**
Learning a foreign language takes time, and you are going to make some mistakes along the way. Making German sounds requires the use of different facial muscles and, just like riding a bike, it takes practice to get it right.

Pronunciation and dictation exercises are found at the end of the **Dritte Stufe** in each chapter. The symbols within slashes below, for example /e/, are from the *International Phonetic Alphabet* and represent sounds.

| CHAPTER | PAGE | LETTER/ COMBINATION | IPA SYMBOL | EXAMPLE |
|---------|------|---------------------|------------|---------|
| Ch. 1 | p. 33 | the long vowel **ä** | /e/ | Mädchen |
| | | the long vowel **e** | /e/ | zehn |
| | | the long vowel **ü** | /y/ | Grüß |
| | | the long vowel **ö** | /ø/ | hören |
| | | the letter **w** | /v/ | wer |
| | | the letter **v** | /f/ | vier |
| Ch. 2 | p. 57 | the vowel combination **ie** | /i/ | spielen |
| | | the diphthong **ei** | /ai/ | schreiben |
| | | the letter **j** | /j/ | Junge |
| | | the letter **z** | /ts/ | zur |
| Ch. 3 | p. 81 | the long vowel **o** | /o/ | Obst |
| | | the long vowel **u** | /u/ | Stuhl |
| | | the letter **s** | /z/ | sieben |
| | | the letter **s** | /s/ | Preis |
| | | the letters **ss** | /s/ | müssen |
| | | the letter **ß** | /s/ | Straße |
| Ch. 4 | p. 109 | the diphthong **eu** | /ɔy/ | teuer |
| | | the diphthong **äu** | /ɔy/ | Verkäufer |
| | | the diphthong **au** | /au/ | bauen |
| | | the final **b** | /p/ | gelb |
| | | the final **d** | /t/ | Rad |
| | | the final **g** | /k/ | sag |
| Ch. 5 | p. 133 | the short vowel **i** | /ɪ/ | schick |
| | | the short vowel **ä** | /ɛ/ | lässig |
| | | the short vowel **e** | /ɛ/ | Bett |
| | | the short vowel **a** | /a/ | haben |
| | | the letter combination **sch** | /ʃ/ | Schule |
| | | the letter combination **st** | /ʃt/ | Stiefel |
| | | the letter combination **sp** | /ʃp/ | Spitze |
| Ch. 6 | p. 157 | the letter combination **ch** | /ç/ | ich |
| | | the letter combination **ch** | /x/ | doch |
| | | the letter **r** | /r/ | rund |
| | | the final **er** | /ɐ/ | super |

| CHAPTER | PAGE | LETTER/ COMBINATION | IPA SYMBOL | EXAMPLE |
|---|---|---|---|---|
| Ch. 7 | p. 185 | the short vowel **o** | /ɔ/ | wolkig |
| | | the short vowel **u** | /ʊ/ | uns |
| | | the letter **l** | /l/ | Lehrer |
| | | the letter combination **th** | /t/ | Mathe |
| | | the letter combination **pf** | /pf/ | Pfennig |
| Ch. 8 | p. 209 | the short vowel **ö** | /œ/ | können |
| | | the short vowel **ü** | /Y/ | Stück |
| | | review diphthong **ei** | /ai̯/ | Eier |
| | | review vowel combination **ie** | /i/ | wieder |
| | | review letter **z** | /ts/ | Zeit |
| Ch. 9 | p. 233 | review long vowel **ü** | /y/ | für |
| | | review long vowel **ö** | /ø/ | blöd |
| | | review letter **s** | /z/ | Senf |
| | | review letter **s** | /s/ | es |
| | | review letters **ss** | /s/ | besser |
| | | review letter **ß** | /s/ | Spaß |
| Ch. 10 | p. 261 | review short vowel **o** | /ɔ/ | Onkel |
| | | review long vowel **o** | /o/ | Oma |
| | | review short vowel **u** | /ʊ/ | Gruppe |
| | | review long vowel **u** | /u/ | Musik |
| | | review combination **ch** | /ç/ | Pech |
| | | review combination **ch** | /x/ | Buch |
| Ch. 11 | p. 285 | review **r** | /r/ | Bruder |
| | | review **er** | /ɐ/ | meiner |
| | | review vowel **a** | /a/ | Vater |
| | | review diphthong **eu** | /ɔy/ | heute |
| | | review diphthong **äu** | /ɔy/ | Verkäufer |
| | | review diphthong **au** | /au̯/ | Strauß |
| Ch. 12 | p. 309 | review letter **w** | /v/ | weiß |
| | | review letter **v** | /f/ | viel |
| | | review letter **j** | /j/ | Juli |
| | | review short vowel **ä** | /ɛ/ | häßlich |
| | | review short vowel **e** | /ɛ/ | Sessel |
| | | review long vowel **ä** | /e/ | Käse |
| | | review long vowel **e** | /e/ | dem |

# GERMAN-ENGLISH VOCABULARY

This vocabulary includes almost all words in this textbook, both active (for production) and passive (for recognition only). Active words and phrases are practiced in the chapter and are listed in the **Wortschatz** section at the end of each chapter. You are expected to know and be able to use active vocabulary. An entry in black, heavy type indicates that the word or phrase is active. All other words—some in the opening dialogs, in exercises, in optional and visual material, in the **Landeskunde, Zum Lesen** and **Kann ich's wirklich?** sections—are for recognition only. The meaning of these words and phrases can usually be understood from the context or may be looked up in this vocabulary.

With some exceptions, the following are not included: proper nouns, forms of verbs other than the infinitive, and forms of determiners other than the nominative.

Nouns are listed with definite article and plural form, when applicable. The numbers in the entries refer to the chapter where the word or phrase first appears or where it becomes an active vocabulary word. Vocabulary from the preliminary chapter is followed by a page reference only.

The following abbreviations are used in this vocabulary: adj (adjective), pl (plural), pp (past participle), sep (seperable-prefix verb), sing (singular), and conj (conjunction).

## A

ab *from, starting at,* 4; ab und zu *now and then,* 10
**der Abend, -e** *evening,* 2; **am Abend** *in the evening,* 2; jeden Abend *every evening,* 10
abends *evenings,* 6
**der Abenteuerfilm, -e** *adventure movie,* 10
**aber** *but,* 3; Aber sicher! *Sure!,* 11
**abheben** (sep) *to pick up,* 11; **den Hörer abheben** *to pick up the receiver,* 11
**abräumen** (sep) *to clean up, clear off,* 7; **den Tisch abräumen** *to clear the table,* 7
abschmecken (sep) *to taste,* 12
abwaschen (sep) *to wash up,* 12
**Ach** Oh!, 2; **Ach ja!** *Oh yeah!,* 1; Ach so! *Oh, I see!,* 1; Ach was! *Give me a break!,* 5; Ach wo! *Oh no!,* 4
**acht** *eight,* 1
achten *to pay attention (to),* 11
Achtung! *Attention!,* 6
**achtzehn** *eighteen,* 1
**achtzig** *eighty,* 3
der Ackerbau *agriculture,* 6
**der Actionfilm, -e** *action movie,* 10
das Adreßbuch, ̈er *address book,* 11
ähnlich *similar,* 11
die Ahnung: Keine Ahnung! *I have no idea!,* 9
aktiv *active,* 12
die Aktivität, -en *activity,* 12
aktuell *current,* 5
die Algebra *algebra,* 4

alle *all, everyone,* 2
allein *alone,* 8
aller *of all,* 8
allerdings *admittedly,* 7
alles *everything,* 2; Alles klar! *O.K.!,* 10; **Alles Gute zum Geburtstag!** *Best wishes on your birthday!,* 11; **Alles Gute zum Muttertag!** *Happy Mother's Day!,* 11
allgemein *general,* 4; im allgemeinen *in general,* 10
der Alptraum, ̈e *nightmare,* 10
als *as,* 6; als letzter *the last,* 12
also *well then,* 2; Also, auf geht's! *Well, let's go!,* 9
**alt** *old,* 3
älter *older,* 3
das Altpapier *recycled paper,* 7
die Altstadt, ̈e *historical part of downtown,* 12
**am=an dem** *at the,* 2; **am ...platz** *on ... Square,* 9; **am Abend** *in the evening,* 2; **am ersten (Juli)** *on the first (of July),* 11; **am liebsten** *most of all,* 10; Am liebsten sehe ich Krimis. *I like detective movies the best.,* 10; **am Montag** *on Monday,* 4; **am Nachmittag** *in the afternoon,* 2; **am Wochenende** *on the weekend,* 2
der Amerikaner, - *American (male),* 9
die Amerikanerin, -nen *American (female),* 9
amerikanisch *American (adj),* 8
**die Ampel, -n** *traffic light,* 9; an der Ampel *at the traffic light,* 9;

**bis zur Ampel** *until you get to the traffic light,* 9
amtlich *official,* 9
an *to, at,* 4; an der Ampel *at the traffic light,* 9; ansonsten *otherwise,* 11; an welchem Tag? *on which day?,* 11
die Ananas, - *pineapple,* 8
das Andenken, - *souvenir,* 11
**andere** *other,* 2
ändern *to change,* 9
anfallen (sep): alles was anfällt *anything that comes up,* 12
**das Angebot, -e** *offer,* 5; Angebot der Woche *weekly special,* 8
angefangen (pp) *started,* 7
angeln *to fish,* 10
**anprobieren** (sep) *to try on,* 5
anrösten *to brown,* 12
**anrufen** (sep) *to call* (phone), 11; Ruf mal an! *Give me a call!,* 11
anschauen (sep) *to look at,* 6
ansehen (sep) *to look at,* 9
ansonsten *otherwise,* 11
anstrengend *exhausting,* 7
die Antwort, -en *answer,* 1
antworten *to answer,* 2
der Anwalt, ̈e *lawyer,* 10
die Anwendung, -en *application,* 1
die Anzeige, -n *ad,* 10
**anziehen** (sep) *to put on, wear,* 5
der Anzug, ̈e *suit,* 5
**der Apfel, ̈** *apple,* 8
**der Apfelkuchen, -** *apple cake,* 6
das Apfelküchle - *(see p. 298),* 12
**der Apfelsaft, ̈e** *apple juice,* 3; **ein Glas Apfelsaft** *a glass of apple juice,* 3

der Apfelstrudel, - *apple strudel*, 8
**der Apparat, -e** *telephone*, 11
**der April** *April*, 7
die Arbeit *work*, 7
die Arbeitsliste, -n *work list*, 12
ärgerlich *annoying*, 6
**die Armbanduhr, -en** *wristwatch*, 11
der Ärmel, - *sleeve*, 5
der Ast, ⸚e *branch*, 8
   **auch** *also*, 1; **Ich auch.** *Me too.*, 2
   auf *on; to*, 1; Also, *auf geht's! Well, let's go!*, 9; **auf dem Land** *in the country*, 3; auf dem Weg *on the way*, 6; auf der Straße *on the street*, 9; auf einer Fete *at a party*, 12; auf englisch *in English*, 10; auf Schritt und Tritt *all the time*, 10; **Auf Wiederhören!** *Goodbye! (on the telephone)*, 11; **Auf Wiedersehen!** *Goodbye!*, 1; auf deutsch *in German*, 9; auf der rechten Seite *on the right (hand) side*, 9
   aufdringlich *pushy*, 7
der Aufdruck, -e *design*, 5
   aufhängen (sep) *to hang up*, 12; die Wäsche aufhängen *to hang up the laundry*, 7
   aufhören (sep) *to stop*, 3
   **auflegen** (sep) *to hang up (the telephone)*, 11; **den Hörer auflegen** *to hang up (the receiver)*, 11
die Aufnahme, -n *admittance*, 2
   aufpassen: Paß auf! *Watch out!*, 6; **Paßt auf!** *Pay attention!*, p. 8
   **aufräumen (sep)** *to clean up*, 7; **mein Zimmer aufräumen** *to clean my room*, 7; **meine Klamotten aufräumen** *to pick up my clothes*, 7
**der Aufschnitt** *cold cuts*, 8
**das Auge, -n:** *eye*; **blaue (grüne, braune) Augen** *blue (green, brown) eyes*, 3
der August *August*, 7
   aus *from*, 1; *made of*, 9; **aus Baumwolle** *made of cotton*, 12; aus Holz *made of wood*, 12; aus Kunststoff *made of plastic*, 12; aus Leder *made of leather*, 12; aus Seide *made of silk*, 12
   ausbacken (sep) *to bake until done*, 12
der Ausdruck, ⸚e *expression*, p. 8
   ausgeben (sep) *to spend (money)*, 8
   ausgehen (sep) *to go out*, 11
der Ausländer, - *foreigner*, 9

ausleihen (sep) *to rent*, 10
auspacken (sep) *to unpack*, 8
ausräumen (sep) *to clean, clear out*, 12; den Geschirrspüler ausräumen *to unload the dishwasher*, 12
ausreichend *sufficient, passing (grade)*, 4
die Aussage, -n *statement*, 9
   **aussehen** (sep) *to look like, to appear*, 3; **Der Rock sieht ... aus.** *The skirt looks...*, 5; **er/sie sieht aus** *he/she looks like*, 5; **Wie sieht er aus?** *What does he look like?*, 3; **Wie sehen sie aus?** *What do they look like?*, 3
   aussprechen (sep) *to pronounce*, 1; richtig aussprechen *to pronounce correctly*, 1
die Ausstellung, -en *exhibit*, 10
der Austauschschüler, - *exchange student*, 9
die Auswahl *selection*, 11
   auswählen (sep) *to select*, 4
**das Auto, -s** *car*, 1; Auto fahren *to drive (a car)*, 9; **mit dem Auto** *by car*, 1
   außerdem *in addition*, 7
   außerhalb *outside of*, 6

## B

backen *to bake*, 8
**der Bäcker, -** *baker*, 8; **beim Bäcker** *at the baker's*, 8
**die Bäckerei, -en** *bakery*, 8
das Backpulver *baking powder*, 12
das Bad, ⸚er *pool*, 12
   **baden** *to swim*, 6; **baden gehen** *to go swimming*, 6
der Badepark, -s *park with swimming facilities*, 12
**der Bahnhof, ⸚e** *train station*, 9
   bald *soon*, 11
der Ball, ⸚e *ball*, 12
der Ballon, -s *balloon*, 11
die Banane, -n *banana*, 3
**die Bank, -en** *bank*
das Basilikum *basil*, 12
das Basisstück, -e *basic item*, 5
**der Basketball, ⸚e** *basketball*, 2
   **basteln** *to do crafts*, 2
   bauen *to build*, 5
**die Baumwolle** *cotton*, 5; **aus Baumwolle** *made of cotton*, 12
   bayrisch *Bavarian (adj)*, 9
   beantworten *to answer*, 9
der Becher, - *cup*, 6
der Bedarf *need*, 12
   bedeuten *to mean*, 10; Was bedeutet ... ? *What does...mean?*, p. 8

bedruckt *printed*, 5
befriedigend *satisfactory (grade)*, 4
beginnen *to begin*, 11
begleiten *to accompany*, 9
begonnen (pp) *begun*, 10
begrüßen *to greet*, 1
behalten *to keep*, 6
bei *at*, 1; bei meinen Freunden *at my friends'*, 10; **beim Bäcker** *at the baker's*, 8; **beim Metzger** *at the butcher's*, 8; **Hier bei ...** *The ...residence.*, 11
beide *both*, 5
beim=bei dem *at the*, 2
das Beispiel, -e *example, model*, p. 5; zum Beispiel *for example*, 10
bekannt *familiar*, 12
der Bekannte *acquaintance (male)*, 7
**bekommen** *to get, to receive*, 4; **Ich bekomme ...** *I'll have...*, 6; **Was bekommen Sie?** *What would you like?*, 5
belegen: mit Tomaten belegen *to top with tomatoes*, 8
beliebt *popular*, 6
die Belletristik *fiction*, 10
bemalt *painted*, 11
die Bemerkung, -en *remark*, 4
benutzen *to use*, 11
Benutzung, -en *use*, 4
**bequem** *comfortable*, 3
die Beratung, -en *advice*, 11
bereit *ready*, 10
bereiten *to prepare*, 12
der Berg, -e *mountain*, 10
der Bericht, -e *report*, 10
der Berliner, - *here: jelly-filled roll*, 9
die Berliner (pl) *residents of Berlin*, 9
berühmt *famous*, 7
beschäftigt *occupied, busy*, 8
beschattet *tailed, shadowed*, 10
beschreiben *to describe*, 9
die Beschreibung, -en *description*, 12
**besetzt** *busy (telephone)*, 11
besichtigen *to visit, to sightsee*, 9; **die Stadt besichtigen** *to visit the city*, 12
besonder *special*, 7
**besonders** *especially*, 8; **besonders gern** *especially like*, 10
besprechen *to discuss*, 12
**besser** *better*, 8
best *best*, 1
**bestimmt** *certainly, definitely*, 5
bestreuen *to sprinkle*, 8
**besuchen** *to visit*, 2; **Freunde besuchen** *to visit friends*, 2
**das Bett, -en** *bed*, 3; **das Bett machen** *to make the bed*, 7
die Beurteilung, -en *evaluation*, 4
der Beutel, - *bag*, 8

bevor *before*, 2
bewohnbar *inhabitable*, 3
die Bewölkung *cloudiness*, 7
bieten: anbieten (sep) *to offer*, 7
das Bild, -er *picture*, 11
**billig** *cheap*, 4
**bin: ich bin** *I am*, 1
die Biologie (Bio) *biology*, 4
die Biologielehrerin, -nen *biology teacher (female)*, 1
die Birne, -n *pear*, 8
bis *until*, 1; **Bis bald!** *See you soon!*, 9; **Bis dann!** *Till then! See you later!*, 1; **bis zum ...platz** *until you get to ... Square*, 9; **bis zur ...straße** *until you get to ... Street*, 9; **bis zur Ampel** *until you get to the traffic light*, 9
**bist: du bist** *you are*, 1
bitte *please*, 3; Bitte? *Excuse me?*, 1; **Bitte (sehr, schön)!** *You're (very) welcome!*, 3; **Bitte?** *Yes? Can I help you?*, 5
**bißchen: ein bißchen** *a little*, 5; **ein bißchen mehr** *a little more*, 8;
blättrig *flaky*, 8
blau *blue*, 3; **in Blau** *in blue*, 5
bleiben *to stay*, 7
**der Bleistift, -e** *pencil*, 4
der Blick, -e *view*, 7
**blöd** *dumb*, 2
**blond** *blonde*, 3
der Blouson, -s *short jacket*, 5
**bloß** *only*, 4
die Blume, -n *flower*, 7; **die Blumen gießen** *to water the flowers*, 7
das Blumengeschäft, -e *florist shop*, 8
der Blumenkohl *cauliflower*, 8
**der Blumenstrauß, ⁻e** *bouquet of flowers*, 11
**die Bluse, -n** *blouse*, 5
blutig *bloody*, 10
die Bockwurst, ⁻e *bockwurst*, 6
die Bowle, -n *punch*, 12
die Bratkartoffeln (pl) *fried potatoes*, 6
die Bratwurst, ⁻e *bratwurst*, 8
**brauchen** *to need*, 5; **ich brauche ...** *I need...*, 5; **ich brauche noch ...** *I also need...*, 8
die Brauerei, -en *brewery*, 7
**braun** *brown*, 3; **in Braun** *in brown*, 5
**das Brettspiel, -e** *board game*, 2; **ein Brettspiel spielen** *to play a board game*, 12
**die Brezel, -n** *pretzel*, 8
der Brief, -e *letter*, 2
**die Briefmarke, -n** *stamp*, 2;

**Briefmarken sammeln** *to collect stamps*, 2
**die Brille, -n** *a pair of glasses*, 3
bringen *to bring*, 1
**das Brot, -e** *bread*, 8; **Ich habe Brot gekauft.** *I bought bread.*, 8
das Brötchen, - *hard roll*, 8
**der Bruder, ⁻** *brother*, 3
die Brühe, -n *broth*, 12
**brutal** *brutal, violent*, 10
**brutalste** *the most brutal*, 10
**das Buch, ⁻er** *book*, 4
die Buchhandlung, -en *bookstore*, 10
bügeln *to iron*, 7
der Bummel *stroll*, 9
**das Bundesland, ⁻er** *federal state (German)*, 1
bunt *colorful*, 6
**der Bus, -se** *bus*, 1; **mit dem Bus** *by bus*, 1
**die Butter** *butter*, 8
**das Butterschmalz** *shortening*, 12

## C

das Café, -s *café*, 6; **in ein Café/ins Café gehen** *to go to a/the café*, 6
der Cappuccino, -s *cappuccino*, 6
**die CD, -s** *compact disc*, 11
der Champignon, -s *mushroom*, 8
die Chance, -n *chance*, 10
**Chanukka** *Hanukkah*, 11; **Frohes Chanukka-Fest!** *Happy Hanukkah!*, 11
charmant *charming*, 3
die Chemie *chemistry*, 4
chic *smart (looking)*, 12
der Chor, ⁻e *choir*, 4
die Clique, -n *clique*, 10
der Club, -s *club*, 2
**die Cola, -s** *cola*, 3
**die Comics** (pl) *comic books*, 2; **Comics sammeln** *to collect comics*, 2
**die Couch, -en** *couch*, 3
**der Cousin, -s** *cousin (male)*, 3
die Currywurst, ⁻e *curry sausage*, 6

## D

da *there*, 1; **da drüben** *over there*, 4; **da hinten** *there in the back*, 4; **da vorn** *there in the front*, 4
dabei *with*, 4
das Dach, ⁻er *roof*, 7
dafür *for it*, 5
dahin *there*, 10
die Dame, -n *lady*, 5
damenhaft *ladylike*, 5
damit *with it; so that*, 7
**danach** *after that*, 4

**Danke!** *thank you!*, 3; **Danke (sehr, schön)!** *Thank you (very much)!*, 3
**dann** *then*, 4
darauf *on it*, 12
darüber *about it*, 5
**das** *the* (n); *that*, 1; **Das ist ...** *That's...*, 1; **Das ist alles.** *That's all.*, 8; **Das sind...** *Those are...* (with plurals), 3
**daß** *that* (conj), 9; **ich finde es gut/schlecht, daß ...** *I think it's good/bad that...*, 9; **ich finde, daß ...** *I think that...*, 9; ich glaube, daß ... *I think that...*, 9
dasselbe *the same*, 11
dauern *to last*, 9
dazugeben *to add*, 12
**decken: den Tisch decken** *to set the table*, 7
**dein** *your*, 3; **deinem Vater** *to, for your father*, 11; **deiner Mutter** *to, for your mother*, 11
**dem** *the* (masc, neuter, dat case), 11
**den** *the* (masc, acc case), 5
denken *to think*, 3
**denn** (particle), 1
**denn** *because, for* (conj), 8
**der** *the* (m), 1; *to the* (fem, dat case), 11
des *of the*, 4
desillusioniert *disillusioned*, 10
**deutsch** *German* (adj), 9
**Deutsch** *German* (language), p. 4; (school subject), 4; **Ich habe Deutsch.** *I have German.*, 4
der Deutsche, -n *German (male)*, 2
die Deutsche *German (female)*, 2
die Deutschen (pl) *German people*, 2
**der Deutschlehrer, -** *German teacher (male)*, 1
**die Deutschlehrerin, -nen** *German teacher (female)*, 1
der Dezember *December*, 7
**dich** *you* (acc), 7
**die** *the*, 1
**der Dienstag** *Tuesday*, 4
dies- *this, these*, 2
das Diktat, -e *dictation*, 1
der Dinosaurier, - *dinosaur*, 10
dir *to you*, 3
direkt *direct(ly)*, 6
der Dirigent, -en *conductor (music)*, 6
**die Disko, -s** *disco*, 6; **in eine Disko gehen** *to go to a disco*, 6
diskutieren *to discuss*, 10
**DM = Deutsche Mark** *German mark* (monetary unit), 4
**doch** (particle), 1
Doch! *Oh yes!*, 2

der **Donnerstag** *Thursday,* 4
  donnerstags *Thursdays,* 6
  **doof** *dumb,* 10
  **dort** *there,* 4; **dort drüben** *over there,* 4;
die Dose, -n *can,* 7
das Dotter, - *egg yolk,* 12
  **drei** *three,* 1
  **dreimal** *three times,* 7
  **dreißig** *thirty,* 3
  **dreiundzwanzig** *twenty-three,* 3
  **dreizehn** *thirteen,* 1
  drin *in it,* 9
  dritte *third,* 8
  **du** *you* (sing), 2
  **dumm** *dumb, stupid,* 10
  dunkelblau *dark blue,* 5; **in Dunkelblau** *in dark blue,* 5
  durch *through,* 9; *divided by,* 3
der Durst *thirst,* 6


**E**

  eben (particle), 5
  echt *real,* 5
  **eckig** *with corners,* 12
  **ehrlich** *honestly,* 5
das **Ei**, -er *egg,* 8
der Eierkuchen, - 9
  eigen *own* (adj), 10
  eigentlich *actually,* 5
die Eigentumswohnung, -en *condominium,* 3
  **ein** *a, an,* 3; **ein paar** *a few,* 3; **eine Eins (Zwei, Drei, Vier, Fünf, Sechs)** (German grades), 4
  **einen** *a, an* (masc, acc case), 5; **Einen Pulli in Grau, bitte.** *A sweater in gray, please.,* 5
  einfach *simple, easy,* 1; **Also, einfach!** *That's easy!,* 1
das Einfamilienhaus, ⸚er *single-family house,* 3
  einfarbig *solid color,* 5
  eingeladen (pp) *invited,* 11
  eingelegt (pp) *docked (boat),* 9
  einige *some,* 9
der Einkauf, ⸚e *purchase,* 8
  **einkaufen** *to shop,* 8; **einkaufen gehen** *to go shopping,* 8
der Einkaufsbummel *shopping trip,* 8
das Einkaufszentrum, die Einkaufszentren *shopping center,* 6; **ins Einkaufszentrum gehen** *to go to the shopping center/mall,* 6
der Einkaufszettel, - *shopping list,* 8
  **einladen** (sep) *to invite,* 11; **er/sie lädt ... ein** *he/she invites,* 11
die Einladung, -en *invitation,* 11

  **einmal** *once,* 7
  **eins** *one,* 1
der Eintritt *admission,* 2
  **einundzwanzig** *twenty-one,* 3
  einverstanden *agreed,* 8
der Einwohner, - *inhabitant,* 6
die Einwohnerzahl, -en *population,* 1
  einzeln *single individual,* 6
der Einzelpassagier, -e *individual passenger,* 9
das **Eis** *ice cream,* 6; **ein Eis essen** *to eat ice cream,* 6
der **Eisbecher**, - *a dish of ice cream,* 6
die Eissporthalle, -n *skating rink,* 12
  EL=Eßlöffel, - *tablespoon,* 8
die Elektronik *electronics,* 7
die Elektrotechnik *electrical engineering,* 10
  **elf** *eleven,* 1
  **Eltern** (pl) *parents,* 3
der Emmentaler *Emmentaler* (cheese), 12
das Ende *end,* 5
  endgültig *final,* 10
  **eng** *tight,* 5
  engagiert *occupied,* 10
die Engländer (pl) *English people,* 1
der Engländer, - *English person (male),* -
die Engländerin, -nen *English person (female),* -
  englisch *English* (adj), 4; **auf englisch** *in English,* 10
  **Englisch** *English* (school subject), 4; (language), 9
  entscheiden *to decide,* 9; **sie entscheidet sich für** *she decides on,* 11
  entschließen *to decide,* 9
  **Entschuldigung!** *Excuse me!,* 9
  **er** *he,* 2; *it,* 3
das Erdbeereis *strawberry ice cream,* 9
die Erdbeere, -n *strawberry,* 8
der Erdbeerkuchen, - *strawberry cake,* 8
die **Erdkunde** *geography,* 4
die Erdnußbutter *peanut butter,* 8
  erfüllen *to fulfill,* 7
  ergänzen *to complete,* 9
  erkennen *to recognize,* 10
  erklären *to explain,* 5
  ermittelt von *compiled by,* 10
  ernst: im Ernst? *seriously?,* 10
  erst *first,* 6
  ersten: **am ersten (Juli)** *on the first (of July),* 11
  erwarten *to expect,* 12
  erwecken *to awaken,* 10
  erweisen *to grant,* 10
  erzählen *to tell,* 10; **Erzähl weiter!** *Keep on talking!,* 10
  **es** *it,* 3

  **essen** *to eat,* 3; **er/sie ißt** *he/she eats,* 6
der Essig *vinegar,* 12
der Estragon *tarragon,* 12
  etwa *approximately,* 12
  **etwas** *something,* 7; **Noch etwas?** *Anything else?,* 9
  **euch** *you* (pl, acc case), 7
  europäisch *European* (adj), 10
die Europareise, -n *trip to Europe,* 11
der Eßlöffel, - *tablespoon,* 8
der **Eßtisch**, -e *dining table,* 12


**F**

das **Fach**, ⸚er *school subject,* 4
die Fachsprache, -n *technical lingo,* 12
der Fächer, - *fan,* 11
  **fahren** *to go, ride, drive (using a vehicle),* 9; **er/sie fährt** *he/she drives,* 9; **in die Stadt fahren** *to go downtown (by vehicle),* 11; **wir fahren Rad** *we're riding bikes,* 10
der Fahrpreis, -e *fare,* 4
die Fahrpreisermäßigung, -en *reduced fare,* 4
das Fahrrad, ⸚er *bicycle,* 7
die Fahrt, -en *drive* 2; **Auto fahren** *to drive (a car),* 9
  fällen *to fall,* 4
  falsch *false,* 11
die **Familie**, -en *family,* 3
das Familienmitglied, -er *family member,* 11
das Familientreffen, - *family reunion,* 12
  **Fang mit ... an!** *Begin with...,* 9
das Fantasybuch, ⸚er *fantasy book,* 10
der Fantasyfilm, -e *fantasy film,* 10
der **Fantasyroman**, -e *fantasy novel,* 10
die **Farbe**, -n *color,* 5; **Wir haben das in allen Farben.** *We have that in all colors.,* 5
  fast *almost,* 12
  faul *lazy,* 7
der **Februar** *February,* 7
  fehlen *to be missing,* 4; **Was fehlt hier?** *What's missing?,* 5
  feiern *to celebrate,* 11
der **Feiertag**, -e *holiday,* 11
  feiertags *holidays,* 10
  feingehackt *finely chopped,* 12
die Feinmechanik *precision mechanics,* 10
das **Fenster**, - *window,* p. 8; **die Fenster putzen** *to clean the windows,* 7
die Ferien (pl) *vacation,* 1
das Ferngespräch, -e *long distance call,* 11

das Fernsehen *television,* 2; **Fernsehen schauen** *to watch television,* 2; im Fernsehen *on television,* 5

die Fernsehsendung, -en *television show,* 9

fertig *finished,* 7

**fesch** *stylish, smart,* 5

das Fest, -e *festivity,* 11

die Fete, -n *party,* 5; auf einer Fete *at a party,* 12

feurig *fiery,* 6

**der Film, -e** *movie,* 10; **einen Film sehen** *to see a movie,* 6

die Filmart, -en *type of movie,* 10

der Filmverleih, -e *movie rental,* 10

**finden** *to think about,* 2; **Das finde ich auch.** *I think so, too.,* 2; **Das finde ich nicht.** *I disagree.,* 2; **Ich finde es gut/schlecht, daß ...** *I think it's good/bad that...,* 9; **ich finde (Tennis) ...** *I think (tennis) is...,* 2; **Ich finde den Pulli stark!** *The sweater is awesome!,* 5; **Ich finde es toll!** *I think it's great!,* 9; **Wie findest du (Tennis)?** *What do you think of (tennis)?,* 2

die Firma, die Firmen *firm, company,* 9

**der Fisch, -e** *fish,* 8

die Fläche, -n *surface, area,* 1

die Flasche, -n *bottle,* 7

**das Fleisch** *meat,* 8

die Fleischbrühe, -n *meat broth,* 12

die Fliese, -n *tile,* 12

die Flöte, -n *flute,* 2

die Floßfahrt, -en *rafting trip,* 9

der Fluß, ̈sse *river,* 1

folgende *following,* 9

die Form, -en *form,* 5

das Foto, -s *photo,* 3

das Fotoalbum, die Fotoalben *photo album,* 3

das Fotogeschäft, -e *photo store,* 9

die Frage, -n *question,* 1

fragen *to ask,* 9

Französisch *French* (school subject), 4

**Frau** *Mrs.,* 1; **die Frauen** *women,* 3

frei: **Wir haben frei.** *We are off (out of school).,* 4

freilich *of course,* 9

**der Freitag** *Friday,* 4

freitags *Fridays,* 6

freiwillig *voluntary,* 7

der Freiwillige, -n *volunteer,* 4

**die Freizeit** *free time, leisure time,* 2

das Freizeitinteresse *free time interest,* 12

der Freizeitpark, -s *amusement park,* 10

das Freizeitvergnügen, - *enjoyment of leisure time.* 12

die Fremdsprache, -n *foreign language,* 4

die Freude, -n *joy, happiness,* 11

freuen *to be happy, glad,* 7; Freut mich! *It's a pleasure!,* 8

Sie freut sich darüber. *She is happy about it.,* 11; wir freuen uns *we're very happy, pleased,* 12

**der Freund, -e** *friend (male),* 1; **Freunde besuchen** *to visit friends,* 2

der Freundeskreis, -e *peer group,* 9

die Freundin, -nen *friend (female),* 1

freundlich *friendly,* 9

**frisch** *fresh,* 8

froh *happy,* 11

fröhlich *happy, cheerful,* 11

die Frucht, ̈e *fruit,* 8

das Fruchteis *ice cream with fruit,* 6

**der Frühling** *spring* (season), 2; **im Frühling** *in the spring,* 2

führen *to lead,* 12

füllen *to fill,* 12

**fünf** *five,* 1

**fünfundzwanzig** *twenty-five,* 3

**fünfzehn** *fifteen,* 1

**fünfzig** *fifty,* 3

**für** *for,* 7

**Für wen?** *For whom?,* 7

**furchtbar** *terrible, awful,* 5; **furchtbar gern** *to like a lot,* 10

fürs=für das *for the,* 2

**füttern** *to feed,* 7; **die Katze füttern** *to feed the cat,* 7

der Fuß, ̈e *foot,* 1; **zu Fuß** *on foot,* 1

**der Fußball** *soccer,* 2; **Ich spiele Fußball.** *I play soccer.,* 2

## G

**ganz** *really,* 3

ganz *not broken,* 4; *whole,* 9; die ganze Zeit *the whole time,* 12; Ganz einfach! *Quite simple!,* 9; **Ganz klar!** *Of course!,* 4

gar (particle), 3; **gar nicht gern** *not to like at all,* 10

die Garderobe, -n *wardrobe,* 5

**der Garten,** ̈ *yard, gardens,* 9

der Gast, ̈e *guest,* 12

der Gastgeber, - *host,* 12

das Gebäude, - *building,* 7

**geben** *to give,* 11; **er/sie gibt** *he/she gives,* 11; Was gibt es hier zu essen? *What is there to eat here?,* 9; Was gibt's? *What's up?,* 1

geboren *born,* 4

gebrüht *simmered,* 8

gebucht *booked,* 9

gebunden *bound,* 10

das Geburtsdatum (pl -daten) *date of birth,* 4

die Geburtsstadt, ̈e *place of birth,* 6

**der Geburtstag, -e** *birthday,* 11; **Alles Gute zum Geburtstag!** *Best wishes on your birthday!,* 11; **Herzlichen Glückwunsch zum Geburtstag!** *Best wishes on your birthday!,* 11; **Ich habe am ... Geburtstag.** *My birthday is on...,* 11

das Geburtstagsgeschenk, -e *birthday present,* 8

die Geburtstagskarte, -n *birthday card,* 11

der Geburtstagskuchen, - *birthday cake,* 12

gefährdet *endangered,* 11

gefahren (pp) *driven,* 10

gefährlich *dangerous,* 9

gefallen *to be pleasing,* 5; **Er/Sie/Es gefällt mir.** *I like it.,* 5; **Sie gefallen mir.** *I like them.,* 5

gefettet *oiled,* 12

gefüllt *filled,* 12

gegenseitig *reciprocal(ly),* 5

gegessen (pp) *eaten,* 9

gehackt *chopped,* 8

**gehen** *to go,* 2; **Das geht nicht.** *That won't work.,* 7; **Es geht.** *It's okay.,* 6; nach Hause gehen *to go home,* 3,6; Geht er noch? *Is it still working?,* 4; **Wie geht's (denn)?** *How are you?,* 6

gekauft (pp) *bought,* 8; **Ich habe Brot gekauft.** *I bought bread.,* 8; **Was hast du gekauft?** *What did you buy?,* 8

geknotet *knotted,* 5

gekocht *cooked,* 12

gelb *yellow,* 4; **in Gelb** *in yellow,* 4

**das Geld** *money,* 4

gelesen (pp) *read,* 10; **Was hast du gelesen?** *What did you read?,* 10

gemacht (pp) *done,* 10; **Was hast du am Wochenende gemacht?** *What did you do on the weekend?,* 10

gemahlen *ground,* 12

gemalt *painted,* 11

gemeinsam *common,* 11

gemischt *mixed,* 8

**das Gemüse** *vegetables*, 8; **im Obst- und Gemüseladen** *at the produce store*, 8

**der Gemüseladen**, ⸚ *produce store*, 8

genau *exact(ly)*, 6; genauer lesen *reading for detail*, 6

genießen *to enjoy*, 6

**genug** *enough*, 9; **Ich habe genug.** *I have enough.*, 9

geöffnet *open*, 6

**gepunktet** *polka-dot*, 12

gerade *just*, 8

**geradeaus** *straight ahead*, 9; **Fahren Sie geradeaus!** *Drive straight ahead.*, 9

das Gericht, -e *dish* (food), 6

**gern (machen)** *to like (to do)*, 2; **gern haben** *to like*, 4; **Gern geschehen!** *My pleasure!*, 9; **nicht gern (machen)** *to not like (to do)*, 2; **nicht so gern** *not to like very much*, 2; **Siehst du gern Horrorfilme?** *Do you like to watch horror movies?*, 10; **besonders gern** *especially like*, 10

gesagt (pp) *said*, 10

gesalzen *salted*, 8

das Geschäft, -e: ein Geschäft machen *to make a deal*, 7

geschehen: **Gern geschehen!** *My pleasure!*, 9

**das Geschenk, -e** *gift*, 11

**die Geschenkidee, -n** *gift idea*, 11

der Geschenkladen, ⸚ *gift shop*, 11

die Geschenkliste, -n *gift list*, 11

die Geschenkwaren (pl) *gifts*, 9

**die Geschichte** *history*, 4

geschickt *clever, talented*, 12

**das Geschirr** (pl) *dishes*, 7; **das Geschirr spülen** *to wash the dishes*, 7

der Geschirrspüler, - *dishwasher*, 12; den Geschirrspüler ausräumen *to unload the dishwasher*, 12

geschlossen *closed*, 10

der Geschmack *taste*, 8

**die Geschwister** (pl) *brothers and sisters*, 3

gesehen (pp) *seen*, 10; **Was hast du gesehen?** *What did you see?*, 10

gesetzt *sat*, 10

das Gespräch, -e *conversation*, 7

die Gesprächsnotiz, -en *message*, 11

**gesprochen** (pp) *spoken*, 10; **Worüber habt ihr gesprochen?** *What did you (pl) talk about?*, 10; Worüber sprichst du mit deinen Freunden? *What do you talk about with your friends?*, 10

---

die Geste, -n *gesture*, 7

**gestern** *yesterday*, 8; **gestern abend** *yesterday evening*, 8;

**gestreift** *striped*, 12

gesund *healthy*, 8

das Getränk, -e *beverage*, 11

gewachsen *grown*, 8

gewinnen *to win*, 2

**das Gewitter**, - *storm*, 7

gewöhnlich *usually*, 11

das Gewürz, -e *spice*, 8

gewürzt *spiced*, 8

**gießen** *to water*, 7; **die Blumen gießen** *to water the flowers*, 7

die Gitarre, -n *guitar*, 2

Gitarrenklänge *guitar music*, 6

gitterförmig *criss cross*, 8

**das Glas**, ⸚er *glass*, 3; **ein Glas Apfelsaft** *a glass of apple juice*, 3; **ein Glas (Mineral) Wasser** *a glass of (mineral) water*, 3; ein Glas Tee *a glass of tea*, 6

die Glatze, -n *bald head*, 3; **eine Glatze haben** *to be bald*, 3

**glauben** *to believe*, 2; **ich glaube** *I think*, 2; ich glaube, daß ... *I think that...*, 9; Ich glaube schon. *I believe so.*, 7

gleich *equal*, 3; *same*, 10

**das Glück** *luck*, 4; **So ein Glück!** *What luck!*, 4

der Glücksklee *clover* (symbol for good luck), 11

das Glücksschwein, -e *good luck pig* (symbol for good luck), 11

**das Golf** *golf*, 2

**der Grad** *degree(s)*, 7; **zwei Grad** *two degrees*, 7; **Wieviel Grad haben wir?** *What's the temperature?*, 7

das Gramm *gram*, 7

grau *gray*, 3; **in Grau** *in gray*, 5

grausam *cruel*, 10

**groß** *big*, 3

**die Größe, -n** *size*, 5

die Großeltern (pl) *grandparents*, 3

die Großmutter (Oma), ⸚ *grandmother*, 3

der Großvater (Opa), ⸚ *grandfather*, 3

grün *green*, 3; **in Grün** *in green*, 5

das Grundstück, -e *piece of land*, 3

grüner *greener*, 8

**die Gruppe, -n** *group*, 10

der Gruselroman, -e *horror novel*, 10

grüßen: **Grüß dich!** *Hi!*, 1

gültig *valid*, 4

die Gültigkeit *validity*, 6

günstig *advantageous; low-priced*, 4

die Gurke, -n *cucumber*, 8

---

**der Gürtel**, - *belt*, 5

gut *good*, 4; **Gut!** *Good! Well!*, 6; **Gut! Mach' ich!** *Okay, I'll do that!*, 7

der Gutschein, -e *gift certificate*, 11

das Gymnasium, die Gymnasien (German secondary school), 4

**das Gyros** *gyros*, 9

## H

**das Haar, -e** *hair*, 3

**haben** *to have*, 4; **er/sie hat** *he/she has*, 4; **Haben Sie das auch in Rot?** *Do you also have that in red?*, 5

**das Hackfleisch** *ground meat*, 8

der Haferbrei *oatmeal*, 9

**das Hähnchen**, - *chicken*, 8

halb *half*, 6; **halb (eins, zwei, usw.)** *half past (twelve, one, etc.)*, 6

der Halbbruder, ⸚ *half brother*, 3

halbieren *to halve*, 12

das Halbjahr, -e *half a year*, 4

die Halbschwester, -n *half sister*, 3

die Hälfte, -n *half*, 12

**Hallo!** *Hi! Hello!*, 1

der Hals, ⸚e *neck*, 8

das Halstuch, ⸚er *scarf*, 11

**halt** (particle), 6

halten *to hold*, 7

der Hamster, - *hamster*, 7

der Handball *handball*, 2

der Hauptbahnhof, ⸚e *main train station*, 4

hauptsächlich *mainly*, 6

**die Hauptstadt**, ⸚e *capital*, 1

das Haus, ⸚er *house*, 3; **zu Hause sein** *to be at home*, 6; **nach Hause gehen** *to go home*, 6; **zu Hause helfen** *to help at home*, 7

die Hausarbeit, -en *chores*, 7

**die Hausaufgaben** (pl) *homework*, 2; **Hausaufgaben machen** *to do homework*, 2

der Haushalt, -e *household*, 7

**das Haustier, -e** *pet*, 3

die Hauswirtschaft *home economics*, 4

häßlich *ugly*, 3

**He!** *Hey!*, 2

das Heft, -e *notebook*, 4

heiß *hot*, 7

**heißen** *to be called*, 1; **er heißt** *his name is*, 1; **ich heiße** *my name is*, 1; **sie heißt** *her name is*, 1; **Wie heißt das Mädchen?** *What's the girl's name?*, 1; **Heißt sie ...?** *Is her name ...?*, 1; **Wie heißt der Junge?** *What's the boy's name?*, 1; **Wie heißt du?** *What's your name?*, 1

**helfen** *to help*, 7; **zu Hause helfen** *to help at home*, 7
hell *light*, 5
hellblau *light blue*, 5; **in Hellblau** *in light blue*, 5
hellgrau *light gray*, 5
hellgrün *light green*, 5
**das Hemd, -en** *shirt*, 5
herausnehmen *to take out*, 12
**der Herbst** *fall* (season), 2; **im Herbst** *in the fall*, 2
**der Herd, -e** *stove*, 12
**Herr** *Mr.*, 1
herzlich: Herzliche Grüße! *Best regards!*, 1; Herzlich willkommen bei uns! *Welcome to our home!*, 12; Herzlichen Glückwunsch zum Geburtstag! *Best wishes on your birthday!*, 11
**heute** *today*, 7; **heute morgen** *this morning*, 8; **heute nachmittag** *this afternoon*, 8; **heute abend** *tonight, this evening*, 7
**hier** *here*, 3; **Hier bei ...** *The... residence.*, 11; **Hier ist ...** *This is...*, 11; hier vorn *here in front*, 5
hierher *over here*, 11
**die Hilfe, -n** *help*, 7
hin *to*, 8
hinten *back there*, 4; **da hinten** *there in the back*, 4
**das Hobbybuch, ⸚er** *hobby book*, 10
hoch *high*, 10
hochbegabt *very talented*, 10
hoffen *to hope*, 9
**holen** *to get, fetch*, 8
**das Holz** *wood*, 12; **aus Holz** *out of wood*, 12
**der Honig** *honey*, 8
**hören** *to hear*, 1; Hör gut zu! *Listen carefully*, p. 6; Hört zu! *Listen!*, p. 8; Musik hören *to listen to music*, 2
**der Hörer, -** *receiver*, 11; **den Hörer abheben** *to pick up the receiver*, 11; **den Hörer auflegen** *to hang up (the telephone)*, 11
**der Horrorfilm, -e** *horror movie*, 10
**die Hose, -n** *pants*, 5
**das Hotel, -s** *hotel*, 9
**hübsch** *pretty*, 5
**das Hufeisen, -** *horse shoe*, 11
**der Hund, -e** *dog*, 3
**hundert** *a hundred*, 3
**der Hunger** *hunger*, 9

## I
**ich** *I*, 2; **Ich auch.** *Me too.*, 2; **Ich nicht.** *I don't.*, 2

**die Idee, -n** *idea*, 9
**ihm** *to, for him* (masc, neuter, dat case), 11
**ihn** *it, him* (masc, acc case), 5
ihnen *them* (pl, dat case), 12
Ihnen *you* (formal, dat case), 5
**ihr** *her* (poss adj), 3
**ihr** *their* (poss adj), 2
**ihr** *to, for her* (fem, dat case), 11
**ihr** *you* (pl, subj pron), 2
im=in dem *in the*, 1; im Fernsehen *on television*, 5; **im Frühling** *in the spring*, 2; **im Herbst** *in the fall*, 2; **im Januar** *in January*, 7; im Kino *at the movies*, 10; im Konzert *at the concert*, 10; **(einmal) im Monat** *(once) a month*, 7; **im Sommer** *in the summer*, 2; **im Supermarkt** *at the supermarket*, 8; **im Winter** *in the winter*, 2
**der Imbißstand, ⸚e** *snack stand*, 6
**die Imbißstube, -n** *snack bar*, 9
**immer** *always*, 7
in *in*, 1; **in Blau** *in blue*, 5; **in Braun** *in brown*, 5; **in Gelb** *in yellow*, 5; **in Grau** *in gray*, 5; **in Grün** *in green*, 5; **in Hellblau** *in light blue*, 5; **in Rot** *in red*, 5; **in Schwarz** *in black*, 5; **in Weiß** *in white*, 5
der Individualist, -en *individualist*, 9
die Industrie, -n *industry*, 1
die Informatik *computer science*, 4
die Information, -en *information*, 10
der Ingenieur, -e *engineer*, 10
die Innenstadt, ⸚e *downtown*, 5; **in der Innenstadt** *in the city, downtown*, 9
ins=in das *in the, into the*, 2; **zu the**, 6
die Insel, -n *island*, 6
insgesamt *all together*, 8
**das Instrument, -e** *instrument*, 2
**interessant** *interesting*, 2
**das Interesse, -n** *interest*, 2; Hast du andere Interessen? *Do you have any other interests?*, 2
interessieren *to interest*, 10
irgend- *any*, 11
irgendetwas *anything*, 6
irgendwann *anytime*, 11
irgendwelch- *some*, 8
irgendwie *somehow*, 8
**ist:** er/sie/es ist *he/she/it is*, 1; sie ist aus *she's from*, 1

## J
ja *yes*, 1; **Ja klar!** *Of course!*, 1
**die Jacke, -n** *jacket*, 5

**das Jahr, -e** *year*, 1; **Ich bin ... Jahre alt.** *I am...years old.*, 1
**der Januar** *January*, 7; **im Januar** *in January*, 7
**die Jeans, -** *jeans*, 5
die Jeans-Tasche, -n *denim school bag*, 4
jed- *every*, 5; jeden Abend *every evening*, 10; **jeden Tag** *every day*, 7
jeglich- *any*, 8; jeglicher Art *every kind*, 9
**jetzt** *now*, 1
**joggen** *to jog*, 12
**der Jogging-Anzug, ⸚e** *jogging suit*, 5
der Joghurt *yogurt*, 8
das Joghurteis *yogurt ice cream*, 8
die Jugend *youth*, 10
der Jugendclub, -s *youth club*, 9
der Jugendliche, -n *young adult*, 7
das Jugendzentrum, die Jugendzentren *youth center*, 12
**der Juli** *July*, 7
jung *young*, 10
**der Junge, -n** *boy*, 1
**der Juni** *June*, 7

## K
**der Kaffee** *coffee*, 8; eine Tasse Kaffee *a cup of coffee*, 6
der Kaiser, - *emperor*, 6
der Kaiserschmarren (Austrian and southern German dish), 8
das Kalb, ⸚er *veal*, 8
**der Kalender, -** *calendar*, 11
die Kalorie, -n *calorie*, 8
**kalt** *cold*, 7
der Kanal, ⸚e *canal*, 1
das Kaninchen, - *rabbit*, 7
die Kanzlei, -en *law office*, 10
das Kapitel, - *chapter*, 1
**kaputt** *broken*, 3
die Kapuze, -n *hood (of coat)*, 5
**die Karte, -n** *card*, 2
das Kartenspiel, -e *card game*, 2
**die Kartoffel, -n** *potato*, 8
der Kartoffelsalat, -e *potato salad*, 12
**der Käse, -** *cheese*, 8
**das Käsebrot, -e** *cheese sandwich*, 6
der Käsekuchen, - *cheese cake*, 6
die Kasse, -n *cashier*, 10
**die Kassette, -n** *cassette*, 4
die Kastagnette, -n *castanet*, 11
der Kasten, - *box, container*, 9
die Kastenform, -en *bread pan*, 12
**die Katze, -n** *cat*, 3; **die Katze füttern** *to feed the cat*, 7
**kaufen** *to buy*, 5
das Kaufhaus, ⸚er *department store*, 5
kegeln *to bowl*, 10

GERMAN-ENGLISH VOCABULARY

**kein** *no, none, not any,* 9; **Ich habe keine Zeit.** *I don't have time.,* 7; **Ich habe keinen Hunger mehr.** *I'm not hungry any more.,* 9; **kein(en) ... mehr** *no more...,* 9; **Kein Problem!** *No problem!,* 11; **Keine Ahnung!** *I have no idea!,* 9; Nein danke, keinen Kuchen mehr. *No thanks. No more cake.,* 9; **Ich möchte kein(e)(en) ... mehr.** *I don't want another....,* 9

**der Keks, -e** *cookie,* 3; **ein paar Kekse** *a few cookies,* 3

**der Kellner, -** *waiter,* 6

**kennen** *to know, be familiar* or *acquainted with,* 10

**kennenlernen** *to get to know,* 12

**die Kerze, -n** *candle,* 11

**das Kilo=Kilogramm, -** *kilogram,* 8

**das Kind, -er** *child,* 8

**die Kinderkirche** *Sunday school,* 8

**das Kino, -s** *cinema,* 6; **im Kino** *at the movies,* 10; **ins Kino gehen** *to go to the movies,* 6

**die Kinokarte, -n** *movie ticket,* 9

**das Kinoprogramm, -e** *movie guide,* 10

**die Kirche, -n** *church,* 6

**die Kirschtorte, -n** *cherry cake,* 10

**die Kiwi, -s** *kiwi,* 8

**die Klamotten** (pl) *casual term for clothes,* 5; **meine Klamotten aufräumen** *to pick up my clothes,* 7

**Klar!** *sure,* 2; *clear,* 9; **Alles klar!** *O.K.!,* 10

**Klasse!** *Great! Terrific!,* 2

**die Klasse, -n** *grade level,* 4

**die Klassenarbeit, -en** *test, exam,* 4

**der Klassenkamerad, -en** *classmate,* 3

**das Klassenzimmer, -** *classroom,* p. 8

**der Klassiker, -** *classicist,* 11

**klassisch** *classical,* 10

**das Klavier, -e** *piano,* 2; **Ich spiele Klavier.** *I play the piano.,* 2

**das Kleid, -er** *dress,* 5

**klein** *small,* 3

**die Kleinigkeit, -en** *small thing,* 11

**klug** *clever,* 9

**die Knoblauchzehe, -n** *garlic clove,* 8

**der Knochen, -** *bone,* 8

**kochen** *to cook,* 2

**kommen** *to come,* 1; **er kommt aus** *he's from,* 1; **ich komme** *I come,* 1; **ich komme aus** *I'm from,* 1; **Komm doch mit!** *Why don't you come along?,* 7; **Komm mit nach ...** *Come along to...,* 1; es kommt ganz darauf an *it really depends,* 12; **sie kommen aus** *they're from,* 1; **sie kommt aus** *she's from,* 1; **Wie komme**

ich zum (zur) ... ? *How do I get to...?,* 9; **Wie kommst du zur Schule?** *How do you get to school?,* 1; Wie kommt man dahin? *How do you get there?,* 9

**die Komödie, -n** *comedy,* 10

**der Komponist, -en** *composer,* 11

**die Konditorei, -en** *confectioner's,* 8

**können** *to be able to,* 7; **Kann ich bitte Andrea sprechen?** *Could I please speak with Andrea?,* 11; **Kann ich's wirklich?** *Can I really do it?,* 1; **Was kann ich für dich tun?** *What can I do for you?,* 7; **Kann ich etwas für dich tun?** *Can I do something for you?,* 7

**das Kontingent, -e** *allotment,* 9

**das Konzert, -e** *concert,* 6; **im Konzert** *at the concert,* 10; **ins Konzert gehen** *to go to a concert,* 6

**der Kopf, ⸚e** *head,* 1

**der Kopfsalat, -e** *head lettuce,* 8

**der Korb, ⸚e** *basket,* 7

**kosten** *to cost,* 4; **Was kostet ... ?** *How much does...cost?,* 4

**köstlich** *delicious,* 8

**das Kotelett, -s** *cutlet,* 8

**die Kräuter** (pl) *herbs,* 12

**kriegen** *to get,* 10

**der Kriegsfilm, -e** *war movie,* 10

**der Krimi, -s** *detective movie,* 10

**der Krug, ⸚e** *jug,* 12

**die Kruste, -n** *crust,* 8

**die Küche, -n** *kitchen,* 12; **in der Küche** *in the kitchen,* 12

**der Kuchen, -** *cake,* 3; **ein Stück Kuchen** *a piece of cake,* 3

**die Kugel, -n** *scoop (of ice cream),* 6

**kühl** *cool,* 7

**kühler** *cooler,* 7

**der Kühlschrank, ⸚e** *refrigerator,* 12

**die Kuckucksuhr, -en** *cookoo clock,* 12

**der Kuli, -s** *ballpoint pen,* 4

**kulturell** *cultural,* 10

**der Kümmel** *caraway,* 8

**die Kunst, ⸚e** *art,* 4

**der Kunststoff, -e: aus Kunststoff** *out of plastic,* 12

**der Kurpark, -s** *spa park,* 12

**kurz** *short,* 3

**die Kusine, -n** *cousin (female),* 3


**L**

**lachen** *to laugh,* 11

**der Laden, ⸚** *store,* 8; **im Obst- und Gemüseladen** *at the produce store,* 8

**die Lampe, -n** *lamp,* 12

**das Land, ⸚er** *country,* 3; **auf dem Land** *in the country,* 3

**die Landeshauptstadt, ⸚e** *state capital,* 1

**lang** *long,* 3

**länger** *longer,* 7

**der Langlauf** *cross country,* 9

**langweilig** *boring,* 2

**lässig** *casual,* 5

**die Last, -en** *burden,* 7

**das Latein** *Latin,* 4

**laufen** *to run,* 2; **Rollschuh laufen** *to roller skate,* 9; **Schlittschuh laufen** *to ice skate,* 12

**das Leben, -** *life,* 10

**die Lebensmittel** (pl) *groceries,* 8

**die Leber** *liver,* 9

**der Leberkäs** (see p. 229), 9

**lecker** *tasty, delicious,* 6

**das Leder: aus Leder** *made of leather,* 12

**legen** *to put, lay,* 8

**leger** *casual,* 5

**der Lehrer, -** *teacher (male),* 1

**die Lehrerin, -nen** *teacher (female),* 1

**leicht** *easy,* 10

**leid: Es tut mir leid.** *I'm sorry.,* 9

**leider** *unfortunately,* 3; **Ich kann leider nicht.** *Sorry, I can't.,* 7

**das Leinen** *linen,* 5

**die Lektüre** *reading,* 10

**lernen** *to study, learn,* 8

**lesen** *to read,* 10; **er/sie liest** *he/she reads,* 10; richtig lesen *to read correctly,* 1

**der Leserbrief, -e** *letter to the editor,* 9

**der Lesetrick, -s** *reading trick,* 1

**letzt-** *last,* 8; **letzte Woche** *last week,* 8; **letztes Wochenende** *last weekend,* 8

**die Leute** (pl) *people,* 9

**das Licht, -er** *light,* p. 8

**lieb** *nice,* 7

**lieber (mögen)** *to prefer,* 10; **Ich sehe Komödien lieber.** *I like comedies better.,* 10

**Liebe(r) ...** *Dear...,* 1

**der Liebesfilm, -e** *romance,* 10

**der Liebesroman, -e** *romance novel,* 10

**Lieblings-** *favorite,* 4

**das Lieblingsessen, -** *favorite food,* 4

**das Lied, -er** *song,* 10

**liegen** *to lie,* 1

**lila** *purple,* 5

**die Limo, -s (Limonade, -n)** *lemon drink,* 6

**link** *left, left hand,* 10; **nach links** *to the left,* 9; **auf der linken Seite** *on the left (side),* 9

**der Linseneintopf, ⸚e** *lentil soup,* 9

**die Liste, -n** *list,* 10

**der Liter, -** *liter,* 8

**locker** *loose, easy going,* 5

logisch *logical*, 4

los: Los geht's! *Let's start!*, 1; Was ist los? *What's happening?*, 5

die Lust: Lust haben *to feel like*, 7

**lustig** *funny*, 10

lustigste *funniest*, 10

## M

**machen** *to do*, 2; **Das macht (zusammen) ...** *That comes to...*, 6; **Gut! Mach' ich!** *Okay, I'll do that!*, 7; **Machst du Sport?** *Do you play sports?*, 2; Macht nichts! *It doesn't matter!* 4; die Hausaufgaben machen *to do homework*, 2

**das Mädchen**, - *girl*, 1

**mähen** *to mow*, 7; **den Rasen mähen** *to mow the lawn*, 7

die Mahlzeit, -en *meal*, 8

**der Mai** *May*, 7; **im Mai** *in May*, 7

die Maisstärke *corn starch*, 12

der Majoran *majoram*, 12

**mal** *(particle)*, 1

malen *to paint*, 2

man *one, you (in general), people*, 1

**manchmal** *sometimes*, 7

der Mandelkuchen, - *almond cake*, 12

die Mandel, -n *almond*, 12

mangelhaft *unsatisfactory (grade)*, 4

**der Mann**, ⸚er *man*, 3

der Mantel, ⸚ *coat*, 5

die Margarine *margarine*, 12

der Marienkäfer, - *lady bug*, 11

**die Mark**, - *mark (German monetary unit)*, 4

der Markt, ⸚e *market*, 6

**der Marktplatz**, ⸚e *market square*, 9

die Marmelade, -n *jam, jelly*, 8

**der März** *March*, 7; **im März** *in March*, 7

der Maschinenbau *machine building industry*, 10

die Masse, -n *mass*, 12

die Mathearbeit, -en *math test*, 4

**die Mathematik (Mathe)** *math*, 4

die Matheprüfung, -en *math exam*, 6

die Mauer, -n *wall*, 12

die Maultaschen (pl) *(Southern German dish)*, 9

Mau Mau *(card game)*, 2

die Maus, ⸚e *mouse*, 7

das Meer, -e *ocean*, 6

das Meerschweinchen, - *guinea pig*, 7

**das Mehl** *flour*, 8

**mehr** *more*, 2; **Ich habe keinen Hunger mehr.** *I'm not hungry anymore.*, 9

die Mehrwegflasche, -n *refund bottle*, 7

**mein** *my*, 3; **meinem Vater** *to, for my father*, 11; **meiner Mutter** *to, for my mother*, 11

meinen: **Meinst du?** *Do you think so?*, 5

die Meinung, -en *opinion*, 2

meisten *most*, 9

meistens *mostly*, 5

die Melone, -n *melon*, 3

der Mensch, -en *person*, 7; Mensch! *Oh man!*, 2

das Messer, - *knife*, 10

der Metzger, - *butcher*, 8; **beim Metzger** *at the butcher's*, 8

**die Metzgerei**, -en *butcher shop*, 8

**mich** *me*, 7

**die Milch** *milk*, 8

mild *mild*, 8

die Million, -en *million*, 7

**das Mineralwasser** *mineral water*, 3

minus *minus*, 3

die Minute, -n *minute*, 8

mir *to me*, 3

miserabel *miserable*, 6

der Mist: So ein Mist! *That stinks! What a mess!*, 4

**mit** *with, by*, 1; **mit Brot** *with bread*, 6; **mit dem Auto** *by car*, 1; **mit dem Bus** *by bus*, 1; **mit dem Moped** *by moped*, 1; **mit dem Rad** *by bike*, 1; **mit der U-Bahn** *by subway*, 1; **mit Senf** *with mustard*, 9; **mit Zitrone** *with lemon*, 6

mitarbeiten (sep) *to work with*, 7

mitgebracht (pp) *brought with*, 12

die Mithilfe *cooperation*, 7

**mitkommen (sep)** *to come along*, 7

mitnehmen (sep) *to take with*, 10

der Mitschüler, - *classmate (male)*, 1

die Mitschülerin, -nen *classmate (female)*, 1

der Mittag *noon*, 8

die Mittagspause, -n *midday break*, 9

die Mitternacht *midnight*, 10

mittler- *middle*, 6

**der Mittwoch** *Wednesday*, 4; **am Mittwoch** *on Wednesday*, 4

**die Möbel (pl)** *furniture*, 3

**möchten** *would like to*, 3; **Ich möchte ... sehen.** *I would like to see...*, 5; **Was möchtest du essen?** *What would you like to eat?*, 3; **Ich möchte noch ein(e)(en) ...** *I'd like another....*, 9; **Ich möchte kein(e)(en) ... mehr.** *I don't want another....*, 9

**die Mode**, -n *fashion*, 10

das Modegeschäft, -e *clothing store*, 5

der Modekenner, - *fashion expert*, 5

**modern** *modern*, 12

modisch *fashionable*, 5

mogeln *to cheat*, 2

**mögen** *to like, care for*, 10

möglich *possible*, 4

möglichst ... *as...as possible*, 12

**der Moment**, -e *moment*, 3; **Einen Moment, bitte!** *Just a minute, please.*, 11; **im Moment gar nichts** *nothing at the moment*, 3

**der Monat**, -e *month*, 7; **(einmal) im Monat** *(once) a month*, 7

**das Monster**, -s *monster*, 1

**der Montag** *Monday*, 4; **am Montag** *on Monday*, 4

**das Moped**, -s *moped*, 1; **mit dem Moped** *by moped*, 1

**morgen** *tomorrow*, 7

**der Morgen**, - *morning*, 2; **Guten Morgen!** *Good morning!*, 1; **Morgen!** *Morning!*, 1

**der Müll** *trash*, 7; **den Müll sortieren** *to sort the trash*, 7

der Mülleimer, - *trash can*, 12

die Münchner (pl) *residents of Munich*, 9

mündlich *oral*, 4

**die Münze**, -n *coin*, 11; **Münzen einstecken** *to insert coins*, 11

**das Museum, die Museen** *museum*, 9

**die Musik** *music*, 2; **klassische Musik** *classical music*, 10; **Musik hören** *to listen to music*, 2

**das Musikprogramm**, -e *music program*, 10

**das Müsli** *muesli*, 8

**müssen** *to have to*, 7; **ich muß** *I have to*, 7

**die Mutter**, ⸚ *mother*, 3

die Mutti *mom*, 3

**der Muttertag** *Mother's Day*, 11; **Alles Gute zum Muttertag!** *Happy Mother's Day!*, 11

## N

Na? *Well?*, 2; Na ja. *Oh well*, 5; na dann *well then*, 9; Na klar! *Of course!*, 5

**nach** *after*, 2; **nach der Schule** *after school*, 2; **nach links** *to the left*, 9; **nach rechts** *to the right*, 9; **nach der Pause** *after the break*, 4; **nach Hause gehen** *to go home*, 3

die Nachbarschaft *neighborhood*, 8

nacherzählen *to retell*, 3

nachfolgend- *following*, 7

nachher *later, afterwards*, 3

die Nachhilfe *tutoring*, 7

die Nachhilfestunde, -n *tutoring lesson*, 7

der Nachmittag, -e *afternoon*, 2; **am Nachmittag** *in the afternoon*, 2

nächste *next*, 6; **die nächste Straße** *the next street*, 9

die Nacht, ⸚e *night*, 6

die Nähe: **in der Nähe** *nearby*, 3

der Name, -n *name*, 1

der Namenstag, -e *name day*, 11

**Natürlich!** *Certainly!*, 11

**naß** *wet*, 7

**nehmen** *to take*, 5; **er/sie nimmt** *he/she takes*, 5; **ich nehme ...** *I'll take...*, 5; **Nehmt ein Stück Papier!** *Take out a piece of paper.*, p. 8

**nein** *no*, 1

nennen *to name*, 5

nett *nice*, 2

**neu** *new*, 3

**neun** *nine*, 1

**neunundzwanzig** *twenty-nine*, 3

**neunzehn** *nineteen*, 1

**neunzig** *ninety*, 3

neuste *newest*, 10

nicht *not*, 2; **Nicht besonders.** *Not really.*, 6; **nicht gern haben** *to dislike*, 4; **nicht schlecht** *not bad*, 4; **Ich nicht.** *I don't.*, 2; **Nicht zu lang?** *Not too long?*, 5

nichts *nothing*, 2; **Nichts, danke!** *Nothing, thank you!*, 3; **Nichts mehr, danke!** *Nothing else, thanks!*, 9

**nie** *never*, 7

**noch** *yet, still*, 2; **Haben Sie noch einen Wunsch?** *Would you like anything else?*, 8; **Ich brauche noch ...** *I also need...*, 8; **Möchtest du noch etwas?** *Would you like something else?*, 9; **noch ein** *more, another*, 9; **Noch einen Saft?** *Another glass of juice?*, 9; **Noch etwas?** *Anything else?*, 9; **Ich möchte noch ein(e)(en) ...** *I'd like another...*, 9

normalerweise *usually*, 10

**die Note, -n** *grade*, 4

**das Notizbuch, ⸚er** *notebook*, 1

**der November** *November*, 7; **im November** *in November*, 7

**die Nudelsuppe, -n** *noodle soup*, 6

**null** *zero*, 1

die Nummer, -n *number*, 1

nun *now*, 6

nur *only*, 2

## O

ob *whether* (conj), 9

oben *upstairs; up there*, 3

**das Obst** *fruit*, 3

der Obst- und Gemüseladen, ⸚ *fresh produce store*, 8; **im Obst- und Gemüseladen** *at the produce store*, 8

der Obstkuchen, - *fruit cake*, 8

der Obstsalat, -e *fruit salad*, 8

obwohl *although* (conj), 7

oder *or*, 1

der Ofen, ⸚ *oven*, 12

öffnen: Öffnet eure Bücher auf Seite ... ! *Open your books to page...*, p. 8

**oft** *often*, 7

ohne *without*, 5

Oje! *Oh no!*, 6

**der Oktober** *October*, 7; **im Oktober** *in October*, 7

**das Öl, -e** *oil*, 12

**die Oma, -s** *grandmother*, 3

**der Onkel, -** *uncle*, 3

**der Opa, -s** *grandfather*, 3

**die Oper, -n** *opera*, 10

die Optik *optics*, 10

die Orange, -n *orange*, 3

**der Orangensaft** *orange juice*, 3

das Orchester, - *orchestra*, 4

organisieren *to organize*, 11

die Originalfassung, -en *original version*, 10

der Ort, -e *place, location*, 9

**das Ostern** *Easter*, 11; **Frohe Ostern!** *Happy Easter*, 11

österreichisch *Austrian* (adj), 9

## P

das Paar, -e *pair*, 5; **paar: ein paar** *a few*, 3

das Päckchen, - *packet*, 12

das Paddel, - *paddle*, 12

die Pailletten (pl) *beads*, 5

das Papier *paper*, p. 8

der Paprika *bell pepper*, 8

**das Parfüm, -e** *perfume*, 11

**der Park, -s** *park*, 9; **in den Park gehen** *to go to the park*, 12

der Partner, - *partner (male)*, p. 7

die Partnerin, -nen *partner (female)*, 6

der Passant, -en *passer-by*, 9

**passen** *to fit*, 5; **der Rock paßt prima!** *The skirt fits great!*, 5; **Was paßt zusammen?** *What goes together?*, 1; **aufpassen: Paßt auf!** *Pay attention!*, p. 8; **Paß auf!** *Watch out!*, 6

passieren: Was passiert hier? *What's happening here?*, 1

die Pastellfarben (pl) *pastel colors*, 5

**die Pause, -n** *break*, 4; **nach der Pause** *after the break*, 4

**das Pech** *bad luck*, 4; **So ein Pech!** *Bad luck!*, 4

die Perle, -n *bead*, 5

die Person, -en *person*, 3

persönlich *personally*, 11

der Pfadfinder, - (similar to Boy Scout), 6

**Pfd.=Pfund** *pound*, 8

der Pfeffer *pepper*, 12

**der Pfennig, -** (smallest unit of German currency; 1/100 of a mark), 4

die Pflaume, -n *plum*, 8

pflegen *to do regularly*, 9

die Pflicht, -en *duty*, 7

der Pflichtunterricht *mandatory class*, 4

**das Pfund, - (Pfd.)** *pound*, 8

**phantasievoll** *imaginative*, 10

phantastisch *fantastic*, 3

die Physik *physics*, 4

pikant *spicy*, 8

der Pilz, -e *mushroom*, 6

**die Pizza, -s** *pizza*, 6

der Plan, ⸚e *plan*, 6

planen *to plan*, 6

die Planung, -en *planning*, 10

der Platz, ⸚e *place, spot*, 1; **am ...platz** *on ... Square*, 9; **bis zum ...platz** *until you get to ... square*, 9

der Pokalsieg, -e *victory*, 9

**die Politik** *politics*, 10

populär *popular*, 11

populärste *most popular*, 11

das Portemonnaie, -s *wallet*, 8

die Portion, -en *portion*, 12

**die Post** *post office*, 9

**das Poster, -** *poster*, 11

die Postkarte, -n *postcard*, 1

**die Praline, -n** *fancy chocolate*, 11

der Präsident, -en *president*, 9

der Preis, -e *price*, 4

das Preisplakat, -e *poster with prices*, 8

**preiswert** *reasonably priced*, 4; **Das ist preiswert.** *That's a bargain.*, 4

**Prima!** *Great!* 1; **Prima Idee!** *Great idea!*, 7

die Prise, -n: eine Prise Salz *a pinch of salt*, 12

probieren *to try* (with foods), 5

das Problem, -e *problem*, 8

Prost! *Cheers!*, 12

das Prozent, - *percent*, 5

die Prüfungsvorbereitung, -en *preparation for a test*, 7

Pst! *Ssh!*, 12

der Pulli, -s (Pullover, -) *pullover, sweater*, 5

das Putenschnitzel, - *turkey cutlets*, 8

**putzen** *to clean*, 7; **die Fenster putzen** *to wash the windows*, 7

das Putzmittel, - *cleaning agent*, 7

## Q

der Quadratkilometer, - *square kilometer*, 1
die Qualität *quality*, 5
der Quark (milk product), 8
Quatsch! *Nonsense!*, 7

## R

das Rad, ⁼er *bike*, 1; **mit dem Rad** *by bike*, 1; **Wir fahren Rad.** *We're riding bikes.*, 10
radeln *to ride a bike*, 7
radfahren *to ride a bike*, 2
der Radiergummi, -s *eraser*, 4
das Radieschen, - *radish*, 8
das Radio, -s *radio*, 11
der Rasen, - *lawn*, 7; **den Rasen mähen** *to mow the lawn*, 7
raten: Rate! *Guess!*, 2; Rate mal! *Guess!*, 1
das Rathaus, ⁼er *city hall*, 9
der Rechner, - *calculator*, 4
recht: Du hast recht! *You're right!*, 4
recht- *right, right hand*, 7; **nach rechts** *to the right*, 9
die Rechtschreibung *spelling*, 8
reden *to talk*, 5
reduziert *reduced*, 5
das Regal, -e *bookcase*, 3
die Regel, -n *rule*, 2
regelmäßig *regularly*, 7
der Regen *rain*, 7
die Regie *director* (of a film), 10
regnen: Es regnet. *It's raining.*, 7
regnerisch *rainy*, 7
das Reich, -e *empire*, 6
reich *rich*, 8
die Reihe, -n *row*, 10
der Reim, -e *rhyme*, 11
rein *pure*, 6
das Reisebüro, -s *travel agency*, 9
reiten *to ride horseback*, 2
das Reitturnier, -e *riding tournament*, 12
die Religion, -en *religion* (school subject), 4
das Restaurant, -s *restaurant*, 9
richtig *correct(ly)*, 1
riechen *to smell*, 8
Riesen- *gigantic*, 8
der Rock, ⁼e *skirt*, 5
die Rolle, -n *role*, 9
der Rollschuh, -e *roller skate*, 2
die Rollschuhbahn, -en *roller skating course*, 9
Rollschuh laufen *to roller skate*, 9; ich laufe Rollschuh *I roller skate*, 9
der Roman, -e *novel*, 10
der Rosenkohl *Brussel sprouts*, 9

die Rosine, -n *raisin*, 8
rot *red*, 3; **in Rot** *in red*, 5
Ruhe! *Quiet!*, 4
der Ruhetag, -e *day of rest*, 6
der Rührteig, -e *batter*, 12
rund *round*, 12
runter *down*, 3

## S

das Sachbuch, ⁼er *non-fiction book*, 10
die Sache, -n *thing*, 5
der Saft, ⁼e *juice*, 3
saftig *juicy*, 6
der Saftstand, ⁼e *juice stand*, 9
sagen *to say*, 2; **Sag, ...** *Say...*, 1; **Sag mal ...** *Say...*, 2; so sagt man das *here's how you say it*, 1; Was sagst du dazu? *What do you say to that?*, 9; **Was sagt der Wetterbericht?** *What does the weather report say?*, 7; Wie sagt man ... auf deutsch? *How do you say...in German?*, p. 8;
sagenhaft *great*, 6
sagte *said*, 10
die Sahne *cream*, 8
die Saison, -s *season*, 5
der Salat, -e *lettuce*, 8; *salad*, 12
das Salz *salt*, 12
sammeln *to collect*, 2; **Comics sammeln** *to collect comics*, 2; **Briefmarken sammeln** *to collect stamps*, 2
der Samstag *Saturday*, 4; **am Samstag** *on Saturdays*, 4
der Sänger, - *singer (male)*, 10
die Sängerin, -nen *singer (female)*, 10
der Satz, ⁼e *sentence*, 1; Sätze bauen *to form sentences*, 1
sauberer *cleaner*, 7
saubermachen *to clean*, 12
sauer *annoyed*, 2
säuerlich *sour*, 12
saugen: Staub saugen *to vacuum*, 7
das Schach *chess*, 2
Schade! *Too bad!*, 4
die Schale, -n *serving dish*, 8
schauen *to look*, 2; Schau! *Look!*, 1; Schau mal! *Take a look!*, 1; **Schauen Sie!** (formal) *Look!*, 4; Schaut auf die Tafel! *Look at the board!*, 12; **Fernsehen schauen** *to watch television*, 2
der Schauer, - *(rain) shower*, 7
das Schaufenster, - *store window*, 12
der Schauspieler, - *actor*, 10
die Schauspielerin, -nen *actress*, 10

die Scheibe, -n *slice*, 8
scheinen *to shine*, 7; **Die Sonne scheint.** *The sun is shining.*, 7
schenken *to give (a gift)*, 11; **Schenkst du deinem Vater einen Kalender zum Geburtstag?** *Are you giving your father a calendar for his birhtday?*, 11; **Was schenkst du deiner Mutter?** *What are you giving your mother?*, 11
scheußlich *hideous*, 5
schick, chic *smart (looking)*, 5
schimpfen *to complain*, 7
der Schinken *ham*, 6
das Schlagzeug *drums; percussion*, 2
schlecht *bad(ly)*, 4
der Schlittschuh, -e *ice skate*, 12; **Schlittschuh laufen** *to ice skate*, 12
das Schloß, die Schlösser *castle*, 12
schmalzig *corny, mushy*, 10
schmecken: **Schmeckt's?** *Does it taste good?*, 6; **Wie schmeckt's?** *How does it taste?*, 6
der Schmuck *jewelry*, 11
der Schnee *snow*, 7
schneien: **Es schneit.** *It's snowing.*, 7
schneiden *to cut*, 8
schnell *fast*, 7
das Schnitzel, - *schnitzel*, 9
das Schokoladeneis *chocolate ice cream*, 6
die Schokoladenstücke (pl) *pieces of chocolate*, 12
schon *already*, 1; schon bekannt *already known*, 2; Schon gut! *That's okay!*, 1
schön *pretty, beautiful*, 3
schöner *more beautiful, prettier*, 5
schönste *most beautiful*, 5
der Schornsteinfeger, - *chimney sweep*, 11
der Schrank, ⁼e *cabinet*, 3
schreiben *to write*, 1; richtig schreiben *to write correctly*, 1; Schreibt euren Namen auf! *Write down your names.*, p. 8; Schreib ... auf! *Write down...!*, 12
der Schreibtisch, -e *desk*, 3
der Schreibwarenladen, ⁼ *stationery store*, 4
schriftlich *written*, 4
der Schritt, -e *step*, 10; auf Schritt und Tritt *all the time*, 10
die Schule, -n *school*, 4; **nach der Schule** *after school*, 2; **Wie kommst du zur Schule?** *How do you get to school?*, 1

der Schüler, - *pupil, student (male)*, 3
die Schülerin, -nen *pupil, student (female)*, -
der Schülerausweis, -e *student I.D.*, 4
der Schulhof, ⸚e *school yard*, 4
das Schuljahr, -e *school year*, 4
**die Schulsachen** (pl) *school supplies*, 4
**die Schultasche, -n** *schoolbag*, 4
die Schulter, -n *shoulder*, 8
die Schüssel, -n *bowl*, 12
der Schutzumschlag, ⸚e *dust jacket (on a book)*, 10
    **schwarz** *black*, 3; **in Schwarz** *in black*, 5
das Schwein, -e *pig*, 8
der Schweinebraten, - *pork roast*, 8
das Schweineschnitzel, - *pork cutlet*, 9
die Schweinshaxe, -n *pork shank*, 7
das Schweinswürstel, - *little pork sausage*, 8
    schwer *difficult, hard*, 11
**die Schwester, -n** *sister*, 3
**das Schwimmbad,** ⸚er *swimming pool*, 6; **ins Schwimmbad gehen** *to go to the (swimming) pool*, 6
    **schwimmen** *to swim*, 2
**der Science-fiction-Film, -e** *science fiction movie*, 10
    **sechs** *six*, 1
    **sechsundzwanzig** *twenty-six*, 3
    **sechzehn** *sixteen*, 1
    **sechzig** *sixty*, 3
der See, -n *lake*, 1
die See *sea*, 4
    **segeln** *to go sailing*, 2
    **sehen** *to see*, 10; Am liebsten sehe ich Krimis. *I like detective movies the best.*, 10; **er/sie sieht** *he/she sees*, 10
    sehenswert *worth seeing*, 9
    **sehr** *very*, 2; **Sehr gut!** *Very well!*, 6
    **seid: ihr seid** *you (pl) are*, 1
die Seide, -n *silk*, 5; **aus Seide** *made of silk*, 12
    **sein** *to be*, 1; **er ist** *he is*, 1; **er ist aus** *he's from*, 1; **ich bin aus** *I am from*, 1; **sie sind** *they are*, 1; **sie sind aus** *they're from*, 1; **du bist** *you are*, 1
    **sein** *his*, 3
    seit *since, for*, 10
die Seite, -n *page*, 6; *side*, 9; auf der rechten Seite *on the right (hand) side*, 9
    selber *myself*, 7
    selbst *yourself*, 7
    Selbstgemachtes *homemade*, 11
    selten *seldom*, 7

die Semmel, -n *roll*, 8
**der Senf** *mustard*, 6; **mit Senf** *with mustard*, 9
    **sensationell** *sensational*, 10
    separat *separate*, 7
**der September** *September*, 7
der Sessel, - *armchair*, 12
    setzen *to sit down*, 6; Setzt euch! *Sit down!*, p. 8
**die Shorts** *pair of shorts*, 5
    sich *oneself*, 5
    **Sicher!** *Certainly!*, 3; **Ich bin nicht sicher.** *I'm not sure.*, 5
    sichern *to secure*, 9
    **sie** *she*, 2
    **sie** (pl) *they*, 2
    **Sie** *you* (formal), 2
    **sie** *it* (with objects), 3
    **sie** (pl) *they* (with objects), 3; *them* (with objects), 5
    **sieben** *seven*, 1
    **siebenundzwanzig** *twenty-seven*, 3
    **siebzehn** *seventeen*, 1
    **siebzig** *seventy*, 3
    **sind: sie sind** *they are*, 1; **Sie** (formal) **sind** *you are*, 1; **wir sind** *we are*, 1
    singen *to sing*, 10
    sitzen *to be sitting*, 10
    Skat (German card game), 2
    Ski laufen *to ski*, 2
    **so** *so, well, then*, 1; so groß wie *as big as*, 6; **so lala** *so so*, 6; so oft wie möglich *as often as possible*, 10; so sagt man das *here's how you say it*, 1
    sobald *as soon (as)*, 10
**die Socke, -n** *sock*, 5
**das Sofa, -s** *sofa*, 12
    **sollen** *should, to be supposed to*, 8
**der Sommer** *summer*, 2; **im Sommer** *in the summer*, 2
    sommerleicht *summery (clothing)*, 5
das Sonderangebot, -e *sale*, 4
    sondern *but*, 5
die Sonne *sun*, 7
    **sonnig** *sunny*, 7
**der Sonntag** *Sunday*, 4
    sonntags *Sundays*, 8
    sonst *otherwise*, 2; an sonsten *otherwise*, 11; **Sonst noch etwas?** *Anything else?*, 8
die Sorge, -n *worry*, 8
    **sorgen** *to care (for), to take care of*, 6
    **sortieren** *to sort*, 7; **den Müll sortieren** *to sort the trash*, 7
    soviel *as much*, 9
    sowieso *anyway*, 5
    Sozialkunde *social studies*, 4

    Spanisch *Spanish* (class), 4; (language), 10
    **spannend** *exciting, thrilling*, 10
der Spargel *asparagus*, 8
    sparsam *thrifty*, 7
    spät *late*, 6; **Wie spät ist es?** *What time is it?*, 6
    später *later*, 2
das Spätprogramm, -e *late show*, 10
das Spatzenbrett, -er (cutting board to make Spätzle), 12
die Spätzle (pl) (see p. 298), 12
**der Spaß** *fun*, 2; Hat es Spaß gemacht? *Was it fun?*, 10; **(Tennis) macht keinen Spaß.** *(Tennis) is no fun.*, 2; **(Tennis) macht Spaß.** *(Tennis) is fun.*, 2; Viel Spaß! *Have fun!*, 9
der Speck *bacon*, 12
die Speisekarte, -n *menu*, 6
    spektakulärste *most spectacular*, 10
die Spezialität, -en *specialty*, 9
das Spiel, -e *game*, 10
    **spielen** *to play*, 2; **Ich spiele Fußball.** *I play soccer.*, 2; **Ich spiele Klavier.** *I play the piano.*, 2; **Spielst du ein Instrument?** *Do you play an instrument?*, 2
der Spieler, - *player*, 12
der Spießbraten, - *roast*, 6
der Spinat *spinach*, 9
    **Spitze!** *Super!*, 2
die Spitzenqualität *top quality*, 8
    sponsern *to sponsor*, 10
    spontan *spontaneous(ly)*, 9
**der Sport** *sports*, 2; *physical education*, 4; **Machst du Sport?** *Do you play sports?*, 2
die Sportart, -en *type of sport*, 9
die Sporthalle, -n *indoor gym*, 6
    sportlich *sportive*, 5
die Sportmode *sportswear*, 9
die Sprache, -n *language*, 5
    **sprechen** *to speak*, 4; **sprechen über** *to talk about, discuss*, 10; **er/sie spricht über** *he/she talks about*, 10; **Kann ich bitte Andrea sprechen?** *Could I please speak with Andrea?*, 11
**das Spülbecken, -** *sink*, 12
    **spülen** *to wash*, 7; **das Geschirr spülen** *to wash the dishes*, 7
die Spülmaschine, -n *dishwasher*, 12; die Spülmaschine ausräumen *to unload the dishwasher*, 12
**die Stadt,** ⸚e *city*, 9; **in der Stadt** *in the city*, 3; in die Stadt fahren *to go downtown (by vehicle)*, 11; **in die Stadt gehen** *to go downtown*, 6

das Stadtmuseum *city museum,* 9
der Stadtplan, ⁼e *city map,* 9
   stark *great, awesome,* 5
**der Staub** *dust,* 7; **Staub saugen** *to vacuum,* 7
   stehen: Steht auf! *Stand up!,* p. 8; Wie steht's mit dir? *How about you?,* 10
der Stehimbiß, -sse *fast food stand,* 9
   stellen *to put,* 10
**die Stereoanlage, -n** *stereo,* 3
der Stiefbruder, ⁼ *stepbrother,* 3
**der Stiefel, -** *boot,* 5
die Stiefmutter, ⁼ *stepmother,* 3
die Stiefschwester, -n *stepsister,* 3
der Stiefvater, ⁼ *stepfather,* 3
   stimmen *to be correct,* 3; **Stimmt (schon)!** *Keep the change.,* 6; **Stimmt!** *That's right! True!,* 2; **Stimmt nicht!** *Not true!; False!,* 2
   stimmungsvoll *full of atmosphere,* 6
das Stirnband, ⁼er *headband,* 5
**die Straße, -n** *street,* 9; auf der Straße *on the street,* 9; **bis zur ...straße** *until you get to ... Street,* 9; **die erste (zweite, dritte) Straße** *the first (second, third) street,* 9; **in der ...straße** *on ... Street,* 3
der Streifen, - *stripe,* 5
   streng *strict,* 7
**das Stück, -e** *piece,* p. 8; **ein Stück Kuchen** *a piece of cake,* 3
die Stufe, -n *level,* 1
**der Stuhl, ⁼e** *chair,* 3
die Stunde, -n *hour,* 9
**der Stundenplan, ⁼e** *class schedule,* 4
   **suchen** *to look for, search for,* 4; **ich suche ...** *I'm looking for...,* 5
   **super** *super,* 2
**der Supermarkt, ⁼e** *supermarket,* 8; **im Supermarkt** *at the supermarket,* 8
   süß *sweet,* 8
die Süßspeise, -n *dessert,* 9
das Süßwarengeschäft, -e *candy store,* 11
die Szene, -n *scene,* 9

### T

**das T-Shirt, -s** *T-shirt,* 5
die Tafel, -n *(chalk)board,* p. 8; Geht an die Tafel! *Go to the board,* p. 8
**der Tag, -e** *day,* 2; eines Tages *one day,* 10; **Guten Tag!** *Hello!,* 1; **Tag!** *Hello!,* 1; **jeden Tag**

   *every day,* 7
   täglich *daily,* 10
**die Tante, -n** *aunt,* 3
   **tanzen** *to dance,* 2; **tanzen gehen** *to go dancing,* 6
das Taschengeld *pocket money,* 7
**der Taschenrechner, -** *pocket calculator,* 4
die Tasse, -n *cup,* 3; eine Tasse Kaffee *a cup of coffee,* 6
   tauschen *to switch, trade,* 9; Tauscht die Rollen aus! *Switch roles.,* 8
die Technik *technology,* 4
**der Tee** *tea,* 3; **ein Glas Tee** *a (glass) cup of tea,* 6
der Teelöffel (TL) *teaspoon,* 8
der Teig *dough,* 8
   teilweise *partly,* 12
**das Telefon, -e** *telephone (on the telephone),* 11
   **telefonieren** *to call,* 11
**die Telefonnummer, -n** *telephone number,* 11
die Telefonzelle, -n *telephone booth,* 11
der Teller, - *plate,* 11
   **Tennis** *tennis,* 2
**der Teppich, -e** *carpet,* 12
der Termin, -e *appointment,* 9
   **teuer** *expensive,* 4
der Teufel, - *devil,* 10
der Text, -e *text,* 12
**das Theater, -** *theater,* 9; ins Theater gehen *to go to the theater,* 12
das Theaterstück, -e *(stage) play,* 10
das Thema, die Themen *topic,* 10
der Thymian *thyme,* 12
das Tier, -e *animal,* 7
**der Tisch, -e** *table,* 12; **den Tisch abräumen** *to clear the table,* 7; **den Tisch decken** *to set the table,* 7
der Tischtennis *table tennis,* 2
der Titel, - *title,* 10
   **Tja ...** *Well...,* 2
   tödlich *deadly,* 10
die Toilette, -n *toilet,* 12
   **toll** *great, terrific,* 2; Ich finde es toll! *I think it's great!,* 9
**die Tomate, -n** *tomato,* 8
das Tor, -e *gate,* 12
**die Torte, -n** *layer cake,* 8
das Training *training,* 1
**die Traube, -n** *grape,* 8
der Traumjob, -s *dream job,* 10
   **traurig** *sad,* 10
   traurigste *saddest,* 10
der Treff *meeting place,* 10
   treffen *to meet,* 9
   treiben: Ich treibe Sport. *I do sports.,* 9

   **trinken** *to drink,* 3
   **trocken** *dry,* 7
die Trompete, -n *trumpet,* 2
der Tropfen, - *drop,* 12
   trotzdem *nevertheless,* 5
   trüb *overcast,* 7
   **Tschau!** *Bye! So long!,* 1
   **Tschüs!** *Bye! So long!,* 1
   **tun** *to do,* 7; **Es tut mir leid.** *I'm sorry.,* 9
die Tür, -en *door,* p. 8
**der Turnschuh, -e** *sneaker, athletic shoe,* 5
   tust: du tust *you do,* 9
die Tüte, -n *bag,* 5
   typisch *typical,* 7

### U

**die U-Bahn**=Untergrundbahn *subway,* 1; **mit der U-Bahn** *by subway,* 1
**die U-Bahnstation, -en** *subway station,* 9
   üben *to practice,* p. 9
   über *about,* 4
   **überhaupt: überhaupt nicht** *not at all,* 5; **überhaupt nicht gern** *strongly dislike,* 10
   überließ *left (to someone else),* 10
die Überraschung, -en *surprise,* 12
   übertreffen *to outdo, surpass,* 5
   übrigens *by the way,* 3
die Übung, -en *exercise,* 11
   Uhr *o'clock,* 1; **um 8 Uhr** *at 8 o'clock,* 4; **um ein Uhr** *at one o'clock,* 6; **Wieviel Uhr ist es?** *What time is it?,* 6
die Uhrzeit *time (of day),* 6
   um *at,* 1; *around,* 9; **um 8 Uhr** *at 8 o'clock,* 4; **um ein Uhr** *at one o'clock,* 6; **Um wieviel Uhr?** *At what time?,* 6
die Umfrage, -n *survey,* 1
   umgeben *to surround,* 10
   umhören *to listen around,* 7
die Umrechnungstabelle, -n *conversion table,* 5
   umsteigen *to change lines (on a bus, subway, etc.),* 4
**die Umwelt** *environment,* 10
   unbedingt *absolutely,* 11
   **unbequem** *uncomfortable,* 3
   **und** *and,* 1
   unfreundlich *unfriendly,* 11
   **ungefähr** *about, approximately,* 7
   ungenügend *unsatisfactory (grade),* 4
   ungewöhnlich *unusual,* 12
   unheimlich *incredibly, incredible,* 8
die Uni, -s (Universität, -en), *university,* 2

unlogisch *illogical,* 4
die Unordnung *disorder,* 8
    unregelmäßig *irregularly,* 8
    **uns** *us,* 7
    unser *our,* 4
    unten *below, downstairs,* 10
    unter *below, under,* 8
    unterbrechen *to interrupt,* 10
    unterhalten *to entertain,* 11
    unterheben *to fold in,* 12
die Unterrichtsveranstaltung, -en
    *school-sponsored activity,* 4
die Unterschrift, -en *signature,* 4
    unterstützen *to support,* 10
    unterwegs *on the way,* 10
    usw. = und so weiter *etc., and so forth,* 10

# V

die Vanille *vanilla,* 6
das Vanilleeis *vanilla ice cream,* 6
**der Vater,** ∸ *father,* 3; **deinem Vater** *to, for your father,* 11; **meinem Vater** *to, for my father,* 11
**der Vatertag** *Father's Day,* 11; **Alles Gute zum Vatertag!** *Happy Father's Day!,* 11
    verabreden *to make a date,* 6
die Veranstaltung, -en *event,* 10
    **verbringen** *to spend (time),* 10; **Wie verbringst du deine Freizeit?** *How do you spend your free time?,* 10
    verdienen *to earn,* 7
    verdünnt *diluted,* 12
der Verein, -e *club,* 9
    verfeinern *to improve,* 8
die Vergünstigung, -en *benefit,* 10
der Verkauf *sale,* 6
der Verkäufer, - *sales clerk (male),* 4
die Verkäuferin, -nen *sales clerk (female),* 4
der Verlag, -e *publishing house,* 7
    verlegt: auf (time expression) verlegt *postponed until,* 6
    verlieren *to lose,* 2
    vermeiden *to avoid,* 7
    verrühren *to blend,* 12
der Vers, -e *verse,* 11
    verschenkt *given away,* 11
    **verschieden** *different,* 11
    versteckt: versteckte Sätze *hidden sentences,* 3
    versuchen *to try,* 10
    verteilen *to distribute,* 8
der Verwandte, -n *relative (male),* 11
die Verwandte, -n *relative (female),* 11
    verwenden *to use,* 10
    **Verzeihung!** *Excuse me!,* 9
**das Video, -s** *video cassette,* 10
das Videospiel, -e *video game,* 2

die Viehzucht *cattle raising,* 6
**viel** *a lot,* 2; **Viel Spaß!** *Have fun!,* 9; **viel zu** *much too,* 5; **viele** *many,* 2; **viele Grüße** *best regards,* 9; **Vielen Dank!** *Thank you very much!,* 9
die Vielfalt *diversity,* 5
    **vielleicht** *probably,* 11
    **vier** *four,* 1
    viermal *four times,* 7
das Viertel, - *quarter,* 6; **Viertel nach** *a quarter after,* 6; **Viertel vor** *a quarter till,* 6
    vierundzwanzig *twenty-four,* 3
    **vierzehn** *fourteen,* 1
    **vierzig** *forty,* 3
der Vogel, ∸ *bird,* 7
    **Volleyball** *volleyball,* 2
das Vollkornbrot, -e *whole grain bread,* 8
**die Vollkornsemmel, -n** *whole wheat roll,* 9
    vom=von dem *from the,* 8
    von *of,* 1; *from,* 3; **von 8 Uhr bis 8 Uhr 45** *from 8:00 until 8:45,* 4
    vor *before,* 1; *in front of,* 9; vor allem *especially,* 9; **zehn vor ...** *ten till...,* 6
    voraus *in advance,* 9
    vorbeigehen *to go by,* 7
    vorbeikommen *to come by,* 9
    vorbeigekommen *came by,* 8
    vorbereiten *to prepare,* 12
die Vorbereitung, -en *preparation,* 12
    **vorgestern** *day before yesterday,* 8
der Vormittag *before noon,* 2
    vorn *ahead,* 4; hier vorn *here in front,* 5; **da vorn** *there in the front,* 4
**der Vorort, -e** *suburb,* 3; **ein Vorort von** *a suburb of,* 3
der Vorschlag, ∸e *suggestion,* 12
    vorstellen *to introduce,* 1
die Vorstellung, -en *introduction,* 10
die Vorwahlnummer, -n *area code,* 11
die Vorzeit, -en *pre-history,* 10

# W

    wählen *to choose,* 10; die Telefonnummer wählen *to dial the telephone number,* 11
das Wahlpflichtfach, ∸er *required elective,* 4
    Wahnsinn! *Crazy!,* 11
    wahr *true,* 11
    während *while,* 6
    **wahrscheinlich** *probably,* 11
der Walnußkern, -e *walnut,* 8
    **wandern** *to hike,* 2

**wann?** *when?,* 2; **Wann hast du Geburtstag?** *When is your birthday?,* 11
    war: ich war *I was,* 8; **Ich war beim Bäcker.** *I was at the baker's.,* 8
die Ware, -n *ware,* 5
    **waren: wir waren** *we were,* 8; **sie waren** *they were,* 8; **Sie (formal) waren** *you were,* 8
    warm *warm,* 7
    warmhalten *to keep warm,* 12
    warst: du warst *you were,* 8; **Wo warst du?** *Where were you?,* 8
    wart: ihr wart *you (plural) were*
    warten *to wait,* 2; ich warte auf *I'm waiting for,* 10
    warum? *why?,* 7
    **was?** *what?,* 1; **Was ist los?** *What's up?,* 4; **Was gibt's?** *What's up?,* 1; **Was ist das?** *What is that?,* p. 8; **Was noch?** *What else?,* 2
    was für? *what kind of?,* 10; **Was für Filme magst du gern?** *What kind of movies do you like?,* 10; **Was für Musik hörst du gern?** *What kind of music do you like?,* 10
die Wäsche *laundry,* 12; die Wäsche aufhängen *to hang up the laundry,* 7
die Waschmaschine, -n *washing machine,* 12
**das Wasser** *water,* 3; **ein Glas (Mineral)Wasser** *a glass of (mineral) water,* 3
    wasserscheu *afraid of water,* 12
der Wecken, - *roll,* 8
    weg *away,* 7
der Weg, -e: den Weg zeigen *to give directions,* 9
    wegbringen *to take, bring away,* 7
    weggebracht (pp) *brought away,* 7
der Weichkäse, - *soft cheese,* 8
**das Weihnachten** *Christmas,* 11; **Fröhliche Weihnachten!** *Merry Christmas!,* 11
    weil *because* (conj), 8
    weit *far,* 3; *wide,* 5; **weit von hier** *far from here,* 3
    weiter *farther,* 7
das Weizenmehl *wheat flour,* 12
    **weiß** *white,* 3; **in Weiß** *in white,* 5
die Weißwurst, ∸e *(southern German sausage specialty),* 9
    **welch-** *which,* 2; an welchem Tag? *on which day?,* 11; **Welche Fächer hast du?** *Which subjects do you have?,* 4

die Welt *world*, 8
**wem?** *to whom?, for whom?*, 11
**wen?** *whom?*, 7; **Wen lädst du ein?** *Whom are you inviting?*, 12
wenden *to turn (to)*, 9
wenig *few*, 7
wenn *when, if* (conj), 5
**wer?** *who?*, 1; **Wer ist das?** *Who is that?*, 1
die Werbung *advertisement*, 4
werden *to become*, 5
Werken *shop* (school subject), 4
die Weste, -n *vest*, 5
**der Western,** - *western* (movie), 10
**das Wetter** *weather*, 7; **Wie ist das Wetter?** *How's the weather?*, 7
der Wetterbericht, -e *weather report*, 7
wichtig *important*, 7
**wie?** *how?*, 1; **Wie alt bist du?** *How old are you?*, 1; **Wie bitte?** *Excuse me?*, 8; **Wie blöd!** *How stupid!*, 4; **wie oft?** *how often?*, 7
wieder *again*, 9
**Wiederhören** *Bye!* (on the telephone), 11; **Auf Wiederhören!** *Goodbye!* (on the telephone), 11
**Wiedersehen!** *Bye!*, 1; **Auf Wiedersehen!** *Goodbye!*, 1
wiederverwertet *reused*, 7
**wiegen** *to weigh*, 8
die Wiener (Würstchen), - *sausage*, 6
**wieviel?** *how much?*, 8; **Wieviel Grad haben wir?** *What's the temperature?*, 7; **Wieviel Uhr ist es?** *What time is it?*, 6
willkommen: Herzlich willkommen bei uns! *Welcome to our home!*, 12
windig *windy*, 7
**der Winter** *winter*, 2; **im Winter** *in the winter*, 2
**wir** *we*, 2
wird *becomes*, 7
**wirklich** *really*, 5
die Wirkung, -en *effect*, 8
wischen *to mop*, 12
**wissen** *to know* (a fact, information, etc.), 9; **Das weiß ich nicht.** *That I don't know.*, 9; **Ich weiß nicht.** *I don't know.*, 5; **Weißt du noch?** *Do you still remember?*, 7; **Weißt du, wo das Museum ist?** *Do you know where the museum is?*, 9
witzig *funny*, 10
**wo?** *where?*, 1

wobei *in doing so, in the process of*, 7
**die Woche, -n** *week*, 6; **(einmal) in der Woche** *(once) a week*, 7
**das Wochenende, -n** *weekend*, 2; **am Wochenende** *on the weekend*, 2
die Wochenendheimfahrerin, -nen *student (female) who goes home on weekends*, 3
**woher?** *from where?*, 1; **Woher bist du?** *Where are you from?*, 1; **Woher kommst du?** *Where are you from?*, 1
**wohin?** *where (to)?*, 6; **Wohin geht's?** *Where are you going?*, 7
das Wohlergehen *welfare*, 8
**wohnen** *to live*, 3; **Wo wohnst du?** *Where do you live?*, 3
die Wohnung, -en *apartment*, 3
**das Wohnzimmer,** - *living room*, 12; **im Wohnzimmer** *in the living room*, 12
der Wolf, ⁻e *wolf*, 12
**wolkig** *cloudy*, 7
**wollen** *to want (to)*, 6
die Wollwurst, ⁻e *(southern German sausage specialty)*, 8
das Wort, ⁻er *word*, 2
**das Wörterbuch, ⁻er** *dictionary*, 4
der Wortschatz *vocabulary*, 1
worüber? *about what?*, 10; **Worüber habt ihr gesprochen?** *What did you (pl) talk about?*, 10; Worüber sprichst du mit deinen Freunden? *What do you talk about with your friends?*, 10
wunderbar *wonderful*, 4
**der Wunsch, ⁻e** *wish*, 5; **Haben Sie einen Wunsch?** *May I help you?*, 5; **Haben Sie noch einen Wunsch?** *Would you like anything else*, 8
würde *would*, 10
würdest: du würdest *you would*, 7
der Würfel, - *cube*, 12
**die Wurst, ⁻e** *sausage*, 8
**das Wurstbrot, -e** *bologna sandwich*, 6
das Würstchen, - *sausage link*, 9

## Z

z.B.=zum Beispiel *for example*, 10
zahlen *to pay*, 6; **Hallo! Ich möchte/will zahlen!** *The check please!*, 6

die Zahlen (pl) *numbers*, p. 9
zart *tender*, 8
**zehn** *ten*, 1
**zeichnen** *to draw*, 2
die Zeichnung, -en *drawing*, 6
zeigen *to show*, 3; den Weg zeigen *to give directions*, 9
die Zeile, -n *line*, 11
**die Zeit** *time*, 4; die ganze Zeit *the whole time*, 12; **Ich habe keine Zeit.** *I don't have time.*, 7
**die Zeitschrift, -en** *magazine*, 10
**die Zeitung, -en** *newspaper*, 10
das Zeug *stuff*, 4
das Zeugnis, -se *report card*, 4
das Ziel, -e *goal*, 2
**ziemlich** *rather*, 4
**das Zimmer,** - *room*, 3; **mein Zimmer aufräumen** *to clean my room*, 7
der Zimt *cinnamon*, 12
**die Zitrone, -n** *lemon*, 12; **mit Zitrone** *with lemon*, 6
der Zitronensaft, ⁻e *lemon juice*, 8
**der Zoo, -s** *zoo*, 12; **in den Zoo gehen** *to go to the zoo*, 12
**zu** *too*, 5; *to*, 7; **zu Fuß** *on foot*, 1; **zu Hause** *at home*, 3; **zu Hause helfen** *to help at home*, 7; zu Hause sein *to be at home*, 6
die Zubereitung, -en *preparation (of food)*, 8
**der Zucker** *sugar*, 8
**zuerst** *first*, 4
der Zug, ⁻e *train*, 4
zuhören *to listen*, p. 6
**zuletzt** *last of all*, 4
zum = zu dem *to the*, 2; zum Beispiel *for example*, 10
zur = zu der *to the*, 1
zurück *back*, 4
zurückkommen *to come back*, 12
zusammen *together*, 2
zusammenlegen *to fold (the wash)*, 12
zusammentun *to join*, 11
der Zuschauer, - *viewer*, 7
die Zutaten (pl) *ingredients*, 8
**zwanzig** *twenty*, 1
**zwei** *two*, 1
**zweimal** *twice*, 7
zweite *second*, 4
**zweiundzwanzig** *twenty-two*, 3
**die Zwiebel, -n** *onion*, 12
zwischen *between*, 9
**zwölf** *twelve*, 1
zynisch *cynical(ly)*, 10

# ENGLISH-GERMAN VOCABULARY

This vocabulary includes all of the words in the **Wortschatz** sections of the chapters. These words are considered active—you are expected to know them and be able to use them.

Idioms are listed under the English word you would be most likely to look up. German nouns are listed with definite article and plural ending, when applicable. The number after each German word or phrase refers to the chapter in which it becomes active vocabulary. To be sure you are using the German words and phrases in the correct context, refer to the chapters in which they appear.

The following abbreviations are used in the vocabulary: sep (separable-prefix verb), pl (plural), acc (accusative), dat (dative), masc (masculine), and poss adj (possessive adjective).

## A

**a, an** *ein(e)*, 3
**about** *ungefähr*, 7
**action movie** *der Actionfilm, -e*, 10
**actor** *der Schauspieler, -*, 10
**actress** *die Schauspielerin, -nen*, 10
**adventure movie** *der Abenteuerfilm, -e*, 10
**after** *nach*, 2; **after school** *nach der Schule*, 2; **after the break** *nach der Pause*, 4
**after that** *danach*, 4
**afternoon** *der Nachmittag, -e*, 2; **in the afternoon** *am Nachmittag*, 2
**again** *wieder*, 9
**along: Why don't you come along!** *Komm doch mit!*, 7
**already** *schon*, 1
**also** *auch*, 1; **I also need...** *ich brauche noch ...*, 8
**always** *immer*, 7
**am: I am** *ich bin*, 1
**and** *und*, 1
**another** *noch ein*, 9; **I don't want any more....** *Ich möchte kein(e)(en) ... mehr.*, 9; **I'd like another....** *Ich möchte noch ein(e)(en) ...* , 9
**anything: Anything else?** *Sonst noch etwas?*, 8
**appear** *aussehen (sep)*, 5
**apple** *der Apfel, :*, 8
**apple cake** *der Apfelkuchen, -*, 6
**apple juice** *der Apfelsaft, :*, 3; **a glass of apple juice** *ein Glas Apfelsaft*, 3
**approximately** *ungefähr*, 7
**April** *der April*, 7
**are: you are** *du bist*, 1; (formal) *Sie sind*, 1; (pl) *ihr seid*, 1; **we are** *wir sind*, 1
**armchair** *der Sessel, -*, 12
**art** *die Kunst*, 4
**at: at 8 o'clock** *um 8 Uhr*, 4; **at one o'clock** *um ein Uhr*, 6; **at the baker's** *beim Bäcker*, 8; **at the butcher's** *beim Metzger*, 8; **at the produce store** *im Obst- und Gemüseladen*, 8; **at the supermarket** *im Supermarkt*, 8; **At what time?** *Um wieviel Uhr?*, 6
**August** *der August*, 7
**aunt** *die Tante -n*, 3
**awesome** *stark*, 5; **The sweater is awesome!** *Ich finde den Pulli stark!*, 5
**awful** *furchtbar*, 5

## B

**bad** *schlecht*, 4; **badly** *schlecht*, 6; **Bad luck!** *So ein Pech!*, 4
**baker** *der Bäcker, -*, 8; **at the baker's** *beim Bäcker*, 8
**bakery** *die Bäckerei, -en*, 8
**bald: to be bald** *eine Glatze haben*, 3
**ballpoint pen** *der Kuli, -s*, 4
**bank** *die Bank, -en*, 9
**bargain: that's a bargain** *das ist preiswert*, 4
**basketball** *Basketball*, 2
**be** *sein*, 1; **I am** *ich bin*, 1; **you are** *du bist*, 1; **he/she is** *er/sie ist*, 1; **we are** *wir sind*, 1; (pl) **you are** *ihr seid*, 1; (formal) **you are** *Sie sind*, 1; **they are** *sie sind*, 1
**be able to** *können*, 7
**be called** *heißen*, 1
**beautiful** *schön*, 3
**because** *denn, weil*, 8
**bed** *das Bett, -en*, 3; **to make the bed** *das Bett machen*, 7
**believe** *glauben*, 9
**belt** *der Gürtel, -*, 5
**best: Best wishes on your birthday!** *Herzlichen Glückwunsch zum Geburtstag!*, 11
**better** *besser*, 8
**big** *groß*, 3
**bike** *das Fahrrad, :er*, 1; **by bike** *mit dem Rad*, 1

**biology** *Bio (aie Biologie)*, 4
**biology teacher (female)** *die Biologielehrerin, -nen*, 1
**birthday** *der Geburtstag, -e*, 11; **Best wishes on your birthday!** *Herzlichen Glückwunsch zum Geburtstag!*, 11; **Happy Birthday!** *Alles Gute zum Geburtstag!*, 11; **My birthday is on....** *Ich habe am ... Geburtstag.*, 11; **When is your birthday?** *Wann hast du Geburtstag?*, 11
**black** *schwarz*, 3; **in black** *in Schwarz*, 5
**blond** *blond*, 3
**blouse** *die Bluse, -n*, 5
**blue** *blau*, 3; **blue (green, brown) eyes** *blaue (grüne, braune) Augen*, 3; **in blue** *in Blau*, 5
**board game** *das Brettspiel, -e*, 2
**bologna sandwich** *das Wurstbrot, -e*, 6
**book** *das Buch, :er*, 4
**bookcase** *das Regal -e*, 3
**boot** *der Stiefel, -*, 5
**boring** *langweilig*, 2
**bought** *gekauft*, 8; **I bought bread.** *Ich habe Brot gekauft.*, 8
**bouquet of flowers** *der Blumenstrauß, :e*, 11
**boy** *der Junge, -n*, 1
**bread** *das Brot, -e*, 8
**break** *die Pause, -n*, 4; **after the break** *nach der Pause*, 4
**broken** *kaputt*, 3
**brother** *der Bruder, :*, 3; **brothers and sisters** *die Geschwister (pl)*, 3
**brown** *braun*, 3; **in brown** *in Braun*, 5
**brutal** *brutal*, 10
**bus** *der Bus, -se*, 1; **by bus** *mit dem Bus*, 1
**busy (telephone)** *besetzt*, 11
**but** *aber*, 3
**butcher shop** *die Metzgerei, -en*, 8; **at the butcher's** *beim Metzger*, 8

butter *die Butter*, 8
buy *kaufen*, 5; **What did you buy?**
*Was hast du gekauft?*, 8
by: **by bike** *mit dem Rad*, 1; **by bus**
*mit dem Bus*, 1; **by car** *mit dem
Auto*, 1; **by moped** *mit dem Moped*,
1; **by subway** *mit der U-Bahn*, 1
Bye! *Wiedersehen! Tschau! Tschüs!*, 1;
(on the telephone) *Wiederhören!*, 11

## C

cabinet *der Schrank*, ̈e, 3
café *das Café*, -s, 6; **to the café** *ins
Café*, 6
cake *der Kuchen*, -, 3; **a piece of
cake** *ein Stück Kuchen*, 3
calendar *der Kalender*, -, 11
call *anrufen* (sep), *telefonieren*, 11
can *können*, 7
capital *die Hauptstadt*, ̈e, 1
car *das Auto*, -s, 1; **by car** *mit dem
Auto*, 1
cards *Karten*, 2
care for *mögen*, 10
carpet *der Teppich*, -e, 12
cassette *die Kassette*, -n, 4
casual *lässig*, 5
cat *Katze*, -n, 3; **to feed the cat** *die
Katze füttern*, 7
Certainly! *Natürlich!*, 11; *Sicher!*, 3
chair *der Stuhl*, ̈e, 3
change: **Keep the change!** *Stimmt
(schon)!*, 6
cheap *billig*, 4
check: **The check please!** *Hallo! Ich
möchte/will zahlen!*, 6
cheese *der Käse*, -, 8
cheese sandwich *das Käsebrot*, -e, 6
chess *Schach*, 2
chicken *das Hähnchen*, -, 8
Christmas *das Weihnachten*, -, 11;
**Merry Christmas!** *Fröhliche
Weihnachten!*, 11
church *die Kirche*, -n, 9
cinammon *der Zimt*, 12
cinema *das Kino*, -s, 6
city *die Stadt*, ̈e, 9; **in the city** *in
der Stadt*, 3
city hall *das Rathaus*, ̈er, 9
class schedule *der Stundenplan*, ̈e, 4
classical music *klassische Musik*, 10
clean: **to clean the windows** *die
Fenster putzen*, 7; **to clean up my
room** *mein Zimmer aufräumen*
(sep), 7
clear: **to clear the table** *den Tisch
abräumen* (sep), 7
clothes (casual term for) *die
Klamotten* (pl), 5; **to pick up my
clothes** *meine Klamotten aufräumen* (sep), 7

cloudy *wolkig*, 7
coffee *der Kaffee*, 8; **a cup of coffee**
*eine Tasse Kaffee*, 6
coin *die Münze*, -n, 11
cold *kalt*, 7
cold cuts *der Aufschnitt*, 8
collect *sammeln*, 2; **to collect comics**
*Comics sammeln*, 2; **to collect
stamps** *Briefmarken sammeln*, 2
color *die Farbe*, -n, 5
come *kommen*, 1; **I come** *ich
komme*, 1; **That comes to....** *Das
macht (zusammen) ...* , 6; **to come
along** *mitkommen* (sep), 7
comedy *die Komödie*, -n, 10
comfortable *bequem*, 3
comics *die Comics*, 2; **to collect
comics** *Comics sammeln*, 2
compact disc *die CD*, -s, 11
concert *das Konzert*, -e, 6; **to go to a
concert** *ins Konzert gehen*, 6
cookie *der Keks*, -e, 3; **a few cookies**
*ein paar Kekse*, 3
cool *kühl*, 7
corners: **with corners** *eckig*, 12
corny *schmalzig*, 10
cost *kosten*, 4; **How much does...
cost?** *Was kostet ... ?*, 4
cotton *die Baumwolle*, 12; **made of
cotton** *aus Baumwolle*, 12
couch *die Couch*, -es, 3
country *das Land*, ̈er, 3; **in the
country** *auf dem Land*, 3
cousin (female) *die Kusine*, -n, 3;
**cousin (male)** *der Cousin*, -s, 3
crime drama *der Krimi*, -s, 10
cruel *grausam*, 10

## D

dance *tanzen*, 2; **to go dancing**
*tanzen gehen*, 6
dark blue *dunkelblau*, 5; **in dark
blue** *in Dunkelblau*, 5
day *der Tag*, -e, 1; **day before yesterday** *vorgestern*, 8; **every day**
*jeden Tag*, 7; **day before yesterday**
*vorgestern*, 8
December *der Dezember*, 7
definitely *bestimmt*, 5
degree *der Grad*, -, 7
Delicious! *Lecker!*, 6
desk *der Schreibtisch*, -e, 3
detective movie *der Krimi*, -s, 10
dial *wählen*, 11; **to dial the number**
*die Nummer wählen*, 11
dictionary *das Wörterbuch*, ̈er, 4
different *verschieden*, 11
dining table *der Eßtisch*, -e, 12
directly *direkt*, 4
disagree: **I disagree.** *Das finde ich
nicht.*, 2

disco *die Disko*, -s, 6; **to go to a
disco** *in eine Disko gehen*, 6
dishes *das Geschirr*, 7; **to wash the
dishes** *das Geschirr spülen*, 7
dislike *nicht gern haben*, 4; **strongly
dislike** *überhaupt nicht gern*, 10
do *machen*, 2; *tun*, 7; **do crafts**
*basteln*, 2; **do homework** *die
Hausaufgaben machen*, 2; **Do you
have any other interests?** *Hast
du andere Interessen?*, 2; **Do you
need help?** *Brauchst du Hilfe?*, 7;
**Do you play an instrument?**
*Spielst du ein Instrument?*, 2; **Do
you play sports?** *Machst du
Sport?*, 2; **Do you think so?**
*Meinst du?*, 5; **Does it taste good?**
*Schmeckt's?*, 6; **What did you do
on the weekend?** *Was hast du am
Wochenende gemacht?*, 10
dog *der Hund*, -e, 3
done *gemacht*, 10
downtown *die Innenstadt*, 9; **to go
downtown** *in die Stadt gehen*, 6
draw *zeichnen*, 2
dress *das Kleid*, -er, 5
drink *trinken*, 3
drive *fahren*, 9; **he/she drives** *er/sie
fährt*, 9
dry *trocken*, 7
dumb *blöd*, 2; *doof, dumm*, 10

## E

Easter *das Ostern*, -, 11; **Happy
Easter!** *Frohe Ostern!*, 11
easy *einfach*, 1; **That's easy!** *Also,
einfach!*, 1
eat *essen*, 3; **he/she eats** *er/sie ißt*,
6; **to eat ice cream** *ein Eis essen*, 6
egg *das Ei*, -er, 8
ehrlich *honestly*, 5
eight *acht*, 1
eighteen *achtzehn*, 1
eighty *achtzig*, 3
eleven *elf*, 1
enough *genug*, 9
environment *die Umwelt*, 10
eraser *der Radiergummi*, -s, 4
especially *besonders*, 6; **especially
like** *besonders gern*, 10
evening *der Abend*, 1; **in the
evening** *am Abend*, 2
every: **every day** *jeden Tag*, 7
exciting *spannend*, 10
Excuse me! *Entschuldigung!,
Verzeihung!*, 9
expensive *teuer*, 4
eye *das Auge*, -n, 3; **blue (green,
brown) eyes** *blaue (grüne,
braune) Augen*, 3

## F

fall *der Herbst*, 2; in the fall *im Herbst*, 2
family *die Familie, -n*, 3
fancy chocolate *die Praline, -n*, 11
fantasy novel *der Fantasyroman, -e*, 10
far *weit*, 3; far from here *weit von hier*, 3
fashion *die Mode*, 10
father *der Vater, ÷*, 3; to, for your father *deinem Vater*, 11; to, for my father *meinem Vater*, 11
Father's Day *der Vatertag*, 11; Happy Father's Day! *Alles Gute zum Vatertag!*, 11
favorite *Lieblings-*, 4
February *der Februar*, 7
feed *füttern*, 7; to feed the cat *die Katze füttern*, 7
fetch *holen*, 8
few: a few *ein paar*, 3; a few cookies *ein paar Kekse*, 3
fifteen *fünfzehn*, 1
fifty *fünfzig*, 3
five *fünf*, 1
first *erst-*, 11; first of all *zuerst*, 4; on the first of July *am ersten Juli*, 11; the first street *die erste Straße*, 9
fit *passen*, 5; The skirt fits great! *Der Rock paßt prima!*, 5
flower *die Blume, -n*, 7; to water the flowers *die Blumen gießen*, 7
foot: on foot (I walk) *zu Fuß*, 1
for *für*, 7; *denn* (conj), 8
forty *vierzig*, 3
four *vier*, 1
fourteen *vierzehn*, 1
for whom? *für wen?*, 8
free time *die Freizeit*, 2
fresh *frisch*, 8
fresh produce store *der Obst- und Gemüseladen, ÷*, 8
Friday *der Freitag*, 4
friend (male) *der Freund, -e*, 1; (female) *die Freundin, -nen*, 1; to visit friends *Freunde besuchen*, 2
from *aus*, 1; *von*, 4; from 8 until 8:45 *von 8 Uhr bis 8 Uhr 45*, 4
from where? *woher?*, 1; I'm from *ich bin (komme) aus*, 1; Where are you from? *Woher bist (kommst) du?*, 1
front: there in the front *da vorn*, 4
fruit *das Obst*, 8; a piece of fruit *Obst*, 3
fun *der Spaß*, 2; (Tennis) is fun. *(Tennis) macht Spaß.*, 2; (Tennis) is no fun. *(Tennis) macht keinen Spaß.*, 2
funny *lustig*, 10
furniture *die Möbel* (pl), 3

## G

garden(s) *der Garten, ÷*, 9
geography *die Erdkunde*, 4
German mark (German monetary unit) *DM = Deutsche Mark*, 4
German teacher (male) *der Deutschlehrer, -*, 1; (female) *die Deutschlehrerin, -nen*, 1
get *bekommen*, 4; *holen*, 8
gift *das Geschenk, -e*, 11
gift idea *die Geschenkidee, -n*, 11
girl *das Mädchen, -*, 1
give *geben*, 11; he/she gives *er/sie gibt*, 11
give (a gift) *schenken*, 11
glass *das Glas, ÷er*, 3; a glass (cup) of tea *ein Glas Tee*, 6; a glass of (mineral) water *ein Glas (Mineral)Wasser*, 3; a glass of apple juice *ein Glas Apfelsaft*, 3
glasses: a pair of glasses *eine Brille, -n*, 3
go *gehen*, 3; to go home *nach Hause gehen*, 3
golf *Golf*, 2
good *gut*, 4; Good! *Gut!*, 6
Good morning! *Guten Morgen! Morgen!*, 1
Goodbye! *Auf Wiedersehen!*, 1; (on the telephone) *Auf Wiederhören*, 11
grade *die Note, -n*, 4
grade level *die Klasse, -n*, 4
grades: a 1, 2, 3, 4, 5, 6 *eine Eins, Zwei, Drei, Vier, Fünf, Sechs*, 4
gram *das Gramm, -*, 8
grandfather *der Großvater (Opa), ÷*, 3
grandmother *die Großmutter (Oma), ÷*, 3
grandparents *die Großeltern* (pl), 3
grape *die Traube, -n*, 8
gray *grau*, 3; in gray *in Grau*, 5
Great! *Prima!*, 1; *Sagenhaft!*, 6; *Klasse! Toll!*, 2
green *grün*, 3; in green *in Grün*, 5
groceries *die Lebensmittel* (pl), 8
ground meat *das Hackfleisch*, 8
group *die Gruppe, -n*, 10
guitar *die Gitarre, -n*, 2
gyros *das Gyros, -*, 9

## H

hair *die Haare* (pl), 3
half *halb*, 6; half past (twelve, one, etc.) *halb (eins, zwei usw.)*, 6
hang up (the telephone) *auflegen* (sep), 11

Hanukkah *Chanukka*, 11; Happy Hanukkah! *Frohes Chanukka Fest!*, 11
have *haben*, 4; he/she has English *er/sie hat Englisch*, 4; I have German. *Ich habe Deutsch.*, 4; I have no classes on Saturday. *Am Samstag habe ich frei.*, 4; I'll have... *Ich bekomme ...*, 6
have to *müssen*, 7; I have to *ich muß*, 7
he *er*, 2; he is *er ist*, 1; he's from *er ist (kommt) aus*, 1
hear *hören*, 2
Hello! *Guten Tag! Tag! Hallo! Grüß dich!*, 1
help *helfen*, 7; to help at home *zu Hause helfen*, 7
her *ihr* (poss adj), 3; her name is *sie heißt*, 1
hideous *scheußlich*, 5
hike *wandern*, 2
him *ihn*, 5
his *sein* (poss adj), 3; his name is *er heißt*, 1
history *die Geschichte*, 4
hobby book *das Hobbybuch, ÷er*, 10
holiday *der Feiertag, -e*, 11
homework *die Hausaufgabe, -n*, 2; to do homework *Hausaufgaben machen*, 2
horror movie *der Horrorfilm, -e*, 10
horror novel *der Gruselroman, -e*, 10
hot *heiß*, 7
hotel *das Hotel, -s*, 9
how much? *wieviel?*, 8; How much does... cost? *Was kostet ... ?*, 4
how often? *wie oft?*, 7
how? *wie?*, 1; How are you? *Wie geht's (denn)?*, 6; How do I get to...? *Wie komme ich zum (zur) ... ?*, 9; How do you get to school? *Wie kommst du zur Schule?*, 1; How does it taste? *Wie schmeckt's?*, 6; How old are you? *Wie alt bist du?*, 1; How's the weather? *Wie ist das Wetter?*, 7
hunger *der Hunger*, 9
hungry: I'm hungry. *Ich habe Hunger.*, 9; I'm not hungry any more. *Ich habe keinen Hunger mehr.*, 9

## I

I *ich*, 2; I don't. *Ich nicht.*, 2
ice cream *das Eis*, 6; a dish of ice cream *ein Eisbecher*, 6
ice skate *Schlittschuh laufen*, 12
idea: I have no idea! *Keine Ahnung!*, 9
imaginative *phantasievoll*, 10

**in** *in*, 2; **in the afternoon** *am Nachmittag*, 2; **in the city** *in der Stadt*, 3; **in the country** *auf dem Land*, 3; **in the evening** *am Abend*, 2; **in the fall** *im Herbst*, 2; **in the kitchen** *in der Küche*, 12; **in the living room** *im Wohnzimmer*, 12; **in the spring** *im Frühling*, 2; **in the summer** *im Sommer*, 2; **in the winter** *im Winter*, 2

**insert** *einstecken*, 11; **to insert coins** *Münzen einstecken (sep)*, 11

**instrument** *das Instrument, -e*, 2; **Do you play an instrument?** *Spielst du ein Instrument?*, 2

**interesting** *interessant*, 2

**interest** *das Interesse, -n*, 2; **Do you have any other interests?** *Hast du andere Interessen?*, 2

**invite** *einladen (sep)*, 11; **he/she invites** *er/sie lädt ... ein*, 11

**is: he/she is** *er/sie ist*, 1

**it** *er, es, sie*, 3; *ihn*, 5

## J

**jacket** *die Jacke, -n*, 5

**January** *der Januar*, 7; **in January** *im Januar*, 7

**jeans** *die Jeans, -*, 5

**jewelry** *der Schmuck*, 11

**jog** *joggen*, 12

**jogging suit** *der Jogging-Anzug, ⁻e*, 5

**juice** *der Saft, ⁻e*, 3

**July** *der Juli*, 7

**June** *der Juni*, 7

**just: Just a minute, please.** *Einen Moment, bitte.*, 11

## K

**keep: Keep the change!** *Stimmt (schon)!*, 6

**kilogram** *das Kilo, -*, 8

**kitchen** *die Küche, -n*, 12; **in the kitchen** *in der Küche*, 12

**know** (a fact, information, etc.) *wissen*, 9; **I don't know.** *Ich weiß nicht.*, 5

**know** (be familiar or acquainted with) *kennen*, 10

## L

**lamp** *die Lampe, -n*, 12

**last** *letzt-*, 8; **last of all** *zuletzt*, 4; **last week** *letzte Woche*, 8; **last weekend** *letztes Wochenende*, 8

**Latin** *Latein*, 4

**lawn** *der Rasen, -*, 7; **to mow the lawn** *den Rasen mähen*, 7

**layer cake** *die Torte, -n*, 8

**leather** *das Leder*, 12; **made of leather** *aus Leder*, 12

**left: to the left** *nach links*, 9

**lemon** *die Zitrone, -n*, 12

**lemon drink** *die Limo, -s*, 3

**lettuce** *der Salat*, 8

**light blue** *hellblau*, 5; **in light blue** *in Hellblau*, 5

**like** *gern haben*, 4; *mögen*, 10; **I like it.** *Er/Sie/Es gefällt mir.*, 5 **I like them.** *Sie gefallen mir.*, 5; **like an awful lot** *furchtbar gern*, 10; **not like at all** *gar nicht gern*, 10; **not like very much** *nicht so gern*, 2

**like (to do)** *gern (machen)*, 2; **to not like (to do)** *nicht gern (machen)*, 2

**listen (to)** *hören*, 2; *zuhören, p. 6*

**liter** *der Liter, -*, 8

**little** *klein*, 3; **a little** *ein bißchen*, 5; **a little more** *ein bißchen mehr*, 8

**live** *wohnen*, 3

**living room: in the living room** *im Wohnzimmer*, 12

**long** *lang*, 3

**look** *schauen*, 2; **Look!** *Schauen Sie!*, 4

**look for** *suchen*, 5; **I'm looking for** *ich suche*, 5

**look like** *aussehen (sep)*, 5; **he/she looks like** *er/sie sieht ... aus*, 5; **The skirt looks....** *Der Rock sieht ... aus.*, 5; **What do they look like?** *Wie sehen sie aus?*, 3; **What does he look like?** *Wie sieht er aus?*, 3

**lot: a lot** *viel*, 2

**luck: Bad luck!** *So ein Pech!*, 4; **What luck!** *So ein Glück!*, 4

## M

**made: made of cotton** *aus Baumwolle*, 12; **made of leather** *aus Leder*, 12; **made of plastic** *aus Kunststoff*, 12; **made of silk** *aus Seide*, 12; **made of wood** *aus Holz*, 12

**magazine** *die Zeitschrift, -en*, 10

**make** *machen*, 2; **to make the bed** *das Bett machen*, 7

**man** *der Mann, ⁻er*, 3

**many** *viele*, 2

**March** *der März*, 7

**mark** *die Mark, -*, 4

**market square** *der Marktplatz, ⁻e*, 9

**math** *Mathe (die Mathematik)*, 4

**may: May I help you?** *Haben Sie einen Wunsch?*, 5

**May** *der Mai*, 7

**maybe** *vielleicht*, 11

**me** *mich*, 7; **Me too.** *Ich auch.*, 2

**meat** *das Fleisch*, 8

**mess: What a mess!** *So ein Mist!*, 4

**milk** *die Milch*, 8

**mineral water** *das Mineralwasser*, 3

**minute: Just a minute, please.** *Einen Moment, bitte.*, 11

**miserable** *miserabel*, 6

**modern** *modern*, 12

**moment** *der Moment, -e*, 3

**money** *das Geld*, 4

**month** *der Monat, -e*, 7

**moped** *das Moped, -s*, 2; **by moped** *mit dem Moped*, 1

**more** *mehr*, 9

**morning** *der Morgen*, 1; **Morning!** *Morgen!*, 1

**most of all** *am liebsten*, 10

**mother** *die Mutter, ⁻*, 3

**Mother's Day** *der Muttertag*, 11; **Happy Mother's Day!** *Alles Gute zum Muttertag!*, 11

**movie** *der Film, -e*, 10; **to go to the movies** *ins Kino gehen*, 6

**movie theater** *das Kino, -s*, 6

**mow** *mähen*, 7; **to mow the lawn** *den Rasen mähen*, 7

**Mr.** *Herr*, 1

**Mrs.** *Frau*, 1

**much** *viel*, 2; **much too** *viel zu*, 5

**museum** *das Museum, die Museen*, 9

**music** *die Musik*, 2; **to listen to music** *Musik hören*, 2

**mustard** *der Senf*, 6; **with mustard** *mit Senf*, 6

**my** *mein*, 3; **my name is** *ich heiße*, 1; **to, for my father** *meinem Vater*, 11 **to, for my mother** *meiner Mutter*, 11

## N

**name** *der Name, -n*, 1; **her name is** *sie heißt*, 1; **his name is** *er heißt*, 1; **my name is** *ich heiße*, 1; **What's the boy's name?** *Wie heißt der Junge?*, 1; **What's the girl's name?** *Wie heißt das Mädchen?*, 1; **What's your name?** *Wie heißt du?*, 1

**nearby** *in der Nähe*, 3

**need** *brauchen*, 5; **I need** *ich brauche*, 5

**never** *nie*, 7

**new** *neu*, 3

**newspaper** *die Zeitung, -en*, 10

**next: the next street** *die nächste Straße*, 9

**nine** *neun*, 1

**nineteen** *neunzehn*, 1

**ninety** *neunzig*, 3

**no** *kein*, 9; **No more, thanks!** *Nichts mehr, danke!*, 9

**non-fiction book** *das Sachbuch, ⁻er*, 10

**none** *kein*, 9

**noodle soup** *die Nudelsuppe, -n,* 6

**not** *nicht,* 2; **not at all** *überhaupt nicht,* 5; **not like at all** *gar nicht gern,* 10; **Not really.** *Nicht besonders.,* 6; **Not too long?** *Nicht zu lang?,* 5

**not any** *kein,* 9

**notebook** *das Notizbuch,* 1; *das Heft, -e,* 4

**nothing** *nichts,* 3; **nothing at the moment** *im Moment gar nichts,* 3; **Nothing, thank you!** *Nichts, danke!,* 3

**novel** *der Roman, -e,* 10

**November** *der November,* 7

**now** *jetzt,* 1

**number** *die (Telefon)nummer,* 11; **to dial the number** *die Nummer wählen,* 11

### O

**o'clock: at 8 o'clock** *um 8 Uhr,* 4; **at one o'clock** *um ein Uhr,* 6

**October** *der Oktober,* 7

**Of course!** *Ja klar!,* 1; *Ganz klar!,* 4

**offer** *das Angebot, -e,* 5

**often** *oft,* 7

**Oh!** *Ach!,* 1; **Oh yeah!** *Ach ja!,* 1

**oil** *das Öl,* 12

**Okay! I'll do that!** *Gut! Mach' ich!,* 7; **It's okay.** *Es geht.,* 6

**old** *alt,* 3; **How old are you?** *Wie alt bist du?,* 1

**on: on ... Square** *am ...platz,* 9; **on ... Street** *in der ...straße,* 3; **on foot (I walk)** *zu Fuß,* 1; **on Monday** *am Montag,* 4; **on the first of July** *am ersten Juli,* 11; **on the weekend** *am Wochenende,* 2

**once** *einmal,* 7; **once a month** *einmal im Monat,* 7; **once a week** *einmal in der Woche,* 7

**one** *eins,* 1

**one hundred** *hundert,* 3

**onion** *die Zwiebel, -n,* 12

**only** *bloß,* 4

**opera** *die Oper, -n,* 10

**orange juice** *der Orangensaft, ⁼e,* 3

**other** *andere,* 2

**oven** *der Ofen, ⁼,* 12

**over there** *dort drüben,* 4; **over there in the back** *da hinten,* 4

**overcast** *trüb,* 7

### P

**pants** *die Hose, -n,* 5

**parents** *die Eltern* (pl), 3

**park** *der Park, -s,* 12; **to go to the park** *in den Park gehen,* 12

**pencil** *der Bleistift, -e,* 4

**people** *die Leute* (pl), 9

**perfume** *das Parfüm, -,* 11

**pet** *das Haustier, -e,* 3

**physical education** *der Sport,* 4

**piano** *das Klavier, -e,* 2; **I play the piano** *Ich spiele Klavier.,* 2

**pick up** *aufräumen* (sep), 7; **to pick up my clothes** *meine Klamotten aufräumen,* 7; **to pick up the telephone** *abheben* (sep), 11

**piece** *das Stück, -e,* 3; **a piece of cake** *ein Stück Kuchen,* 3; **a piece of fruit** *Obst,* 3

**pizza** *die Pizza, -s,* 6

**plastic** *der Kunststoff, -e,* 12; **made of plastic** *aus Kunststoff,* 12

**play** *spielen,* 2; **I play soccer.** *Ich spiele Fußball.,* 2; **I play the piano.** *Ich spiele Klavier.,* 2; **to play a board game** *ein Brettspiel spielen,* 12

**please** *bitte,* 3

**pleasure: My pleasure!** *Gern geschehen!,* 9

**pocket calculator** *der Taschenrechner, -,* 4

**politics** *die Politik,* 10

**polka-dot** *gepunktet,* 12

**post office** *die Post,* 9

**poster** *das Poster, -,* 11

**potato** *die Kartoffel, -n,* 8

**pound** *das Pfund, -,* 8

**prefer** *lieber (mögen),* 10

**pretty** *hübsch,* 5; *schön,* 3

**pretzel** *die Brezel, -n,* 8

**probably** *wahrscheinlich,* 11

**produce store** *der Obst- und Gemüseladen, ⁼,* 8; **at the produce store** *im Obst- und Gemüseladen,* 8

**Pullover** *der Pulli, -s,* 5

**put on** *anziehen* (sep), 5

### Q

**quarter: a quarter after** *Viertel nach,* 6; **a quarter to** *Viertel vor,* 6

### R

**railroad station** *der Bahnhof, ⁼e,* 9

**rain** *der Regen,* 7; **It's raining** *Es regnet.,* 7

**rainy** *regnerisch,* 7

**rather** *ziemlich,* 4

**read** *lesen,* 10; **he/she reads** *er/sie liest,* 10; **What did you read?** *Was hast du gelesen?,* 10

**really** *ganz,* 3; *wirklich,* 5; **Not really.** *Nicht besonders.,* 6

**receive** *bekommen,* 4

**receiver** *der Hörer, -,* 11

**red** *rot,* 3; **in red** *in Rot,* 5

**refrigerator** *der Kühlschrank, ⁼e,* 12

**religion** *die Religion, -en,* 4

**residence: The ... residence** *Hier bei ... ,* 11

**right: to the right** *nach rechts,* 9

**roll** *die Semmel, -n,* 8

**romance** *der Liebesfilm, -e,* 10; **romance novel** *der Liebesroman, -e,* 10

**room** *das Zimmer, -,* 3; **to clean up my room** *mein Zimmer aufräumen* (sep), 7

**round** *rund,* 12

### S

**sad** *traurig,* 10

**salt** *das Salz,* 12

**Saturday** *der Samstag,* 4

**sausage** *die Wurst, ⁼e,* 8

**say** *sagen,* 1; **Say!** *Sag mal!,* 2; **What does the weather report say?** *Was sagt der Wetterbericht?,* 7

**school** *die Schule, -n,* 4; **after school** *nach der Schule,* 2; **How do you get to school?** *Wie kommst du zur Schule?,* 1

**school subject** *das Fach, ⁼er,* 4

**school supplies** *die Schulsachen* (pl), 4

**schoolbag** *die Schultasche, -n,* 4

**science fiction movie** *der Science-fiction-Film, -e,* 10

**search (for)** *suchen,* 4

**second** *zweit-,* 11; **the second street** *die zweite Straße,* 9

**see** *sehen,* 10; **he/she sees** *er/sie sieht,* 10; **See you later!** *Bis dann!,* 1; **to see a movie** *einen Film sehen,* 6; **What did you see?** *Was hast du gesehen?,* 10

**sensational** *sensationell,* 10

**September** *der September,* 7

**set** *decken,* 7; **to set the table** *den Tisch decken,* 7

**seven** *sieben,* 1

**seventeen** *siebzehn,* 1

**seventy** *siebzig,* 3

**she** *sie,* 2; **she is** *sie ist,* 1; **she's from** *sie ist (kommt) aus,* 1

**shine: the sun is shining** *die Sonne scheint,* 7

**shirt** *das Hemd, -en,* 5

**shop** *einkaufen* (sep), 8; **to go shopping** *einkaufen gehen,* 8

**short** *kurz,* 3

**shortening** *das Butterschmalz,* 12

**shorts: pair of shorts** *die Shorts, -,* 5

**should** *sollen,* 8

**silk** *die Seide,* 12; **made of silk** *aus Seide,* 12

singer (female) *die Sängerin,*
*-nen,* 10
singer (male) *der Sänger, -,* 10
sink *das Spülbecken, -,* 12
sister *die Schwester, -n,* 3; brothers
and sisters *die Geschwister* (pl), 3
six *sechs,* 1
sixteen *sechzehn,* 1
sixty *sechzig,* 3
size *die Größe, -n,* 5
skirt *der Rock, ⸚e,* 5
small *klein,* 3
smart (looking) *fesch, schick, chic,* 5
snack bar *die Imbißstube, -n,* 9
sneaker *der Turnschuh, -e,* 5
snow *der Schnee,* 7; It's snowing *Es
schneit.,* 7
so *so,* 2; So long! *Tschau! Tschüs!,*
1; so so *so lala,* 6
soccer *der Fußball,* 2; I play soccer.
*Ich spiele Fußball.,* 2
sock *die Socke, -n,* 5
soda: lemon-flavored soda *die Limo,
-s (die Limonade, -n),* 3
sofa *das Sofa, -s,* 12
something *etwas,* 7
sometimes *manchmal,* 7
song *das Lied, -er,* 10
sorry: I'm sorry. *Es tut mir leid.,* 9;
Sorry, I can't. *Ich kann leider
nicht.,* 7
sort *sortieren,* 7; to sort the trash
*den Müll sortieren,* 7
spend (time) *verbringen,* 10
sports *der Sport,* 2; Do you play
sports? *Machst du Sport?,* 2
spring *der Frühling,* 2; in the spring
*im Frühling,* 2
square *der Platz, ⸚e,* 9; on ... Square
*am ...platz,* 9
stamp *die Briefmarke, -n,* 2; to
collect stamps *Briefmarken
sammeln,* 2
state: German federal state *das
Bundesland, ⸚er,* 1
stereo *die Stereoanlage -n,* 3
stinks: That stinks! *So ein Mist!,* 4
store *der Laden, ⸚,* 8
storm *das Gewitter, -,* 7
stove *der Herd, -e,* 12
straight ahead *geradeaus,* 9
street *die Straße, -n,* 9; on ... Street
*in der ...straße,* 3
striped *gestreift,* 12
stupid *blöd,* 5
subject (school) *das Fach, ⸚er,* 4;
Which subjects do you have?
*Welche Fächer hast du?,* 4
suburb *der Vorort, -e,* 3; a suburb of
*ein Vorort von,* 3
subway *die U-Bahn,* 1; by subway
*mit der U-Bahn,* 1

subway station *die U-Bahnstation,
-en,* 9
sugar *der Zucker,* 8
summer *der Sommer,* 2; in the
summer *im Sommer,* 2
sun *die Sonne,* 7; the sun is shining
*die Sonne scheint,* 7
Sunday *der Sonntag,* 4
sunny *sonnig,* 7
Super! *Spitze!, Super!,* 2
supermarket *der Supermarkt, ⸚e,* 8;
at the supermarket *im
Supermarkt,* 8
supposed to *sollen,* 8
sure: I'm not sure. *Ich bin nicht
sicher.,* 5
sweater *der Pulli, -s,* 5
swim *schwimmen,* 2; to go swimming *baden gehen,* 6
swimming pool *das Schwimmbad,
⸚er,* 6; to go to the (swimming)
pool *ins Schwimmbad gehen,* 6

## T

T-shirt *das T-Shirt, -s,* 5
table *der Tisch, -e,* 12; to clear the
table *den Tisch abräumen* (sep), 7;
to set the table *den Tisch decken,* 7
take *nehmen,* 5; he/she takes *er/sie
nimmt,* 5; I'll take *ich nehme,* 5
talk about *sprechen über,* 10; he/she
talks about *er/sie spricht über,* 10
What did you (pl) talk about?
*Worüber habt ihr gesprochen?,* 10
taste *schmecken,* 6; Does it taste
good? *Schmeckt's?,* 6; How does it
taste? *Wie schmeckt's?,* 6
Tasty! *Lecker!,* 6
tea *der Tee,* 6; a glass (cup) of tea
*ein Glas Tee,* 6
teacher (male) *der Lehrer, -,* 1;
(female) *die Lehrerin, -nen,* 1
telephone *das Telefon, -e, der
Apparat, -e,* 11; pick up the telephone *abheben* (sep), 11
telephone booth *die Telefonzelle,
-n,* 11
telephone number *die
Telefonnummer, -n,* 11
television *das Fernsehen,* 2; to
watch TV *Fernsehen schauen,* 2
temperature: What's the temperature? *Wieviel Grad haben wir?,* 7
ten *zehn,* 1
tennis *Tennis,* 2
terrible *furchtbar,* 5
terrific *Klasse, prima, toll,* 2
thank *danken,* 3; Thank you (very
much)! *Danke (sehr, schön)!,* 3;
*Vielen Dank!,* 9; Thank you!
*Danke!,* 3

that *daß* (conj), 9; That's all. *Das
ist alles.,* 8; That's... *Das ist ...,* 1
the *das, der, die,* 1; *den* (masc, acc),
5; *dem* (masc, neuter, dat), 11
theater *das Theater, -,* 9
then *dann,* 4
there *dort,* 4
they *sie,* 2; they are *sie sind,* 1;
they're from *sie sind (kommen)
aus,* 1
think: Do you think so? *Meinst
du?,* 5; I think *ich glaube,* 2; I
think (tennis) is... *Ich finde
(Tennis) ...,* 2; I think so too.
*Das finde ich auch.,* 2; I think it's
good/bad that.... *Ich finde es
gut/schlecht, daß ...,* 9; I think
that... *Ich finde, daß ...,* 9 What
do you think of (tennis)? *Wie
findest du (Tennis)?,* 2
third *dritte,* 9
thirteen *dreizehn,* 1
thirty *dreißig,* 1
this: this afternoon *heute nachmittag,* 8; This is... *Hier ist ...* (on the
telephone), 11; this morning *heute
morgen,* 8
three *drei,* 1
three times *dreimal,* 7
thrilling *spannend,* 10
Thursday *der Donnerstag,* 4
tight *eng,* 5
till: ten till two *zehn vor zwei,* 6
time *die Zeit,* 4; At what time? *Um
wieviel Uhr?,* 6; I don't have time.
*Ich habe keine Zeit.,* 7; What time
is it? *Wie spät ist es?, Wieviel Uhr
ist es?,* 6
to, for her *ihr,* 11
to, for him *ihm,* 11
today *heute,* 7
tomato *die Tomate, -n,* 8
tomorrow *morgen,* 7
tonight *heute abend,* 7
too *zu,* 5; Too bad! *Schade!,* 4
tour *besichtigen,* 12; to tour the city
*die Stadt besichtigen,* 12
train station *der Bahnhof, ⸚e,* 9
trash *der Müll,* 7; to sort the trash
*den Müll sortieren,* 7
true: Not true! *Stimmt nicht!,* 2;
That's right! True! *Stimmt!,* 2
try on *anprobieren* (sep), 5
Tuesday *der Dienstag,* 4
twelve *zwölf,* 1
twenty *zwanzig,* 1
twenty-one *einundzwanzig,* 3; (see
p. 79 for numbers 21-29)
twice *zweimal,* 7
two *zwei,* 1

## U

ugly  *häßlich*, 3
uncle  *der Onkel*, -, 3
uncomfortable  *unbequem*, 3
unfortunately  *leider*, 7; Unfortunately I can't.  *Leider kann ich nicht.*, 11
until: from 8 until 8:45  *von 8 Uhr bis 8 Uhr 45*, 4; until you get to ... Square  *bis zum ...platz*, 9; until you get to ... Street  *bis zur ...straße*, 9; until you get to the traffic light  *bis zur Ampel*, 9
us  *uns*, 7

## V

vacuum  *Staub saugen*, 7
vegetables  *das Gemüse*, 8
very  *sehr*, 2; Very well!  *Sehr gut!*, 6
video cassette  *das Video, -s*, 10
violent  *brutal*, 10
visit  *besuchen*, 2; to visit friends  *Freunde besuchen*, 2
volleyball  *Volleyball*, 2

## W

want (to)  *wollen*, 6
war movie  *der Kriegsfilm, -e*, 10
warm  *warm*, 7
was: I was  *ich war*, 8; I was at the baker's.  *Ich war beim Bäcker.*, 8; he/she was  *er/sie war*, 8
wash  *spülen*, 7; to wash the dishes  *das Geschirr spülen*, 7
watch  *schauen*, 2; to watch TV  *Fernsehen schauen*, 2
water: to water the flowers  *die Blumen gießen*, 7
water  *das Wasser*, 3; a glass of (mineral) water  *ein Glas (Mineral)Wasser*, 3
we  *wir*, 2
wear  *anziehen (sep)*, 5

weather  *das Wetter*, 7; How's the weather?  *Wie ist das Wetter?*, 7; What does the weather report say?  *Was sagt der Wetterbericht?*, 7
Wednesday  *der Mittwoch*, 4
week  *die Woche, -n*, 7
weekend  *das Wochenende, -n*, 2; on the weekend  *am Wochenende*, 2
weekly special  *das Angebot der Woche*, 8
weigh  *wiegen*, 8
were: Where were you?  *Wo warst du?*, 8; we were  *wir waren*, 8; they were  *sie waren*, 8; (pl) you were  *ihr wart*, 8; (formal) you were  *Sie waren*, 8
western (movie)  *der Western*, -, 10
wet  *naß*, 7
what?  *was?*, 2; What can I do for you?  *Was kann ich für dich tun?*, 7; What else?  *Noch etwas?*, 9
what kind of?  *was für?*, 10; What kind of movies do you like?  *Was für Filme magst du gern?*, 10; What kind of music do you like?  *Was für Musik hörst du gern?*, 10; What will you have?  *Was bekommen Sie?*, 6
when?  *wann?*, 2
where?  *wo?*, 1; Where are you from?  *Woher bist (kommst) du?*, 1
where (to)?  *wohin?*, 6
which  *welch-*, 2
white  *weiß*, 3; in white  *in Weiß*, 5
who?  *wer?*, 1; Who is that?  *Wer ist das?*, 1
whole wheat roll  *die Vollkornsemmel, -n*, 9
whom  *wen*, 7; *wem*, 11
why?  *warum?*, 8; Why don't you come along!  *Komm doch mit!*, 7
wide  *weit*, 5
window  *das Fenster*, -, 7; to clean the windows  *die Fenster putzen*, 7
winter  *der Winter*, 2; in the winter  *im Winter*, 2

with  *mit*, 6; with bread  *mit Brot*, 6; with corners  *eckig*, 12; with lemon  *mit Zitrone*, 6; with mustard  *mit Senf*, 9
woman  *die Frau, -en*, 3
wood: made of wood  *aus Holz*, 12
work: That won't work.  *Das geht nicht.*, 7
would like (to)  *möchten*, 3; I would like to see....  *Ich möchte ... sehen.*, 5; What would you like to eat?  *Was möchtest du essen?*, 3; What would you like?  *Was bekommen Sie?*, 5; Would you like anything else?  *Haben Sie noch einen Wunsch?*, 8
wristwatch  *die Armbanduhr, -en*, 11
write  *schreiben*, p. 8

## Y

year  *das Jahr, -e*, 1; I am...years old.  *Ich bin ... Jahre alt.*, 1
yellow  *gelb*, 5; in yellow  *in Gelb*, 5
yes  *ja*, 1; Yes?  *Bitte?*, 5
yesterday  *gestern*, 8; yesterday evening  *gestern abend*, 8; the day before yesterday  *vorgestern*, 8
you  *du*, 2; you are  *du bist*, 1; (pl) you are  *ihr seid*, 1; (formal) you are  *Sie sind*, 1
you (formal)  *Sie*, 2
you (plural)  *ihr*, 2
you (pl, acc pronoun)  *euch*, 7
you (acc pronoun)  *dich*, 7
you're (very) welcome!  *Bitte (sehr, schön)!*, 3
your  *dein*, 3; to, for your father  *deinem Vater*, 11; to, for your mother  *deiner Mutter*, 11

## Z

zoo  *der Zoo, -s*, 12; to go to the zoo  *in den Zoo gehen*, 12

# GRAMMAR INDEX

**NOTE:** For a summary of the grammar presented in this book see pages 326–336.

## ABBREVIATIONS

| | | | | | |
|---|---|---|---|---|---|
| acc | *accusative* | dir obj | *direct object* | prep | *preposition* |
| comm | *command* | indir obj | *indirect object* | pres | *present* |
| conv past | *conversational past* | inf | *infinitive* | pron | *pronoun(s)* |
| dat | *dative* | interr | *interrogative* | ques | *question(s)* |
| def | *definition* | nom | *nominative* | sep pref | *separable prefix* |
| def art | *definite article* | pers | *person* | sing | *singular* |
| indef art | *indefinite article* | plur | *plural* | subj | *subject* |

## A

accusative case: def art, p. 123; indef art, p. 123; p. 230; third pers pron, sing, p. 128; third pers pron, plur, p. 180; first and second pers pron, p. 180; following **für**, p. 180; p. 297; following **es gibt**, p. 229

article: *see* definite article, indefinite articles

**anziehen:** pres tense forms of, p. 131

**aussehen:** pres tense forms of, p. 132

## C

case: *see* nominative case, accusative case, dative case

class: def, p. 24

command forms: **du**-commands, p. 200; p. 297; **Sie**-commands, p. 227

conjunctions: **denn** and **weil**, p. 206; **daß**, p. 232

## D

dative case: introduction to, p. 283; following **mit**, p. 283; word order with, p. 284; *see also* indirect objects

definite article: to identify class, p. 24; p. 74; acc, p. 123; dat, p. 283; nom and acc, p. 303

direct object: def, p. 123; *see also* accusative case

direct object pronouns: p. 128; p. 180

**du**-commands: p. 200; p. 297

## E

**ein:** nom, p. 72; acc, p. 123; p. 230; dat, p. 283

**ein**-words: **mein(e)**, **dein(e)**, p. 78; acc, p. 230; **kein**, p. 231; p. 307; dat, p. 283

**es gibt:** p. 229

**essen:** pres tense forms of, p. 155

## F

**fahren:** pres tense forms of, p. 227

**für:** prep followed by acc, p. 180; p. 297

future: use of **morgen** and present tense for, p. 183

## G

**gefallen:** p. 125; p. 132

## H

**haben:** pres tense forms, p. 100

## I

indefinite articles: **ein**, nom, p. 72; acc, p. 123; p. 230; nom and acc, p. 303

indirect object: def, p. 283; *see also* dative case

indirect object pronouns: p. 283

infinitive: use with **wollen**, p. 150; use with **müssen**, p. 175; in final position following modals, p. 309

interrogative pronouns: nom form **wer**, p. 23; acc form **wen**, p. 180; dat form **wem**, p. 283

interrogatives: **wo**, **woher**, **wie**, p. 23; **was**, p. 48; **worüber**, p. 259

## K

**kein:** p. 231; p. 307

**können:** pres tense of, p. 179; p. 297

## L

**Lieblings-:** p. 102

## M

**möchte**-forms: pres tense, p. 71; p. 155; p. 307

modal auxiliary verbs: **möchte**-forms, p. 71; **wollen**, p. 150; **müssen**, p. 175; **können**, p. 179; **sollen**, p. 199; **mögen**, p. 250

**mögen:** pres tense forms of, p. 250

**müssen:** pres tense forms of, p. 175; p. 302

## N

**nehmen:** pres tense forms of, p. 132
**noch ein:** p. 230; p. 307
nominative case: def, p. 123; *see also* subject
nouns: classes of, p. 24; plural of, p. 106
noun phrases: def, p. 123

## P

past tense of: **sein**, p. 207
possessives: **mein(e), dein(e)**, nom, p. 78; **sein(e), ihr(e)**, p. 79; dat, p. 304
plural formation: p. 106
prefix: see separable prefixes
preposition: **für**, p. 180; **über**, use with **sprechen**, p. 259; **mit**, p. 283
present tense: of **sein**, p. 26; of **spielen**, p. 46; of the **möchte**-forms, p. 71; of **haben**, p. 100; of **anziehen**, p. 131; of **nehmen, aussehen**, p. 132; of **wollen**, p. 150; of **essen**, p. 155; of **müssen**, p. 175; of **können**, p. 179; of **sollen**, p. 199; of **wissen**, p. 222; of **mögen**, p. 250; of **sehen**, p. 253; of **lesen, sprechen**, p. 259
present tense verb endings: p. 50; verbs with stems ending in **d, t**, or **n**, p. 55; verbs with stems ending in **eln**, p. 56
pronouns: personal pron sing, p. 26; personal pron plur, p. 48; **er, sie, es, sie** (pl), p. 75; p. 107; third pers sing, acc, p. 128; third pers, plur, p. 180; first and second pers, p. 180; dat, p. 283; nom and acc, p. 303; dat, p. 304

## Q

questions: asking and answering ques, p. 23; ques beginning with a verb, p. 23; ques beginning with a ques word, p. 23
question words: **wer, wo, woher, wie**, p. 23; **was**, p. 48; **worüber**, p. 259; **wem**, p. 304

## S

**sein:** pres tense forms of, p. 26; simple past tense forms of, p. 207
separable prefix verbs: **anziehen, anprobieren, aussehen**, p. 131; **aufräumen, abräumen, mitkommen**, p. 176
**Sie**-commands: p. 227
**sehen:** present tense forms of, p. 253
**sollen:** present tense forms of, p. 199
**sprechen:** present tense forms of, p. 259
stem-changing verbs: **nehmen, aussehen**, p. 132; **essen**, p. 155; **fahren**, p. 227; **sehen**, p. 253; **lesen, sprechen**, p. 259
subject: def, p. 123; *see also* nominative case

## V

verbs: with sep pref, **anziehen, anprobieren, aussehen**, p. 131; **aufräumen, abräumen, mitkommen**, p. 176; with vowel change in the **du**- and **er/sie**-form, **nehmen, aussehen**, p. 132; **fahren**, p. 227; **sehen**, p. 253; **lesen, sprechen**, p. 259
verb-final position: in **weil**-clauses, p. 206; in clauses following **wissen**, p. 222; in **daß**-clauses, p. 232
verb-second position: p. 54; p. 151; p. 309

## W

**wissen:** pres tense forms of, p. 222; p. 299
**wollen:** pres tense forms of, p. 150; p. 302
word order: ques beginning with a verb, p. 23; ques beginning with a ques word, p. 23; verb in second position, p. 54; p. 151; p. 309; in **denn**- and **weil**-clauses, p. 206; verb-final in clauses following **wissen**, p. 222; p. 299; verb-final in **daß**-clauses, p. 232; with dat case, p. 284

## ACKNOWLEDGMENTS [continued from page T6]

*Hilton Hotel:* Advertisement, "Kulinarische Highlights Im München City Hilton."

*Immobilien:* Advertisement, "Immobilien T. Kurcz," from *Südwest Presse: Schwäbisches Tagblatt,* July 14, 1990.

*Institut Rosenberg:* Advertisement, "Institut Rosenberg," from *Süddeutsche Zeitung,* July 10–11, 1993, p. 40.

*IVT-Immobiliengesellschaft der Volksbank Tübingen mbH & Co.:* "Auf dem Lande" and "2-Zi.-Eigentumswohnung" from "Immobilienverbund-Volksbanken Raiffeisenbanken" from *Südwest Presse: Schwäbisches Tagblatt,* Tübingen, July 14, 1990.

*Jahreszeiten Verlag GmbH:* "DAS WEISSE HEMD" from *Petra,* May 1992, p. 52.

*K+L Ruppert:* Advertisements, "Kurz Und Gut!" and "Qualitäts-Garantie."

*Kabarett Mon Marthe:* Text and photograph to "Reiner Kröhnert," from *Kabarett Mon Marthe: Das Programm bis Juni 1993.*

*Karsten Jahnke Konzertdirektion:* Advertisement of upcoming concert tours from *Konzerte: Karsten Jahnke Präsentiert Konzertübersicht 1993,* no. 248.

*Kriegbaum Aktuell:* Advertisement, "Stark Reduziert!," from *Südwest Presse: Schwäbisches Tagblatt,* Tübingen, June 27, 1990.

*Liberty Diskothek Café:* Advertisement, "Liberty Diskothek Café," from *in münchen,* no. 30/31, July 25–August 7, 1991.

*Mädchen:* Recipe, "Pizzateig," from *Mädchen,* March 1993, no. 13, p. 62.

*Messe Stuttgart Kongress-U. Tagungsburo.:* "Hanns-Martin-Schleyer-Halle" from *Veranstaltungskalender der Messe Stuttgart, März 1992.*

*Müller Brot:* Advertisements, "Der Mensch ist, wie er ißt" and "HOTLINE."

*Neuen Zürcher Zeitung:* Advertisements, "The Addams Family," "Das verlorene Halsband der Taube," "JFK," "Little Man Tate," and "Prince of Tides," from *Neuen Zürcher Zeitung,* Zurich, March 3, 1992, no. 52, p. 16.

*OK-PUR:* From "MTV News" and "OK-PUR TAGESTIP: The Romeos" from *OK-PUR,* June 22, 1993.

*Quick-Schuh GmbH & Co. KG, Mainhausen:* "Stundenplan" (class schedule) from *Quick-Schuh.*

*QUICK Verlag GmbH:* Advertisement, "Milchbars," from *QUICK,* August 8, 1991, no. 33. Copyright © 1991 by QUICK Verlag GmbH.

*Dr. Rall GmbH, Reutlingen:* Advertisement, "Tübingen-Lustnau Am Herrlesberg," from *Südwest Presse: Schwäbisches Tagblatt,* Tübingen, July 14, 1990.

*Sator Werbe-Agentur:* Advertisement, "Bahrenfelder Forstaus," from *Hotels und Restaurants 93/94,* Hamburg Das Tor zur Welt.

*Hartmut Schmid:* Game, "Schach," from *Südwest Presse: Schwäbisches Tagblatt,* Tübingen, July 13, 1990.

*Schneider & Händle, Werbeagentur Deutschland:* Advertisement, "Der mit dem Wolf tanzt," from *1. Ludwigsburger: Sommernachts Open-Air-Kino,* text by Frank Schneider, illustration by Gernot Händle.

*Schwäbisches Tagblatt:* Advertisement, "UNI Sommerfest," from *Südwest Presse: Schwäbisches Tagblatt,* Tübingen, June 23, 1990.

*Spar Öst Warenhandels-AG:* From flyer, "Spar Supermarkt: NEUERÖFFNUNG, July 1, 1993."

*Stadt Bietigheim-Bissingen, Presseamt und Stadtarchiv:* Captions from *Stadt Bietigheim-Bissingen.*

*Südwest Presse:* Advertisement, "Eninger Hot Jazz Festival," *Schwäbisches Tagblatt,* Tübingen, June 23, 1990.

*Tiefdruck Schwann-Bagel GmbH:* Adaption of advertisement, "Hobby," from *JUMA Das Jugendmagazin,* 2/90, p. 47, February 1990. Advertisement, "Mode '91" from *JUMA Das Jugendmagazin,* 3/91, p. 31, July 1991. "Christoph, 12," "Nils, 19 Jahre," from *JUMA Das Jugendmagazin,* 4/91, pp. 7 and 22, October 1991. Pictures & captions from "Polo mit Eskimorolle" from *JUMA Das Jugendmagazin,* 1/92, pp. 2–3, January 1992. "Traumhaus" from *JUMA Das Jugendmagazin,* 1/92, p. 16, January 92. "...in Dänemark," from *JUMA Das Jugendmagazin,* 3/92, p. 42, July 1992. "Geschenke," "Hallo Heiko!," "Hallo Sven!," "Hallo Tina!," "Im Geschenkladen sucht," "Im Supermarkt läuft Ben," and "Stefan wird Im Schreibwarengeschäft," from *JUMA Das Jugendmagazin,* 2/93, pp. 21, 23, 38, 39, 40, and 42, April 1993.

*Turner Broadcasting:* Advertisement, "The Wall," from *Der besondere Film.*

*United International Pictures GmbH:* Advertisement, "Jurassic Park," from *Kino Magazin,* February 1993.

*Verkehrsamt Stuttgart:* Captions from *Stuttgart.*

*Verlag DIE ABENDZEITUNG, GmbH & Co. KG:* Movie advertisements, "Beethoven," "Mein Vetter Winnie," "Vater der Braut," from *Abendzeitung,* May 1992, p. 34. Movie advertisement, "Schtonk," from *Abendzeitung,* June 4, 1992, p. 31.

*Verlag Mohr, Georg Siebeck, publisher:* Advertisement, "Wohnung," from *Südwest Presse: Schwäbisches Tagblatt,* Tübingen, July 14, 1990.

*VIPP Video:* "Video Hits" from *Bravo,* 44/1991, p. 67, October 1991.

# PHOTOGRAPHY CREDITS

Abbreviations used: (t) top, (c) center, (b) bottom, (l) left, (r) right, (i) inset.

**FRONT COVER:** (bl) Nawrocki Stock Photo, Inc., **BACK COVER:** (tl) Fridmar Damm/Leo de Wys, Inc., (tr) David Frazier Photolibrary, **FRONT AND BACK COVER COLLAGE:** HRW Photo by Andrew Yates

Chapter Opener photos: Scott Van Osdol

All photographs by George Winkler/Holt, Rinehart and Winston, Inc. except:

**TABLE OF CONTENTS:** Page v(bl), vi(tl), vi(cl), vi(bl), vii(br), viii(cr), viii(bl), viii(br), ix(b), x(tl), x(c), x(b), xi(t), xi(b), xii(tl),xii(cl), xii(cr), xii(b), (all) Michelle Bridwell/Frontera Fotos.

**Preliminary Chapter:** (background), (all) Eric Beggs. Page 1(tl), 1(tc), Westlight; 1(tr), FPG International; 4(tl), DPA Photoreporters; 4(tr), Westlight; 4(cl), Robert Young Pelton/Westlight; 4(bl), Dallas & John Heaton/Westlight; 4(br), Westlight; 5(l), 5(c), 5(br), Bettmann Archive; 5(tr), AP/Wide World Photos, Inc.; 5(b), Archive Photo; 7(tl), 7(tr), Michelle Bridwell/Frontera Fotos; 10(cl), 10(b), AP/Wide World Photos, Inc.; 10(tr), I. George Bilyk.

**UNIT ONE:** Page 12–13, Jose Fuste Raga/The Stock Market; 14(tl), Kaki/Helga Lade/Peter Arnold, Inc.; 14(c), D. Assmann/Helga Lade/Peter Arnold, Inc. **Chapter One:** Page 20, 21(tl), 21(bl), 21(br), Michelle Bridwell/Frontera Fotos; 21(tr), Viesti Associates, Inc.; 28, Michelle Bridwell/Frontera Fotos; 34–35(background), Courtesy of Lufthansa German Airlines, New York; 35(bl), 36, HRW Photo. **Chapter Two:** Page 41(b), Michelle Bridwell/Frontera Fotos; 44, HRW Photo by Michelle Bridwell; 47, HRW Photo by Richard Hutchings; 48, Harbrace Photo by Oscar Buitrago; 51, (all) Michelle Bridwell/Frontera Fotos; 58(t), Comstock; 61, (all) Viesti Associates, Inc. **Chapter Three:** Page 69(tl), 69(bli), 69(bci), 69(bri), Michelle Bridwell/Frontera Fotos; 69(br), Viesti Associates, Inc.; 70(l), PhotoEdit; 70(cl), 70(cr), Viesti Associates, Inc.; 76, (all) Michelle Bridwell/Frontera Fotos; 76(tl), Courtesy of Scandinavia Contemporary Interiors/Michelle Bridwell/Frontera Fotos; 77(top row), Viesti Associates, Inc.; 77(second row), (2,3,4) Viesti Associates, Inc.; 77(third row), (5) Viesti Associates, Inc.; 77(fourth row), (all), 85, 86, (all) Michelle Bridwell/Frontera Fotos.

**UNIT TWO:** Page 88, 89, 90, (all) R. Robert/Helga Lade/Peter Arnold, Inc. **Chapter Four:** Page 93(b),

107(t), (all) Michelle Bridwell/Frontera Fotos; 107(b), HRW Photo by Michelle Bridwell. **Chapter Five:** Page 125, 129, 131, (all) Michelle Bridwell/Frontera Fotos; 131(l), Courtesy of Texas Clothier/Michelle Bridwell/Frontera Fotos; 137, David Vance/The Image Bank. **Chapter Six:** Page 158–159(background), Rolf Nobel/Visum.

**UNIT THREE:** Page 164, 165, Comstock. **Chapter Seven:** Page 173(top row), (1,2) Michelle Bridwell/Frontera Fotos; 173(second row), (1,2,3) Michelle Bridwell/Frontera Fotos; 173(third row), (4) Viesti Associates, Inc.; 183, (all) PhotoEdit; 186, 187(tl), Viesti Associates, Inc.; 187(b), Michelle Bridwell/Frontera Fotos; 188 (5), Michelle Bridwell/Frontera Fotos. **Chapter Eight:** Page 193(tr), 194(tl), Michelle Bridwell/Frontera Fotos; 197(top left panel), (all) Michelle Bridwell/Frontera Fotos; 197(right panel: top), Michelle Bridwell/Frontera Fotos; 197(right panel: bottom), HRW Photo by Sam Dudgeon; 197(center panel), HRW Photo by Sam Dudgeon; 197(bottom panel), (1) Viesti Associates, Inc.; (2), HRW Photo by Sam Dudgeon; (3,4t), Viesti Associates, Inc.; (4b), HRW Photo by Sam Dudgeon; (5), Viesti Associates, Inc.; (6t), HRW Photo by Sam Dudgeon; (6b), Viesti Associates, Inc.; 198(tr), Viesti Associates, Inc. **Chapter Nine:** Page 226(t), 226(b), composite photographs, Munich Square: George Winkler; people: Michelle Bridwell/Frontera Fotos; 232, Thomas Kanzler/Viesti Associates, Inc.; 237(top row) (2,3) Michelle Bridwell/Frontera Fotos; 237(bottom row) (1), Michelle Bridwell/Frontera Fotos.

**UNIT FOUR:** Page 240–241(background), 242(tl), S.K./Helga Lade/Peter Arnold, Inc. **Chapter Ten:** Page 249(top row), (all) Motion Picture & TV Photo Archive; 249(center row) (l) Motion Picture & TV Photo Archive; 249(c), 249(r), Everett Collection; 249(bottom row), (all) Motion Picture & TV Photo Archive; 251, Marko Shark; 256, 259, (all) Michelle Bridwell/Frontera Fotos; 260, Thomas Kanzler/Viesti Associates, Inc. **Chapter Eleven:** Page 268, 269, (all) Michelle Bridwell/Frontera Fotos; 281(t), Courtesy of Wicks & Sticks/Michelle Bridwell/Frontera Fotos; 281(top row), (1) Michelle Bridwell/Frontera Fotos; (2) Viesti Associates, Inc.; (3) Michelle Bridwell/Frontera Fotos; (4) Viesti Associates, Inc.; (5) Michelle Bridwell/Frontera Fotos; 281(bottom row), 283, 285, 288, (all) Michelle Bridwell/Frontera Fotos. **Chapter Twelve:** Page 300(top row), (r) Michelle Bridwell/Frontera Fotos; 300(bottom row), (l) Viesti Associates, Inc.; 303(tr), 310(background), 310(t), 310(b), 311(c), (all) Michelle Bridwell/Frontera Fotos.

# ILLUSTRATION AND CARTOGRAPHY CREDITS

**Beier, Ellen:** 9

**Böhm, Eduard:** 45, 46, 49, 71, 72, 106, 113, 121, 155, 175, 181, 199, 202, 231, 254, 278, 279, 298, 305, 307

**Carlson, Susan:** xviii, 2, 3

**Cooper, Holly:** i, v, vi, viii, x, xii, xiv, 6, 22, 60, 71, 77, 97, 99, 121, 124, 125, 132, 133, 136, 138, 145, 156, 157, 160, 175, 190, 199, 228, 265, 304, 305

**Kell, Leslie:** 11, 146, 225, 236, 265

**Krone, Mike:** 279, 284, 290, 299

**Maryland Cartographics:** 1, 13, 89, 165, 241

**McLeod, George:** 22, 23, 30, 49, 70, 74, 108, 148, 174, 181, 223, 289, 302

**Piazza, Gail:** 45, 53, 80, 100

**Rummonds, Tom:** 8, 37, 84, 126, 127, 145, 149, 179, 180, 184, 200, 208, 273, 274

**Rushing, Riki:** 225, 313

**Williamson, Reagan:** 27

**Wilson, John:** 221, 223, 238

# NOTIZEN

# NOTIZEN

# NOTIZEN

# NOTIZEN

# NOTIZEN

# NOTIZEN

# NOTIZEN

# NOTIZEN

# NOTIZEN

*NOTIZEN*